INTERNATIONAL FINANCE

McGraw-Hill Series in Finance

CONSULTING EDITOR

Charles A. D'Ambrosio, *University of Washington*

Brealey and Myers: Principles of Corporate Finance
Campbell: Financial Institutions, Markets, and Economic Activity
Christy and Clendenin: Introduction to Investments
Coates: Investment Strategy
Edmister: Financial Institutions: Markets and Management
Francis: Investments: Analysis and Management
Francis: Management of Investments
Garbade: Securities Markets
Haley and Schall: The Theory of Financial Decisions
Hastings and Mietus: Personal Finance
Henning, Pigott, and Scott: International Financial Management
Lang and Gillespie: Strategy for Personal Finance
Levi: International Finance: Financial Management and the International Economy
Martin, Petty, and Klock: Personal Financial Management
Robinson and Wrightsman: Financial Markets: The Accumulation and
 Allocation of Wealth
Schall and Haley: Introduction to Financial Management
Sharpe: Portfolio Theory and Capital Markets
Stevenson: Fundamentals of Finance
Troelstrup and Hall: The Consumer in American Society:
 Personal and Family Finance

McGraw-Hill Finance Guide Series

CONSULTING EDITOR

Charles A. D'Ambrosio, *University of Washington*

Bowlin, Martin, and Scott: Guide to Financial Analysis
Farrell: Guide to Portfolio Management
Gup: Guide to Strategic Planning
Riley and Montgomery: Guide to Computer-Assisted Investment Analysis
Smith: Guide to Working Capital Management
Weston and Sorge: Guide to International Finance

INTERNATIONAL FINANCE

FINANCIAL MANAGEMENT AND THE INTERNATIONAL ECONOMY

Maurice Levi

Bank of Montréal Professor
University of British Columbia

McGraw-Hill Book Company

New York   St. Louis   San Francisco   Auckland   Bogotá
Hamburg   London   Madrid   Mexico   Montreal   New Delhi
Panama   Paris   São Paulo   Singapore   Sydney   Tokyo   Toronto

This book was set in Times Roman by Graphic Technique, Inc.
The editors were Bonnie E. Lieberman and Scott Amerman;
the production supervisor was Phil Galea.
The drawings were done by Felix Cooper.
R. R. Donnelley & Sons Company was printer and binder.

INTERNATIONAL FINANCE

Financial Management and the International Economy

890 DOCDOC 898

ISBN 0-07-037481-3

Library of Congress Cataloging in Publication Data

Levi, Maurice D., date
    International Finance.

    (McGraw-Hill series in finance)
    Includes bibliographies and indexes.
    1. International finance.   2. International
business enterprises—Finance.   I. Title.   II. Series.
HG3881.L455   1983   332'.042   82-9954
ISBN 0-07-037481-3   AACR2

TO KATE

CONTENTS

PREFACE

Courses in international finance are offered both in departments of economics and in schools of business. The topics covered and the levels of analysis are, however, very different. Instructors of students of economics tend to concentrate on the more macroeconomic issues of the balance of payments, the international financial adjustment process, the adequacy of international reserves, transfer problems, and impacts of economic policies in an open environment. These topics are not of direct interest to the student of business. The economist does, however, treat these topics in a relatively rigorous manner using tools that are familiar to a student who has taken a course in economics.

Students of business, whether concentrating in finance or concentrating in international business, often have a more practical interest. Consequently, courses offered in business programs are concerned with topics such as where to borrow and invest, what different types of bonds can be used to raise capital, how exchange rates affect cash flows, what can be done to avoid foreign exchange risk, and the general management problems of multinational enterprises. Despite adequate levels of preparation, generally including an introduction to economics and finance, the student of business often receives a rather descriptive treatment of these topics which fails to build on the foundations of previous courses. For this reason, many second-year M.B.A. students and undergraduate business majors with solid backgrounds in, for example, marginal revenue-cost analysis or the advantages of portfolio diversification feel they move sideways rather than forward into international finance.

In addition to proceeding from an appropriate background, the coverage of topics in a good international finance text written for business students should be from the perspective of business management. This book builds on an economics and finance background that should be common to every student of economics or business who moves into a course in international finance. Furthermore, since some students will be familiar with lower-level college mathematics, those topics which can be treated with calculus or involve what are primarily mathematical manipulations are covered in appendixes. However, no background in mathematics is required other than straightforward algebra to understand the main part of the text, and the appendixes can be ignored, since they are not necessary for understanding the text. Only the kernel of knowledge provided in an introduction to economics is required. Some degree of familiarity with the material covered in a conventional introduction to finance is valuable but not essential, and when "difficult" concepts are used, a short review is presented.

The topics in this text are covered from the perspective of a person who wishes to know how the international environment will affect the firm. However, it is important that managers also understand international financial developments on an overall macroeconomic level. Such an understanding enables managers to project economic changes and to adjust to what they expect to occur. Because of this double level of interest in the forces behind events and the consequences of these events for the firm, this book includes a section on the international finance of the economy. However, even at this macroeconomic level, a managerial perspective is taken.

In order for different instructors to have some flexibility in planning the contents of their course, a text is required which deals with the core of the theory and practice of international finance. This core can and perhaps should be augmented with readings that the instructor feels are appropriate. The text would then form the backbone of a course that involves an accompanying but short list of supplementary readings. The text should nevertheless provide sufficient material for a one-semester course. It is hoped that this book achieves the goal of providing a sufficient core for a full course in international finance while leaving room for some supplementary readings.

The more difficult sections of the book are marked with an asterisk. These can be avoided or left for a second reading, for they are not essential for understanding the subsequent material.

This book evolved over a number of years while I was teaching at the University of British Columbia and also at the School of Business Administration of the Hebrew University, Jerusalem, and the School of Business Administration of the University of California, Berkeley. Parts of the text were written while I was visiting the Department of Economics at the Massachusetts Institute of Technology.

An author's debts are a pleasure to acknowledge, and I have incurred many that I would find difficult to repay. The help that was offered by reviewers of the numerous different drafts was immensely important in improving the final product. Charles D'Ambrosio meticulously examined each chapter and provided wise advice on the presentation of material. Laurence D. Booth of the University of Toronto conscientiously and carefully checked voluminous portions of the manuscript and generously gave the benefit of his professional and critical judgment. His advice on the appropriate coverage of topics was of great value. Richard Brealey of the London Business School helped me avoid numerous errors and confusions and offered perceptive and valuable comments on virtually every aspect of the text. Detailed and valuable comments were also received from James Hugon of Portland State University and from J. Fred Weston of the University of California, Los Angeles. The coordination of reviews and numerous other editorial jobs involved in producing this book was most professionally handled by Bonnie E. Lieberman and the expert staff at McGraw-Hill.

I have had the good fortune of obtaining help from individuals at universities I visited while writing this book, especially from David Babbel at the University of California at Berkeley and from Donald Lessard at MIT. Alan Shapiro provided generous help while he was visiting and teaching at the University of British Columbia. Leonard Back of Citibank helped in obtaining material, and Thomas Campbell of the Federal Reserve Bank of New York offered generous advice.

I would like to thank my colleagues at the University of British Columbia—Gary Bortz, Michael Brennan, Robert Heinkel, Alan Kraus, and Peter Lusztig—who provided input at various stages. A vital contribution was made by my good friend and colleague Eduardo Schwartz; he gave constant and invaluable advice on numerous topics. I received superbly professional and indispensable help in improving the presentation of material from Barbara Brett. Too numerous to mention individually but of great importance were the students in my graduate and undergraduate courses in international finance at the University of British Columbia. Their comments and reactions were a crucial ingredient in various revisions of the text.

An immeasurable debt is owed to my teachers of international finance at the University of Chicago: Robert Z. Aliber, Arthur Laffer, Lloyd Metzler, Robert A. Mundell, and the late Harry G. Johnson. Financial assistance was provided by the Canadian Ministry of Industry, Trade, and Commerce and the Division of International Business Studies at the University of British Columbia. Their help is most gratefully appreciated. It is to Kate Birkinshaw, who helped in every stage of preparing this book, that I owe my greatest and sincerest thanks. She provided the input and environment that made this book a shared labor of love.

Maurice Levi

CHAPTER 1

THE NATURE OF INTERNATIONAL RISKS AND THE PLAN OF THIS BOOK

THE SCOPE OF INTERNATIONAL FINANCE

It is difficult to escape being constantly confronted with the phenomenal impact of international trade on our standard of living and daily lives. In the department store we find cameras and electrical equipment from Japan and clothing from Hong Kong. On the street we find automobiles from Germany, Japan, Britain, Sweden, and France using gasoline from Venezuela, Saudi Arabia, Great Britain, Mexico, and Kuwait. At home we drink tea from India, coffee from Brazil, whiskey from Scotland, beer from Germany, and wine from France. It is sometimes difficult to believe that every item which has reached us from some other land has involved international investments and the movement of money along the channels of the payments network that is the subject of this book on international finance.

The network of payments and the international investments have elevated the study of finance to a multinational scale. Events in distant lands, whether they involve changes in the prices of oil and gold, election results, the outbreak of war, or the establishment of peace, have effects which instantly reverberate around the globe. We see the consequences of events in the stock markets and interest rates of an increasingly integrated and interdependent economic environment. The links between the money and capital markets have become so close as to make it almost futile to concentrate on any individual part. It is these developments which have made it imperative that every actual and aspiring manager of a business concern take a good look into the exciting and dynamic field of international finance.

BENEFITS OF STUDYING INTERNATIONAL FINANCE

A knowledge of international finance can help in two very important ways. First, it can help the manager decide how international events will affect a firm and which steps can be taken to insulate the firm from the more harmful effects. Second, it can help the manager to anticipate the path of events and to make profitable decisions before the events occur. Among the events that will affect the firm and which the manager must anticipate are changes in exchange rates, interest rates, inflation rates, and national incomes, as well as the prospects for change in different political environments. These events are intricately linked, and it is crucial that the links be understood if profitable decisions are to be made and harmful effects avoided.

We are concerned with the problems faced by any firm whose performance is affected by the international environment. Our analysis is relevant to more than the giant multinational corporations (MNCs) that have received so much attention in the media. It is just as valid for a company with a domestic focus that happens to export a little of its output or buys inputs from abroad. Even companies that operate only domestically but compete with firms producing abroad and selling in their local market are affected by international developments. For example, U.S. clothing or automobile manufacturers with limited or zero overseas sales will find U.S. sales and profit margins affected by exchange rates which influence the dollar prices of imported clothing and automobiles.

What makes international finance different from domestic finance are the additional risks of involvement in different currencies and in different political jurisdictions or countries. Dealing with different currencies gives rise to exchange rate risk, and dealing with different countries entails political risk.

We can do little more than indicate the nature of the risks in this introduction. The reader should not, therefore, be disturbed if some of what is stated in this introductory chapter is not immediately understood.

EXCHANGE RATE AND POLITICAL RISKS

There are frequent periods when each day we hear about the plight of the dollar or the currency of some other major trading country. Tensions in Europe or in other politically sensitive parts of the world, changes in the price of oil or gold, interest rate patterns, and the prospect of economic booms or busts all spill over into the foreign currency markets and influence the prices of foreign exchange.

Changes in exchange rates means changed fortunes for those who are *exposed to foreign exchange risk*. Exposure to exchange rate risk means that changes in the price of foreign currencies will affect either the value of existing foreign currency assets/liabilities or the value of foreign income not yet even earned.

Exposure on Existing Foreign Assets/Liabilities

Existing assets that are not sold and liabilities that are not repaid are affected by exchange rates as a result of being "denominated" in a foreign currency. By denomination in a foreign currency we mean that the asset or liability has a stated or market value given in a foreign currency. Foreign bank notes and bonds are generally denominated in a foreign currency. In addition, from a U.S. perspective, a pound sterling bank account in London or Canadian stocks that trade on the Toronto Stock Exchange are denominated in foreign currency. So, too, is any real asset, such as property, owned abroad which has a market value in terms of foreign currency.

Exchange rate risk exists because the value of foreign-currency-denominated assets or liabilities must be "translated" into the domestic currency for tax or accounting purposes. By translation into domestic currency we mean, from a U.S. perspective, the conversion of foreign currency values into U.S. dollars. This requires multiplying foreign currency values by the exchange rate. For example, if the exchange rate is 2 U.S. dollars ($2) per pound sterling, a bank balance of 100 pounds (£100) in London translates into U.S. $200 (2 × 100 = 200). Uncertainty about the exchange rate that will exist at the time of translation means an uncertain dollar value of existing assets or liabilities in U.S. accounting statements.

The uncertainty of asset/liability values in domestic currency, because of uncertainty in exchange rates, is called *translation risk* and results from *translation exposure*. It is a risk only in the sense that it affects the measurements in accounts. However, when the assets are actually sold or when liabilities are repaid, the transactions occur at exchange rates that cannot be precisely known in advance. This uncertainty is *transaction risk*, which is merely the eventual realization of translation risk. We can summarize this:

> Translation risk results from uncertainty in exchange rates at which the value of foreign currency assets or liabilities is converted or translated into domestic currency for inclusion in financial statements. Transaction risk results from uncertainty in exchange rates when assets are actually sold or liabilities repaid, that is, when the transactions occur.

Exposure on Future Foreign Income

Existing assets and liabilities face translation risk only with regard to amounts appearing in accounts; they face transaction risk only when gains or losses are realized. Another risk from changes in exchange rates that is faced all the time is the effect on the value of foreign income that is not yet earned or payments that are not yet made. This risk is relevant for exporters and importers for whom exchange rate changes mean changes in future profitability. For example, even if a U.S. exporter has no foreign currency assets or liabilities, a fall in the foreign currency value of the dollar should increase sales. This is because it will reduce the price of U.S. exports faced by foreign buyers.

For example, if the exchange rate is 2 German marks (DM2) per dollar, a $10 bottle of bourbon whiskey will cost DM20 in Germany. If the dollar falls to only DM1.6, a $10 bottle of whiskey will cost only DM16, and more bottles are likely to be sold. The profitability of U.S. whiskey exporters will therefore be affected by exchange rates independently of any foreign currency assets or liabilities these exporters have to translate or transact. The risk faced by exporters vis-à-vis their future income has been called *economic risk* and results from *economic exposure*. Importers whose importation costs, sales revenues, and, therefore, corporate income depend on exchange rates also face economic risk. In summary:

Economic risk results from the effect that exchange rates have on export prices and quantities and hence on future corporate income. It also results from the effect of exchange rates on the prices and quantities sold of imported goods.

Complexities in Exchange Rate Risk

The subject of international finance, and hence the contents of this book, involves the study of the different kinds of foreign exchange risks and the ways they can be avoided. It spells out the effects of exchange rates on translated and transacted values of foreign currency assets/liabilities of different kinds, the effect on exporter and importer profitability, and so on. It shows how companies can select the currency and country in which to borrow and thereby reduce their risks. It also shows how the forward exchange market (in which currencies can be bought and sold for future delivery) can be used for reducing risks. But international finance goes even further than this.

Whether, for example, a fall in the value of the dollar will affect the profitability of exporters depends on whether the fall in the foreign currency price of the dollar will really make U.S. exports cheaper abroad. If the decline in the dollar merely reflects higher inflation in the U.S. than elsewhere, then the fall in the foreign exchange value of the dollar could be offset by higher prices in the U.S.

For example, if a fall in the dollar from DM2 to DM1.6 occurs while the price of a bottle of bourbon whiskey for export from the United States goes from $10.00 to $12.50, a bottle of whiskey will continue to cost Germans DM20. This is because the dollar price multiplied by the exchange rate, which gives the mark price, is unchanged. Our example should indicate that in order to determine the effect of changes in exchange rates, we must examine inflation and how inflation and exchange rates are related. This requires that we examine the economy as a whole.

Translation and transaction risks also depend on interest rates and on how asset and liability market values are connected to the exchange rate. For example, if foreign-currency-denominated assets tend to increase in market value when the currency is falling in value, the owner of the asset might find that the increased market value in units of foreign currency compensates for the fall in the value of the foreign currency. Similarly, a high interest rate might compensate for a fall in a currency value on foreign-interest-yielding assets or liabilities. At this point we can do little more than point out the difficulties of defining risk and note that we can show that economic risk depends on a principle known as *purchasing power parity*, while translation or transaction risks depend on this and on another principle known as the *Fisher-open principle*.

Foreign Exchange Hedging and Speculation

Because of translation and transaction risks, it is important where a company borrows or invests and in which currency it invoices exports or imports. However, the risks can be avoided by purchasing or selling foreign currencies for delivery in the future. For example, foreign export revenue can be sold for dollars with the exchange of dollars for foreign currency arranged for the day the receipts are due.

This can be done in the forward exchange market for a couple of years or more into the future and helps in avoiding translation and transaction exposure—but not economic exposure.

When translation or transaction risk is avoided by using the forward market, we say that the company is *hedged* or *covered*. When currencies are bought and sold for future delivery and there is no matching export revenue, import payment, and so on, the activity is called *speculation*. International finance and this book are concerned with speculation as well as the more conservative behavior of hedging. A market where a lot of hedging occurs is the Eurocurrency market, of which the Eurodollar market is a part. Eurodollars are U.S.-dollar-denominated bank accounts held outside the United States.

Political Risk

Foreign exchange risks are only part of the extra risks of the international financial environment. The other important additional risk is political risk. Political risk involves the possibility of expropriation, confiscation, or the destruction of property by revolution or war, and it should be considered in the capital budgeting decision for investment in physical plant and equipment. There are ways of reducing political risks via insurance, borrowing where investment occurs, engaging in a joint venture, holding back technical expertise, and so on. Exchange rate risks faced in overseas capital projects can also be reduced by borrowing abroad or by the shareholders of the firm holding a diversified portfolio of currencies.

This review of risks should serve to introduce you to some of the types of problems that should be covered in a book on international finance and international financial management. Additional problems that should be covered involve the factors affecting exchange rates and whether changes in exchange rates can be forecasted, the connected question of the efficiency of foreign exchange markets, the different natures of fixed and flexible rates, the balance of payments accounts, international taxation, and so on. We have emphasized the risks not because we believe that managers should always try to avoid them. Indeed, the very nature of business involves taking risks in a calculated fashion, especially when doing business overseas. We have emphasized risk only because this has enabled us to show the additional dimensions of international finance and discuss some of the topics covered in this book.

TOPICS COVERED IN THIS BOOK

Part 1, consisting of Chapters 2 and 3, explores the foreign exchange markets. Chapter 2 explains the nature of bank note markets and bank draft markets, with the former involving the paper currency in our wallets and the latter involving checks. It is shown that the profit motive of professional foreign exchange dealers, taking the form of arbitrage, helps to ensure that little or no opportunity for profitable trading in currencies exists for the ordinary person or company. The managerial lesson in this chapter is that for firms other than large banks, it can pay to shop around for the best price of the currency they wish to buy or sell, but it does not pay to buy and sell currencies for profit.

Chapter 3 examines the forward and futures exchange markets and shows how they work, and it discusses the meaning of forward premiums and discounts. The conventions for quoting forward rates and the distinction between forwards and currency futures are given.

Part 2, consisting of Chapters 4 to 6, focuses on the international economic environment and the factors which can make exchange rates move up and down. This is done so that the reader does not make international financial decisions in a vacuum. Chapter 4 looks at the structure and meaning of the international balance of payments accounts, which is where the factors behind the supplies of and demands for currencies are recorded. The interpretation of the accounts depends on whether a country has fixed or flexible exchange rates. Chapter 5 examines the fixed exchange rate system and how it restores balance when imbalances appear in international payments. This involves looking at the gold standard and also the dollar-exchange standard and understanding how they work. Chapter 6 examines the workings of flexible exchange rates. In particular, it shows the conditions required for stable currency values and the factors to include in exchange rate forecasting models. The arguments for and against flexible exchange rates are presented. Chapter 6 gives a brief history of the international financial system and, in an appendix, provides an account of the factors affecting the effectiveness of monetary and fiscal policy to aid in forecasting.

With the nature of the foreign exchange markets and the international financial system explained in Parts 1 and 2, the reader will be familiar with the environment in which decisions must be made. Parts 3, 4, and 5 are concerned with the decision making itself.

Part 3, consisting of Chapters 7 to 10, looks at decisions in the money market in which securities of up to 1-year maturity are traded. Chapter 7 develops the criteria for making short-term investment and borrowing decisions in which translation or transaction risk can be avoided by hedging in the forward market. The chapter also develops the interest parity theorem, which shows how interest rates in different countries are linked to spot and forward exchange rates. Chapter 8 examines an active market for borrowing and investing, the Eurocurrency market. Chapter 8 also looks at the nature of international banks, which are where Eurocurrencies are held in the form of bank deposits.

Chapter 9 describes the methods available to exporters and importers for avoiding foreign exchange risk on receivables and payables. We have seen that when exporters and importers (or borrowers and investors) avoid risk, they are hedging and that the opposite of hedging is speculation. The chapter explains the way to speculate and how the speculators and the hedgers collectively determine the forward exchange rate. The chapter also describes the documentation involved in international trade, including the letter of credit and the bill of exchange. An example is given to show the numerous steps involved in shipping and paying for goods from abroad.

Chapter 10 examines the problems of the management of working capital on a multinational scale as well as some systems that have been designed to overcome the problems. The chapter looks at how corporate costs and earnings can be allocated among divisions of a multinational corporation by selecting internal transfer prices for goods and services that are exchanged between corporate divisions.

Part 4, consisting of Chapters 11, 12, and 13, examines the conditions required for changes in exchange rates to be "real" and the effect these have. By real changes in exchange rates we mean changes that will have effects on the appearance of accounts, export revenues, and so on, and which are not offset by inflation or compensated for by interest rates. Chapter 11 explains the principle of purchasing power parity, which is the basis for determining real changes in exchange rates. The chapter also shows the result of combining purchasing power parity with another principle, that of interest parity, and derives a principle known as *Fisher-open*, which links real interest rates (which are net of inflation) between countries. The chapter also examines methods of exchange rate forecasting and the record of some forecasting firms. The ability to make valuable forecasts is closely tied to the efficiency of the foreign exchange markets, and the empirical evidence on market efficiency is examined.

Chapter 12 provides operational definitions of real changes in exchange rates that are relevant for fixed and financial assets and for changes in operational profitability. Chapter 13 shows what real exchange rate changes mean for the sales, costs, and profitability of exporters and importers.

Part 5 considers decisions in the long-term capital market. Chapter 14 looks at the bond decision and where bonds should be sold. The effect of the international diversification of equities is shown by referring to a model of capital asset pricing. The chapter also looks at capital structure, in the form of debt versus equity, in different countries. Chapter 15 is devoted to the capital budgeting decision for overseas investment and the problems brought about by the giant multinational corporations which have been the result of this type of investment.

SUMMARY

1 Every good or service reaching us from abroad has involved international finance. Knowledge of the subject can help managers avoid harmful effects of international events and profit from the events.

2 Foreign exchange exposure means that exchange rates can affect the value of existing foreign assets and liabilities or the amount of income received from the sale of exports or purchase of imports.

3 Existing foreign assets and liabilities are affected by exchange rates because they are denominated—that is, have values stated—in units of foreign currency. These foreign currency values must be translated into the firm's home currency by multiplying by the exchange rate. Since exchange rates move up and down, there is translation risk. This is a risk only in the sense that *measured* amounts of existing assets or liabilities in home currency units depend on exchange rates.

4 When assets are sold or liabilities repaid at exchange rates that are not known in advance, there is transaction risk.

5 Exporters and importers are affected by economic risk. This is because their future profitability is affected by exchange rates even if they have no foreign assets or liabilities.

6 The extent of economic risk depends on the extent to which exchange rates reflect

inflation. If falls in currency values are matched by inflation, profitability may not be affected.

7 Translation and transaction risks also depend on how inflation and exchange rates are linked. In addition, they depend on whether or not interest rates compensate for eventual changes in exchange rates.

8 When foreign exchange risk is avoided by using forward exchange markets or by borrowing, the firm or individual is hedged or covered. The opposite of hedging is speculation.

9 Political risks are also added by dealing internationally. They can be reduced by insurance, joint ventures with foreign firms, and so on.

10 International finance is the study of foreign exchange risks and political risk. In addition, it covers the nature of foreign exchange rate systems, the balance of international payments, and so on.

BIBLIOGRAPHY

Aliber, Robert Z.: *Exchange Risk and Corporate International Finance*, The Macmillan Press Ltd., New York, 1978.

Coombs, Charles: *The Arena of International Finance*, John Wiley & Sons, New York, 1976.

Dufey, Gunter, and Ian Giddy: *The International Money Market*, Prentice-Hall, Inc., Englewood Cliffs, N.J., 1978.

Dunning, John H. (ed.): *Economic Analysis and the Multinational Enterprise*, Frederick A. Praeger, Inc., New York, 1974.

Eitman, David K., and Arthur I., Stonehill: *Multinational Business Finance*, 2d ed. Addison-Wesley Publishing Co., Reading, Mass., 1979.

Grubel, Herbert, G.: *International Economics*, Richard D. Irwin, Inc., Homewood, Ill., 1977.

Henning, Charles N., William Piggot, and Robert H. Scott: *International Financial Management*, McGraw-Hill Book Company, New York, 1978.

Jacque, Laurent L.: *Management of Foreign Exchange Risk*, Lexington Books, Lexington, Mass., 1978.

Lessard, Donald R. (ed.): *International Financial Management: Theory and Applications*, Warren, Gorham and Lamont, Boston, 1979.

Mundell, Robert A.: *International Economics*, The Macmillan Company, Ltd., New York, 1968.

Robinson, Richard: *International Business Management*, Holt, Rinehart and Winston, New York, 1973.

Rodriguez, Rita, and E. Eugene Carter: *International Financial Management*, 2d ed., Prentice-Hall, Inc., Englewood Cliffs, N.J., 1979.

Stern, Robert: *The Balance of Payments: Theory and Economic Policy*, Aldine Publishing Company, Chicago, 1973.

Tarleton, Jesse: "Recommended Courses in International Business for Graduate Business Students," *Journal of Business*, October 1977, pp. 438–447.

Vernon, Raymond, and Louis Wells, Jr.: *Manager in the International Economy*, 3d ed., Prentice-Hall, Inc., Englewood Cliffs, N.J., 1976.

Weston, J. Fred, and Bart W. Sorge: *Guide to International Financial Management*, McGraw-Hill Book Company, New York, 1977.

Parallel Material for Case Courses

Aharoni, Yair: *The Foreign Investment Decision Process*, Harvard Graduate School of Business Administration, Boston, 1966.

Carlson, Robert, S., H. Lee Remmers, Christine R. Hekman, David K. Eitman, and Arthur Stonehill: *International Finance: Cases and Simulation*, Addision-Wesley Publishing Co., Reading, Mass., 1980.

Feiger, George, and Bertrand Jacquillat: *International Finance: Text and Cases*, Allyn and Bacon Inc., Boston, 1982.

Zernoff, David B., and Jack Zwick: *International Financial Management*, Prentice-Hall, Inc., Englewood Cliffs, N.J., 1969.

INTRODUCING THE FOREIGN EXCHANGE MARKETS

CHAPTER 2

BANK NOTES AND SPOT MARKETS

To the ordinary person, international finance is synonymous with exchange rates, and indeed, a large part of the study of international finance is a study of exchange rates. What is not always known to those with a limited knowledge of international finance is the number of exchange rates that exist at the same moment between the same two currencies. There are exchange rates for *bank notes*, which are the Federal Reserve notes with pictures of former U.S. presidents, and, for example, the equivalent Bank of England notes containing pictures of the queen. There are also exchange rates between checks stating dollar amounts and those stating amounts in pounds or other currency units. Furthermore, the rates on these checks depend on whether they are issued by banks—*bank drafts*—or by corporations and on the amounts they involve.

A definition that is valid for all exchange rates is as follows:

An *exchange rate* is the number of units of one currency required in order to purchase one unit of a different currency.

We will begin by looking at the exchange rate for that form of money with which we are most familiar: the bank notes of different countries.

THE FOREIGN BANK NOTE MARKET

The earliest experience that many of us have of dealing with foreign currency is on our first overseas vacation. When not traveling abroad, most of us have very little to do with foreign exchange, which is not used in the course of ordinary commerce, especially in the United States. The foreign exchange with which we deal when on vacation involves bank notes, and, quite frequently, foreign-currency-denominated traveler's checks. Table 2.1 gives the exchange rates on bank notes facing a traveler on October 8, 1981. It is worth taking a look at how these retail bank note rates are quoted.

The first column of Table 2.1 gives the exchange rates in terms of the number of units of each foreign currency that must be *offered to the bank* to buy a U.S. dollar. For example, it takes 1.22 Canadian dollars (Can$1.22) or 0.54 United Kingdom pounds (£0.54) to buy a U.S. dollar. The second column gives the number of units of each foreign currency that will be *received from the bank* when buying the foreign currency with U.S. dollars. For example, the traveler will receive Can$1.18 or £0.52 for each U.S. dollar. We recall that these rates are for bank notes for the international traveler.

The rates of exchange posted for travelers in bank and currency exchange windows or international tourist centers are the most expensive or unfavorable that exist. They are expensive in the sense that the buying and selling prices on individual currencies can differ by a large percentage—frequently as much as 5 to 6 percent. The difference between buying and selling prices is called the *spread*. Table 2.1 shows that the spreads can indeed be large. They are generally in the range of 4 to 6 percent. For example, the 2-cent difference between the buying price and the selling price on the British pound is a spread of nearly 4 percent.

The experience we have of exchanging currencies on vacation should not lead us

TABLE 2.1
EXCHANGE RATES ON FOREIGN BANK NOTES
Traveler's Dollar—October 8, 1981
(Foreign Currency per U.S. Dollar)

	Bank buys	Bank sells
Australia (dollar)	0.88	0.84
Austria (schilling)	15.85	15.00
Belgium (franc)	37.80	36.00
Canada (dollar)	1.22	1.18
Denmark (kroner)	7.22	6.88
Finland (markkaa)	4.50	4.25
France (franc)	5.70	5.40
Germany (Deutsche mark)	2.25	2.15
Greece (drachma)	58.00	55.00
Hong Kong (dollar)	6.15	5.85
Ireland (pound)	0.64	0.61
Israel (shekel)	13.85	13.10
Italy (lira)	1200.00	1140.00
Japan (yen)	232.00	222.00
Mexico (peso)	25.85	24.75
Netherlands (guilder)	2.52	2,40
Norway (kroner)	5.95	5.65
South Africa (rand)	0.98	0.92
Spain (peseta)	98.00	92.00
Sweden (krona)	5.55	5.25
Switzerland (franc)	1.90	1.82
United Kingdom (pound)	0.54	0.52

to believe that large-scale international finance faces similar costs. The bank note market used by travelers involves large spreads because generally only small amounts are traded, which nevertheless require as much paperwork as bigger commercial trades. Another reason why the spreads are large is that each bank and currency exchange must hold many different currencies to be able to provide customers with what they want, and these notes do not earn interest. This involves an opportunity or inventory cost as well as some risk from changes in exchange rates. Moreover, bank robbers, in which the United States does not have a monopoly, specialize in bank notes; therefore, those who hold large amounts of them are forced to take security precautions—especially when moving bank notes from branch to branch.[1]

While the exchange of bank notes between the ordinary private customer and the bank or currency exchange takes place in the retail market, the banks trade their surpluses of notes between each other in the wholesale market. The wholesale market involves firms which specialize in buying and selling foreign bank notes with commercial banks and currency exchanges. These are *bank note wholesalers*. They exist only in leading banking centers and do not have names that are readily recognized by the general public.

As an example of the workings of the wholesale market, during the summer a British bank might receive large numbers of German marks from Germans traveling in Britain. The same British bank may also be selling large amounts of Italian lire to the British leaving for vacations in Italy. The British bank will sell its surplus German marks to a bank note wholesaler in London, who might then transport the mark notes back to Germany or to a non-German bank in need of mark notes. The British bank will buy lire from a wholesaler who may well have transported the lire from Italy (or bought them from banks in Europe which in turn bought them from Italians engaged in the popular sport of smuggling lire out of the country to avoid exchange controls). The spreads on the wholesale level are less than the retail bank note spreads, generally well below 2 percent, because larger amounts are generally traded.

Because of the large retail spreads on bank notes, the banks and currency exchanges which deal in the retail market do not have to continually revise their exchange rates. They will continue to profit even if exchange rates change by small amounts during the day. Normally, on the small amounts that are traded at branch banks and currency exchanges, quotations are fixed at rates received in the morning from the head office and maintained all day unless different instructions are received. During more volatile times, quotations might be received twice a day, with a morning rate and an afternoon rate. These are the procedures in cities where foreign bank notes are continually being exchanged, such as New York City, the capitals of Europe and Asia, and the larger Canadian cities. But even in these places, there are times when there will be departures from normal practices.

---

[1]Because banks face a lower risk of theft of traveler's checks and because the companies that issue them, which are often themselves banks, will quickly credit the bank that accepts them, many banks give a more favorable exchange rate on checks than on bank notes. The spread might be as much as 2 percent lower than for bank notes.

If, for example, a customer wants to buy foreign bank notes at a small branch bank, the customer will probably be directed to the main branch or told that he or she must wait a couple of days before receiving the notes. In all but the very largest U.S. cities, foreign notes are not kept in local banks' inventories at all; they must be received from a bank note wholesaler or from banks in New York City, Chicago, Los Angeles, San Francisco, or some other large center. The wait could easily be a week. The purchase of less commonly exchanged bank notes—for example, the bank notes of small African nations or Soviet-bloc countries—will involve a wait even in New York City or in the capitals of Europe or Asia. Exchange rates will be determined by the bank on each separate transaction, usually as a markup over the wholesale cost.

If a customer wants to sell a very large amount of foreign bank notes—for example, thousands of dollars' worth—there will also be a departure from the normal procedure of buying at the posted rate of the day. The manager will probably call the head office to check the most recent rate on the foreign exchange market. (If the customer is not well known—for example, if he or she is a foreign tourist at a local department store or hotel—the banker might also call the police. Counterfeit and stolen bank notes have a habit of showing up in foreign financial centers.)

THE SPOT FOREIGN EXCHANGE MARKET

The bank note market is also known as the *cash market*. Far larger than the cash market is the *spot foreign exchange market*, which is involved with the exchange of currencies in the form of checks drawn on different currency-denominated bank accounts.

In the spot market, instructions to exchange currencies take the form of *bank drafts*, which are checks issued by banks. Delivery or *value* from the bank drafts is "immediate"—usually in 1 or 2 days. This distinguishes the spot market from the forward or futures exchange market, which involves the planned exchange of currencies for value at some date in the future—after a number of days or even years.

> The spot foreign exchange market involves the exchange of bank drafts for value within 1 or 2 business days.

There are a number of other special features of the spot market. We will explain them after more carefully describing the nature of the delivery period of spot foreign exchange.

Delivery Period

When available, bank notes of the major western countries are exchanged for each other instantaneously over the bank counter. However, when U.S. dollars are exchanged in the form of bank drafts with non–North American currencies, this will generally not provide value until 2 business days after the initiation of the transaction. With the currencies of the North American continent, the Canadian dollar and the Mexican peso, delivery is slightly quicker, with an exchange providing value after 1 business day. This means there is a distinction between the value date and the initiation date of transactions. The distinction can be illustrated by an example.

Suppose that a financial executive of an American corporation, Amcorp, calls his or her bank, Ambank National, a large currency-dealing bank in New York City, to buy £1 million. Suppose that the call is placed on Thursday, October 8, 1981, and that the British pounds are to be used to settle Amcorp's debt to Britcorp. Ambank will quote an exchange rate at which it will sell Amcorp £1 million. If Amcorp approves of this rate, then the foreign exchange department of Ambank will request details for making payment in Britain. These details will include the bank at which Britcorp is to be paid and the account number.

The spot exchange rate that is quoted by Ambank National on October 8 will be binding and will not be changed even if market conditions subsequently change. A confirmation of the order of £1 million at the agreed exchange rate—for example, $2 per pound—will be sent out to Amcorp on Thursday, October 8. Because of the intervening weekend, 2 business days later is Monday, October 12, and on this day Ambank will debit Amcorp's account at the bank by $2 million. On the same day, October 12, Britbank will credit Britcorp's account by £1 million. The transaction is complete for the payer and the payee, with Britcorp receiving the £1 million and Amcorp having paid the dollar equivalent, $2 million.

Bank Settlement

Our description of the transaction in the example is complete only for the payer and the payee. We have not yet described the settlement between the banks. This settlement is necessary because Britbank needs to be compensated for the £1 million it has credited to Britcorp's account.

In order to keep our example straightforward, we can begin by assuming that the banks settle by maintaining deposits with each other. Banks at which other banks maintain deposits are called *correspondents*, so let us first assume that Britbank maintains a correspondent account directly at Ambank. On October 12, at the same time that Ambank debits the account of Amcorp by $2 million, it will credit $2 million to the account that Britbank maintains with it. This is seen in Ambank's account in part *a* of Table 2.2. Britbank, with its extra $2 million in the United States, will credit Britcorp on the same date, October 12, with £1 million. Thus Britbank has received $2 million at Ambank and an extra liability of £1 million to Britcorp. This is seen in Britbank's account in part *a* of Table 2.2. If Britbank decides that it does not want the dollars, it will sell them to another bank for pounds. There will very likely be further effects and adjustments in both countries as a result of these transactions.

If Britbank does not maintain a deposit directly at Ambank but does maintain one with another bank in New York City, the settlement in dollars will probably

TABLE 2.2
TWO EXAMPLES OF BANK CLEARING

(a) Britbank maintains deposit at Ambank

Britbank

Assets		Liabilities	
At Ambank	+$2,000,000	Britcorp	+£1,000,000
($2,000,000 @ $2/£)	+£1,000,000		+£1,000,000
	0		

Ambank

Assets	Liabilities	
	Amcorp	-$2,000,000
	Britbank	+$2,000,000
0		0

(b) Ambank maintains deposit at Britbank

Britbank

Assets	Liabilities	
	Britcorp	+£1,000,000
	Ambank	-£1,000,000
0		0

Ambank

Assets		Liabilities	
At Britbank	-£1,000,000	Amcorp	-$2,000,000
(£1,000,000 @ $2/£)	-$2,000,000		-$2,000,000

involve the New York Clearing House.[2] The Clearing House settles interbank payments for foreign exchange transactions. Before 1981 the New York Clearing House took an extra business day to settle between banks. In other words, our transaction on October 8 would have been settled between banks in New York on October 13 (or later if October 13 had not been a business day). Because of the day required to clear between banks via the New York Clearing House, the U.S. banks used to restrict the use of funds by depositors of dollars from foreign transactions until they had received "Federal Funds" (which meant that the banks had been credited with the dollars by the U.S. Federal Reserve).[3]

Since October 1, 1981, the settlements in U.S. dollars from foreign exchange transactions have been completed on the value date of the transaction—October 12 in our example. Same-day settlement has been permitted through the use of the computerized Clearing House Interbank Payments System (CHIPS). The debiting and crediting take place in *escrow accounts*, which are accounts that the leading banks hold at the New York Clearing House. Each bank has its escrow account increased or decreased each day by the amount of receipts from other banks minus payments to other banks.[4] The introduction of same-day settlement via CHIPS means only that banks settle on the value date for foreign transactions, with the value date still 1 or 2 business days after the initiation of the transaction.

If Ambank maintains an account directly with Britbank, rather than the reverse, the steps for settlement are similar to those already described. When Amcorp pays Britcorp, Ambank will charge Amcorp for the pounds it has purchased by debiting Amcorp's account by \$2 million. At the same time, Ambank's own account at Britbank will be debited by £1 million. This is seen in Ambank's account in part *b* of Table 2.2. Also, at the same time, Britbank will credit Britcorp's account with the £1 million debited from the account of Ambank. This is seen in Britbank's account in part *b* of Table 2.2. The only difference between this case, where Ambank keeps an account with Britbank, and the reverse is which bank finds its currency mix changed. When Britbank maintains an account at Ambank, Britbank gains dollar assets and pound liabilities. Ambank merely shifts dollars from Amcorp's account to Britbank's account. When it is Ambank that keeps an account at Britbank, Ambank will have its dollar liabilities and pound assets reduced. In the latter case of Ambank keeping pounds with Britbank, the pound is the *vehicle currency*. In the former case of Britbank maintaining a dollar account at Ambank, it is the dollar. The former case is the more usual practice, with more than \$100 billion of interbank

---

[2] We say that settlement between banks will *probably* involve the New York Clearing House because banks could also settle the same day via the Federal Reserve wire transfer service, Fedwire, or on the next business day by clearing checks via ordinary Federal Reserve clearing. The New York Clearing House is generally used for clearing transactions involving foreign exchange.

[3] What was true for foreign transactions before October 1981 was also true for domestic transactions settled via the New York Clearing House; that is, there was a day between a deposit and the receipt of usable Federal Funds. However, many large domestic payments have for some time been settled the same day via Fedwire or another payments system called Bankwire.

[4] The role of escrow accounts in bank clearing is the same in international transactions as it is in domestic transactions. The reader who is not familiar with how bank clearing works can consult an economics textbook or a money and banking textbook.

clearing each day, and so the U.S. dollar is the leading vehicle currency for settling international transactions.

If Ambank does not maintain an account directly with Britbank but instead has an account at some other London bank—its correspondent—the settlement will occur between the London correspondent bank and Britbank via the Clearing House in London. The clearing will take place on the value date of the transaction, so the timing and events are very much like those described earlier vis-à-vis the clearing by CHIPS.

Banks that are active in the foreign exchange market, including the correspondent banks, do not enter the market to cover each and every order from customers. Rather, they allow themselves an amount of flexibility in terms of each currency, and they enter the market only when their holdings exceed or are below what they have deemed acceptable. The size of an acceptable currency holding is an internal managerial decision. Banks are conservative institutions and prefer to avoid being heavily exposed to foreign exchange risk. We have stated that exposure means that a firm or individual will be affected if there is a change in exchange rates. A bank *will* be affected if it has promised foreign exchange that it does not have. It will also be affected if it has not yet sold foreign exchange that it has agreed to purchase. The active banks enter the market only when they feel their exposure exceeds a comfortable level. The smaller inactive banks in the foreign exchange market will generally avoid having any exposure at all. They will enter the market on each and every order from a customer to ensure that they have bought or sold in the market whatever they have agreed to supply to or purchase from the customer.

Since the fall of 1977 many banks have used a computer-based telegraphic transfer system which is replacing cables. The system is based in Brussels and is known as the Society for Worldwide International Financial Telecommunications (SWIFT). This is likely to be only a step toward a fully integrated computer system. SWIFT is used for transmitting messages between banks in a standard format. It is not itself a system for settling between banks; settlement requires a clearing house such as CHIPS, described earlier.

Market Organization

The U.S. foreign exchange market is an informal arrangement of the larger commerical banks and foreign exchange brokers; they are linked to each other by telephone, telex, telegraph, and even letters. Together, the banks and brokers, including their counterparts overseas, form the exchange market. Because of the speed of communication, significant events have virtually instantaneous impacts everywhere in the world despite the huge distances separating the market participants. This is what makes the foreign exchange market just as efficient, in terms of utilizing information, as a conventional stock or commodity market that is housed under a common roof. The volume and efficiency of the market are revealed in the extremely narrow spreads between buying and selling prices. These spreads can be smaller than a tenth of a percent of the value of a contract and are therefore about one-fiftieth or less of the spread experienced with bank notes by the international traveler.

The banks and foreign exchange brokers, in conjunction with their counterparts abroad, collectively determine exchange rates. Each dealer gets "a feel for where the market is going" and takes positions to buy or sell on the basis of this feeling and according to orders received from clients. The feel for the market in each currency, as well as a desire to balance the books, is what determines the position the banker is prepared to take. If it is decided that the bank's pound position should be balanced and, further, customers wish to sell pounds, the bank will enter the market to sell these pounds.

Once the desired amount of buying or selling of a currency has been determined, the banker will call foreign exchange dealers at other banks and "ask for the market." The caller does not say whether he or she wants to buy or sell or state the amount to be traded. The caller might say, " What's your market in sterling?" This means, "At what price are you willing to buy and at what price are you willing to sell British pounds for U.S. dollars?" In replying, a foreign exchange dealer must attempt to determine whether the caller really wants to buy or to sell and what his or her own position is. This is a subtle and tricky game involving human judgment. Bluff and counterbluff are used. A good trader, with a substantial order in pounds, may ask for the market in Canadian dollars. After placing a small order he or she might say, "And by the way, what's the market in British sterling?" Dealers are not averse to having their assistants place the really large and really small orders, just to confuse the other side and obtain favorable quotes. A difference in quotation of the fourth decimal place can mean thousands of dollars on a large order. It is rather like massive-stakes poker.

If the banker who has been called wants to sell pounds, he or she will quote on the side that is felt to be cheap for pounds, given this banker's feel of the market. For example, if the banker feels that other banks are selling pounds at \$1.8852/£, he or she might quote \$1.8850/£ as the selling price. In fact, the banker will quote the buying price and the selling price. Having considered the two-way price, the caller will state whether he or she wishes to buy or sell and the amount. Once the rate has been quoted, convention determines that it must be honored whatever the decision of the caller and the amount involved. The caller has about 1 minute to decide and it is fair game to change the rate after this time. Good judgment of the counterparty and good judgment of the direction of the market are essential in this billion-dollar game. It is important to be accurate and constantly in touch with events.

Once the caller has stated his or her intent and the deal has been consummated by telephone, papers of confirmation are exchanged. Settlement will take place on the value date at the agreed-upon exchange rate in the way we have described. The currencies will be cleared through the banks' clearing accounts, and the clients' accounts will be adjusted. The exchange rate faced by the client is determined by the retail bank draft market (involving customers and their banks), and the rate between the banks is determined in the wholesale arena. This retail-wholesale division of the market is not unlike that for bank notes, except that large corporate clients are given spreads similar to those given to other banks. Even very small differences between rates quoted from other banks and rates offered to the client can produce large profits on the massive amounts involved.

Foreign exchange brokers who intermediate between banks will be called in when banks are unable to make a market between themselves. Foreign exchange brokers (of which there are eight in New York) are involved only when deals are not struck privately.

The procedure for dealing with brokers is different from that of banks dealing with each other. A bank will call a broker and state how much foreign exchange it wants to buy or to sell and the rate at which it is willing to buy or sell. This means that it will not ask for a two-way market but will offer to buy or sell a given amount. The broker will communicate to other banks what rates and amounts are available, always showing the best quotes to the potential counterparties. If the two sides of the market are consistent so that a bank will meet the exchange rate demanded by another bank, a trade will be made. Until an agreement has been struck, each of the two parties does not know the identity of the other. When the contract is made, the broker provides the names of the two parties and receives a fee from each of them. It is this fee which makes dealing via brokers more expensive than direct exchange and which therefore explains why larger banks try to make a market between themselves before engaging a broker's services.

The informal nature of the U.S. foreign exchange market is similar to that of markets in Canada, Britain, and many other countries. In France, Germany, and some other countries, including those in Scandinavia, the procedure is rather more formal, with bank representatives, including a representative of the central bank, meeting daily in the same room. Contracts are exchanged directly, although an informal market coexists in which much of the transactions occur. The formal meeting place provides official settlement exchange rates for certain transactions. Nevertheless, the formal structure that we have described is almost universally the backbone of the market for foreign exchange.[5]

Conventions for Spot Exchange Quotations

In virtually every professional enterprise, especially in the realm of finance and economics, there are special conventions and a particular jargon. This is certainly true in the foreign exchange market, where practices in the quotation of exchange rates make the quotes difficult to interpret unless the jargon and conventions are well understood.

Let us concentrate on the spot exchange rates and consider Figure 2.1. The table quotes rates from *The Wall Street Journal* of October 9, 1981; the rates are the previous day's exchange rates, quoted toward the end of the trading day at 3:00 p.m., Eastern time.

Since, as the table states, the rates are those charged by Bankers Trust Company of New York on sales of more than $1 million to other banks, the rates are wholesale interbank rates involving large drafts. Retail rates to corporate clients will generally be less favorable than these interbank rates.

Figure 2.1 gives rates in two ways—as the number of U.S. dollars per foreign

---

[5] Technical details are always changing. Nevertheless, Paul Einzig's *A Dynamic Theory of Forward Exchange* (Macmillan and Company, London, 1962) gives a timeless account of the goings-on in a part of this lively market.

Foreign Exchange

Thursday, October 8, 1981

The New York foreign exchange selling rates below apply to trading among banks in amounts of $1 million and more, as quoted at 3 p.m. Eastern time by Bankers Trust Co. Retail transactions provide fewer units of foreign currency per dollar.

Country	U.S. $ equiv. Thurs.	U.S. $ equiv. Wed.	Currency per U.S. $ Thurs.	Currency per U.S. $ Wed.
Argentina (Peso)				
Financial	.000126	.000135	7900.00	7425.00
Australia (Dollar)	1.1550	1.1547	.8658	.8660
Austria (Schilling)	.0647	.0642	15.45	15.58
Belgium (Franc)				
Commercial rate	.027156	.026916	36.82	37.152
Financial rate	.02469	.024490	40.49	40.832
Brazil (Cruzeiro)	.009225	.009225	108.40	108.40
Britain (Pound)	1.8930	1.8800	.5282	.5319
30-Day Forward	1.8933	1.8790	.5281	.5322
90-Day Forward	1.8960	1.8803	.5274	.5318
180-Day Forward	1.9000	1.8828	.5263	.5311
Canada (Dollar)	.8339	.8342	1.1991	1.1988
30-Day Forward	.8312	.8309	1.2031	1.2034
90-Day Forward	.8281	.8279	1.2075	1.2078
180-Day Forward	.8238	.8239	1.2138	1.2136
China (Yuan)	.5787	.5741	1.7280	1.7419
Colombia (Peso)	.0178	.0178	56.14	56.14
Denmark (Krone)	.1409	.1399	7.0924	7.1471
Ecuador (Sucre)	.03518	.03518	28.425	28.425
Finland (Markka)	.2301	.2279	4.3451	4.3873
France (Franc)	.1809	.1795	5.5275	5.5700
30-Day Forward	.1803	.1785	5.5475	5.6000
90-Day Forward	.1795	.1776	5.5700	5.6300
180-Day Forward	.1785	.1770	5.6025	5.6500
Greece (Drachma)	.01805	.01795	55.41	55.703
Hong Kong (Dollar)	.1661	.1658	6.02	6.03
India (Rupee)	.1121	.1106	8.92	9.04
Indonesia (Rupiah)	.00158	.00158	630.00	630.00
Ireland (Pound)	1.6028	1.6143	.6239	.6194
Israel (Shekel)	.0787	.0787	13.54	13.54
Italy (Lira)	.000845	.000845	1183.00	1184.00
Japan (Yen)	.004372	.004385	228.70	228.05
30-Day Forward	.004407	.004417	226.90	226.37
90-Day Forward	.004472	.004484	223.60	223.00
180-Day Forward	.004566	.004575	219.00	218.55
Lebanon (Pound)	.2181	.2181	4.585	4.585
Malaysia (Ringgit)	.4308	.4308	2.321	2.321
Mexico (Peso)	.03949	.0395	25.32	25.31
Netherlands (Guilder)	.4102	.4071	2.4374	2.4562
New Zealand (Dollar)	.8340	.8344	1.1990	1.1985
Norway (Krone)	.1733	.1722	5.7705	5.8083
Pakistan (Rupee)	.1016	.1016	9.84	9.84
Peru (Sol)	.002208	.002208	452.83	452.83
Philippines (Peso)	.1247	.1247	8.022	8.022
Portugal (Escudo)	.01577	.01563	63.39	63.99
Saudi Arabia (Riyal)	.2945	.2945	3.3950	3.3950
Singapore (Dollar)	.4762	.4755	2.1000	2.0130
South Africa (Rand)	1.0640	1.0650	.9398	.9389
South Korea (Won)	.001468	.001468	681.00	681.00
Spain (Peseta)	.01067	.0105	93.67	94.79
Sweden (Krona)	.1834	.1820	5.4536	5.4938
Switzerland (Franc)	.5367	.5326	1.8630	1.8775
30-Day Forward	.5393	.5349	1.8540	1.8695
90-Day Forward	.5448	.5399	1.8355	1.8520
180-Day Forward	.5531	.5483	1.8080	1.8235
Taiwan (Dollar)	.0263	.0263	38.00	38.00
Thailand (Baht)	.04347	.04347	23.00	23.00
Uruguay (New Peso)				
Financial	.0882	.0882	11.33	11.33
Venezuela (Bolivar)	.2331	.2331	4.29	4.29
West German (Mark)	.4535	.4500	2.2050	2.2220
30-Day Forward	.4551	.4514	2.1974	2.2152
90-Day Forward	.4591	.4553	2.1780	2.1963
180-Day Forward	.4645	.4606	2.1530	2.1710
SDR	1.16118	1.16168	.861191	.860824

Special Drawing Rights are based on exchange rates for the U.S., West German, British, French and Japanese currencies. Source: International Monetary Fund.

FIGURE 2.1

Exchange rates on bank drafts: Wholesale spot and forward rates. (Reprinted by permission of *The Wall Street Journal* © Dow Jones & Company Inc., Oct. 9, 1981, all rights reserved.)

unit, which is called *US$ equivalent*, and as the number of units of foreign *currency per US$*. To a close approximation, the figures in the second two columns are merely the reciprocals of the figures in the first two columns. The large New York banks, when dealing among themselves, quote most rates as currency per US$ and no longer use the alternative form. The convention of using currency per US$ dates to the fall of 1979, when New York went on what is known as *European terms*. For example, on October 8, 1981, the dollar would have been quoted as 5.4536 Swedish kronor (S. Kr5.4536) or DM2.2050.[6]

The table gives only the rates for selling and not for buying foreign exchange. It is customary for newspapers and even some dealers to quote only the banks' selling rates, but dealers will generally give two-way quotations. The selling rates of banks are called *offer* or *ask rates*. In order to obtain the *buying* or *bid rates*, the newspaper rates must be adjusted, and we must guess the amount of adjustment, since data for both sides of the market are not made available. If US$ equivalent quotations were used, bid rates would be below ask rates; that is, the U.S. bank would buy foreign currency for less U.S. dollars than the amount at which it would sell the foreign currency. For example, Bankers Trust might sell West German marks at $0.4535 each and buy them at $0.4530.

We should note that the buy or bid rate is below the ask or offer rate by $0.0005, or 5 points. A *point* refers to the last digit of the quotation. We must be careful, since two, three, four, five, or more decimal places could be involved. For example, Japanese yen might have an ask or offer rate of $0.004372 and a bid rate of $0.004367; in this case, there is also a 5-point spread.

Since the convention of quoting rates in New York was changed to European terms, the previously higher selling prices and lower buying prices look like they are reversed. With quotation as the amount of currency per US$, the bank's selling or ask rate looks as if it is *below* the buying or bid rate. Usually, if an institution sells below its buying prices, it will incur losses. Of course, the banks do profit from exchanging currencies, and this unusual-looking price structure reflects the nature of the rate quotation.

With quotations in US$ equivalent, we subtract points from the selling rate to obtain the buying rate. However, to obtain buying rates with the currency per US$ quotation, we *add* points to the selling rates. For example, we might guess that Bankers Trust had been buying German marks at DM2.2055 per US$ while selling them at the quoted DM2.2050 per US$, which means that there is a 0.0005 or 5-point bid-ask spread. This 5-point spread for the bank on a $1 million two-way transaction in marks will provide a profit of about $500. For large transactions the spread might be as small as 4 points or even 2 points.

It is important that we distinguish between bid and ask exchange rates, even if it seems that the differences are so small as to be almost irrelevant. The bid-ask spread is what gives banks their profits from dealing in foreign exchange. For example, even if the banks charge only 0.0002 of the value of transactions, the revenue to the

---

[6]There are a couple of exceptions. The British pound and, more rarely, the Australian and New Zealand dollars, the South African rand, and the Canadian dollar will be quoted in New York in U.S. $ equivalent. In Britain, quotations of sterling are given in the same terms, which means, from the British view, foreign currency per £.

banks in New York on their transactions of $100 billion each day is $20 million. This is not all profit, as banks face costs, but it does indicate the importance of spreads to banks. Another way of viewing the importance of spreads is to consider their implication for investments made abroad for only a short period. For example, if a company invests abroad for 1 month and must therefore buy the foreign currency today and sell it after 1 month, a 0.1 percent spread when put on an annual basis by multiplying by 12 involves an annualized cost of 1.2 percent. If the extra interest available abroad is smaller than 1.2 percent, the spread will eliminate the advantage. The shorter the period for which funds are moved, the more relevant spreads become.

THE CONCEPT OF TRIANGULAR ARBITRAGE

Exchange rates between currencies are linked together by the presence or potential presence of *triangular arbitrage*. This can be defined as follows:

Triangular arbitrage is the buying and selling of one currency for another, ending with a return to the original currency, for the purpose of making a profit.

Because of triangular arbitrage or the possibility of it, a limited number of exchange rates will allow us to compute the remaining rates. This makes some exchange rates redundant and gives rise to the *redundancy theorem*. With full redundancy, transaction costs must be zero, which means that the bid and ask prices of currencies are equal. In the spot market, with its narrow spreads, this is often a reasonable approximation, but for bank notes, spreads are so large that we never observe triangular arbitrage taking place. Even in the spot market the spreads will generally prevent profitable arbitrage.

Triangular Arbitrage: Zero Transaction Costs

In a world with only four different currencies, there are 12 different exchange rates. For example, suppose the four currencies are U.S. dollars ($), British pounds or sterling (£), German marks (DM), and Japanese yen (¥). For a holder of dollars, the relevant spot exchange rates are $S(\$/£)$, $S(\$/DM)$, and $S(\$/¥)$, where

$S(\$/£)$ is defined as the number of U.S. dollars needed to purchase a British pound in the spot exchange market. More generally, $S(i/j)$ is the number of units of currency i needed to buy a unit of currency j in the spot market.

For a holder of pounds, the relevant spot exchange rates are $S(£/\$)$, $S(£/DM)$, and $S(£/¥)$, that is, the number of pounds needed to buy a unit of each of the other currencies on the spot market.

All the possible exchange rates between the four currencies are given in Table 2.3, which we might call the exchange rate table or *matrix*. By reading across the table on, for example, the row for £, we find the number of pounds per dollar $S(£/\$)$, the number of pounds per German mark, $S(£/DM)$, and so on.

TABLE 2.3
TABLE OF POSSIBLE EXCHANGE RATES

Currency sold	Currency purchased			
	$	£	DM	¥
$	1	$S(\$/£)$	$S(\$/DM)$	$S(\$/¥)$
£	$S(£/\$)$	1	$S(£/DM)$	$S(£/¥)$
DM	$S(DM/\$)$	$S(DM/£)$	1	$S(DM/¥)$
¥	$S(¥/\$)$	$S(¥/£)$	$S(¥/DM)$	1

We see from Table 2.3 that with four currencies we have 12 nontrivial exchange rate entries. These exchange rates are, however, not all independent, and many rates are redundant. The most obvious cause of redundancy is that once we know the price of, for example, dollars in terms of British pounds, or $S(£/\$)$, this immediately suggests knowing the price of British pounds in terms of dollars, $S(\$/£)$. Indeed, *when there are no brokerage or transaction costs*, we have

$$S(\$/£) = \frac{1}{S(£/\$)} \tag{2.1}$$

or, more generally, $S(i/j) = 1/[S(j/i)]$. For example, with 0.50 pound per dollar, there are 2 dollars per pound. Taking advantage of Equation (2.1) would halve the number of relevant exchange rates. Equation (2.1) is equivalent to saying that if an apple costs 50 cents, then a dollar costs 2 apples. But with exchange rates, the possible manipulations go further than this.

The possible exchange rates between U.S. dollars, British pounds, German marks, and Japanese yen are shown in Table 2.3. Let us suppose that the actual rates are the rates given in Table 2.4, which is obtained from *The Wall Street Journal* and the *Financial Times* of London. From Table 2.4, a person who is holding a U.S. dollar could exchange it for DM2.205. With £0.239/DM, this person could use the DM2.205 to obtain £0.527: $2.205 \times 0.239 = 0.527$. This amount of pounds could then be converted back into U.S. dollars at a rate of $1.893/£ and give $0.9976:

TABLE 2.4
TABLE OF ACTUAL EXCHANGE RATES

Currency sold	Currency purchased			
	$	£	DM	¥
$	1	1.893	0.453	0.00437
£	0.526	1	0.239	0.00231
DM	2.205	4.190	1	0.00966
¥	228.2	433.5	103.5	1

Source: Financial Times, London, Oct. 9, 1981, and *The Wall Street Journal*, Oct. 9, 1981.

2.205 × 0.239 × 1.893 = 0.9976. More generally, using Table 2.3, a person with a dollar could get $S(DM/\$)$ marks, which would buy $S(DM/\$) \cdot S(\pounds/DM)$ British pounds. This could be converted into

$$S(DM/\$) \cdot S(\pounds/DM) \cdot S(\$/\pounds) \qquad (2.2)$$

dollars.

The product or chain of exchange rates in Equation (2.2) gives the number of dollars remaining after starting with $1 and exchanging it through German marks and British pounds back into dollars. It is the result of moving around the exchange markets in the triangular manner shown in Figure 2.2. In this figure, we begin at the dollar sign and follow the arrows clockwise back to the dollar sign.

Clearly, when $S(DM/\$) \cdot S(\pounds/DM) \cdot S(\$/\pounds) > 1$, the triangular pattern of exchanges is profitable, and a financial manager could take $1 and convert it at no risk into more than $1 by merely buying and selling. And if $1 becomes more than $1, $1 million can be turned around even better.

Unfortunately, the opportunity for profiting from triangular arbitrage can disappear while you blink. This is because there are many exchange dealers around the world who are ready to jump at the tiniest opportunity. The activity of these extremely alert and eagle-eyed exchange dealers sets up forces that very rapidly eliminate the original profit opportunities. In terms of our example, buying German marks with dollars would cause the marks to become more expensive, which means a fall in the value of $S(DM/\$)$—the first term in Equation (2.2). There would then be an increase in the price of the pound in terms of German marks as people buy the pounds, and this means a fall in the value of the second term, $S(\pounds/DM)$. Finally, there would be a fall in the value of $S(\$/\pounds)$ as a result of attempts to sell the pounds for dollars. This means that efforts to move around the triangle reduce the value of all the exchange rates in the chain in Equation (2.2). Indeed, professional arbitrage will continue until $1 cannot be converted into more than $1 (as in our specific example), that is, until

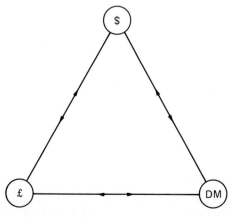

FIGURE 2.2
Triangular arbitrage.

$$S(DM/\$) \cdot S(£/DM) \cdot S(\$/£) \leqslant 1 \qquad (2.3)$$

For the nonprofessional, which means virtually anyone working outside of the foreign exchange rooms of the larger international banks, arbitrage opportunities will occur for such short times that there is little point in even looking at triangular arbitrage. Indeed, if it were not for transaction costs in buying and selling currencies, we could assume that it is the "equal to" part of Equation (2.3) that holds.[7]

We can prove that we will come very close to the equality in condition (2.3) if we consider a person who performs a triangular arbitrage in the reverse or counter-clockwise direction. For example, with the values in Table 2.4 a person could buy £0.526 for $1. This could be used to purchase DM2.20 ($0.526 \times 4.190 = 2.20$), which would then buy dollars at $0.453/DM. This suggests that for $1 this person can obtain, via triangular arbitrage in a counterclockwise direction in Figure 2.2, $0.9984 ($0.526 \times 4.190 \times 0.453 = 0.9984$).

More generally, a dollar will obtain $S(£/\$)$ pounds. This will buy $S(£/\$) \cdot S(DM/£)$ Deutsche marks, which will be converted into

$$S(£/\$) \cdot S(DM/£) \cdot S(\$/DM)$$

dollars. Clearly, this must be less than or equal to unity, as in our specific example. If it were not, holders of dollars would be able to profit from arbitrage by buying British pounds, using these to buy German marks, and then buying dollars for German marks. If the expression is less than or equal to unity, we have $S(£/\$) \cdot S(DM/£) \cdot S(\$/DM) \leqslant 1$. Since we learned earlier that $S(£/\$) = 1/[S(\$/£)]$, $S(DM/£) = 1/[S(£/DM)]$, and $S(\$/DM) = 1/[S(DM/\$)]$, we have by substitution and rearrangement

$$S(DM/\$) \cdot S(£/DM) \cdot S(\$/£) \geqslant 1 \qquad (2.4)$$

Equation (2.4) is consistent with Equation (2.3), which we say must hold from triangular arbitrage in a clockwise direction, only if the equalities rather than the inequalities hold in these relationships. This is the only way that the chain of exchange rates can be both greater than or equal to unity and less than or equal to unity. This means that triangular arbitrage that can proceed in two directions around the triangle ensures that

$$S(DM/\$) \cdot S(£/DM) \cdot S(\$/£) = 1 \qquad (2.5)$$

In our example we do not have an exact value of unity. This is because our numbers contain transaction costs, which we have not yet explicitly introduced.[8]

---

[7] Since most currencies are exchanged directly for the dollar and not for other currencies, actual triangular arbitrage as we describe it will be uncommon. However, we will observe the relationships we compute *as if* direct arbitrage takes place.

[8] In our example the clockwise and counterclockwise arbitrage both result in a number below unity. This is what we would expect from costs of transacting.

The *chain rule* in Equation (2.5) that we have derived from triangular arbitrage with no transaction costs shows how some exchange rates can be derived from others. The exchange rate $S(\$/DM)$ can be derived by putting $S(DM/\$) = 1/[S(\$/DM)]$, which gives, from Equation (2.5),

$$S(\$/DM) = S(\$/£) \cdot S(£/DM) \tag{2.6}$$

In our example, $S(\$/DM) = 1.893 \times 0.239 = 0.452$, which agrees very closely with the number of dollars per German mark in Table 2.4. In addition,

$$S(£/DM) = S(\$/DM)/S(\$/£) \tag{2.7}$$

and

$$S(\$/£) = S(\$/DM)/S(£/DM) \tag{2.8}$$

which can be checked from Table 2.4. We have learned that from any two exchange rates we can find another.[9]

We recall that these results come about because of the ability to arbitrage between currencies in a triangular pattern and because the market is "efficient" in the sense that this occurs until no arbitrage opportunities remain.[10] We note that efficiency, as given by Equation (2.5), requires that arbitrage can go in both directions around the triangle.[11] We also need the absence of transaction costs. But before studying the implications of these costs, we should examine Table 2.5, derived from Equations (2.6) to (2.8) and the rule that $S(i/j) = 1/[S(j/i)]$.

The important feature to note about the exchange rates in Table 2.5 is that they are entirely formed from just three exchange rates: $S(\$/£)$, $S(\$/DM)$, and $S(\$/¥)$. In other words, once we know the value of each currency against the dollar, we know the value of each currency against any other. In general, the $n(n - 1)$ possible exchange rates can all be obtained from only the $(n - 1)$ exchange rates against the nth currency. The other exchange rates are redundant. When we form exchange rates from other exchange rates in the manner of Equations (2.6) to (2.8), the exchange rates that are formed are called *cross rates*.

---

[9]More generally,

$$S(i/j) = S(i/k) \cdot S(k/j)$$

or

$$S(i/j) = S(k/j)/S(k/i)$$

or

$$S(i/j) = S(i/k)/S(j/k)$$

Similarly, $S(i/k)$, $S(k/j)$, and so on, can be written in different ways.

[10]Redundancy in exchange rates can occur without arbitrage. It can instead be achieved by people who already wish to move money between currencies for other reasons, as has been shown by Alan V. Deardorff in "One-Way Arbitrage and Its Implications for the Foreign Exchange Markets," *Journal of Political Economy*, vol. 87, April 1979, pp. 351–364.

[11]Mathematically, there is nothing to prevent us from expanding Equation (2.5) and writing, for example, $S(DM/\$) \cdot S(£/DM) \cdot S(Fr/£) \cdot S(\$/Fr) = 1$, or even more. Arbitrage would not, however, be this circular.

TABLE 2.5
SPOT EXCHANGE RATES WITH ARBITRAGE

Currency sold	Currency purchased			
	$	£	DM	¥
$	1	$S(\$/£)$	$S(\$/DM)$	$S(\$/¥)$
£	$1/[S(\$/£)]$	1	$S(\$/DM)/S(\$/£)$	$S(\$/¥)/S(\$/£)$
DM	$1/[S(\$/DM)]$	$S(\$/£)/S(\$/DM)$	1	$S(\$/¥)/S(\$/DM)$
¥	$1/[S(\$/¥)]$	$S(\$/£)/S(\$/¥)$	$S(\$/DM)/S(\$/¥)$	1

There is no rule that the exchange rates should all be expressed only against the dollar in order to obtain other exchange rates. Any currency would do from a conceptual point of view. For example, every entry in Table 2.5 can be found from any row of Table 2.3. However, as a practical matter, it is important that the chief currency for determining other rates be one that is widely traded and held. At the beginning of the twentieth century, the pound sterling was heavily used, but after the 1944 Bretton Woods Agreement (which is described in Chapter 6), the dollar emerged as the standard for other currency values. We might also note that it is possible to find all exchange rates even without knowing the values of currencies against an nth currency. Instead, we can use the values of currencies against a commodity such as gold, or even against a purely international money such as Special Drawing Rights, or SDRs (which are described in Chapter 6). But this is not the place to deal with these alternatives. Let us now turn to the links between exchange rates in the presence of brokerage or transaction costs.

Triangular Arbitrage with Transaction Costs

Defining the Costs of Transacting We saw earlier that in reality, the price at which we can buy a foreign currency is different from the price at which we can sell it. For example, the ask price that must be paid for a German mark will exceed the bid price received from a sale. In addition, the buyer or seller of a currency might have to pay a lump-sum fee or commission for the transaction. For our purposes, we can think of both the bid-ask spread and the exchange dealer's fee as two parts of the total cost of transacting. They both provide revenue for the dealers in foreign currencies and cause those who need to exchange currencies to lose in going back and forth. Let us define buy and sell rates:

$S(\$/ask£)$ is the total price that must be *paid to the bank* or exchange dealer to buy pounds with dollars. $S(\$/bid£)$ is the number of dollars *received from the bank* or exchange dealer for the sale of pounds for dollars.

We define transaction costs as follows:

Let c stand for the average cost of a one-way transaction in the foreign exchange market.

This means, for example, that

$$S(\$/\text{ask£}) = (1 + c)S(\$/£) \qquad (2.9)$$

where $S(\$/£)$ is the *middle* rate—the exchange rate between dollars and pounds if there were no transaction costs. We might also write

$$S(\$/\text{bid£}) = (1 - c)S(\$/£) \qquad (2.10)$$

If we do this, c is defined as the average transaction cost in percentage terms. For example, if $c = 0.001$, then the costs are $1/10$ of 1 percent to buy or to sell. This is clear because with $S(\$/\text{ask£})$ and $S(\$/\text{bid£})$ written as in Equations (2.9) and (2.10), we know that

$$S(\$/\text{ask£}) - S(\$/\text{bid£}) = 2cS(\$/£)$$

or

$$c = \frac{S(\$/\text{ask£}) - S(\$/\text{bid£})}{2S(\$/£)}$$

We see that in Equations (2.9) and (2.10), we are defining the cost of transacting as one-half of the difference between the buying price and the selling price, where this difference is presented as a percentage of the middle exchange rate. For example, if we could buy pounds for $S(\$/\text{ask£}) = 1.8930$ U.S. dollars and sell them for a net of $S(\$/\text{bid£}) = 1.8910$ U.S. dollars, c would be $0.0020/(2 \times 1.8920) = 0.0005$, or $1/20$ of 1 percent.

In reality, c will depend on the amount transacted. It ranges from $1/50$ of 1 percent, $c = 0.0002$, for large interbank transactions to 2 percent, $c = 0.020$, for small retail transactions.

Transaction costs produce a range for every exchange rate within which there is no profit from arbitrage after costs have been considered. This is true even if the costs are the professionals' own internal costs, such as the costs of time and paperwork. Expressed differently, once we have transaction costs, the cross exchange rates no longer follow exact rules as in Equations (2.6) to (2.8) but instead move within a range determined by the transaction costs of direct exchanges. Moreover, the range of possible movement of the cross rates is wider than that for directly quoted exchange rates. We will prove this result in the following section, which is marked with an asterisk to denote that it can be skipped, for it is not required for understanding subsequent material.

The Range of Cross-Rate Movements* Starting from the dollar sign and arbitraging around the triangle in Figure 2.2, an arbitrager can buy German marks, sell these for pounds, and then sell the pounds for dollars. Arbitrage should take place until the forces it sets up make it no longer profitable. Arbitragers who start with dollars should participate until no more than \$1 can be returned, that is until[12]

$$\frac{1}{S(\$/\text{askDM})} \cdot S(\pounds/\text{bidDM}) \cdot S(\$/\text{bid}\pounds) \leqslant 1 \tag{2.11}$$

Using the definitions of middle exchange rates and transaction costs as used in Equations (2.9) and (2.10), we can rewrite our arbitrage inequality (2.11) as

$$\frac{1}{S(\$/\text{DM})(1+c)} \cdot (1-c)S(\pounds/\text{DM}) \cdot (1-c)S(\$/\pounds) \leqslant 1$$

which can be rearranged into

$$S(\pounds/\text{DM}) \cdot S(\$/\pounds) \cdot \frac{(1-c)^2}{(1+c)} \leqslant S(\$/\text{DM}) \tag{2.12}$$

If we now consider the arbitrager who goes counterclockwise we can consider when he or she will profit from buying pounds with dollars, selling these pounds for Deutsche marks, and then moving back into dollars. This should continue until the forces the arbitrage sets up make it unprofitable to continue, that is, until

$$\frac{1}{S(\$/\text{ask}\pounds)} \cdot \frac{1}{S(\pounds/\text{askDM})} \cdot S(\$/\text{bidDM}) \leqslant 1 \tag{2.13}$$

Once again the definitions of middle rates and transaction costs in Equations (2.9) and (2.10) allow us to write condition (2.13) as

$$\frac{1}{S(\$/\pounds)(1+c)} \cdot \frac{1}{S(\pounds/\text{DM})(1+c)} \cdot S(\$/\text{DM})(1-c) \leqslant 1$$

which by rearrangement gives

$$S(\pounds/\text{DM}) \cdot S(\$/\pounds) \cdot \frac{(1+c)^2}{(1-c)} \geqslant S(\$/\text{DM}) \tag{2.14}$$

If we combine conditions (2.12) and (2.14), we produce the limits on the possible variation in the middle value of the exchange rate between dollars and German marks. These limits come about because it is profitable to arbitrage whenever conditions (2.12) and (2.14) do not hold and give us the following:

---

[12] We note that taking reciprocals of exchange rates must be performed carefully. If it takes \$2.00 to buy £1.00 it could take £1.05 to buy \$2.00. What we do know is that $S(\$/\text{ask}\pounds) \equiv 1/[S(\pounds/\text{bid}\$)]$. This is because the act of buying pounds with dollars is the same as selling dollars for pounds. In general, $S(j/\text{ask}i) \equiv 1/[S(i/\text{bid}j)]$, $S(j/\text{bid}i) \equiv 1/[S(i/\text{ask}j)]$.

$$S(\pounds/\mathrm{DM}) \cdot S(\$/\pounds) \cdot \frac{(1+c)^2}{(1-c)} \geqslant S(\$/\mathrm{DM}) \geqslant \frac{(1-c)^2}{(1+c)} \cdot S(\pounds/\mathrm{DM}) \cdot S(\$/\pounds) \quad (2.15)$$

Whenever the exchange rate $S(\$/\mathrm{DM})$ falls outside the range in expression (2.15), where c is the transaction cost (explicit or implicit), arbitragers should get busy. If, for example, $c = 0.001$ of $1/10$ of 1 percent, then $(1+c)^2/(1-c) = 1.003$ and $(1-c)^2/(1+c) = 0.997$. This means that the exchange rate $S(\$/\mathrm{DM})$ can move over a range of $6/10$ of 1 percent without resulting in profitable arbitrage. The explicit transaction costs which the nonprofessional pays to the professional ensure that exchange rates are never outside of the range in expression (2.15).

For the financial manager of a corporation which does not deal primarily in foreign exchange, transaction costs will be larger than the internal costs faced by large banks. The banks' own very low internal costs for time consumed, paperwork, and so on, set the range of variation that the rest of us will observe. There is no point in looking for arbitrage opportunities unless we are working in one of these banks. This means that markets are efficient in the sense that exchange rates move in such a narrow range that no arbitrage profit remains for the nonprofessional.

What we have said does not mean that financial managers should not shop around for the best exchange rate. With exchange rates moving within a range, different banks will be offering very slightly different prices. It is worthwhile for a corporate executive to make a number of telephone calls before making a deal. The financial manager who is working for an importing or exporting firm that needs to buy or sell foreign currencies will gain from being careful. Efficiency does not rule out successful shopping for the ordinary manager. It does, however, rule out gains from trying to be a currency arbitrager.

The conditions we have derived are valid not only for conventional or spot exchange rates but also for *forward* exchange rates. In order to complete our account of the foreign exchange markets, we must examine the market for forward exchange.

SUMMARY

1 The bid-ask or buy-sell on foreign bank notes is high because of inventory costs and other costs of note handling. Exchange rates are often fixed each business day rather than changed continually.

2 The spot foreign exchange market is the market in which bank drafts are exchanged. In this market currencies are received in bank accounts one or two business days after they are ordered.

3 Banks settle between themselves on the same day their customers receive and pay for foreign exchange. Before 1981 the settlement between banks generally added a day before usable Federal Funds were received.

4 Banks use clearing houses to clear balances between themselves if they do not maintain accounts directly with each other. There is more than $100 billion of clearing for international transactions in New York on normal days.

5 The U.S. foreign exchange market consists of a complex network of informal linkages between banks and foreign exchange brokers. The linkages are also international. When

banks are dealing with each other, they quote two-way exchange rates. Intentions are revealed only after rates have been quoted. When banks deal with a foreign exchange broker they state their intentions, and the broker looks for a counterparty. A number of European countries maintain a formal market.

6 Exchange rates are generally quoted in European terms, in units of foreign currency per U.S. dollar. This convention dates from 1979. Newspapers quote only selling rates. When exchange rates are quoted in European terms, we must add points to selling rates to obtain buying rates. The British pound and some other currencies are still quoted in U.S. terms.

7 In the absence of transaction costs, the number of pounds for a dollar, for example, is the reciprocal of the number of dollars for a pound. When there are transaction costs, this rule does not work precisely.

8 In the absence of transaction costs, the many possible cross exchange rates between n different currencies can be obtained by just knowing the $(n - 1)$ values of the currencies against the remaining nth currency. Any standard will do for measurement.

9 When transaction costs are considered, triangular arbitrage ensures only bands around currency values. It pays to shop for the best deal within the variations across different exchange dealers' prices.

10 Arbitrage is profitable only for professionals. The linkages between different currencies are the same in the forward market as in the spot market.

QUESTIONS

1 Do you think that because of the costs of moving bank notes back to their country of circulation, buying bank notes could sometimes be cheaper than buying bank drafts? Could there be a seasonal pattern in exchange rates for bank notes? [*Hint*: Think of what is involved in shipping U.S. dollars arising from Americans spending summers in Europe versus Europeans vacationing in America.]

2 How can companies that issue and sell traveler's checks charge a relatively low fee? How do they profit?

3 Compute the percentage spread on South African rands and Canadian dollars from Table 2.1. Why do you think the spread on Canadian dollars is lower?

4 What steps are involved in settling a purchase made in Britain with a credit card issued by a U.S. bank? How do you think the spread between rates used in credit card payments compares with that for foreign bank notes?

5 Does the use of U.S. dollars as a vehicle currency put U.S. banks at an advantage for making profits? Why do you think the U.S. dollar has become a common vehicle currency?

6 Why do you think that banks give two-way rates when dealing with each other? Why don't they state their intentions as they do when dealing with foreign exchange brokers?

7 Check a recent business newspaper or the business page for spot exchange rates. Form an $n \times n$ exchange rate matrix by computing the cross rates, and check whether $S(\$/£) = 1/[S(£/\$)]$ and so on.

8 Derive the chain-rule condition without transaction costs in Equation (2.5), starting at pounds rather than dollars.

9 Obtain the range for $S(£/\$)$ when there are transaction costs. Start the arbitrage at pounds.

10 Complete the following exchange rate matrix. Assume that there are no transaction costs.

Currency sold	Currency purchased				
	$	**£**	**Sw Fr**	**DM**	**¥**
$	1	2.0	0.6	0.5	0.005
£		1			
Sw Fr			1		
DM				1	
¥					1

11 Given that there are 0.25 U.S. dollars ($0.25) to 1.00 French franc (Fr1.00) and 2.00 French Francs (Fr2.00) to 1.00 Swiss franc (Sw Fr1.00) where these are middle exchange rates, and given transaction costs of 0.1 percent, that is, 0.001 of the transaction, what exchange values are possible between the dollar and the Swiss franc?

12 Why do you think exchange rates are stated in terms of U.S. dollars? Do you think the reason is the volume of trade that occurs in U.S. dollars?

BIBLIOGRAPHY

Aliber, Robert Z. (ed.): *The International Market for Foreign Exchange*, Frederick A. Praeger, Inc., New York, 1969.

Corporate Foreign Exposure Management, Citibank, New York, 1975.

Deardorff, Alan V.: "One-Way Arbitrage and Its Implications for the Foreign Exchange Markets," *Journal of Political Economy,* vol. 87, April 1979, pp. 351–364.

Einzig, Paul: *A Textbook on Foreign Exchange*, Macmillan and Company, London, 1966.

Frenkel, Jacob A., and Richard M. Levich: "Covered Interest Arbitrage: Unexploited Profits?" *Journal of Political Economy*, vol. 83, spring 1975, pp. 325–338.

Grubel, Herbert G.: *International Economics*, Richard D. Irwin, Homewood, Ill., 1977, chap. 10.

Kubarych, Roger M.: *Foreign Exchange Markets in the United States*, Federal Reserve Bank of New York, 1978.

Reihl, Heinz, and Rita M. Rodriguez: *Foreign Exchange Markets*, McGraw-Hill Book Company, New York, 1977.

Rodriguez, Rita M., and E. Eugene Carter: *International Financial Management*, 2d ed. Prentice-Hall, Inc., Englewood Cliffs, N.J., 1979, chap. 5.

Syrett, W. W.: *A Manual of Foreign Exchange*, 6th ed., Sir Isaac Pitman, London, 1960.

CHAPTER 3

FORWARD EXCHANGE AND CURRENCY FUTURES

It would be difficult to overstate the importance of forward exchange and currency futures. Indeed, a financial manager of a firm with overseas interests may find himself or herself as much involved with future exchange as with spot exchange. Forward exchange and currency futures are valuable for avoiding risks arising from changes in currency values when importing, exporting, borrowing, or investing. Forwards and futures are also used by speculators. This chapter explains the nature of these extremely important markets, while later chapters, especially Chapters 7 and 9, show how the markets can be effectively used.

FORWARD EXCHANGE

What Is Forward Foreign Exchange?

We have already indicated in the previous chapter that there is a market for forward exchange that exists alongside the spot market for bank notes and drafts. Because the 1- or 2-day delivery period for spot transactions is so short, when comparing spot rates with forward or future exchange rates, we can usefully think of spot rates as exchange rates for undelayed transactions. On the other hand, forward or future exchange rates involve an arrangement to delay the exchange of currencies until some future date. A useful working definition is:

> The forward or future exchange rate is the rate that is contracted today for the delivery of a currency at a specified date in the future, at a price agreed upon today.

In the case of both forward and future exchange, payment is not made until delivery.

Our definition applies to both *forward exchange* and *currency futures*. However, there are institutional differences between these two that can cause confusion. These differences should be cleared up before we deal with each of them separately.

Forward Exchange versus Currency Futures

If we look back at Figure 2.1, we note that for Britain, Canada, France, Japan, Switzerland, and West Germany, we are given exchange rates for 30-day, 90-day, and 180-day forwards. Although they are not quoted in the table, 30-day rates, 90-day rates, 180-day rates, and so on, can also be found for many other currencies. In addition, there are rates for maturities other than 30 days, 90 days, and so on. These forward exchange rates are quoted by Bankers Trust Company, a bank. They should be distinguished from currency futures.

Currency futures do not involve commercial banks. Moreover, they are traded in a limited number of formal futures exchanges—such as the IMM (International Monetary Market) in Chicago—which are physical locations rather like stock exchanges. The currency futures are contracts drawn up between the futures dealers and their clients. Forward exchange contracts, on the other hand, are drawn up between banks and their clients. They frequently involve two banks. The market does not have a physical being but instead is similar to the spot market, with an informal structure of telephone and cable linkages. To summarize what we have said:

Forward exchange contracts involve agreements between banks and their clients, who are frequently other banks. They are made in informal markets. Currency futures involve agreements between futures dealers and their customers. They trade in a specialized formal futures exchange.[1]

How Forward Exchange Works

Figure 2.1 tells us that on October 8, 1981, a client dealing in over $1 million in bank draft form could have purchased spot U.K. sterling from Bankers Trust at $1.8930/£. This would have meant delivery of the sterling to the client's account on October 12, 1981, two business days after the order. If, however, this client wished to have the pounds in about 30 days rather than "immediately," then it would have been necessary to pay $1.8933/£, which is $0.0003 or 3 points more than the rate for spot delivery. The term *point* in the forward exchange market has the same meaning as in the spot market. A point is the last digit in the exchange rate quotation.

In a similar way, Figure 2.1 gives the exchange rate for the delivery of Canadian dollars in 30 days as Can$1.2031/$. This is a lower value of the Canadian dollar (that is, more Canadian dollars per U.S. dollar) than the spot rate of Can$1.1991/$. Forward exchange contracts state the date on which the foreign currency will be

---

[1] The reader is warned that in trading, foreign exchange dealers in banks will call their contracts both futures and forwards, knowing that their counterparts understand what they mean. We shall keep a careful distinction between the two to avoid confusion.

received. There is no need to worry about clearing or delivery delays beyond this date. Checks can be written immediately against the funds.

When we must pay more for forward delivery than for spot delivery of a foreign currency, as we do in the case of sterling in Figure 2.1, we say that the foreign exchange is at a *forward premium*. When we can pay less for forward delivery than for spot delivery, as we do in the case of the Canadian dollar in Figure 2.1, we say that the forward currency is at a *forward discount*.[2] Let us carefully define these terms.

Forward Exchange Premiums and Discounts

In order to define premiums and discounts on forward exchange, let us express the forward exchange rate in terms similar to those used for spot rates:

Define F_n ($\$/\pounds$) as the *n*-year forward exchange rate of dollars to pounds.

In Figure 2.1, $F_{1/4}(\$/\pounds) = \$1.8960/\pounds$, $F_{1/2}(\$/\pounds) = \$1.9000/\pounds$, and so on. More generally, F_n (i/j) is the *n*-year forward rate of currency i to currency j.

The *n*-year forward exchange premium or discount of pounds versus dollars, on an annual basis, is defined as follows:

$$\text{Premium}/\text{Discount (}\pounds \text{ vs. } \$) = \frac{F_n(\$/\pounds) - S(\$/\pounds)}{nS(\$/\pounds)} \tag{3.1}$$

Generally, this is multiplied by 100 to put it in percentage terms. We also convert forward premiums and discounts into annual terms by dividing by n, because this is invariably the way interest rates are quoted, and we wish to be able to compare forward premiums in these same terms. Using the values in Figure 2.1, we find that (3.1) is positive and equal to 0.0019 or 0.19 percent for the 1-month forward pound premium. That is,

$$\text{Premium}/\text{Discount (}\pounds \text{ vs. } \$) = \frac{1.8933 - 1.8930}{^1/_{12} \times 1.8930} = 0.0019$$

This is a premium on the pound versus the dollar, because the pound costs approximately one-fifth of 1 percent (per annum) more for forward delivery than for spot delivery.[3]

---

[2] Some people would say that when the spot Canadian dollar is worth less than a U.S. dollar, as it is in Figure 2.1, it is at a discount. This is totally different from a forward discount. Indeed, we often observe that the Canadian dollar is at a forward premium while it is *at a discount against the U.S. dollar*. Conventions are hard to change, so the reader is warned to be careful of the misleading common use of terms.

[3] More generally, the *n*-year premium/discount of currency i versus currency j is

$$\text{Premium}/\text{Discount (}i \text{ vs. } j) = \frac{F_n(j/i) - S(j/i)}{nS(j/i)}$$

Note that for the premium of i versus j, the j and i are reversed in the exchange rate terms.

When the pound is at a forward premium against the dollar, then this is precisely the same as saying that the dollar is at a forward discount against the pound. Clearly, when pounds cost more for forward delivery than for spot delivery against dollars, dollars must cost less against pounds. Indeed, the n-year annualized forward premium/discount of the dollar versus the pound is

$$\text{Premium/Discount (\$ vs. £)} = \frac{F_n(\pounds/\$) - S(\pounds/\$)}{nS(\pounds/\$)} \qquad (3.2)$$

which from Figure 2.1 gives a discount (since the value is negative) of -0.0023 or -0.23 percent for 1 month, or $n = {}^1/_{12}$ year forward.[4]

The fact that most currencies are quoted in European terms (number of units of foreign currency per U.S. dollar rather than the other way around) does not affect our definition of premiums or discounts. The n-year annualized premium/discount of, for example, the dollar versus the Deutsche mark is

$$\text{Premium/Discount (\$ vs. DM)} = \frac{F_n(\text{DM}/\$) - S(\text{DM}/\$)}{nS(\text{DM}/\$)} \qquad (3.3)$$

Equations (3.3), (3.1), and (3.2) show that we always obtain the premium or discount of the currency given before "versus" and after the oblique. As always, a discount of, for example, dollars versus marks will be a premium of marks versus dollars.[5] Table 3.1 gives the forward premiums and discounts of all forward currencies quoted in Figure 2.1.

Forward premiums and discounts are known by other names. Frequently, the term *spot-forward spread* or just *forward spread* is used. Some market traders refer to premiums or discounts as forward *pickups* or *markdowns*. We shall stick with "premiums" and "discounts." These terms will be understood by almost everyone who deals in the forward market.

Conventions in Quoting Forward Exchange

It is easy to see from Figure 2.1 that forward exchange quotations are common in a limited number of currencies—those that are most heavily traded. This was clearly shown in a survey of 44 New York banks by the Federal Reserve Bank of New York in April 1977. The percentages of overall turnover activity in the major currencies are given in Table 3.2, which shows that over 88% of the turnover activity is in the six currencies in which most international trade is conducted, and for which forwards are quoted in Figure 2.1. The exchange rate quotations in Figure 2.1 also show that forward exchange quotations, even on the heavily traded currencies, are provided only for specific and relatively short periods. The table, however, hides the variety of dates and features that appear on different forward exchange contracts.

---

[4] There is a small difference between the numerical value of the pound-versus-dollar premium and the numerical value of the dollar-versus-pound discount, that is, 0.0019 versus 0.0023. This is because of bid-ask spreads and because of the base-selection problem in taking percentage differences.

[5] In the event that forward rates and spot rates are equal, we say that the forward currency is *flat*.

TABLE 3.1
PREMIUM (+) OR DISCOUNT (−) PERCENTAGES ON FORWARD EXCHANGE VIS-À-VIS U.S. DOLLARS

Pound sterling (£ prem./$ disc.)			Canadian dollar (Can$ prem./$ disc.)			French franc (Fr prem./$ disc.)		
30 days	90 days	180 days	30 days	90 days	180 days	30 days	90 days	180 days
+0.19	+0.63	+0.74	−3.89	−2.78	−2.43	−3.98	−3.10	−2.65
−0.23	−0.61	−0.72	+4.00	+2.80	+2.45	+4.34	+3.08	+2.71

Table 3.1 is derived from Figure 2.1 using the formula Premium/Discount $(i \text{ vs. } j) = \dfrac{F_n(j/i) - S(j/i)}{nS(j/i)} \cdot 100$,

where n is the number of years forward. The discounts/premiums on the U.S. dollar (bottom row) do not precisely equal the negative of the foreign exchange premiums/discounts (top row) because of the base-selection problem in computing percentage differences and because of bid-ask spreads.

The 30-day, 90-day, and 180-day quotations in Figure 2.1 are for interbank transactions, and banks do tend to deal among themselves in terms of these "even" dates. However, when dealing with their customers, banks will draw up contracts for periods of a couple of days up to a couple of years, and these periods do not have to be in even multiples of 30 or anything else. On October 8, 1982, a corporate buyer of sterling might well want to take delivery of pounds on June 22, 1983, to meet a sterling obligation that will come due on that date. Forward currency is bought or sold for the value date, June 22, 1983, and this is the day that usable funds will be obtained. Since in the case of most currencies the spot market value date is already 2 business days in the future, the shortest forward contracts are for a period of 3 days.

Sometimes buyers and sellers of forward exchange are not precisely sure when they will need their foreign currency or when they will receive it. For example, a U.S.

TABLE 3.2
THE IMPORTANCE OF DIFFERENT CURRENCIES IN THE NEW YORK FOREIGN EXCHANGE MARKET, IN PERCENTAGES

German mark	27.3
Canadian dollar	19.2
Pound sterling	17.0
Swiss franc	13.8
French franc	6.3
Netherlands guilder	5.7
Japanese yen	5.3
Belgian franc	1.5
Italian lira	1.1
All other	2.8
	100.0

Source: Survey by the Federal Reserve Bank of New York, April 1977.

TABLE 3.1
(Continued)

Japanese yen (¥ prem./$ disc.)			Swiss franc (Sw Fr prem./$ disc.)			Deutsche mark (DM prem./$ disc.)		
30 days	90 days	180 days	30 days	90 days	180 days	30 days	90 days	180 days
+9.61	+9.15	+8.88	+5.81	+6.04	+6.11	+4.23	+4.94	+4.85
−9.45	−8.92	−8.48	−5.80	−5.90	−5.90	−4.14	−4.90	−4.72

importer may know that he or she must pay a British producer 30 days after delivery of the goods, but the exact date of delivery may not be known; delivery might be "towards the end of May." To take care of this, banks will sell forward exchange with some flexibility, allowing the buyer to take delivery of foreign exchange "during the last 10 days of June" or according to some other flexible scheme. Flexibility will cost the buyer a little more, but it will relieve the buyer of considerable worry in case he or she needs the foreign currency before an agreed-upon forward date or has to take delivery of foreign exchange before the agreed forward date of sale of the foreign currency.

The conventions used in quoting forward rates need explanation, since there are two different methods in common use. Forward currencies are quoted both *outright* and as *swaps*. Outright quotations are similar in form to spot exchange rate quotations; they involve the rate of exchange expressed as so many units of one currency for another. European terms—the number of foreign units per dollar—are used for the same currencies that have European-term spot rate quotations. Let us first deal with outright quotations and ask what you would have heard if you had called Bankers Trust on October 8, 1981, for forward quotations and the bank had given you the rates in outright form.

An outright quotation on 30-day British sterling could have been given as 1.8923/33. This means that the bank will buy sterling at $1.8923/£ and sell it at a price 10 points higher, or $1.8933/£. (We note that banks generally quote their "bid" first and then their "ask.") Again, as in the spot market, when the bank quotes its buying and selling rates, it will stand ready to either buy or sell, and the inquirer does not have to specify beforehand what he or she intends to do. Because the first two decimal places could well be assumed to be already known, the outright quotation could be just 23/33. A 30-day quote on Deutsche marks, because European terms are used, could be 2.1984/74 or 84/74, meaning that the bank will buy marks at DM2.1984/$ and sell them at the higher mark value of DM2.1974/$.

When forward rates are quoted in swap rather than outright form, the person who calls a bank will be given the spot exchange rate and an amount in points which must be either added to or subtracted from the spot rate to obtain the forward rate. The need to add or subtract depends both on whether U.S. or European terms are used and on whether the foreign exchange is at a premium or discount. Experience tells banks and their clients what is meant by each quotation. We can learn by examples.

A person who calls Bankers Trust and is given the quotation for forward sterling in terms of swaps would hear "Spot 1.8920/30; 30-day 2 over 3; 90-day 28 over 30; 180-day 66 over 70." We can write this as follows:

Spot	**30-day**	**90-day**	**180-day**
1.8920/30	2/3	28/30	66/70

These quotations correspond to the values in Table 3.3. The reader will observe that the swaps provide the same selling rates as those that are quoted outright in Figure 2.1 and that spreads become larger as we move forward.

Table 3.3 is obtained by adding the swap points to the spot bid and offer quotations. We add because on October 8, 1981, sterling was at a premium against the dollar. If sterling had been at a discount, the swap points would have been subtracted. You might well wonder how you are supposed to know whether there is a premium or discount on sterling. Often the bank will tell. If it does not, it is possible to determine this from the order of the swap points. As an example, if the bank quotes

Spot	**30-day**	**90-day**	**180-day**
1.8920/30	5/4	22/20	30/26

you can see that the forward swap points have higher numbers before the oblique, and so the client should know that sterling is at a discount. This is because bank spreads always increase on more distant forwards, and this is what happens when we subtract swap points to obtain Table 3.4. If we had added rather than subtracted the swap points, we would have made the bank's buying and selling rates move toward each other at more distant forwards, which is never the case. We learn to add when the order of swap points is ascending and the exchange quotation is in U.S. terms.

When European terms are used, the rule of ascending versus descending order

TABLE 3.3
BIDS AND OFFERS ON STERLING
(U.S. Dollars/£ Sterling)

Type of exchange	Bank buys/bids	Bank sells/offers
Spot	1.8920	1.8930
30-day	1.8922	1.8933
90-day	1.8948	1.8960
180-day	1.8986	1.9000

TABLE 3.4
BIDS AND OFFERS ON STERLING
(U.S. Dollars/£ Sterling)

Type of exchange	Bank buys/bids	Bank sells/offers
Spot	1.8920	1.8930
30-day	1.8915	1.8926
90-day	1.8898	1.8910
180-day	1.8890	1.8904

must be reversed. An example will illustrate this. If Deutsche marks are quoted

Spot	**30-day**	**90-day**	**180-day**
2.2060/50	72/76	255/270	488/520

you can see that the forward swap points are higher after the oblique, and so these points must be subtracted to obtain the outrights. These are given in Table 3.5. We see that the procedure provides the quoted forward outright selling prices for the mark listed in Figure 2.1 and gives the required larger spreads on more distant forwards. We learn that with European terms, when forward swap points are in ascending order and higher after the oblique, we must subtract them from the spot rates. What we do for U.S. terms we reverse for European terms. This is summarized in Table 3.6—and it can make life difficult. Only those with experience can do business without mistakes. Nevertheless, mistakes do occur, and banks honor their agreements. A law of survival holds. Those brokers who make more than a couple of errors are no longer brokers. As a consequence, exchange brokers are young—the majority are under 35—and excel in accurate and quick thinking.

The pieces of paper providing forward contracts give the agreed-upon forward exchange rate in outright terms. In addition to the exchange rate, the contracts contain the following information:

1 Name of the primary party
2 Name of the counterparty
3 Value date
4 Total dollar value of contract
5 Specifics for delivery of foreign exchange and dollars, including details of location, bank accounts, and so on

The majority of forward contracts do not exist as outright agreements but instead take the form of swaps. According to the 1977 survey conducted by the Federal Reserve Bank of New York, while spot transactions made up 55 percent of bank foreign exchange turnover in the 44 commercial banks surveyed, swaps made up 40 percent, leaving only 5 percent for outright forward agreements. The two different methods of quoting forward rates that we have described correspond to these two types of agreements. The outright agreements, generally between banks and

TABLE 3.5
BIDS AND OFFERS ON DEUTSCHE MARKS
(Deutsche Marks/Dollar)

Type of exchange	Bank buys/bids	Bank sells/offers
Spot	2.2060	2.2050
30-day	2.1988	2.1974
90-day	2.1805	2.1780
180-day	2.1572	2.1530

TABLE 3.6
CONVERTING SWAP TO OUTRIGHT QUOTATION
This table tells us whether to add swap points to the spot exchange rate or subtract swap points to obtain the outright forward rate. It also tells us whether this gives a forward rate that is at a premium or a forward rate that is at a discount on the foreign currency.

Point order	Terms	
	European	U.S.
Ascending	Subtract swap/ foreign premium	Add swap/ foreign premium
Descending	Add swap/ foreign discount	Subtract swap/ foreign discount

nonbank customers, are for a straightforward purchase or sale of a forward currency. Swaps, which could be between banks or between a bank and a large corporation, involve two exchanges and, consequently, two contracts.[6]

We can define swaps as follows:

A foreign exchange swap is an agreement to both buy and sell foreign exchange at prespecified contracted exchange rates, where the buying and selling are separated in time.

The most common form of swap is to have the original trade as a spot exchange and the second trade as a forward exchange. Indeed, this is the reason the method of adding points to the spot rate to obtain the forward rate is called a *swap quotation*. Such swaps are called *spot-forward* swaps where the trader buys (sells) on the spot market while simultaneously selling (buying) on the forward market, hence reversing the original exchange. When the reversal is on adjacent days, the term *rollover* is used. Large banks also do *forward-forward* swaps, which involve buying and selling with the offsetting contracts both being forward exchange agreements.

Swaps are very valuable to those who are investing or borrowing abroad. For

---

[6] While swap agreements will invariably be quoted in swap form, outright agreements could also be quoted in swap form. Conventions for quoting rates must be distinguished from the forms of contract even though there is close correspondence.

example, a person who invests in a foreign treasury bill can use a spot-forward swap to avoid foreign exchange risk. The investor sells forward the maturity value of the bill at the same time the spot foreign exchange is purchased. Since a known amount of the investor's local currency will be delivered according to the forward contract, no uncertainty from exchange rates is faced. In a similar way, those who borrow in foreign money markets can buy forward the foreign currency needed for repayment at the same time they convert the borrowed foreign funds on the spot market. The value of swaps to international investors and borrowers helps explain their popularity.

While valuable to investors and borrowers, the swap is not very useful to importers and exporters. Payments and receipts in international trade are frequently delayed. However, it is an outright forward purchase of foreign exchange that is valuable to the importer, not a swap. Similarly, the exporter needs to make an outright forward sale of foreign exchange. This is not, however, the place to present the details of these uses of forward exchange or the details of the value of forward exchange to borrowers and investors. You must wait until Part 3.

Swaps are popular with banks because it is difficult to avoid risk while trading in specific future days with so many markets to worry about—there are different markets for each future day. On some days a bank will be *long* in foreign exchange, which means that it has agreed to purchase more foreign currency than it has agreed to sell or already holds more than it wants. On other days, it will be *short*, having agreed to sell more than it had agreed to buy. If, for example, bank A considers itself long on current holdings of British pounds (because it holds more than it wants) and short on 30-day forwards (because of net forward sales), it will find another bank, bank B, in the reverse position. Bank A will sell pounds spot and buy pounds forward, and bank B will do the opposite. In this manner, both banks can balance their spot versus forward positions while economizing on the number of transactions that will achieve this. The use of only even-dated contracts leaves some exposure to remaining long and short positions from day to day. These are then covered with rollover swaps. In this way swap agreements allow the banks to exchange their surpluses and shortages of individual currencies to offset spot and forward trades with their customers. It should be no surprise that matching customer trades with appropriate swaps is a complex and dynamic problem.[7]

CURRENCY FUTURES

What Is a Currency Future?

Currency futures are traded in a formal marketplace such as the International Monetary Market (IMM) of the Chicago Mercantile Exchange. The IMM began

[7]The reader is referred to the many other accounts of this dynamic market. *Foreign Exchange Markets in the United States*, by Roger Kubarych (Federal Reserve Bank of New York, 1978) is an excellent source which replaces the classic account, *The New York Foreign Exchange Market*, written by Alan Holmes and Francis Schott and published in 1965 by the same bank. Other valuable sources include Paul Einzig, *A Dynamic Theory of Forward Exchange*, Macmillan and Company, London, 1966; Rita Rodriguez and E. Eugene Carter, *International Financial Management*, 2d ed., Prentice-Hall, Inc., Englewood Cliffs, N.J., 1979, chap. 5; and David Eiteman and Arthur Stonehill, *Multinational Business Finance*, 2d ed., Addison-Wesley Publishing Company, Reading, Mass., 1973.

dealing in the leading currencies in 1972, and since then, other markets in North America and Europe have considered opening or have opened futures markets.[8]

Currency futures are relatively homogeneous contracts that are traded like conventional commodity futures. In order to keep the contracts homogeneous so that a market is made, it is necessary to have relatively few value dates. At the Chicago IMM, there are four value dates of contracts—the third Wednesday in the months of March, June, September, and December. Contracts are traded in whole units—£25,000, Can$100,000, and so on. This enables the traders to keep track of prices and buy in terms of numbers of contracts. Some of the currencies that are traded, along with their contract size as of late 1981, are shown in Table 3.7.

Because of the homogeneity required to make a market in currency futures, these contracts are not quite as valuable as forward contracts in offsetting planned purchases or sales of foreign exchange and hence in avoiding foreign exchange risk. The value date on the contract will only rarely coincide with the firm's needs. In addition, since fractions of contracts are not traded, the precise amount which the firm might wish to offset cannot be handled. Forward contracts with banks, unlike currency futures, allow greater flexibility. Forward contracts can be written for the exact date on which foreign funds are to be received or paid and for the exact amount. Because of this greater flexibility, most importers and exporters, as well as larger borrowers and lenders, prefer forward exchange contracts with banks to currency futures. Currency futures are most valuable to speculators, who can take any profit by selling back their contract. Speculation with forward exchange requires reversing original transactions and waiting for contracts to mature.

Both buyers and sellers of currency futures make futures contracts with the exchange rather than with each other. In doing this, it is necessary to post a *margin* and pay the broker a fee. The margin is posted to ensure that bad deals are honored, and it must be supplemented if the equity position falls below a certain level, called the *maintenance level*. If, for example, the margin on sterling is $3000 on each contract and the maintenance level is $2500, then if the value of the contract falls on the futures market by more than $500, the full amount of the decline in value must be added to the margin account. Falls in the contract value which leave more than $2500 of equity will not require action. Margin adjustment is done on a daily basis.

Banks require no margin from their larger clients for forward exchange contracts. They will, however, generally reduce the client's existing line of credit. For example, if a bank has granted a client a $1 million line of credit and the customer trades $10 million forward, the bank is likely to reduce the credit line by, perhaps, $500,000, or 5 percent of the contract. In more volatile times, a credit-line reduction of up to 10 percent is likely. For customers without credit lines, the bank will require that a margin be established within a special account. The margin on forward contracts earns interest at prevailing market rates. It is therefore not a cost to those buying or selling currency futures. Instead, the margin serves as a security to the bank. The procedure for maintaining the margin in the forward contract

---

[8] The Chicago IMM is the largest currency futures exchange in the United States. Currency futures are also exchanged on the COMEX commodities exchange in New York and on the American Board of Trade as well as in centers outside the United States.

TABLE 3.7
THE MARKET FOR CURRENCY FUTURES

British pound (IMM)—£25,000; dollars per pound

Date	Open	High	Low	Settle	Open interest
Dec.	1.8910	1.9090	1.8820	1.9085	11,643
Mar. 1982	1.8930	1.9135	1.8855	1.9135	953
June	1.9060	1.9175	1.9010	1.9170	133

Canadian dollar (IMM)—Can$100,000; dollars per Canadian dollar

Date	Open	High	Low	Settle	Open interest
Dec.	.8295	.8298	.8280	.8291	5,629
Mar. 1982	.8242	.8255	.8237	.8252	761
June	–	–	–	.8207	215
Sept.	–	–	–	.8182	83

Japanese yen (IMM)—¥1.25 million; cents per yen

Date	Open	High	Low	Settle	Open interest
Dec.	.4440	.4461	.4428	.4458	7,425
Mar. 1982	.4540	.4559	.4528	.4555	746
June	–	–	–	.4630	1

Swiss franc (IMM)—Sw Fr125,000; dollars per franc

Date	Open	High	Low	Settle	Open interest
Dec.	.5350	.5445	.5349	.5438	12,603
Mar. 1982	.5422	.5500	.5422	.5449	1,243
June	–	–	–	.5560	67
Sept.	–	–	–	.5580	3

West German mark (IMM)—DM125,000; dollars per mark

Date	Open	High	Low	Settle	Open interest
Dec.	.4528	.4590	.4527	.4588	10,920
Mar. 1982	.4590	.4643	.4590	.4643	765
June	–	–	–	.4680	85
Sept.	–	–	–	.4720	3

depends on the bank's relationship with the customer. Margin will be *called*—requiring supplementary funds to be deposited in the margin account—if large, unfavorable movements occur.

As in many commodity futures markets, daily price variation limits are established on currency futures. For example, if the value of the pound in the forward market suddenly and dramatically fell by 10 percent, the futures price would be allowed to fall by only about 2 percent, the daily limit. It would be allowed to fall again on the next trading day. If this were still insufficient, the maximum allowable price movement would be raised on the next 2 days, by 150 and 200 percent of the original limit, and finally, if the limit were achieved for 4 days in a row, it would be removed. The limit is supposed to give participants a chance to maintain their margins and to cool off when conditions are uncertain, but it often means that no market exists at times when the equilibrium price is beyond the allowable movement.

Table 3.7 shows that in the Chicago IMM, exchange rates are quoted in U.S. terms—as so many dollars per foreign currency unit. "Open interest" refers to the number of outstanding contracts. Liquidation occurs when a holder of a currency future sells it back to the dealer instead of holding it to maturity.

Since the table is for October 8, the December contracts are the only remaining contracts for that year. We see that the number of outstanding contracts drops off substantially after December. The market is relatively "thin" when we go more than a couple of contracts into the future. Contracts go forward 12 months. Table 3.8 summarizes the nature of currency futures and forward contracts.

TABLE 3.8
FORWARD CONTRACTS VERSUS CURRENCY FUTURES

	Forward contracts	Currency futures
Counterparty	Commercial bank	Futures exchange
Maturity date	Any date	Third Wednesday of March, June, September, or December
Maximum length	1 or 2 years, occasionally more	12 months
Contracted amount	Any value	Multiples of £25,000, Can$100,000, etc.
Secondary market	Must offset with bank	Can sell to exchange
Margin requirement	Line of credit, 5%–10% on account	Fixed sum, e.g., $3000
Contract variety	Swap or outright form	Outright
Major users	Primarily hedgers	Used frequently by speculators

The Link between the Futures and Forward Markets

The market for currency futures is small compared with the market for forwards. A daily volume of over $1 billion in currency futures is not very common, but in the forward market the trading volume can exceed 20 or even 50 times this amount.[9] Despite the relatively large difference in the sizes of the two markets, there is a mutual interdependence between them; each one is able to impact on the other. This interdependence is the result of the action of arbitragers who take offsetting positions in the two markets when prices differ. The most straightforward type of arbitrage involves outright forward and futures positions.[10]

If, for example, the 3-month forward buying price of pounds were $1.8960/£ while the selling price on the same date on the Chicago IMM were $1.8980/£, an arbitrager could buy forward from a bank and sell forward on the IMM. The arbitrager would make $0.0020/£ so that on each contract for £25,000, he or she could make a profit of $50. However, we should remember that since the futures market requires maintenance or "settling-up" as daily contract prices vary, the arbitrage involves risk which can allow the futures and forward rates to differ. It should also be clear that the degree to which middle exchange rates on the two markets can deviate will depend very much on the spreads between buying and selling prices. Arbitrage will ensure that the ask price of forward currency does not significantly exceed the bid price of currency futures and vice versa. However, the prices can differ a little due to risk from settling-up. We should also note that the direction of influence is not invariably from the rate set on the larger forward market to the small futures market. When there is a move on the Chicago IMM that results in a very large number of margins being called, the scramble to close positions with sudden buying or selling can spill over into the forward market.

Currency Options

It is important to recognize that neither forward exchange contracts nor currency futures are *options*. With an option, the holder has the choice of whether or not to exercise an agreement. For example, an American call option on the stock of the XYZ company might give the holder the right to buy a certain number of shares of XYZ at, for example, $50 per share before a particular date.[11] If the market price of XYZ's shares is below $50 on the expiry date, then the option has no value, and it will not be exercised. It will be thrown away.

Forward exchange and currency futures contracts must be exercised. It is true that a currency future can be sold back to the futures exchange. Indeed, as can be

[9] See Rolf von Pfefer, "The Influence of the IMM," *Euromoney*, January 1980, pp. 89–91. This shows how the currency futures can affect the forward exchange rate.

[10] There can also be arbitrage involving offsetting swaps in the two markets. We can note that even without any arbitrage, the rates for forward contracts and currency futures will be kept in line by users of these markets choosing between them if the rates differ just a little.

[11] A call option gives the right to *purchase* a stock at a certain price. A put option gives the right to *sell* at a certain price. American options can be exercised on any day before the final exercise date, while a European option can be exercised only on a particular date. For more on the types of options and the factors affecting their value, see Richard Brealey and Stewart Myers, *Principles of Corporate Finance*, McGraw-Hill Book Company, New York, 1981, pp. 422–442.

seen from open-interest figures, this is a common practice. In addition, a forward contract can be offset by going into a reverse agreement with a bank. For example, if on October 8 a company has agreed to buy £1 million at $F_{1/4}(\$/£)$ for delivery on January 8 and a month later, on November 8, it decides it does not need the pounds, it can sell them forward 2 months at the rate $F_{1/6}(\$/£)$. The purchase and sale of pounds will cancel—and the company will earn or lose the amount $\$[F_{1/6}(\$/£) - F_{1/4}(\$/£)] \times 1,000,000$. However, all outstanding forward contracts and currency futures must be honored by both parties on the delivery date. That is, the bank, its customers, the futures exchange, and those holding outstanding futures must settle. There is no option allowing a party to settle only if it is to that party's advantage.

There is an interesting example of the creation of a pseudo call provision in the currency markets. This was done in December 1979 to help a large U.S. insurance broker, Marsh and McLennan Company, in its attempt to take over a British insurance company, C. T. Bowring and Company (a member of Lloyds of London).[12]

Marsh and McLennan made a cash-and-share takeover bid for C. T. Bowring and Company that required it to promise to pay £130 million. At the time of making its offer, it did not know whether the bid would succeed. Rather than take a chance on the exchange rate that might prevail on the takeover settlement date, Marsh and McLennan wanted to buy a call option for £130 million that it could exercise only if its effort did succeed. Bankers Trust agreed to provide an option which could be exercised on or before June 15, 1980, 6 months after the original agreement. The company made its request to a number of banks and stated that it paid a "slight premium" for its option. The bid did succeed, and the option was duly exercised.

According to Marsh and McLennan, many banks were surprised at the request for pounds, based on a contingency. However, we can note that conventional currency options, which began trading in Philadelphia and Montreal in 1982, can be used more generally to avoid downside risk by buying/selling currencies which are to be paid/received in the future.

Who Uses Forwards and Futures?

Forward exchange contracts are valuable for a number of purposes. The users of forward markets are:

1 Those who invest abroad
2 Those who borrow abroad
3 Importers
4 Exporters
5 Speculators

The investors, borrowers, importers, and exporters use the forward market to reduce their foreign exchange risks or exposure. This behavior we have already described as *hedging* or *covering*. Speculators, who also trade in currency futures,

---

[12] This interesting case is described in "Marsh and McLennan Insures Takeover Exposure with Call Provision," Business International, *Money Report*, June 13, 1980.

use the forward and currency futures markets to purposely take risks or an exposed position in the hope of profiting from exchange rate movements.

As we have already indicated in our discussions of swaps, the investor who wishes to avoid risks when sending funds abroad will, at the same time that spot foreign exchange is purchased, sell forward the foreign exchange to be received on the investment. In this way, the investor is able to calculate the amount his or her investment will yield in terms of the domestic currency, whatever happens to spot rates. As we have also indicated, the borrower from abroad will, at the same time that the borrowed funds are converted to domestic currency on the spot market, buy forward foreign exchange to cover the repayments on the debt. This makes it possible to calculate the costs of borrowing in different national markets, independent of what might happen to exchange rates. Importers use the forward market to obtain the currencies needed to pay for their purchases in foreign markets. In a similar way, international travelers could buy currency needs ahead of time to be sure of the cost. This is not, however, very common. Exporters can sell forward their foreign exchange proceeds for their domestic currency, despite the delay until payment. Any change in the spot exchange rate between the time that import or export prices are set and the time of settlement will be irrelevant if the foreign currency has been purchased or sold forward. By using the forward market in this way, importers and exporters can avoid risks of changes in exchange rates.

Speculators take positions in the forward exchange market according to the forward rates that currently prevail and their beliefs about future spot rates. For example, speculators will buy forward currencies for which they expect spot values in the future to exceed the current forward price for the same date. It is too early in this book to look at the details of speculation in the forward market or at the specifics of the employment of forward exchange by borrowers, investors, importers, and exporters. This should be left until we have examined the international economic environment in which exchange rates are determined. Our brief sketch has been given here only to reveal the potential importance of the currency forwards and futures.

The factors that affect exchange rates are summarized in the statistics of the balance of payments. The precise way in which exchange rates are determined by these factors depends upon the type of exchange rate system that is in effect. There are two general types of systems that have existed—those with *fixed rates* and those with *flexible rates*. We must examine the workings of these systems and the nature of the balance of payments before we can turn to the detailed account of managerial decision making in the frequently complex international economic environment.

SUMMARY

1 Forward exchange and currency futures allow the purchase or sale of foreign exchange for a future date at a precontracted exchange rate. Both exist in a limited number of currencies.

2 Forward exchange contracts are made by banks in a market similar to the spot market. Currency futures are made in a formal market, where they are traded like commodity futures.

3 Forward contracts can be made for any value date but rarely extend more than 2 years forward. Bankers tend to concentrate on even dates—30 days, 90 days, 180 days—when trading among themselves.

4 A forward premium exists on the foreign currency when forward foreign exchange is more expensive than spot foreign exchange. The forward premium on foreign currency is the discount on domestic currency.

5 Forward exchange rates are quoted outright and as swaps. Swap quotations involve the spot rate and the swap points to be added or subtracted. The need to add or subtract depends on whether there is a forward premium or a discount and on whether European or U.S. terms are used. The presence of a premium or discount can be judged by the order of swap points and the European or U.S. terms of quotation.

6 Swaps involve a double trade—usually a spot trade reversed by a forward trade. They are heavily exchanged between banks in even-dated form so that the banks can keep down their foreign exchange exposure in an efficient manner.

7 Swaps are particularly valuable to international borrowers and investors. They are not so valuable to importers and exporters.

8 Currency futures are traded in specialized markets in numbers of standard contract units. Margins are posted and maintained.

9 Forward exchange and futures contracts are not options. All outstanding contracts must be honored.

10 Forward markets are used by investors, borrowers, importers, exporters, and speculators. The speculators also use currency futures and take those risks which others wish to avoid.

QUESTIONS

1 Using the spot rates in Figure 2.1 and the currency futures prices in Table 3.7, compute the premiums or discounts on the foreign currency futures for Canada and Japan for 90 days and 180 days. How do they compare with the forward premiums given in Table 3.1 over comparable periods?

2 Why do banks quote only even-dated forward rates, for example, 30-day rates and 90-day rates, rather than uneven-dated rates? How would you prorate the rates of uneven-dated maturities?

3 Compute the outright forward quotations from the following swap quotations of Canadian dollars in European terms.

Spot	30-day	90-day	180-day
1.1910/05	10/9	12/10	15/12

4 When would spreads widen quickly as we move forward in the forward market? Select two sets of actual quotations from a volatile time and from a stable time.

5 Could a bank that trades forward exchange ever hope to balance the buys and sells of forward currencies for each future date? How do swap contracts help?

6 Why do banks operate a forward exchange market in only a limited number of currencies? Does it have to do with the ability to balance buy orders with sell orders, and is it the same reason why they rarely offer contracts of over 2 years?

7 Why is the "open interest" smaller on the March 1982 contracts than on the December contracts in Table 3.7? Do the numbers for open interest suggest that many contracts are sold before maturity?

8 Why do you think that futures markets were developed when banks already offered forward contracts? What might currency futures offer which forward contracts did not?

9 Do you think that limits on daily price movements for currency futures make these contracts more or less risky or liquid? Could the limitation on price movement make the futures contracts difficult to sell during highly turbulent times?

10 How could arbitrage take place between forward exchange contracts and currency futures? Would this arbitrage be unprofitable only if the futures and forward rates were exactly the same?

11 Does the need to hold a margin make forward and futures deals less desirable than if there are no margin requirements? Does your answer depend on the interest paid on margins?

12 How does a currency option differ from a forward contract? How does the option differ from a currency future?

BIBLIOGRAPHY

Einzig, Paul A.: *The Dynamic Theory of Forward Exchange*, 2d ed., Macmillan and Company, London, 1967.

Eiteman, David K., and Arthur I. Stonehill: *Multinational Business Finance*, 2d ed., Addison-Wesley Publishing Company, Reading, Mass., 1979, pp. 47–49.

International Monetary Market of the Chicago Mercantile Exchange: *The Futures Market in Foreign Currencies*, the Chicago Mercantile Exchange, Chicago, Ill.

International Monetary Market of the Chicago Mercantile Exchange: *Trading in International Currency Futures*, the Chicago Mercantile Exchange, Chicago, Ill.

International Monetary Market of the Chicago Mercantile Exchange: *Understanding Futures in Foreign Exchange*, the Chicago Mercantile Exchange, Chicago, Ill.

Kubarych, Roger M.: *Foreign Exchange Markets in the United States*, Federal Reserve Bank of New York, 1979.

Rodriguez, Rita M., and E. Eugene Carter: *International Financial Management*, 2d ed., Prentice-Hall, Inc., Englewood Cliffs, N.J., 1979, Chap. 5.

Waldner, Stanley C.: "How Chicago's Foreign Exchange Futures Market Has Worked," *Euromoney*, May 1974, pp. 20–24.

PART TWO

ECONOMIC ENVIRONMENT*

*This part, consisting of Chapters 4, 5, and 6, is included for use in courses in which the international financial environment as well as international financial management is covered. In courses dealing exclusively with international financial management, the reader may skip Part 2 and move directly to Part 3.

CHAPTER 4

THE BALANCE OF INTERNATIONAL PAYMENTS

THE IMPORTANCE OF THE BALANCE OF PAYMENTS STATISTICS

The financial manager can decide, on the basis of the situation that he or she faces at the time, in which country to borrow or invest. However, this puts the manager in a static or passive role of looking at events only after they have already unfolded. Alternatively, a manager can adopt an active or dynamic stance and form an opinion on where the economy and other economies are heading. What is likely to happen to spot exchange rates and forward rates will be most important. The job of the financial manager is then to decide not just where to borrow or invest, but how this should be done and whether she or he should speculate. For example, if the manager believes that a foreign currency will fall in value and thinks that the interest rate on loans denominated in that currency is not high enough to reflect this belief, then this is where borrowing should occur. The payment of the debt will be cheap if the currency in which the debt is denominated does indeed fall. Similarly, investment should be in countries in which exchange rates are believed likely to improve, if this belief is not already reflected in interest and dividend rates in those countries.

If we can learn what makes exchange rates change, we will be able to make better business decisions. The values of exchange rates are determined in the international financial environment of the economy as a whole, and it is therefore essential that this environment be explained. An understanding of the macroeconomy will help us avoid reacting to events only after they have already unfolded, and it can provide great payoffs. If you wish to anticipate events and react intelligently to them, the picture of the economy in its international environment is most important. That picture is seen regularly in the publication of the balance of payments statistics.

DEFINING THE BALANCE OF PAYMENTS

The balance of payments account is a statistical record of the flow of payments between residents of one country and the rest of the world in a given time period.

Our definition makes it clear that the balance of payments is a flow of so much per period of time. In this sense the balance of payments is like national income, and indeed, the part of the balance of payments account that records the values of exports and imports appears in the national income account.

Balance of payments accounting uses the system of double-entry bookkeeping, which means that every debit or credit in the account is also represented as a credit or debit somewhere else. An easy way of seeing how this works is to take a couple of straightforward examples.

Suppose that an American corporation sells $2 million worth of U.S.-manufactured jeans to Britain and that the British buyer pays from a U.S. dollar account that is kept in a New York bank. We will then have the double entry:

	Million dollars	
	Credits (+)	Debits (−)
Export (of jeans)	+2	
Foreign private assets in the United States		−2

We can think of the export of the jeans as allowing Americans—initially represented by the New York bank—to reduce their indebtedness to Britain. We find that the account, with double-entry bookkeeping, shows not just the flow of jeans but also the flow of payments.

With the balance of payments, a record is maintained of *all* transactions that affect the supply or demand of a currency in the foreign exchange markets. There is just as much demand for dollars when non-Americans buy U.S. jeans as there is when they are buying U.S. stocks, bonds, real estate, bank balances, or businesses, and all of these transactions must be recorded. By keeping track of the value of items sold and the methods by which payments are made, we keep track of the supply and demand of the currency. We also ensure that the books indeed balance.

As a second example, suppose that an American corporation purchases $5 million worth of denim cloth from a British mill and that the British mill puts the $5 million it receives into a bank account in New York. We have the double entry:

	Million dollars	
	Credits (+)	Debits (−)
Imports (of cloth)		−5
Foreign private assets in the United States	+5	

The balance of payments treats the deposit of money from the British mill as extra assets held by foreigners in the United States. Alternatively, the deposit of money is viewed as a demand for dollars which matches the supply of dollars that results from the American corporation's payment for the cloth. In a similar way, every entry in the balance of payments will appear twice.

Since all sources of potential demand for dollars by foreigners or supply of dollars to foreigners are included, there are many types of entries. We need a rule for determining which are credits and which are debits. The rule is that any international transaction that gives rise to a demand for U.S. dollars is recorded as a credit in the U.S. balance of payments, and the entry takes a positive sign. Any transaction that gives rise to a supply of dollars in the foreign exchange market is a debit and the entry takes a negative sign. Opposite signs will appear in other countries' balance of payments accounts. A more precise way of expressing this rule is with the following definition:

> Credit transactions are a demand for U.S. dollars and result from purchases by foreigners of goods, services, goodwill, financial and real assets, gold, or foreign exchange from Americans. Debit transactions are a supply of U.S. dollars and result from purchases by Americans of goods, services, goodwill, financial and real assets, gold, or foreign exchange from foreigners.

The full meaning of our definition will become clear as we study the U.S. balance of payments in Table 4.1. The summary can be divided into two major categories of entries.[1] The first of these gives the balance of payments on current account and is formed from lines 1–9. The second category includes the balance on (regular) capital account and the settling transactions and is formed from lines 10–28. We shall consider separately these two categories.

THE CURRENT ACCOUNT BALANCE

The current account of the balance of payments is a record of the value of trade in goods and services and of transfers (or goodwill) between a country and the rest of the world.

The current account corresponds to the goods, services, and "goodwill" in our definition of credits and debits. Purchases from abroad are imports, and sales abroad are exports. The factors that affect the sales of goods/merchandise alone are different from those affecting services and goodwill (that is, transfers), and we should therefore consider each item on its own.

Exports and Imports of Merchandise   Exports or imports of merchandise are what we most immediately consider when we think of the balance of international payments. Exports of heavily traded items such as wheat, aircraft, or computers

---

[1]The format of Table 4.1 replaced the format of the balance of payments statistics given until June 1976. We give a summary of the actual table by combining some entries. Before 1976, a number of payments balances were given, including "basic balance," "official reserves transactions balance," "balance on current and long-term capital," and "liquidity balance," as well as those still included. Because of the demonetization of gold and the move of flexible exchange rates, the balances were scrapped. For a full list of reasons for the changes, see "Report of the Advisory Committee on the Presentation of the Balance of Payments Statistics" in U.S. Department of Commerce, *Survey of Current Business*, June 1976, pp. 18–25.

TABLE 4.1
SUMMARY FORMAT OF THE U.S. BALANCE OF PAYMENTS, 1980
(U.S. International Transactions)

Line (credits, +; debits, −)			Billions of dollars
1 Exports			+341
2 Goods/merchandise		+222	
3 Services		+119	
4 Imports			−334
5 Goods/merchandise		−249	
6 Services		−85	
7 Unilateral transfers (net)			−7
8 U.S. government		−6	
9 Private		−1	
10 U.S. assets abroad (net)			−85
11 Official reserves		−1	
12 Gold	0		
13 SDRs	−1		
14 IMF	0		
15 Currencies	0		
16 U.S. government		−5	
17 Loans	−9		
18 Repayments	+4		
19 U.S. private		−71	
20 Direct investment	−21		
21 Foreign securities	−51		
22 Foreign assets in the U.S. (net)			+48
23 Foreign official*		+16	
24 Foreign private		+32	
25 Direct investment	+8		
26 U.S. securities	+24		
27 Allocation of SDRs			+1
28 Statistical discrepancy			+36
Memoranda:			
29 Balance of (merchandise) trade (lines 2 + 5)			−27
30 Balance of goods and services (lines 1 + 4)			+7
31 Balance on current account (lines 30 + 7)			0
32 Balance on (regular) capital account† (line 16 + 19 + 24 + 27)			−43
33 Increase in U.S. official reserve assets			+8
34 Increase in foreign official reserve assets in U.S.*			−15
35 The balance of payments† (lines 33 + 34)			−7

*We exclude some U.S. government liabilities such as military sales contracts.
†These items do not occur in the official account. Numbers are rounded so that additions are correct.
Source: Survey of Current Business, March 1981.

provide large amounts of foreign exchange earnings. In Table 4.1 we find that the
United States earned $222 billion from merchandise exports in 1980. Imports of
items such as oil, automobiles, TVs, and clothing account for a major use of foreign
exchange, and in 1980, imports of merchandise exceeded exports by $27 billion.
This is the merchandise deficit in line 29, and it is often referred to as the *balance of
trade*.

The volume of U.S. exports will depend upon:

1 U.S. prices versus the prices of comparable goods abroad. If inflation in the United States exceeds inflation elsewhere, then, *ceteris paribus*, U.S. goods become less competitive, and export volume will decline.

2 The foreign exchange value of the U.S. dollar. For a particular level of domestic and foreign prices of goods entering international trade, the higher the foreign exchange value of the U.S. dollar, the more expensive are U.S. exports and the lower their level.

3 Foreign incomes. When foreign buyers experience an increase in their real incomes, the result is an improvement in the export market for American raw materials and manufactures.

4 Domestic incomes. When a country experiences reduced demand, this can encourage domestic producers to become more aggressive in foreign markets.

U.S. imports will respond to the same factors that affect exports, with the direction of response being reversed. The relative preferences of the consumers in different countries and "comparative advantages" lie behind such things as relative prices, which in turn affect exports and imports. For those readers who have never learned about comparative advantage or who have forgotten, a review is included as an appendix to this chapter.

Exports and Imports of Services　　Alongside sales and purchases of merchandise are sales and purchases of services. These are frequently called *invisibles*. Because of barriers that prevent or inhibit the international movement of labor, the importance of services in international commerce tends to be smaller than that of merchandise for most economies. The most important services that enter into international trade are travel, shipping, banking and insurance, consulting, and so on. These items tend to respond to the same economic factors that affect merchandise—domestic versus foreign prices, exchange rates, incomes abroad, and incomes at home.

There is a second category of service exports and imports that is quite different from the "performed services" such as travel or consulting. This is debt service. By debt service exports we mean the interest and dividends that Americans receive from abroad, and by imports we mean the interest and dividends paid abroad. In the twentieth century, the U.S. export of debt service has exceeded imports quite substantially. That is, the United States has earned a considerable amount more from its investments abroad than foreigners have earned from their investments in the United States. For example, in 1980, U.S. service export earnings of interest and dividends amounted to $76 billion (of the total of $119 billion in service exports), while at the same time service import earnings amounted to $44 billion (of the total of $85 billion in service imports). Service export earnings are derived from past direct and security investments abroad, and service import earnings are from past foreign direct and security investments at home.

Since debt service earnings and payments are derived from past investments, they do not respond very much to current changes in economic variables. In this sense the debt service component of total services is very different from performed services.

Table 4.1 shows that in 1980, the United States earned a surplus on services or invisibles of $34 billion. This more than offset the $27 billion merchandise deficit, leaving a surplus on goods and services of $7 billion, as shown on line 30.

Unilateral Transfers (Net) We have already observed that double-entry bookkeeping is used in the balance of payments, and so a flow of goods or services, for example, will correspond to a flow of payments. It is the nature of all trade that the items being traded flow in one direction while the corresponding payments flow in the other. This pattern of two-way flows has to be considered differently when we look at transfers. *Transfers* are payments made abroad or received from abroad for which there is no corresponding flow of goods or services. They are therefore unilateral or unrequited flows, and they can take the form of nonmilitary grants, foreign aid, financial assistance, private gifts, donations, or inheritances. These are shown in net amounts on line 7 in Table 4.1.

Transfers are included in the account as if we were exporting or importing goodwill, with inflows being a sale or export of goodwill (a credit) and outflows being an import (a debit). By including transfers as a trade in goodwill, we preserve double-entry bookkeeping, since the payment for or receipt from the transfer, which will appear elsewhere in the account, will be matched by the transfer item itself.

The value of unilateral transfers depends both on a country's own generosity and on the generosity of its friends. It also depends on the number of expatriates who send money to relatives or receive money from relatives. Poorer countries, from which large numbers typically leave for job opportunities elsewhere, receive net earnings on unilateral transfers. India and Pakistan, for example, receive net inflows on transfers. Richer countries—such as the United States, Canada, Britain, and Australia—which have foreign aid programs and have taken immigrants generally have net outflows on transfers.

The current account balance is the result of exports and imports of goods, services, and goodwill; it is the balance of goods and services plus transfers. The current account therefore consists of lines 1–9 in Table 4.1. In 1980, the current account was virtually balanced, as shown in line 31. The $7 billion debit from net outbound transfers (an import of goodwill) offsets the $7 billion surplus on goods and services. Until June 1976, the balance on current account would have appeared on line 10 in the summary format we have in Table 4.1, but after the downgrading of all balances at that time, the balance has been given only as a memorandum item.

THE CAPITAL ACCOUNT BALANCE

The capital account is a record of investment and payment flows between a country and the rest of the world.

The format used in presenting the U.S. balance of payments no longer shows the distinction in the capital account (lines 10–28) between the "official settling" transactions—those which the government uses to fill any imbalance in international payments—and "regular" transactions—which are the remaining transactions. However, we can use a straightforward procedure to separate these two parts. Moreover, it is important that we do this to get an idea of the overall balance of payments, since the settling transactions show the size and form of any ultimate surplus or deficit that the government had to fill. The settling transactions are themselves the result of any imbalance in the regular transactions.

In Table 4.1, the capital account is given in lines 10–28. Lines 12–15 and line 23 are for the settling transactions. The remainder, lines 16–21 and 24–28, are for the capital account regular transactions.[2] We can consider the regular transactions of the capital account before we consider the settling transactions.[3]

Regular Transactions

In terms of our definition of credits and debits, regular transactions of the capital account, in lines 16–21 and 24–28, result from the purchase or sale of financial and real assets. In the U.S. accounts, these purchases and sales are divided according to whether they are made by U.S. residents or by foreigners and are given on a net basis.

U.S. Assets Abroad (Net)   Line 17 shows that the U.S. government made loans to foreign governments of $9 billion. This means that the U.S. government purchased foreign financial assets, which from our definition of credits versus debits is a debit for the U.S. Line 18 shows that $4 billion of previous loans was repaid, since the $4 billion is a plus. Repayments reduce U.S.-held financial assets and are a credit.

Private investment is divided according to whether it is direct or in securities. With direct investment, the ownership is sufficiently extensive to give Americans a measure of control. Government statisticians have chosen the level of 10 percent ownership to represent control. Original as well as incremental inflows of funds, where more than 10 percent ownership is involved, are considered direct investment (or divestment when funds are brought home). A large part of direct investment involves sending funds to overseas subsidiaries and branches of multinationals.

It can well be that amounts that appear as direct investments are really more in the nature of speculation. On a number of occasions in the 1960s and 1970s, U.S.-based multinationals which expected falls in the value of a currency moved funds into stronger currencies. This was done by extending credit to their subsidiaries or branches or by reducing or increasing their remittances from them. In the data we observe, it is difficult to distinguish investment for expansion from investment for speculation. In 1980 we find a $21 billion debit (that is, a $21 billion outflow) for direct investment (line 20 of Table 4.1).

When assets purchased by Americans involve less than 10 percent ownership, they are included in U.S. private purchases of foreign securities. These are shown in

---

[2] Regular transactions also include all the transactions on current account. This means that with regular transactions we include all the original entries (that is, excluding totals) other than the settling transactions of lines 12–15 and line 23.

[3] The terminology of settling and regular transactions is used by Robert A. Mundell in "The Balance of Payments," in David Sills (ed.), *International Encyclopedia of the Social Sciences*, Crowell Collier and Macmillan, Inc., New York, 1968. This is reprinted as Chapter 10 in Robert Mundell, *International Economics*, Macmillan and Co., New York, 1968.

line 21. This is also called portfolio investment and includes stocks as well as bonds. In the detailed format of the balance of payments, the portfolio investments in foreign securities are separated into long-term and short-term investments, with the division being a maturity of 1 year. This distinction between long-term and short-term investments is very important in countries which believe that the quick response of short-term investments—including so-called hot money—to financial and political events can produce swings in exchange rates.

Direct investment depends on whether there is an advantage in having a business abroad. This advantage could be a greater availability of materials and skills abroad, the need to expand, political risks, diversification gains, tax incentives, or some other factor. The amount of foreign security investment depends on the difference in expected returns between foreign stocks and bonds and domestic stocks and bonds. The expected returns from foreign securities consist of the dividend on stocks (or the interest on bills or bonds), the expected change in the securities' local currency market value, and the expected change in the exchange rate. Because funds will flow between countries until the expected returns in different locations are equal, the advantage that exists for investing in a particular location will be more obvious from statistics in the accounts on the amounts flowing than from statistics on interest yields.[4]

Foreign Assets in the U.S. (Net)   This item is similar to the category "U.S. assets abroad" but refers to the flows of foreign-owned funds. The data are given in net terms and are divided into direct investment and security investment. Direct investment by foreigners in the United States occurs when funds flow into companies that are considered to be controlled by foreigners. The $8 billion of direct investment in the United States is small compared with the security or portfolio investment of $24 billion. Total private investment in the United States is below U.S. investment abroad, and so during 1980 Americans added to their net claims abroad.

Allocation of Special Drawing Rights (SDRs)

In line 27 of Table 4.1 we find approximately $1 billion as an allocation of SDRs. The specific details of SDRs, or Special Drawing Rights, are left to our discussion of international financial institutions. However, we can say that Special Drawing Rights are reserves created by the International Monetary Fund (IMF) and allocated, when they are approved by a sufficient number of members, among participating countries by making ledger entries in the countries' accounts at the IMF. In 1980, the United States was given a little over $1 billion in SDRs as its allocation of newly created reserves. We see that SDRs appear in the balance of payments because they contribute to a country's foreign exchange reserves.

The statistical discrepancy—the item just below SDRs—is neither a regular

---

[4]This point is made, for example, by Fischer Black in "The Ins and Outs of Foreign Investment," *Financial Analysts Journal*, May–June 1978, pp. 1–7.

transaction nor a settling transaction. Instead, it is derived from the difference between settling transactions and the balance on regular transactions. It results from errors in recording regular transactions. A discussion of this discrepancy is therefore best left until we have explained settling transactions and the nature of the errors in measuring regular transactions.

Settling Transactions

The settling transactions consist of lines 12–15, 23 and also line 33 in Table 4.1. The value of these transactions gives the overall deficit or surplus in the balance of payments. You might well wonder why such important statistics are in different parts of the account and are not given special attention. The answer is that some members of the 1976 Advisory Committee on the Presentation of the Balance of Payments Statistics believed that no individual balance can give a clear picture. These members therefore decided to downplay all types of balances and to avoid the use of the words "deficit" and "surplus." There appears to have been an important split within the advisory committee, and as a compromise some balances are still included but relegated to memoranda items. Only balances associated with current transactions are given in the official statistics. It is still possible, however, to derive the capital account balance and the overall surplus or deficit.

The reason the settling transactions give the ultimate or overall balance of payments follows from the identity

$$B \equiv \Delta R \qquad (4.1)$$

where B = overall balance of payments
  ΔR = change in total official reserves

Equation (4.1) says that the balance or, more precisely, the *im*balance in the balance of payments is given by the change in the official reserves. The change in official reserves fills the difference between the amount of currency that private suppliers offer and the amount the private demanders want to purchase. Since it is by no means obvious why this is the balance of payments, we should explain reserves and their role in the international financial system. A full explanation will have to wait until our discussion of fixed exchange rates, but we can nevertheless provide an outline of the argument.

The official reserves of the United States include gold, SDRs, the reserve position at the IMF, and the government holdings of foreign currencies. These items are important because each of them can be used by the government to buy dollars in the world's currency markets. The SDRs and the position at the IMF allow the purchase of dollars from official agencies in foreign countries, and the gold and foreign currencies can be used in the private market.

Fixed exchange rates, which prevailed for almost every currency until the early to mid-1970s, require a country's central bank to buy that amount of its currency not taken up in the private markets —the excess supply. If the central bank did not buy its currency, the price could fall below the official fixed value. Similarly, to maintain fixed rates, central banks must sell their own currency when there is excess demand at the official rate. This will prevent the price from rising. It is the official reserves which must be used to buy and sell the country's currency. Moreover, the dollar value of the change in official reserves equals the amount of dollars that were bought or sold. For example, if there were an excess supply of $2 billion that private buyers did not want, the United States would be forced to buy $2 billion worth of dollars and to use up $2 billion in gold, foreign currencies, SDRs, or reserves at the IMF. Alternatively, if there were an excess demand for $2 billion, the United States would provide (sell) $2 billion worth of dollars and in return receive $2 billion in gold or foreign currencies and so on. This is why the change in official reserves is the ultimate balance—or *im* balance—of payments. It is the excess of dollars offered up or demanded in international trade between the United States and the rest of the world. Since maintaining fixed exchange rates involves foreign governments as well as the monetary authority of the United States, foreign official changes in holdings of dollars, in line 23, should also be included within the overall balance.

When the United States made the dollar inconvertible into gold and exchange rates generally became flexible, changes in official reserves lost some of their significance, and the 1976 Advisory Committee on the Presentation of the Balance of Payments Statistics decided to no longer give them as *the* balance of payments. In the words of the advisory committee:[5]

> . . . The offical reserve transactions balance has less importance under present circumstances than it did, with all its flaws, before August 1971, when the dollar became inconvertible, or before March 1973, when generalized floating began.

But as the report continued:

> Some members, however, believe that the official reserve transactions balance continues to be useful. . . . In the end, the arguments against the continued publication of the official reserve transactions balance and the other overall balances prevailed.

This author sympathizes with those whose arguments did not prevail. Since foreign exchange market intervention still takes place, the size of the change in official reserves is still important. This is because a change in the value of a currency is not fully meaningful until we add the amount of official intervention, as given by changes in the official reserves. The changes in official reserves tell us how the exchange rate might have moved had there been no interference. For example, if the U.S. dollar loses 10 percent against British pounds when U.S. official reserves have fallen and British dollar holdings have gone up, this means that the monetary authorities were buying dollars for pounds and yet the dollar still fell. It would have

---

[5]See "Report of the Advisory Committee on the Presentation of the Balance of Payments Statistics" in U.S. Department of Commerce, *Survey of Current Business*, June 1976, p. 25.

fallen even further without the intervention. We discover that the same change in exchange rates can have different implications, depending on the associated change in official reserves, that is, the settling transactions. We therefore include the settling transactions as line 35 in Table 4.1. This is the sum of lines 33 and 34. We find that in 1980 the United States experienced a balance of payments deficit of $7 billion.

Statistical Discrepancy

Until 1976 the *statistical discrepancy* was called *errors and omissions*, which gives a better idea of its meaning. The discrepancy exists because there are two ways of reaching the balance of payments, and one of these involves errors. We can explain the two ways of arriving at the balance of payments as follows. Let us consider the identity

$$B \equiv B_c + B_k \tag{4.2}$$

where B_c = true balance on the current account
  B_k = true balance on the (regular) capital account

and, as before, B is the overall balance or imbalance on settling transactions.

The identity exists because the balance on settling transactions, B, is what settles the imbalance on the current and regular capital accounts, that is, all the regular transactions. The regular transactions consist of all current account transactions and all transactions of the capital account except settling transactions.

The data on B, which is the change in official reserves as shown in Equation (4.1), are provided from the government's records on its holdings of gold, foreign currencies, IMF balances, and SDRs. It can be assumed, therefore, that the data for the left-hand side of Equation (4.2) are accurately measured. However, the data for the items on the right-hand side of Equation (4.2) are a different story. Current and capital account measurement involves potential errors. Errors might appear because of differences between the time that entries are made for the current account and the time the associated payments appear in the capital account. It is customary for the U.S. Department of Commerce to collect data on exports and imports of goods and services from customs agents; the data on these current account items are reported as the goods cross the border or as the services are rendered. The payments for these goods or services, which are a financial flow, will appear only afterward. This may be in a subsequent report of the balance of payments statistics.

Another reason for errors is that many entries are data estimates. For example, data on travel expenditures are estimated from questionnaire surveys of a limited number of travelers. The average expenditure discovered in a survey is multiplied by the number of travelers. A further reason for measurement error is that illegal transactions, which affect foreign exchange supply and demand despite their illegality, do not explicitly enter the accounts. We can therefore have flows of funds without any associated measured flow of goods or services. Finally, we can have unreported flows of capital.

From Table 4.1 we have that B, the settling transaction or change in official reserves, is an overall deficit of $7 billion. This is found from line 33 plus line 34 and is given as line 35. The balance of payments accounts in their official form have a minus in front of surpluses. This is because the accountant views gains in official reserves as resulting from the purchase of gold or foreign exchange, which is a debit item by definition. However, according to a mathematical and perhaps intuitive view, *positive* amounts indicate surpluses. As a result, we have altered the official format within the memoranda items and have placed pluses with surpluses and minuses with deficits.

While the change in reserves, the B on the left-hand side of Equation (4.2), shows a deficit of $7 billion, the balances on the right-hand side show $B_c = 0$ (line 31) and $B_k = -43$ (line 32). There is therefore an overall *measured* deficit on regular transactions of $43 billion. This, however, is significantly rectified by the statistical discrepancy. When we add the error of $36 billion to the right-hand side of Equation (4.2), we have $0 - 43 + 36 = -7$. This is the overall deficit of $7 billion, which agrees with the official reserves. The $36 billion discrepancy is included for the purpose of making the two methods of measuring the overall balance—via official reserves and via regular transactions—agree with each other.

The measurement error in the balances on regular transactions can be massive. The $36 billion in 1980 is sufficient to convert an awful *measured* deficit from regular transactions of $43 billion into a relatively small deficit of $7 billion, where the actual value is known from the accurately measured official reserves. What at first looks like a frighteningly large deficit turns out to be relatively modest. It is just as well that we do not have to rely on measurements of the regular current and capital transactions and that we can instead check the result against the settling transactions, the changes in reserves. The discrepancy is determined residually from B and $(B_c + B_k)$ and may be very significant.

It is generally believed that the capital account contains a greater measurement error than the current account. This is deduced from the observation by econometricians that the statistical discrepancy fits the theory of short-term capital flows very well.

OTHER COUNTRIES' BALANCE OF PAYMENTS*

There are some differences between the balance of payments format used by the United States and the formats used by other countries. This has been especially true since 1976, when the United States adopted its new format. In making foreign investment decisions, it is wise to examine other countries' balance of payments statistics to judge whether their currencies are healthy, and it is therefore valuable to be able to read other countries' accounts. We can briefly look at Canada and the United Kingdom. These countries are among the major locations of U.S. direct investment, as shown in Table 4.2.

Canadian Balance of International Payments

Each of the entries in Table 4.3 generally has an obvious equivalent entry in the U.S. account (Table 4.1). The primary differences in the Canadian format are the

TABLE 4.2
U.S. DIRECT INVESTMENT ABROAD
(Book Value at Year-End, 1979)

	Billions, US$
Canada	40.2
United Kingdom	23.5
West Germany	13.5
Other European countries	45.6
Latin America	35.1
Australia and New Zealand	7.7
Japan	6.2
Other countries	15.0
Total	186.8

Source: U.S. Department of Commerce, *Survey of Current Business*, August 1981.

division of capital transactions into long-term and short-term components and the explicit statement of balances.

A prominent feature of the Canadian balance of payments is the large deficit on services. There is a travel deficit for 1980 of Can$2 billion and an interest and dividend deficit of Can$5 billion. The travel deficit reflects the propensity of Canadians to vacation in the warmer climes, and the interest and dividend deficit reflects the large foreign ownership of Canadian industry and securities. The interest and dividend is unlikely to change very quickly. It is met with capital inflows and a merchandise surplus, with the former aggravating the problem for the future.

United Kingdom Balance of Payments

The format of the United Kingdom account is more like the Canadian than the U.S. account in that balances are given for current and capital transactions. The account also distinguishes merchandise from the remainder of the current account by using the labels "visible" and "invisible." In Table 4.4., we find that as in the United States, there is a healthy surplus in the invisibles, or services. Service earnings are made in the financial and insurance industries on the basis of the role of London as a financial center. Other services are travel, shipping, and royalties.

Formats for presenting the balances of payments reveal further variations, but they are sufficiently close to Tables 4.1, 4.3, and 4.4 to enable us to understand their major components. More important for the financial manager is understanding how to interpret the statistics and determine what, if anything, they imply for the future course of exchange rates.

INTERPRETING THE INTERNATIONAL FINANCIAL STATISTICS

We have explained the meaning of the current and capital items that appear in the balance of payments. But what do we learn from the balance of payments? The

TABLE 4.3
CANADIAN BALANCE OF INTERNATIONAL PAYMENTS, 1980
(Summary Format)

Line (credits, +; debits, −)		Billions, Can$	
1 Merchandise exports		+76	
2 Travel receipts	+3		
3 Interest and dividend receipts	+2		
4 Freight and shipping receipts	+4		
5 Other service receipts	+5		
6 Total service receipts		+14	
7 Transfer receipts/withholding tax		+2	
8 Merchandise imports		−68	
9 Travel payments	−5		
10 Interest and dividend payments	−7		
11 Freight and shipping payments	−4		
12 Other service payments	−9		
13 Total service payments		−25	
14 Transfer payments/official contributions		−1	
15 Total current account balance (lines 1 + 6 + 7 + 8 + 13 + 14)			−2
16 Direct investment in Canada	+1		
17 Direct investment by Canadians	−3		
18 Portfolio transactions: Canadian securities	+5		
19 Portfolio transactions: foreign securities	0		
20 All other long-term capital	−1		
21 Balance of capital movements in long-term forms (lines 16 to 20)		+2	
22 Residents' holdings of short-term funds abroad	+1		
23 Nonresidents' holdings of Canadian funds	+1		
24 Other short-term transactions	−1		
25 Balance of capital movements in short-term forms (lines 22 to 24)		+1	
26 Total net capital balances (lines 21 + 25)			+3
27 Total current and capital account balance (lines 15 + 26)			+1
28 Errors and omissions		−2	
29 Allocation of SDRs		*	
30 Net official monetary payments		−1	

*Under $1 billion.
Source: Quarterly Estimates of the Canadian Balance of International Payments, 1st quarter, 1981.

answer is that on their own, the balance of payments statistics have become a very poor description of the international performance of national economies. We have already noted this in our brief explanation of the meaning of foreign exchange reserves and of the reasons some government statisticians have been reluctant to publish any bottom-line balances in the payments accounts. It will be useful to review and to extend our earlier discussion by looking at the meaning of the statistics under fixed exchange rates and under flexible exchange rates.

TABLE 4.4
BALANCE OF PAYMENTS OF THE UNITED KINGDOM, 1979
(Summary Format)*

Line (credits, +; debits, −)	Billions, £ sterling		
1 Exports	+41		
2 Imports	−44		
3 Visible balance (lines 1 + 2)		−3	
4 Credits	+22		
5 Debits	−21		
6 Invisible balance (lines 4 + 5), of which:		+1	
7 *Services balance*	+3		
8 *Interest, profits, and dividends balance*	0		
9 *Transfers balance*	−2		
10 Current balance (lines 3 + 6)			−2
11 Total investment and other capital transactions	+1		
12 Balancing item	+2		
13 Balance for official financing (lines 10 + 11 + 12)			+1
14 Official financing (minus line 13)			−1

*Numbers are rounded for conformable totals.
Source: United Kingdom Central Statistical Office, *Annual Abstract of Statistics*, 1981 ed.

Fixed Rates

Many countries still fix the value of their currency according to the currency of another country, the U.S. dollar being the most popular choice. Table 4.5 shows the situation recorded in a survey by the International Monetary Fund for August 31, 1981, and a more detailed summary is given in Appendix 4.3.

For those countries that fix exchange rates, the balance of payments statistics are the best or even the only means for judging international performance. The most important balance is the change in official reserves, since this is the amount the central banks were forced to buy or sell to keep exchange rates fixed. The amount they buy or sell is the excess or deficiency in private transactions in that currency. The other balances are also valuable in showing the origin of the excess or deficiency, for example, whether the imbalance originates in the current account or in the capital account. However, if the statistical discrepancy is large, balances other than the change in official reserves could give a misleading view.

Flexible Rates

If exchange rates were truly flexible, in the sense that central banks never intervened in the foreign exchange markets to buy or sell their currency, then the change in official reserves would always be zero. Clearly, if the banks do not buy or sell their currency, their reserves will remain constant. In such a case the exchange rate becomes the result of the forces in the free or private currency market, and we must look there to judge the international performance of a country. For this reason,

TABLE 4.5
EXCHANGE ARRANGEMENTS
(As of August 31, 1981)

| Currency pegged to | | | | | Exchange rate adjusted according to a set of indicators | Cooperative exchange arrangements | Other |
U.S. dollar	French franc	Other currency	SDR	Other currency composite			
Bahamas	Benin	Equatorial Guinea (Spanish peseta)	Burma	Algeria	Brazil	Belgium	Afghanistan
Barbados	Cameroon		Guinea	Austria	Colombia	Denmark	Argentina
Burundi	C. African Rep.		Guinea-Bissau	Bangladesh	Peru	France	Australia
Chile	Chad		Iran	Botswana	Portugal	Germany	Bahrain
Costa Rica	Comoros	Gambia, The (pound sterling)	Jordan	Cape Verde		Ireland	Bolivia
Djibouti	Congo		Kenya	China, P. R.		Italy	Canada
Dominica	Gabon		Malawi	Cyprus		Luxembourg	Ghana
Dominican Rep.	Ivory Coast	Lesotho (South African rand)	Mauritius	Fiji		Netherlands	Greece
Ecuador	Madagascar		São Tomé & Principe	Finland			Guyana
Egypt	Mali		Seychelles	Kuwait			Iceland
El Salvador	Niger	Swaziland (South African rand)	Sierra Leone	Malaysia			India
Ethiopia	Senegal		Viet Nam	Malta			Indonesia
Grenada	Togo		Zaïre	Mauritania			Israel
Guatemala	Upper Volta		Zambia	Norway			Japan
Haiti				Papua New Guinea			Korea
Honduras				Singapore			Lebanon
Iraq				Solomon Islands			Maldives
Jamaica				Sweden			Mexico
Lao P.D. Rep.				Tanzania			Morocco
Libéria				Tunisia			New Zealand
Libya				Zimbabwe			Nigeria
Nepal							Philippines
Nicaragua							Qatar

Oman
Pakistan

Panama
Paraguay
Romania
Rwanda
Somalia

St. Lucia
St. Vincent
Sudan
Surinam
Syrian Arab Rep.

Trinidad & Tobago
Venezuela
Yeman Arab Rep.
Yeman, P.D. Rep.

Saudi Arabia
South Africa

Spain
Sri Lanka
Thailand
Turkey
Uganda

U. Arab Emirates
United Kingdom
United States
Uruguay
Western Somoa

Yugoslavia

Source: International Financial Statistics, October 1981.

TABLE 4.6
INDEXES OF FOREIGN CURRENCY PRICES OF THE U.S. DOLLAR
(May 1970 = 100)

	End of period											
	1978				1979				1980			
	I	II	III	IV	I	II	III	IV	I	II	III	IV
Trade-weighted average against 22 OECD currencies*	84.1	82.1	79.2	78.5	80.3	80.9	79.8	81.6	89.3	81.0	82.0	85.0
Trade-weighted average against 10 currencies†	77.4	77.1	73.2	71.3	73.0	72.4	70.5	70.7	77.2	70.2	70.9	74.5
Selected currencies:‡												
Canada	105.4	104.7	110.2	110.4	108.1	108.7	108.1	108.8	110.9	107.2	109.0	111.2
France	83.0	81.6	78.5	75.7	77.8	77.6	74.3	72.8	81.1	74.0	76.1	81.8
Germany	55.7	57.1	53.4	50.3	51.4	50.7	48.0	47.7	53.4	48.4	49.9	53.9
Italy	135.5	135.9	130.9	131.9	133.5	132.4	127.5	127.8	142.8	133.4	137.1	147.9
Japan	62.0	57.0	52.7	54.2	58.3	60.5	62.2	66.8	69.6	60.6	59.1	56.6
Netherlands	59.6	61.5	58.0	54.2	55.4	55.9	53.2	52.5	58.6	53.1	54.1	58.6
Switzerland	43.2	43.0	35.7	37.5	39.1	38.4	35.5	36.6	42.4	37.5	38.1	40.7
United Kingdom	129.4	129.1	121.8	118.1	116.1	110.8	109.3	108.0	110.9	101.7	100.6	100.7

*Australia, Austria, Belgium-Luxembourg, Canada, Denmark, Finland, France, Germany, Greece, Iceland, Ireland, Italy, Japan, the Netherlands, New Zealand, Norway, Portugal, Spain, Sweden, Switzerland, Turkey, United Kingdom. Data: U.S. Department of the Treasury.
†Belgium, Canada, France, Germany, Italy, Japan, the Netherlands, Sweden, Switzerland, United Kingdom. Data: Federal Reserve Board.
‡Data: The International Monetary Fund.
Source: U.S. Department of Commerce, *Survey of Current Business,* March 1981.

balance of payments statisticians have replaced statistics on balances with statistics on the path of exchange rates since 1976.

We find in Table 4.6 and Figure 4.1 that the behavior of exchange rates is shown not by the rates themselves but by an index based at 100 in 1970. When this index moves above 100, the U.S. dollar has gained vis-à-vis other countries' currencies, and when it is below 100, the U.S. dollar has lost. We find from Table 4.6 that by 1980 the U.S. dollar had gained in relation to the currencies of Canada and Italy, had remained the same vis-à-vis the British pound, and had fallen against the other currencies shown. When judged against currencies in general, the dollar fared very poorly in the latter half of the 1970s. This is seen most easily from the top chart in Figure 4.1, which gives the trade-weighted averages.

The trade-weighted average of a currency is formed by applying a percentage weight to the separate currency movements. This is done according to the fraction of U.S. trade with each country compared with the total trade of the United States. For example, if 25 percent of the total U.S. trade with the Organization for Economic Cooperation and Development (OECD) countries is with Canada and 10 percent is with the United Kingdom, the weights applied will be 0.25 and 0.10, respectively. Trade-weighted averages, in a system of truly flexible rates, are probably the best means for judging international economic performance. However, as Table 4.5 makes very clear, many countries continue to maintain flexible fixed rates, making exchange rate movements an inaccurate statistic for judging performance. Since the late 1970s, many countries have had a mixed exchange rate system which contains elements of fixed rates and elements of flexible rates. The mixed system is commonly known as the *managed float* or the *dirty float*. In this system the central bank officially allows a flexible rate but intervenes to smooth out day-to-day movements.

Performance in the hybrid dirty float system is difficult to judge. We must combine the movement in the currency value with the change in official reserves. Frequently, however, the views from both will be mutually reinforcing. For example, as the Canadian dollar fell in value during 1978, as shown in Table 4.6, the Bank of Canada ran down its foreign exchange reserves. This means that the Bank of Canada was buying its own currency with U.S. dollars (a major reserve for Canada) to keep up the value of the Canadian dollar. Nevertheless, the Canadian currency fell. We conclude that the Canadian dollar's poor performance would have been understated if we had judged only by the movement of the exchange value index. Similarly, the pound sterling gained in value against the dollar from 1978 to 1980 as British official reserves rose. The Bank of England was therefore selling pounds and buying dollars, and yet the pound rose in value. Again, the two effects are reinforcing. Indeed, reserve movements and currency movements tend to reinforce each other when central banks engaged in dirty floating attempts to slow movements in currency values. In principle, however, a country could gain reserves while its currency fell and vice versa.

Because most central banks, including the U.S. Federal Reserve—the central bank of the United States—do intervene in the foreign exchange markets, we must keep track of both the balance of payments statistics and the path of exchange rates.

FIGURE 4.1

The path of the dollar. (*From U.S. Department of Commerce*, Survey of Current Business, *March 1981.*)

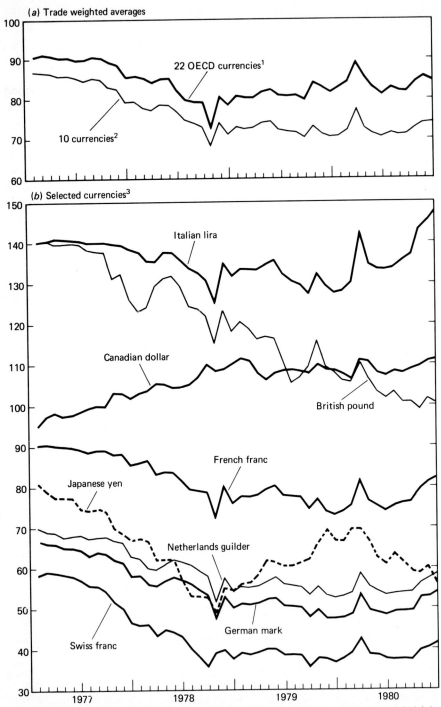

(*a*) Trade weighted averages

22 OECD currencies[1]

10 currencies[2]

(*b*) Selected currencies[3]

Italian lira

Canadian dollar

British pound

French franc

Japanese yen

Netherlands guilder

German mark

Swiss franc

1977 1978 1979 1980

1. Australia, Austria, Belgium - Luxembourg, Canada, Denmark, Finland, France, Germany, Greece, Iceland, Ireland, Italy, Japan, the Netherlands, New Zealand, Norway, Portugal, Spain, Sweden, Switzerland, Turkey, United Kingdom. Data: U.S. Department of the Treasury.

2. Belgium, Canada, France, Germany, Italy, Japan, the Netherlands, Sweden, Switzerland, United Kingdom. Data: Federal Reserve Board.

3. Data: International Monetary Fund.

NOTE — Data are for end of month.

Only if rates were truly flexible could we safely avoid the published value of the balance on line 35 of Table 4.1, because only then would it be zero.

GOALS OF INTERNATIONAL ECONOMIC POLICY

There is a generally held feeling that surpluses in the balance of payments are good and deficits are bad. But is this accurate? An argument can be made that the reverse is true and that if it were possible, we should avoid surpluses and have deficits. This argument is worth exploring. We can begin by asking if we should aim for a surplus.

Consider what it means to have a trade surplus, with merchandise exports exceeding imports, and to have this surplus continue indefinitely. It means that we are producing goods for foreigners to enjoy in excess of the amount they produce for us. But why should one country manufacture goods for the pleasure of another in excess of what it receives in return? No, surpluses mean we are living below our means. We could enjoy more of our own products and still keep the books in balance.

There is another way of viewing this which is the view that was taken in the 1960s by some countries outside the United States. If, for example, France were running a trade surplus with the United States, the United States would be enjoying the products of France—perhaps wine or cheese—in excess of what the French were receiving in return. The excess of French exports over French imports would appear as dollar ledger entries in U.S. banks, and in U.S. Treasury bills. What is more, France would have to earn these dollars if it needed to add to its foreign exchange reserves, since it must do this under fixed exchange rates to accommodate a general expansion of trade. And to raise reserves, France would have to maintain surpluses.

This view was taken by former French President Charles de Gaulle, who saw the United States as profiting from its position of being the provider of a large element of foreign exchange reserves—the U.S. dollar. De Gaulle, along with some other leaders outside the United States, argued that the United States was earning "seigniorage" by being the world's central banker. *Seigniorage* is the profit from making *fiat money*, which is money whose buying power exceeds its cost of production. All central banks profit from their own citizens holding their fiat money, but the United States was in a position to have foreigners hold it too.

This is not the best place to discuss seigniorage, which in actual fact was probably never large, but our discussion should show that having a surplus might mean giving away your products and living below your means. In the same way, deficits mean living above your means. A deficit means enjoying the products and resources of other nations in excess of the products you provide for them. This is marvelous as long as you can get away with it, but as with every person or firm that lives beyond its means, a day of reckoning will come when the credit will run out. This makes continuous deficits as undesirable as continuous surpluses.

Since continuous deficits and continuous surpluses are both to be avoided, the obvious solution is to try to keep a balance. A country might not wish to take the steps needed to achieve that balance year in and year out; it might prefer to balance over each 5- or 10-year period. With flexible exchange rates the balance will be achieved each year in the sense that reserves will remain constant. The question is, then, whether to achieve this balance by having flexible exchange rates or to keep rates fixed and use other means of achieving long-term balance. This is the billion-dollar question that must be answered by every government.

THE NET INTERNATIONAL INVESTMENT POSITION

The capital account of the balance of payments presents the record of the *flows* of funds into and out of the United States. Capital inflows result from the sale of financial and real assets, gold, and foreign exchange to foreigners. Outflows result from the purchase of these assets from foreigners. The inflows and outflows are added to and subtracted from *stocks* of outstanding international assets and liabilities/indebtedness. The account that shows the stocks of assets and liabilities can be written in the form of Table 4.7, which gives the international investment position of the United States at the end of 1980.[6]

When capital leaves the United States for investment overseas, it is added to U.S. assets abroad. The debit that will appear in the balance of payments will therefore be matched by an increase in the value of assets shown in Table 4.7. Similarly, inflows of capital produce credits in the balance of payments and increases in U.S. liabilities to foreigners. In order to judge the solvency of a country, the investment position as in Table 4.7 should be consulted rather than the balance of payments. Table 4.7 shows a positive value of $123 billion of the U.S. net investment position. The earnings on this excess of assets over liabilities produce the net debt service surplus of the United States that appears in the current account of the balance of payments.

There is a link between the balance of payments of Table 4.1 and the investment position of Table 4.7, but that link is imperfect. For example, the direct investment during 1980 given in line 20 of Table 4.1 will have contributed $21 billion to the direct assets of $213 billion in Table 4.7. However, the total investment position is also affected by (1) unrepatriated earnings and (2) changes in market values and exchange rates. These factors make the international investment position change from year to year in a way that is not completely explained by the balance of payments.

In order to evaluate the prospects for a currency devaluation under fixed exchange rates, it is not sufficient to evaluate the balance of payments accounts, since these accounts tell only whether conditions are getting better or worse. They do not give any idea of how good or bad the situation is at that moment. Such information is given by the net investment position of the country and, most importantly, the reserve stock of the central bank. The central bank should be able to defend its currency as long as it has sufficient reserves. If, for example, the bank can afford 20 years of substantial deficits with its stock of reserves, a devaluation can be considered unlikely. On the other hand, if reserves will meet existing deficits for only a couple of years, a devaluation can be considered imminent.

---

[6]The official format gives assets and liabilities in a column format rather than in the more conventional balance sheet format shown here. The official statistics also involve more detail.

TABLE 4.7

INTERNATIONAL INVESTMENT POSITION OF THE UNITED STATES, DECEMBER 31, 1980

(Billions of Dollars)

U.S. government assets:		
Official reserves	27	
Other assets	64	
Total government assets		91
Direct investment		213
Foreign securities:		
Bonds	43	
Stocks	19	
Total		62
Unaffiliated foreigners		34
Assets of U.S. banks		204
Total private assets		513
Total U.S. assets abroad		604

Foreign official assets		176
Foreign private assets:		
Direct investment		65
U.S. securities:		
Bonds	19	
Stocks	64	
Total		74
Liabilities to nonbank unaffiliated foreigners		29
Liabilities of U.S. banks		121
U.S. Treasury securities		16
Total foreign private assets		305
U.S. net investment position		123
Total foreign assets in the U.S.		604

Source: U.S. Department of Commerce, *Survey of Current Business*, August 1981.

SUMMARY

1 The balance of payments is a record of a country's flow of payments with other countries. It is a flow, being so much per period of time, and is published quarterly in the United States.

2 Balance of payments accounting uses double-entry bookkeeping procedures. This means that each credit entry has a corresponding debit elsewhere in the account, and vice versa.

3 For the United States, credit entries give rise to a demand for dollars, and debit entries give rise to a supply of dollars. Credits result from sales of items to foreigners and debits from purchases from foreigners.

4 The current account includes trade in goods and services and unilateral transfers. The goods or merchandise component alone gives the balance of trade as the excess of exports over imports. If exports exceed imports, this component is in surplus, and if imports exceed exports, it is in deficit. Services include not only performed services but also debt service—the flow of interest and dividend payments. Unilateral transfers are flows of money not matched by any other physical flow, and double-entry bookkeeping requires that we have an offsetting flow that can be marked down as goodwill.

5 The capital account is a record of investment and payment flows. The format of the balance of payments statistics adopted in 1976 includes settling transactions within this account along with regular transactions. The settling transactions or balancing items constitute the overall change in official reserves. The regular transactions involve direct investments and security investments, with security investments divided into long- and short-term investments. Direct investment means more than 10 percent ownership.

6 A statistical discrepancy is included because the balance given by the accurately recorded figures on official reserves will rarely agree with regular transactions. The discrepancy is partially due to mismeasurement of short-term capital flows.

7 The balance of payments shows the strength of international economic performance only when there are fixed exchange rates. When exchange rates are truly flexible, we should examine changes in currency values.

8 Trade-weighted indexes of currency values allow an overall evaluation of international economic performance with flexible rates. Since many countries have a managed-float currency, we must examine both the balance of payments accounts and the path of exchange rates.

9 Persistent surpluses grant seigniorage to others. Persistent deficits will run a country into debt, and credit will stop. Balance should therefore be the object of international economic policy. The balance can be achieved over a period of time with fixed exchange rates or continuously with flexible rates.

10 The international investment position is a record of the stock of foreign assets and liabilities/indebtedness. It is relevant for determining the likelihood of a currency devaluation.

QUESTIONS

1 Since gold is a part of official reserves, how would the balance of payments statistics show the sale of domestically mined gold to the country's central bank? What happens if the mining company sells the gold to foreign private buyers?

2 Can all countries collectively enjoy a surplus, or must all surpluses and deficits cancel against each other? What does gold mining and the creation of paper reserves (such as SDRs) at the IMF mean for the world's balance?

3 If overall balance was achieved with a current account deficit and a capital account

surplus, would this be preferable to a current account surplus and a capital account deficit?

4 What does a capital inflow mean with regard to the balance of payments during the period of inflow versus the payments balance during subsequent periods of debt service?

5 If the balance of payments of Alaska was prepared, what would it look like? How about the balance of payments of New York City? What do you think the net investment position of these locations will be? Should we worry if Alaska is in great debt?

6 The size of the Canadian economy is about 10 percent of the size of the United States economy. What does a comparison of Tables 4.1 and 4.3 tell you about the importance of international trade to these economies?

7 Britain converted to a flexible exchange rate in 1972. If you wanted to predict the path of the value of the pound over the next 5 years, what order of importance would you give to the following information?

a Inflation rates for the United Kingdom and the United States for the last 5 years

b Past movements in exchange rates

c Recent U.K. balance of payments and foreign exchange reserve statistics

d Recent and planned growth rates for money supplies

e Interest rates in the United States and in the United Kingdom

8 Why is it true by definition that if exchange rates are truly flexible, the balance of payments must be zero? Why, then, are the balances for Canada and the United Kingdom not zero when these countries claimed to have flexible rates?

9 If the overall level of interest rates in all countries went up, how would this affect the U.S. balance of payments? [*Hint*: The United States has net interest earnings.]

10 Label the appropriate items in Table 4.3 and Table 4.4 with B_c, B_k, and B. Compute the true balances, assuming that all errors of measurement are in the country's capital account.

BIBLIOGRAPHY

Bame, Jack J.: "Analyzing U.S. International Transactions," *Columbia Journal of World Business*, fall 1976, pp. 72–84.

Caves, Richard E., and Ronald W. Jones: *World Trade and Payments: An Introduction*, Little, Brown and Company, Boston, 1973, chap. 5.

Grubel, Herbert G.: *International Economics*, Richard D. Irwin, Inc., Homewood, Ill., 1977, chap. 13.

Heller, H. Robert: *International Monetary Economics*, Prentice-Hall, Inc., Englewood Cliffs, N.J., 1974, chap. 4.

Mundell, Robert A.: "The Balance of Payments" in David Sills (ed.), *International Encyclopedia of the Social Sciences*, Crowell Collier and Macmillan, Inc., New York, 1968. Reprinted as Chapter 10 in Robert Mundell, *International Economics*, The Macmillan Company, New York, 1968.

"Report of the Advisory Committee on the Presentation of the Balance of Payments Statistics," in U.S. Department of Commerce, *Survey of Current Business*, June 1976, pp. 18–25.

Stern, Robert M.: *The Balance of Payments: Theory and Economic Policy*, Aldine Publishing Company, Chicago, 1973, chap. 1.

Stern, Robert M., et al.: "The Presentation of the U.S. Balance of Payments: A Symposium," *Essays in International Finance*, no. 123, international finance section, Princeton University, Princeton, N.J., August 1977.

APPENDIX 4.1: The U.S. Balance of Payments, 1979 and 1980 (Millions of Dollars)

Line	(Credits, +; debits, −)[1]	1979	1980[p]
1	Exports of goods and services[2]	286,521	340,887
2	Merchandise, adjusted, excluding military[3]	182,068	221,781
3	Transfers under U.S. military agency sales contracts	7,194	7,470
4	Travel	8,335	9,985
5	Passenger fares	2,156	2,582
6	Other transportation	9,793	11,041
7	Fees and royalties from affiliated foreigners	5,042	5,728
8	Fees and royalties from unaffilitated foreigners	1,150	1,265
9	Other private services	4,291	4,645
10	U.S. government miscellaneous services	522	362
	Receipts of income on U.S. assets abroad:		
11	Direct investment	37,815	37,068
12	Interest, dividends, and earnings of unincorporated affiliates	19,401	20,253
13	Reinvested earnings of incorporated affiliates	18,414	16,815
14	Other private receipts	25,861	36,436
15	U.S. government receipts	2,294	2,525
16	Transfers of goods and services under U.S. military grant programs, net	305	635
17	Imports of goods and services	−281,560	−333,810
18	Merchandise, adjusted, excluding military[3]	−211,454	−249,135
19	Direct defense expenditures	−8,469	−10,779
20	Travel	−9,413	−10,384
21	Passenger fares	−3,100	−3,533
22	Other transportation	−10,466	−10,981
23	Fees and royalties to affiliated foreigners	−471	−505
24	Fees and royalties to unaffiliated foreigners	−235	−252
25	Private payments for other services	−2,779	−2,980
26	U.S. government payments for miscellaneous services	−1,714	−1,767
	Payments of income on foreign assets in the United States:		
27	Direct investment	−6,033	−8,853
28	Interest, dividends, and earnings of unincorporated affiliates	−2,303	−3,005
29	Reinvested earnings of incorporated affiliates	−3,730	−5,848
30	Other private payments	−16,361	−22,140
31	U.S. government payments	−11,066	−12,501
32	U.S. military grants of goods and services, net	−305	−635
33	Unilateral transfers (excluding military grants of goods and services), net	−5,666	−6,959
34	U.S. government grants (excluding military grants of goods and services)	−3,524	−4,506
35	U.S. government pensions and other transfers	−1,187	−1,287
36	Private remittances and other transfers	−955	−1,165
37	U.S. assets abroad, net [increase/capital outflow (−)]	−61,774	−84,502
38	U.S. official reserve assets, net[4]	−1,133	−8,155
39	Gold	−65	
40	Special drawing rights	−1,136	−16

APPENDIX 4.1: The U.S. Balance of Payments, 1979 and 1980 (Millions of Dollars) (Continued)

Line	(Credits, +; debits, −)[1]	1979	1980[P]
41	Reserve position in the International Monetary Fund	−189	−1,667
42	Foreign currencies	257	−6,472
43	U.S. government assets, other than official reserve assets, net	−3,783	−5,111
44	U.S. loans and other long-term assets	−7,651	−9,697
45	Repayments on U.S. loans[5]	3,852	4,308
46	U.S. foreign currency holdings and U.S. short-term assets, net	16	278
47	U.S. private assets, net	−56,858	−71,236
48	Direct investment	−24,319	−20,592
49	Equity and intercompany accounts	−5,904	−3,777
50	Reinvested earnings of incorporated affiliates	−18,414	−16,815
51	Foreign securities	−4,643	−3,188
	U.S. claims on unaffiliated foreigners reported by U.S. nonbanking concerns:		
52	Long-term	−2,029[12]	n.a.
	Short-term		
	U.S. claims reported by U.S. banks, not included elsewhere:		
54	Long-term	−25,868[13]	−46,608[13]
55	Short-term		
56	Foreign assets in the United States, net [increase/capital inflow (+)]	37,575	47,626
57	Foreign official assets in the United States, net	−14,271	16,179
58	U.S. government securities	−21,891	11,827
59	U.S. Treasury securities[6]	−22,356	9,640
60	Other[7]	465	2,187
61	Other U.S. government liabilities[8]	−714	1,375
62	U.S. liabilities reported by U.S. banks, not included elsewhere	7,219	−84
63	Other foreign official assets[9]	1,116	3,061
64	Other foreign assets in the United States, net	51,845	31,446
65	Direct investment	9,713	8,204
66	Equity and intercompany accounts	5,984	2,357
67	Reinvested earnings of incorporated affiliates	3,730	5,848
68	U.S. Treasury securities	4,830[14]	2,693[14]
69	U.S. securities other than U.S. Treasury securities	2,942	7,443
	U.S. liabilities to unaffiliated foreigners reported by U.S. nonbanking concerns:		
70	Long-term	1,692[12]	n.a.
71	Short-term		
	U.S. liabilities reported by U.S. banks, not included elsewhere:		
72	Long-term[10]	32,668	10,687
73	Short-term[10]		
74	Allocations of special drawing rights	1,139	1,152

APPENDIX 4.1: The U.S. Balance of Payments, 1979 and 1980 (Millions of Dollars) (Continued)

Line	(Credits, +; debits, −)[1]	1979	1980[p]
75	Statistical discrepancy (sum of above items with sign reversed)	23,765	35,605
	Memoranda:		
76	Balance on merchandise trade (lines 2 and 18)	−29,386	−27,354
77	Balance on goods and services (lines 1 and 17)[11]	4,961	7,077
78	Balance on goods, services, and remittances (lines 77, 35, and 36)	2,819	4,625
79	Balance on current account (lines 77 and 33)[11]	−706	118
	Transactions in U.S. official reserve assets and in foreign official assets in the United States:		
80	Increase (−) in U.S. official reserve assets, net (line 38)	−1,133	−8,155
81	Increase (+) in foreign official assets in the United States (line 57 less line 61)	−13,556	14,804

Source: *Survey of Current Business*, March 1981.
General notes:
[p] Preliminary.
n.a. Not available.

1. Credits, +: exports of goods and services; unilateral transfers to United States; capital inflows [increase in foreign assets (U.S. liabilities) or decrease in U.S. assets]; decrease in U.S. official reserve assets.

Debits, −: imports of goods and services; unilateral transfers to foreigners; capital outflows [decrease in foreign assets (U.S. liabilities) or increase in U.S. assets]; increase in U.S. official reserve assets.

2. Excludes transfers of goods and services under U.S. military grant programs (see line 16).

3. Excludes exports of goods under U.S. military agency sales contracts identified in Census export documents, excludes imports of goods under direct defense expenditures identified in Census import documents, and reflects various other adjustments (for valuation, coverage, and timing) of Census statistics to balance of payments basis.

4. For all areas, amounts outstanding on December 31, 1980, were as follows, in millions of dollars: line 38, 26,756; line 39, 11,160; line 40, 2,610; line 41, 2,852; line 42, 10,134.

5. Includes sales of foreign obligations to foreigners.

6. Consists of bills, certificates, marketable bonds and notes, and nonmarketable convertible and nonconvertible bonds and notes.

7. Consists of U.S. Treasury and Export-Import Bank obligations, not included elsewhere, and of debts securities of U.S. government corporations and agencies.

8. Includes, primarily, U.S. government liabilities associated with military sales contracts and other transactions arranged with or through foreign official agencies.

9. Consists of investment in U.S. corporate stocks and in debt securities of private corporations and state and local governments.

10. Beginning with estimates for the second quarter of 1978, the distinction between short- and long-term liabilities is discontinued.

11. Conceptually, the sum of lines 79 and 74 is equal to "net foreign investment" in the National Income and Product Accounts (NIPAs). However, the foreign transactions account in the NIPAs (a) includes adjustments to the international transactions accounts for the treatment of gold, (b) excludes capital gains and losses of foreign affiliates of U.S. parent companies from the NIPA's measure of income receipts from direct investment abroad, and from the corresponding income payments, and (c) beginning with last quarter 1973, excludes shipments and financing of military orders placed by Israel under Public Law 93-199 and subsequent similar legislation. Line 77 differs from "net exports of goods and services" in the NIPAs for the same reasons with the exception of the military financing, which is excluded, and the additional exclusion of U.S. government interest payments to foreigners. The latter payments, for NIPA's purposes, are excluded from "net exports of goods and services" but included with transfers in "net foreign investment."

12. Because of the introduction of new reporting forms for nonbank claims and liabilities, the maturity breakdown is available only on a limited basis.

13. Because of the introduction of new reporting forms for bank-related transactions, the maturity breakdown is available only on a limited basis.

14. Includes foreign-currency-denominated notes sold to private residents abroad.

APPENDIX 4.2: A Review of Comparative Advantage

INTUITIVE EXPLANATION

Comparative advantage is not one of the most intuitive results in economics, and it can require a little thought to leave the reader convinced of the validity of the argument. Discovered by the English stockbroker-millionare David Ricardo, the idea helps answer the following questions:

> Suppose that the United States is much more efficient than Japan in producing food and marginally more efficient than Japan in producing steel. Suppose also that food and steel are the only items produced and required in both countries. In a totally free-trade world:
> 1 Should and would Japan produce anything at all?
> 2 If Japan does produce something, would both countries simultaneously be better off?

Obviously, the world must be better off as a whole if Japan produces something rather than nothing. Otherwise, some of the resources of the world will be idle. Even if they are relatively inefficiently used, these resources can make a positive contribution to world output. Consequently, Japan should produce something, and presumably that something should be the output which Japan can produce *relatively* more efficiently vis-à-vis the United States, even if in absolute terms it is less efficient in producing that output. By assumption Japan is relatively or comparatively more efficient in producing steel; that is, in producing that output, Japan is by assumption only marginally less efficient than the United States. If Japan produces steel, this can release factors of production in the United States for food, and the world's overall output can be larger. Therefore, with some distribution of world output, both countries can be simultaneously better off.

TABLE 4A.1
INPUT/OUTPUT UNDER AUTARKY REGIME*

Output	United States	Japan
Number of people per ton of output		
Food	10	25
Steel	4	5
Millions of people employed/output		
Food	60	50
Steel	60	50
Autarky output, millions of tons		
Food	6	2
Steel	15	10

Autarky means existing in isolation.

TABLE 4A.2
INPUT/OUTPUT UNDER FREE TRADE

Output	United States	Japan
Millions of people employed/output		
Food	88	0
Steel	32	100
Trading output, millions of tons		
Food	8.8	0
Steel	8	20
Consumption amounts under trading division		
Food	6.4	2.4
Steel	16	12

AN EXAMPLE

In case you remain unconvinced from the preceding argument or were not already convinced from an introductory economics course, we can show comparative advantage with an example.

Suppose that the total number of workers or available people power in the United States and Japan and also the efficiency of these people for the given stock of land and capital with which they can work are as given in Table 4A.1. The bottom rows of Table 4A.1 give the total output of food and steel in each country if half of the working population is employed in each activity. For example, 60 million Americans can produce 6 million tons of food when 10 people are required per ton, and the other 60 million who work can produce 15 million tons of steel. We have in Table 4A.1 a total world output of food of 8 million tons and a total world output of steel of 25 million tons.

Suppose now that all the Japanese workers devote their energies to producing steel and that, for example, 88 million Americans produce food and the remaining 32 million working Americans produce steel. The effect of this is shown in Table 4A.2. We find that with Japan specializing in steel, the output in which it has a comparative although not absolute advantage, total output for the two countries combined is 8.8 million tons of food and 28 million tons of steel. The combined output of both items has increased by 10 percent or more, merely by having Japan concentrate on its comparative advantage, steel, and the United States concentrate on its comparative advantage, food.

The United States and Japan can both be richer if they trade certain amounts between themselves. One such trading division would be for the United States to sell Japan 2.4 million tons of food and to buy from Japan 8 million tons of steel, giving a relative "price" or "terms of trade" of 0.3 ton of food per ton of steel. The United States and Japan would then end up consuming the amounts in the bottom rows of Table 4A.2, all of which exceed what they could consume under autarky as shown in Table 4A.1.

APPENDIX 4.3: Summary of Exchange Rate Systems

Country	1a	1b	1c	1d	1e	1f	1g	2	3	4	5	6	R1	R2
Afghanistan								●					●	●
Algeria						●							●	●
Argentina							●							●
Australia							●							●
Austria						●								●
Bahamas	●								●				●	●
Bahrain						●								
Bangladesh						●			●	●	●		●	●
Barbados	●												●	●
Belgium and Luxembourg					●				●		●	●		
Benin			●											●
Bolivia	●													
Botswana						●							●	●
Brazil							●		●	●	●	●	●	●
Burma						□●							●	●
Burundi	●												●	●
Cameroon			●											●
Canada								●						
Cape Verde						●							●	●
Central African Rep.			●										●	●
Chad			●										●	●
Chile	●													●
China, People's Rep. of							●						●	●
Colombia							●		●	●	●	●	●	●
Comoros			●										●	●
Congo			●										●	●

Exchange Arrangement

1. Exchange rate maintained within relatively narrow margins in terms of:
   - a U.S. dollar
   - b pound sterling
   - c French franc
   - d South African rand or Spanish peseta
   - e A cooperative exchange arrangement (under mutual intervention system)
   - f A composite of currencies
   - g A set of indicators
2. Exchange rate not maintained within relatively narrow margins as in a – g above, or otherwise determined (see country pages)
3. Separate exchange rates for some or all capital transactions and/or some or all invisibles
4. Import rate(s) different from export rate(s)
5. More than one rate for imports
6. More than one rate for exports

Payments Restrictions

1. Restrictions on payments for current transactions
2. Restrictions on payments for capital transactions

Country	a	b	c	d	e	f	g	2	3	4	5	6	P1	P2
Ivory Coast			●											●
Italy					●				●				●	●
Israel								●						●
Ireland					●									●
Iraq	●												●	●
Iran							□	●					●	●
Indonesia								●					—	—
India								●					●	●
Iceland								●	●				●	●
Hong Kong								●					—	—
Honduras	●												—	●
Haiti	●													●
Guyana	●												●	●
Guinea-Bissau							□	●					●	●
Guinea							□	●					●	●
Guatemala	●													●
Grenada	●								●	●	●		●	●
Greece								●					●	●
Ghana								●	●	●	●	●	●	●
Germany, Fed. Rep. of					●									—
The Gambia		●												●
Gabon			●											●
France					●									●
Finland						●								●
Fiji						●								●
Ethiopia	●										●		●	●
Equatorial Guinea				●					●				●	●
El Salvador	●												●	●
Egypt	●								●	●	●		●	●
Ecuador	●								●				—	—
Dominican Republic	●								●	●	●	●		●
Dominica	●												—	●
Djibouti	●												—	—
Denmark					●								—	●
Cyprus						●							●	●
Costa Rica								●	●				—	—

Exchange Arrangement.

1. Exchange rate maintained within relatively narrow margins in terms of:
   - a U.S. dollar
   - b pound sterling
   - c French franc
   - d South African rand or Spanish peseta
   - e A cooperative exchange arrangement (under mutual intervention system)
   - f A composite of currencies
   - g A set of indicators
2. Exchange rate not maintained within relatively narrow margins[4] as in a – g above, or otherwise determined (see country pages)
3. Separate exchange rates for some or all capital transactions and/or some or all invisibles
4. Import rate(s) different from export rate(s)
5. More than one rate for imports
6. More than one rate for exports

Payments Restrictions

1. Restrictions on payments for current transactions (P1)
2. Restrictions on payments for capital transactions (P2)

Exchange Arrangement
1. Exchange rate maintained within relatively narrow margins in terms of:
   - *a* U.S. dollar
   - *b* pound sterling
   - *c* French franc
   - *d* South African rand or Spanish peseta
   - *e* A cooperative exchange arrangement (under mutual intervention system)
   - *f* A composite of currencies
   - *g* A set of indicators
2. Exchange rate not maintained within relatively narrow margins[4] as in *a – g* above, or otherwise determined (see country pages)
3. Separate exchange rates for some or all capital transactions and/or some or all invisibles
4. Import rate(s) different from export rate(s)
5. More than one rate for imports
6. More than one rate for exports

Payments Restrictions
1. Restrictions on payments for current transactions
2. Restrictions on payments for capital transactions

Country	1a	1b	1c	1d	1e	1f	1g	2	3	4	5	6	PR1	PR2
Niger			●										●	●
Nicaragua	●								●		●	●	●	●
New Zealand								●						●
Netherlands Antilles	●													●
Netherlands					●									
Nepal	●									●	●	●	●	●
Morocco						●							●	●
Mexico								●						
Mauritius						□ ●				●			●	●
Mauritania						●							●	●
Malta						●							●	●
Mali			●											●
Maldives								●						
Malaysia						●								
Malawi						□ ●							●	●
Madagascar			●										●	●
Libyan Arab Jamahiriya	●													●
Liberia	●													
Lesotho				●						●				●
Lebanon								●						
Lao People's Dem. Rep.	●									●			●	●
Kuwait						●								
Korea								●						●
Kenya						□ ●					●		●	●
Jordan						□ ●								●
Japan								●						
Jamaica	●												●	●

	Nigeria	Norway	Oman	Pakistan	Panama	Papua New Guinea	Paraguay	Peru	Philippines	Portugal	Qatar	Romania	Rwanda	St. Lucia	St. Vincent and Grenadines	São Tomé and Principe	Saudi Arabia	Senegal	Seychelles
Exchange Arrangement																			
1. Exchange rate maintained within relatively narrow margins in terms of: *a* U.S. dollar	—	—	●	●	●	—	●	—	—	—	—	●	●	●	●	—	—	—	—
b pound sterling	—	—	—	—	—	—	—	—	—	—	—	—	—	—	—	—	—	—	—
c French franc	—	—	—	—	—	—	—	—	—	—	—	—	—	—	—	—	—	●	—
d South African rand or Spanish peseta	—	—	—	—	—	—	—	—	—	—	—	—	—	—	—	—	—	—	—
e A cooperative exchange arrangement (under mutual intervention system)	—	—	—	—	—	—	—	—	—	—	—	—	—	—	—	—	—	—	—
f A composite of currencies	—	●	—	—	—	●	—	—	—	—	—	—	—	—	—	□ ●	—	—	□ ●
g A set of indicators	—	—	—	—	—	—	—	●	—	●	—	—	—	—	—	—	—	—	—
2. Exchange rate not maintained within relatively narrow margins[4] as in *a* – *g* above, or otherwise determined (see country pages)	●	—	—	—	—	—	—	—	●	—	●	—	—	—	—	—	●	—	—
3. Separate exchange rates for some or all capital transactions and/or some or all invisibles	—	—	—	—	—	—	●	●	—	—	—	●	—	—	—	—	—	—	—
4. Import rate(s) different from export rate(s)	—	—	—	—	—	—	●	●	—	—	—	●	—	—	—	—	—	—	—
5. More than one rate for imports	—	—	—	—	—	—	●	—	—	—	—	●	—	—	—	—	—	—	—
6. More than one rate for exports	—	—	—	—	—	—	●	●	—	—	—	●	—	—	—	—	—	—	—
Payments Restrictions																			
1. Restrictions on payments for current transactions	●	—	—	●	—	—	—	—	●	●	—	●	●	●	●	●	—	—	—
2. Restrictions on payments for capital transactions	●	●	—	●	—	●	●	—	●	●	—	●	●	●	●	●	—	●	—

	Sierra Leone	Singapore	Solomon Islands	Somalia	South Africa	Spain	Sri Lanka	Sudan	Suriname	Swaziland	Sweden	Syrian Arab Rep.	Tanzania	Thailand	Togo	Trinidad and Tobago	Tunisia	Turkey
Exchange Arrangement																		
1. Exchange rate maintained within relatively narrow margins in terms of: *a* U.S. dollar	—	—	—	●	—	—	—	●	●	—	—	●	—	—	—	●	—	—
b pound sterling	—	—	—	—	—	—	—	—	—	—	—	—	—	—	—	—	—	—
c French franc	—	—	—	—	—	—	—	—	—	—	—	—	—	—	●	—	—	—
d South African rand or Spanish peseta	—	—	—	—	—	—	—	—	—	●	—	—	—	—	—	—	—	—
e A cooperative exchange arrangement (under mutual intervention system)	—	—	—	—	—	—	—	—	—	—	—	—	—	—	—	—	—	—
f A composite of currencies	□ ●	●	●	—	—	—	—	—	—	—	●	—	●	●	—	—	●	—
g A set of indicators	—	—	—	—	—	—	—	—	—	—	—	—	—	—	—	—	—	—
2. Exchange rate not maintained within relatively narrow margins[4] as in *a* – *g* above, or otherwise determined (see country pages)	—	—	—	—	●	●	●	—	—	—	—	—	—	—	—	—	—	●
3. Separate exchange rates for some or all capital transactions and/or some or all invisibles	—	—	—	—	●	—	—	●	—	●	—	●	—	—	—	—	—	●
4. Import rate(s) different from export rate(s)	—	—	—	—	—	—	—	●	—	—	—	●	—	—	—	—	—	●
5. More than one rate for imports	—	—	—	—	—	—	—	●	—	—	—	●	—	—	—	—	—	●
6. More than one rate for exports	—	—	—	—	—	—	—	●	—	—	—	●	—	—	—	—	—	●
Payments Restrictions																		
1. Restrictions on payments for current transactions	●	—	—	●	●	—	●	●	—	—	—	●	●	—	●	—	●	●
2. Restrictions on payments for capital transactions	●	—	●	●	●	●	●	●	●	●	●	●	●	●	●	●	●	●

Key and Footnotes

● indicates that practice exists.
□ indicates that the composite is the SDR.

| | Exchange Arrangement — 1. Exchange rate maintained within relatively narrow margins in terms of: | | | | | | | 2. Exchange rate not maintained within relatively narrow margins[4] as in a–g above, or otherwise determined (see country pages) | 3. Separate exchange rates for some or all capital transactions and/or some or all invisibles | 4. Import rate(s) different from export rate(s) | 5. More than one rate for imports | 6. More than one rate for exports | Payments Restrictions — 1. Restrictions on payments for current transactions | 2. Restrictions on payments for capital transactions |
	a U.S. dollar	b pound sterling	c French franc	d South African rand or Spanish peseta	e A cooperative exchange arrangement (under mutual intervention system)	f A composite of currencies	g A set of indicators							
Zimbabwe						●							●	●
Zambia						□ ●					●		●	●
Zaire						□ ●							●	●
Yugoslavia								●					●	●
Yemen, Peop. Dem. Rep.	●												●	●
Yemen, Arab Rep.	●													
Western Samoa								●		●			●	●
Viet Nam						□ ●			●				●	●
Venezuela	●								●					
Uruguay								●						
Upper Volta			●											●
United States								●						
United Kingdom								●						
United Arab Emirates								●						
Uganda						□ ●							●	●

Source: Annual Report on Exchange Arrangements and Exchange Restrictions, 1981, International Monetary Fund, Washington, D.C.

CHAPTER 5

THE INTERNATIONAL FINANCIAL ENVIRONMENT WITH FIXED EXCHANGE RATES

In our description of the international economic environment we will take the view of the financial executive who is interested in forecasting exchange rates, or at least in understanding when and why they change. This will, of course, require that we give an account of the nature of the international environment, since foreign currency values are determined in that environment. In the previous chapter we described how the various factors that affect exchange rates are recorded in the balance of international payments statistics. However, as we have noted, the balance of payments statistics take on a different meaning and importance according to whether exchange rates are fixed or flexible. In this chapter we will look at how fixed exchange rates are affected by economic events. In the following chapter we will take on the task of explaining changes in a flexible system, where exchange rates are determined in a free market and without government involvement.

Understanding what causes exchange rates to change is particularly important to the financial executive who is considering investing or borrowing abroad. For example, there is an advantage to avoiding investment in countries whose currencies may suffer an unexpected decline. An awareness of the factors affecting exchange rates and of the implications of changes is also important when forecasting cash flows from international operations. Exporting and importing firms will experience changes in both product prices and volumes from changes in exchange rates, and cash planning therefore requires close scrutiny of economic developments. This chapter is devoted to explaining how exchange rates are determined in a fixed-rate system. We will postpone the question of how good exchange rate forecasts can be. The question of forecasting accuracy is closely connected to the "efficiency" of the foreign exchange market—a term we will define—and we will leave the question unanswered until we have developed the necessary tools.

We can begin our explanation of the fixed exchange rate system by recalling that when markets move out of equilibrium, there is generally a force or automatic adjustment mechanism working toward restoring that equilibrium. In the theory of supply and demand the mechanism is the market price, which falls with excess supply and rises with excess demand to restore the equality of market supply and demand. In the Keynesian theory in macroeconomics, a key mechanism is the adjustment of national income. When withdrawals (savings, taxes, imports) exceed injections (investment, government spending, exports) the leakages from the circular flow of income reduce the gross national product (GNP) and therefore savings, again restoring equality between withdrawals and injections. These various adjustment mechanisms re-establish equilibrium, if market conditions are stable.

Fixed exchange rates exhibit a number of different, simultaneously operating adjustment mechanisms which work to remove deficits (or surpluses) in the balance of payments. The mechanisms collectively serve a role that is similar to the role of prices in the theory of supply and demand. Generally, however, they do not work as well as price adjustment mechanisms, and balance of payments adjustment under fixed exchange rates is rarely complete. Because there is no rapidly working automatic adjustment to restore international financial balance under fixed exchange rates, the government frequently feels the need for economic policy action to speed the return to equilibrium. This need is akin to that for monetary and fiscal policy for stabilizing the domestic economy.

With so many countries still fixing their exchange rate to other currencies and so many countries with a managed or dirty float, the mechanisms for eliminating imbalances in the fixed exchange rate system remain a lively topic of debate. The debate centers on the effectiveness of the automatic adjustment mechanisms and on whether they need to be supplemented with discretionary government policies.

We will begin our account of the effectiveness of automatic adjustment mechanisms with the so-called price-level mechanism, which will work in all fixed-rate systems. We will explain the specifics of the various systems and agreements as we proceed, but a quick survey will give an overview. Until 1914 the world was on a "gold standard." Immediately after the First World War there was a period of flexible exchange rates, followed in 1926 by an attempt to return to the gold standard. The gold standard was abandoned with the depression of 1929–1933, and from the depression until 1944 there were widespread foreign exchange controls. In 1944 a "gold-exchange standard" emerged with the Bretton Woods Agreement, and it lasted until it was replaced in 1968 by a "dollar standard," which survived until just after the Smithsonian Agreement in 1972, when many countries abandoned fixed rates. Exchange rates remained fixed within parts of Europe, with the "snake" followed by the European Monetary System of 1980. Let us begin to describe the price-level adjustment by showing how it worked under the gold standard.

ADJUSTMENT VIA THE PRICE LEVEL

The Gold Standard Adjustment Mechanism

The price-level adjustment that existed with the gold standard exchange system is known as the *price-specie adjustment mechanism*. This mechanism was explained as early as 1752.[1] In order to explain the mechanism, it is easiest to begin with a world in which every country uses the same money and to let that common money be gold. This is the most primitive kind of fixed exchange rate system, since 1 ounce of one country's gold can be exchanged for 1 ounce of another country's gold. If gold is the only money, it can be used for making purchases from people at home or from people in another country. Everyone will recognize and accept the common money. If the residents of one country purchase more from the foreigners than they sell to the foreigners, they will send more gold out of the country than flows in. The deficit country's money supply will decline. Similarly, in the other country there will be more gold flowing in than flowing out. This leaves us with a conclusion that is central to a discussion of fixed exchange rates—that is, that deficits reduce the supply of money and surpluses raise it.

In the minds of the eighteenth-century classical economists who described the workings of the gold standard, the fall in the money supply in the deficit country would cause a general fall in prices. At the same time, the increase in the money supply in the surplus countries (in the world we are describing, one country's deficit must represent other countries' surpluses) would cause a general increase in prices. The link between money supply and prices that the classical economists had in mind is the *quantity theory of money*. Many readers already have seen the quantity equation favorably or unfavorably reviewed in some introductory or intermediate course in economics. The level of controversy that surrounds the quantity equation is such that opinions are, in general, strongly held one way or the other.

In the case the reader has not previously met the quantity equation, he or she can start by imagining a primitive economy in which there are 1000 pieces of paper saying "this is one dollar" and where 100 fruits are produced and sold each year. The fruits are the only output that the people have and need, and they can be used as food, for heat, and for everything else. If each "dollar" is used on the average once a year, then 1000 pieces of paper will be traded one way, and 100 fruits will be traded the other way. On the average, each fruit must be worth $10 if 1000 dollars are paid for 100 fruits.

If the number of dollars is doubled and the dollars are still used on the average once a year, then 2000 dollars will go one way, and 100 fruits will go the other way in each year. The fruits must cost an average of $20 if 2000 dollars are paid for 100 fruits. We find that twice the money supply means twice the price level. The quantity theory holds in the same way for the less primitive economies in which we live, which produce diverse national products rather than homogeneous fruits.[2]

We can now complete our description of the gold standard adjustment mechanism. The supply of money in a deficit country will decline because more gold flows out to buy foreign goods than flows in for local products. It follows from the

[1] The price-specie adjustment system is described by David Hume in "Of the Balance of Trade," in "Of Money," *Political Discourses*, 1752. This is reprinted in Richard Cooper, *International Finance*, Penguin Books, Baltimore, 1969.
[2] It is likely that the reader will recognize the importance of the constant velocity and output assumed in our argument. The quantity theory requires only that velocity is "stable" and that output is inflexible. These are subject to much testing, and evidence abounds. Since, however, our purpose is to quickly review the quantity equation, we need not go any further.

quantity theory that the price level will also decline. At the same time, the surplus countries' money supplies will increase from net inflows of gold, and so will their prices. We will therefore find prices in deficit countries falling in relation to prices in surplus countries. The fall in relative prices will make the deficit country's exports more competitive and make them increase. In addition, domestically produced goods will appear cheaper than foreign goods to local residents. Imports will therefore decline. With exports increasing and imports decreasing, the deficit country's deficit will decline. As long as the deficit exists, the deficit country's money supply will continue to fall and the surplus country's money supply will continue to rise until balance is restored. This is the price-specie adjustment mechanism. Expressed succinctly, a deficit causes a declining money supply and lower prices, which in turn stimulate exports, reduce imports, and thereby eliminate the deficit.

The price-specie adjustment mechanism, which works via changes in relative prices *between* countries, is augmented by an adjustment mechanism affecting relative prices *within* each country. In the deficit country, for example, the prices of nontraded goods will decline according to the quantity theory, but the prices of goods which enter international trade will remain unchanged. This is because prices of traded goods are determined by world supply and demand, not by deficits and surpluses in balances of payments. The fall in the relative prices of nontraded goods in the deficit country will encourage local consumers to switch from the traded goods to the nontraded goods. At the same time, local producers will find it relatively more profitable to produce traded goods. The switch in consumer spending will free more exports, and the producers will produce more export items. These effects will be reinforced by developments in the surplus countries. The prices of nontraded goods there will rise in relation to the prices of traded goods, switching consumers toward traded goods and producers away from them. Altogether, we will find more exports from deficit countries, fewer imports, and an improved balance of payments.[3]

The gold standard that was in existence until 1914 and returned for a brief period from 1926 to 1929 did not exist in a world in which only gold was used for exchange. Instead, it existed in a world in which gold was used alongside paper (or fiat) money. (*Fiat money* is money whose face or stated value is greater than its intrinsic value.) The central banks maintained the value of paper money in terms of gold by agreeing to exchange the paper money for gold at a fixed price, for example, $25 per ounce or £5 per ounce. This gold standard reveals the same price-specie adjustment mechanism that is found in the gold-only world we have already described, *if* deficits continue to reduce the supply of money. But do deficits reduce the money supply when we have both gold and paper money in circulation?

Gold Standard with Paper Money

When central banks or governments stood ready to exchange gold for paper money at a fixed rate of exchange, they had to make sure that they had sufficient gold on

---

[3] For an account of this and other fixed exchange rate adjustment systems, see Rudiger Dornbusch, *Open Economy Macroeconomics*, Basic Books, Inc., New York, 1980, or Leland Yeager, *International Monetary Relations: Theory, History, and Policy*, 2d ed., Harper & Row, Inc., New York, 1976, chap. 5.

hand for those occasions when many people wished to return paper money for gold. Prudent banking would have required a minimum reserve ratio of gold, and this was established in the United States by a law requiring the Fed (the U.S. Federal Reserve) to back its notes with gold.

The maintenance of a minimum reserve gave rise to the same adjustment mechanism as in the gold-only world we have just described. Deficits between countries were still met with gold, since gold was the money that was acceptable everywhere. If a country had a deficit, it therefore lost gold. To maintain the required reserve ratio of paper money to gold, the central bank was forced to reduce the amount of paper money in circulation. Deficits therefore reduced money supplies and, according to the quantity theory of money, also prices. Similarly, the governments of surplus countries could print more money (which was desirable, because they could spend it and obtain more goods than were represented by the cost of the paper), and prices would rise.

While the automatic adjustment mechanism could still exist in a combined gold-and-paper-money gold standard system, in practice the mechanism can be more or less effective than in a gold-only system. It is more effective to the extent that the existence of fractional reserves magnifies the effects of changes in gold reserves. For example, if a country maintains a 25 percent gold reserve and runs a deficit of $1 billion, it will lose $1 billion in gold. To maintain the required reserve ratio, it must reduce the money supply by $4 billion. The adjustment mechanism is therefore enhanced.

Arguing for a less effective gold standard when we have paper money plus gold, rather than gold only, the government may be tempted to abandon the required reserve ratio when the maintenance of that ratio runs counter to other objectives. If a deficit is not allowed to reduce the money supply because, for example, the government thinks the reduction will raise interest rates or unemployment to intolerable levels, the adjustment mechanism is lost. If, at the same time, the surplus countries with rising gold reserves do not print more paper money because of, for example, a fear of inflation, then both causes of a relative price-level adjustment are lost; we lose the lower prices in the deficit country and the higher prices elsewhere. The policy of not allowing a change in reserves to change the supply of money is known as *sterilization* or *neutralization policy*. As goals of full employment became common in the twentieth century, many countries abandoned their efforts to maintain the required reserve ratio and focused on their local economic ills.

As a result of sterilization, the gold standard was not allowed to work. This is perhaps the most powerful criticism of the system. But that does not explain whether it *could have* worked. Some economists, most notably Robert Triffin, have said that it could not work.[4] Central to this view is the notion that prices are rigid downward (a feature of Keynesian economics) and that therefore deficits from gold outflows cannot be self-correcting, because prices cannot fall. Critics of the gold

[4] Robert Triffin, "The Myth and Realities of the So-called Gold Standard," in *The Evolution of the International Monetary System: Historical Reappraisal and Future Perspective*, Princeton University Press, Princeton, N.J., 1964. This is reprinted in Richard Cooper, *International Finance*, Penguin Books, Baltimore, 1969.

standard support this with evidence on the parallel movement of prices in surplus and deficit countries, rather than the reverse movement implied by the gold standard. It is true that without a decline in *absolute* prices, improving the balance of deficit countries is more difficult. However, it is *relative* prices which are relevant (including those of nontraded versus traded goods *within* the country), and these could decline if surplus countries' prices rise to a greater extent than those of deficit countries. If, therefore, prices are flexible upward and surplus countries' prices rise faster than those of the deficit country, we still have an automatic adjustment mechanism, although it is weaker than the mechanism that might have existed if absolute prices could fall. The other common criticism of the gold standard—that gold flows were frequently sterilized—is a valid criticism, but it is as much a criticism of the government for not allowing the gold standard to operate as it is of the gold standard itself.

A number of twentieth-century economists and politicians have favored a return to the gold standard. What appeals to the proponents of this system is the discipline that the gold standard placed on the expansion of the money supply and the check that this therefore placed on that creeping evil, inflation. The economists who prefer a return to the gold standard include Jacques Rueff and Michael Heilperin.[5] The politicians include late French President Charles de Gaulle and President Reagan. A return to the gold standard, or some standard based on gold, would make exchange rate forecasting a relatively straightforward task. The exchange rate in normal times would vary within limits known as *gold points*, which are set by the buying or selling prices of gold at the central banks and by the cost of shipping the precious metal from country to country. Larger changes in exchange rates would occur when countries changed the price of their currency in terms of gold, and this would be a reasonably predictable event. Countries that were running out of reserves would raise the price of gold, while countries which were gaining reserves might lower it. These conclusions are not obvious, and an explanation is provided in an appendix.

The Gold-Exchange and Dollar Standards

With a gold standard, exchange rates, or at least their range of potential variation, are determined indirectly via the conversion price of each currency vis-à-vis gold. When the gold standard came to an end with the depression of 1929–1933, the exchange rate system which eventually replaced it in 1944 (after war and general disarray) offered direct determination of exchange rates. The system adopted in 1944 is called the *gold-exchange standard*. This direct method of determining exchange rates allowed movement in exchange rates between the "support points." At these support points the central banks purchased and sold their currency for U.S. dollars to ensure that the exchange rate did not move beyond these points. In return

---

[5]See Jacques Rueff, "Gold Exchange Standard: A Danger to the West," *The Times* (London), June 27–29, 1961, reprinted in Herbert G. Grubel (ed.), *International Monetary Reform: Plans and Issues,* Stanford University Press, Palo Alto, Calif., 1963, and Michael Heilperin, "The Case for Going Back to Gold," *Fortune*, September 1962, also reprinted in Grubel.

for foreign central banks fixing or "pegging" their currencies to the U.S. dollar, the United States fixed the price of the dollar to gold, and so the gold-exchange standard involved:

1 The United States offering to exchange U.S. dollars for gold at an official rate, which for a long time was $35 per ounce
2 Other countries offering to exchange their currencies for dollars at an offical or *parity* exchange rate

We will deal later with the history of the international financial system, but we can note that the ability to convert (foreign) *privately* held gold to dollars by the United States lasted until 1968, and the ability to convert foreign *officially* held gold lasted until 1971. With only the second part of the gold-exchange standard remaining in effect—that part involving the exchange of foreign currencies for dollars—the fixed exchange system from 1968 on is best described as a dollar standard. (We pick the date 1968 because there was little official exchange of dollars for gold between 1968 and 1971, even though it was formally allowed.) A price-level adjustment mechanism somewhat like the price-specie adjustment mechanism of the gold standard is present in both the gold-exchange and dollar standards. This price-level mechanism in the gold-exchange and dollar standards originates in the common feature of the convertibility of foreign currencies for the dollar.

Price-Level Adjustment under Gold-Exchange and Dollar Standards

As we have said, under the gold-exchange standard and the dollar standard, countries which fixed or, more precisely, "pegged" their exchange rates to the U.S. dollar were required to keep the actual rate close to (within 1 percent of) the selected or "parity" value. In order to ensure that the exchange rate vis-à-vis the dollar remained within the required 1 percent of official parity, it was necessary for central banks to intervene whenever free-market forces would have created an exchange rate that was outside the range. This intervention took the form of buying and selling the local currency for U.S. dollars at the upper and lower support points around official parity. The support points meant adding to or reducing central bank official reserves whenever the uncontrolled exchange rate would have moved beyond the official limits. We can illustrate the way these fixed exchange standards operated by using a diagram.

Suppose that the Bank of England has decided, as it did from 1949 to 1967, that it wishes to peg the value of the pound sterling at a central value of $2.80. The upper and lower support points that the bank must maintain are $2.8280/£ and $2.7720/£. These are shown on the vertical axis of Figure 5.1, which gives the spot price of pounds in terms of dollars. The horizontal axis gives the quantity of pounds, and so the diagram has the usual price and quantity axes so familiar from the theory of supply and demand. We have added to the diagram conventionally sloping supply and demand curves for pounds drawn against the price of pounds (measured in terms of dollars).

FIGURE 5.1
The workings of the gold-exchange and dollar standards.

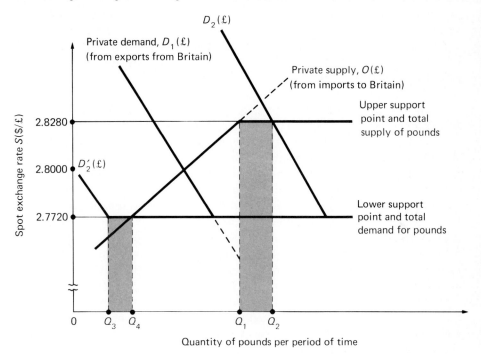

With the gold-exchange and dollar standards the Bank of England stood ready to buy pounds at the lower support point and sell pounds at the upper support point. This made the demand for pounds perfectly elastic at the lower support point and the supply perfectly elastic at the upper support point, ensuring that rates fell in the allowable range.

The supply of pounds rises when the British sell pounds in order to obtain foreign exchange to pay for imports into Britain. In order to draw the supply curve of pounds with an upward slope as we have with $O(£)$—where the $O(£)$ notation helps prevent confusion with spot rates—we can think of what happens to the desire of the British to purchase imports as we raise the value of the pound. As we move up the vertical axis to higher values of the pound, imports become cheaper in Britain. For example, a pair of U.S.-made jeans at $28 per pair is £10 at $2.8000/£ but only £9.90 at $2.8280/£. We will therefore have more imports at higher values of $S(\$/£)$ and expect more pounds to be offered, which is why we call $O(£)$ an *offer curve*.[6]

---

[6] There is a good chance that there will not be more pounds offered. More *jeans* (and other imports) will be purchased, but if, for example, the dollar price of the imports remains fixed, then purchasing more jeans for fewer pounds each could mean *fewer* pounds being supplied/offered. Indeed, if the import price elasticity of demand is in the inelastic range (<1), the price of imports in terms of pounds will fall by more than the quantity of imports will rise, and the amount of pounds supplied will fall. This will give a downward-sloping supply curve rather than the conventional upward slope. We see that the situation is potentially complex, and we must postpone an analysis of it.

The demand for pounds exists because pounds are needed to purchase British exports such as goods, services, or capital. If we think of goods and services but not of capital, we can say that as the pound becomes cheaper and we move down the vertical axis, British goods become cheaper to non-British people, and more will be exported from Britain. This will raise the demand for British pounds. This gives the downward slope to the demand curve.[7] We have drawn the original demand for pounds, $D_1(£)$, intersecting the supply or offer curve, $O(£)$, within the 1 percent range of the official parity.

Suppose that for some exogenous reason there is an increase in demand for British exports. This might, for example, be because of a general economic expansion outside of Britain or a change in taste toward British goods. This will shift the demand curve for pounds to the right, from D_1 (£) to D_2 (£), and the demand for pounds will then intersect the private supply or offer curve at an exchange rate above the allowed ceiling. In order to prevent this, the Bank of England must, according to the gold-exchange and dollar standards, intervene at the upper support point of $2.8280/£ and supply, in exchange for dollars, the pounds necessary to keep the rate from moving above this level. In terms of Figure 5.1, the Bank of England will supply Q_1Q_2 pounds for dollars. This, with the private supply of OQ_1 pounds sterling and the demand curve of $D_2(£)$, would leave the rate at $2.8280. Because the Bank of England will supply whatever number of pounds is required at the upper support point, the supply curve of pounds becomes flat at this point, like the heavily drawn line in Figure 5.1. This is a feature of the gold-exchange and dollar standards; the supply curve of the local currency becomes perfectly elastic at the upper support point.[8]

Suppose that instead of rising to $D_2(£)$, the demand for pounds falls to $D_2'(£)$ as a result of, perhaps, a general slowdown in economic activity outside of Britain or a feeling that the quality of British goods and services has deteriorated. According to private supply and demand, the price of the pound will fall below the lower support point, and to prevent this from happening, the Bank of England will enter the market and purchase pounds. It will purchase Q_3Q_4 pounds with $(2.7720 \times Q_3Q_4)$ in U.S. dollars. The dollar amount is given by the shaded area above Q_3Q_4; it represents the decline in dollar reserves of the Bank of England. It is hence the deficit in the balance of payments, measured in U.S. dollars. Because the Bank of England must demand whatever number of pounds is not wanted by private buyers, the demand for pounds that includes both private and official demand has a flat section at the lower support point. Total demand is the heavily drawn line in Figure 5.1. This is another feature of the gold-exchange and dollar standards: the demand for local currencies becomes perfectly elastic at the lower support point.

In order to understand the price-level adjustment mechanism of the gold-

---

[7] There is no ambiguity here. More British exports at the same pound price or at a higher pound price means more pounds demanded.

[8] While in Figure 5.1 the Bank of England supplies Q_1Q_2 pounds, it will be buying Q_1Q_2 times 2.8280 in dollars, which is the shaded area above Q_1Q_2 in the figure. The amount Q_1Q_2 is the gain in the Bank of England's foreign exchange reserves (its balance of payments surplus, valued in terms of pounds), and the area above Q_1Q_2 is the official British balance of payments surplus, valued in terms of dollars.

FIGURE 5.2
The price-level adjustment mechanism of the gold-exchange and dollar
standards.

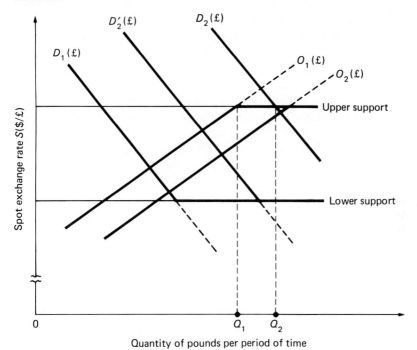

If the demand for pounds moves to $D_2(£)$ and exceeds the supply at the upper
support point, the Bank of England must sell pounds in exchange for dollars.
Ceteris paribus, this increases the British money supply and prices. Higher
prices make British exports decline, shifting the demand for pounds back
toward $D_2'(£)$. Higher prices also increase imports into Britain, and the offer
curve shifts from $O_1(£)$ toward $O_2(£)$. Shifts in demand and supply move
exchange rates toward their allowable range.

exchange and dollar standards, we refer to Figure 5.2. Suppose that after starting
with $O_1(£)$ and $D_1(£)$ and a privately determined exchange rate within the allowed
range, we find that there is an increase in private demand for pounds to $D_2(£)$. As
before, the Bank of England will be required to supply Q_1Q_2 pounds. These pounds
will increase the money supply in Britain; they will enter the system as the Bank of
England sells pounds for dollars. If we again employ the quantity theory of money,
the increase in the number of pounds in circulation will raise British prices. At each
exchange rate on our vertical axis, this will lower the competitiveness of British
goods. Exports will fall, and imports will increase.

The decline in British exports will mean a lower demand for pounds, and the
demand curve will move back. We can assume that it will move to $D_2'(£)$. The
increase in British imports will mean a larger supply of pounds to the foreign
exchange market, and the private supply curve will move to the right. We can move

it to $O_2(£)$. With the demand and supply at $D_2'(£)$ and $O_2(£)$, the free-market rate of exchange will return to the allowed range. We find that intervention by a central bank affects the supply of money, local prices, and exports and imports and thus restores free-market equilibrium. For example, a balance of payments surplus raises the supply of money and hence prices; as a result of this, exports are reduced, imports are increased, and the surplus is thereby eliminated. Of course, if there is sterilization of the balance of payments surplus and the money supply is not allowed to increase, the price-level adjustment mechanism will not work. Sterilization will eventually result in a continued growth in foreign exchange reserves and a need to revise the parity exchange rate. This makes exchange rate forecasting a potentially highly rewarding activity for the financial executive, since the bank's need to change the parity value becomes clearly apparent in the foreign exchange reserve statistics. It is quite worthwhile to see how forecasting can be done.

Forecasting with Fixed Exchange Rates

We have already noted that when exchange rates are determined on a gold standard, changes in rates will follow large changes in gold reserves. For example, countries which are losing reserves will eventually be forced to raise the price of gold in terms of their own currency. This means a fall in the foreign exchange value of the currency. To take an example, if Britain was losing gold and raised its gold price from £20 per ounce to £25 per ounce while the U.S. price remained fixed at $40 per ounce, the exchange rate would change from[9]

$$S(\$/£) = \frac{\$40/\text{ounce}}{£20/\text{ounce}} = \$2/£$$

to

$$S(\$/£) = \frac{\$40/\text{ounce}}{£25/\text{ounce}} = \$1.60/£$$

This is a devaluation of the pound. By keeping track of gold reserves, a financial executive could see that the central bank might be forced to raise the price of gold, that is, to devalue. The exact date would be difficult to predict, but actions based on such an assumption are unlikely to result in losses. A country that is losing reserves might manage not to devalue, but it certainly would not revalue, that is, raise the value of its currency by reducing the price of gold set by the central bank. This means that the financial manager would discover either that she or he was correct and a devaluation did occur or that the exchange rate remained as before. Thus there is an opportunity for a one-way bet, and the worst that is likely to happen is that no speculative gain will be made.

The "par" or middle exchange rate in a gold-exchange or dollar standard will respond to changes in reserve positions in a way that is similar to the response in a

---

[9]The exact link between gold prices and exchange rates is given in Appendix 5.1.

gold standard. The reserves held to defend the currency in a gold-exchange or dollar standard are made up of U.S. dollars, assets readily convertible to dollars, and gold. When these reserves are getting low, chances are that a devaluation, that is, a reduction in par value, will eventually take place. Indeed, speculation that a devaluation will occur is likely to make it occur. For example, prior to the 1980 devaluation of the Mexican peso, speculators had decided that a peso devaluation was imminent. They therefore sold pesos, and the Mexican authorities were required to purchase them at the lower support point. The pesos were purchased with U.S. dollars, and hence the Mexican reserves were lowered. Eventually, reserves were so much reduced that the Mexicans were forced to devalue. The speculators' beliefs were vindicated. In a sense, their expectations were self-fulfilling.

The need to reduce the value of a currency in a country experiencing deficits and declining reserves depends on the ability of the central bank to borrow additional reserves. There are arrangements between central banks for exchanging currency reserves, and there are many lines for borrowing from international institutions such as the International Monetary Fund (which we will discuss later). The borrowing arrangements include central bank swaps, which should be carefully distinguished from the swaps we discussed in Chapter 3. Those swaps involved going between spot exchange and forward exchange. Central bank swaps involve, for example, the U.S. government making U.S. dollars available to the Bank of Canada when Canadian foreign exchange reserves are low. The Bank of Canada will temporarily swap these U.S. dollars for Canadian dollars. The swap of U.S. dollars for Canadian dollars will be reversed later, according to the original agreement. Often the swap will be reversed only after a number of years to allow the borrowing country to correct its balance of payments. Central banks also frequently borrow from private banks. The Bank of Canada, for example, borrowed heavily from both Canadian and U.S. commercial banks during the late 1970s and early 1980s despite the fact that the exchange rate was supposed to be flexible. The ability of central banks to borrow from other central banks and from private banks and international institutions makes the forecasting of exchange rates more difficult. Revisions of par values can be delayed many years by countries with good credit ratings.

Another factor making exchange rate forecasting under fixed rates more difficult is the degree of urgency in reactions to surpluses and deficits. Countries that are facing a deficit and losing reserves will eventually be forced into a devaluation because their reserves and ability to borrow will eventually be gone. On the other hand, the countries enjoying surpluses will be under no pressure to revalue their currencies and may instead allow reserves to keep growing. A revaluation would allow their citizens to enjoy cheaper goods from abroad and lower inflation. This, however, does not seem to be as strong an incentive to change the currency value as running out of reserves.

INCOME ADJUSTMENT*

The price-level adjustment mechanism requires flexibility of prices in order to operate. The macroeconomic revolution marked by the publication of *The General*

Theory of Employment, Interest and Money by John Maynard Keynes, while focusing on a closed economy, spilled over into international finance and introduced an alternative adjustment mechanism that works if price flexibility does not exist.[10] This alternative adjustment mechanism, popularized by the followers of Keynes, involves automatic adjustment via changes in national income. Like the price-level adjustment mechanism, the income adjustment system operates on the current account. The most straightforward way of describing Keynesian adjustment is to employ a Keynesian income-expenditure model and show how variations in national income work to correct balance of payments surpluses and deficits.

A straightforward model which will reveal the important features of income adjustment consists of the following equations:

$$Y \equiv C + I_0 + (Ex_0 - Im) \tag{5.1}$$

$$C = C_0 + c \cdot Y \tag{5.2}$$

$$Im = Im_0 + m \cdot Y \tag{5.3}$$

In these equations, Y is the national income or GNP, C is aggregate consumption of goods and services, I_0 is the given amount of aggregate investment or capital formation, Ex_0 is the given amount of exports, and Im is imports.

The national income accounting identity is given by Equation (5.1), where, because it is not relevant for our purposes, we have omitted government spending. Y is the total value of *domestically produced* goods and services. Because it is difficult for government statisticians to separate consumption and investment of domestic goods from consumption and investment of imported goods, especially when domestic goods have imported components, C and I refer to the *total* consumption and investment of goods and services. In addition, exports, Ex_0, include re-exports, that is, items from abroad that are resold after reprocessing or used as inputs in exported products. Because Y refers to domestic production only, as the relevant output/income of a nation, and because C, I_0, and Ex_0 include imports, we must subtract imports, Im, to ensure the identity of (5.1). This is the most convenient approach from the viewpoint of a national income statistician, because records of imports exist with customs agents, and records of consumption and investment contain total amounts and do not show imported components separated from domestic components.

Equation (5.2) is the consumption function. The "intercept," C_0, is the part that does not depend on income. The effect of national income on consumption is given by the marginal propensity to consume, c, which will be between zero and unity. Since C represents all consumption, it includes the imports, Im, and the import equation itself is Equation (5.3). We assume that investment and exports are exogenous, or at least exogenous in relation to national income in the economy we are examining.

In order to discover how automatic adjustment via national income works, we

[10] John Maynard Keynes, *The General Theory of Employment, Interest and Money*, Macmillan and Company, London, 1936.

can begin with an intuitive explanation. Suppose the balance of payments is initially in balance and that there is an exogenous increase in exports, Ex. This means an increase in national income via Equation (5.1), which itself indirectly further increases income via the extra induced consumption in Equation (5.2). The higher national income will increase imports via Equation (5.3). We find that the initial increase in exports that moved the balance of payments into surplus will induce an increase in imports, which will tend to offset the effect of exports. This is an automatic adjustment working via income. It is not apparent from our intuitive explanation that this adjustment, while tending to restore balance, will not be complete. In order to see this, we can employ our model.

If we substitute Equations (5.2) and (5.3) in the national income accounting identity, Equation (5.1), we obtain

$$Y = C_0 + c \cdot Y + I_0 + \mathrm{Ex}_0 - \mathrm{Im}_0 - m \cdot Y \qquad (5.4)$$

By gathering terms, we can write Y as a function of exogenous terms:

$$Y = \frac{1}{1 - c + m} \cdot (C_0 + I_0 + \mathrm{Ex}_0 - \mathrm{Im}_0) \qquad (5.5)$$

The item in front of the open parenthesis, $1/(1 - c + m)$, is the "multiplier." We can note that the larger the "marginal propensity to import," m, the smaller will be the multiplier. The multiplier depends on the leakages from the circular flow of income, and by having imports, we add a leakage abroad, m, to the leakage into savings given by the marginal propensity to save, $1 - c$. The more leakages we have, the smaller the increase in income from any exogenous shock.

Let us allow exports to increase exogenously from Ex_0 to $\mathrm{Ex}_0 + \Delta \mathrm{Ex}$ and the corresponding increase in GNP to be from Y to $Y + \Delta Y$. We can therefore write

$$Y + \Delta Y = \frac{1}{1 - c + m} \cdot (C_0 + I_0 + \mathrm{Ex}_0 + \Delta \mathrm{Ex} - \mathrm{Im}_0) \qquad (5.6)$$

Subtracting each side of Equation (5.5) from Equation (5.6), we have

$$\Delta Y = \frac{1}{1 - c + m} \cdot \Delta \mathrm{Ex} \qquad (5.7)$$

The value of ΔY in Equation (5.7) gives the effect on national income of an exogenous change in exports. To find the induced effect on imports of this change in national income, we can use ΔY from Equation (5.7) in the import equation, Equation (5.3). Putting Equation (5.3) in terms of the new level of imports, $\mathrm{Im} + \Delta \mathrm{Im}$, after an increase in income to $Y + \Delta Y$, we have

$$\mathrm{Im} + \Delta \mathrm{Im} = \mathrm{Im}_0 + m \cdot (Y + \Delta Y) \qquad (5.8)$$

Subtracting Equation (5.3) from Equation (5.8) on both sides gives

$$\Delta \text{Im} = m \cdot \Delta Y \qquad (5.9)$$

and substituting ΔY from Equation (5.7) in Equation (5.9) gives

$$\Delta \text{Im} = \frac{m}{1 - c + m} \cdot \Delta \text{Ex} \qquad (5.10)$$

Equation (5.10) tells us that the automatic adjustment working via national income will raise imports by $m/(1 - c + m)$ times the initial increase in exports. The value of $m/(1 - c + m)$ is, however, below unity. [Since the marginal propensity to consume is below unity, that is, $c < 1, (1 - c) > 0$. We hence have m divided by itself *plus* the positive number $(1 - c)$. When a number is divided by a total larger than itself, the result is below unity. For example, if $c = 0.8$ and $m = 0.2$, imports will increase by only a half of any exogenous increase in exports. If $c = 0.4$ and $m = 0.2$, the offset is only a quarter.] What we have is an adjustment process via national income that is not complete. While an exogenous change in exports will change imports in the same direction, imports will change by less than the initial change in exports, and so initial effects persist.

Income and income adjustment are relevant to the financial manager who is trying to forecast movements in exchange rates. If a country's national income is growing more rapidly than that of others *as a result of growth in exports*, then the country's foreign exchange reserves will increase, and eventually the currency will probably increase in value. Induced increases in imports resulting from export growth will only partially dampen the growth of reserves and the need to eventually revalue the currency. When a nation's income is growing from a growth in domestic investment, I_0, or from growth in consumption or imports, C_0 or Im_0, then foreign exchange reserves will shrink, and eventually the exchange value of the currency will have to be reduced. The growth in income will raise imports but not exports, since these are determined primarily by the incomes of other nations.

There is an additional force, also working via changes in national income, that will help complete the automatic adjustment process. This force is induced by changes in the money supply, which in turn affect interest rates, the rate of investment, national income, and imports. The process works as follows. If we start in balance and an exogenous increase in exports does not induce a sufficient rise in imports to offset the increase in exports, a surplus will remain. Under fixed exchange rates this will require the central bank to supply its currency to prevent the price from rising. This is an increase in the supply of money. A money supply increase tends to lower the rate of interest. Lower interest rates stimulate investment, I, which will in turn both directly and indirectly work toward raising the national income, Y. Higher income will raise imports, Im, via Equation (5.3), helping to close the gap that began the process of adjustment.[11]

---

[11] When we introduce the money supply into the adjustment mechanism, we are getting close to the *monetary approach* to the balance of payments. We will save our presentation of this approach until we have explained the other automatic adjustment mechanisms under fixed exchange rates.

The force that we have just described involves a lowering of interest rates via the money supply. The effect of interest rates, working via investment and income on imports and the current account, is in addition to the effect they have on capital flows and the capital account. Since capital flows are highly responsive to interest rate differentials, this mechanism is likely to be the most effective one that exists under fixed exchange rates. We shall examine this effect on the capital account and then combine it with the effect on the current account, including the price-level and income adjustment mechanisms we have given.

INTEREST ADJUSTMENT

The automatic interest rate adjustment mechanism relies on the effect of the balance of payments on the money supply. We have seen that if the effects are not sterilized, a balance of payments deficit should reduce the supply of money, and a surplus should raise it. This was most obvious in a gold-only world, where a deficit meant gold—that is, money supply—outflows, and a surplus meant gold inflows. The effect on the money supply was less direct in the actual gold standard of the early twentieth century, where paper currency and gold were exchangeable at fixed prices in the central banks, but as we have seen, the effect still existed provided the gold reserve ratio was maintained. We have also seen that the gold-exchange and dollar standards, the other fixed exchange rate standards we explained, also produce falls in money supplies after deficits and increases after surpluses. Here this is achieved via intervention by the government. A deficit requires the local monetary authority to purchase its currency to keep the value up. Thus money is withdrawn from circulation. Similarly, a surplus requires the central bank to sell its currency and hence increase the supply of money. With this we can explain the interest rate adjustment mechanism.

The interest rate adjustment mechanism via the capital account involves the following. If a deficit occurs, it will reduce the money supply and raise the interest rate. The deficit means surpluses elsewhere. Therefore the money supplies of other countries will be rising. This will reduce their interest rates. For both reasons there is a rise in interest incentives in favor of the deficit country. This will make investment (in securities, and so on) in that country appear relatively more attractive, given the rates of interest in other countries. The resultant inflows on the capital account will improve the balance of payments, causing an increase in foreign exchange reserves.[12]

Interest rates are relevant to the financial manager who is making exchange rate forecasts when sterilization is occurring, which means that interest rates and the money supply are being manipulated by the central bank. Increases in interest rates in relation to levels in other countries will improve the balance of payments and cause an inflow of reserves. The reverse will occur in countries which experience

---

[12] The interest adjustment mechanism will be blunted if there is a Keynesian liquidity trap, which means that the demand for money is perfectly elastic, and increases in the money supply do not affect interest rates. In practice the liquidity trap is unlikely to be a problem, because even if it did exist, it was limited to the depression, and its existence at that time is not certain.

declining interest rates. This can help in forecasting. If a financial manager believes, for example, that because of domestic concerns a central bank will attempt to maintain low interest rates, then there is a good chance that there will be deficits, declining reserves, and an eventual devaluation. If a central bank is maintaining high interest rates to fight inflation, then a revaluation could eventually occur, and the revaluation itself will help the war against inflation by lowering import prices.

We have introduced a number of adjustment mechanisms that work simultaneously. It is useful to combine these into a coherent form and to examine the circumstances that determine which types of adjustments will dominate.

COMBINED EFFECTS*

A diagrammatic representation of the combined automatic adjustment mechanisms under fixed exchange rates is developed in Figure 5.3. The vertical axis gives the

Figure 5.3
Combining the fixed exchange rate automatic adjustment mechanisms.

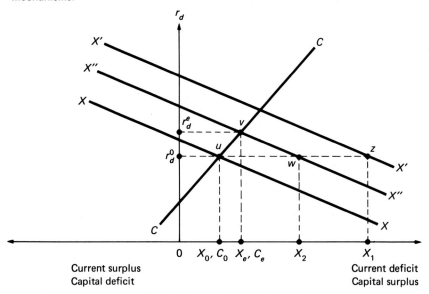

Current surplus
Capital deficit

Current deficit
Capital surplus

Quantity of dollars per period of time

XX represents the balance of payments current account. Lower r_d means more spending, including spending for imports, and therefore a worsening current account. CC represents the capital account. For given foreign interest rates, a higher domestic rate means more capital inflows and an improving capital account. Therefore, while XX slopes down, CC slopes up. The overall balance is where XX and CC meet.

domestic interest rate, r_d. The horizontal axis gives the capital and current account surpluses and deficits. Moving to the right along the horizontal axis means a capital account improvement and a current account deterioration. This reversal of direction for measuring the two accounts is required in order to identify the overall balance.[13] The scales of the capital and current account measurements are equal, and so at each point on the axis, the size of the surplus/deficit on the capital account equals the size of the deficit/surplus on the current account.

The XX line represents equilibrium in the current account of the overall balance. It is shown as sloping downward vis-à-vis the domestic interest rate, r_d, because at lower interest rates we expect more investment spending, hence more national income, higher imports, and therefore a smaller surplus or larger deficit on the current account. XX is drawn for given levels of prices and national income. As prices fall, we expect the current account to improve, via increasing exports/ decreasing imports, and XX to shift to the left. Similarly, as income falls, we expect imports to fall, and hence an improvement in the current account. This means that XX will shift to the left.

Line CC gives the net capital inflows or outflows. It is drawn for a given foreign interest rate, and it slopes upward because higher domestic interest rates, that is, a movement up the vertical axis, mean higher interest differentials, which will raise capital inflows or reduce capital outflows.[14]

The CC line and the initial XX line, drawn at initial prices and income, intersect at point u in Figure 5.3. This is the equilibrium for the balance of payments. The initial deficit in the current account, given by the XX line, is equal to the initial surplus in the capital account, given by CC, with $0X_0 = 0C_0$ at r_d^0. Suppose that we begin at this equilibrium with a balanced balance of payments and that there is then an exogenous decline in the amount of exports. The line which gives the current account surplus or deficit at different levels of the domestic interest rate will move to the right. Let it move to $X'X'$. At the original interest rate, r_d^0, there will be a balance of payments deficit: the capital inflows at the original interest rate will remain in surplus at $0C_0$, given off the CC line; the current account deficit will increase to the amount $0X_1$, given off the $X'X'$ line. The overall balance of payments will be in deficit by the excess of the current account deficit over the capital account inflow. This is given by distance C_0X_1, or by the distance between point u and point z.

The newly created deficit will, under a system of fixed exchange rates, cause a decline in the money supply of the deficit country, if the deficit is not sterilized. To the extent that the fall in the money supply will reduce prices, this will raise exports, decrease imports, and improve the current account at each interest rate. XX will

---

[13] We do not include unilateral transfers explicitly in our analysis. We can therefore think of the current acount as the result of exports and imports of goods and services.

[14] By taking the foreign interest rate as given, we do not allow adjustment in the foreign country. A model that allows adjustment in both countries and is like the one developed here can be found in Lloyd A. Metzler, "The Process of International Adjustment under Conditions of Full Employment: A Keynesian View," in Richard E. Caves and Harry G. Johnson (eds.), *Readings in International Economics*, Richard D. Irwin, Homewood, Ill., 1968.

shift back from $X'X'$ toward the original position. This is the effect of the price-level adjustment mechanism.

The fall in exports which originally shifted XX will also set up an income adjustment. The decline in exports will, via the Keynesian multiplier process, cause a fall in national income. This will reduce imports and improve the current account, hence moving XX back toward its original position. Let us suppose that the combined effects of the price and income adjustment mechanisms move line XX back as far as $X''X''$. We can consider next how the interest rate adjustment mechanism will simultaneously add to the automatic adjustment of the price-level and income mechanisms. We have already seen that the deficit from the initial shift in XX causes a decline in the money supply. This will raise interest rates above r_d^0 to, let us say, r_d^e. The higher domestic interest rate will raise capital inflows and move us *along* the CC or capital flow line toward point v. In addition, the higher interest rate will lower investment and hence reduce income. The result will be reduced imports and an improvement in the current account. This is shown by a movement *along* the $X''X''$ line from point w to point v in Figure 5.3.[15]

At v, with a higher domestic interest rate, we again have overall balance. The current account deficit of $0X_e$ is equal to the capital account surplus of $0C_e$. This is the new equilibrium toward which the shift of $X'X'$ to $X''X''$ (from the price and income adjustment processes) and the movement along $X''X''$ and CC (from the interest adjustments on the current and capital accounts) tend to push us. At any moment after the shock to the balance of payments we will be in disequilibrium. These forces will, however, work toward a restoration of overall balance.

We can use Figure 5.3 to illustrate the determinants of the relative effectiveness of the different adjustment processes. In the short run we expect the price-level adjustment and income adjustment mechanisms to be rather slow in restoring equilibrium, and so XX will move very little toward its original position. We expect that in the short run the major adjustment will occur via interest rates, which can move very quickly. Over time, however, we expect price-level adjustments and income adjustments to take place, moving $X'X'$ back all the way to XX. Interest rates can then move back toward their original level, and so the interest adjustment has meant only a temporary increase in interest rates.

If capital flows are sensitive to interest rate differentials, CC will be flat in relation to XX as in part a of Figure 5.4, and the interest rate adjustment will be along CC and hence in the capital account. (We see in part a of Figure 5.4 that the movement from u to v, in moving to the new equilibrium, exceeds the movement from w to v.) If, however, capital flows are insensitive to interest rates, the CC line will be relatively steep as in part b of Figure 5.4, and the interest adjustment will be more along XX than along CC. We expect that between major developed countries, such as the United States, Canada, Britain, or Germany, the CC line is nearly flat. This means that large changes in capital flows will result from small changes in the

---

[15] The interest rate effect that moves us *along* XX works via the effect of interest rates on investment and hence on income and imports. This is to be distinguished from the alternative Keynesian income adjustment that does not rely on interest rates and hence *shifts* XX instead of moving us along it.

FIGURE 5.4
Relative effectiveness of different fixed exchange rate
automatic adjustment mechanisms.

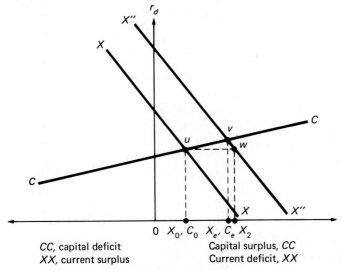

CC, capital deficit   Capital surplus, CC
XX, current surplus   Current deficit, XX

(a) Interest sensitive capital flows

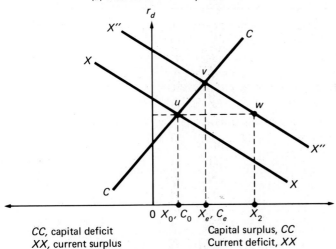

CC, capital deficit   Capital surplus, CC
XX, current surplus   Current deficit, XX

(b) Interest insensitive capital flows

In part a, capital flows are sensitive to interest rates, and most
of the adjustment occurs in the capital account. In part b, with a
steeper CC, adjustment is more evenly shared between the
current account and the capital account.

interest incentive. This is another way of saying that we expect the most effective short-run fixed exchange rate automatic adjustment mechanism between developed countries to be interest adjustment. (It also means that when exchange rates are flexible, the primary cause of short-run movements in exchange rates is variations in interest rates. The primary cause of long-run movements in exchange rates is the inflation rate.)

When countries with undeveloped capital markets find themselves in a balance of payments disequilibrium, we expect the adjustment will be more evenly shared among the different adjustment mechanisms. For example, increases in interest rates in Angola or in Ecuador will not lead to massive inflows of capital, so the country will have to rely on price-level or income adjustment to correct imbalances in its international payments, or it will be forced to periodically revise its exchange rate.

We should mention that filling deficits via capital inflows, when capital flows are sensitive to interest rates, is a short-run blessing. In the long run, capital inflows must be serviced. That is, there will be payments of interest which will appear as a debit in the invisible or service part of the current account. This means that in the future, the current account will be in a larger deficit unless the investment from overseas provides more output for export. If there are no extra exports from foreign investment, the country will have larger and larger current account deficits, and there will be a need for bigger capital inflows to cover the debt service. This has been the experience of countries such as Canada which borrowed heavily in the past and now have a large service deficit.

THE MONETARY APPROACH TO THE BALANCE OF PAYMENTS

During the late 1960s and the 1970s a new view of the balance of payments adjustment mechanism became popular among certain economists. This view is known as the *monetary approach* to the balance of payments. If any individual economist is to be credited with the original statement of this view, it is Robert Mundell, but the concept has been extended by numerous other economists.[16] The

---

[16] Mundell's ideas are presented in *International Economics,* Macmillan and Company, New York, 1968, especially Chapters 17 and 18. The development of the monetary approach and some of the tests of the implications can be found in Jacob Frenkel and Harry Johnson (eds.), *The Monetary Approach to the Balance of Payments,* Allen & Unwin, Ltd., London, 1976. In particular, see the paper by Michael Mussa, "Tariffs and the Balance of Payments," in the Frenkel and Johnson volume. Other papers which explain the monetary approach are Harry Johnson, "The Monetary Approach to the Balance of Payments: A Nontechnical Guide," *Journal of International Economics,* vol. 7, August 1977, pp. 251–268; Mordechai Kreinin and Lawrence Officer, "The Monetary Approach to the Balance of Payments: A Survey," *Princeton Studies in International Finance,* no. 43, Princeton University, Princeton, N.J., November 1979; and Stephen Magee, "The Empirical Evidence on the Monetary Approach to the Balance of Payments and Exchange Rates," *American Economic Review,* vol. 66, May 1976, pp. 163–170. A paper by Jacob Frenkel, Thorvaldur Gylfason, and John Helliwell, "A Synthesis of Monetary and Keynesian Approaches to Short-Run Balance of Payment Theory," *Economic Journal,* vol. 90, September 1980, pp. 582–592, shows how monetary and Keynesian approaches are special cases of a more general theory and can both be derived from it.

monetary approach explains the balance of payments in terms of differences between the supply of money and the demand for money. The supply of a nation's currency is under the control of the nation's central bank, and the demand for money is by the public.

We can show the workings of the monetary approach by taking, as an example, the effect on the balance of payments of an increase in national income. The demand for money depends on income, and when the national income rises, there is a greater demand for money. For a given supply of money, the increase in demand will mean that the public will try to satisfy this excess demand by

1 Reducing the fraction of income that is spent on consumption
2 Selling bonds and other securities to get more cash

The first of these, reduced spending, will help the balance of payments by putting downward pressure on prices and by reducing imports as a direct part of reduced consumption in general. This will mean an improvement in the current account. The second part, selling securities, will lower bond prices, raise interest rates, cause more capital inflows (less outflow), and improve the balance of payments on the capital account. Thus we find that according to the monetary approach to the balance of payments, when national income rises, there is a balance of payments improvement. On the other hand, an increase in income in the Keynesian approach means more imports, both directly via Equation (5.3) and via induced effects, worsening the balance of payments. These outcomes are summarized in Appendix 5.2. This appendix reveals only some of the complexities of Keynesian and monetary adjustment, but it shows how different the conclusions can be.

To take another example of the workings of the monetary approach, let us see what happens when the nation's price level rises. This will reduce the real supply of money. If the real supply of money and the demand for money were initially in equilibrium, real supply will be less than real demand after the price level increases. To restore real cash balances, the public, as before, will spend less on goods and services and will sell bonds. The former action will improve the current account as imports are reduced, and the latter action will improve the capital account, since falling bonds prices are translated into rising interest rates. However, according to a Keynesian, a higher price level makes local goods less competitive and worsens the current account.

So far, we have used the monetary approach to reveal what happens after there are changes that affect the *demand* for money. The monetary approach can also be used to show the effects of changes in the *supply* of money. What happens is this. If the supply of money is initially equal to the demand and is then raised, there will be an excess supply. To try to eliminate the excess supply of money, the public will buy goods and bonds. The buying of goods will raise prices and worsen the current account by increasing imports. The buying of bonds will lower interest rates and worsen the capital account. The balance of payments is hence worsened by the creation of too much money.

The monetary approach is used by its proponents to explain why some countries have persistent deficits. If too much money is created, deficits will occur. With fixed exchange rates the central bank must purchase its own currency to prevent it from falling in value on the foreign exchange market. This will tend to reduce the money supply, because the central bank will be buying what it created. Persistent deficits occur because the central bank reintroduces the money in an attempt to keep a higher supply of money in circulation. Therefore, the countries with deficits are the countries which persist in adding to their money supply.

WHY STUDY AUTOMATIC ADJUSTMENT MECHANISMS?

The economy is always in disequilibrium somewhere. Our analysis does not tell us precisely where equilibrium will be, but it does tell us the direction and therefore helps in forecasting. Knowing where we are going is important because it is the future, and not the past, that is relevant in making decisions. While that future is uncertain, it does help to have an idea of what it will probably look like. In this way an understanding of the forces that direct us can help in effective managerial decision making.

We must rely on the automatic adjustment mechanisms presented so far if exchange rates are fixed. An adjustment mechanism that we have not yet called into play involves automatic variations in exchange rates, as in the system of flexible exchange rates.

SUMMARY

1 An automatic adjustment mechanism is a force that tends to restore equilibrium after a disturbance. The gold standard, the gold-exchange standard, and the dollar standard are fixed exchange rate systems that existed before exchange rates became more flexible.

2 The gold standard involved the settlement of international transactions in gold and the open offer to exchange domestic paper money for gold at a fixed price. A deficit meant the outflow of gold. The reduction in reserves reduced the local money supply and put downward pressure on prices in the deficit country, via the quantity theory. The fall in prices stimulated exports and lowered imports. In the surplus (foreign) countries, the money supplies were rising, raising the prices in those countries. This led to a reduction of relative prices in the deficit country. In addition, changes in relative prices within each country helped eliminate a deficit or surplus.

3 If the discipline of the gold standard was maintained (by always maintaining fractional gold reserve ratios), the changes in the money supply were larger than the changes in gold reserves. This could make the price adjustment system more effective.

4 This price-specie adjustment mechanism could be frustrated by neutralization or sterilization policies. These policies severed the link between gold flows and the money supply, and the remainder of the adjustment mechanism was lost.

5 Critics of the gold standard argue that prices in surplus and deficit countries showed parallel movement rather than the reverse movement implied by the gold standard. Downward price rigidity is responsible. However, an adjustment of relative prices will still occur if prices go up by more in surplus countries than in deficit countries. Another

criticism of the gold standard is that governments do not allow it to work. This is as much a criticism of government as it is of the gold standard.

6 The gold-exchange standard required countries to fix the price of their currency either to gold or to the U.S. dollar. For most of the period of the gold-exchange standard (1944–1968), the dollar was fixed at $35 an ounce, and other countries fixed their currencies to the dollar.

7 To maintain the fixed exchange rate in terms of the dollar, central banks were forced to purchase or sell their local currency at the support points on either side of the parity value. If the free-market exchange rate would have been above the upper support point, the central bank sold its currency and purchased dollars. This raised its official reserves and meant a surplus in the balance of payments. It also raised the supply of money. At the lower support point the central bank purchased the local currency with dollars, which reduced official reserves and resulted in a deficit in the balance of international payments. This lowered the money supply. Surpluses therefore raise money supplies under fixed exchange rates, and deficits lower money supplies.

8 Keynesian income adjustment involves a mechanism that restores equilibrium even if prices are inflexible. For example, if exports decline, causing a deficit, there will be a multiplier decline in national income, reducing consumption (including imports) and tending to restore equilibrium. The mechanism is, however, incomplete.

9 While income adjustment is incomplete, there is an additional mechanism working via income that is indirect and follows from changes in the money supply and interest rates. While a deficit persists, the supply of money will decline, raising the interest rate, reducing investment, lowering income and imports, and hence helping to restore equilibrium.

10 Price and income adjustments, including indirect adjustment via the supply of money and investment, work on the current account. In countries with well-developed capital markets, adjustment via the capital account is the most effective mechanism. Deficits, which cause the money supply to decline and interest rates to rise, also raise capital inflows. This restores overall balance.

11 The relative effectiveness of different adjustment mechanisms depends on the interest sensitivity of capital flows versus price and income adjustment. If adjustment is completed quickly via interest adjustment and flows of capital, the other adjustments will follow later. Re-establishing equilibrium via capital flows can create problems. Capital inflows provide a once-and-for-all improvement. In successive periods the extra foreign debt must be serviced, and this will contribute to larger deficits in future current accounts.

12 In the monetary approach to the balance of payments, deficits are considered the result of an excess supply of money. Anything which reduces the demand for money or raises the supply causes deficits.

13 Increases in income or prices which raise the demand for money will, for a given supply of money, raise interest rates and cause inflows of capital, reduced demand, and therefore an improvement in both the capital and current accounts. These conclusions run counter to the predictions of many people.

14 Persistent deficits occur if a central bank refuses to allow deficits to eliminate themselves by lowering the money supply. When central banks do not frustrate the automatic adjustment, it is valuable for a financial manager to understand this adjustment process in order to predict exchange rate trends.

15 The ability to forecast the eventual movement of exchange rates in fixed exchange rate systems gives speculators a one-way bet. Reductions in reserves should eventually cause devaluations, and increases should cause revaluations. Reserve growth will be reduced by reductions in national income or interest rates. Predicting the timing of eventual changes

in exchange rates is made difficult by the ability of central banks to borrow foreign exchange reserves.

QUESTIONS

1 How can government objectives such as the maintenance of full employment hinder the functioning of the gold standard? Would adjustment via income or via interest rates be inhibited in the same way?

2 Why might historical patterns of prices show parallel movements between deficit and surplus countries? Could gold discoveries and common movements in national incomes cause this?

3 Use Figure 5.2 to show the effect of a fall in demand for British goods in terms of (a) the balance of payments measured in pound units and (b) the balance of payments measured in dollar units. Show also the movements in curves that the deficit and contraction in money supply will create in restoring equilibrium.

4 If the marginal propensity to consume *domestic* goods is 0.6 and the marginal propensity to consume all goods, including imports, is 0.8, what deficit will persist after Keynesian income adjustment if exports exogenously increase by $1 billion? Will changes in *foreign* national incomes improve adjustment?

5 How will the fraction of adjustment occurring via capital flows be influenced by a tax on interest paid to foreigners?

6 If international capital markets are perfect and capital flows respond to the tiniest differential, will the adjustment occur in the current account or in the capital account? [*Hint*: Use Figure 5.3 with a CC line that shows infinite flows of capital as r_d moves.]

7 What determines the *slope* of XX in Figure 5.4? What determines the size of the *shift* in XX?

8 Describe the effects on the balance of payments of a fall in income and a fall in the price level. Give both monetary and Keynesian views.

9 How would you use interest rate and national income forecasts made available by government or industry in forecasting exchange rate movements? Would you need interest rate and income forecasts for a number of countries? How might the central banks frustrate your effort to obtain good forecasts? Could the ability of the central banks to borrow reserves present a problem?

10 Use Appendix 5.1 to compute the gold points, assuming that the world has returned to the gold standard with the following prices:

$$P_G^{US}(\text{ask}) = \$1005$$
$$P_G^{US}(\text{bid}) = \$1000$$
$$P_G^{UK}(\text{ask}) = £402$$
$$P_G^{UK}(\text{bid}) = £400$$

The cost of shipping gold between the United States and the United Kingdom, c_G, is 0.0005 of the value of transported gold. In which direction would gold arbitrage occur if the exchange rate between currencies was $2.55/£, and what is the profit per dollar of arbitrage?

BIBLIOGRAPHY

Caves, Richard E., and Ronald W. Jones: *World Trade and Payments: An Introduction*, Little, Brown and Company, Boston, 1973, part 4.

Dornbusch, Rudiger: *Open Economy Macroeconomics*, Basic Books, Inc., New York, 1980.

Frenkel, Jacob A., and Harry G. Johnson (eds.): *The Monetary Approach to the Balance of Payments*, Allen & Unwin, Ltd., London, 1976.

—— and —— (eds.): *The Economics of Exchange Rates: Selected Readings*, Addison-Wesley Publishing Company, Reading, Mass., 1978.

Grubel, Herbert G.: *International Economics*, Richard D. Irwin, Homewood, Ill., 1977, part 4.

Heller, H. Robert: *International Monetary Economics,* Prentice-Hall, Inc., Englewood Cliffs, N.J., 1974, chaps. 7 and 8.

Johnson, Harry G.: "The Monetary Approach to the Balance of Payments: A Nontechnical Guide," *Journal of International Economics*, August 1977, pp. 251–268.

Metzler, Lloyd A.: "The Process of International Adjustment under Conditions of Full Employment: A Keynesian View," in Richard E. Caves and Harry G. Johnson (eds.), *Readings in International Economics*, Richard D. Irwin, Homewood, Ill., 1968.

Mundell, Robert A.: *International Economics*, Macmillan and Company, New York, 1968, chaps. 17 and 18.

Stern, Robert M.: *The Balance of Payments: Theory and Economic Policy*, Aldine Publishing Company, Chicago, 1973, chaps 4–6.

Triffin, Robert: "The Myth and Realities of the So-called Gold Standard," in *The Evolution of the International Monetary System: Historical Reappraisal and Future Perspective*, Princeton University Press, Princeton, N.J., 1964. Reprinted in Richard Cooper, *International Finance*, Penguin Books, Baltimore, 1969.

Yeager, Leland: *International Monetary Relations: Theory, History, and Policy*, 2d ed., Harper & Row, Inc., New York, 1976.

APPENDIX 5.1: Gold Points

Gold points are the extreme values between which the exchange rate can vary in a gold-standard world. The width of the range within which exchange rates can move is determined by the potential for arbitrage profit from shipping gold between central banks. (Arbitrage, we recall, means buying something and then selling it in a different market to take advantage of price differences.) The traditional gold points allowed exchange rates to vary within a range of a percent or two of the middle value. This idea of a range was carried into the fixed exchange rate standard adopted in 1944. We hence obtain a historical perspective by a study of gold-point determination.

Suppose that the U.S. Federal Reserve (the Fed) and the Bank of England both offer to exchange their paper money for gold at fixed prices. Let us define these prices as follows:

$$P_G^{US}(\text{ask}) = \text{Federal Reserve selling price of gold, in dollars}$$
$$P_G^{US}(\text{bid}) = \text{Federal Reserve buying price of gold, in dollars}$$
$$P_G^{UK}(\text{ask}) = \text{Bank of England selling price of gold, in pounds}$$
$$P_G^{UK}(\text{bid}) = \text{Bank of England buying price of gold, in pounds}$$

In order to determine the potential variation of the exchange rate between U.S. dollars and U.K. pounds, we can look at the behavior of arbitragers, who move gold and paper money solely for profit. For each dollar used to buy gold in the United States, an arbitrager will receive $1/P_G^{US}$ (ask) ounce of the precious metal. This can be shipped to Britain. Let us define the shipping cost as follows:

The shipping cost is represented by c_G, which is the fraction of the total value of gold shipped between the United States and the United Kingdom that is paid for shipping. For example, the cost c, is 0.01 if shipping costs are 1 percent of the value of the cargo.

Let us define the bid and ask exchange rates as before

$S(\$/\text{bid}£)$ is the number of dollars received from the sale of pounds for dollars, and $S(\$/\text{ask}£)$ is the number of dollars that must be paid to buy pounds with dollars.

An arbitrager who takes a dollar and buys $1/P_G^{US}$ (ask) ounce of gold in the United States will have

$$(1 - c_G)/P_G^{US}(\text{ask})$$

ounce of gold after meeting the costs of shipping this gold to the United Kingdom. At the buying price of gold in the United Kingdom, this amount of gold will bring

$$(1 - c_G) \cdot \frac{P_G^{UK}(\text{bid})}{P_G^{US}(\text{ask})} \tag{5A.1}$$

in British pounds sterling. At the selling price of pounds for dollars, $S(\$/\text{bid}£)$, the number of pounds in (5A.1) will fetch

$$(1 - c_G) \cdot \frac{P_G^{UK}(\text{bid})}{P_G^{UK}(\text{ask})} \cdot S(\$/\text{bid}£) \tag{5A.2}$$

in U.S. dollars. Each dollar that the arbitrager uses to buy gold in the United States will return the number of dollars in (5A.2) when the full arbitrage is complete. There is a profit if

$$(1 - c_G) \cdot S(\$/\text{bid}£) \cdot \frac{P_G^{UK}(\text{bid})}{P_G^{US}(\text{ask})} > 1 \tag{5A.3}$$

that is, if more than a dollar is received from each original dollar. The prices of gold are those of the central banks, and we can take them as fixed. When (5A.3) holds, gold will be sent from the United States to the United Kingdom, and the pounds that are received for the gold will be sold for dollars. This will tend to lower $S(\$/\text{bid}£)$ until arbitrage is no longer profitable. This requires that the arbitrage will exist until

$$(1 - c_G) \cdot S(\$/\text{bid}£) \cdot \frac{P_G^{UK}(\text{bid})}{P_G^{US}(\text{ask})} \leqslant 1$$

or

$$S(\$/\text{bid}£) \leqslant \frac{P_G^{\text{US}}(\text{ask})}{P_G^{\text{UK}}(\text{bid})} \cdot \frac{1}{(1 - c_G)} \tag{5A.4}$$

Arbitragers in the United Kingdom will wish to take pounds and perform the reverse arbitrage. They will purchase $1/P_G^{\text{UK}}(\text{ask})$ ounce of gold for each pound, ship the gold to the United States, and have, after shipping,

$$(1 - c_G)/P_G^{\text{UK}}(\text{ask})$$

ounce of gold, which they will send to the Federal Reserve for

$$(1 - c_G) \cdot \frac{P_G^{\text{US}}(\text{bid})}{P_G^{\text{UK}}(\text{ask})}$$

in U.S. dollars. These dollars can be sold for pounds at $S(\$/\text{ask}£)$, and so each original pound will return

$$\frac{(1 - c_G)}{S(\$/\text{ask}£)} \cdot \frac{P_G^{\text{US}}(\text{bid})}{P_G^{\text{UK}}(\text{ask})} \tag{5A.5}$$

pounds. When the value of (5A.5) exceeds unity, the arbitrage will be profitable. The gold prices are fixed, but the selling of dollars for pounds will raise the value of $S(\$/\text{ask}£)$ and lower the value of (5A.5) until

$$\frac{(1 - c_G)}{S(\$/\text{ask}£)} \cdot \frac{P_G^{\text{US}}(\text{bid})}{P_G^{\text{UK}}(\text{ask})} \leqslant 1$$

Only then will the arbitrage originating in the United Kingdom come to a stop. We can therefore claim that arbitrage ensures that

$$S(\$/\text{ask}£) \geqslant \frac{P_G^{\text{US}}(\text{bid})}{P_G^{\text{UK}}(\text{ask})} \cdot (1 - c_G) \tag{5A.6}$$

We find that when each central bank does nothing more than offer to buy and sell its currency for gold, a range of values will be established within which the exchange rate can vary. The bid and ask exchange rates can vary between the limits of $S(\$/\text{bid}£)$ in (5A.4) and $S(\$/\text{ask}£)$ in (5A.6). No rate quotation can lie outside this range without forces pushing it back. We can say that

$$\frac{P_G^{\text{US}}(\text{bid})}{P_G^{\text{UK}}(\text{ask})} \cdot (1 - c_G) \leqslant S(\$/£) \leqslant \frac{P_G^{\text{US}}(\text{ask})}{P_G^{\text{UK}}(\text{bid})} \cdot \frac{1}{(1 - c_G)}$$

where $S(\$/£)$ stands for the exchange rate, whether it be a bid rate or an ask rate. For example, if the gold prices of the central banks are

$$P_G^{\text{US}}(\text{ask}) = \$40.20$$
$$P_G^{\text{US}}(\text{bid}) = \$40.00$$
$$P_G^{\text{UK}}(\text{ask}) = £20.10$$
$$P_G^{\text{UK}}(\text{bid}) = £20.00$$

and $c = 0.01$, the exchange rate must be in the range

$$1.97 \leqslant S(\$/£) \leqslant 2.03$$

The ends of the range are the gold points. In this case the gold points are $\$1.97/£$ and $\$2.03/£$. We find that the gold points result from both the bid-ask spreads on gold prices and the cost of shipping gold between the two countries.

APPENDIX 5.2. Implications of Monetary and Keynesian Approaches to the Balance of Payments

Exogenous change	Monetary approach	Keynesian approach
Income increase	$Y\uparrow \Rightarrow MD\uparrow \Rightarrow MD > MS \Rightarrow$ (1) $C\downarrow \Rightarrow Im\downarrow, P\downarrow \Rightarrow (Ex - Im)\uparrow$ (2) Bond sales $\Rightarrow r\uparrow \Rightarrow$ capital inflow ∴ Balance improves	$Y\uparrow \Rightarrow Im\uparrow \Rightarrow (Ex - Im)\downarrow$ ∴ Balance worsens
Increase in price level	$P\uparrow \Rightarrow (MS/P)\downarrow \Rightarrow (MD/P) > (MS/P) \Rightarrow$ (1) $C\downarrow \Rightarrow Im\downarrow, P\downarrow \Rightarrow (Ex - Im)\uparrow$ (2) Bond sales $\Rightarrow r\uparrow \Rightarrow$ capital inflow ∴ Balance improves	$P\uparrow \Rightarrow Im\uparrow, Ex\downarrow \Rightarrow (Ex - Im)\downarrow$ ∴ Balance worsens
Decrease in interest rates	$r\downarrow \Rightarrow (MD/P)\uparrow \Rightarrow (MD/P) > (MS/P) \Rightarrow$ (1) $C\downarrow \Rightarrow Im\downarrow, P\downarrow \Rightarrow (Ex - Im)\uparrow$ (2) Capital outflows ∴ Current account improves; Capital account worsens	$r\downarrow \Rightarrow$ (1) $I\uparrow \Rightarrow Y\uparrow \Rightarrow Im\uparrow \Rightarrow (Ex - Im)\downarrow$ (2) Capital outflows ∴ Current account worsens; Capital account worsens
Depreciation/devaluation of currency	No effect on MD or MS ∴ No effect	$S(\$/\pounds)\downarrow \Rightarrow Ex\uparrow, Im\downarrow \Rightarrow (Ex - Im)\uparrow$ ∴ Balance improves

Key: Y = national income, MD = money demand, MS = money supply, C = consumption, I = investment, P = price level, (MD/P) = real money demand, (MS/P) = real money supply, Ex = exports, Im = imports.

6

THE FLEXIBLE EXCHANGE RATE ENVIRONMENT: BRINGING US UP TO DATE

Par currency values under fixed exchange rates were set by the central banks. Central bankers allowed a currency to be devalued or revalued only if there was a significant decline or increase in foreign exchange reserves. Predicting changes in exchange rates, other than the relatively minor fluctuations within the allowable limits, therefore involved judging when a central bank would decide that a revision of the par value was in order. Since central banks hold reserves and can borrow from each other, from private banks, and from the International Monetary Fund, devaluations and revaluations were far apart and frequently delayed. Adjustments to payments imbalances came about through the slow and painful mechanisms of changes in price levels, interest rates, and income rather than through revisions in exchange rates.

With a commitment to full employment solidly entrenched in almost every economy by the early 1970s, the suffering required to re-establish balance of payments equilibrium under fixed exchange rates became politically infeasible. Adjustments were therefore postponed, and corrective action was frequently halted or reversed before it had a chance to take effect. In such an environment, it was necessary to adopt an exchange rate system in which adjustment did not require obvious economic hardship. Such a system required greater flexibility in exchange rates. In 1970, Canada floated, that is, made flexible, the Canadian dollar, having held it fixed since 1960, and in 1972, Britain floated the pound. Other currencies followed, and by the mid-1970s most of the major currencies (but few minor currencies) were floating vis-à-vis the U.S. dollar.

With flexible exchange rates, the job of forecasting involves examining those factors which influence the demands for and supplies of foreign exchange. Before we show why this is so and describe the factors to examine when forecasting, we should note that since the U.S. dollar is the rate against which other currencies are quoted, it is the *other* countries which decide whether their particular exchange rate will float. The decision is not made by the United States. As we said in the previous chapter, under fixed exchange rates most of the intervention is by the foreign central banks, and it is therefore *their* decision to continue to intervene or to allow the rate to float.[1] In this sense, foreign currencies are fixed against the dollar, and the dollar is not itself fixed to other currencies. We see that it is a matter of the organization of the system.

THE FLEXIBLE EXCHANGE RATE SYSTEM

How Flexible Exchange Rates Work

Flexible exchange rates occur when the central banks do not select parity values or intervene in the foreign exchange market; therefore the exchange market is "free" and uncontrolled. The determination of flexible rates is then as straightforward as supply and demand. Indeed, the exchange rate is the rate at which the supply of and demand for a currency are equal. For example, in Figure 6.1, the value of the pound sterling will be $S_1(\$/£)$ if the supply of and demand for pounds are $O_1(£)$ and $D_1(£)$. If for some reason the demand for pounds increases to $D_2(£)$, then at the original exchange rate of $S_1(\$/£)$ there will be an excess demand for pounds. This will put upward pressure on the price of the pound, and $S(\$/£)$ will increase until it reaches $S_2(\$/£)$. That exchange rate will remain until there is a further change in supply or demand. It is that straightforward.

Because there is no intervention by central banks, with *truly* flexible exchange rates, there can be no change in foreign exchange reserves. This means that the balance of payments must by definition always be balanced, since the deficit or surplus *is* the change in foreign exchange reserves. However, rarely if ever are rates truly flexible. As we have already said, most countries have adopted managed floats, which are also called dirty floats. In a managed or dirty float, the central bank buys and sells its currency from day to day in the hope of smoothing out fluctuations without affecting underlying trends. The central banks engaged in this activity argue that if the foreign exchange market was not managed, it would become volatile and hinder international trade. However, rarely does the record show that the management of the exchange rate has been only for stabilization purposes, since if it was, then over a calendar quarter or year the net change in foreign exchange reserves would be very small. In fact, reserves are frequently run down for lengthy periods, as in the case of Canada from 1979 to 1980, or increased for lengthy periods, as in the case of Britain over the same period.

Managed floats are a hybrid of fixed and flexible exchange rates, and they introduce considerable complexity into the system. But even truly flexible rates, in some circumstances, are not as straightforward as our discussion of Figure 6.1

---

[1]The U.S. Federal Reserve System frequently cooperates with foreign central banks in buying and selling dollars for foreign exchange. However, the primary responsibility for fixing rates rests with the foreign central banks.

FIGURE 6.1
The uncontrolled foreign exchange market.

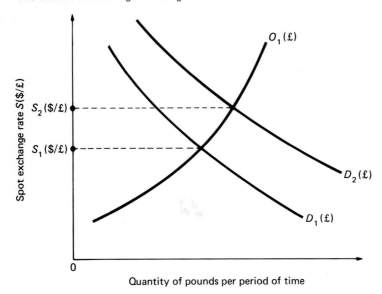

With flexible exchange rates the value of S ($/£) is determined where
the supply equals demand. With O_1 (£) and D_1 (£) the value of S ($/£)
will be S_1 ($/£). If demand rises to D_2 (£), the value of S ($/£) will rise to
S_2 ($/£). In Figure 6.1 the exchange rate is stable.

indicated. For example, if the foreign exchange market is unstable, forecasting
becomes extremely difficult. We should examine the conditions that cause an
unstable foreign exchange market.

Flexible Exchange Rates and Stability

What do we mean by "stability"?

> A foreign exchange market is stable if the exchange rate will tend toward a finite
> equilibrium value when conditions change. It is unstable if the rate does not
> approach an equilibrium.[2]

The exchange rate in Figure 6.1 is in a stable equilibrium, because if it were to
momentarily change, forces would eventually return it to its equilibrium value. This
stability exists because as we move down along the supply curve from higher to
lower prices, the supply curve intersects the demand curve from above. If the slope

[2] In actuality we can have stability, instability, and metastability. To explain these by analogy, a ball
on a concave table will find the lowest point and remain there. This is a stable equilibrium. A ball
balanced on the top of a convex table, if disturbed, will roll until it falls off. This is an unstable
equilibrium. A ball on a completely flat table will stay wherever it is put. This is a metastable equilibrium.

of the supply curve is sufficiently changed so that the curve intersects the demand curve from below, the system becomes unstable. Such a possibility can occur in foreign exchange markets. We hinted at this in the previous chapter, but it will take a moment to develop the argument fully.

In Figure 6.1 the quantity of pounds is on the horizontal axis, and the price of pounds (in terms of dollars) is on the vertical axis. The demand for pounds in terms of dollars results from Americans (or others using dollars when making their payments) demanding British goods, services, claims, currency, or gold, as we said in Chapter 5. Let us concentrate on the goods and services, since the exchange rate in itself is not the primary determinant of the demand for British claims, currency, or gold.[3] Figure 6.1 shows that as pounds become cheaper, Americans (and others) will buy more British goods and services, that is, British exports. If the price of British exports in terms of pounds is given, more purchases of British products because of a cheaper pound means that more pounds are wanted. Therefore the demand for pounds goes up as the price of the pound, $S(\$/£)$, falls. We therefore have no ambiguity about the slope of $D(£)$, which will be downward as in Figure 6.1.

The supply of pounds results from the desire of the British to buy foreign goods and services, claims, and gold, but again we will concentrate on the goods and services. As the value of the pound increases, that is, as $S(\$/£)$ goes up, the British will find that foreign goods and services become cheaper. They will therefore want more of them. But how much more? If, for example, the pound increases in value by 10 percent, making foreign items 10 percent cheaper (for a given dollar price), but the British want only 5 percent more goods, they will actually be spending fewer pounds than before. This is because while they are buying 5 percent more goods than before, each item requires 10 percent fewer pounds, and that is approximately 5 percent fewer pounds to be supplied or offered. Therefore, the supply curve of pounds might not slope upward. In this particular case, as the price of pounds goes up, the supply of pounds, that is, the number offered, goes down, and so we have a downward-sloping supply curve.

The example of a 10 percent increase in the value of the pound (or fall in the value of the dollar) causing a 5 percent increase in British demand for imports is a case of an inelastic demand; that is, demand elasticity is less than 1.0. In fact, the absolute value of the import elasticity is as follows:

$$\text{Import demand elasticity, } \eta_{\text{Im}} = -\frac{\text{percentage change in quantity}}{\text{percentage change in price}}$$

$$= -\frac{5}{-10} = 0.5$$

The minus in the demand elasticity definition allows us to think of η_{Im} as positive. This situation corresponds to the upper section of the supply curve of pounds in

---

[3]The demand for claims, that is, financial securities, depends on the expected future course of exchange rates and on the interest rate differential between countries. The spot exchange rate that exists *today* has no direct bearing on interest differentials or on the path of exchange rates *in the future* and is therefore unimportant in the security decision.

FIGURE 6.2
The offer curve of pounds.

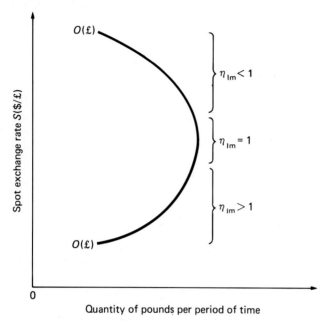

The supply or offer curve of pounds could have an upward slope or a downward slope. When import demand is elastic, there will be an upward slope, and when it is inelastic, there will be a downward slope.

Figure 6.2.[4] If the demand for imports into Britain increases by 10 percent when the prices fall by 10 percent from a 10 percent pound appreciation, then the same amount will be spent after the pound appreciation as before. In this case the demand elasticity of imports is unity, and since the quantity of pounds supplied does not change with the exchange rate, we are on a vertical section of the supply curve for pounds.[5] This is shown in the middle section of Figure 6.2. Similarly, if the demand for imports increases by more than 10 percent when the foreign exchange value of the dollar falls by 10 percent, British import demand will be elastic, and $\eta_{Im} > 1$. We will then have an increase in the number of pounds offered as $S(\$/£)$ goes up, and the result will be an upward-sloping supply curve. This is shown in the lower section of Figure 6.2.

[4]For a 10 percent increase in the value of pounds to cause a 10 percent fall in the pound price of imports, it is necessary that import prices *in terms of dollars* do not change along with the exchange rate. This will be the case if Britain is a small part of the total market for the goods that it buys or if import production costs are constant.

[5]Hence when the elasticity of demand for *imports* equals unity, that is, when $\eta_{Im} = 1$, the elasticity of supply of *pounds* is zero. Similarly, as we shall see, when $\eta_{Im} > 1$, the elasticity of supply of pounds is positive, and when $\eta_{Im} < 1$, it is negative. In reality, an individual offer curve will not have all the slopes. Figure 6.2 is drawn as it is to avoid having a separate figure for each elasticity.

FIGURE 6.3
Stable and unstable exchange equilibriums.

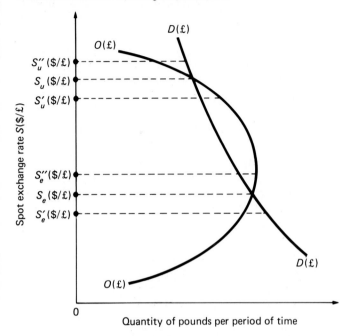

The exchange rate S_e ($/£) is stable. If the rate falls below this
level, there is an excess demand for pounds, and the rate will
return to S_e ($/£). If the rate goes above this level, there is an
excess supply of pounds, and S($/£) will fall. S_u ($/£) represents an
unstable equilibrium. Temporary deviations from this level do not
set up forces tending to restore equilibrium.

When we add the demand curve for pounds to the offer curve, as shown in Figure
6.3, we discover that because of the backward-bending section on the offer curve
there are potentially two different types of equilibrium exchange rates, corresponding to S_e($/£) and S_u($/£). While both represent equilibriums in the sense of supply
equaling demand, only the lower exchange rate, S_e($/£), is stable. We can see this by
asking what happens if the actual exchange rate temporarily deviates from S_e($/£)
and then asking the same thing with regard to the rate S_u($/£).

If the exchange rate temporarily drops from S_e($/£) to S'_e($/£), there will be an
excess demand for pounds. This will push up the price of pounds toward the
equilibrium value. Similarly, if the rate temporarily rises to S''_e($/£), there will be an
excess supply of pounds, and this will push the rate back to the equilibrium. Hence
S_e($/£) represents a stable equilibrium.

At the equilibrium rate S_u($/£) we have a different situation. While this
represents an equilibrium with supply equal to demand, and while the rate will be
unchanged as long as nothing happens, any slight change in the rate will result in a
larger movement away from equilibrium. For example, if the rate temporarily falls

from $S_u(\$/£)$ to $S'_u(\$/£)$, there will be an excess supply of pounds. This will lower $S(\$/£)$ to below $S'_u(\$/£)$, causing an even greater excess supply, which will lower $S(\$/£)$, and so on. Similarly, above $S(\$/£)$ there is an excess demand, so the rate rises, and so on. We have an unstable equilibrium at $S_u(\$/£)$.

An individual supply curve of a currency will not necessarily have both an upward-sloping section and a downward-sloping section; instead, it may be either upward-sloping or downward-sloping. If the downward slope of the supply curve is such that as we travel along the curve from higher to lower prices, it cuts the demand curve from below, then the equilibrium is unstable.[6] This then becomes an important question: Are the exchange markets stable? If they are unstable, then governments do have a case for fixing their exchange rate. In addition, in unstable markets, corporate treasurers should try to avoid foreign exchange risk, and they will have a difficult time making forecasts.

If we could be sure that import demand is price-elastic, that is, responds by more than the percentage change in exchange rates, then we would know that $O(£)$ slopes upward. This would ensure that the market is stable.[7] Because of the importance of the price elasticities of demand for imports and exports, they have been a topic of considerable research. Some of the initial research produced elasticity estimates which were small and indicated that exchange markets could be unstable, but these original results were later discovered to be smaller than their "true values."[8] We can reasonably assume here that the exchange markets are stable.

Forecasting with Flexible Exchange Rates

The difficulty of forecasting devaluations and revaluations with fixed exchange rates is the difficulty of judging when central banks will give in to market forces and revise their parity values. However, because the need to change the rate builds up over time, it is not difficult to forecast in which direction the rate will go when eventually it is changed. With a flexible exchange rate system the rates are moving continuously, and the financial executive does not have the advantage of watching foreign exchange reserves move to the point of requiring exchange rate revision. However, with flexible rates the complex political and human factors behind central bank decisions are not part of the forecasting problem—if the rate is "clean." Instead, in a flexible system with rates changing continuously, the forecasting problem involves examining the factors which affect the free-market supply of and demand for foreign currencies. We have mentioned the important factors in the previous chapter, so we need to give only a brief review here. Before we do so, we

---

[6] It is straightforward to verify that if $O(£)$ slopes downward but nevertheless cuts $D(£)$ from above, then the equilibrium is still stable. This means that a downward slope is a necessary but not sufficient condition for an unstable equilibrium.

[7] Even if the supply curve of a currency slopes downward, there is still a chance that the market is stable, since, as we noted earlier, the supply curve must cut demand from below for an unstable equilibrium. The stability conditions are derived in Appendix 6.1.

[8] For a survey of import and export elasticities, see Robert M. Stern, Jonathan Francis, and Bruce Schumacher, *Price Elasticities in International Trade: An Annotated Bibliography*, The Macmillan Press, Ltd., London, 1976. See also Maurice Levi, "World-Wide Effects and Import Elasticities," *Journal of International Economics*, vol. 6, May 1976, pp. 203–214.

FIGURE 6.4
Effect of inflation, income, etc.

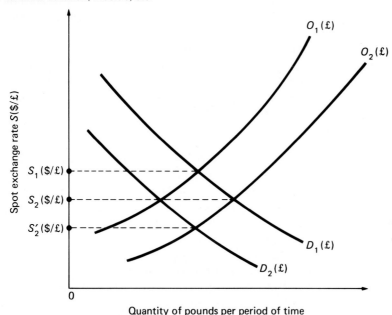

More rapid inflation in Britain than elsewhere will lower the demand for pounds and raise the supply. The same will occur from a relative decline in British interest rates. Increasing the British money supply or national income raises the supply of pounds while increasing foreign money supplies or national income raises demand. Resource discoveries in Britain raise the demand for pounds or lower the supply.

should remember that in order to know in advance which way the exchange rate will move, we must be able to correctly anticipate the factors affecting currency supplies and demands. Alternatively, we must be able to make use of other people's forecasts of these factors.[9]

General Inflation   When wages and prices increase, a country's goods become harder to sell in world markets. If all other factors remain constant, there will be a fall in exports and an increase in imports, and the exchange rate will decline. Figure 6.4 shows inflation in Britain lowering the demand for pounds from $D_1(£)$ to $D_2(£)$ and raising the supply from $O_1(£)$ to $O_2(£)$. Together these results will lower the value of sterling from $S_1($/£)$ to $S_2'($/£)$. We recall that relative prices affect international trade, and so the fall in the demand for pounds from the fall in the demand for British goods and services will result from more rapid inflation in Britain than in the United States. If all countries experience similar rates of inflation, exchange rates will remain unaffected.

If the financial manager can forecast differences in inflation rates, he or she will go a long way toward explaining movements in currency values. We will see this

[9] We will leave the question of the ability to achieve good forecasts until later. Forecasting accuracy is covered in Part 4 when we introduce concepts of market efficiency.

again when we examine the purchasing power parity theorem, but we will leave this until later. Since inflation will depend on the monetary policy and perhaps also the fiscal policy of government, the ability to forecast these politically based decisions in different countries will help the financial manager in predicting the path of exchange rates. The anticipation of political decisions such as the resolve to control inflation or to tolerate high unemployment is extremely complex. However, forecasters have been known to examine such factors as the educational backgrounds of officials and their advisers, as well as their past records, in forming judgments of what decisions the officials will make.

National Income   We have seen, in our presentation of the Keynesian approach in the previous chapter, how increases in national income will increase the demand for imports. If, for example, the British national income was to rise, with the pound floating against the dollar, this would raise the number of pounds offered on the foreign exchange market. This is shown in Figure 6.4 with a movement of the pound offer curve from $O_1(\pounds)$ to $O_2(\pounds)$. This will lower $S(\$/\pounds)$ to $S_2(\$/\pounds)$, with the original demand curve, and hence reduce the dollar value of sterling. If *foreign* national incomes rise, this will raise the demand for British goods, move the demand curve for pounds to the right, and raise the exchange value of sterling.

It should be apparent that the relative growth in national incomes will affect currency values in the same way as relative inflation. If British incomes are rising faster than incomes abroad, then the offer curve of pounds will move further to the right than the demand curve, and $S(\$/\pounds)$ will fall. If instead the United States and other countries are booming while the British economy is depressed, then the pound will appreciate against other currencies. We discover that the ability to forecast general levels of demand can be an important skill in tracking movements of exchange rates.

Interest rates   In the previous chapter we saw how interest rates can affect relative currency demands via the current and capital accounts. If British interest rates were to rise because of an increase in the Bank of England's minimum lending rate (MLR—equivalent to the Federal Reserve discount rate), then the demand for pounds would also rise. For a given offer curve of pounds, this would raise the value of $S(\$/\pounds)$. It goes without saying that the relative interest rates are relevant. If the interest rates in the United States and other countries move alongside the rates in Britain, there will be no change in the exchange rate.[10]

Interest differentials are only part of the foreign investment decision. Currency supplies and demands also depend on the expected path of exchange rates and on the difference between current spot rates and forward exchange rates. This is because changes in exchange rates can affect final yields. However, we will leave the details of this until the next chapter.

---

[10] There are currencies which are affected by the overall level of interest rates rather than only by interest differentials. Canada has a large foreign debt to service and pays more interest abroad than Canadian residents receive in return. This is a current account deficit on services. If the overall level of interest rates were to fall, the payments abroad would fall more than receipts from abroad, hence improving the value of the Canadian dollar.

Money Supply   In our brief explanation of the monetary approach to the balance of payments, we introduced a way in which the money supply could influence flexible exchange rates directly (as well as indirectly via inflation). An increase in the money supply will create an excess supply of money and will cause more spending and more bonds to be bought. For example, if the British money supply is increased, the extra spending for foreign goods and services will increase the offer of pounds. $O(\pounds)$ will move from $O_1(\pounds)$ to $O_2(\pounds)$ in Figure 6.4, lowering the value of $S(\$/\pounds)$. The extra spending on bonds from an increased supply of pounds will raise British bond prices and lower British interest rates, causing some people to use the extra pounds to buy foreign bonds. This will increase the offer of pounds.

Because the relative growth rates in money supplies will affect exchange rates, an ability to sense the determination of different central banks to control their money supplies could help in exchange rate forecasting. For example, correctly anticipating the will of the British government to control the money supply despite painfully high interest rates (in 1980) would have helped in forecasting the gains made by the pound. Similarly, anticipation of the fight to control the money supply in the United States during 1981 would have helped in forecasting the great gains made by the U.S. dollar. It should be clear that the money supply, national income, inflation, and interest rates are all closely linked within an economy, and so the different factors we have so far included will involve forecasts that are interdependent.

Resource Discoveries and Political Developments   Because the world has proved to be vulnerable to key resource shortages and to political developments, we should not leave our account of the factors moving exchange rates without some mention of these. When the supply of oil from major suppliers such as those in the Middle East becomes insecure, the demand for the currencies of countries which are relatively self-sufficient in oil rises. Previous oil crises tended to favor the United States, Canada, Great Britain, and Norway and to hurt the currency values of energy-importing nations such as Japan and Germany. Similarly, major oil and gas discoveries helped the currencies of the countries in which the discoveries were made. The British pound made great strides from 1979 to 1980 as North Sea oil made Britain a net supplier of energy. Announcements of discoveries of oil and gas off the Canadian east coast and the Arctic have raised the value of the Canadian dollar at different times. It is not a straightforward matter to predict political crises or discoveries of oil, but the financial executive who is tuned in to political and resource developments can have an edge in predicting in which direction things will go. For example, it was not too difficult to predict the recovery of the pound from the development of North Sea oil, yet it was not until the oil was actually flowing that the pound gained from $1.60/\pounds$ to over $2.40/\pounds$ in a couple of years before subsequently falling back.

ARGUMENTS FOR AND AGAINST FIXED AND FLEXIBLE EXCHANGE RATES

The potential instability of foreign exchange markets has been used as an argument against flexible exchange rates on the grounds that we would not achieve balance in international payments. This view holds that markets could be in an unstable equilibrium, like $S_u(\$/£)$ in Figure 6.3. As we have seen, this requires inelastic demand and is an empirical question. The belief that equilibrium is unstable, often known as *elasticity pessimism*, has become less common as carefully derived elasticity estimates have (not surprisingly) shown that demand elasticities are sufficiently large for equilibrium to be stable. However, there are numerous other arguments for and against fixed and flexible exchange rates which remain hot topics of debate.

Arguments for Flexible Exchange Rates[11]

Better Adjustment   Perhaps the most important argument for flexible exchange rates is that they provide a much smoother adjustment mechanism than do fixed exchange rates. An incipient deficit with flexible exchange rates will merely cause a decline in the foreign exchange value of the currency rather than require a recession to reduce income or prices, as would fixed exchange rates. We should note, however, that the decline in the value of a nation's currency still cures a balance of payments deficit by reducing real (price-level-adjusted) income and wages. We can make our products more competitive either by reducing prices in local currency or by reducing the foreign exchange value of that currency. For political and social reasons it is impractical to reduce local currency wages, so instead we can reduce the international value of the currency.

We can see how a currency devaluation or depreciation reduces real wages in two ways. First, it means more expensive imports, which raises the cost of living and thereby reduces the buying power of given local wages. Second, when the wages or incomes of the workers in different countries are ranked in terms of a common currency, the fall in the value of a currency will mean that wages and incomes in the respective country fall vis-à-vis those in other countries. It should hence be clear that a decline in the value of a currency via flexible exchange rates is an alternative to a decline in local currency wages and prices to correct payments deficits. The preference for flexible exchange rates, on the grounds of better adjustment, is based on the potential for averting adverse worker reaction by only indirectly reducing real wages.

Better Confidence   It is claimed as a corollary to better adjustment that if flexible exchange rates prevent a country from having large persistent deficits, then there will be more confidence in the international financial system. More confidence means fewer attempts by individuals or central banks to readjust currency portfolios, and this gives rise to calmer foreign exchange markets.

Better Liquidity   Flexible exchange rates do not require central banks to hold foreign exchange reserves, since there is no need to intervene in the foreign exchange

---

[11] The classic case for flexible exchange rates has been made by Milton Friedman in "The Case for Flexible Exchange Rates," in *Essays in Positive Economics*, University of Chicago Press, Chicago, 1953, and by Egon Sohmen in *Flexible Exchange Rates: Theory and Controversy*, University of Chicago Press, Chicago, 1969.

market. This means that the problem of having insufficient liquidity (international foreign exchange reserves) does not exist with truly flexible rates, and competitive devaluations aimed at securing a larger share of an inadequate total stock of reserves will not take place.

Gains from Freer Trade   When deficits occur with fixed exchange rates, tariffs and restrictions on the free flow of goods and capital invariably abound. If, by maintaining external balance, flexible rates avoid the need for these regulations, which are costly to enforce, then the gains from trade and international investment can be enjoyed.

Increased Independence of Policy   Maintaining a fixed exchange rate can force a country to follow the same economic policy as its major trading partners. For example, suppose that the United States allows a rapid growth in the money supply, as it did during the Vietnam war. This will tend to push up U.S. prices and lower interest rates (in the short run), the former causing a deficit or deterioration in the current account and the latter causing a deficit or deterioration in the capital account. If, for example, the Canadian dollar is fixed to the U.S. dollar, the deficit in the United States will most likely mean a surplus in Canada. This will put upward pressure on the Canadian dollar, forcing the Bank of Canada to sell Canadian dollars and hence increase the Canadian money supply. In this case an increase in the U.S. money supply causes an increase in the Canadian money supply. It was for this reason that the United States was accused of "shipping" its inflation to the rest of the world. However, if exchange rates are flexible, all that will happen is that the value of the U.S. dollar will decrease against other currencies.

The advantage of flexible rates in allowing independent policy action has been put in a different way in the so-called optimum currency area argument. An optimum currency area is an area within which exchange rates should be fixed. The concept has been developed primarily by Robert Mundell and Ronald McKinnon[12] and can be explained by asking what it would mean for the European Economic Community (EEC) to have a common currency, that is, for the EEC currencies to be truly fixed to each other.[13] We can begin by asking what would happen if, for example, Britain suffered a fall in demand for its exports and the result was high unemployment, while the remainder of the EEC was booming.

Offsetting the fall in demand and easing the unemployment in Britain would require an expansion in the money supply. With a common currency throughout the

---

[12] See Robert Mundell, "A Theory of Optimum Currency Areas," *American Economic Review*, vol. 51, September 1961, pp. 657–665, and Ronald McKinnon, "Optimum Currency Areas," *American Economic Review*, vol. 53, September 1963, pp. 717–725. See also Harry Johnson and Alexander Swoboda (eds.), *Madrid Conference on Optimum Currency Areas*, Harvard University Press, Cambridge, Mass., 1973.

[13] Truly fixed exchange rates are the same as a common currency because one country's money will be exchanged for a fixed number of units of another country's money just as two $5 bills are exchanged for a $10 bill. The United States has dozens of fixed exchange rates (that is, has a common currency), with New York dollars (that is, those issued by the New York Fed as shown to the left of center on the note) being exchanged at a fixed exchange rate (that is, 1.0) for San Francisco dollars, Boston dollars, St. Louis dollars, and so on.

EEC, this would involve the risk of inflation in the economies with full employment. We see that Britain cannot have an independent policy. If, however, Britain has its own currency, then the money supply can be expanded to take care of Britain's problem. Moreover, even if the discretionary policy action is not taken, having a separate currency with a flexible exchange value means that this adjustment can be achieved automatically. The fall in demand for British exports would lower the external value of the pound, and the lower value would then stimulate export sales. In addition, a lower pound would encourage investors to build plants in Britain and take advantage of the cheap British wages, vis-à-vis those in other countries.

The optimum currency area argument can be taken further. Why not have a separate currency with a flexible exchange rate for Wales, which is part of Britain? Then a fall in the demand for coal or steel, major products of Wales, would cause a fall in the value of this hypothetical Welsh currency, stimulating other industries to locate in Wales. A separate currency would also allow discretionary policies to solve the economic difficulties specific to the region. And if Wales, then why not Cardiff, a city in Wales, or even parts of Cardiff? Extending the argument to the United States, why shouldn't there be a separate northeastern dollar or a separate northwestern dollar? Then if, for example, there is a fall in the demand for the timber of the northwest, the northwestern dollar will decline in value, and other industries will be encouraged to move to the northwest. But what limits this?

We can begin our answer by saying that there is no need to have a separate northwestern dollar if the people in the northwest are prepared to move to where opportunities are plentiful so that unemployment does not occur. We need a separate currency for areas from which factors of production cannot move or prefer not to move. This prompted Robert Mundell to argue that the optimum currency area is the "region." A region is defined as an area within which factors of production are mobile and from which they are immobile. Mundell argued that if currency areas are smaller than existing countries, then there is considerable inconvenience in converting currencies, and there is exchange rate risk in local business activity. In addition, thin currency markets can experience monopolistic private speculation. Mundell therefore limited the optimum currency area to something larger than a nation. This makes the problem one of asking which countries should have fixed exchange rates.

The notion that the optimum number of currency areas is limited by the risk and inconvenience of having too many different currencies is a leading argument in the case against flexible rates. We will begin with this when we give the negative side of the flexible rates argument.

The Case against Flexible Rates

Flexible Rates Cause Uncertainty and Inhibit International Trade and Investment It is claimed by proponents of fixed rates that if exporters and importers do not know the future exchange rate, they will stick to local markets. This means a lower level of exploiting the advantages of international trade and making overseas investments, and it is a burden on everyone. To counter this argument, a believer in a flexible system can say the following:

1 Flexible rates do not necessarily fluctuate wildly, and fixed rates do change— often dramatically.[14] There have been numerous well-publicized occasions when so-called fixed exchange rates have been changed by as much as 25 percent. Many changes have taken place in the fixed value of British pounds, Deutsche marks, Israeli shekels, French francs, and Mexican pesos. In addition, there have been periods of relative stability of flexible exchange rates. For example, the Canadian dollar varied within a range of about 2 percent for a period of years in the early 1970s.

2 The forward exchange market can be used to avoid foreign exchange risk, and this market is cheap to use. An exporter or importer who has not been lucky enough to invoice in his or her own currency can buy or sell the foreign exchange forward. Since exporters and importers will in any case face spot exchange transaction costs, the costs of hedging in the forward market will matter only if forward exchange transaction costs are much higher than spot costs. In fact there is very little difference between spot and forward transaction costs. This is a powerful argument against this criticism of flexible rates.

Flexible Rates Cause Destabilizing Speculation   A highly controversial argument is that under flexible exchange rates, speculators will cause wide swings in the value of different currencies. These swings are the result of the movement of "hot money." (The expression is used because of the speed at which the money moves in response to news items.) There are two counterarguments that can be made:

1 To be destabilizing, speculation will, in general, have to result in losses. The argument goes like this. To cause destabilization, a speculator must buy when the price is high to make it go higher and sell when it is low to make it go lower. In this way the variations in rates will be higher than they would otherwise be, as is illustrated in Figure 6.5. If the rate without speculation follows the path shown, then to make the rate vary by more than this, pounds must be purchased when $S(\$/\pounds)$ would have been at A [making $S(\$/\pounds)$ rise to A'], sold when $S(\$/\pounds)$ would have been at B [making $S(\$/\pounds)$ fall to B'], and so on. But this means buying high and selling low, which is a sure recipe for a quick exit from any speculative game.[15]

If speculators are to make a profit, they must sell pounds when $S(\$/\pounds)$ would have been at A [forcing $S(\$/\pounds)$ toward A''] and buy pounds when $S(\$/\pounds)$ would have been at B [forcing $S(\$/\pounds)$ toward B'']. In this way speculators will dampen variations in exchange rates and stabilize the market.

---

[14] Occasionally, proponents of fixed exchange rates refer to flexible rates as a "fluctuating exchange rate system." There is no such thing as a system of fluctuating rates, and those people who use this term are confusing "flexible"—which means able to move—with "fluctuation"—which means actual movement.

[15] Special circumstances can be established whereby destabilizing speculation can be profitable. For an account of these, see Robert M. Stern, *The Balance of Payments*, Aldine Publishing Company, Chicago, 1973.

FIGURE 6.5
Stabilizing and destabilizing currency speculation.

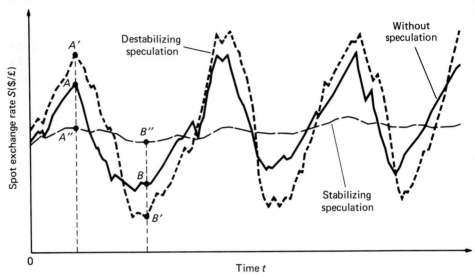

With destabilizing speculation we expect variations in exchange rates to be larger than they would otherwise be. Profitable speculation involving buying high and selling low should, however, reduce variability.

2 Speculation with fixed exchange rates is destabilizing and it can be profitable too. When a country is running out of foreign exchange reserves, its currency is likely to be under selling pressure, with the exchange rate at its lower support point. When speculators see this, they will sell the currency. Under fixed rates the central bank will purchase the currency sold by the speculators at the lower support price and use up foreign exchange reserves. This will make the shortage of reserves even worse, causing other holders of the troubled currency to sell. This will further lower foreign exchange reserves and eventually force the central bank to reset the rate at a lower level. This is highly destabilizing speculation. It is also profitable.

With fixed exchange rates the speculators know in which direction the rate will move. For example, when the pound sterling was pegged at \$2.8000/£ and experiencing downward pressure in the early and mid-1960s, a revaluation of the pound was exceedingly unlikely. By selling pounds the worst that could have happened was that the rate would not have changed. And if it had changed, there would have been a pound devaluation, and the speculator could have bought back the pounds later at a lower price. Similarly, when the Deutsche mark was fixed to the dollar and under heavy buying pressure in the late 1960s, everybody could have been confident that the mark would not be devalued. If anything, it would have been revalued, and a profit would have been made by buying Deutsche marks. The worst that could have happened was that the rate would not have changed. And so fixed-rate speculation is destabilizing, and because it provides one-way bets, it is also profitable.

Flexible Exchange Rates Will Not Work for Small Open Economies[16]   This is a valid argument that has been made by a number of economists, including Robert Mundell. The argument begins by noting that a depreciation or devaluation of a currency will help the balance of payments if it reduces the relative prices of locally produced goods and services. However, a depreciation or devaluation will raise the prices of imports. This will increase the cost of living, which will put upward pressure on wages. If, for example, a 1 percent depreciation or devaluation raises import costs by a full 1 percent and most goods are imported (the country is a "banana republic" which produces a narrow range of outputs and imports most consumption goods), then if real wages are maintained, nominal wages must rise by the amount of depreciation. If wages rise 1 percent when the currency falls by 1 percent, the effects are offsetting, and changes in exchange rates, whether in flexible or pegged values, will be ineffective. In such a case the country may as well fix the value of its currency to the currency of the country which supplies the most imports.

Every country produces some of its consumer goods and services locally. Housing is always local (and often accounts for over 25 percent of consumption), and in many places most services, perishable foods, and so on, are too. This means that while the open-economy case is relevant, it is unlikely to make changes in exchange rates completely ineffective. However, it is possible that even though some goods and services are produced locally, a depreciation will raise the prices of competing import items, allowing local producers to raise their prices. With this effect it is presumed that there is a lack of competition between local producers, but the effect could be relevant in some small countries.

Flexible Exchange Rates Are Inflationary   Rigid adherence to the gold standard involved a constraint on monetary authorities. They had to keep their money supplies and inflation under control. It is claimed by proponents of fixed rates that the dollar-exchange standard also involved discipline, since poor performance was readily apparent in statistics on declining foreign exchange reserves. This, it is said, gave the central bank public support for strong action. Flexible exchange rates, according to this argument, allow conditions to deteriorate without providing evidence to support strong corrective action. However, this argument against flexible exchange rates fails to recognize that the exchange rate itself is daily evidence of poor economic performance. The need for corrective action is apparent to everyone. It is true that the problem can creep up rather than appear suddenly and dramatically. However, in order to believe that flexible rates are more inflationary than fixed rates, it is necessary to believe that central bankers

---

[16] By an open economy we mean a country which trades extensively with others. Openness can be judged from the value of imports or exports compared with the GNP. Thus Holland, for example, is more open than the United States.

are more concerned with evidence of declining reserves than with evidence of a declining currency value or that central bankers are better able to act on evidence of declining reserves.

INTERMEDIATE SOLUTIONS

Fixed and flexible exchange rates are only two alternatives defining the extremes of exchange rate systems. In between these extremes are a number of other systems which have been tried or suggested. We can look at two of the more prominent of these.

Wider Bands

A move toward more flexibility was tried for a very short while after December 1971, when the International Monetary Fund members decided at a meeting at the Smithsonian Institute in Washington, D.C., to allow the range of fluctuation of exchange rates to be 2¼ percent on either side of the official value. This gave a 4½ percent total range of variation before the central bank would intervene, compared with the 2 percent range that existed from 1944 to 1971. The intention was to reduce the uncertainty about future exchange rates and at the same time allow more adjustment. The wider the band, the closer the system came to being a flexible rate system.

The wider band was not tried by many of the major countries. Canada had opted for a completely floating rate before the Smithsonian meeting, and Britain and the other major European countries floated their currencies (some of which remained fixed to each other) shortly afterward.

Crawling Peg

The crawling peg is an automatic system for revising the central value—the value around which the rate can fluctuate. This proposal can be combined with a wider band.[17] The crawling peg requires the central bank to intervene whenever the exchange rate approaches a support point. However, the central value, around which the support points are set, is revised according to the average exchange rate over the previous weeks or months. If the rate is allowed to remain at or near, for example, the lower support point, the new central value will be revised downward. In this way the rate can drift up or down gradually, giving some degree of certainty without completely frustrating long-term fundamental trends.

The wider band and crawling peg proposals came at a time when the international financial system was undergoing great strain. The background to the crisis in the international financial system and where this system might yet go are both important topics for the executive who wishes to understand the changing international environment.

---

[17] For an account of alternative adjustment systems see John Williamson, "Surveys in Applied Economics: International Liquidity," *Economic Journal*, vol. 83, September 1973, pp. 685–746.

TWENTIETH-CENTURY INTERNATIONAL FINANCIAL HISTORY

The Story before Bretton Woods

We have on a few occasions already touched on the evolution of the international financial system. A complete account was left until now so that we would be familiar with the workings of the systems which will be described.

As we have already noted, the gold standard, which involved the exchange of national currencies for the international medium gold, came to an end (after an earlier temporary suspension) during the depression of 1929–1933. The beginnings of the gold standard cannot so easily be identified, because the system was not deliberately devised; it evolved with general practice.

For a gold standard to work, it is necessary that deficit countries allow the pressure of deficits on their gold reserves to slow monetary growth. It is just as necessary that the surplus countries allow their increased gold reserves to liberalize their monetary policies. However, in practice, the burden of both types of adjustment was considered so great that frequently there was reluctance to behave in this way. Many countries began to manipulate exchange rates for their own domestic objectives. For example, the French devalued the franc in 1926 to stimulate their economy, and the undervalued currency contributed to the problems of the British pound. Then in 1928 the French decided to accept only gold and no more foreign exchange for reserves. When in 1931 the French decided that they would not accept any more pounds sterling and also that they would exchange their existing sterling holdings for gold, there was little the British could do other than make sterling inconvertible into gold. This they did in 1931. The ability to exchange currencies for gold is the central feature of the gold standard, and when other countries found their holdings of pounds no longer convertible, they followed Britain. By 1934 only the U.S. dollar could be exchanged for gold.

Since a full recovery from the depression of 1929–1933 did not take place until the onset of World War II, the conditions for any formal reorganizing of the international financial order were not present. The depression had provided an environment in which self-interested policies of "beggar thy neighbor"—competitive devaluations and increased tariff protection—followed the model established earlier by France. Since no long-lasting effective devaluations were possible and the great interruption of world trade eliminated the gains from international trade, such an environment hindered economic growth. When the war replaced the depression, no cooperation was possible, and it was not until July of 1944 that, with victory imminent in Europe, the representatives of the United States, Great Britain, and other allied powers met in the rural surroundings of Bretton Woods, New Hampshire, to hammer out a new international financial order to replace the failed gold standard.

Bretton Woods and the IMF

Of paramount importance to the representatives at the 1944 meeting at Bretton Woods was the prevention of another breakdown of the international financial order, such as the breakdown which followed the peace after World War I. From 1918 until well into the 1920s the world had witnessed a rise in protectionism on a grand scale to protect jobs for those returning from the war, competitive devaluations designed for the same effect, and massive hyperinflation as the inability to raise conventional taxes gave rise to the hidden tax of inflation. A system was required that would keep countries from changing exchange rates for competitive advantage. This meant that some sort of control on rate changes was needed, as well as a reserve base for deficit countries. The reserves were to be provided via an institution created for this purpose. The International Monetary Fund (IMF) was established to collect and allocate reserves in order to implement the Articles of Agreement signed at Bretton Woods.

The Articles of Agreement required member countries (of which there were 143 by September 28, 1981) to:

1 Promote international monetary cooperation
2 Facilitate the growth of trade
3 Promote exchange rate stability
4 Establish a system of multilateral payments
5 Create a reserve base

The reserves were contributed by the member countries according to a quota system (since then many times revised) based on the national income and importance of trade in different countries. Of the original contribution, 25 percent was in gold—the so-called gold tranche position—and the remaining 75 percent was in the country's own currency. A country was allowed to borrow up to its gold tranche contribution without IMF approval and an additional 100 percent in four steps, each with additionally stringent conditions established by the IMF. These conditions were to ensure that corrective macroeconomic policy actions would be taken.

The lending facilities have been expanded over the years. Standby arrangements were introduced in 1952, enabling a country to have funds appropriated ahead of the need so that currencies would be less open to attack during the IMF's deliberation of whether help would be made available. Other extensions of the IMF's lending ability took the form of:

1 The Compensating Financing Facility, introduced in 1963 to help countries with temporarily inadequate foreign exchange reserves as a result of events such as crop failures.

2 The Extended Fund Facility of 1974, providing loans for countries with structural difficulties that take longer to correct.

3 The Trust Fund from the 1976 decision to allow the sale of gold that was no longer to have a formal role in the international financial system. The proceeds of gold sales are used for special development loans.

4 The Supplementary Financing Facility, also known as the Witteveen Facility after the managing director of the IMF. It replaced the 1974–1976 Oil Facility, which was established to help countries with temporary difficulties resulting from oil price increases. This gives standby credits.

5 The Buffer Stock Facility, which grants loans to enable countries to purchase crucial inventories.

These facilities have been supplemented by the 1980 decision allowing the IMF to borrow in the private capital market, when necessary.

The most important feature of the Bretton Woods Agreement was the decision to have the U.S. dollar freely convertible into gold and to have the values of other currencies fixed in U.S. dollars. The exchange rates were to be maintained within 1 percent on either side of the official parity, with intervention required at the support points. This required the United States to maintain a reserve of gold and other countries to maintain a reserve of U.S. dollars. Because the initially selected exchange rates could have been incorrect for balance of payments equilibrium, each country was allowed a revision of up to 10 percent within a year of the initial selection of the exchange rate. In this basic form the system survived until 1971.

The central place of the U.S. dollar was viewed by John Maynard Keynes, who was the British representative at Bretton Woods, as a potential weakness. Keynes preferred an international settlement system based on a new currency unit—the Bancor. However, the U.S. plan was accepted, and it was not until the 1960s that the inevitable collapse of the Bretton Woods arrangement was recognized by a Yale economist, Robert Triffin.[18] According to the *Triffin paradox*, in order for the stock of world reserves to grow along with world trade, the providers of reserves—primarily the United States but also Great Britain—must run balance of payments deficits. These deficits are the means by which other countries can accumulate dollar and pound reserves. Although the reserve country deficits are needed, the more they occur, the more the holders of dollars (and pounds) will doubt the ability of the Federal Reserve (and Bank of England) to convert dollars (and pounds) into gold at the agreed price. This built-in paradox means that the system is doomed.

Among the more skeptical holders of dollars was France, which began in 1962 to exchange dollars for gold despite the objection of the United States. Not only were the French doubtful about the future value of the dollar, but they also objected to the prominent role of the United States in the Bretton Woods system. Part of this distaste for a powerful United States was political, and part was based on the seigniorage gains that France believed accrued to the United States by virtue of the U.S. role as the world's banker. *Seigniorage* is the profit from making money and depends on the ability to have people hold your currency or other assets at a noncompetitive yield. Every government which issues legal-tender currency can ensure that it is held by its own citizens, even if it offers no yield at all. For example, U.S. citizens will hold Federal Reserve notes and give up goods or services for them, even though the paper the notes are printed on costs very little to provide. The United States was in a special position because its role as the leading provider of foreign exchange reserves meant that it could ensure that foreign central banks as well as U.S. citizens would hold U.S. dollars. However, most reserves were and are kept in securities such as treasury bills, which yield interest. If the interest that is paid on the reserve assets is a competitive yield, then the seigniorage gains to the

---

[18] Robert Triffin, *Gold and the Dollar Crisis*, Yale University Press, New Haven, Conn., 1960.

United States from foreigners holding U.S. assets is small. Indeed, with sufficient competition from (1) alternative reserves of different currencies and (2) alternative investments in the United States, the gains should be a normal and fair return on the assets.[19] Nevertheless, the French continued to convert their dollar holdings into gold. This led other countries to worry about whether sufficient gold would remain for them after the French had finished selling dollars.

By 1968, the run on gold was of such a scale that at a March meeting in Washington, D.C., a two-tier gold-pricing system was established. While the official U.S. price of gold was to remain at $35 per ounce, the private-market price of gold was to be allowed to find its own level.

After repeated financial crises, including a devaluation of the pound from $2.80/£ to $2.40/£ in 1967, some relief came in 1970 with the allocation of Special Drawing Rights (SDRs).[20] The SDRs are book entries that are credited to the accounts of IMF member countries according to their established quotas. They can be used to meet payments imbalances, and they provide a net addition to the stock of reserves without the need for any country to run deficits or mine gold. From 1970 to 1972, approximately $9.4 billion worth of the SDRs (or paper gold) was created, and there was no further allocation until January 1, 1979, when SDR 4 billion was created. Similar amounts were created on January 1, 1980, and on January 1, 1981, bringing the total to over SDR 20 billion. A country can draw on its SDRs as long as it maintains an average of more than 30 percent of its cumulative allocation, and a country is required to accept up to 3 times its total allocation. Interest is paid to those who hold SDRs and by those who draw their SDRs, with the rate based on an average of money market interest rates in the United States, the United Kingdom, Germany, Japan, and France.

The SDR was originally set equal in value to the gold content of a U.S. dollar in 1969, that is, 0.888571 gram or 1/35 ounce. The value was later revised and based on 16 major currencies, and since January 1, 1981, the SDR has been valued in terms of 5 currencies as follows:

U.S. dollar	(42%)
German mark	(19%)
U.K. pound	(13%)
Japanese yen	(13%)
French franc	(13%)

The currency basket and the weights are to be revised every 5 years according to the importance of each country in international trade. The value of the SDR is quoted daily.

If the SDR had arrived earlier, it might have prevented or postponed the collapse of the Bretton Woods system, but by 1971, the fall was imminent. With only two

[19] For an account and estimates of seigniorage gains, see the papers in Robert Mundell and Alexander Swoboda, *Monetary Problems of the International Economy*, University of Chicago Press, Chicago, 1969.
[20] See Fritz Machlup, *Remaking the International Monetary System: The Rio Agreement and Beyond*, Johns Hopkins Press, Baltimore, 1968, for the background to the creation of SDRs.

major revisions of exchange rates in the 1950s and 1960s—the floating of the Canadian dollar during the 1950s and the devaluation of sterling in 1967—events suddenly began to rapidly unfold. On August 15, 1971, the United States responded to a record $30 billion trade deficit by making the dollar inconvertible into gold. A 10 percent surcharge was placed on imports, and a program of wage and price controls was introduced. Many of the major currencies were allowed to float against the dollar, and by the end of 1971 most had appreciated, with the Deutsche mark and the Japanese yen both up 12 percent. The dollar had begun a decade of decline.

The International System since 1971

On August 15, 1971, the United States made it clear that it was no longer content to support a system based on the U.S. dollar. The costs of being a reserve currency country were perceived as having begun to exceed any benefits in terms of seigniorage. The largest countries, called the "group of ten," were called together for a meeting at the Smithsonian Institute in Washington, D.C. As a result of the Smithsonian Agreement, the United States raised the price of gold to $38 per ounce (that is, devalued the dollar). Each of the other countries in return devalued its currency by an amount of up to 10 percent. The band around the new official parity values was increased from 1 percent to 2¼ percent on either side. The stronger European Economic Community (EEC, or Common Market) countries preferred to keep their own exchange rates within a narrower range of each other—1⅛ percent each way—while jointly allowing the 4½ percent band vis-á-vis the dollar. The so-called snake within the tunnel became the worm within the snake within the tunnel when the allowable range of some EEC countries was narrowed even further.

The dollar devaluation was insufficient to restore stability to the system. By 1973 the dollar was under heavy selling pressure even at its devalued or depreciated rates, and in February 1973, the price of gold was raised 10 percent, from $38 to $42.22 per ounce. By the next month most major currencies were floating. This was the unsteady state of the international financial system as it approached the oil crisis of the fall of 1973.

The rapid increase in oil prices after the oil embargo worked to the advantage of the U.S. dollar. Since the United States was relatively self-sufficient in oil at that time, the U.S. dollar was able to weather the worst of the storm. The strength of the dollar allowed the United States to remove controls on capital outflows in January 1974. This opened the way for large-scale U.S. lending to companies and countries in need—and came just in time. The practice of paying for oil in U.S. dollars meant that the buyers needed dollars and that the sellers—principally the members of the Organization of Petroleum Exporting Countries (OPEC)—needed to invest their receipts. And so the United States began to recycle petrodollars, taking them in from OPEC on one side of the account and lending them to the oil buyers on the other.

It was not until 1976, at a meeting in Jamaica, that the system that had begun to emerge in 1971 was approved, with ratification coming later, in April 1978. Flexible exchange rates, already extensively used, were deemed to be acceptable to the IMF members, and central banks were permitted to intervene and manage their floats to prevent undue volatility. Gold was officially demonetized, and half of the IMF's gold holdings was returned to the members. The other half was sold, and the proceeds were to be used to help poor nations. Individual countries were allowed to sell their gold holdings, and the United States, the IMF, and some other countries began sales. IMF sales were completed by May of 1980.

In March 1979 the European snake ("joint float") was extended into the long-awaited European Monetary System (EMS). Consisting of the European Common Market countries other than Britain (and with Italy given special dispensation), the EMS was based on the newly created European Currency Unit (ECU). The ECU is the same as the European Unit of Account (EUA), which was previously used in the Common Market, and it is a currency basket equivalent to the sum of 3.66 Belgian francs (B Fr3.66), 0.217 Danish krone (D Kr0.217), Fr1.15, 0.00759 Irish pound (£Ir0.00759), 109 Italian lire (Lit109), 0.14 Luxembourg franc (Lux Fr0.14), 0.286 Dutch guilder (f0.286), £0.0885, and DM0.828. The ECU is therefore rather like the SDR, except that it is designed for use within Europe and is therefore based only on European currencies. ECUs are used as reserves by participating central banks, which borrow and lend them. Participating countries must maintain exchange rates within 2¼ percent on either side of a central par value (except Italy, which is allowed 6 percent deviations). This is done through intervention in the foreign exchange market. Countries must use their foreign exchange reserves or borrow currencies from each other. The borrowing is arranged and supervised by the European Monetary Co-operation Fund (EMCF), Europe's own equivalent of the IMF.[21]

Other Institutions

The International Bank for Reconstruction and Development (IBRD), commonly known as the World Bank, was, like the IMF, also a product of the Bretton Woods Agreement. It is not a bank in the sense of accepting deposits and providing payment services between countries. Rather, it is a lending institution that borrows from governments by selling them its bonds and then uses the proceeds for development in undeveloped (or developing) nations. The president of the World Bank until 1980 was Robert MacNamara. By trying to ensure that World Bank loans were tied to population control programs, he embroiled the World Bank in controversy. In June 1981 the former head of the Bank of America, A. W. Clausen, became president.

World Bank or IBRD loans have a maturity of up to 20 years. Interest rates are determined by the (relatively low) cost of funds to the bank. Many developing countries do not meet the conditions for World Bank loans, so in 1960 an affiliated organization, the International Development Agency (IDA) was established to help even poorer countries. Credits, as the loans are called, have terms of up to 50 years

---

[21] For a more detailed account of the EMS, the ECU, and so on, see *International Letter*, Federal Reserve Bank of Chicago, March 16, 1979. This gives a full account of the workings of the snake in the tunnel.

and carry no interest charges. A second affiliate of the World Bank is the International Finance Corporation (IFC). This was established in 1956 to help stimulate economic growth in the private sector of developing nations by drawing capital into equity investment.

The Bank of International Settlements (BIS) predates the Bretton Woods Agreement and dates back to the end of World War I. Located in Basel, Switzerland, it serves as a membership organization of central banks. It is here that major policy decisions can be introduced to discover how others will react. A similar consulting and advisory institution is the Paris-based Organization for Economic Co-operation and Development (OECD), which was established in 1961. The OECD publishes a large volume of economic statistics for its members and makes forecasts of members' GNP, inflation, and so on, to help in planning.

An agreement which should have important implications for economic well-being and standards of living but which has often faced an uphill struggle against protectionist sentiment is the General Agreement on Tariffs and Trade (GATT). This agreement sets guidelines for commercial policy specifically concerning tariffs and quotas. GATT also is used in mediations concerning commercial disputes over the acceptability of cheap loans for exporters, dumping (selling abroad at lower prices than at home), and other issues. There have been some successes at tariff cuts from this agreement, most notably those in Geneva in 1947; in the "Kennedy round," which extended from 1962 to 1967; and in the "Tokyo round," which was based on the so-called Swiss formula and extended from 1973 to 1979.[22]

The international financial system evolved rapidly over the latter half of the twentieth century. It appears that a mixed system of managed flexible rates, crawling pegs, and fixed rates is likely to continue in the foreseeable future, but judging from the past, if anything remains certain, it is that further changes will take place.

SUMMARY

1 Other currencies float against the U.S. dollar rather than vice versa. This leaves the decision to float with the foreign central banks.

2 Flexible exchange rates are determined by the supply of and demand for a currency. Since a flexible rate ensures that these are equal, the change in reserves should be zero, and the balance of payments should always be balanced. However, central banks have frequently intervened to iron out daily variations and have often intervened on a long-term basis. The managed float involves exchange rate adjustments alongside changes in reserves.

3 Foreign exchange markets could be stable or unstable. They are unstable when, as the price falls, the supply or offer curve cuts the demand curve from below. This can occur only if the demand for imports is inelastic, since the demand for a currency, derived from the demand for exports, will always slope downward. This makes estimates of the price elasticity of demand important for government economists and corporate executives.

4 Currencies under flexible exchange rates are depreciated by rates of inflation that are

---

[22] For an account of GATT, see Richard Caves and Ronald Jones, *World Trade and Payments: An Introduction*, Little, Brown and Company, Boston, 1973, especially pp. 279–290.

higher than in other countries. They are also depreciated if the growth in national income and in the supply of money is greater than elsewhere and if interest rates are lower than elsewhere. Exchange rates have been susceptible to resource discoveries and political developments. An ability to forecast such events can be extremely valuable in exchange rate forecasting.

5 The potential for an unstable foreign exchange market is only the first of many arguments against flexible exchange rates. Arguments *for* flexible rates include better adjustment (by finding a more acceptable way of reducing real wages), better confidence, more adequate foreign exchange reserves (by doing away with the need to hold any), more freedom for economic policy instruments, and the creation of more policy independence.

6 An optimum currency area is an area within which exchange rates ought to be fixed. The optimum currency area argument provides an alternative viewpoint with regard to the debate of fixed rates versus flexible rates. Having many small currency areas improves automatic adjustment and allows local monetary policy. However, currency areas add uncertainty and introduce costs of exchanging currencies in local trade. The optimum currency area is the region, which is the area within which there is factor mobility. It is generally claimed that this area is at least as large as a country.

7 The case *against* flexible exchange rates includes the argument that they cause uncertainty and inhibit international trade. Counterarguments are that fixed rates, as they have worked in practice, have also been uncertain and that forward exchange contracts allow exporters and importers to avoid exchange risk for only the extra cost of forward currency versus spot currency.

8 Another argument against flexible rates is that they allow destabilizing speculation. However, this requires that speculators incur losses, and in any case, speculation with fixed rates is destabilizing as well as profitable.

9 A valid argument against flexible rates is that they will not work for small open economies because wages are likely to be forced up along with prices of imports, offsetting the effect of the devaluation or depreciation. Another argument is that flexible rates are inflationary.

10 Alternatives to fixed rate systems and flexible rate systems include a fixed rate with a wide band and a crawling peg. These combine attributes of both fixed rate systems and flexible rate systems.

11 The gold standard involved the exchange of gold for local currencies at a fixed price, with international transactions settled by shipping gold. The system came to an end with the depression of 1929–1933.

12 The IMF, the World Bank, and the gold-exchange standard were established in the Bretton Woods Agreement of 1944. The IMF and the World Bank survive, but many of the major countries have moved to flexible exchange rates.

13 According to the Triffin paradox, the collapse of the gold-exchange standard was inevitable, because growing reserves require continuing deficits, which lower the acceptability of the reserves. SDRs offer a remedy for the Triffin paradox.

14 The United States has been the primary recycler of petrodollars. Oil producers invest their dollars, and oil users borrow them.

15 The OECD is an advisory service for 24 western economies. GATT is used in mediations concerning commercial disputes and tries to achieve freer trade.

QUESTIONS

1 As an exporter or importer, would you feel more inclined to venture abroad under flexible rates rather than under fixed rates? Is the probability of a change in the exchange rate offset by the potential size of the change if it does occur?

2 How predictable is tomorrow's exchange rate in a system of flexible rates? Is it more or less predictable than in a system of fixed rates?

3 Why can speculators make profits with less risk with fixed rates? From whom do they make their profits?

4 Explain how you would go about setting up a procedure for forecasting exchange rates. What variables would you emphasize in your procedure?

5 Assume that you are going to poll the following groups:
   a Central bankers
   b Academic economists
   c Practicing business executives
   d Consumer advocates
   How do you think each group would weigh the arguments for and against flexible rates? What does each group have to gain or lose from more flexibility?

6 Why do we observe deficits or surpluses under "flexible" rates? Does this tell us something of the management of the rates?

7 Should Appalachia have its own currency? Should the members of the European Common Market (EEC) have separate currencies?

8 Will *re*valuations or appreciations work for small open economies? Why is there asymmetry in the effect of a revaluation and a devaluation?

9 List some reasons why you believe it is important for a corporate executive to understand the workings of the international financial system. Could such an understanding help in forecasting?

10 Do you think that the collapse of the Bretton Woods system would have been less likely had surplus countries expanded their economies to ease the burden of adjustment on the countries with deficits?

11 How would you go about trying to estimate the seigniorage gains to the United States? [*Hint:* They depend on the quantity of U.S. dollars held abroad, the competitive rate of interest that would be paid on these, and the actual rate of interest.]

12 Why do you think some EEC countries wanted a snake in the tunnel? Does your answer have to do with optimum currency areas?

13 Australia and New Zealand do extensive trading with each other. Should they have fixed exchange rates?

14 Why have central bankers frequently intervened in the foreign exchange market under a system of flexible exchange rates? If they have managed to smooth out fluctuations, have they made profits for their citizens?

15 Which argument for fixed exchange rates do you think would be most compelling for Fiji? [*Hint:* Fiji's major "export" is tourism, and most manufactures and other consumer goods are imported.]

BIBLIOGRAPHY

Brittan, Samuel: *The Price of Economic Freedom: A Guide to Flexible Rates*, Macmillan and Company, London, 1970.

Dornbusch, Rudiger: *Open Economy Macroeconomics*, Basic Books, Inc., New York, 1980.

Frenkel, Jacob A., and Harry G. Johnson: *The Economics of Exchange Rates: Selected Readings*, Addison-Wesley Publishing Company, Reading, Mass., 1978.

Friedman, Milton: "The Case for Flexible Exchange Rates," in *Essays in Positive Economics*, University of Chicago Press, Chicago, 1953.

Grubel, Herbert G.: *International Economics*, Richard D. Irwin, Homewood, Ill., 1977, chap. 22.

Heller, H. Robert: *International Monetary Economics*, Prentice-Hall, Inc., Englewood Cliffs, N.J., 1974, chap. 6.

Johnson, Harry G.: "The Case for Flexible Exchange Rates, 1969," in George N. Halm (ed.), *Approaches to Greater Flexibility of Exchange Rates: The Burgenstock Papers*, Princeton University Press, Princeton, N.J., 1970. Reprinted in Robert E. Baldwin and J. David Richardson, *International Trade and Finance: Readings*, Little, Brown and Company, Boston, 1974.

McKinnon, Ronald I.: "Optimum Currency Areas," *American Economic Review*, September 1963, pp. 717–724.

Mundell, Robert A.: *International Economics*, Macmillan and Company, New York, 1978, chap. 12.

Sohmen, Egon: *Flexible Exchange Rates: Theory and Controversy*, rev. ed., University of Chicago Press, Chicago, 1969.

Willett, Thomas D., and Edward Tower: "The Concept of Optimum Currency Areas and the Choice between Fixed and Flexible Exchange Rates," in George N. Halm (ed.), *Approaches to Greater Flexibility of Exchange Rates: The Burgenstock Papers*, Princeton University Press, Princeton, N.J., 1970.

Yeager, Leland B.: *International Monetary Relations: Theory, History and Policy*, 2d ed., Harper & Row, Inc., New York, 1976.

APPENDIX 6.1: The Condition for Stability in Foreign Exchange Markets

We consider the case of the stability of $S(\$/£)$ by looking at conditions in only the United States and the United Kingdom. The demand for dollars which results from U.S. exports will depend on the price of the U.S. dollar in terms of British pounds. We can write this as $\text{Ex}(1/S)$; that is, U.S. exports are a function of $1/[S(\$/£)] = S(£/\$)$. The supply of dollars results from U.S. imports. The imports depend on the price of pounds in terms of dollars, which we can write as $\text{Im}(S)$. If imports into the United States from Britain are priced in terms of pounds, we must multiply by $S(\$/£)$ to put the value in dollars, and so we can write the excess demand for dollars, E, as

$$E = \text{Ex}(1/S) - S \cdot \text{Im}(S) \qquad (6A.1)$$

where E = excess demand for dollars
$\quad$ Ex = U.S. exports in dollars
$\quad$ Im = U.S. imports in pounds
$\quad$ S = $S(\$/£)$

Differentiating Equation (6A.1), we have

$$\frac{dE}{dS} = \frac{\delta \text{Ex}}{\delta(1/S)} \cdot \frac{d(1/S)}{dS} - S \cdot \frac{\delta \text{Im}}{\delta S} - \text{Im}$$

or

$$\frac{dE}{dS} = -\left(\frac{1/S}{\text{Ex}} \cdot \frac{\delta \text{Ex}}{\delta 1/S} \right) \cdot \frac{\text{Ex}}{S} - \left(\frac{S}{\text{Im}} \cdot \frac{\delta \text{Im}}{\delta S} \right) \cdot \text{Im} - \text{Im} \qquad (6A.2)$$

We can define the elasticity of demand for exports, η_{Ex}, and the elasticity of demand for imports, η_{Im}, as follows:

$$\eta_{Ex} = -\left(\frac{1/S}{Ex} \cdot \frac{\delta Ex}{\delta 1/S}\right) \quad \text{and} \quad \eta_{Im} = -\left(\frac{S}{I} \cdot \frac{\delta Im}{\delta S}\right)$$

These elasticities use *values*, Ex and Im, and not *quantities* of exports and imports, and therefore it is implicitly assumed that the price of output in local currency does not change with exchange rates. This requires that supplies of exports and imports must be perfectly elastic. Using these definitions in Equation (6A.2), we have

$$\frac{dE}{dS} = \eta_{Ex} \cdot \frac{Ex}{S} + \eta_{Im} \cdot Im - Im$$

where we have defined the elasticities as positive. If the balance of payments had initially been in balance, then

$$Ex = S \cdot Im \quad \text{or} \quad \frac{Ex}{S} = Im$$

This enables us to write the following equation:

$$\frac{dE}{dS} = (\eta_{Ex} + \eta_{Im} - 1) \cdot Im \tag{6A.3}$$

The stability of the foreign exchange market requires that as the value of the dollar goes up (S falls), the excess demand for dollars must fall (E falls). Similarly, it requires that as the dollar falls in value (S goes up), the excess demand for dollars must rise (E goes up). This means that for stability, E and S move in the same direction ($dE/dS > 0$). This means that for stability,

$$\frac{dE}{dS} = (\eta_{Ex} + \eta_{Im} - 1) \cdot Im > 0 \tag{6A.4}$$

That is,

$$\eta_{Ex} + \eta_{Im} - 1 > 0$$

or

$$\eta_{Ex} + \eta_{Im} > 1 \tag{6A.5}$$

We discover that for stability, the average elasticity of demand must exceed 0.5. For instability,

$$\eta_{Ex} + \eta_{Im} < 1$$

For metastability, we need $\eta_{Ex} + \eta_{Im} = 1$. Condition (6A.5) is generally known as the Marshall-Lerner condition, after Alfred Marshall and Abba Lerner, who independently derived the inequality. We can note that the stability condition also applies to the price adjustment mechanism described in the previous chapter.

APPENDIX 6.2: The Effects of Macroeconomic Policy

It can be extremely valuable for those effecting macroeconomic policies, as well as for those who are affected by them, to know what the policies will do. For example, it is important for a corporate executive to know whether an expansionary monetary or fiscal policy is likely to work. There are circumstances which favor monetary policy and others which favor fiscal policy, but because of additional considerations or an inadequate understanding, the government might mistakenly take an expansionary policy action that will not subsequently raise sales or general demand. It is very important for the executive to know which circumstances will make certain policies ineffective so that the plant is not expanded and debt is not incurred at the wrong time. The key factors which determine whether different policies will or will not be effective are the exchange rate system in effect and possible conflicting targets facing the policy maker.

When exchange rates are fixed, that is, pegged, we can add devaluation policy to monetary and fiscal policies for stimulating the economy. Devaluation can be effective in raising output and improving the balance of payments only if there is unemployment. Another policy alternative available with any exchange rate regime involves the imposition of import tariffs or export subsidies. The effectiveness of this depends on the type of exchange rate system and also on the amount of unemployment. In this appendix, designed for those readers with a course in macroeconomics, we will derive these conclusions and try to throw some light on the impacts of policies in order to help the corporate executive and citizen forecast what will happen after economic policies have been put into effect.

POLICY EFFECTIVENESS

By effectiveness we mean the extent to which policies can influence aggregate demand and national output. With fixed exchange rates we can consider four different policies for stimulating the economy: monetary policy, fiscal policy, devaluation policy, and tariff policy. Many of the macroeconomic policy conclusions concerning the effectiveness of policy can be derived from the income-expenditure model or *IS-LM* framework that is frequently the kernel of courses in macroeconomics. For those who have forgotten their macroeconomics, we will begin with a brief review of *IS* and *LM*.

A Review of IS and LM

The *IS* curve (which some authors refer to as the *EE* curve) gives the combination of the interest rate, r, and the national income, Y, at which the goods market is in equilibrium. This means that the injections into the circular flow of income (investment, government spending, and exports) equal the withdrawals (savings, tax payments, and imports). The *IS* curve, as shown in Figure 6A.1, slopes downward because at lower interest rates, r, there is more investment—an injection. To maintain balance between injections and withdrawals, we need more savings—a withdrawal—and this will occur at a higher national income (which we measure as *real* GNP). If a lower r needs a higher Y for equilibrium, the *IS* curve must slope downward.

FIGURE 6A.1
Goods, money, and external equilibrium.

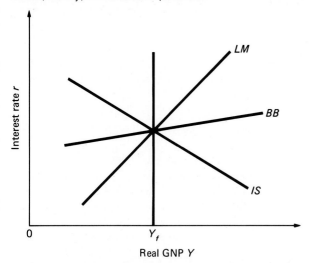

IS gives equilibrium in the market for goods and is where
withdrawals equal injections into the circular flow of income.
LM gives equilibrium in the money market where the
demand for and supply of money are equal. *BB* gives
equilibrium in the balance of payments where deficits
(surpluses) in the current account equal surpluses (deficits)
in the capital account. Y_f is full employment output. The
figure represents overall equilibrium.

Any stimulation of demand from extra government spending, tax cuts, extra exports, or
reduced imports will shift *IS* to the right. This is because at the same *r* there will be more
injections into spending, and for balance to be restored we need more withdrawals. This will
occur at a higher *Y*, which will increase savings, tax payments, and imports—all withdrawals.
Any comparable reduction in demand from reductions in government spending, investment,
exports, or other factors will shift *IS* to the left. We need reduced withdrawals to match the
reduced injections. This is achieved at a lower income level.

The *LM* curve (which some authors refer to as the *MM* curve) gives the combination of *r*
and *Y* at which the supply of and demand for money are equal. The supply of money is
determined by the central bank, and so for a constant supply we need to keep a constant
demand. At a higher *r*, the demand for money falls because of the higher opportunity cost. To
keep a constant demand, we need to offset the effect of the higher *r* by having a higher income,
which raises the transactions demand for money. Therefore, equilibrium requires that a
higher *r* be matched by a higher *Y*, which means that *LM* will have an upward slope.

If the money supply is increased, *LM* shifts downward and to the right. This is because the
extra supply must be matched by extra demand. This can be caused by a lower *r* (downward
shift) or a higher *Y* (rightward shift). A decrease in the money supply shifts *LM* upward and
to the left. This is because the reduction in supply must be matched with a reduced demand
for money, and this requires a higher interest rate or a lower income.

We have put a point, Y_f, on Figure 6A.1 showing the full employment level of the real
national income, or GNP, which is on the horizontal axis. To the right of Y_f we have

"overemployment," which is inflationary, and to the left we have unemployment (which used to be generally thought of as deflationary).

Introducing the Balance of Payments

We have added a line, *BB*, to the conventional *IS-LM* diagram for the "closed" economy (that is, an economy without international trade). This is the line of equilibrium in the balance of payments. *BB* is drawn with an upward slope. This is because at higher interest rates the balance of payments will improve, and there are two reasons for this.

   1 A higher *r* results in a lower aggregate demand, which reduces purchases, including imports.
   2 A higher *r* will encourage higher capital inflows for given foreign rates of interest.

The first of these effects means an improvement in the current account, and the second means an improvement in the capital account. In order to prevent a balance of payments surplus from resulting from these two forces, at higher values of *r* we need a higher *Y*. The higher *Y* will mean more imports, helping to eliminate the surplus caused by the higher *r*. Because the higher *r* has two effects—on the current account and on the capital account—we need a substantial increase in *Y* (with effects on the current account) to compensate for a higher *r*; hence *BB* will be quite flat.

   On the *BB* line itself, the balance of payments is in balance. Below the line the interest rate is too low or the income (and hence imports) is too high for balance, and we have a deficit. Above the line, because of capital inflows or low imports, we have a surplus. A currency devaluation or depreciation will shift the *BB* line downward and to the right, and the reverse is true for a revaluation or appreciation. This is because a devaluation or depreciation will make the country's goods more competitive and thereby improve the current account balance. This will require the country to have lower interest rates at any income level so that a weaker capital account can offset the improved current account.

TABLE 6A.1
SHIFTS IN *IS-LM* DIAGRAM*

	Rightward shift	**Leftward shift**
IS	Expansionary fiscal policy or increase in net exports from devaluation or depreciation	Contractional fiscal policy or decrease in net exports from revaluation or appreciation
LM	Increase in money supply	Decrease in money supply
BB	Devaluation or depreciation or increase in tariffs/subsidies	Revaluation or appreciation or decrease in tariffs/subsidies
Y_f	Determined by real factors	Determined by real factors

*This table does not show *LM* shifting with exchange rates. If devaluations/depreciations raise the price level, that is, reduce the real supply of money, then *LM* will shift to the left.

The factors causing shifts in the lines in the *IS-LM* diagram are summarized in Table 6A.1. This is a useful reference for the directions of shifts from all the policy changes we will discuss.

Policy Effectiveness with Fixed Rates

The *IS-LM* framework can provide a graphic account of the difficulty in applying monetary policy in a fixed exchange rate system. Consider the policy objective of raising national income to its full employment level. Suppose the economy begins at E_1 in parts *a* to *c* of Figure 6A.2. This is an equilibrium in the goods and money markets and involves a balance of international payments, but it also involves output below the full employment level and therefore some unemployment. Let us assume that the importance of imports in total consumption is relatively small and that therefore devaluations and revaluations do not have a major impact on the price level and hence on *real* cash balances. In other words, *LM* does not shift with exchange rates.

Monetary Policy   By monetary policy we mean changes in the supply of money. Our question concerning the effectiveness is this: Will we be able to use changes in the money supply to affect aggregate demand? The answer is that when we have fixed exchange rates, the effort to increase the supply of money will itself be difficult. This means that even if monetary policy works in a closed economy, it will not be a useful policy for an open economy. Let us begin by assuming that the money supply is increased and then show why it will eventually decline.

An increase in the money supply pushes *LM* downward and to the right. This occurs because to match the higher supply, the demand must be higher, requiring a higher income or a lower interest rate. In part *a* of Figure 6A.2, *LM* moves to *LM'*. The new intersection of *IS* and *LM* is below the *BB* line, in an area of balance of payments deficit, since *r* is too low. The deficit will mean downward pressure on the foreign exchange value of the currency, and with fixed exchange rates this requires the central bank to buy back its currency to support the price. This will lower the money supply, causing *LM* to shift back from *LM'* to *LM*. We find that attempts to change the money supply are frustrated when central banks support the value of the currency. Monetary policy does not offer a solution to unemployment when there are fixed exchange rates. The only effect of monetary policy with fixed exchange rates is to change the asset composition of the central bank. For example, if the money supply is expanded via open-market purchases of securities, central bank assets will involve more securities and less foreign exchange reserves.

We can note that if the monetary authority was to persist in attempting to increase the money supply to reduce unemployment, there would be persistent deficits. This is the view of the proponents of the monetary approach to the balance of payments.

Fiscal Policy   An increase in the fiscal deficit (more spending or less taxes) will push *IS* to the right to *IS'* in part *b* of Figure 6A.2. This is because the higher injections must be matched by more withdrawals, such as savings, and this requires a higher income or higher interest rates. The new *IS* curve cuts the *LM* curve above *BB*, in an area of balance of payments surplus. This puts upward pressure on the exchange value of the currency, forcing the central bank to supply more money in order to keep the rate at the upper support limit. If the balance of payments surplus is not neutralized in some way, this raises the money supply, forcing the *LM* line to *LM'*. We find that fiscal policy does work to raise real GNP because it is simultaneously able to raise the money supply.

FIGURE 6A.2
Policy effectiveness with fixed rates.

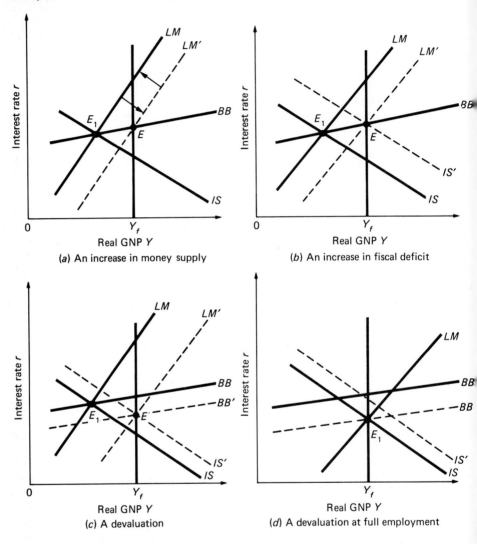

(a) An increase in money supply

(b) An increase in fiscal deficit

(c) A devaluation

(d) A devaluation at full employment

Part a shows that an increase in the money supply will eventually be reversed as the lower interest rates cause a deficit, forcing the central bank to buy its currency.

Part b shows that an increased fiscal deficit will raise interest rates, cause a capital account surplus, and hence cause the central bank to supply its currency to maintain fixed rates.

Part c shows a devaluation raising exports and hence shifting IS. This causes a current account surplus, which raises the money supply as the central bank sells its currency, shifting LM to the right.

Part d shows that a devaluation at full employment will cause inflation unless it is accompanied by an expenditure-reducing policy.

Currency Devaluation   Suppose that the currency is devalued in order to help raise the GNP. This will shift *BB* downward to *BB'* in part *c* of Figure 6A.2, because balance of payments equilibrium can be reached with a lower *r* and consequently a poorer capital account, since the current account will improve from the devaluation. At the same time, the devaluation will mean, via the effect of switching expenditures from foreign goods to domestic goods, that exports will rise and imports will fall, pushing *IS* to *IS'*. The new intersection of *IS* and *LM* will be above *BB'*, both because the intersection moves upward and because *BB* moves downward. The area above *BB'* represents a surplus in the balance of payments. This will require the central bank to increase the money supply, causing *LM* to shift to the right to *LM'*. The shift in *LM* will continue as long as there is a balance of payments surplus and hence money being injected, that is, when *IS* and *LM* intersect above *BB*. The shift will therefore continue until *IS* and *LM* intersect on the new *BB* line. We discover that a devaluation will be effective in raising the GNP and employment, both because it stimulates extra local demand and because it increases the money supply.

If an economy has full employment, a devaluation will be inflationary and will not help the balance of payments. For a devaluation—a policy designed to switch expenditures from foreign goods to domestic goods—to work, it must be accompanied by an expenditure-reducing policy. This can be shown in terms of *IS* and *LM*. Suppose that we begin with *IS* and *LM* intersecting at E_1 in part *d* of Figure 6A.2. This involves full employment and equilibrium in the money and goods markets, but not in the balance of payments, which is in deficit because we are below the *BB* line. Suppose that a devaluation is employed to correct the deficit. This will shift *BB* downward to *BB'*. This shift would be a solution if it were the only thing that happened, but the devaluation will also raise exports and reduce imports. This will shift the *IS* curve to *IS'*. The *LM* curve will be cut at a *Y* above the full employment real GNP, Y_f, and this effect is inflationary. For the devaluation to work, it must be accompanied by a restrictive (fiscal) policy to keep *IS* from shifting.

The conclusion that at full employment a devaluation for improving the balance of payments must be accompanied by expenditure reduction can also be reached by applying the *absorption principle*. According to the absorption principle, the balance of payments deficit is the difference between what is produced (real GNP) and what is used or "absorbed" by the economy. It can be stated in terms of the national income accounting identity that we used in presenting the income adjustment with fixed exchange rates:

$$Y \equiv C + I + (\text{Ex} - \text{Im}) \tag{6A.6}$$

This previously appeared as Equation (5.1). We will recall that *C*, *I*, and Ex refer to total amounts of consumption, investment, and exports, including the imported components of each item. Absorption is what we use via consumption and investment (and will include government spending if we choose to consider the government), so we can write

$$A \equiv C + I$$

where *A* is absorption. We see that Equation (6A.6) becomes

$$Y \equiv A + (\text{Ex} - \text{Im})$$

or, alternatively,

$$(\text{Ex} - \text{Im}) \equiv Y - A \tag{6A.7}$$

We see that the merchandise surplus or deficit, (Ex − Im), of the balance of payments can be identically written as the difference between aggregate production and aggregate absorption. This tells us that to improve the balance of payments, we could:

1 Reduce absorption. This means trying to reduce A more than Y.
2 Raise output. This means trying to increase Y more than A.

The policy which follows the first route is an expenditure-reducing policy. It can be effected via a restrictive monetary or fiscal policy. The second route requires an expenditure-switching policy so as to get more demand and output of local products without more total spending or absorption. This can be achieved by a devaluation or by a tariff/subsidy designed to switch spending from foreign goods to domestic products while keeping total spending constant.[23]

Tariff Policy   A general tariff on all imports and an equal subsidy on all exports will have effects that are very similar to the effects of a devaluation of the currency. Both raise the prices of imports and reduce the prices of exports. An import tariff–export subsidy policy is hence an expenditure-switching policy, and the same conclusions concerning the effectiveness of a devaluation apply; that is, BB will shift downward and IS upward and to the right. This will help the balance of payments and raise the GNP and employment, provided the economy has unemployed resources. If the economy is at full employment, an import tariff and export subsidy increase will be inflationary and will not improve the balance of payments unless accompanied by an expenditure-reducing policy.

Policy Effectiveness with Flexible Rates

When there are flexible exchange rates, there is no BB line, since the balance of payments is always in balance. Devaluation policy cannot be used. However, when there is a fall in the rate of interest or an increase in income, there will be downward pressure on the exchange rate. This helps us determine the effects of policy. In particular:

Monetary Policy   An expansion of the money supply will shift LM to the right to LM' and lower the interest rate. This will cause capital outflows and a currency depreciation. The depreciation will shift IS to the right from the expenditure-switching effect. This is shown in part a of Figure 6A.3. Monetary policy is effective in raising the GNP if the economy is not already at capacity.

Fiscal Policy   An increase in the fiscal deficit will shift the IS curve to IS' in part b of Figure 6A.3. As a result, the interest rate and income will increase. If the positive effect of interest rates on the capital account dominates the negative effect of income and hence imports in the current account, the foreign exchange value of the currency will appreciate.

---

[23] The absorption principle and the conclusions we have reached by using it were originally developed by Sidney Alexander and Harry G. Johnson. See Sidney Alexander, "Effects of a Devaluation on the Trade Balance," *IMF Staff Papers*, vol. 2, April 1952, pp. 263–278, or Harry G. Johnson, "Towards a General Theory of the Balance of Payments," in his book *International Trade and Economics Growth*, George Allen & Unwin, Ltd., London, 1958. Both of these papers are reprinted in Richard Caves and Harry G. Johnson (eds.), *Readings in International Economics*, Richard D. Irwin, Homewood, Ill., 1968. The reader is also referred to Robert M. Stern, *The Balance of Payments: Theory and Economic Policy*, Aldine Publishing Company, Chicago, 1973, chap. 10.

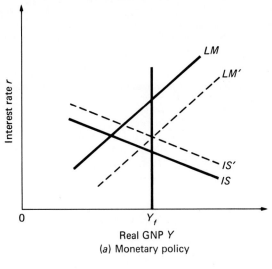

(a) Monetary policy

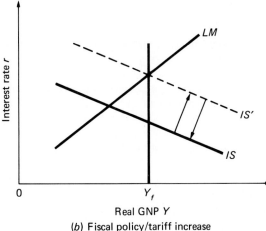

(b) Fiscal policy/tariff increase

FIGURE 6A.3
Policy effectiveness with flexible rates.
　　Part *a* shows that an increase in the money supply will lower interest rates, causing the exchange rate to depreciate. This will encourage exports, discourage imports, and shift *IS* to the right.
　　Part *b* shows that an expansionary fiscal policy will raise interest rates, causing an appreciation. This will discourage exports, encourage imports, and shift *IS* back toward its original position.

This will reduce exports and raise imports, causing a negative switching effect which will shift *IS'* back to *IS*. Fiscal policy is, therefore, ineffective with respect to the GNP.

　　A devaluation is not an option with flexible rates, but a tariff increase can still be tried. This will shift *IS* to *IS'*, raising the interest rate and income. If the positive effect of the higher interest rate on the capital account dominates the negative effect of income on the current account, the currency value will improve. The result will be a negative expenditure-switching effect, and *IS* will shift back toward its original position. Part *b* of Figure 6A.3 shows this situation, and we can conclude that the policy does not raise output.

　　Our discussion of the effects of macroeconomic policies shows that sometimes a policy designed to stimulate the economy will work, and sometimes it will not. A knowledge of when it will work is an important input in corporate planning. Therefore, our conclusions are summarized in Table 6A.2, which shows the effect of different policies on aggregate demand and therefore on sales. There are frequent changes in the direction of economic policy. A

TABLE 6A.2
EFFECTIVENESS OF DIFFERENT MACROECONOMIC POLICIES

| | Macroeconomic policies | | | |
Rate regime	Monetary policy	Fiscal policy	Devaluation	Import tariff/ export subsidy
Fixed rates	Ineffective	Works	Works (inflationary with full employment)	Works (inflationary with full employment)
Flexible rates	Works	Ineffective	–	Ineffective

corporate executive would be well served by considering the conclusions of this table when deciding on the response in terms of production levels, borrowing needs, and so on, when economic policy is altered.

POLICY CONFLICTS

If an economy is suffering from the joint problems of unemployment and a balance of payments deficit, the problems cannot both be resolved by a straightforward expansionary or contractional policy. Expanding the money supply (lowering the interest rate) or running larger fiscal deficits might well work to cure the unemployment problem. However, the extra stimulation of demand will worsen the current account of the balance of payments and, if the interest rate is reduced, also the capital account. Similarly, if an economy is suffering from both inflation and a balance of payments surplus, there is a conflict of objectives. Efforts to reduce demand by reducing the money supply (or raising interest rates) or by reducing fiscal deficits might help bring down inflation, but they will make the balance of payments surplus even larger.

Sometimes the policy objectives will not be in conflict. If there is inflation and an international payments deficit, then both monetary and fiscal constraint will work. If there is unemployment and a surplus, both situations will benefit from economic stimulation. These conclusions are summarized in Table 6A.3. They are also illustrated in terms of the *IS-LM* diagram by the shaded and unshaded areas of Figure 6A.4.

Objectives can be in conflict if we have more objectives than we have policies with which to achieve these objectives. In our situation we have one policy—general expansion or contraction—and two objectives—internal equilibrium and external equilibrium. According

TABLE 6A.3
ECONOMIC CONDITIONS AND APPROPRIATE POLICY

	Unemployment	Inflation
Balance of payments deficit	Policy conflict	Contractional policy
Balance of payments surplus	Expansionary policy	Policy conflict

FIGURE 6A.4
Policy recommendations when *IS* and *LM* intersect in
different regions.

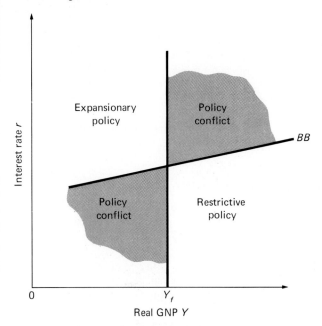

Some economic objectives cannot be reached without
mixing monetary policy and fiscal policy. Above *BB* we have
a surplus, and to the right of Y_f we have inflation. The
inflation requires restrictive policy, but this will aggravate
the surplus. Below *BB* and to the left of Y_f we have
unemployment and a deficit. The stimulation to lower
unemployment will worsen the deficit.

to an important theorem by Jan Tinbergen, we can achieve two targets or objectives with two
economic instruments or policies.[24] If policy makers separate macroeconomic policy into the
two separate components of monetary policy and fiscal policy, they have the two instruments
needed to achieve the two targets of external (balance of payments) equilibrium and internal
(employment and output) equilibrium. Considerations of economic dynamics dictate that
they should do the following:

1 Use monetary policy to correct the external equilibrium.
2 Use fiscal policy to correct the internal equilibrium.

These conclusions follow because monetary policy has a comparative advantage in affecting
the balance of payments, since an increase in interest rates will improve the balance of
payments in two ways—via improved capital inflows and via dampened demand and hence
reduced imports. The first is an improvement in the capital account and the second an

[24]See Jan Tinbergen, *On the Theory of Economic Policy*, North-Holland Publishing Company,
Amsterdam, 1952. Tinbergen's theory extends to *n*-policies or instruments and *n*-objectives or targets.

improvement in the current account. Restrictive fiscal policy has less impact on the balance of payments than monetary policy because its influence is limited to the current account: it cannot directly affect capital flows. It follows that the *comparative* advantage of fiscal policy is in influencing employment, output, and the internal equilibrium.

What these conclusions mean is that if we have unemployment and a balance of payments deficit, the government will be successful if it raises interest rates (monetary policy) to help eliminate the payments deficit and increases government spending or reduces taxes to reduce the unemployment (without, it is hoped, also causing inflation). In the other situation of conflicting targets, when there is inflation and a balance of payments surplus, the government will succeed by reducing interest rates to reduce the payments surplus and by reducing government spending or raising taxes to cool the economy.[25] We see that the appropriate solution to conflicting targets is to mix the instruments of monetary policy and fiscal policy. The problem of reaching multiple objectives has hence been called the *assignment problem*.

QUESTIONS ON THE EFFECTIVENESS OF POLICY

1 If you were an exporter, would you expand your productive capacity if the government in an export market began to use an expansionary monetary policy and the exchange rate was fixed? Would you expand capacity after the introduction of an expansionary monetary policy if the exchange rate was flexible?
2 Answer question 1 with regard to fiscal policy. Consider both exchange rate regimes.
3 If your company produces nontraded goods such as newspapers and local magazines, would you expect a sales increase or a cost increase to result from a devaluation of the currency in your country? Could you be hurt by devaluation?
4 Would it be easier to cure the joint evils of unemployment and inflation with flexible exchange rates? Explain why you might apply a restrictive monetary policy to cure the inflation and an expansionary fiscal policy to ease the unemployment.

BIBLIOGRAPHY ON THE EFFECTIVENESS OF POLICY

Dornbusch, Rudiger: "Monetary Policy under Exchange Rate Flexibility," in *Managed Exchange Rate Flexibility*, conference vol. 20, Federal Reserve Bank of Boston, Boston, 1979.

Dornbusch, Rudiger: "Capital Mobility, Flexible Exchange Rates and Macroeconomic Equilibrium," in E. Claassen and P. Salin (eds.), *Recent Issues in International Monetary Economics*, Elsevier–North Holland Publishing Company, New York, 1976.

Mundell, Robert A.: "The Appropriate Use of Monetary and Fiscal Policy for Internal and External Stability," *IMF Staff Papers*, March 1962, pp. 70–79. Reprinted as Chapter 16 in Robert Mundell's *International Economics*, Macmillan and Company, New York, 1968.

Mussa, Michael L.: "The Exchange Rate, the Balance of Payments and Monetary and Fiscal Policy under a Regime of Controlled Floating," *Scandinavian Journal of Economics*, May 1976, pp. 229–248.

Stern, Robert M.: *The Balance of Payments: Theory and Economic Policy*, Aldine Publishing Company, Chicago, 1973, chap. 10.

---

[25] The pioneering analysis which reached these conclusions was developed by Robert Mundell in "The Appropriate Use of Monetary and Fiscal Policy under Fixed Exchange Rates," *IMF Staff Papers*, March 1962, pp. 70–79. The adventurous reader will be well rewarded by reading Robert Mundell's *International Economics*, Macmillan and Company, New York, 1967, or Rudiger Dornbusch's *Open Economy Macroeconomics*, Basic Books, Inc., New York, 1980.

SHORT-TERM BORROWING
AND INVESTMENT DECISIONS

CHAPTER 7

WHERE TO BORROW AND INVEST—THE INTEREST RATE PARITY THEOREM

With the foreign exchange markets explained in Part 1 and the environment in which the exchange rates are determined explained in Part 2, we can begin a more practical treatment of the problems of international financial management. With our knowledge of the difference between spot and forward markets and the different types of financial environments, we can derive criteria on where a company should borrow and invest. In this chapter and in the next two chapters we will look at short-term borrowing and investing decisions, which involve securities trading in the money markets. We will concentrate on borrowing and investing where forward contracts are used to help avoid foreign exchange risk. We will also show how borrowing and investing can be used for avoiding foreign exchange risk in the presence of foreign exchange flows originating from other activities, such as the buying and selling of goods.

The criteria for borrowing and investing lead us into the interest rate parity theorem. This theorem states that certain forces will work toward making investment yields and borrowing costs equal in different countries and currencies. If yields were made precisely equal, there would be no advantage to shopping around for the best countries in which to borrow or invest. However, as we shall see, there are a number of factors that can allow yield differences to persist, and we must examine these factors before we can understand the nature of the Eurocurrency market (discussed in Chapter 8). We will also discover that the practical problems in working capital management are related to the reasons for persistent yield differences.

As we proceed, and for the remainder of the book, it will be useful at a number of points to develop concepts by referring to a specific example. For this purpose, we shall consider a manufacturing company that makes denim clothing, primarily jeans; the company is called Aviva (Denim Clothing) Corporation.

Aviva Corporation is headquartered in the United States but has sales and a reputation for its denim clothing in many different countries. It buys denim cloth wherever it finds the best price, and it competes with other U.S. and foreign producers of denim clothing. Primarily production is in the United States, but Aviva will consider opening plants elsewhere if this is particularly advantageous. Aviva has uneven cash flows; therefore, on some occasions it has surplus funds to invest, and on other occasions it needs to borrow.

Short-term borrowing and investment take place in the *money market*. This is the market that deals in securities with maturities of less than 1 year. Because there are forward contracts with money market maturities, the money market deserves special treatment. Forward contracts allow money market borrowers and lenders to avoid translation and transaction foreign exchange risk. We will start by asking where Aviva should invest.

THE INVESTMENT AND BORROWING CRITERIA

Determining the Currency of Investment

Suppose that a firm like Aviva Corporation has some funds that it wishes to place in the money market for a period of 3 months. Perhaps it has received a major payment but can wait before paying for a large investment in new equipment. The firm could place these funds in its own domestic money market at an interest rate that can be discovered simply by calling around for the going rates on, for example, commercial paper or treasury bills. Alternatively, it could invest in foreign securities. Should it buy money market securities at home or abroad?

Many countries have well-developed money markets in which instruments such as treasury bills are traded and in which the default risks are relatively small. It might well be possible in some of these markets to obtain interest yields that are higher than those available at home. Simply placing funds in the foreign-currency-denominated securities could, however, involve the firm in foreign exchange risk. If, for example, the value of the foreign currency in which Aviva's treasury bills are denominated happens to fall during the period before maturity, then there will be a foreign exchange loss when the bills mature and are converted back into dollars. Of course, exchange rates could also move the other way so that gains—transaction gains—are made, but the uncertainty of the direction of exchange rate movements might keep many risk-averse firms from investing abroad, even if the foreign interest rates are appreciably higher. However, as we shall see, the existence of the forward exchange market makes avoiding foreign currency issues on the grounds of extra foreign exchange risk completely unjustified.

It is possible for a firm like our Aviva Corporation to invest in a foreign currency money market instrument without incurring any transaction or translation foreign exchange risk. In other words, it is possible to avoid being affected at all by changes in exchange rates. All that is required is the sale on the forward market of the foreign currency proceeds from the investment. Let us see how an exchange-risk-free investment decision is made. We will select for our example 3-month rather than full-year securities to make clear the need to be careful and keep exchange rate movements and interest rates on comparable annualized terms.

For every dollar invested in the domestic (U.S.) money market for 3 months, the investor will receive when the securities mature

$$\left(1 + \frac{r_{US}}{4}\right)$$

dollars, where r_{US} is the annualized interest rate. Interest rates are invariably quoted on a per annum basis, and division by 4 is required to compute the 3-month return. It might seem as if it would be more precise to allow for the nature of compound interest in finding 3-month returns, but since for convenience annualization generally involves multiplying by 4, division by 4 gives the correct return. In general, we multiply r by n, where n is the number of years to maturity (for example, $n = \frac{1}{4}$). The interest rate is in decimal form, and so an 8 percent rate means that $r_{US} = 0.08$.

Suppose that Aviva considers the British money market and that the spot dollar/sterling exchange rate, in the conventional U.S. terms of quotation, is $S(\$/£)$. $S(\$/£)$ gives the number of dollars to buy pounds sterling, and so for $1 our firm will obtain $1/[S(\$/£)]$ in British pounds, assuming that there are no transaction costs. If the annualized British interest rate on 3-month treasury bills is r_{UK}, then for every dollar sent to Britain, our firm will receive after 3 months the number of pounds, $1/[S(\$/£)]$, that was invested (the principal) plus the 3-month interest on this, which is $r_{UK}/4$. That is, it will receive

$$£ \; \frac{1}{S(\$/£)} \cdot \left(1 + \frac{r_{UK}}{4}\right) \tag{7.1}$$

For example, if $S(\$/£) = 1.8930$ and $r_{UK} = 0.1612$, then each dollar invested in Britain will produce

$$£ \; \frac{1}{1.8930}\left(1 + \frac{0.1612}{4}\right) = £0.55$$

This certain number of pounds represents an uncertain number of dollars, but a forward contract can offer a complete hedge and guarantee the number of dollars that will finally be received.

If, at the time of buying the 3-month treasury bills in Britain, Aviva sells forward the amount of pounds to be received at the maturity of the security, that is, the amount in (7.1) or £0.55 in our example, then the number of dollars that will be obtained is set by the forward contract. After 3 months, Aviva will deliver the British pounds and will receive the number of dollars stated in the forward exchange agreement. If, for example, the 3-month forward exchange rate at the time of buying the treasury bills is $F_{1/4}(\$/£)$ in the conventional U.S. terms, then we must multiply (7.1) by this amount to get the number of dollars received for each pound sold forward. We will obtain

$$\frac{F_{1/4}(\$/\pounds)}{S(\$/\pounds)} \cdot \left(1 + \frac{r_{UK}}{4}\right) \tag{7.2}$$

dollars. For example, if $F_{1/4}(\$/\pounds) = 1.8960$, then the number of pounds in (7.1), £0.55, will provide $\$1.8960 \times 0.55 = \$1.0420$ when sold forward for dollars. This is the number of dollars received after 3 months or $\frac{1}{4}$ year for each original dollar sent to the London money market. This means an annual rate of return of

$$4\left(\frac{1.0420 - 1.0000}{1.0000}\right) = 0.1678 \text{ or } 16.78\%$$

It is important to remember that the number of dollars given in (7.2) is a certain amount. The purchase of the spot pounds, the British security, and the forward sale of the British pounds take place at the same time, and so there is no doubt about the number of dollars that will be received. If the exchange rate changes before the security matures, that will make no difference. The exchange rate to be used is already set in the terms of the forward contract, which is part of the swap of pounds for dollars. In terms of our example, it is guaranteed that $1.0420 will be received.

It is now a simple matter to express the rule for deciding where to invest. The U.S. firm should invest in the domestic money market, rather than in the British market, over a 3-month period whenever[1]

$$\left(1 + \frac{r_{US}}{4}\right) > \frac{F_{1/4}(\$/\pounds)}{S(\$/\pounds)} \cdot \left(1 + \frac{r_{UK}}{4}\right)$$

If this inequality holds, there is more to be gained from investing in the domestic money market than from investing in the British money market. There is more to be gained from investing in the British market whenever the reverse inequality holds. Only if

$$\left(1 + \frac{r_{US}}{4}\right) = \frac{F_{1/4}(\$/\pounds)}{S(\$/\pounds)} \cdot \left(1 + \frac{r_{UK}}{4}\right) \tag{7.3}$$

should the firm be indifferent, since the same amount will be received from a dollar invested in either money market.[2]

---

[1] When exchange rates are in European terms, the forward and spot rates must be inverted, and subsequent deduction gives results which are more difficult to interpret. This is left as an exercise at the end of the chapter.

[2] In more general terms, Equation (7.3) can be written as

$$\frac{F}{S} = \frac{1 + r}{1 + r_f}$$

where the form of the exchange rate quotation and the annualization are assumed to be understood. The term r_f is the foreign interest rate.

We can convert Equation (7.3) into a more meaningful equality if we subtract the amount $\left(1 + \frac{r_{\text{UK}}}{4}\right)$ from both sides:

$$\left(1 + \frac{r_{\text{US}}}{4}\right) - \left(1 + \frac{r_{\text{UK}}}{4}\right) = \frac{F_{1/4}(\$/£)}{S(\$/£)}\left(1 + \frac{r_{\text{UK}}}{4}\right) - \left(1 + \frac{r_{\text{UK}}}{4}\right)$$

With cancellation and rearrangement we obtain

$$r_{\text{US}} = r_{\text{UK}} + 4\left(\frac{F_{1/4}(\$/£) - S(\$/£)}{S(\$/£)}\right)\left(1 + \frac{r_{\text{UK}}}{4}\right) \qquad (7.4)$$

We will interpret this below, but before we do, we can note that part of the second right-hand term in Equation (7.4) involves the multiplication of two small numbers, the forward pound premium and $r_{\text{UK}}/4$. The product will frequently be very small. For example, if the forward premium is 5 percent and British interest rates are 10 percent, the cross product term from Equation (7.4) will be 0.00125 (0.05×0.025), or only $\frac{1}{8}$ percent. In order to interpret Equation (7.5), we might therefore temporarily drop the term formed from this product (which means dropping the $r_{\text{UK}}/4$) and write it to an approximation as follows:[3]

$$r_{\text{US}} = r_{\text{UK}} + 4\left(\frac{F_{1/4}(\$/£) - S(\$/£)}{S(\$/£)}\right) \qquad (7.5)$$

The second right-hand term in Equation (7.5) is the annualized (because of the 4) forward premium on pounds. A firm should be indifferent about investing at home or investing abroad if the home interest rate equals the foreign rate plus the annualized forward exchange premium/discount on the foreign currency. The firm should invest at home when the domestic interest rate exceeds the sum of the foreign rate plus the foreign exchange premium/discount, and it should invest abroad when the domestic rate is less than this sum. We discover that a mere comparison of interest rates is not sufficient. In order to determine where to invest, we must add the foreign interest rate to the forward premium or discount. Using the terminology of the previous chapter, we must add the foreign interest rate to the cost of the spot-forward swap of pounds for dollars, where this swap is put on annualized terms.

An Example

Suppose that Aviva Corporation faces the exchange rate and money market situation shown in Table 7.1 and has $5 million to invest for 3 months. Where should it place its funds?

---

[3] When interest rates and forward premiums are high, we should stay with the precise form. We shall follow the practice of using the precise form, which has become increasingly important with high inflation and the resulting high interest rates.

If we compute

$$r_j + 4\left(\frac{F_{1/4}(\$/j) - S(\$/j)}{S(\$/j)}\right)\left(1 + \frac{r_j}{4}\right)$$

for each market, j, we will obtain the annualized yields given in the bottom line of Table 7.1. The country with the highest yield in this example is Britain, which does not have the highest interest rate.

The differences in yields are smaller, in general, than the differences in interest rates, with the premiums on the currencies of the countries with lower interest rates more than compensating for the interest disadvantages vis-a-vis the interest rate in the United States. If Aviva invests $5 million for 3 months in Britain, it will receive

$\$5,000,000 \cdot \left(1 + \frac{0.1548}{4}\right) = \$5,193,500$ without incurring foreign exchange risk.

If the management of Aviva had not looked abroad and had kept the $5 million in

New York, the corporation would have received $\$5,000,000 \cdot \left(1 + \frac{0.1250}{4}\right) =$

$5,156,250. Thus Aviva will receive a reward of $37,250 in 3 months for doing the homework and investing in Britain. It might seem surprising that such an opportunity would exist. However, we will give a number of reasons later in the chapter.

Determining the Country from Which to Borrow

Imagine that Aviva Corporation needs to borrow for a period of 3 months. If the annualized interest rate for domestic borrowing is r_{US}, then the required repayment after 3 months is the principal plus interest, or

$$\left(1 + \frac{r_{US}}{4}\right) \tag{7.6}$$

dollars for each dollar borrowed.

If Aviva has access to the British money market, and if the going spot exchange rate is $S(\$/\pounds)$, then borrowing $1 means borrowing $1/[S(\$/\pounds)]$ in pounds. For example, at the exchange rate $S(\$/\pounds) = 1.8930$, borrowing $1 means borrowing £0.5283. If the annualized interest rate is r_{UK}, then for each dollar borrowed Aviva must repay

$$\frac{1}{S(\$/\pounds)}\left(1 + \frac{r_{UK}}{4}\right) \tag{7.7}$$

pounds. For example, if $r_{UK} = 0.1550$ (the 3-month borrowing rate), Aviva must repay £0.5487. Without a forward exchange contract the number of dollars this would represent when Aviva repays its debt is uncertain. With a forward exchange contract the risk is eliminated.

TABLE 7.1
EXCHANGE AND INTEREST RATES IN MAJOR MONEY MARKETS: YIELDS ON TREASURY BILLS

New York	London			Frankfurt*			Paris			Tokyo†		
r_{US}	r_{UK}	$S(\$/\pounds)$	$F_{1/4}(\$/\pounds)$	r_{GY}	$S(\$/DM)$	$F_{1/4}(\$/DM)$	r_{FR}	$S(\$/Fr)$	$F_{1/4}(\$/Fr)$	r_{JP}	$S(\$/\text{¥})$	$F_{1/4}(\$/\text{¥})$
12.50	14.82	1.8930	1.8960	5.73	0.4535	0.4591	16.75	0.1809	0.1795	5.63	0.004372	0.004472
Covered yield‡												
12.50%	15.48%			10.74%			13.52%			14.91%		

*German treasury bills are for 180 days.
†Japanese treasury bills are for 60 days.

‡Covered yields are computed as $r_j + 4\left(\dfrac{F_{1/4}(\$/i) - S(\$/i)}{S(\$/i)}\right)\left(1 + \dfrac{r_i}{4}\right)$.

Source: The Wall Street Journal, New York, and the Harris Bank, Weekly Review, Oct. 9, 1981.

Suppose that Aviva buys forward the amount of pounds in (7.7) at the price $F_{1/4}(\$/£)$. When the debt is repaid, Aviva will receive the required number of pounds on a forward contract that requires the corporation to pay

$$\frac{F_{1/4}(\$/£)}{S(\$/£)}\left(1 + \frac{r_{UK}}{4}\right) \tag{7.8}$$

in U.S. dollars. The firm should borrow abroad whenever (7.8) is less than (7.6), that is, when

$$\left(1 + \frac{r_{US}}{4}\right) > \frac{F_{1/4}(\$/£)}{S(\$/£)}\left(1 + \frac{r_{UK}}{4}\right)$$

This inequality says that Aviva should borrow in Britain when the dollar amount to be repaid is lower in Britain than in the United States. The borrowing decision criteria are seen to be just the reverse of the investment criteria.

Borrowing and Investing for Arbitrage Profit

Imagine a firm that can borrow funds in its own money market and/or in foreign money markets, as can a large corporation or bank. Suppose that it can borrow for 3 months in New York at an annualized interest rate of r_{US}. Thus for each dollar it borrows, it must repay $(1 + r_{US}/4)$ dollars. The firm can take the borrowed dollars and buy $1/[S(\$/£)]$ pounds. If this is invested at r_{UK} per annum and if the resulting receipts are sold forward, the firm will receive

$$\frac{F_{1/4}(\$/£)}{S(\$/£)}\left(1 + \frac{r_{UK}}{4}\right)$$

dollars. Note that because of the forward cover there is no exchange risk and that the company has begun with no funds of its own. Borrowing in New York and simultaneously investing in London will result in a profit if the number of dollars received from the British investment exceeds the repayment on the U.S. loan, that is, if

$$\left(1 + \frac{r_{US}}{4}\right) < \frac{F_{1/4}(\$/£)}{S(\$/£)}\left(1 + \frac{r_{UK}}{4}\right)$$

The reverse activity, borrowing in London and investing in New York, will be profitable if the reverse inequality holds. As long as either inequality holds, it pays to borrow in one market and lend, or invest, in the other. This is known as *interest arbitrage*.

In should be no surprise that the potential for interest arbitrage helps guarantee that little opportunity for profit remains and that investors and borrowers will be relatively indifferent with regard to choosing a market. This is clear, for example, from the similarity of yields in Figure 7.1. Interest arbitrage is generally limited to

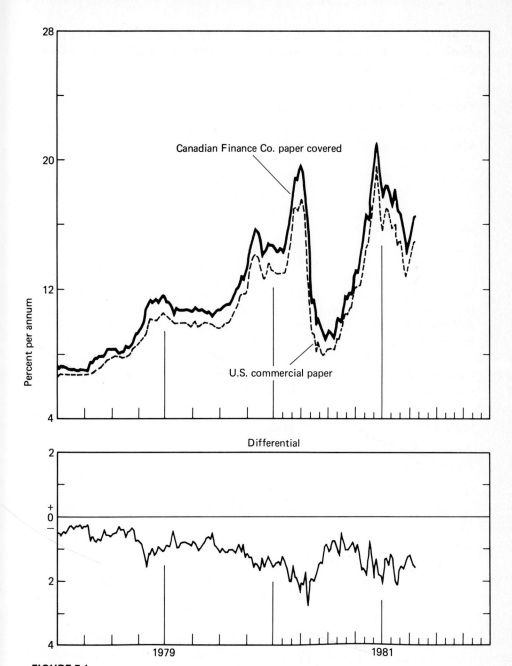

FIGURE 7.1
International opportunities for interest rate arbitrage. (*From* Selected Interest and Exchange Rates; *Weekly Series of Charts*, *Board of Governors*, *Federal Reserve System*, *May 4*, *1981*.)

large-scale commercial banks, which can borrow and invest funds with narrow spreads and do not face any external or explicit transaction costs when buying and selling spot and forward foreign exchange.

THE INTEREST PARITY THEOREM

We have determined that 3-month investors and borrowers would be indifferent with regard to choosing between the United States and Britain if

$$\left(1 + \frac{r_{US}}{4}\right) = \frac{F_{1/4}(\$/£)}{S(\$/£)} \cdot \left(1 + \frac{r_{UK}}{4}\right) \tag{7.9}$$

which in general terms is

$$\frac{(1 + nr_j)}{(1 + nr_i)} = \frac{F_n(j/i)}{S(j/i)} \tag{7.10}$$

We have also determined that when this condition holds, interest arbitrage is not profitable. The interest parity theorem states that equation (7.10) will indeed hold and that there will therefore be no advantage to borrowing or investing in any particular money market or from interest arbitrage.

The interest parity theorem can be considered as part of the law of one price and follows because of money market efficiency. A straightforward demonstration of the theorem can be made by using a graphic analysis.

Interest Parity: A Graphic Presentation

We can represent interest parity by using the framework of Figure 7.2. The annualized sterling premium is drawn on the vertical axis, and the annualized interest advantage of the United States versus Britain is drawn along the horizontal axis. The section above the origin represents a sterling forward premium, and the section below the origin represents a sterling forward discount. To the right of the origin there is a U.S. interest advantage, and to the left there is a U.S. interest disadvantage.

Interest parity, as expressed in Equation (7.9), can be written as

$$(r_{US} - r_{UK}) = 4\left(\frac{F_{1/4}(\$/£) - S(\$/£)}{S(\$/£)}\right)\left(1 + \frac{r_{UK}}{4}\right) \tag{7.11}$$

If the same scale is used on the two axes in Figure 7.2, this parity condition is represented by the 45-degree line. This line traces the points where the two sides of our equation are indeed equal.

Suppose that instead of having the equality in (7.9) we have the following inequality:

$$(r_{US} - r_{UK}) < 4\left(\frac{F_{1/4}(\$/£) - S(\$/£)}{S(\$/£)}\right)\left(1 + \frac{r_{UK}}{4}\right) \tag{7.12}$$

FIGURE 7.2
The interest parity diagram.

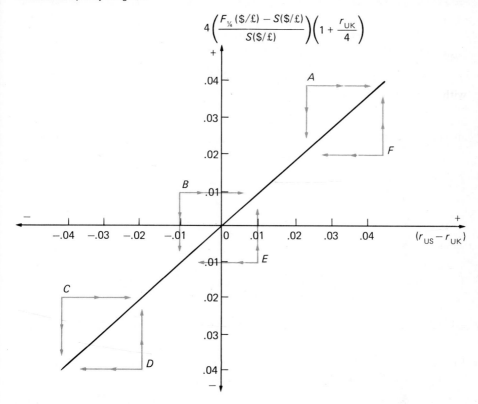

The diagonal is the line of interest parity. On the interest parity line, investors and borrowers are indifferent with regard to choosing between the U.S. and British money markets. Above and to the left of the line there is an incentive to invest in Britain and borrow in the United States. Below and to the right of the line there is an incentive to invest in the United States and borrow in Britain. In situations off the interest parity line, forces are at work pushing us back toward it.

This condition means, for example, that any sterling premium more than compensates for any U.S. interest advantage. Thus

1 Covered investment in Britain yields more than in the United States.
2 Borrowing in the United States is cheaper than covered borrowing in Britain.

It also means that it is profitable for an interest arbitrager to borrow in the United States and make a covered investment in Britain. Since this act of interest arbitrage involves both borrowing in the cheaper market and investing in the higher-yielding market, we can concentrate on the combined rather than the separate effects of borrowing and investing.

The incentive in (7.12) to borrow in the United States and make a covered investment in Britain means an incentive to

1 Borrow in the United States, perhaps by issuing and selling a security—and thus tend to raise r_{US}

2 Buy spot sterling with the borrowed dollars—and thus raise $S(\$/\pounds)$

3 Buy a British security—and thus lower r_{UK}

4 Sell the sterling proceeds forward for U.S. dollars—and thus lower $F_{1/4}(\$/\pounds)$

The inequality in (7.12) can be represented in Figure 7.2 by points such as A, B, and C that are above and to the left of the 45-degree line. The character of these points is summarized in Table 7.2. At point B, for example, U.S. interest rates are lower than British rates, and at the same time the U.S. dollar is at a forward discount. For both reasons there is an advantage to moving funds from the United States into the British money market. The covered margin or advantage of doing this is the interest differential plus what we loosely call the forward pound premium, for a total of 2 percent. In terms of Equation (7.12), the inequality holds because the left-hand side is negative, -0.01, and the right-hand side is positive, $+0.01$. The interest arbitrage, in each of the four steps we have distinguished, will tend to restore interest parity by pushing the situation at B back toward the parity line. The same thing will occur at every other point, and we should show why.

Consider the situation at point A, where there is an incentive to borrow in the United States and invest in Britain. The extra borrowing in the United States to profit from the arbitrage opportunity will put upward pressure on U.S. interest rates. If the borrowing is through money market instruments, efforts to sell them will reduce their prices. For a given coupon or par value, this will raise their yield. We will find r_{US} increasing. The increase in r_{US} can be represented in Figure 7.2 as a force pushing to the right of A, toward the interest parity line.

The second step in interest arbitrage requires the spot sale of the U.S. dollars for British sterling. This will help bid up the spot price of the sterling; that is, $S(\$/\pounds)$ will increase. For any given value of $F_{1/4}(\$/\pounds)$, this will lower the value of

$$\frac{F_{1/4}(\$/\pounds) - S(\$/\pounds)}{S(\$/\pounds)}$$

This is shown in Figure 7.2 by an arrow pointing downward from A, toward the interest parity line.

The pounds that were purchased will be used to invest in a British security. If

TABLE 7.2
POINTS OFF THE INTEREST PARITY LINE*

	Point					
	A	*B*	*C*	*D*	*E*	*F*
Interest differential	+.02	−.01	−.04	−.02	+.01	+.04
Forward premium†	−.04	−.01	+.02	+.04	+.01	−.02
Covered margin	−.02	−.02	−.02	+.02	+.02	+.02

*U.S. advantage = +; U.S. disadvantage = −.
†This is the forward premium multiplied by $(1 + r_{UK}/4)$.

there are enough extra buyers, the price of the security will increase, and the yield will decrease, that is, r_{UK} will fall. This will mean an increase in $(r_{US} - r_{UK})$, which is shown by an arrow that points to the right from A. Again, the movement is back toward the parity line.

Covering the funds moved abroad, which involves the forward sale of sterling, will lower $F_{1/4}(\$/£)$. For any given value of $S(\$/£)$, there will be a lower value of $[F_{1/4}(\$/£) - S(\$/£)]/S(\$/£)$. Thus there is a second force that will also push downward from A and toward the parity line. We can observe, of course, that since all four steps of the arbitrage will occur simultaneously, all the forces shown by the arrows will work simultaneously.

Since points B and C, like point A, indicate profitable opportunities to borrow in the United States and invest in Britain, there will also be changes in interest and exchange rates at these two points, as revealed by the arrows. For example, at point C the interest rate in the United States is 4 percent lower than in the United Kingdom, and there is a 2 percent annual discount on pounds. This will encourage arbitrage flows toward the United Kingdom. As before, there will be borrowing in the United States, and hence an increase in r_{US}; spot purchases of pounds, which will raise $S(\$/£)$; investment in Britain, which will lower r_{UK}; and forward sales of pounds, which will lower $F_{1/4}(\$/£)$. Indeed, at any point above the interest parity line, these forces, shown by the arrows emanating from A, B, and C in Figure 7.2, will be at work. We find that if we are off the interest parity line and above it, the market forces that are set up force us back down toward the line.

Below the interest parity line, forces push us back up. At points such as D, E, and F, interest arbitragers will wish to borrow in the British money market and invest in the U.S. market. For example, at point E, U.S. interest rates are 1 percent higher than U.K. rates, *and* the dollar is at a 1 percent forward premium. Thus the U.S. money market has a 2 percent advantage. This will cause arbitragers to sell British securities, lowering their price and raising r_{UK}. This is shown in Figure 7.2 by an arrow that points to the left. The arbitragers will then sell sterling for dollars, lowering $S(\$/£)$ and causing a movement upward, toward the line. They will also purchase U.S. securities, lowering r_{US} and causing a second movement toward the left. Hedging by buying sterling forward for dollars will raise the forward premium on sterling: $[F_{1/4}(\$/£) - S(\$/£)]/S(\$/£)$. This means that again there will be an upward pressure and movement toward the line, since the forward premium is the primary component on the vertical axis.

We find that above the interest parity line, outflows of funds push us back toward it, and below the line, inflows of funds also push us back toward it. The amount of adjustment in the interest rates vis-à-vis spot or forward exchange rates depends on the "thinness" of the markets. The spot exchange market and the securities markets are generally more active than the forward market. It is likely, therefore, that a large part of the adjustment toward interest parity will take place in the forward rate. As a result, the actual paths followed from points such as A or E back toward the parity line will lie closer to the vertical arrows than to the horizontal ones. We can therefore think of the forward premium as being determined by the interest differential.

In reality, interest parity does not hold precisely. This is apparent from the "interest arbitrage opportunities" shown in Figure 7.1. The failure to achieve interest parity occurs because in actual financial markets

1 There are transactions costs.

2 There are "political risks."

3 There are withholding taxes and potential advantages to foreign exchange earnings.

4 There are liquidity differences between foreign securities and domestic securities.

5 There are participants in the forward market other than investors, borrowers, and interest arbitragers, and these other participants can move forward rates slightly away from interest parity levels.

While the departures from interest parity are not sufficient to make it profitable for individuals and corporations to engage in interest arbitrage, they can be sufficient to make it worthwhile to shop for the highest investment yield or lowest borrowing cost. That is, while arbitrage opportunities will very rarely be found, sufficient departures from interest parity can persist and thus offer advantages through the careful cash management of funds which are in any case to be invested or borrowed. It is therefore instructive to examine the conditions which allow the small departures from interest parity. In this chapter we will examine transaction costs, political risks, taxes, and differential liquidity. In Chapter 9 we will see how, according to certain economists, the existence of other participants in the forward market, such as exporters, importers, and currency speculators, can result in the forward rate being moved slightly away from the level required for interest parity.[4]

WHY COVERED INTEREST DIFFERENCES PERSIST

Interest Parity and Transaction Costs

Transaction costs are the brokerage costs of buying and selling foreign exchange and/or securities.[5] When a decision is being made on where to borrow and invest, the yields that are available or the rates that must be paid should be compared only

---

[4]We have not included foreign exchange risk in our analysis. This is because we are examining covered yields, where the obvious foreign exchange risk has been avoided by using the forward market. Some authors have considered what happens if some foreign exchange risk is not avoided. They include Bradford Cornell ("Spot Rates, Forward Rates, and Market Efficiency," *Journal of Financial Economics*, vol. 5, August 1977, pp. 55–56); Robert Cumby and Maurice Obstfeld ("A Note on Exchange-Rate Expectations and Nominal Interest Differentials," *Journal of Finance*, vol. 36, June 1981, pp. 697–703); Jeffrey Frankel ("The Diversifiability of Exchange Risk," *Journal of International Economics*,vol. 9, August 1979, pp. 379–393); Fred Grauer, Robert Litzenberger, and R. Stehle ("Sharing Rules and Equilibrium under Uncertainty," *Journal of Financial Economics*, vol. 3, June 1976, pp. 233–259); and Pentti Kouri ("International Investment and Interest Rate Linkages," in Robert Aliber (ed.), *The Political Economy of Monetary Reform*, The Macmillan Press, London, 1977).

[5]Transaction costs in foreign exchange are reflected in the bid-ask spread when buying or selling. They are treated extensively by Jacob Frenkel and Richard Levich in "Covered Interest Arbitrage: Unexploited Profits," *Journal of Political Economy*, vol. 83, April 1975, pp. 325–338. Transaction costs in the context of interest arbitrage have also been discussed by William H. Branson in "The Minimum Covered Interest Differential Needed for International Arbitrage Activity," *Journal of Political Economy*, vol. 77, December 1969, pp. 1029–1034. We might also wish to add the cost of the manager's time. However, if the manager's salary is considered a fixed cost, the time required for an extra transaction can be ignored.

after all these costs are included. The costs mean that a covered interest advantage can exist as long as it does not exceed the cost of doing the arbitrage. We can show the revised interest parity condition that allows for transaction costs if we recall the definitions of bid and ask exchange rates. In Chapter 2, $S(\$/ask£)$ and $F_n(\$/ask£)$ were defined as the spot and n-year forward rates for buying pounds with dollars, and $S(\$/bid£)$ and $F_n(\$/bid£)$ were defined as the rates when selling pounds for dollars.

A covered investment in British securities by a holder of U.S. dollars involves a spot purchase and a forward sale of pounds. The return from an original dollar invested in Britain is therefore

$$\frac{F_n(\$/bid£)}{S(\$/ask£)} (1 + r_{UK})$$

if we ignore transaction costs in the securities market.[6] The rule for a holder of U.S. dollars, then, is to invest in Britain whenever

$$\frac{F_n(\$/bid£)}{S(\$/ask£)} \left(1 + \frac{r_{UK}}{n}\right) > \left(1 + \frac{r_{US}}{n}\right) \qquad (7.13)$$

and to invest in the United States when the reverse inequality holds. Since transaction costs will ensure that $F_n(\$/bid£) < F_n(\$/£)$ and $S(\$/ask£) > S(\$/£)$, where $F_n(\$/£)$ and $S(\$/£)$ are the middle rates, the condition for advantageous investment in Britain is made less likely by transaction costs.

In covered borrowing in Britain, the relevant spot rate is the rate at which the borrowed pounds can be sold for dollars, and the relevant forward rate is the rate at which pounds can be purchased for dollars in making repayment. The rule for borrowing is that a U.S.-based borrower should obtain the funds via British pounds whenever

$$\frac{F_n(\$/ask£)}{S(\$/bid£)} \left(1 + \frac{r_{UK}}{n}\right) < \left(1 + \frac{r_{US}}{n}\right)$$

Since $F_n(\$/ask£) > F_n(\$/£)$ and $S(\$/bid£) < S(\$/£)$, this condition is more unlikely than the condition without transaction costs. We find that the incentive to venture abroad for investment or borrowing is reduced by the consideration of transaction costs.

The points of indifference for borrowing and lending when transaction costs are present are different from each other and are also different from the condition that gave us the interest parity line in Figure 7.2. It should be clear that transaction costs allow a certain amount of deviation from interest parity before it becomes worthwhile to venture abroad. In terms of Figure 7.3, when transaction costs are

---

[6]Since transaction costs of buying securities will exist at home and abroad, they are met wherever investment takes place. If the costs are similar in each market, they can be ignored when making yield comparisons.

FIGURE 7.3
Interest parity in the presence of transaction costs, political risks, taxes, or required liquidity premiums.

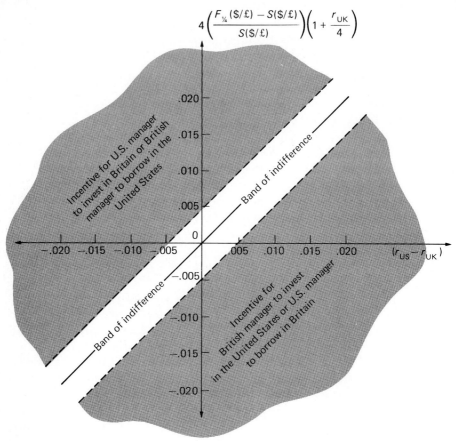

Transaction costs result in a band within which investors, borrowers, and interest arbitragers will be indifferent. With normal currency transaction costs and with 3-month securities, this band could be a full percentage point.

present, it does not pay to invest or borrow abroad as long as exchange rates and interest rates are such that we are within a certain band around the interest parity line. The total range of this band can be substantial when we are considering the money market.

The reason why transaction costs for buying and selling foreign exchange are particularly important in the money market is that while these costs are small, they can become significant when covered interest yields are annualized. For example, as we will show below, a 5-point transaction cost in the spot market and an 8-point cost in the forward market mean that 3-month securities can have covered yield differentials larger than ½ of 1 percent, that is, differentials of over 50 points. Transaction costs are therefore a potentially important cause of deviations from money market interest parity. (They are also of great importance to foreign exchange banks. It is the bid-ask spread that is their bread and butter.)

In order to demonstrate the importance of transaction costs for interest parity, let us use the following definitions:

c_S = proportional transaction costs of buying/selling spot foreign exchange (for example, $c_s = 0.0005$ or 5 points)

c_F = proportional transaction costs of buying/selling forward foreign exchange[7] (for example, $c_f = 0.0008$ or 8 points)

From our definitions of $S(\$/\text{ask}£)$, $F_n(\$/\text{ask}£)$, and so on, we know that $S(\$/\text{ask}£) = (1 + c_S) S(\$/£)$ and that $F_n(\$/\text{bid}£) = (1 - c_F) F_n(\$/£)$.

A U.S. investor will be indifferent with regard to the choice of investing in either domestic 3-month securities or foreign 3-month securities when there is an equality in (7.13) and $n = \frac{1}{4}$, that is, when[8]

$$\frac{F_{1/4}(\$/£)(1 - c_F)}{S(\$/£)(1 + c_S)}\left(1 + \frac{r_{UK}}{4}\right) = \left(1 + \frac{r_{US}}{4}\right) \tag{7.14}$$

Subtracting the amount $\left(1 + \dfrac{r_{UK}}{4}\right)$ from both sides of Equation (7.14) gives

$$\frac{(1 - c_F)}{(1 + c_S)}\frac{F_{1/4}(\$/£)}{S(\$/£)}\left(1 + \frac{r_{UK}}{4}\right) - \left(1 + \frac{r_{UK}}{4}\right) = \left(1 + \frac{r_{US}}{4}\right) - \left(1 + \frac{r_{UK}}{4}\right) \tag{7.15}$$

By factoring and rearranging Equation (7.15), we get

$$r_{US} - r_{UK} = 4\left(\frac{(1 - c_F)}{(1 + c_S)}\frac{F_{1/4}(\$/£)}{S(\$/£)} - 1\right)\left(1 + \frac{r_{UK}}{4}\right) \tag{7.16}$$

We can rewrite Equation (7.16) as

$$r_{US} - r_{UK} = 4\left(\frac{F_{1/4}(\$/£) - S(\$/£)}{S(\$/£)}\right)\left(1 + \frac{r_{UK}}{4}\right)$$
$$- 4\left(\frac{c_S + c_F}{1 + c_S} \cdot \frac{F_{1/4}(\$/£)}{S(\$/£)}\right)\left(1 + \frac{r_{UK}}{4}\right) \tag{7.17}$$

Equation (7.17) is the same as the earlier interest parity condition in (7.11), except that we now have an additional term:

$$- 4\left(\frac{c_S + c_F}{1 + c_S} \cdot \frac{F_{1/4}(\$/£)}{S(\$/£)}\right)\left(1 + \frac{r_{UK}}{4}\right)$$

---

[7] The c used in Chapter 2 could be considered as either c_S or c_F, depending on which market is being studied.

[8] As we have noted, transaction costs for buying securities will be faced wherever securities are purchased. As long as they are approximately the same percentage of the value of the transaction, they cancel out.

When, for example, $c_S = 0.0005$, $c_F = 0.0008$, $r_{UK} = 0.15$, and $F_{1/4}(\$/£) \cong S(\$/£)$, that is, when the pound vis-à-vis the dollar is flat, the extra term has a value of 0.0054, or about ½ of 1 percent. This extra term means that when transaction costs are included, the interest parity line drawn against the axes of Figure 7.2 will be shifted vertically upward by a distance of 0.0054. This is obvious, since the value on the vertical axis must be higher by this amount to preserve parity after costs are met. This is shown by the upper broken line in Figure 7.3. The figure shows that it does not pay for a U.S.-based manager with surplus dollars to invest in Britain unless conditions in the money and exchange markets are as revealed by the points above this line. Points between the upper broken line and the conventional interest parity line are points of indifference for a U.S. manager. The range of indifference is a full one-half of 1 percent of the annualized covered yield differential and is hence not trivial.

If we consider the decision of a British cash manager with surplus pounds, we can follow the same procedure and obtain a range of indifference on the other side of the interest parity line. This is shown in Figure 7.3. Only if the exchange and money market circumstances put us below this range will British cash managers with surplus pounds find it profitable to invest in the United States. Between the lower broken line and the original parity line, the pre-transaction-cost advantage of investing in the United States is not enough to cover the costs of transacting. The British money manager will therefore be indifferent in this region.

We find that when transaction costs are introduced into the management of liquid funds, there is a band or region within which it does not pay to move surplus funds temporarily abroad. The total range in this band is about a full percentage point for realistic values of transaction costs on 3-month-maturity securities. This is seen in Figure 7.3. The range of .01 is clearest along the vertical axis between $-.005$ and $+.005$. If we applied our analysis to the decision of where to borrow funds rather than to the decision of where to invest funds, transaction costs would again provide a band in which it does not pay to borrow abroad. This band would again have a nontrivial size which could keep managers from borrowing abroad unless the advantage exceeded about one-half of 1 percent per annum for 3-month securities.

We are, of course, not likely to move far away from the area of indifference in Figure 7.3 because if we did, arbitrage incentives would be set up. For example, if we are in the area of incentive for Americans to invest surplus funds in Britain, it will be profitable to invest in Britain even if borrowing is required in the United States. Such action will raise r_{US}, lower r_{UK}, raise $S(\$/£)$, and lower $F_{1/4}(\$/£)$ as the pounds are sold forward. All of these are movements back toward the upper broken line. If, on the other hand, we are at any point in the area of indifference, we can remain there indefinitely, for there are no forces pushing in any direction. We find that rather than requiring interest rates and exchange rates to stay on the interest parity line, the presence of transaction costs forces interest rates and exchange rates to be such that (covered) yields remain very similar in different countries.

For people from countries other than the United States and Britain, their choice appears to be symmetrical vis-à-vis the need to incur transaction costs, since they must pay to buy or sell foreign exchange whether they invest their funds in Britain or invest their funds in the United States. For these people, it seems that foreign exchange transaction costs will cancel just like security-buying costs, and we will be left with an interest parity line rather than a band. In other words, it appears that the cash manager can compute investment yields and borrowing costs as if there were no transaction costs. However, since most currencies are traded directly against the U.S. dollar only and are not also traded directly against other currencies, even pounds, there are two costs per transaction for non-American managers of working capital when they are investing or borrowing outside the United States. For example, a Mexican investing in Britain will have to buy spot and sell forward British pounds for U.S. dollars and also buy spot and sell forward U.S. dollars for Mexican pesos. Thus investing in Britain involves two transaction costs in both the spot market and the forward market compared with only one cost in each market when the Mexican invests in the United States. The two transaction costs for going outside the United States can permit U.S. yields to be a little lower than those of other countries without stopping investment in the United States (or they can permit U.S. covered costs to be higher without stopping borrowing). There is a band around the interest parity line between the United States and other countries because of the extra costs when venturing outside the U.S. money market.

Interest Parity and Political Risks

Another reason why the interest parity condition will not hold precisely is that foreign securities face political risks. This means that while funds are invested in a foreign country, they may be frozen, or they may become inconvertible into other currencies, or they may be confiscated. Even if such extremes do not occur, investors might find themselves facing new or increased taxes in the foreign country. Generally, the investment that involves the least political risk is at home. If funds are invested abroad, to the risk of tax or other changes at home is added the risk of changes in another political jurisdiction. It is, of course, possible that for investors in some countries, it might be politically less risky to send funds abroad. This would be true if investors would thereby avoid restrictions or taxes at home. Investing in Switzerland is an example of reducing the potential for risk by moving funds abroad. In these circumstances, a foreign investment might be made even at a covered interest disadvantage. In general, however, we would expect a premium from a foreign investment versus a domestic investment before funds are moved abroad.

In diagrammatic terms, political risks would create a situation very much like the situation created by transaction costs (see Figure 7.3). Only in an area beyond a certain positive covered differential would there be an incentive to send funds abroad. This would, therefore, provide a second cause for a band and add a political risk premium to the width of the band of investor/borrower and arbitrage indifference. The rewards to be gained by moving funds temporarily abroad must cover both the costs of the transactions and a premium for the political risk. If, for example, we refer back to Figure 7.1, we see that Canadian yields are generally a little higher than U.S. yields, even when forward hedging is included, and this can be attributed to a perceived political risk.

Taxes and Interest Parity

If taxes are the same on domestic versus foreign investment and borrowing, then the existence of taxes will make no difference to our investment and borrowing criteria or the interest parity line. Taxes will cancel out when yield comparisons are made. However, if the tax rates depend on the country in which funds are invested or borrowed, the interest parity condition will be affected. There are two ways in which taxes can affect the parity condition. One way involves withholding taxes, and the other way involves differences between the tax rate on income and that on capital gains.

Withholding Taxes   One might think that a potential cause of higher taxes on foreign earnings than on domestic earnings, and hence a band around the interest parity line, is the foreign resident withholding tax. A withholding tax is a tax applied to foreigners at the source of their earnings. For example, if a Canadian resident was to earn $100 in the United States, the payer of that $100 would be required to deduct, as tax, a percentage of earnings (for example, 10 percent). Similarly, the earnings of U.S. residents in Canada might be subject to a withholding tax. Withholding taxes, however, are unlikely to offer a reason for a band around the interest parity line.

As long as the rate of withholding is less than or equal to the tax rate that would be applied to the earnings at home, domestic withholding tax credits will offset the tax withheld. For example, suppose that a resident of the United States pays the equivalent of $10 on $100 of interest or dividends earned in Canada, and the total tax payable on the $100 in the United States is $45. The Internal Revenue Service (IRS) will grant the U.S. resident a $10 credit on taxes paid to the taxing authority in Canada. Only an additional $35 will be payable in the United States. The investor ends up paying a total of $45, which is the same as he or she would have paid on $100 earned at home. Complete or full withholding tax credit leaves no incentive to choose domestic securities rather than foreign securities. Only if withholding tax credits are less than the amount withheld will there be a reason to keep money at home.[9] This means that the interest parity condition is in general not affected, and we have no band around the parity line as a result of withholding taxes.

Capital Gains versus Income Taxes*   Taxes can affect the interest parity condition if the financial manager can obtain a lower tax rate on his or her foreign exchange earnings than on his or her interest earnings. Financial managers who do not make a habit of dabbling in foreign exchange and security markets can sometimes obtain a lower tax rate on foreign exchange earnings.[10] These particular

---

[9]Even when full credit is obtained, interest earnings are lost on the funds withheld compared with what might have been earned if taxes were paid at home at the end of the tax period. This should, however, be a relatively small consideration except when interest rates are high.

[10]For the conditions for capital account treatment of foreign exchange earnings, see Martin Kupferman and Maurice Levi, "Taxation and the International Money Market Investment Decision," *Financial Analysts Journal*, vol. 34, July/August 1978, pp. 61–64. The potential for lower taxes is an important reason for financial managers to cooperate closely with the company's tax accountant.

cash managers can frequently obtain a capital account treatment of their foreign exchange gains or losses. This is valuable if the effective tax rate on capital gains is lower than the income tax rate. The differential tax rates result in an interest parity line that has a slope which is different from the slope of the usual parity line.

Many countries offer lower tax rates on capital gains than on income, but interest earnings are almost invariably treated as income. Let us write the U.S. tax rate on capital gains as τ_k and the U.S. tax rate on income as τ_y, and let us assume that for the particular investment and investor, $\tau_y > \tau_k$. Since all interest earnings on domestic securities held to maturity are considered as income, after paying taxes and ignoring transaction costs, a U.S. investor will get from each dollar invested at home

$$1 + (1 - \tau_y) \frac{r_{US}}{4} \tag{7.18}$$

That is, the investor will lose the fraction τ_y of the interest earned. If he or she instead invests in Britain, then before taxes the U.S. return will be

$$\frac{F_{1/4}(\$/\pounds)}{S(\$/\pounds)} \left(1 + \frac{r_{UK}}{4}\right) = \left(\frac{F_{1/4}(\$/\pounds) - S(\$/\pounds)}{S(\$/\pounds)}\right) \left(1 + \frac{r_{UK}}{4}\right) + \left(1 + \frac{r_{UK}}{4}\right)$$

We have just expanded the total return into the earnings from exchange rates—the first term on the right-hand side—and the principal plus interest. After taxes, if capital gains taxes are paid even on hedged foreign exchange earnings, the investor will receive only $(1 - \tau_y)$ of the interest and $(1 - \tau_k)$ of the gain from the forward premium, that is,

$$1 + (1 - \tau_y) \frac{r_{UK}}{4} + (1 - \tau_k) \left(\frac{F_{1/4}(\$/\pounds) - S(\$/\pounds)}{S(\$/\pounds)}\right) \left(1 + \frac{r_{UK}}{4}\right) \tag{7.19}$$

We have used the income tax rate, τ_y, since all interest, whatever the source, is subject to the income tax rate, τ_y.

We can show the effect of taxes in terms of the graphic presentation of interest parity if we proceed the same way we did when we included transaction costs. A U.S.-based cash manager will be indifferent with regard to investing in the United States or investing in the United Kingdom only if (7.18) and (7.19) are equal, which requires that

$$(r_{US} - r_{UK}) = 4 \cdot \frac{(1 - \tau_k)}{(1 - \tau_y)} \cdot \left(\frac{F_{1/4}(\$/\pounds) - S(\$/\pounds)}{S(\$/\pounds)}\right) \cdot \left(1 + \frac{r_{UK}}{4}\right) \tag{7.20}$$

In comparing Equation (7.20) with Equation (7.11), we see that the differential taxes add $(1 - \tau_k)/(1 - \tau_y)$ to the front of the forward premium term. When capital gains taxes are lower than income taxes

$$\frac{(1 - \tau_k)}{(1 - \tau_y)} > 1$$

For example, if $\tau_k = 0.25$ and $\tau_y = 0.45$, then

$$\frac{(1 - \tau_k)}{(1 - \tau_y)} = 1.36$$

This will change the slope of the interest parity line, which was unity when taxes were not included. The interest parity line will become flatter, with $(r_{US} - r_{UK})$ changing by more than before with each change in the forward premium.

As a practical matter, if many of the firms which invest and borrow abroad cannot obtain capital account treatment of foreign exchange gains, the interest parity line will not be affected. However, this means that those firms which can obtain capital account treatment will find situations off their own parity line.

Liquidity Differences and Interest Parity

The liquidity of an asset can be judged by how quickly and cheaply it can be converted into money. For example, when a domestic asset such as a 90-day security is sold before maturity after only 50 days, domestic security selling transaction costs must be paid that would not have been incurred had the security been held to maturity. If, however, a covered foreign 90-day investment is sold after only 50 days, there are more than security selling costs to be faced. This should be explained carefully.

The brokerage costs for selling the foreign asset are likely to be virtually the same as those for selling the domestic security. However, we face transaction costs when we convert on the spot exchange market the foreign exchange received from the sale of the security. These costs would have not been faced had the asset been held to maturity and the proceeds converted according to the original forward contract. Further, when an asset is sold prior to maturity and the funds are brought home, there is still the matter of honoring the original forward contract to sell the foreign exchange at the maturity of the foreign investment. If cash managers want to avoid the foreign exchange risk that would be faced by leaving the original forward contract in effect, they must cover their position. In our example, if there is a 90-day forward contract and the funds are brought home after only 50 days, the cash manager should buy a new forward exchange contract for 40 days. This purchase of forward foreign exchange will nullify the sale of foreign exchange that was part of the original covered investment. At the conclusion of the full 90-day period, the foreign exchange that was originally sold will be obtained from that bought 40 days previously.

The extra spot and forward exchange costs from the premature sale of a foreign investment require an initial covered advantage of foreign investment to make the initial investment worthwhile. There is hence another reason for a band around the parity line. The amount of extra required return and hence the potential width of the band depend on the likelihood that the funds will be needed early and on whether these funds can be borrowed by using the original covered investment as a guarantee. Since the required extra return depends on the *likelihood* that the funds will be needed, it is clear that this liquidity consideration is different from the transaction costs consideration discussed earlier, which involved *known* amounts of transaction costs. Liquidity does relate to transaction costs, but these are *expected* costs. Clearly, if it is known that funds will not be required, or if it is known that the foreign investment can be used as the guarantee or security for borrowing funds, no foreign yield premium is required.[11] The more uncertainty there is concerning future needs and alternative sources of short-term financing, the higher will be the premiums that should be required before venturing into foreign money markets. This will mean wider bands around the interest parity line.[12]

We will return to the factors which allow departures from interest parity to persist when we deal with the topic of working capital management in Chapter 10. We will find that these same factors—transaction costs, political risks, taxes, and differential liquidity of foreign securities versus domestic securities—are important considerations in the handling of working cash balances. However, before we turn to the question of the management of working capital, we should look at the market in which interest parity is observed to hold most closely. This is the Eurocurrency market. After we have examined Eurocurrencies, the multinational banks which deal in them, and the nature of speculation, we will look at practical ways of managing working capital in the multinational corporation.

SUMMARY

1 Forward exchange markets allow firms to avoid foreign exchange risk when they are involved in short-term borrowing and investing abroad.

---

[11] It might be felt that movements in asset values because of changes in market interest rates also affect the liquidity of domestic investment versus foreign investment. Although the reason is not obvious, this view is not, in general, correct because relative interest rate movements should be offset by exchange rate movements, which are all related according to the interest parity theory.

[12] The development of the interest parity theorem and the reasons for deviations from interest parity that we have presented come from a long line of contributions. Among the more notable contributions are Robert Z. Aliber, "The Interest Parity Theorem: A Reinterpretation," *Journal of Political Economy*, vol. 81, December 1973, pp. 1451–1459; William H. Branson, "The Minimum Covered Interest Differential Needed for International Arbitrage Activity," *Journal of Political Economy*, vol. 77, December 1979, pp. 1029–1034; Alan V. Deardorff, "One-Way Arbitrage and Its Implications for the Foreign Exchange Markets," *Journal of Political Economy*, vol. 87, April 1979, pp. 351–364, Jacob A. Frenkel, "Elasticities and the Interest Parity Theorem," *Journal of Political Economy*, vol. 81, June 1973, pp. 741–747; Jacob A. Frenkel and Richard M. Levich, "Covered Interest Arbitrage: Unexploited Profits?" *Journal of Political Economy*, vol. 83, April 1975, pp. 325–338; Herbert G. Grubel, *Forward Exchange, Speculation, and the International Flow of Capital*, Stanford University Press, Stanford, Calif., 1966; Alan R. Holmes and Francis G. Schott, *The New York Foreign Exchange Market*, Federal Reserve Bank of New York, New York, 1965; Houston H. Stokes, "The Relationship between Arbitrage, Spot Speculation and Forward Speculation," *American Economic Review*, vol. 63, December 1973, pp. 995–998; John M. Keynes, *A Tract on Monetary Reform*, Macmillan and Company, London, 1923; Maurice D. Levi, "Taxation and 'Abnormal' International Capital Flows," *Journal of Political Economy*, vol. 85, June 1977, pp. 635–646; Lawrence H. Officer and Thomas D. Willet, "The Covered-Arbitrage Schedule: A Critical Survey of Recent Developments," *Journal of Money, Credit and Banking*, vol. 2, May 1970, pp. 247–257; and Jerome L. Stein, *The Nature and Efficiency of the Foreign Exchange Market*, Essays in International Finance, no. 40, Princeton University Press, Princeton, N.J., 1962.

2 A firm should be indifferent with respect to investing at home or investing abroad when the domestic interest rate equals the foreign rate plus the annualized forward exchange premium. It should invest at home when the domestic rate exceeds the other two, and it should invest abroad when the domestic rate is lower than the other two.

3 A firm should borrow abroad when the domestic interest rate exceeds the foreign rate plus the forward exchange premium, and it should borrow at home when the domestic interest rate is lower than the foreign rate plus forward premium.

4 Interest arbitrage involves borrowing in one currency to invest in another. It can be done by a firm without funds (and with good credit), and it is profitable as long as there are differences between covered borrowing costs and investment yields.

5 The interest parity theorem states that there will be no advantage to borrowing or lending in one country's money market rather than in that of another. Forces set up by interest arbitragers will move the market toward covered interest parity.

6 Actual interest rates and exchange rates do not generally show precise interest parity. However, the covered yield differential between comparable securities of major countries rarely exceeds 2 percent.

7 Transaction costs in the foreign exchange market can prevent covered interest rates from being equal. They also mean that investors and borrowers should be careful to determine whether the exchange rates they use in yield calculations are the buying rates or the selling rates.

8 Political risks can also allow covered interest rate differentials to differ slightly from zero. They therefore add to the band around interest parity created by transaction costs.

9 Withholding taxes do not affect the interest parity theorem. For those who face differential taxes on income versus capital gains, the relevant interest parity line has a different slope, but since many firms pay the same tax on interest and foreign exchange gains, taxes are unimportant.

10 Covered foreign investments are less liquid than domestic investments, because extra exchange transaction costs are met on liquidating foreign securities. The liquidity relates to expected rather than actual transaction costs.

QUESTIONS

1 Derive the criteria for making covered money market investment decisions when the exchange rates are given in European terms. Derive the equivalent of Equation (7.5).

2 You have been given the following information:

r_{US}	r_{UK}	$S(\$/£)$	$F_{1/4}$
15%	16%	2.000	1.995

where r_{US} = annual interest on 3-month U.S. commercial paper
r_{UK} = annual interest on 3-month U.K. commercial paper
$S(\$/£)$ = number of dollars per pound, spot
$F_{1/4}(\$/£)$ = number of dollars per pound, 3-month forward

On the basis of the precise criteria:

a Where would you invest?

b Where would you borrow?

c How would you arbitrage?

d What is the profit from interest arbitrage per dollar borrowed?

3 a Use the data in question 2 and the precise formula on the right-hand side of Equation (7.4) to compute the yield of investment in Britain. Repeat this, using the approximate formula on the right-hand side of Equation (7.5).

b Compare the error between the precise formula and the approximate formula in **a** above with the error in the situation where $r_{US} = 5$ percent, $r_{UK} = 6$ percent, and $S(\$/£)$ and $F_{1/4}(\$/£)$ are as above.

c Should we be more careful to avoid the use of the "interest plus premium or minus discount" approximation in Equation (7.5) at higher versus lower interest rates?

d If the interest rates and the forward rate in question 2 are for 12 months, is the difference between Equation (7.4) and Equation (7.5) greater than when we are dealing with 3-month rates?

4 Derive the equivalent of Table 7.1 where all covered yields are against sterling rather than dollars. This will require computing appropriate cross spot and forward rates.

5 Draw a figure like Figure 7.2 to show what interest arbitrage will do to the interest rate differential and the forward premiums at points A to F in the table below. If all the adjustment to interest parity occurs in the forward exchange rate, what will $F_{1/12}(\$/£)$ be after interest parity has been restored?

	A	B	C	D	E	F
$S(\$/£)$	2.2200	2.2200	2.2200	2.2200	2.2200	2.2200
$F_{1/12}(\$/£)$	2.2220	2.2150	2.2220	2.2150	2.2180	2.2120
r_{US}(1 month)	13.00%	13.00%	13.00%	13.00%	13.00%	13.00%
r_{UK}(1 month)	15.00%	14.00%	13.00%	12.00%	11.00%	10.00%

6 Suppose that you face the following situation:

r_{US}	r_{GY}	$S(\$/DM)$	$F_{1/2}(\$/DM)$	c_S	c_F	c_{GY}	c_{US}
8%	6%	0.5200	0.5260	0.0008	0.0012	0.0	0.0

where $r_{US} = $ 6-month commercial paper interest rate in United States

$r_{GY} = $ 6-month commercial paper interest rate in Germany

$S(\$/DM) = $ number of dollars per German mark, spot

$F_{1/2}(\$/DM) = $ number of dollars per German mark, 6 months forward

$c_S, c_F = $ proportional costs of transacting in the spot and forward markets, respectively

$c_{GY}, c_{US} = $ proportional securities transaction costs in the two countries

a Where would you invest?

b Where would you borrow?

7 If the transaction costs in the security markets in each country were 0.0025 instead of zero, would this affect your decisions? Why should security transaction costs have little effect on choosing between different securities?

8* Suppose that you face the situation in question 6, except that the effective tax rate on interest income is 50 percent and the effective tax rate on capital gains is 30 percent. Where would you wish to invest, assuming that you pay tax on your returns after any transaction costs have been removed? [Answer requires reading asterisked section.]

9 If banks are as happy to advance loans that are secured by domestic money market investments as they are to advance loans secured by similar foreign covered money market investments, would firms prefer local investments on the grounds of liquidity? How does the importance that should be attached to security liquidity relate to the probability that cash will be needed?

10 Draw the equivalent of Figure 7.3 with a transaction cost band that is based on the information in question 6. Does the band have an equal width, or does it vary with the size of the forward exchange premium? [*Hint*: Use Equation (7.17) in plotting the band.]

BIBLIOGRAPHY

Aliber, Robert Z.: "The Interest Rate Parity Theorem: A Reinterpretation," *Journal of Political Economy*, vol. 81, December 1973, pp. 1451–1459.

Branson, William H.: "The Minimum Covered Interest Differential Needed for International Arbitrage Activity," *Journal of Political Economy*, vol. 77, December 1969, pp. 1029–1034.

Deardorff, Alan V.: "One-Way Arbitrage and Its Implications for the Foreign Exchange Markets," *Journal of Political Economy*, vol. 87, April 1979, p. 351–604.

Frenkel, Jacob A., and Richard M. Levich: "Covered Interest Arbitrage: Unexploited Profits?" *Journal of Political Economy*, vol. 83, April 1975, pp. 325–338.

Kubarych, Roger M.: *Foreign Exchange Markets in the United States*, Federal Reserve Bank of New York, New York, 1978.

Levi, Maurice D.: "Taxation and 'Abnormal' International Capital Flows," *Journal of Political Economy*, vol. 85, June 1977, pp. 635–646.

Llewellyn, David T.: *International Financial Integration: The Limits of Sovereignty*, The Macmillan Press, London, 1980.

Officer, Lawrence H., and Thomas D. Willet: "The Covered-Arbitrage Schedule: A Critical Survey of Recent Developments," *Journal of Money, Credit and Banking*, vol. 2, May 1970, pp. 247–257.

CHAPTER 8

EURODOLLARS, EUROCURRENCIES, AND INTERNATIONAL BANKING

There are few topics in international finance which cause as much disagreement among the experts as do Eurodollars. The most important disagreements center on the roles, in Eurodollar expansion, of the U.S. balance of payments and commercial banks. We will attempt to give a balanced view of these questions, and we will also explain the many aspects of Eurodollars and Eurocurrencies on which there is consensus. After this has been done, we will describe the nature of the banks which deal in the Eurocurrency markets. However, before we begin, we should define what we mean by Eurodollars and Eurocurrencies.

What Are Eurodollars and Eurocurrencies?

Here is a short, accurate definition:

> A Eurodollar deposit is a U.S.-dollar-denominated bank deposit outside the United States.

Hence a dollar-denominated bank deposit in Barclays Bank in London or in Citibank in London is a Eurodollar deposit, while a dollar deposit in Barclays or Citibank in New York is not. Eurocurrency deposits are just the generalization of Eurodollars and include other externally held currencies. For example, a Euromark deposit is a mark-denominated bank deposit held outside of Germany; a Eurosterling deposit is a sterling deposit in Paris, Zurich, New York, Toronto, or a variety of other money market centers.

Table 8.1 gives the Eurocurrency rates that were offered in London on October 30, 1981. There were similar quotations of rates on dollars, sterling, and so on, in

TABLE 8.1
EUROCURRENCY YIELDS IN LONDON, SPOT AND FORWARD RATES, AND COVERED DOLLAR YIELDS

	U.S. dollar	Canadian dollar	British pound	Belgian (financial) franc	French franc	German mark	Italian lira	Dutch guilder	Swiss franc	Japanese yen
Eurocurrency yields										
1 month	15.6250	18.75	15.875	15.125	15.875	11.6875	20.750	12.625	9.75	6.5625
3 months	16.3125	18.75	16.000	15.625	17.750	11.4375	22.250	12.750	10.625	7.2500
6 months	16.6250	18.75	15.875	15.500	18.250	11.3750	23.125	12.625	10.250	7.3750
12 months	16.5000	18.75	15.875	15.000	18.750	11.3125	22.250	12.500	9.625	7.7500
Exchange rates										
Spot rate	1.0	1.2034	1.8510	37.65	5.6550	2.2480	1199	2.4780	1.8340	233.00
1 month forward	1.0	1.2068	1.8498	37.73	5.6595	2.2405	1204	2.4730	1.8347	231.33
3 months forward	1.0	1.2115	1.8499	37.97	5.6775	2.2236	1218	2.4594	1.8188	228.00
6 months forward	1.0	1.2161	1.8520	38.19	5.7150	2.1965	1237	2.4360	1.7920	223.25
12 months forward	1.0	1.2276	1.8605	38.15	5.7650	2.1475	1272	2.3850	1.7330	214.80
Covered yields in U.S. terms										
1 month	15.6250	15.3163	15.0868	12.5485	14.9082	15.7436	15.6804	15.0767	15.2228	15.2728
3 months	16.3125	15.9503	15.7528	12.1222	16.0945	15.9523	15.6632	15.8716	16.0886	16.1809
6 months	16.6250	16.4655	15.9916	12.4526	15.9587	16.3310	16.2707	16.2909	16.2370	16.4317
12 months	16.5000	16.4091	16.4697	13.9862	16.4842	16.5218	15.2341	16.3987	16.5833	16.8797

Source: The Harris Bank, *Weekly Review*, Oct. 30, 1981.

other money markets, such as Frankfurt, Paris, Zurich, and New York.[1] The Eurocurrency market is also called the *offshore currency market*. This is perhaps a better title because part of the market is centered in such places as Singapore, Toronto, Sydney, and Hong Kong. The Singapore market goes separately by the name Asiadollar market. Currencies other than dollars are not heavily traded in Asia. We shall retain the term *Eurocurrency market* even though this does not reflect the links with markets on other continents.

The Nature of the Euromarket

The Eurocurrency market means that in making hedged or covered investment and borrowing decisions such as those described in Chapter 7, there is no need to go to the different currency centers to arrange deals. For example, an American investor could compare covered 3-month yields on dollars, sterling, marks, yen, and various other currencies in London and arrange for investment or borrowing in the currency of his or her choice in that market. Moreover, as we shall see later in this chapter, the multinational nature of banks means that this American, dealing in London in foreign currencies, could easily be trading with an American bank. The larger U.S., British, French, German, and Swiss banks, along with many others, maintain sizable operations in the larger money market Eurocurrency centers.

It should be no surprise that with different Eurocurrencies available within the same jurisdiction, the covered yields or costs are very similar. This is readily apparent from Figure 8.1, in which Eurodollar rates are compared with the interbank sterling rate (the rate banks charge each other for sterling), and from Figure 8.2, in which Eurodollar rates are compared with the covered rates on interbank Deutsche marks and Swiss francs.

The closeness of yields can also be seen if we compute yields and costs, covered against exchange risk, as we did in Chapter 7, in Table 7.1. Again, for each currency we use the generalization of Equation (7.4). The covered yield/cost of funds, measured against U.S. dollars on an n-year security is given by

$$\text{Yield/cost of Eurocurrency, } j = r_j + \frac{F_n(\$/j) - S(\$/j)}{nS(\$/j)} (1 + nr_j)$$

That is, the yield on Eurocurrency j is equal to the interest rate plus the forward premium times $(1 + nr_j)$. Using the Eurocurrency interest rates in Table 8.1, we obtain the London Eurocurrency covered yields or costs in the bottom four rows of Table 8.1. When covered against exchange risk, the yields become relatively close. However, different covered Eurocurrencies do not have precisely the same yields. We find with 12-month Eurocurrencies that the best covered yields are offered on Japanese yen, which happen to offer the lowest interest rate. Over 3 months and 6

---

[1]British pound interest rate quotations in London allow comparison with deposits denominated in other currencies. They are, however, no more a Eurocurrency than an American's deposit in a New York bank is a Eurodollar.

FIGURE 8.1
Eurodollar yields versus covered sterling rate. (*From* Selected Interest Rates and Exchange Rates, *Weekly Series of Charts*, *Board of Governors*, *Federal Reserve System*, *May 4, 1981*.)

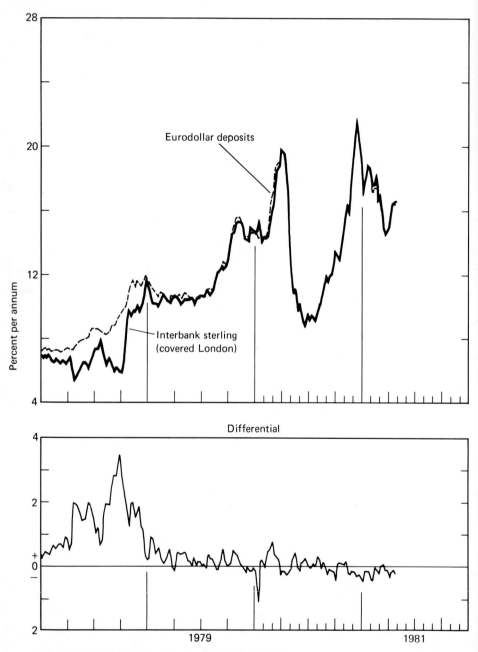

1 Percent on differential scale = 2 percent on rate scale

FIGURE 8.2
Eurodollar rates versus covered rates on interbank Deutsche marks and Swiss francs. (*From Selected Interest Rates and Exchange Rates, Weekly Series of Charts, Board of Governors, Federal Reserve System, May 4, 1981.*)

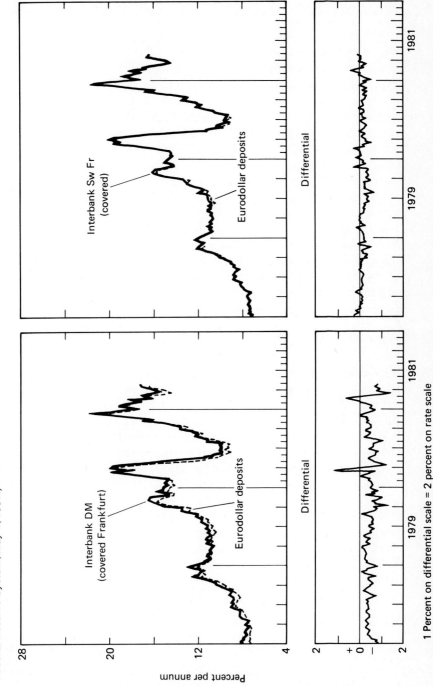

months, Eurodollar deposits hold an advantage. The best Eurocurrency covered yield for 1 month is on the Deutsche mark deposits. The covered yields are much closer than the uncovered interest rates except in the case of the heavily controlled Belgian franc; in Belgium different exchange rates exist for financial and commercial transactions.

Taking the covered rates in Table 8.1 to represent borrowing and investing rates and excluding the Belgian franc, we find that there is a 12-month interest arbitrage advantage from covered borrowing in Italian lire (which have the highest interest rate) and making a covered investment in Japanese yen (which have the lowest interest rate).[2] For every dollar borrowed there will be a before-tax and transaction cost profit of $(0.1688 − 0.1523) or 1.75 cents. Over 1 month the largest interest arbitrage advantage is obtained from covered borrowing in French francs and covered lending in German marks.[3] The gains, however, are relatively small. Indeed, we should expect the apparent gains to be reduced or even eliminated via the borrowing rate–investment yield spread and the costs of transacting.

In the Eurocurrency market, political risk is not a cause of persistent covered yield differentials. We recall from the previous chapter that when we consider financial securities from different countries, we can find an apparent covered interest arbitrage advantage that is not eliminated because this advantage is not sufficient to compensate for the risk of having funds subject to a foreign jurisdiction. However, in the Eurocurrency market different currency denominations are offered in the financial center. We have, for example, both dollar and pound securities being traded side by side in Zurich. The extent to which the yield differential *within* a location is smaller than the differential *between* locations gives us a means of discovering the importance of political risk.[4] For example, the larger differential between dollar and pound securities in London and New York than between dollar and pound Eurocurrencies in Zurich can be attributed to political risk between countries which is not present within a country.

When the security yields in the different currency denominations are both offered in Zurich, the most obvious political risk is the potential for action on the part of the Swiss government. Since this would probably affect all external currencies in the same way, there is no reason for higher risk premiums on a pound securities versus dollar securities in Zurich. Any yield differentials should not, therefore, result from political risks. By comparing market-quoted covered yield differentials, we can see how important the political risks happen to be. Not surprisingly, perhaps, they are not substantial between Eurocurrency deposits denominated in the more important currencies.

---

[2]The quoted rates in Table 8.1 are investment yields, so we cannot be sure of borrowing costs. However, with similar spreads between borrowing costs and investment yields in the different markets, our conclusions would follow.

[3]Since hedging takes place through U.S. dollars, this covered interest arbitrage requires two forward contracts. It is necessary to buy forward French francs against U.S. dollars and sell forward Italian lire against U.S. dollars.

[4]This is the approach taken by Robert Aliber in "The Interest Parity Theorem: A Reinterpretation," *Journal of Political Economy*, vol. 81, December 1973, pp. 1451–1459.

Why Did Eurodollar Deposits Develop?

In order to explain why Eurodollars developed and why later other Eurocurrencies developed, we must explain why holders of U.S. dollars preferred to keep their U.S. dollars in banks in Europe rather than in banks in the United States. We must also explain why borrowers of U.S. dollars arranged their loans with banks in Europe rather than with banks in the United States.

The original establishment of Eurodollar accounts is usually credited to the Soviet Union, although in reality the role of the U.S.S.R. was probably rather small.[5] During the 1950s, the Soviet Union found itself selling gold and some other products in order to earn U.S. dollars. These dollars were to be used to purchase grain and other western products, many of which came from the United States. What was the Moscow Narodny bank to do with its dollars between the time they were received and the time they would be needed? Of course, banks in New York were willing to take them on deposit. This, however, was generally unacceptable to the Soviets because of the risk that the dollars might be frozen if the cold war became hotter. Also, placing dollars in New York banks should have meant that the Soviet government was "making loans" to capitalist banks, which would channel the funds to other capitalist enterprises. So instead of using New York banks as the sole place of deposit for their dollars, the Soviets made their dollars available to banks in Britain and France. The British and French banks took the Soviet-earned dollars and invested them at interest. This partly involved making loans in the United States by buying U.S. treasury bills, private commercial and financial paper, and so on.[6] With the interest earned on these investments, the banks in Europe were able to pay interest on the Soviet deposits.

As intriguing as the covert Soviet role in the creation of Eurodollars may sound, in reality the development and expansion of the Eurocurrency market had its roots in more overt events. We can classify these events as affecting the supply of deposits moving to the Eurodollar market or affecting the demand for loans from Eurodollar banks.

The Supply of Eurodollar Deposits   During the 1960s and 1970s, the U.S. banks and other deposit-taking institutions were subject to limitations on the interest rates they could offer on deposits. The most notable of these limitations came from the U.S. Federal Reserve Board's Regulation Q. With higher interest rates offered on dollars deposited in Europe rather than in the United States, there was an obvious incentive to move funds to banks located in Europe. Many U.S. banks opened European offices to receive these funds. Some restrictions were removed after the mid-1970s, but to the extent that limitations were effective before that time, they

---

[5]See especially Gunter Dufey and Ian Giddy, *The International Money Market*, Prentice-Hall, Inc., Englewood Cliffs, N.J., 1978. Dufey and Giddy attribute the growth of Eurodollars to the freer regulatory environment and the consequent higher yields and lower borrowing costs in Europe, allowing narrower spreads.

[6]The truth, therefore, is that the Soviet government was, via British and French banks, making loans to the U.S. government, defense manufacturers, and so on.

contributed to the flow of dollars abroad. The dollars placed in Europe to avoid U.S. interest ceilings on deposits were reinvested, often back in the United States.

The supply or availability of Eurodollar deposits also grew from the advantage for U.S. banks in moving operations to Europe and avoiding Federal Reserve Regulation M. This regulation required the keeping of reserves against deposits. Until 1969 this regulation did not apply to deposits of European branches of U.S. banks (and since 1978 this regulation has not applied to such deposits). Since reserves mean idle funds, the cost of operations in Europe was reduced—vis-à-vis the cost of operations in the United States. This encouraged U.S. banks to move some of their depositors' accounts—including the accounts of many Americans—to the relatively unregulated European market. Also, the absence of reserve requirements and other troublesome Federal Reserve regulations allowed U.S. banks operating within Europe to offer higher interest rates on dollar deposits. This is clearly revealed in Figure 8.3. During 1979 and 1980, for example, Eurodollar deposits offered about 1 percent more than comparable CDs (certificates of deposit) in the United States.

Since the late 1960s, growth in Eurodollars has come from sources other than Federal Reserve and U.S. government regulations. Post-1960s growth has also come about because Eurodollars are more convenient than dollars in the United States. Europeans and other non-Americans have uneven cash flows in U.S. dollars. On some occasions they have inflows of dollars, and on others they have outflows. They could, of course, sell the dollars for their home currency when their inflows are large and repurchase dollars with the home currency when outflows are large. However, this involves transaction costs, and there is the potential for exchange risk. Alternatively, they could leave their dollars in banks in the United States. However, this means dealing with bankers who are thousands of miles away and unfamiliar with the customers' problems. It is easier to keep the dollars in a bank with offices close by which can respond quickly to the customers' needs. Therefore, the Eurocurrency market has expanded at a rapid rate. It is more convenient to use Eurodollars than to buy and sell foreign currencies as shortages and surpluses arise or keep funds in the currency's distant home market. The convenience is, of course, augmented by the higher yields on Eurodollars.

The Demand for Eurodollar Loans Eurodollars could have developed without a local—that is, European—desire to borrow the funds left on deposit, but the banks would have been required to recycle their Eurodollar holdings back into the U.S. money market. However, as a result of limitations in the 1960s and 1970s on obtaining loans within the United States that did not apply in Europe, a demand for U.S. funds outside the United States was created. This encouraged the growth of Eurodollars on the debit side of the balance sheet. The controls and restrictions on borrowing funds in the United States for reinvestment abroad began with a voluntary restraint program in 1965. This was followed by mandatory controls in 1968. These controls forced many borrowers to seek sources of loans in Europe, and the loans were often arranged with U.S. banks.

Another regulation affecting foreign demand for Eurodollar loans was the U.S.

FIGURE 8.3
Eurodollar versus U.S. interest rates; + favors the Eurodollar investment. (*From* Selected Interest Rates and Exchange Rates, *Weekly Series of Charts*, *Board of Governors*, *Federal Reserve System*, *May 4, 1981.*)

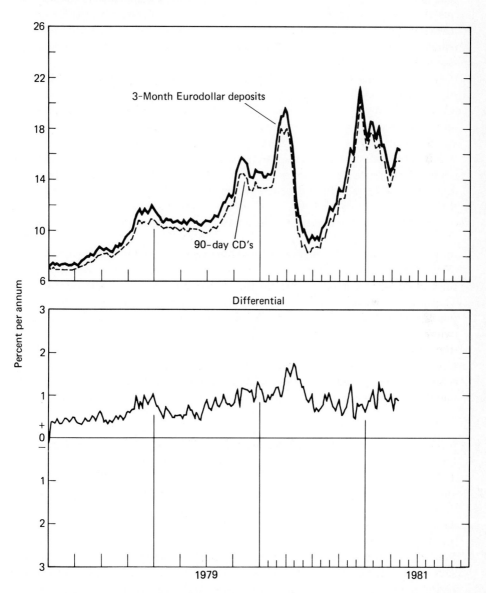

interest equalization tax, introduced in 1963. This was a tax on U.S. residents' earnings on foreign securities. To encourage U.S. residents to lend to foreign borrowers, the foreigners were forced to offer higher yields in order to cover the interest equalization tax. By channeling funds via Eurodollars, the interest equalization tax was avoided, and this allowed lower interest rates to be offered.

With deposits going abroad to escape Regulation Q, banks going abroad to escape Regulation M and the U.S. Fed, and borrowing going abroad to escape the interest equalization tax and credit and direct investment controls, the Eurodollar market expanded very rapidly. (The direct investment controls and the interest equalization tax were removed in 1974, when the market was already well established.)

Considerations of convenience affected the demand for Eurodollars as well as the supply of Eurodollars. Taking Eurodollar loans is often more convenient than taking loans in the United States. The same is true for other currency loans; it is more convenient to arrange for them locally instead of in a currency's home market. Local bankers know the creditworthiness and talents of local borrowers in a way that is rarely possible for distant bankers. Consequently, instead of taking dollar loans in New York, sterling loans in London, and so on, borrowers take loans in the different currencies in the Eurocurrency market.

The Role of Narrow Spreads   In the final analysis, the most important factor affecting the supply of and demand for Eurodollars is the desire of depositors to receive the highest yield and the desire of borrowers to pay the lowest cost. Because of the absence of regulations, the Eurobanks can offer higher yields on deposits than can U.S. banks. At the same time, the Eurobanks can charge lower borrowing costs. The lower interest rates on loans are made possible by the absence of severe regulations and by the sheer size and number of informal contacts among European banks. These factors are important advantages in making large loans. Higher rates to depositors and lower costs to borrowers mean operating on narrower spreads. Nevertheless, the European-based banks are left with profits because of their lower costs. While the growth of the Eurodollar market is best attributed to the ability of the Eurobanks to operate on a narrow spread, this has not always been the accepted explanation.

The Role of U.S. Deficits   During the early period of development of the Eurodollar market, the market's growth was often attributed to the U.S. trade deficits occurring at the time. A trade deficit means that dollars are being received and accumulated by non-Americans. This did not, however, have much to do with the expansion of the Eurodollar deposits. The dollars being held by non-Americans could have been placed in banks within the United States or invested in U.S. financial securities. Eurodollar deposits will grow only if the dollars are kept in Europe. Similarly, the Eurodollar market will not disappear if the United States runs trade surpluses. We need the reasons given above, such as convenience and liberal regulations, for the Eurodollar market to exist. As long as banks located outside the United States can offer smaller spreads than banks within the United States, they will continue to prosper.

TABLE 8.2
THE SIZES OF DIFFERENT EUROCURRENCIES AT THE END
OF 1979

	Size	
Eurocurrencies	**$ billion**	**% of total market**
U.S. dollars	229	34
German marks	128	19
Swiss francs	41	6
British pounds	15	2
French francs	11	2

Source: Federal Reserve Bank of Chicago, *International Letter*, July 4, 1980.

The growth of the other Eurocurrencies, such as the Deutsche mark and the Swiss franc, clearly did not depend on deficits in the respective countries. For example, Germany and Switzerland ran consistent surpluses in the 1960s and 1970s, and yet as Table 8.2 clearly shows, these other offshore currency markets are by no means insignificant.

Determination of Eurodollar Interest Rates

Eurodollar interest rates cannot differ much from rates offered on similar deposits in the United States. As we have indicated, the rate offered to Eurodollar depositors is slightly higher than in the United States, and the rate charged to borrowers is slightly lower. The U.S. money market rates influence the rates for Eurodollars and vice versa, as they are all part of an integrated money market. The total supply of dollars in this well-integrated market, compared with the total demand, determines the rate of interest. As a practical matter, however, each individual bank bases its rates on the rates it observes in the market.

The interest rates charged to borrowers of Eurodollars are based on the London Interbank Offered Rate (LIBOR). This is the rate charged in interbank transactions (that is, when banks borrow from each other), and it is the base rate for non–bank customers. The rate is the average of the lending rates of six leading London lenders of Eurocurrencies. Borrowers are charged on a "LIBOR-plus" basis, with the premium based on the creditworthiness of the borrower. With borrowing maturities of over 6 months, a floating interest rate is charged. Every 6 months or so, the loan is rolled over, and the interest rate is based on the current LIBOR rate. This reduces the risk to both the borrower and the lender (the bank) in that neither will be left with a long-term contract that does not reflect the current interest costs. For example, if interest rates rise after the credit is extended, the lender will lose the opportunity to earn more interest for only 6 months. If interest rates fall after a loan is arranged, the borrower will lose the opportunity to borrow more cheaply for only 6 months. With the lower interest rate risk, credit terms frequently reach 10 years.

The liabilities of the Eurobanks are primarily (over 80 percent) conventional term deposits, which are bank deposits, with a fixed term, such as 30 days or 90 days. The interest rate is fixed for the term of a deposit, and this keeps the maturity of deposits relatively short. There is a penalty for early withdrawal, and it is frequently cheaper to borrow against the Eurodollar deposit than to redeem it prematurely. The rates offered to depositors move with those offered by banks within the United States. The Eurodollar deposit rates tend to be slightly higher because of the lack of regulation, and the borrowing rates are lower.

Not as important as any of the individual Eurocurrency denominations shown in Table 8.2 but nevertheless of some importance are the Eurodeposits denominated in Special Drawing Rights (SDRs). The SDRs were originally introduced as central bank reserve assets by the International Monetary Fund, and they have already been described in conjunction with this institution. Special Drawing Right term deposits were first offered by Chemical Bank in London. As of 1981, the value of SDR-denominated deposits stated in dollar terms was over $2.5 billion. Like the bulk of Eurodeposits denominated in specific currencies, the SDR deposits are term deposits and nonnegotiable.

Approximately 20 percent of the U.S. dollar liabilities of the Eurobanks are not term deposits; they take the form of certificates of deposit (CDs), which are IOUs of the banks. These can be sold on an active secondary market. The CDs are negotiable promises to pay the bearer an amount of U.S. dollars, and they are similar to other U.S.-dollar money and capital market instruments. The only difference is that they are created outside the United States. This allows the banks to offer slightly higher yields because of the lower operating costs. Certificates of deposit in other currencies also exist. Since 1981, some London-based banks have offered SDR-denominated CDs as well as conventional deposits. The banks that first offered the SDR-denominated CDs were Barclays Bank International, Chemical Bank, Hong Kong and Shanghai Bank, Midland Bank International, National Westminster Bank, and Standard Chartered Bank.[7]

Also in 1981, the London branch of the First National Bank of Chicago began offering an extensive range of SDR-denominated assets and liabilities. The bank will make short-term loans denominated in SDRs, which means that holders of SDR assets can hedge against foreign exchange exposure. The hedging is possible because holders of SDR assets can engage in SDR-denominated liabilities by arranging SDR loans. First National Bank of Chicago also trades CDs denominated in SDRs and has thereby established a secondary market. In addition, the bank offers demand accounts in SDRs alongside its interest-bearing time deposits.

An expansion of Eurocurrency operations within the United States has been made possible by rules allowing the establishment of international banking facilities (IBFs). The IBFs are, in effect, a different set of accounts with an existing bank; they date back to late 1981. The facilities can accept foreign currency deposits and are exempt from both U.S. reserve requirements and interest ceilings on deposits as long as the deposits are used exclusively for making loans to foreigners. Two days'

---

[7]See Business International, "Slimmed-Down SDR Makes Comeback; Techniques Include Opening Up Market for Negotiable SDR CD's," *Money Report*, Jan. 16, 1981.

notice for withdrawals is required. These facilities compete with the Eurocurrency banks operating within Europe and will bring some of the offshore business back to the United States.

Eurobanks generally remain well hedged. They accept deposits in many different currencies, and they also have assets in these same currencies. When they balance the two sides of their accounts with equal volumes and maturities of assets and liabilities in each denomination, they are perfectly hedged and therefore unaffected by changes in exchange rates. Sometimes it is difficult to balance the maturities of assets and liabilities, and until 1981 this situation involved the Eurobanks in risk. However, since the end of 1981 the Eurobanks have been able to avoid risk from unbalanced maturities by using the Eurodollar futures market at the International Money Market operated by the Chicago Mercantile Exchange. Since 1982 the banks have also been able to use the Eurodollar futures markets of the Chicago Board of Trade, the New York Futures Exchange, the London International Financial Futures Exchange, and an offshore exchange in Bermuda. It is worthwhile to explain the risk from unbalanced maturities and the way this can be avoided with Eurodollar futures.

Suppose that a bank accepts a 3-month Eurodollar deposit of $1 million on March 1 at 15 percent and at the same time makes a Eurodollar loan for 6 months at 16 percent. In June, when the 3-month deposit matures, the Eurobank must refinance the 6-month loan for the remaining 3 months. If by June the deposit rate on 3-month Eurodollars has risen above 16 percent, the spread on the remaining period of the loan will become negative. To avoid this risk, on March 1 when making the 6-month loan, the bank could sell a 3-month Eurodollar future for June. (On the International Money Market in Chicago, contracts are traded in $1 million denominations for March, June, September, and December.) If by June the Eurodollar rates have gone up, the bank will find that is has made money on the sale of its Eurodollar future. This follows because as in the bond market, purchases of interest rate futures provide a profit when interest rates fall, and sales (short positions) provide a profit when interest rates rise. The profit made by the Eurobank in selling the Eurodollar future will offset the extra cost of refinancing the 6-month Eurodollar loan for the remaining 3 months.

Eurobanks perform "intermediation" when they convert Eurocurrency deposits into, for example, commercial loans. This term is used because the banks are intermediaries between the depositors and the borrowers. If the two sides of the Eurobankers' accounts are equally liquid—that is, if the IOUs they purchase are as marketable as their Eurocurrency deposits—then according to the view of some researchers, the Eurobanks have not created any extra liquidity of "money."[8] However, it could happen that the original foreign currency that was deposited in a Eurobank is redeposited in other Eurobanks before finding its way back to the home country. In this way we can have a total of Eurocurrency deposits that is a multiple of the original deposit. Before demonstrating how we can have a

---

[8]This is the view in Jurg Niehans and John Hewson, "The Euro-Dollar Market and Monetary Theory," *Journal of Money, Credit and Banking*, vol. 8, February 1976, pp. 1–27.

Eurocurrency multiplier we must clearly state that this is a topic of considerable and unending controversy, and there is even some dispute over whether Eurodollar multipliers can be defined at all.[9]

Redepositing and Multiple Eurocurrency Expansion

Let us construct a situation in which multiple expansion of Eurodollars does occur. Assume that a British exporter, Britfirm A, receives a $100 check from an American purchaser of its products and that this check is drawn against a U.S. bank. This is an original deposit of dollars in Europe. Assume that Britfirm A does not need the dollars immediately but that it will need the dollars in 90 days. The $100 is held in Britfirm A's account in a British bank as a dollar term deposit—a Eurodollar. The British bank will, after accepting the check from Britfirm A, send the check to the U.S. bank with which it deals. The British bank will be credited with $100, and the British bank's balance sheet will show this as an asset ("deposit in U.S. bank"). The British bank's balance sheet will also show as a liability the Eurodollar deposit of Britfirm A (see Table 8.3).

The $100 deposit in the British bank probably will not be removed during the term of the deposit, since removing it would involve a substantial interest penalty for Britfirm A. The British bank will therefore look for an investment vehicle that approximately matches the term of Britfirm A's deposit. Suppose that the British bank decides to maintain a cash reserve of 20 percent with an American bank and discovers a British firm, Britfirm B, which wishes to borrow the remaining $80 to settle a payment with an Italian supplier, Italfirm A. The British bank will give to Britfirm B a check for $80 drawn against the British bank's account at the U.S. bank and payable to Italfirm A. After the check has been drawn but before it is deposited by Italfirm A, we have the situation in the top left-hand corner of Table 8.3. (If the dollars are loaned to a U.S. borrower, as they could well be, the effects end here with the bank merely intermediating, that is, serving as go-between for the depositor and the borrower.)

On receiving the check from Britfirm B, Italfirm A will deposit it in its account at the Italian bank, which will in turn send it for collection to the United States. If the Italian bank deals with the same U.S. bank as the British bank, all that will happen in the United States is that $80 will be removed from the British bank's account and credited to the Italian bank's account. The British bank's account with the U.S.

---

[9]The controversy began after the publication of Milton Friedman's article "The Euro-Dollar Market: Some First Principles" (*Morgan Guarantee Survey*, October 1969, pp. 4–14, reprinted with clarifications in Federal Reserve Bank of St. Louis, *Review*, July 1971, pp. 16–24). Friedman treated the Eurodollar multiplier as a conventional domestic banking multiplier and this prompted a criticism from Fred H. Klopstock ("Money Creation in the Euro-Dollar Market—A Note on Professor Friedman's Views," *Monthly Review*, Federal Reserve Bank of New York, January 1970, pp. 12–15). The controversy expanded with the publication of the Niehans and Hewson paper (see note 8 above). Gunter Dufey and Ian H. Giddy have introduced a variety of multipliers (*The International Money Market*, Prentice-Hall, Inc., Englewood Cliffs, N.J., 1978). We will use the conventional multiplier and treat the question in the conventional way, as does Herbert G. Grubel in *International Economics*, Richard D. Irwin, Homewood, Ill., 1977.

TABLE 8.3
CHANGE IN BALANCE SHEETS FROM $100 OF PRIMARY DEPOSITS

		Before drain in cash reserves		
Bank	**Assets**		**Liabilities**	
British bank	Deposit in U.S. bank	+$100	Term deposit of Britfirm A	+$100
	Loan to Britfirm B	+ 80	Check drawn against U.S. bank	+ 80
		+$180		+$180
Italian bank	Deposit in U.S. bank	+$ 80	Term deposit of Italfirm A	+$ 80
	Loan to Italfirm B	+ 64	Check drawn against U.S. bank	+ 64
		+$144		+$144
Dutch bank	Deposit in U.S. bank	+$ 64.00	Term deposit of Dutchfirm A	+$ 64.00
	Loan to Dutchfirm B	+ 51.20	Check drawn against U.S. bank	+ 51.20
		+$115.20		+$115.20
Canadian bank	Deposit in U.S. bank	+$ 51.20	Term deposit of Canafirm A	+$ 51.20
	Loan to Canafirm B	+ 40.96	Check drawn against U.S. bank	+ 40.96
		+$ 92.16		+$ 92.16

		After drain in cash reserves		
Bank	**Assets**		**Liabilities**	
British bank	Deposit in U.S. bank	+$ 20	Term deposit of Britfirm A	+$100
	Loan to Britfirm B	+ 80		
		+$100	Eurodollar deposit	+$100
Italian bank	Deposit in U.S. bank	+$ 16	Term deposit of Italfirm A	+$ 80
	Loan to Italfirm B	+ 64		
		+$ 80	Eurodollar deposit	+$ 80
Dutch bank	Deposit in U.S. bank	+$ 12.80	Term deposit of Dutchfirm A	+$ 64
	Loan to Dutchfirm B	+ 51.20		
		+$ 64.00	Eurodollar deposit	+$ 64
Canadian bank	Deposit in U.S. bank	+$ 10.24	Term deposit of Canafirm A	+$ 51.20
	Loan to Canafirm B	+ 40.96		
		+$ 51.20	Eurodollar deposit	+$ 51.20

bank will be reduced to $20, and it will no longer have the liability of the $80 check. The British bank's account will have the entries shown in the bottom part of Table 8.3; it will show the $100 Eurodollar deposit offset by a $20 reserve and an $80 IOU. (If the British and Italian banks maintain reserves at different U.S. banks, the outcome will be the same after U.S. interbank clearing.) We see that the clearing of Eurodollars takes place in New York, with the banks in the United States merely showing different names of depositors after Eurodollars have been transferred. Originally, they showed the owner of the dollars who paid Britfirm A. Afterward, the U.S. banks showed the British bank and then the Italian bank as the depositor. Since only the names change, nothing happens inside the United States in terms of having more or fewer loans.

After Italfirm A deposits the check in the Italian bank, the Italian bank will have an $80 deposit at the U.S. bank to offset its term Eurodollar liability to Italfirm A. Like its British counterpart, it will not leave the funds idle. Let us suppose that it maintains 20 percent, or $16, in the U.S. bank and lends the balance of $64 to Italfirm B. The Italian bank will draw a check against its U.S. bank account on behalf of Italfirm B. We assume that this check is in turn made payable to Dutchfirm A. We will have the situation in Table 8.3 for the Italian bank before the drain in cash reserves.

If Dutchfirm A deposits the check in a Dutch Eurodollar term account, the Italian bank will be left with $16 in reserves in the U.S. bank. The Dutch bank will be credited with $64. We now assume that it lends $51.20 to Dutchfirm B by drawing a check on Dutchfirm B's behalf to Canafirm A. After Canafirm A deposits the check, the Dutch bank will have only $12.80 in reserves, and the Canadian bank with which the check is deposited will have $51.20. If the Canadian bank lends Canafirm B 80 percent of this, or $40.96, and Canafirm B pays an American company that banks in the United States, then the process of Eurodollar creation will end. The Canadian bank will have its account in its U.S. bank reduced by $40.96 and will be left with 20 percent, or $10.24, against its Eurodollar deposit of $51.20. The books are balanced, and every bank is in its desired position of having a 20 percent reserve backing against its Eurodollar deposit, with the remaining 80 percent out as loans. By the time the Eurodollar creation comes to an end, there is a total of $100.00 + $80.00 + $64.00 + $51.20, or $295.20, in Eurodollars. The original deposit of $100 has grown 2.952 times, and this might be called the "multiplier" vis-à-vis the original $100 base. However, the $295.20 in Eurodollars vis-à-vis the total of *reserves still remaining in Eurobanks*—that is, $20.00 + $16.00 + $12.80 + $10.24, or $59.04—gives a "deposit ratio" of 5, which is what we expect with a reserve ratio of 0.2, since each $1 of reserves supports $5 of deposits.

The interesting magnitude is not the deposit ratio but rather the multiplier, which is the expansion on the base of the original deposit. Only if there are no leakages back to the United States will the multiplier be as large as the deposit ratio. If funds deposited in the Euromarket are loaned back in the United States at the outset, the leakage is immediate and the Eurobank is merely intermediating. The rate of leakage depends on how extensively U.S. dollars are used for settling payments between parties outside the United States. The more any currency is used between offshore parties, the larger the multiplier is likely to be.

When dollar loans offered by commercial banks outside the United States are made to central banks, a leakage back to the United States is almost certain to occur. Central banks tend to hold their dollars in U.S. banks or place them in U.S. treasury bills. This will drain any extra dollar reserves back into the U.S. banking system. However, when many central banks kept dollars at the Bank for International Settlements (BIS) in Basel, Switzerland, in the 1960s, the leakage did not occur. The BIS frequently reinvested in the Eurodollar market and thus contributed to the expansion of Eurodollars.

Estimates of the value of the Eurodollar multiplier vary. As we have seen, the value of the multiplier depends on the definition and on the speed with which funds return to the United States. Fred Klopstock estimates that the leakage back to the United States is so rapid that the multiplier is about 1.05 to 1.09. Alexander Swoboda gives a value of about 2.00, which is close to the estimates of Boyden Lee. John Hewson and Eisuke Sakakibara find a range of 3 to 7, whereas John Makin has produced estimates from 10.31 to 18.45.[10] Clearly, the larger estimates must refer to deposits-to-reserve ratios rather than to the multiplier and are incorrect as multiplier estimates.

ORGANIZATIONAL FEATURES OF INTERNATIONAL BANKING

In our example showing how Eurodollars are created, we did not specify the ties that banks in different countries maintain with each other. Banks are linked in numerous formal and informal ways; for example, there are correspondent accounts and fully owned foreign banks. We briefly mentioned correspondent accounts in Chapter 2. The growth and importance of foreign branches and some other forms of foreign bank organization are shown in Figure 8.4. We should describe these forms and the other popular forms of banking organizations.

Correspondent Banking

An informal linkage between banks in different countries is set up when banks maintain correspondent accounts with each other. Many banks in the United States have correspondent relationships with banks in almost every country in which they do not have their own office. The purpose of maintaining foreign correspondents is to facilitate international payments and collections for customers. The term "correspondent" comes from the mail or cable communications that the banks maintain when settling customer accounts. For example, if Aviva wished to pay a Canadian supplier, it would ask its U.S. bank, which would then communicate with its Canadian correspondent bank by mail or cable. The Canadian bank would credit the account of the Canadian firm, while Aviva's bank would debit Aviva's account and then settle with the Canadian bank.

Correspondent banking allows banks to help their customers who are doing business abroad, without having to maintain any personnel or offices overseas. The relationship between banks is primarily for settling customer payments, but it can extend to providing limited credit for each other's customers and to settling up contacts between local businesspeople and the clients of the correspondent banks.

---

[10]These estimates are found in Boyden E. Lee, "The Eurodollar Multiplier," *Journal of Finance*, September 1973, pp. 867–874; John Hewson and Eisuke Sakakibara, "The Eurodollar Multiplier: A Portfolio Approach," *IMF Staff Papers*, July 1974, pp. 307–328; Fred H. Klopstock, "Money Creation in the Euro-Dollar Market—A Note on Professor Friedman's Views," *Monthly Review*, Federal Reserve Bank of New York, January 1970, pp. 12–15; John H. Makin, "Demand and Supply Functions for Stocks of Eurodollar Deposits: An Empirical Study," *Review of Economics and Statistics*, November 1972, pp. 381–391; and Alexander K. Swoboda, *The Eurodollar Market: An Interpretation*, Essays in International Finance, no. 64, Princeton University Press, Princeton, N.J., 1968.

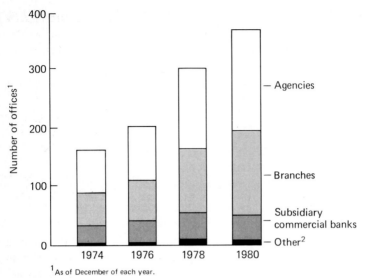

[1] As of December of each year.

[2] New York investment companies and agreement corporations.

FIGURE 8.4
Number of directly owned foreign banks in the United States. (*From International Letter, no. 448, Federal Reserve Bank of Chicago, May 22, 1981.*)

Resident Representatives

In order to provide their customers with help from their own personnel on the spot in foreign countries, banks open overseas business offices. These are not banking offices in the sense of accepting local deposits or providing loans. The primary purpose of these offices is to provide information about local business practices and conditions, including the creditworthiness of potential customers and the bank's clients. The resident representatives will keep in contact with local correspondent banks and provide help when needed. Representative offices are generally small; they have the appearance of an ordinary commercial office rather than a bank.

Bank Agencies

An agency is like a full-fledged bank in every respect except that it does not handle ordinary deposits. The agencies deal in the local money markets and in the foreign exchange markets, arrange loans, clear bank drafts and checks, and channel foreign funds into financial markets. Agencies are common in New York; for example, Canadian and European banks keep busy offices there, with perhaps dozens of personnel dealing in the short-term credit markets and in foreign exchange. Agencies will also often arrange long-term loans for customers, but they deal primarily on behalf of the home office to keep it directly involved in the important foreign financial markets.

Foreign Branches

Foreign branches are operating banks like local banks, except that the directors and owners tend to reside elsewhere. Generally, foreign branches are subject to both local banking rules and the rules at home, but because they can benefit from loopholes, the extra tier of regulations is not necessarily onerous. The books of a foreign branch are incorporated with those of the parent bank, although the foreign branch will also maintain separate books for revealing separate performance, for tax purposes, and so on. The existence of foreign branches can mean very rapid check clearing for customers in different countries, because the debit and credit operations are internal and can be initiated by a telephone call. This can offer a great advantage over the lengthy clearing that can occur via correspondents. The foreign branch also offers bank customers in small countries all the service and safety advantages of a large bank that the local market might not itself be able to support. Partly by penetrating overseas markets, some banks have grown to over $100 billion in assets. In Table 8.4 the world's 20 largest banks are ranked by total assets.

TABLE 8.4
THE WORLD'S 20 LARGEST BANKS*

Rank		Bank and head office	Assets less contra accounts	Total deposits	Capital and reserves
1979	1978				
1	2	Credit Agricole, Paris	104,997	85,560	6024
2	1	BankAmerica Corp., San Franciso	103,919	84,985	3462
3	3	Citicorp, New York	102,742	70,291	3598
4	5	Banque Nationale de Paris, Paris	98,859	97,383	1386
5	4	Deutsche Bank, Frankfurt	91,188	61,825	2942
6	6	Credit Lyonnais, Paris	91,085	88,820	1115
7	7	Societe Generale, Paris	84,914	76,809	1402
8	9	Dresdner Bank, Frankfurt	70,331	66,715	1981
9	19	Barclays Group, London	67,474	58,504	3906
10	8	Dai-Ichi Kangyo Bank, Tokyo	66,581	51,863	2517
11	21	National Westminster Bank, London	64,393	59,043	4175
12	10	Chase Manhattan Corp., New York	61,975	48,456	2027
13	16	Westdeutsche Landesbank Gironzentrale, Dusseldorf	60,080	57,787	1906
14	11	Fuji Bank, Tokyo	59,833	47,597	2485
15	20	Commerzbank, Dusseldorf	58,271	44,658	1442
16	12	Sumitomo Bank, Tokyo	58,022	47,196	2438
17	13	Mitsubishi Bank, Tokyo	57,344	44,776	2307
18	14	Sanwa Bank, Osaka	55,301	43,601	2084
19	15	Norinchukin Bank, Tokyo	53,663	39,902	213
20	17	Banco do Brasil, Brasilia	49,130	16,037	3262

*All amounts are in millions of dollars.
Source: The Banker, June 1980, p. 149.

There would probably be far more extensive foreign branch networks of the large international banks were it not for legal limitations imposed by local governments to protect local banks from aggressive foreign competition. Great Britain has traditionally been liberal in allowing foreign banks to operate and has gained in return from the reciprocal rules that are frequently offered. On the other hand, Canada has been very rigid. Until the 1980 Bank Act was passed, the opening of foreign bank subsidiaries within Canada was prohibited, and branches of foreign banks are still not allowed. The United States is selectively allowing foreign banks to operate. The regulation and supervision of foreign banks within the United States is provided for in the International Banking Act of 1978. This act allows the U.S. comptroller of the currency to grant to foreign banks a license to open branches (or agencies). The foreign banks can open wherever state banking laws allow them to.[11] The banks are restricted to their declared "home state" and are subject to federally imposed reserve requirements when they are federally chartered. They have access to Federal Reserve services and can borrow from the Fed's discount window. Since 1980, the foreign banks that accept retail deposits have been required to provide deposit insurance for customers. Between December 31, 1972, and December 31, 1980, the number of foreign banks in the United States grew from 110 to 369, and the assets rose from $27 billion to $188 billion. The foreign banks are relatively more important in providing commercial and industrial loans than in other investment activities, and by December 1980, they were responsible for more than 14 percent of the business in this area.

Foreign Subsidiaries and Affiliates

A foreign *branch* is part of a parent organization that is incorporated elsewhere. A foreign *subsidiary* is a locally incorporated bank that happens to be owned either completely or partially by a foreign parent. Foreign subsidiaries do all types of banking, and it may be very difficult to distinguish them from an ordinary locally owned bank except perhaps by the name.

Foreign *subsidiaries* are controlled by foreign owners, even if the foreign ownership is partial. Foreign *affiliates* are similar to subsidiaries in being locally incorporated, and so on, but they are joint ventures, and no individual foreign owner has control (even though a *group* of foreign owners might have control).

Consortium Banks

Consortium banks are joint ventures of the larger commercial banks. They can involve a half dozen or more partners from numerous countries. They are primarily concerned with investment, and they arrange large loans and underwrite stocks and bonds. Consortium banks are not concerned with taking deposits, and they deal only with large corporations or perhaps governments. They will take equity positions—part ownership of an investment—as well as make loans, and they are

---

[11] As of 1979, the states allowing the operation of foreign banks were California, Florida, Georgia, Hawaii, Illinois, Massachusetts, New York, Oregon, Pennsylvania, and Washington.

frequently busy arranging takeovers and mergers. Table 8.5 shows the ownership structure of two of the larger consortium banks.

Edge Act and Agreement Corporations

While U.S. banks can participate in investment bank consortia and may operate branches overseas, they cannot themselves have equity—direct ownership—in foreign banking subsidiaries. However, because of a 1919 amendment to the Federal Reserve Act initiated by Senator Walter Edge, U.S. banks are able to establish subsidiaries for doing business "abroad." These subsidiaries, which are federally chartered, can have equity in foreign banks and are known as Edge Act corporations. There are over 100 of them. They profit both from holding stock in subsidiaries overseas and by engaging in investment banking, that is, borrowing and investing. Edge Act corporations engage in almost all the activities of banking: accepting deposits, making loans, exchanging currencies, selling government and corporate securities, and so on. They can invest in equity, while domestic banks are not allowed to. A major impetus to the growth of Edge Act corporations has been that they enable a bank to open an office outside of its home state. The International Banking Act of 1978 allows foreign banks to open Edge Act corporations and accept deposits directly related to international transactions. There is no longer a rule that states that foreign-bank-owned Edge Act corporations will be permitted only if the directors of these corporations are U.S. citizens. Further liberalization of the regulations governing the Edge Act corporation seems likely.

Agreement corporations are a little different from Edge Act corporations. The

TABLE 8.5
TWO LARGE MULTINATIONAL CONSORTIUM BANKS

Midland and International Banks, Ltd.	
Members:	
Midland Bank (Britain)	45.0%
Toronto Dominion Bank (Canada)	26.0%
Standard and Chartered (Britain)	19.0%
Commercial Bank of Australia (Australia)	10.0%
Total assets: £1188 million, Mar. 31, 1980	

Orion Bank, Ltd.	
Members:	
Chase Manhattan Corp. (U.S.A.)	20.0%
National Westminister Bank (Britain)	20.0%
Royal Bank of Canada (Canada)	20.0%
Westdeutsche Landesbank Girozentrale (Germany)	20.0%
Credito Italiano (Italy)	10.0%
Mitsubishi Bank (Japan)	10.0%
Total assets: £1232 million, Dec. 31, 1979	

Source: The Banker, November 1980, p. 187.

TABLE 8.6
THE TOP 10 ARAB BANKS

Rank, by deposits	Banks	US$ millions
1	Rafidain Bank	7818
2	National Commercial Bank	7177
3	National Bank of Abu Dhabi	4492
4	Banque Nationale d'Algerie	4154
5	Arab Bank	4007
6	UBAF Bank	3826
7	BCCI	3566
8	National Bank of Kuwait	3314
9	Riyadh Bank	3307
10	Gulf Bank	3132

Source: *The Banker*, December 1980, p. 153.

authority to establish agreement corporations dates from a 1916 amendment to the Federal Reserve Act. This allows banks which are members of the Federal Reserve System to enter into an agreement with the Fed to engage in international banking. Agreement corporations, unlike the Edge Act corporations, can be chartered by a state government, and they can only engage in international banking, not in general investment activities. There were only six agreement corporations as of 1977.

U.S. International Banking Facilities (IBFs)

We have already mentioned international banking facilities (IBFs) in connection with the Eurodollar market. Since December 3, 1981, U.S. banks have been allowed by the Board of Governors of the Federal Reserve System to establish IBFs as adjunct operations.[12] IBFs are not subject to domestic banking regulations on reserve requirements and interest ceilings, and they can accept deposits only from non-Americans and in minimums of $100,000. The funds obtained cannot be used domestically; they must be used overseas. To ensure that U.S.-based companies and individuals satisfy this requirement, these borrowers must sign a statement when they begin taking loans.

Petrodollar Recycling and Arab Banking

Since the 1973–1974 increases in oil prices, it has been necessary to recycle petrodollars, that is, move them from the recipients to those who need them to pay for imports. This recycling has been carried out almost entirely by the larger banks in London, New York, Paris, Zurich, Frankfurt, and other money centers. The OPEC deposits of petrodollars have allowed the major banks to in turn make loans

[12]See *International Letter*, Federal Reserve Bank of Chicago, June 19, 1981.

to the purchasers of oil—many of them developing nations. This has been handled well by banks with offices located primarily in the key European centers and New York. There are signs, however, that things could quickly change.

After 1975 there was a growth of banks within the Persian Gulf region, and by the end of 1980, banks in this region—many of them in Bahrain—held assets of over $336 billion, up from only $23 billion in 1978. An added impetus to the growth of Arab banks (the names are in Table 8.6) was the freezing of Iranian assets during the 1979–1980 hostage-taking incident. This led some depositors to seek locally managed operations.

SUMMARY

1 Eurodollars are U.S.-dollar deposits or bank CDs held outside the United States. Included within the Eurodollar market are the Asiadollar market and other markets outside Europe. Eurocurrencies are bank deposits held outside the home countries of the currencies. The Eurocurrency market is also known as the offshore currency market. Eurocurrency markets allow investors and borrowers to choose among different currencies of denomination within the same location.

2 Eurocurrency yields are very close when covered for foreign exchange risk. They are similar on different currencies and in different locations.

3 The commonly held view is that Eurodollars came into existence initially as the result of the preferences of Soviet holders of dollar balances. For safety and ideological reasons, they preferred to hold their dollars in Europe. Perhaps more important were the U.S. Federal Reserve System regulations on interest rates on deposits, and on holding reserves; these regulations encouraged a flow of dollars to Europe. The borrowing of these dollars was stimulated by credit and capital flow restrictions in the United States. The convenience of holding deposits in and negotiating loans with local banks, as well as the lower spreads on Eurodollars from the absence of severe regulation, resulted in the later expansion of Eurodollars and other Eurocurrencies.

4 Eurocurrencies result in potential multiple expansions of bank deposits. The size of the multiplier depends on the speed with which funds leak to a currency's home market.

5 Banks can do business abroad via correspondents. They can also post representatives abroad to help clients. If they wish even greater involvement overseas, they can consider opening an agency, which does not accept deposits, open a foreign branch, or buy or establish a subsidiary. Banks can venture abroad as part of a consortium. U.S. banks can establish an Edge Act subsidiary to invest in foreign subsidiary banks or otherwise invest outside the home state or abroad, or they can establish an international banking facility.

QUESTIONS

1 Since a person can open a Eurosterling account with only dollars—by converting the dollars into pounds—or open a Eurodollar account with sterling, what yield differences can exist between different (forward-hedged) Eurocurrencies?

2 Why do you think Eurodollars are the major Eurocurrency? Does it have to do with the amount of business transacted in U.S. dollars?

3 Given the relatively extensive use of dollars in denominating sales contracts in international trade, are Eurodollar multipliers likely to be larger than multipliers for other Eurocurrencies? [*Hint*: Recall that the value of a multiplier has to do with the speed with which funds return to their home.]

4 a What is the Eurodollar creation from a deposit of $2 million when the Eurocurrency banks maintain a 5 percent reserve? Assume that the $2 million is deposited in a London office of Barclays Bank, which makes a loan to British Holdings Ltd., which uses the funds to pay for goods from British Auto Ltd., which in turn places the proceeds in Citibank in London. Assume that Citibank uses its extra dollars to make a loan to Aviva Corporation, which uses the dollars back in the United States.

  b Recompute the change in Eurodollars in **a** above, assuming instead that a 10 percent reserve is maintained.

  c Recompute the change in Eurodollars in **a** above with the 5 percent reserve, assuming that five banks are involved before leakage occurs.

  d What do you think is more important in affecting the size of the Eurodollar multiplier— the size of reserves or the time before a leakage occurs?

5 Give a reason (or reasons) why each of the following might open a Eurodollar account.

  a The government of Iran

  b A U.S. private citizen

  c A Canadian university professor

  d A European-based corporation

  e A U.S.-based corporation

6 Does it make any difference to the individual bank that makes a loan whether the loaned funds will leak to the United States? In other words, does the individual bank lose the funds no matter who borrows the dollars?

7 What is the difference between a foreign branch, a foreign subsidiary, a foreign affiliate, and a foreign agency? Which types of foreign banking will make banks multinational?

8 If the object of U.S. banks moving overseas was purely to help customers, could they have used only correspondent relationships and representative offices? Why then do you believe they have opened branches and purchased subsidiaries?

BIBLIOGRAPHY

Aliber, Robert Z.: "Toward a Theory of International Banking," *Economic Review*, Federal Reserve Bank of San Francisco, spring 1976, pp. 5–8.

Baker, James C., and M. Gerald Bradford: *American Banks Abroad, Edge Act Companies and Multinational Banking*, Frederick A. Praeger, New York, 1974.

Bhattacharya, Anindya: *The Asian Dollar Market*, Frederick A. Praeger, New York, 1977.

Debs, Richard A.: "International Banking," *Monthly Review*, Federal Reserve Bank of New York, June 1975, pp. 122–129.

Dufey, Gunter, and Ian Giddy: *The International Money Market*, Prentice-Hall, Inc., Englewood Cliffs, N.J., 1978.

Einzig, Paul A.: *The Euro-Dollar System*, 5th ed., St. Martin's Press, New York, 1973.

Freedman, Charles: "A Model of the Eurodollar Market," *Journal of Monetary Economics*, April 1977, pp. 139–161.

Friedman, Milton: "The Euro-Dollar Market: Some First Principles," *Morgan Guarantee Survey*, October 1969, pp. 4–14.

Henning, Charles N., William Pigott, and Robert H. Scott: *International Financial Management*, McGraw-Hill Book Company, New York, 1978.

Klopstock, Fred H.: "Money Creation in the Euro-Dollar Market—A Note on Professor Friedman's Views," *Monthly Review*, Federal Reserve Bank of New York, January 1970, pp. 12–15.

Lees, Francis A.: *International Banking and Finance*, John Wiley & Sons, New York, 1974.

McKenzie, George W.: *The Economics of the Euro-Currency System,* John Wiley & Sons, New York, 1976.

McKinnon, Ronald I.: *The Eurocurrency Market*, Essays in International Finance, no. 125, Princeton University Press, Princeton, N.J., 1977.

Moore, Alan: "Will Gulf Investors Use Their Own Bank?" *The Banker*, December 1980, pp. 83–94.

Ricks, David A., and Jeffrey S. Arpan: "Foreign Banking in the United States," *Business Horizons*, February 1976, pp. 84–87.

Robinson, Stuart W., Jr.: *Multinational Banking*, A. W. Sijthoff International Publishing Co., Leiden, The Netherlands, 1972.

CHAPTER 9

AVOIDING AND TAKING EXCHANGE RISKS— HOW TO HEDGE AND SPECULATE

In the previous two chapters we discovered how money market investors and borrowers can avoid foreign exchange translation and transaction risks. There are, however, others exposed to these risks, most notably importers and exporters. In this chapter we will show how foreign exchange translation and transaction exchange risks can be avoided by importers and exporters. (In Chapter 13 we will discuss the other risk faced by importers and exporters, that is, economic risk.) The methods involve forward exchange contracts, borrowing and lending, and many other devices. We will also describe assistance programs for exporters and the actual documentation that is involved in importing and exporting, including the letter of credit and the draft.

There are some who wish to take risks in the hope of making profits. We will show how speculation involves far more than buying currencies that are expected to increase in value and how speculation is best achieved. The hedging activities of investors and borrowers and of importers and exporters, together with the actions of the speculators, determine the forward exchange rate. We will show how this occurs.

HEDGING BY IMPORTERS AND EXPORTERS

Importing and exporting firms can be involved in significant transaction or translation exposure because of the foreign currency denomination of their trade. An importer, for example, does not receive a product immediately after ordering it. Often, the product must first be produced. This may take a number of months. After production is completed, the goods must be shipped, and this again takes time. And after delivery, it is customary for the vending firm to grant the importer a short period of trade credit. The importer may not be required to pay until 6 months, a year, or perhaps even a couple of years after the order has been placed. Yet the price of a product is frequently set at the time the order is placed.

The delay between the placing of an order and the date of settlement exists whether a purchase is made abroad or at home. The chief difference when buying abroad is the foreign currency in which import prices are often denominated. This difference can, however, be made irrelevant by appropriate use of the forward market. We can illustrate the importance of the currency in which prices are denominated and the value of forward exchange contracts if we take as an example the denim clothing producer, Aviva Corporation.

The high-quality denim that Aviva insists on using can be produced by mills in the United States, France, Germany, Great Britain, and Canada. Suppose that the

TABLE 9.1

DENIM CLOTH AND JEAN PRICES FACED BY AVIVA CORPORATION
(Import decisions should be based on the prices in the importer's currency, with foreign currency prices translated at the appropriate forward exchange rate. Failure to buy needed foreign exchange forward or sell foreign currency receivables forward is currency speculation.)

Cost/exchange rate	United States	Canada	Great Britain	France	Germany
		Denim imports			
Denim invoice cost/yard (c.i.f.)	$8	Can$10	£4	Fr45	DM15
Current spot exchange rate, S ($/j)	1	0.8500	2.0000	0.2000	0.5000
Denim cost ($)	$8	$8.50	$8.00	$9.00	$7.50
Expected spot exchange rate, S_1^* ($/j)	1	0.8450	2.0500	0.1900	0.5800
Denim cost ($)	$8	$8.45	$8.20	$8.55	$8.70
Forward exchange rate, F_1 ($/j)	1	0.8400	1.8500	0.1800	0.5500
Denim cost ($)	$8	$8.40	$7.40	$8.10	$8.25
		Jean exports			
Jean invoice price/paid (f.o.b)	$25	Can$30	£15	Fr150	DM50
US$ revenue at expected spot exchange rate	$25	$25.35	$30.75	$28.50	$29.00
US$ revenue at forward exchange rate	$25	$25.20	$27.75	$27.00	$27.50

same weight and quality of denim is available in a given width from the various supplying markets at the prices (including delivery) stated in Table 9.1.[1] Assume that delivery will take 10 months and that the prices are stated in terms of the currency of the manufacturer of the cloth. Assume also that it is conventional to grant 2 months of trade credit in this industry; therefore, payment is not required for a full year. Where should Aviva buy its denim cloth?

If Aviva uses the existing spot exchange rate to convert the foreign currency costs (in Table 9.1) into U.S. dollar amounts, it will find that the German cloth, at $7.50 per yard, appears to be the cheapest. But will Aviva want to buy its basic input in Germany?

Payment is not required for 12 months. During this period before settlement, the exchange rates can easily change. This can, of course, work to the advantage or disadvantage of the firm. If the exchange rates change from their current spot values to the expected rates shown in Table 9.1, American cloth will be cheapest. If Aviva Corporation decides on the German cloth on the basis of current spot rates and the expected exchange rates do indeed materialize, it will end up paying more than the cost of domestically produced cloth. On the other hand, the firm will gain even more from buying in Germany if the price of the Deutsche mark falls against the dollar to a level below the current spot value.

When an importer is deciding on the cheapest source of a product for which payment is to be made in the future, he or she should not use the current spot exchange rates. But the exchange rates that are expected to prevail at the time of payment should also not be used. If costs are converted at these expected rates, the importer might make a costly mistake. He or she might, for example, order at home on the basis of the expected rates in Table 9.1 and find that the rates at the time of settlement are those shown as the forward rates. In such a case the importer will have missed the chance to order the cheaper British cloth.

Whenever current spot rates or even expected spot rates are used, an importer is taking a risk that can be avoided by using the forward exchange market. Indeed, as we shall see, an importer who does not use the forward market is not just an importer; he or she has become a speculator.

At the time of deciding on the best source of denim, Aviva Corporation should use the existing forward exchange rate for the date on which payment is required. This will enable the firm to avoid all foreign exchange risk and is as simple as calling the bank for the forward rate quotations. Once this is done, the importing firm can compare the costs in certain dollar amounts from the various suppliers around the world and select the cheapest source. Forward markets can thus help a firm make

---

[1] Prices for imported goods are generally quoted as prices including delivery, or c.i.f. (import cost, insurance, freight) prices. A c.i.f. import price therefore includes import costs, insurance costs, and other delivery costs which are to be paid by the vendor. If a price were merely c.f. (import cost and freight), the importer would face the cost of insurance. The codes setting out the responsibilities of buyers and sellers have been established by the International Chamber of Commerce and are known as incoterms. We will take imports as involving all costs (that is, c.i.f.) and exports as "free on broad" (that is, f.o.b.). More of the terms are described in the appendix for this chapter.

good business decisions. On the basis of the forward rates shown in Table 9.1, Aviva should decide to buy from the British supplier. The firm will save $0.60 per yard by ordering the British cloth instead of the domestic cloth. There will be no exchange risk because although the invoice price will be stated in British pounds, those pounds will be delivered at the known forward exchange rate. The settlement will, therefore, involve a known number of dollars.

When the sterling payment is made via the forward contract, Aviva may find either that it has gained or that it has lost vis-à-vis the actual spot rate prevailing at the time of transacting. For example, if the actual spot price of the pounds happens to be only $1.7500/£, then the price of £4 per yard will represent only $7. It would have been cheaper, in retrospect, to have waited. On the other hand, if the exchange rate is higher, for example, $1.9500/£, then the cost without the forward contract will be $7.80, or $0.40 more than the cost with a forward contract.

Since waiting to settle at the spot rate prevailing when payment is due means taking a risk that could work either way, it is a gamble vis-a-vis hedging with a forward contract. In other words, the importer who does not buy required foreign exchange on the forward market is a speculator. It is surprising how many importers and exporters avoid forward exchange contracts, saying that they do not want to speculate. In fact, they are engaging in speculation by *avoiding* the forward market.

Before leaving the topic of hedging imports and exports via forward contracts, we should observe that the cost of avoiding foreign exchange risk with forward contracts is smaller than it might appear from casual observation. The price of forward cover is the transaction cost of buying or selling forward. However, it must be remembered that there are also transaction costs in the spot market which must be faced in converting currencies if forward cover is *not* obtained. The relevant cost of forward cover is the *extra* cost of forward exchange over the cost of spot exchange. In terms of our earlier notation, this is $(c_f - c_s)$ per dollar, which is a very small amount (rarely exceeding a very small fraction of a cent per dollar hedged) for added peace of mind.

Since 1982 a new hedging technique has become available with the establishment of currency options markets. An option allows the holder to buy or sell a currency at a stated "strike" price provided this is preferable to the spot rate. This allows exporters and importers, for a price, to reduce their downside risk. For example, one importer can buy "call options" (options to buy) of the needed currency for a particular exchange rate, with that rate good until an expiry date. If the spot price of the foreign currency is above the stated price the importer can "exercise" the option at the stated price. This sets a maximum the importer must pay. If, however, the spot price is below the stated price the importers can pay the more favorable spot price. In the same way exporters can buy "put options" (options to sell) to set a minimum on their receipts. Clearly, an amount must be paid for this "insurance" so that on average the total amount paid/received for a currency—including the cost of the option—with this downside risk protection is not necessarily better than when using forward exchange. We should note that as with forwards the payment for the foreign currency does not take place until the option is exercised, with most options not being exercised.

DOCUMENTATION INVOLVED IN INTERNATIONAL TRADE

The shipment of goods between countries involves more risk than just the exchange rate risk, which is so easily avoided in the forward exchange market. There is also the risk that exporters will not be paid. Because of the risk of nonpayment, procedures and documents have been developed which help to ensure that foreign buyers honor their agreements. We can explain these procedures and documents if we continue using Aviva Corporation as our example. Let us suppose that after considering the foreign currency costs of alternative suppliers of cloth and the forward exchange rates, Aviva decides to buy its cloth from the British denim manufacturer, British Cotton Mills Ltd. The order is placed for 1 million yards at £4 per yard. Aviva will receive the shipment in 10 months, and payment will be due 2 months after delivery.

Having made the agreement with British Cotton Mills, Aviva will go to its bank, Citibank, N.A., in New York, and buy forward (12 months ahead) the £4 million. At the same time it will request a *letter of credit*, which is frequently referred to as an L/C or a credit. An example of a letter of credit issued by Citibank, N.A., in New York is shown in Figure 9.1.[2] The letter of credit is a guarantee by Aviva's bank that if all the relevant documents are presented in exact conformity with the terms of the letter of credit, the British exporter will be paid. The most important part of the letter of credit is shown in the bottom left-hand corner of Figure 9.1. This is the promise by Citibank to make payment, and it makes the letter an "irrevocable negotiation," as noted at the top of the letter. Aviva Corporation will have to pay Citibank, N.A., a fee for the irrevocable letter of credit. Citibank will issue the letter only if it is satisfied with the creditworthiness of Aviva Corporation. If it is unsure, it will require some collateral.

A copy of the letter of credit will be sent to Citibank, N.A., in London. That bank will inform the British exporter's bank, Britbank, which will in turn inform British Cotton Mills of the credit advice. In our example, Citibank is both the "opening bank," as shown in the letterhead, and the "paying bank," as shown by the "drawn on" entry in the letter, while Britbank is the "advising bank." On receiving the credit advice, British Cotton Mills Ltd. can begin producing the denim cloth, confident that even if Aviva Corporation is unable to pay, payment will nevertheless be forthcoming from Citibank, N.A. The actual payment will be made by means of a "draft" (also called a "bill of exchange"), and this will be drawn up by the exporter at a later date—most likely at the time the cloth is delivered. The draft will stipulate that payment is to be made to the exporter or the exporter's bank, and therefore it is different from conventional checks, which are drawn up by those making the payment rather than by those who are to receive payment.

The draft corresponding to the letter of credit in Figure 9.1 is shown in part *a* of

---

[2] The format of the letter of credit shown in Figure 9.1 follows the standard recommended by the International Chamber of Commerce in 1971. The letter in Figure 9.1 was kindly provided by Citibank, N.A. Examples of letters of credit and other documents can be found in Leonard Back, *Introduction to Commercial Letters of Credit*, International Trade Services, Citibank, New York. The letter of credit we have presented is for a straightforward situation.

Citibank, N.A.
NBG LETTER OF CREDIT, DIVISION
111 WALL STREET, NEW YORK, N.Y. 10015

IRREVOCABLE NEGOTIATION DOCUMENTARY CREDIT

CREDIT NUMBER		
OF FNCB		OF ADVISING BANK
900000		

— ADVISING BANK —

MAIL TO:
Britbank Ltd,.
1 Floor Street,
London,
England

FURTHER TO OUR CABLE OF TODAY

MAIL TO:
Aviva (Denim Clothing) Corp.
New York, New York

APPLICANT

— BY ORDER OF —

— BENEFICIARY —

British Cotton Mills Ltd.
London, England

AMOUNT: £4,000,000 (Four Million British pounds sterling)

— EXPIRY —

DATE IN: June 30, (next year) — FOR NEGOTIATION

WE HEREBY ISSUE IN YOUR FAVOR THIS DOCUMENTARY CREDIT WHICH IS AVAILABLE BY NEGOTIATION OF YOUR DRAFT(S) MARKED DRAWN UNDER OUR DOCUMENTARY CREDIT NO. INDICATED ABOVE.

DRAWN AT ☐ SIGHT X ___60___ DAYS SIGHT ☐ _____ DAYS DATE (DRAFTS TO BE DATED SAME DATE AS BILL OF LADING) ☐ _____ OTHER

DRAWN ON ☐ Citibank, N.A., New York, N.Y. . FOR _____ % INVOICE COST

DRAWN ON X Citibank, N.A. London, England (OVERSEAS BANK IF "CREDIT" IN FOREIGN CURRENCY) ____ FOR _____ % INVOICE COST

FOR DRAFTS ON TERM BASIS, DISCOUNT CHARGES FOR ☐ SHIPPERS ☐ BUYERS ACCOUNT

ACCOMPANIED BY THE FOLLOWING DOCUMENTS WHICH ARE INDICATED BY "X".

X COMMERCIAL INVOICE – ORIGINAL AND _2_ COPIES

X CUSTOMS INVOICE – ORIGINAL AND _0_ COPIES

☐ INSURANCE POLICY AND/OR CERTIFICATE (TO BE EFFECTED BY SHIPPER, UNLESS OTHERWISE INDICATED BELOW)

☐ INSURANCE TO INCLUDE WAR RISK

☐ AIR WAYBILL CONSIGNED TO _____

_____ DATED LATEST: _____ 19____

X ON BOARD ORIGINAL OCEAN BILL OF LADING OR CONTAINER BILL OF LADING OR BILL OF LADING BEARING CONTAINER ENDORSEMENT (IF MORE THAN ONE ORIGINAL HAS BEEN ISSUED, ALL ORIGINALS ARE REQUIRED)

ISSUED TO ORDER OF: Citibank, N.A.

MARKED: NOTIFY Aviva Corporation, New York, New York

MARKED: FREIGHT ☐ COLLECT X PAID DATED LATEST: June 20, (current year) 19__

☐ OTHER DOCUMENTS _____

COVERING: MERCHANDISE DESCRIBED IN THE INVOICE(S) AS: 1,000,000 yards of denim cloth

TERMS: ☐ FAS _LOCATION_ ☐ FOB _LOCATION_ X C & F _LOCATION_ ☐ CIF _LOCATION_ ☐ C & I _LOCATION_

SHIPMENT FROM: London, England	PARTIAL SHIPMENTS	X PERMITTED ☐ PROHIBITED
TO: New York, New York	TRANSSHIPMENTS	X PERMITTED ☐ PROHIBITED

X DRAFTS AND DOCUMENTS MUST BE PRESENTED TO NEGOTIATING OR PAYING BANK WITHIN __15__ DAYS AFTER THE DATE OF ISSUANCE OF THE BILLS OF LADING OR OTHER SHIPPING DOCUMENTS BUT WITHIN EXPIRY.

X INSURANCE EFFECTED BY APPLICANT.

NEGOTIATING BANK TO FORWARD ALL DRAFTS AND DOCUMENTS LISTED HEREIN BY AIRMAIL IN A SINGLE MAILING TO CITIBANK, N.A., NBG LETTER OF CREDIT DIVISION 3, P.O. BOX 4566, GRAND CENTRAL STATION, NEW YORK, N.Y. 10017

We hereby engage with drawers and/or bona fide holders that drafts drawn, negotiated and presented in conformity with the terms of this credit will be duly honored on presentation, and that drafts accepted within the terms of this credit will be duly honored at maturity.
The amount of each draft must be endorsed on the reverse of this credit by the negotiating bank.

CITIBANK

AUTHORIZED SIGNATURE

PLACE, DATE, NAME AND SIGNATURE OF ADVISING BANK

EXCEPT AS FAR AS OTHERWISE EXPRESSLY STATED, THIS DOCUMENTARY CREDIT IS SUBJECT TO THE "UNIFORM CUSTOMS AND PRACTICE FOR DOCUMENTARY CREDITS" (1974 REVISION) INTERNATIONAL CHAMBER OF COMMERCE (PUBLICATION 290).

FIGURE 9.1

Irrevocable letter of credit. (*From Citibank, New York*)

Figure 9.2. It was drawn up by the exporter, British Cotton Mills Ltd., and specifies that £4,000,000 is to be paid at the exporter's bank, Britbank. This is a "time" or "usance" draft, because the exporter, British Cotton Mills, is allowing a 60-day credit period. The draft will be sent directly or via Britbank Ltd. to Citibank, N.A., in London, and that bank will "accept" the draft if it and other relevant documents that are presented to the bank are in exact conformity with the letter of credit. If the draft is stamped and signed by an officer of Citibank, it will become a "bankers' acceptance." A banker's acceptance looks like the specimen in part *b* of Figure 9.2.

FIGURE 9.2
The draft and banker's acceptance.

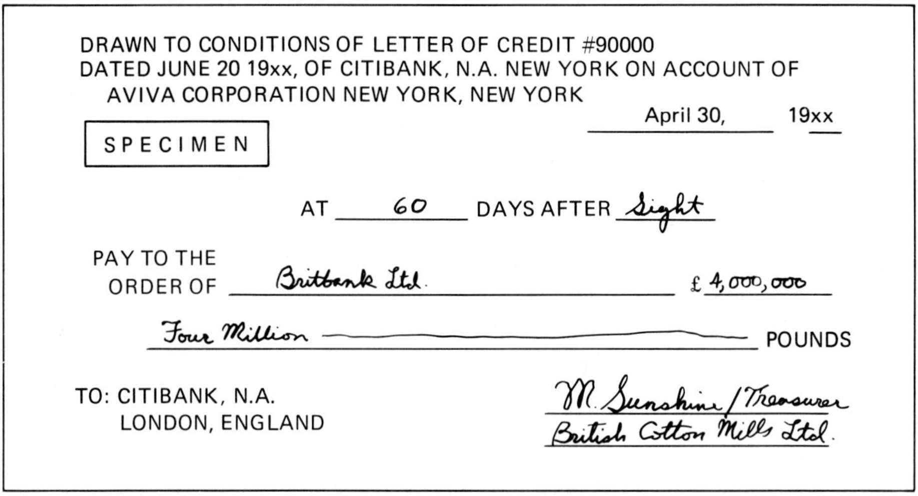

(a)

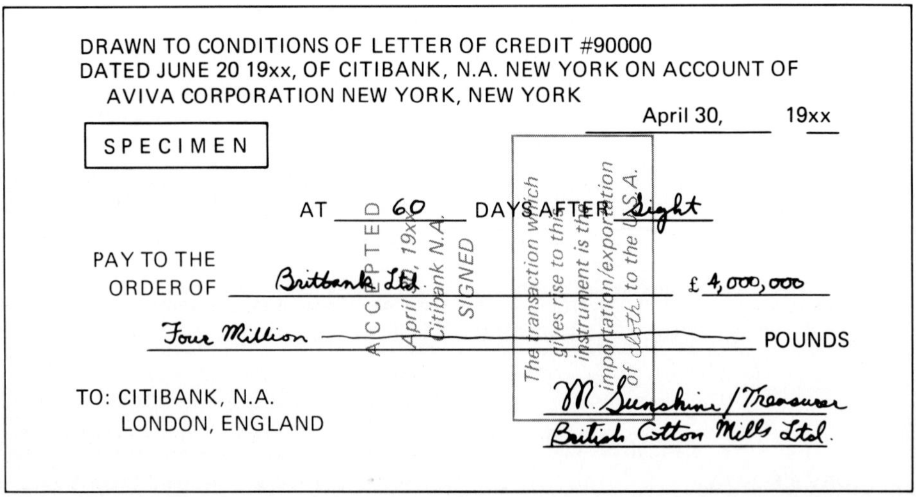

(b)

British Cotton Mills Ltd. can sell the accepted draft at a "discount" to reflect the interest cost of the money advanced, but not to reflect any risk, since the draft has been guaranteed by a reputable bank. Alternatively, British Cotton Mills Ltd. can wait until payment is made to Britbank Ltd. and its account with the bank is credited. This will occur on June 30—2 months after the date on which the draft was accepted (April 30) and a year after the date of the sales contract.[3]

Citibank in London will forward the documents to New York. Citibank in New York will require payment from Aviva Corporation on June 30 of the dollar amount in the forward contract agreed to in the previous year for the purchase of £4 million. At the same time that Aviva's account is debited by Citibank in New York, Citibank will give the documents to Aviva. The New York and London offices of Citibank will then settle their accounts with each other. British Cotton Mills will have been paid via Britbank; Aviva will have paid Citibank in New York; Citibank in New York will have paid Citibank in London; and Citibank in London will have paid Britbank. Aviva will have the papers to receive the cloth. The transaction is complete. The steps are summarized in Figure 9.3.

We have considered the straightforward case of an irrevocable letter of credit drawn up by the importer's bank, and a draft that is accepted by the importer's bank and becomes a banker's acceptance. A variety of other situations can exist. For example, if the exporter's bank, Britbank Ltd., "confirms" the letter of credit, then that bank will itself pay British Cotton Mills Ltd. and then obtain reimbursement from Citibank. The letter in Figure 9.1 is an "unconfirmed letter of credit" because there is no accompanying confirmation from Britbank. Because the letter of credit in Figure 9.1 requires that certain documents be presented, it is a "documentary credit." This is shown in the first line below the boxes at the top of the letter. The accompanying draft is referred to as a "documentary draft." A "clean draft" does not require a letter of credit or other supporting documents and is used only when there is complete trust—for example, when goods are shipped between different divisions of the same multinational. If the documents are delivered upon the *acceptance* of a draft, the draft is an "acceptance draft," and if the documents are delivered upon the *payment* of a draft, the draft is a "payment draft."

The most important document that is required before a bank will accept a draft is the *bill of lading*. A bill of lading, or B/L, is issued by the carrier and shows that the carrier has originated the shipment of merchandise. The B/L can serve as the title to the goods, which are owned by the exporter until payment is made. Then, via the participating banks, the bill of lading is sent to the importer to be used for claiming the merchandise. An *order bill of lading* is a bill which gives title to a stated party. It can be used by that party as collateral for loans.

If instead of importing cloth Aviva is exporting its jeans, then it is in the position of British Cotton Mills Ltd. described in our previous example. It will receive a copy of a letter of credit from the buyer of the jeans and will draw up a draft—its bill. If the draft is denominated in sterling, Aviva can sell the sterling forward for dollars if it wishes to avoid foreign exchange transaction risk. Using the forward market is

[3] When payment is made upon the presentation of a draft, the draft is a "sight draft." When payment is made after sight, the draft is a "time draft" (as in part *a* of Figure 9.2).

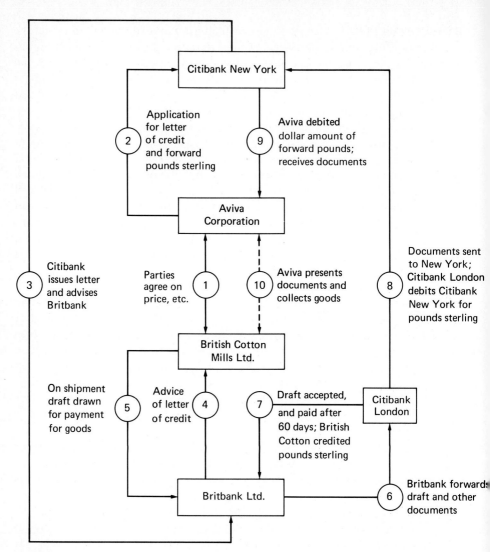

FIGURE 9.3
The steps in international trade. (*Adapted from Leonard A. Back*, Introduction to
Commercial Letters of Credit, *Citibank*, *New York*.)

one of the cheapest and most straightforward ways of avoiding foreign exchange
risk. But there are other ways of hedging, or avoiding risk, and in some
circumstances these can prove to be more valuable.

OTHER IMPORTER AND EXPORTER HEDGING TECHNIQUES

Forward exchange contracts are frequently so easy to draw up that other means
need not be considered. However, a comprehensive list of hedging procedures
should include the following.

Selecting the Currency of Trade

The need to hedge or cover transaction exchange risk can be completely avoided if exporters or importers are in a position to denominate their sales or purchases in their own currency. In our example, if Aviva can negotiate the price of its denim cloth in terms of U.S. dollars, it need not face any transaction exchange risk on its imports. Indeed, in general, when business convention or the power that a firm holds in negotiating its purchases and sales results in the expression of prices in terms of the home currency, the firm that trades abroad will face no more transaction risk than the firm with strictly domestic interests. However, even when trade can be denominated in the importers' or exporters' local currency, only part of the uncertainty is resolved. For example, an American exporter who charges for his or her products in U.S. dollars will still find the level of sales dependent on the exchange rate and hence face economic risk. This is because the quantity the exporter sells depends on the price the foreign buyer must pay, and that is determined by the rate of exchange between the dollar and the buyer's own currency. Moreover, the extent to which sales change from a change in the exchange rate will depend on the buyer's elasticity of demand for the product. We therefore discover that even when all trade is in local currency, some foreign exchange exposure—economic exposure—will remain. This will be covered in Chapter 13. We can also note that only one side of an international deal can be hedged by stating the price in the importer's or exporter's currency. If the importer has his or her way, the exporter will face the exchange risk, and vice versa. There is a way, however, to share the risk, and this involves mixing the currency used for billing.

Mixing the Currency of Trade

If Aviva was to buy 1 million yards of denim from Britain at $8 per yard, the British mill would take the exchange risk. If instead Aviva agreed to make payment at £4 per yard, then it would be the firm that accepted the risk. In between these two extreme positions is the possibility of setting the price at, for example, $4 plus £2 per yard. Payment would be made in a mixture of currencies. If this were done and the exchange rate between dollars and sterling varied, the risk for Aviva would involve only half of the funds payable—those that are payable in pounds. Similarly, the British mill would face risk on only the dollar component of its receivables.

The mixing of currencies in denominating sales contracts can go further than a simple sharing between the units of currency of the importer and exporter. It is possible, for example, to express a trade agreement in terms of a composite currency unit—a unit that is formed from many different currencies. A prominent composite unit is the Special Drawing Right, or SDR. We have already shown that this unit is constructed by taking a weighted average of the major world currencies. Although the SDR is itself an official international financial instrument, it is used privately as a unit of contract because of its relatively even movement vis-à-vis the movement of any individual currency.

Besides the official SDR unit, there are private currency "baskets" or "cocktails" which are also designed to move smoothly. They are formed by various weighted averages of a number of different currencies. The composite currency units will reduce risk because the exchange rate movements tend to cancel or offset each other. However, they cannot eliminate risk as can a forward contract, and they themselves would be difficult to hedge forward. It is perhaps because of this that cocktails and baskets are not as common in denominating trade, where forward hedging is frequently available, as they are in denominating long-term debt, where forward hedging is frequently not available.

A large fraction of the world's trade is, by convention and for convenience, conducted in U.S. dollars. This is an advantage for American importers and exporters in that it helps them avoid exchange rate risk. When, however, the U.S. dollar is used in an agreement between two non-American parties, *both* parties experience exchange risk. This situation occurs often. For example, a Japanese firm may purchase Canadian raw materials at a price denominated in U.S. dollars. Often both parties can hedge—for example, by engaging in forward exchange contracts. The Japanese importer could buy and the Canadian exporter would sell the U.S. dollars forward against their own currencies. In the case of some of the smaller countries where foreign business is often expressed in dollar terms, there might not be a regular forward market in the country's currency. However, the denomination of trade in U.S. dollars might still be seen as a way of reducing uncertainty if the dollar is less volatile in value than the currency of each party involved in a trade agreement.

Borrowing and Lending Abroad ("Swaps")

There is a very important alternative to using the forward market for hedging against exchange risk, and it involves borrowing and investing abroad. We have learned, for example, that if Aviva Corporation buys its denim in Britain, it can avoid exchange risk through forward buying of the required British pounds. Alternatively, Aviva can buy the pounds immediately and invest them in Britain. The corporation should select an investment that matures or can be sold at the time that payment is due. Aviva should buy and invest an amount of pounds that will produce, at maturity, the number of pounds required for the payment for the denim. If, for example, the payment is due in a year, Aviva should buy and invest today

$$£\frac{1}{(1 + r_{UK})}$$

for each pound it will require. If the required £4,000,000 is due in a year and $r_{UK} = 16$ percent, Aviva must purchase £3,448,276. This means that they must sell $\$S(\$/£)/(1 + r_{UK})$ for each required pound. If $S(\$/£) = 2.0000$, \$6,896,552 must be sold for the required number of pounds to be invested immediately in Britain.

One favorable aspect of covering with forward contracts is that the funds do not have to be found until later, when payment is due. However, even if Aviva does not yet have the number of dollars it needs and it still wishes to avoid risk by investing abroad, it may borrow the needed dollars in the United States. When interest is included, each pound received from the investment in Britain and used to pay for the denim imports will require eventual payment in the United States of

$$\$\ \frac{S(\$/\pounds)\ (1 + r_{US})}{(1 + r_{UK})} \tag{9.1}$$

In our example, in which $r_{UK} = 16$ percent, and $S(\$/\pounds) = 2.0000$, if $r_{US} = 12$ percent, then expression (9.1) is $7,724,138, which is the amount to be paid after a year.

We should recall that this alternative of hedging by investing abroad involves:

1 Borrowing, if necessary, at home
2 Buying the foreign exchange on the spot market
3 Investing the foreign exchange
4 Repaying the domestic debt

Clearly, if the value in expression (9.1) is the same as the forward exchange price of the pounds for a year ahead, $F_1(\$/\pounds)$, the importer will be indifferent with regard to the choices of buying forward and going through this foreign investment hedging procedure. Indifference with regard to methods therefore requires that

$$S(\$/\pounds)\ \frac{(1 + r_{US})}{(1 + r_{UK})} = F_1(\$/\pounds)$$

We should recognize this as the interest parity condition. We find that when interest parity holds, the importer should not care whether he or she buys forward or borrows at home and invests abroad to obtain the required foreign exchange for the time of settlement. In either case the number of dollars paid—for the forward currency or to repay the debt—is exactly the same.

An exporter can also use a borrowing and lending technique to avoid foreign exchange risk. The exporter does the reverse of the importer. When Aviva is to receive foreign exchange for its jeans, it can sell it forward. Alternatively, it can

1 Borrow, if necessary abroad
2 Sell the foreign exchange on the spot market
3 Invest or otherwise employ the proceeds at home
4 Repay the foreign debt with the export earnings

Since the foreign debt will be repaid with the foreign exchange proceeds from export earnings, Aviva will not have any foreign exchange transaction risk. The amount that is borrowed should be such that the amount needed to repay the debt is equal to the export revenues that are to be received. If, for example, payment is due in a year, Aviva should borrow

$$\pounds\ \frac{1}{(1 + r_{UK})}$$

for each pound it is due to receive. This number of pounds will be exchanged for

$S($/£)/(1 + r_{UK})$, which will produce

$$\$S(\$/£) \frac{(1 + r_{US})}{(1 + r_{UK})} \tag{9.2}$$

at the time that payment for the jeans is received. The alternative is to sell the foreign exchange receipts for the jeans on the forward market at $F_1(\$/£)$. Clearly, an exporter will be indifferent with regard to the choices of using the forward market and borrowing at home and investing abroad when $F_1(\$/£)$ equals expression (9.2), that is, when the interest parity condition holds. The borrowing and lending procedure is, not surprisingly, also called a "swap," but it is different from the currency swap we discussed earlier. Currency swaps involve both spot and forward currencies, whereas only spot currency is involved with hedging via borrowing and lending.

Buying Inputs in Export Markets

In general, foreign exchange risks are avoided when net payables or receivables are equated to zero. This is what happens when an importer buys forward foreign exchange, since what the importer will receive in the future is what he or she has agreed to pay. Similarly, an exporter who sells forward foreign exchange agrees to sell what is to be received. The denomination of trade in your own currency obviously and directly eliminates foreign exchange receivables and payables. In only a slightly less obvious manner, the method of borrowing and lending also eliminates net amounts of foreign exchange payables and receivables. The importer who invests abroad creates a receipt from the investment to offset (or swap) his or her import payables, and the exporter who borrows abroad creates a payable on the loan to offset (or swap) what he or she will receive from exports.

Although this is not always available as a means of reducing foreign exchange transaction or translation exposure, a firm that can buy its inputs where it sells its goods can offset payables against receivables. Aviva Corporation, for example, might buy its denim cloth in the countries where it sells its jeans. If about one-half of the wholesale value of jeans is the value of the material, then on each pair of jeans the firm has only about one-half of the foreign exchange exposure of the jeans themselves. Aviva could buy the denim in the various markets in rough proportion to the volume of sales in those markets.

The risk-reducing technique of buying inputs where outputs are sold has a clear disadvantage vis-à-vis the alternative ways of reducing foreign exchange exposure and risk. Aviva should buy its denim where the material is cheapest, and it should not pay more for its cloth just to avoid foreign exchange risks. However, after an input source has been chosen according to the best price, there will be some automatic hedging occurring in that currency. For example, if Aviva settles on buying its denim in Britain because the cloth is cheapest there, the total value of the jeans that it sells in that market should be netted aginst its denim purchases. Only the net pound sterling payables (or receivables) will require some form of hedging.

Using forward markets is one of the most straightforward ways of covering and avoiding the foreign exchange risks involved in importing and exporting goods and services. The alternatives we have mentioned (mixing and selecting the currency of trade, investing or borrowing abroad, and so on) are of greatest value when forward markets do not exist. Moreover, many international trade agreements specify that delivery is to be made over many years, whereas forward agreements rarely extend beyond a couple of years. In situations where forward market covering is not available, the alternatives we have discussed could be of great value. This will be made even clearer when we deal with long-term decisions and show how borrowing abroad brings gains from reductions not only in foreign exchange transaction risk but also in political risk.

THE EXPORT-IMPORT BANK (EX-IM BANK)

Exchange rate hedging via forward contracts, money market borrowing and investing, and so on, will help firms avoid foreign-exchange-related risk. It will not, however, help firms avoid other risks involved in international trade—in particular, the risk of nonpayment. While this risk to the exporter is reduced by the documentation procedures described earlier, a risk of nonpayment remains for the exporter who operates without a letter of credit. Before turning to the speculator to complete our account of the actors in the forward market, we will take a brief look at the institution that helps U.S. exporters without a letter of credit, and banks, face risk of nonpayment.

The Export-Import Bank is an independent agency of the executive branch of the U.S. government. Originally established in 1934 and rechartered in 1945, the Export-Import Bank will:

1 Guarantee that U.S. banks are repaid for funds advanced in connection with financing U.S. exports. This allows exporters who pay an insurance fee to sell receivables to a U.S. commercial bank without having them heavily discounted for risk. Frequently, it is the commercial bank itself which will apply for receivables insurance on behalf of the exporter. The Export-Import Bank will guarantee both short-term and medium-term (up to 5 years) obligations of the foreign buyer of U.S. exports.

2 Make loans to foreign buyers of U.S. goods. The borrowed dollars are paid directly to the U.S. exporter, and the foreign buyer makes repayment. Often, private lenders are involved in making the loans.

3 Provide loans for foreign financial institutions, which will in turn make loans to foreign buyers of U.S. goods and services. Half of the required funds are made available for the foreign financial institutions.

4 Finance initial development costs for large overseas capital projects to be built by U.S. firms. This covers plan preparations, feasibility studies, and so on.

5 Provide insurance against political and business risks to U.S.-owned capital equipment that is leased or in use abroad. The Export-Import Bank will also help finance leasing deals.

It should be noted that the Export-Import Bank provides no insurance against foreign exchange risk. This risk can be avoided by using the forward market, swaps, and so on.

Another institution that helps U.S. exporters and works closely with the Export-Import Bank is the Private Export Funding Corporation (PEFCO). PEFCO is a private lending organization that provides loans for foreign buyers of U.S. goods and services. PEFCO was started in 1970 by a group of commercial banks and large export manufacturers. The loans made by PEFCO are guaranteed by the Ex-Im Bank. The loans supplement funds already available from the Ex-Im Bank. PEFCO raises its funds through the sale of the foreign repayment obligations that it has guaranteed and through the sale of secured notes on the U.S. securities market.

Many countries have an export-import bank or an equivalent institution. In Britain the financing and guaranteeing are handled by the Export Credits Guarantee Department, and in Canada the job is done by the Export Development Corporation. At times, these export-aiding institutions have been instrumental in gaining contracts for their nation's companies. For example, the G. Heilman Brewing Company bought equipment from the British manufacturer Robert Morton and Company because of good credit terms obtained with the help of the Export Credits Guarantee Department.[4] Credit was found for 7.75 percent—half the rate prevailing at that time. Despite the potential importance of export credits, the budget of the Export-Import Bank faced substantial trimming in 1981.

THE BEST WAYS TO SPECULATE

Having considered investors and borrowers in the previous two chapters and also the importers and exporters, we can now turn to another actor frequently found in the forward exchange market: the speculator. When many think of the active participants in the foreign exchange market, they have an image of quiet, tidy men in vested suits moving massive amounts of money and providing themselves with handsome profits. The phrase "the gnomes of Zurich" was coined by a former British chancellor of the exchequer when his country faced what he perceived as an outright attack on its currency by those ever-hungry and apparently heartless individuals. In spite of the images of evil we might have, we should attempt to objectively analyze the nature of speculation and the role speculation plays in determining exchange rates. Before we do this, we should describe the ways to speculate.

There are two traditional ways to speculate in foreign exchange: spot speculation and forward speculation. The distinction between spot speculation and forward speculation has been made by Sho Tsiang, and while forward speculation is generally more common, we should describe both.[5]

---

[4]See "Export Credit Competition Expands to Sales to Developed Countries," *Money Report*, Business International, Feb. 13, 1981.

[5]See Sho C. Tsiang, "Spot Speculation, Forward Speculation and Arbitrage: A Clarification and Reply," *American Economic Review*, vol. 63, December 1973, pp. 999–1002. See also the use made of the distinction between the two forms of speculation by E. Dwight Phaup in "A Reinterpretation of the Modern Theory of Forward Exchange Rates," *Journal of Money, Credit and Banking*, vol. 13, November 1981, pp. 477–484.

Spot Speculation

Spot speculation involves *un*covered interest arbitrage. In order to describe the nature of this, let us begin by considering speculating in pounds.

If we think that the pound will gain in value, we can buy spot pounds. For each pound that we wish to have in 1 year's time, we should purchase today $1/(1 + r_{UK})$ pound, which can be invested in Britain. This means that every pound we want for next year will cost

$$\frac{S(\$/\pounds)}{(1 + r_{UK})}$$

dollars today. If we do not wish to pay this today, or if we are unable to pay today, we might borrow these dollars in the United States. The payment in dollars in 1 year, at the time of receiving the pound, will be

$$\$S(\$/\pounds)\frac{(1 + r_{US})}{(1 + r_{UK})}$$

This can be thought of as the cost of acquiring £1 for 1 year ahead.

Let us define the value of the pound a speculator thinks will prevail on the spot market in n years' time.

$S_n^*(\$/\pounds)$ is the spot exchange rate the speculator expects n years ahead. The asterisk refers to the fact that this is an expectation about the future.

A spot speculator will borrow in the United States to receive pounds in 1 year if the speculator's expectation is such that

$$S_1^*(\$/\pounds) > S(\$/\pounds) \cdot \frac{(1 + r_{US})}{(1 + r_{UK})}$$

If the expectation is realized, the value of the pound which is to be received, when converted at the future spot rate, will exceed the number of dollars owed on the loan taken out to buy the pound. The speculation will provide a profit. If the realized spot rate next year is smaller than $\$S(\$/\pounds) \cdot [(1 + r_{US})/(1 + r_{UK})]$, that is, the amount owed on the loan, the speculator will lose.

Borrowing to buy pounds in the way we have just described is going "long" in pounds (and "short" in dollars). The reverse form of spot speculation—going short in pounds—involves borrowing in Britain. For each pound the speculator wishes to be short next year, it is necessary to borrow $£1/(1 + r_{UK})$ this year. The borrowed pounds can be immediately converted into $S(\$/\pounds)/(1 + r_{UK})$ dollars and invested at r_{US}. The invested dollars will provide

$$\$S(\$/\pounds)\frac{(1 + r_{US})}{(1 + r_{UK})}$$

next year when the pounds on the British loan must be repaid. If the speculator thinks that

$$S_1^*(\$/£) < S(\$/£) \cdot \frac{(1 + r_{US})}{(1 + r_{UK})}$$

that is, that the pound will not be worth as many dollars as will be coming due on the funds invested in the United States, the short-pound spot speculation will be profitable. If the expected pound spot price, that is, $S_1^*(\$/£)$, does materialize, the pounds owed in Britain can be paid out of the funds from the dollar investment and a profit will remain. However, if the pound has a spot value that is greater than

$$\$S(\$/£) \cdot \frac{(1 + r_{US})}{(1 + r_{UK})}$$

next year, the short speculation will be unprofitable.

It should be clear from the interest parity theorem described in Chapter 7 that $S(\$/£) \cdot [(1 + r_{US})/(1 + r_{UK})]$ will not differ by much from the forward exchange rate. This means that the condition for deciding on spot speculation differs little from the condition used in deciding on forward speculation, which we will describe next.

Forward Speculation

Speculation in the forward exchange market should be based upon a comparison of the forward exchange rate and the speculator's view of where the future spot exchange rate will be. Since we have written $S_n^*(\$/£)$ as the spot exchange rate that the speculator expects n years ahead, we can make the following statement:

> Abstracting from any risk premia, a forward speculator will sell pounds for delivery n years forward when $F_n(\$/£) > S_n^*(\$/£)$. A forward speculator will buy pounds n years forward when $F_n(\$/£) < S_n^*(\$/£)$.

For example, if $F_1(\$/£) = 1.8500$ and the speculator thinks that in 1 year the spot rate will be $\$1.8550/£$, that is, that $S_1^*(\$/£)$ equals 1.8550, the speculator will buy pounds forward at the forward rate—$F_1(\$/£) = 1.8500$—in the hope of selling each of the purchased pounds at $\$1.8550/£$. The expected profit is $\$0.005$ per pound purchased, or $\$5000$ per £1,000,000. If forward and spot transaction costs are respectively 8 points and 5 points (as in Chapter 7, where $c_S = 0.0005$ and $c_F = 0.0008$), the cost of buying forward £1,000,000 and selling this amount spot will be $£(c_S + c_F) \times 1,000,000 = £1300$. At $S_1(\$/£) = 1.8550$, the cost will be $\$2411.50$, leaving a profit from the expected $\$5000$ gain. Alternatively, if the speculator's expectation is that $S_1^*(\$/£)$ equals 1.8450, he or she will sell pounds forward at $F_1(\$/£) = 1.8500$ in the hope of being able to buy them for delivery on the spot market in 1 year at their expected price of $\$1.8450/£$. When the pounds are delivered to satisfy the forward contract at the forward rate—$F_1(\$/£) = 1.8500$—there will be a profit of $0.005 per pound sold ($1.8500 − $1.8450), or $5000 per £1,000,000. We should note that these expected profits may be insufficient to compensate for the risk involved.

If we ignore transaction costs, the speculator will profit from selling pounds forward at $F_n(\$/£)$ when

$$F_n(\$/£) > S_1(\$/£)$$

where $S_1(\$/£)$ is the *actual* (not expected) spot rate prevailing in a year's time, when the forward contract matures. This is because the pounds sold forward can be bought on the spot market for less than the amount at which they are to be sold according to the contract. The speculator will lose from *selling* pounds forward if

$$F_n(\$/£) < S_1(\$/£)$$

Similarly, the speculator will profit from *buying* pounds forward at $F_n(\$/£)$ if $F_n(\$/£) < S_1(\$/£)$ and lose if $F_n(\$/£) > S_1(\$/£)$. A speculator who buys pounds forward for dollars is going long in pounds and short in dollars, and a speculator who sells pounds forward for dollars is going short in pounds and long in dollars.

It is important to note, as we stated in Chapter 6, that in the course of going long and short, forward speculators are generally stabilizing the foreign exchange markets, and in that sense they serve a useful function. It is also important to observe that the criteria for how to speculate and decide on a long or short position do not involve the current spot exchange rate, $S(\$/£)$. The decision involves only the forward rate and the expected spot rate. Even if an individual firmly believes that spot rates will improve, this is not sufficient reason to buy forward, since the forward rate probably already reflects that belief. One thing we can be quite sure of in this world is that there are few obvious bargains. If a country is managing its economy well and its exchange rate is appreciating, its currency is likely to be at a forward premium. Buying that currency forward will be profitable only if the actual spot rate appreciates by *more than* the amount already visible in the forward rate. If it appreciates by less than this, forward purchases will involve losses despite the improved currency value.

Before going on to combine the various actors in the forward market with a general explanation of the forward exchange rate, we can note that speculative activity is frequently combined with the other activities of importing and exporting or investing and borrowing. In particular, if an importer or a firm that borrows abroad does not buy forward foreign exchange and an exporter or a firm that invests abroad does not sell foreign exchange, these actors are also speculators.

DETERMINING THE FORWARD EXCHANGE RATE*

The various actors who use the forward exchange market will collectively determine the forward exchange rate. A useful framework that we can use to combine the

FIGURE 9.4
Forward exchange schedules: importers/exporters and investors/borrowers.

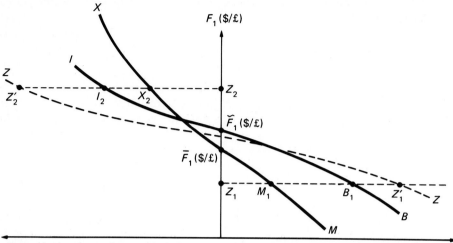

IB represents net forward pound purchases and sales by investors, borrowers, and interest arbitragers, and *XM* represents net forward pound purchases and sales by importers and exporters. *ZZ* is the horizontal sum of *IB* and *XM*, with, for example, $Z_2X_2 + Z_2I_2 = Z_2Z_2'$.

behavior of the various participants has been developed by Herbert Grubel.[6] In Figure 9.4, the vertical axis gives the forward price of the British pound vis-à-vis the dollar, and the horizontal axis gives the purchases and/or sales of forward pounds against the dollar. To the right of the origin there are net purchases of the British currency on the forward market, and to the left there are net sales.

The point $\tilde{F}_1(\$/£)$ on the vertical axis is the particular forward rate at which, given the spot exchange rate and interest rates, the interest parity condition holds; that is,

$$\tilde{F}_1(\$/£) = S(\$/£) \frac{(1 + r_{\text{US}})}{(1 + r_{\text{UK}})}$$

When the actual forward rate, $F_1(\$/£)$, moves above this value, there is an advantage to investing in Britain and to borrowing in the United States. Either activity will, when covered in the forward exchange market, give rise to forward sales of pounds. Similarly, as $F_1(\$/£)$ moves below $\tilde{F}_1(\$/£)$, an advantage is created for investing in the United States and borrowing in Britain. When covered, these

---

[6] Herbert Grubel, *Forward Exchange, Speculaton and the International Flow of Capital*, Stanford University Press, Stanford, Calif., 1966. E. Dwight Phaup (ibid.) has questioned Grubel's approach on the grounds that forward speculation will not be used when spot speculation is cheaper.

activities give rise to forward purchases of pounds. Only at $\bar{F}_1(\$/\pounds)$ is there no incentive to move funds.

Line IB is the investment/borrowing schedule. Since there are more forward sales as $F_1(\$/\pounds)$ moves higher and more forward purchases as $F_1(\$/\pounds)$ moves lower, line IB slopes downward from left to right.

We should note that if potentially unlimited arbitrage took place at interest rates above and below line IB, then IB would be horizontal, and the only forward rate we would ever observe would be the parity rate, $\tilde{F}_1(\$/\pounds)$. Many economists therefore claim that the parity rate is the rate that we will observe. This author, however, believes that there is a spread between borrowing and investing interest rates facing interest arbitragers and therefore that other actors will also influence the forward rate. We will allow a downward slope on IB. Question 6 at the end of the chapter considers the case of an unlimited supply of arbitrage funds.

Even after we have accepted the idea that IB has a downward slope, we still have to decide whether IB is a straight line or whether it gets flatter or steeper as we move away from the forward rate for interest parity, $\tilde{F}_1(\$/\pounds)$. Making IB steeper as in Figure 9.4 means that less additional foreign borrowing/investing will follow from any additional opportunities that exist. This will be true if many rush to take advantage of initial benefits but thereafter further interest in borrowing or lending abroad begins to dry up. Allowing the tails of IB to become flatter implies the reverse. A priori, it is difficult to know which situation is more likely.

If importers and exporters do not wish to speculate, then, as we have shown, they can use the forward exchange market.[7] If they do cover their foreign exchange risks in this way, the exchange rate that is relevant in their importing and exporting decisions is the forward rate and not the spot rate or the expected spot rate. This was brought out in our example with Aviva Corporation. The forward rate determines where they should buy their inputs and what they receive for exports.

If U.S. importers and exporters use forward rates in their calculations, then as the forward price of pounds goes up, imports from Britain become less attractive. This should mean a reduction in imports.[8] This will mean fewer pounds bought forward at higher forward rates and vice versa. Similarly, for a firm that has limited output to allocate, as the forward price of the pounds goes up, more will be sold in Britain, since it will become more profitable to sell in that market. Forward sales of pounds will therefore increase. Similar reactions to changes in forward rates will occur with British importers and exporters. From all these joint effects we have that an increase in the forward price of pounds will result in fewer forward purchases of pounds (from U.S. imports and British exports) and more forward sales (from U.S. exports and British imports). When covered imports equal covered exports, the net purchase/sales of traders will be zero. This will occur at $\bar{F}_1(\$/\pounds)$ in Figure 9.4. This has been assumed to be below $\tilde{F}_1(\$/\pounds)$. As the forward exchange rate moves above

---

[7]They can, as we have seen, also try to denominate in their own currency or cover risks through borrowing/investing.

[8]As seen in Chapter 6, if price increases exceed quantity reductions—that is, if import demand is inelastic—the value of import spending could actually increase. In the analysis here, however, we ignore this possibility.

this level, $\bar{F}_1(\$/£)$, there will be net sales, and vice versa. We have the downward-sloping line XM giving net forward purchases and sales by importers and exporters.

To find the combined effect of investing and borrowing and of exporting and importing, we must add the amounts involved horizontally. For example, at the relatively low forward rate of Z_1 in Figure 9.4, there will be $Z_1 M_1$ of net forward pound purchase from net U.S. imports from Britain. There will also be $Z_1 B_1$ of purchases from net borrowing in Britain. The total of these is the distance $Z_1 Z_1'$, which gives the aggregate purchases. Similarly, at the high forward rate of Z_2, there will be $Z_2 X_2$ of sales from a net export surplus with Britain. Further, at Z_2 there will be $Z_2 I_2$ of sales from net investment in Britain. The total of these two is the distance $Z_2 Z_2'$. From selecting various forward rates and horizontally adding IB and XM, we obtain the combined effect given by line ZZ.

Line ZZ shows net sales and purchases of pounds by borrowers and investors and importers and exporters. If they were the only participants, the only viable forward rate would be where ZZ crosses the vertical axis. By an obvious tautology, somebody's purchase is another's sale. According to the way Figure 9.4 is structured, if the forward rate is where ZZ cuts the vertical axis, we have net pound purchases by Americans who borrowed abroad (or by British people who invested in the United States) being matched by net pound sales from net American exports (or British imports). We have, however, yet to include the speculators.

Figure 9.5 shows line ZZ from Figure 9.4, and a new line, VV, which represents purchases and sales of pounds by speculators. We should observe that for the speculators we have reversed the intrepretation of the horizontal axis. As we move to the right of the origin along VV, we have forward sales of pounds, and to the left we have purchases. This switching of direction is required for a convenient interpretation of equilibrium.

If the "middle view" of speculators is that the future spot exchange rate in Britain will be $S_1^*(\$/£)$, then when the forward rate equals this amount, speculators will neither wish to buy forward exchange nor wish to sell forward exchange. VV therefore cuts the vertical axis at the point $S_1^*(\$/£)$. As the forward rate falls below this value, we have $F_1(\$/£) < S_1^*(\$/£)$, and speculators will buy forward. We therefore move downward and to the left along VV as $F_1(\$/£)$ falls, remembering that the left-hand segment refers to forward buying by speculators. When the forward rate moves above $S_1^*(\$/£)$, speculators will sell forward. We therefore move up along VV.

We are now in a position to identify the equilibrium forward rate when all the actors in the forward exchange market are included. Equilibrium will occur at point E with the forward rate $F_1^e(\$/£)$. There will be net purchases $—OQ—$ of forward British pounds by investers/borrowers and importers/exporters taken all together. This will be matched by an equal amount of net sales by speculators. As Figure 9.5 shows, the equilibrium forward exchange rate falls between the rate required for interest parity—$\tilde{F}_1(\$/£)$, which in Figure 9.4 is above the ZZ line on the vertical axis—and the rate required for speculator indifference—$S_1^*(\$/£)$. The forward rate that we observe in the market might not be the interest parity rate. We have discovered another cause of disparity to add to the causes discussed previously in Chapter 7. Similarly, we find that the forward rate can deviate from the speculators'

FIGURE 9.5
Determining the forward exchange rate.

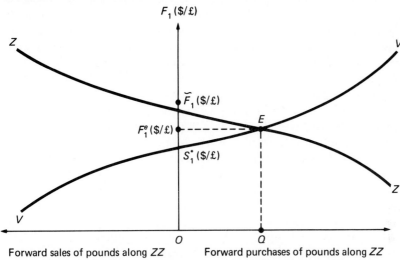

Forward sales of pounds along *ZZ*   Forward purchases of pounds along *ZZ*
Forward purchases of pounds along *VV*   Forward sales of pounds along *VV*

ZZ gives net forward exchange purchases and sales of borrowers, investors, exporters, and importers. *VV* gives the sales and purchases of forward exchange by speculators. The forward market clears at *E*, where (small) interest arbitrage and speculative opportunities could persist. The flatter *ZZ* is from, for example, the availability of interest arbitrage funds, the closer the equilibrium forward rate is to the rate for interest parity. The flatter *VV* is, the closer the equilibrium rate is to expectations of future rates.

expectations of the future spot rate.[9] For example, many people could believe that the foreign currency will rise in value, and yet the forward market might not reflect this. We find that profitable opportunities can persist for speculators in the forward markets, as can the opportunities for arbitrage.[10] The arbitrage is limited, by assumption, by the availability of funds for the arbitragers. If there were no limit and interest rates for borrowing were constant no matter how much was borrowed, *ZZ* would cut the vertical axis at $F_1^e(\$/£)$, and the interest parity condition would hold exactly.

---

[9] We note that this conclusion follows from the allowance of some slope in *IB* and *VV*. If we take the supply of funds for interest arbitrage or for speculaton to be unlimited, then the equilibrium forward rate will be for arbitrage indifference or speculator indifference depending on which line is flat.

[10] The conclusion that opportunities for successful speculation can persist is perhaps surprising and has been subjected to testing. It does appear from the empirical evidence that profitable speculation can occur. For example, a number of profitable rules have been discovered by Paul Boothe ("Estimating the Structure and Efficiency of the Canadian Foreign Exchange Market 1971–78," unpublished Ph.D. dissertation, University of British Columbia, 1981). Profitable speculation is also shown to persist in David Longworth, "Testing the Efficiency of the Canadian-U.S. Exchange Market under the Assumption of No Risk Premium," *Journal of Finance*, vol. 36, March 1981, pp. 43–49. These results are consistent with the empirical findings of M. Beenstock (*The Foreign Exchanges*, The Macmillan Press, London, 1978). Beenstock finds that *VV* is relatively inelastic compared with *ZZ* in his estimates of the elasticities of these two schedules.

As in the spot market, the rate that will in practice exist in the forward market will come not from diagrams on paper but from the informal market of banks. The banks will be buying and selling forward contracts with borrowers and lenders, importers and exporters, and speculators. It is the job of the banks to collectively find the rate that will balance the speculators with the hedgers, that is, the rate $F_1^e(\$/\pounds)$, and in doing this, the banks are able to avoid taking a speculative position. The beauty of the workings of markets is that somehow they tend to achieve clearing prices, and the forward market is no exception.

Anybody considering a career in the foreign exchange market should note that reaching market clearing prices requires a frenetic level of activity. Foreign exchange markets are free markets, not only in terms of the free entry and exit of funds but in terms of foreign exchange traders as well.[11]

SUMMARY

1 There are a variety of actors in the forward exchange market. Besides borrowers, investors, and interest arbitragers, we find importers, exporters, and speculators. Speculators use the forward market to gain an exposed position in foreign exchange. The others do the reverse. They use the forward market to cover or hedge positions that would otherwise be exposed.

2 Importers can buy and exporters can sell forward foreign exchange to help avoid foreign exchange risk. The forward market gives the importer a way to shop around and compare prices in terms of his or her own currency.

3 The primary documents involved in importing and exporting are the letter of credit and the draft. Letters of credit are issued on behalf of buyers of goods (importers) and help the sellers (exporters) avoid the risk of not being paid.

4 Actual payment is effected by the draft (or bill of exchange). Drafts are either sight drafts or time drafts and can be accepted by the company or a bank. Those accepted by a bank are called banker's acceptances, and they can be traded in a well-established market.

5 Forward exchange contracts are not the only means available to importers and exporters for avoiding foreign exchange risk. When forward markets do not exist, perhaps because the delivery and settlement period is too long or because the currency is traded too thinly, importers and exporters can try to denominate their trade in their home currency. Of course, both sides cannot succeed. However, they can compromise with a mixed currency basket or currency cocktail denomination. Importers can avoid exchange risk by borrowing at home and investing abroad, and exporters can borrow abroad and invest at home. Exporters can buy their inputs in their export markets, and all traders can hope that business in a large number of currencies will leave them well diversified.

6 The Export-Import Bank guarantees obligations of U.S. banks made in connection with export sales. It also helps directly in financing export trade.

7 The Private Export Funding Corporation also helps finance trade. It works in conjunction with the Export-Import Bank.

8 Spot speculators compare the spot rate that they expect with the cost of buying or selling with *un*covered arbitrage. Forward speculators will buy forward when the spot price that

---

[11]The fact that speculators can choose the cheaper of spot and forward speculation can be shown to make the above conclusions dependent on a spread between the borrowing and lending rates facing arbitragers.

they expect exceeds the forward price, and they will sell forward when the forward price exceeds the spot price that they expect.

9 Any borrower or importer whose contract is denominated in foreign currency is a speculator if he or she does not buy forward, and so is an exporter or investor who does not sell forward.

10 The forward exchange rate is determined by all the actors collectively. In general, if each group of actors has limited access to funds, the forward exchange rate will be where neither interest arbitragers nor speculators are indifferent. Some profitable (but rather small) opportunities can remain. The forward rate is ultimately determined by banks.

QUESTIONS

1 Why is an importer who invoices in the foreign currency and does not buy the currency forward a speculator? Does this conform with most people's view of a speculator?

2 Suppose that you were importing small electric transformers, that delivery from all suppliers would take approximately 6 months, and that you faced the situation shown in the table below:

	United States	Canada	Great Britain	France	Germany
Local cost	$20,000	Can$22,000	£10,000	Fr82,000	DM38,000
$S\,(\$/j)$	1	0.84	2.00	0.20	0.50
$S^*_{1/2}\,(\$/j)$	1	0.82	2.05	0.19	0.52
$F_{1/2}\,(\$/j)$	1	0.83	2.02	0.21	0.54
$S_{1/2}\,(\$/j)$	1	0.80	2.00	0.23	0.51

a Where would you buy if you decided on forward hedging?

b Where would you buy if you decided on being unhedged (and you did not know $S_{1/2}(\$/j)$ for another 6 months)?

c If you were a speculator, in which currencies would you go long and in which would you go short?

d What is the profit/loss from your chosen speculations per million units of foreign exchange?

e Could we have $S^*_{1/2}(\$/j) \neq F_{1/2}(\$/j)$ as in the table? If so, give an intuitive explanation.

3 Assume that you are importing German transformers and that you face the following situation.

r_{US}	r_{GY}	$S\,(\$/DM)$	$F_{1/2}\,(\$/DM)$
12%	8%	0.5000	0.5100

a How would you hedge? Would you buy Deutsche marks forward, or would you buy spot and invest in Germany for 6 months?

b Would it make any difference if you currently had no funds but could borrow or invest at the above rates?

4 Why are letters of credit not used in domestic trade whereas banker's acceptances are used? Does it have to do with risk?

5* What would the forward exchange rate be in Figure 9.5 if there were no speculators? Could there be situations where $F_1(\$/£)$ is higher without speculators than with speculators and where $F_1(\$/£)$ is lower without speculators than with speculators?

6* Redraw Figure 9.5 to show the situation where interest arbitragers have unlimited funds available to them. Who will then determine the forward exchange rate?

7* Redraw Figure 9.5 to show the situation where ZZ is unchanged but speculators are prepared to risk unlimited funds when they perceive a speculative opportunity. Who will then determine the forward exchange rate?

8* What kind of argument concerning the level of speculative activity will make VV steeper as we move farther away from $S_1^*(\$/£)$? Do you think that a VV that becomes flatter farther away from $S_1(\$/£)$ makes good sense?

9 How would you rank the various means of hedging that are available to importers and exporters in terms of what should be tried first, second, and so on?

10* If the interest rates in the United States exceed those in Britain, where would you place the spot rate, $S(\$/£)$, on the vertical axis in Figure 9.5? What would the final position of speculators versus hedgers be if, in Figure 9.5, $S_1^*(\$/£) > \tilde{F}_1(\$/£)$?

BIBLIOGRAPHY

Adler, Michael, and Bernard Dumas: "Portfolio Choice and the Demand for Forward Exchange," *American Economic Review*, May 1976, pp. 332–339.

Back, Leonard A.: *Introduction to Commercial Letters of Credit*, Citibank, New York.

Grubel, Herbert G.: *Forward Exchange, Speculation and the International Flow of Capital*, Stanford University Press, Stanford, Calif., 1966.

Grubel, Herbert G.: *International Economics*, Richard D. Irwin, Homewood, Ill., 1977.

Harrington, J. A.: *Specifics on Commercial Letters of Credit and Bankers' Acceptances*, Scott Printing Corp., Jersey City, N.J., 1974.

Kennen, Peter B.: "Trade, Speculation and the Forward Exchange Rate," in R. E. Baldwin et al. (eds.), *Trade Growth and the Balance of Payments*, Rand McNally Inc., Chicago, 1965.

Letters of Credit, Books 2 and 3, The American Bankers' Association, Washington, D.C., 1968.

Levi, Maurice D.: "Underutilized Forward Markets or Rational Behavior?" *Journal of Finance*, September, 1979, pp. 1013–1017.

Shapiro, Alan C., and David P. Rutenberg: "Managing Exchange Risks in a Floating World," *Financial Management*, summer 1976, pp. 48–58.

Watson, Alasdair: *Finance of International Trade*, The Institute of Bankers, London, 1976.

APPENDIX: International Commercial and Financial Abbreviations[12]

COMMERCIAL ABBREVIATIONS

a.a.r.:	Against all risks (marine)
A/R:	All risks or against all risks (marine)
A.T.:	American terms
A/V:	Ad valorem

---

[12] Adapted from Leonard Back, *Introduction to Commercial Letters of Credit*, Citibank, New York.

B.E.:	Bill of exchange
B/L:	Bill of lading
B.M.:	Board measure
Carr. pd.:	Carriage paid
c. & f.:	Cost and freight
c.i.f.:	Cost, insurance, freight
c.i.f. & c.:	Cost, insurance, freight, and commission
c.i.f.c. & i.:	Cost, insurance, freight, commission, and interest
c.i.f.i. & e.:	Cost, insurance, freight, interest, and exchange
C/R:	Company's risk
D/O:	Delivery order
E. & O.E :	Errors and omissions excepted
Ex.:	Out of
f.a.b.:	Free on board (French/German/Spanish)
F.A.S.:	Free alongside
f.c.s.:	Free of capture and seizure
f.o.b.:	Free on board
f.o.d.:	Free of damage
f.o.r.:	Free on rails at point of destination
f.p.a.:	Free of particular average
F.P.A.A.C.:	Free of particular average (American conditions)
F.P.A.E.C.:	Free of particular average (English conditions)
G/A:	General average
Grs.T.:	Gross ton
H.M.C.:	Her Majesty's Customs
Kd:	Knocked down
l.t.:	Long ton
M.I.P.:	Marine insurance policy
n.o.p.:	Not otherwise provided for
N/B:	Mark well (*nota bene*)
O/R:	Owner's risk
o.r.b.:	Owner's risk of breakage
S/D:	Sight draft
S.D.B.L.:	Sight draft, bill of lading attached
S/N:	Shipping note
S.P.A.:	Subject to particular average
s.t.:	short ton

FINANCIAL ABBREVIATIONS

A/S:	After sight
A/S:	At sight
A/T:	American terms
B/E:	Bill of exchange
B/P:	Bills payable
B/R:	Bills receivable
C.W.O.:	Cash with order
D/N:	Debit note
D/S:	Days (after) sight
L/A:	Letter of authority
L/C:	Letter of credit
R/ A:	Refer to acceptor
R/D:	Refer to drawer
S/A:	Sociedad Anomina—corporation (Spanish/French/German)
S/D:	Sight draft
S.D.B.L.:	Sight draft, bill of lading attached
S/D D/P:	Sight draft documents against payment
W.B.:	Waybill
W/R:	Warehouse receipt

CHAPTER 10

MULTINATIONAL DIMENSIONS OF CASH MANAGEMENT

For most corporations, both the inflow and outflow of funds are frequently uncertain. It is therefore important for companies to maintain a certain degree of liquidity. The amount of liquidity, as well as form it should take, constitutes the topic of working cash (or working capital) management. Liquidity can take a number of forms, including coin and currency, bank deposits, overdraft facilities, and short-term readily marketable securities. These involve different degrees of opportunity cost, in terms of foregone earnings available on less liquid investments. However, there are such highly liquid short-term securities in sophisticated money markets that virtually no funds have to remain completely idle. There are investments with maturities that extend no further than "overnight" or the next day, and there are overdraft facilities which allow firms to hold minimal cash balances. This makes part of the cash management problem similar to the problem of where to borrow and invest.

The objectives of effective working capital management in an international environment are both to allocate short-term investments and cash balance holdings between countries to maximize overall corporate returns and to borrow in different money markets to achieve the minimum cost. These objectives are to be pursued under the conditions of maintaining the required liquidity and minimizing any risks that might be incurred. The problem of having numerous currency and country choices for investing and borrowing, which is the extra dimension of international finance, is shared by firms with local markets and firms with international markets for their product. For example, a firm that produces and sells only within the United States will still have an incentive to earn the highest yield, or borrow at the lowest cost, even if that means venturing abroad to Eurocurrency or foreign money markets. There *are* additional problems faced by firms that have a multinational orientation of production and sales. These include the question of local versus head office management of working capital and the forms of liquidity within different countries. We will examine these problems in this chapter. However, we should remember that most of the questions on where to hold funds and where to borrow in the international money markets are relevant for any profit-maximizing firm.

Money markets (where working cash balances are held and borrowed) are different from capital markets (where securities with maturities of more than 1 year are traded) because we can use forward cover in a money market to avoid foreign exchange risk. In Chapter 7 we saw how to avoid risk in the money market, choose the investment with the highest risk-free yield, and borrow at the lowest risk-free cost. We also saw that because firms the world over search for the highest yield or lowest cost, any advantage one country has over another for investing or borrowing tends to be eliminated, leaving yields and costs approximately equal in different countries. This follows from the interest parity theorem we presented in Chapter 7.

If the interest parity condition held precisely, there would be no problem of where to borrow or invest. Temporary surpluses, covered in the forward market, could be invested anywhere, and temporary shortages could be met by borrowing anywhere. However, as we saw in Chapter 7, the interest parity condition does not hold precisely. Indeed, the reasons for interest disparity are the same reasons why careful working capital management is important. We will briefly review these reasons and how they affect cash management.

INTEREST DISPARITY AND CASH MANAGEMENT

It might be thought that with covered interest disparity, a firm wishing to invest or borrow should compute the covered yields or costs and act accordingly. However, the covered interest disparity is unlikely to offer a significant opportunity after a firm considers the transaction costs, differential liquidities, and so on, that allow the disparity to persist.

When we explain what the reasons for disparity imply for cash management, we will also discuss money management techniques when there is no forward market in which to hedge exchange risk. We will see how borrowing and investing to create offsetting foreign exchange payables or receivables can reduce risk.

Absence of Forward Markets

In general, when there is no forward market or other means for covering net receivables or payables, if funds are received in a particular currency and there is an anticipated need for that currency in the near future, the funds should be invested locally. In that way the funds, when they are needed, will be in the correct currency. For example, if a firm with an operation in South Korea receives 2 million won (W2 million) in payment for sales from its subsidiary in South Korea and needs approximately this quantity of won to meet a payment in a month or two, the funds should be left in South Korea—if expected yields are not much higher elsewhere. When the expected yields are only a little higher in other countries, any extra yields from only temporarily converting out of won may not be sufficient to compensate for the transaction costs of conversion and for the risk that unanticipated changes may take place in exchange rates while funds are not held as won. We will remember, however, that if there *is* a forward market and we do not have any of the conditions required for interest disparity—transaction costs, tax and political risk effects, and so on—any extra yield will make the conversion worthwhile because foreign exchange risks are avoided.

We have already explained in the previous chapter that even where there is no forward market and payables are due in the future, it could be worthwhile to purchase the foreign currency immediately and hold it in a local liquid form in order to avoid the risk that it will cost more later when it is needed. This may be done even where there is a forward market, and the cost should be the same as long as interest parity holds. Similarly, when foreign currency receivables are due in the near future, it can be worthwhile to hedge against foreign currency risk by borrowing foreign currency to create an offsetting payable. When this is done, the borrowed funds are converted into the firm's home money at the known currency spot exchange rate. Later, when the foreign currency receivables come in, they are used immediately to settle what is owed from the borrowing. The exchange rate at the time of settlement is irrelevant, because the created payable on the foreign currency debt is just matched by the foreign currency receivables. Clearly, because some foreign currency receipts might already match payments in the same currency, only the difference, or *net* payables or receivables, will require some foreign borrowing or the immediate purchase of the foreign exchange. This is often easier said than done, since the offsetting of foreign currency payables and receivables is rarely precise, with amounts and their timing frequently unknown.

The Reasons for Interest Disparity

Transaction costs are an obvious reason to keep funds in the original currency rather than move them into some other currency. This reason will hold even when there is no foreign exchange risk. Transaction costs are the reason we gave in Chapter 8 for holding some Eurocurrency deposits. Money managers may try to avoid the costs of switching out of and back into the needed currency.

Political risk is a reason to keep funds in the company's home country rather than in the country in whose currency the funds are denominated. This is because the home jurisdiction is generally the most friendly one. The reduction in political risk that results from moving funds home must, of course, be balanced against the extra costs this entails when the funds must later be converted back into the foreign currency. Between most developed countries, the transaction costs of temporarily moving funds home are likely to exceed the reduction in political risk, and so cash balances should be maintained in the foreign countries. However, the political situation in some third world countries might be considered sufficiently volatile, and so only minimal working balances should be maintained in those countries.

Liquidity considerations argue in favor of keeping funds in the currency in which they are *most likely* to be needed in the future. This might not be the currency in which the funds arrive or the company's home currency. The liquidity factor is hence different from transaction costs, which imply that funds should be kept in the

TABLE 10.1
FACTORS AFFECTING WORKING CAPITAL MANAGEMENT

Factor	Implication
Absence of forward markets	Keep funds in the currency received if an anticipated future need exists.
Transaction costs	Keep funds in the currency received.
Political risk	Move funds to the domestic market.
Liquidity requirements	Keep funds where they will most likely be needed in the future.
Overdraft facilities	Allow minimum working balances.

currency in which they arrive, and it is also different from political risk, which implies that funds should be kept at home. We use the words "most likely" because it is the uncertainty of cash flows that is responsible for the need to maintain liquidity. If inflows and outflows were *perfectly* predictable, a firm could arrange the maturities of long-term securities so that each security matures at the precise time the funds are needed. Complete certainty would do away with the so-called transaction and precautionary needs for holding money balances; the "speculative motive" concerns only the maturity of the securities.[1] However, even with uncertainty in the timing and amounts of cash inflows and outflows, extremely liquid money market investments and overdraft facilities at banks have allowed firms to keep most of their funds in interest-bearing or money market instruments.

Taxes can be an extremely complex consideration in working capital management, as we showed in Chapter 7. However, for firms that are heavily involved in dealing in many countries, foreign exchange gains and interest earnings will face similar taxes. There is therefore little need to favor any particular market. The factors affecting the location of working capital are summarized in Table 10.1.

MULTINATIONALS AND WORKING CAPITAL MANAGEMENT

We have stated that most working capital does not remain idle; it is invested in liquid instruments that earn interest, and only a limited amount remains in zero-interest bank deposits. The potential gain from using the liquid instruments of other

[1] The transaction, precautionary, and speculative motives are common categories within the theory of money demand. The transaction motive is related to normal company turnover and exists to reduce the transaction costs of buying and selling securities to meet ongoing needs. The precautionary motive involves holding money to help ensure that uncertain expenses are covered. Clearly, if all flows are certain, transaction motive needs are met with planned maturities and without having to sell securities, and the precautionary motive does not exist. The speculative motive involves holding "cash" if interest rates are expected to rise, that is, if security prices are expected to fall, but since some interest is better than none, speculation should merely involve shortening the maturities of investments to maintain lower risk. For more on the motives for holding money, see Rudiger Dornbusch and Stanley Fischer, *Macroeconomics*, 2d ed., McGraw-Hill Book Company, New York, 1981, or Robert Gordon, *Macroeconomics*, Little Brown and Company, Boston, 1979.

countries when yield advantages more than cover additional costs, risk, illiquidity, and perhaps taxes is not limited to multinational firms. Nor is the ability to borrow short-term funds abroad. A multinational firm which has operations in a number of countries might find it easier to take advantage of international opportunities than would a strictly domestic firm, but this is likely to be as much a function of size as of multinational character. This means that our foregoing presentation is relevant for any firm.

There are problems concerning working capital management in the international arena that are unique to multinationals. These problems have to do with the *need* to simultaneously manage cash flows in numerous currencies as opposed to a *desire* to move funds into or out of different currencies to maximize profits. In addition to dealing with the need to manage funds in numerous currencies, the multinational faces problems in allocating interdivisional costs and revenues between different parts of its operations. This gives rise to international dimensions of transfer pricing that are far more complex than those faced by firms with purely local operations. The problems resulting from the need to simultaneously manage cash balances in different currencies should be considered separately from the problems in setting interdivisional transfer prices.

MANAGING MULTIPLE CASH BALANCE POSITIONS

The multinational faces uncertain inflows and outflows of funds within its different countries of operation. If there were no transaction costs, illiquidities, or unavoidable political and foreign exchange risks, liquid balances could be concentrated within a limited number of financial centers and then moved to where they were needed. The opportunities for this are generally limited by the costs, illiquidity, and risks, and as a result, liquid balances must be held in each currency of operation. There are various forms in which liquid balances can be held, ranging from bank notes and coin to marketable money market securities, but not every country offers the same choices for allocating cash. Some general factors which affect the composition of working capital include the types of financial instruments available and the advantages of centralized cash management.

Available Securities and Banking Efficiency

We have already noted that in those countries where overdraft facilities are available in the banks, there will be very little need for liquidity that does not earn interest. The countries with overdraft facilities tend also to be the countries which have a choice of money market sources and uses of funds. Because of overdraft facilities and profitable investment opportunities, a multinational should keep a high fraction of its total liquidity in financial securities in countries with developed money markets. This partly explains why multinationals maintain their liquidity in places such as New York, Toronto, London, Frankfurt, Zurich, Sydney, Paris, Hong Kong, Singapore, and Tokyo and keep much lower balances in smaller financial centers. Since the leading currencies are often accepted outside the home countries—dollars being used extensively outside the United States and pounds outside Britain—it is frequently possible to avoid holding the rarer currencies and to make *all* payments in the well-known currencies. This allows multinationals to concentrate working capital in a couple of centers. With Eurocurrency bank deposits and multinational banks, payments can be effected quickly via local banks, even if outside rather than local currencies are used. For example, a British-based multinational which banks with Chase Manhattan can pay a Belgian supplier in U.S. dollars by writing, in London, a U.S.-dollar-denominated check. The check can be cashed quickly at Chase Manhattan in Brussels.

In deciding on how much working capital to hold in countries without developed financial centers, a firm should take into account the delays in converting funds into the local currency, as well as any potential restrictions on re-exchanging these funds. As we stated earlier, the exchange of major currencies is generally completed within 2 business days, but it can take longer to move funds into rarer currencies. If an important payment is due, especially if it is to a foreign government for taxes or to a local supplier of a crucial input, excess cash balances should be held, even if these mean opportunity costs in terms of higher interest earnings available elsewhere. When the cash needs in local currencies are known well ahead of time, arrangements can be made in advance for receiving the needed currency, but substantial allowances for potential delay should be made. When one is used to dealing in North America, Europe, and other developed areas, it is too easy to believe that banking is efficient everywhere, but the delays that can be faced in banks in, for example, the Middle East and Africa can be exceedingly long, uncertain, and costly.

It is useful for a firm to denominate as many payments and receipts as its counterparties will allow in units of a major currency and to have bills payable in major financial centers, where the banking and money markets are more predictable. This means that the multinational should keep bank accounts and perhaps a small office in a number of centers even if it has no primary business in those centers. Contracts for payment due to the multinational should stipulate not only the payment date and the currency in which payment is to be made but also the branch or office at which the payment is due. Penalties for late payment can help ensure that payments are made on time. The speed of collection of payments can be increased by using post office box numbers whenever they are available. Similarly, if a firm banks with a large-scale multinational bank, it can stipulate that payment should be made at a foreign branch of the bank. The head office accounts will be credited quickly.

There can be an element of speculation in working capital management, with an incentive to keep the minimum amount of cash in what are generally believed to be depreciating currencies. However, when interest is being earned on working capital, these currencies tend to offer compensating high interest rates, according to the interest parity theorem, and so it is appropriate to reduce holdings of depreciating currencies only if compensation is viewed as insufficient.

In forming and utilizing cash budgeting plans, an important component involves the decision on how much centralization or "pooling" is advisable. Centralization is achieved by keeping funds in a major-currency financial center. The funds are ready for movement to where funds are needed. Centralization can also be achieved by persuading counterparties, when possible, to make payments and accept receipts in one of the major currencies. We should look at the advantages of centralized cash management and how it can be done.

Advantages of Centralized Cash Management

By keeping cash in a central location and in a limited number of leading currencies, a multinational can keep cash holdings to a minimum. Working capital can be moved to where it is needed rather than left idle in each separate country. If cash is centralized in a major-currency center, the money markets can be used for the surplus cash balances. The limits set by uncertainties and delays in moving funds to where they are needed require that some balances be maintained everywhere, but the more centralized the holdings, the lower the opportunity costs. Cash budgeting will help in determining the appropriate local balances and the timing of conversions to meet needed payments.

The primary advantage of centralized working capital management is that it reduces the variance of total cash needs. This is because cash surpluses and deficiencies in different locations do not move in a perfectly parallel fashion. As a result, the variance of total cash flows is smaller than the sum of the variances of flows for individual countries. For example, when there are large cash balance outflows in Belgium, it is not likely that there will also be unusually large outflows in Britain, the United States, France, Holland, Germany, and so on. If a firm is to have sufficient amounts in each individual country, it must maintain a large reserve in each. However, if the total cash needs are pooled in, for example, the United States, then when the need in Belgium is unusually high, it can be met from the central pool because there will not be unusually high drains in other countries at the same time. We should note that it is not a question of pooling the *currencies* in, for example, U.S. dollars, since deposits denominated in different currencies can be held by the head office in the form of local Eurocurrencies, or they can be allocated elsewhere. Instead, it is a question of centralizing the *management* of funds. We should also note that the conclusion that centralization reduces cash needs follows from the fact that the needs of individual countries are imperfectly correlated. This will be shown later in the context of imports and exports.

Centralized management of working capital offers advantages in addition to the reduction in total cash needs. If the centralized management can take a broad view of international money markets—a view that local individual management might not be able to take—it can select the best yields or the lowest cost of borrowed funds. In addition, to the extent that some foreign exchange transaction costs reveal returns to scale, it helps to deal with larger sums rather than have each separate division of the multinational exchanging small amounts of funds at a high cost per dollar exchanged. However, probably more important than any of these is the fact that the multinational corporation can avoid funds transfer costs if it uses transfer pricing or if it offsets company settlements. We will leave transfer pricing until the end of the chapter and deal first with the offsetting of company settlements, which is known as *netting*.

Netting Payments

Netting can be a purely intracompany operation, or it can involve settlements between the company and other companies. Here is an example of potential intracompany netting. Suppose that the U.S. operation of Aviva Corporation has sold £8 million worth of jeans to its British sales subsidiary and has purchased £10 million worth of denim cloth from a British denim-manufacturing subsidiary. Settlement with both subsidiaries is required on the same date. It would be advantageous in this situation to net the payable of £8 million against the receipt of £10 million and to purchase only the balance of £2 million. The £8 million owed by the British sales subsidiary to the head office would not have to be converted, with the consequent transaction costs, into dollars; instead, it could be applied with the purchased £2 million directly to pay the British denim-manufacturing subsidiary. If netting were not done, £8 million would have to be sold for dollars, £10 million would have to be bought with dollars, and transaction costs would be incurred on the full £18 million. When netting involves outsiders, the idea is to purchase or sell only the net amounts of currencies the entire corporation needs or has in excess.

The period of time over which netting is done is closely tied to the question of whether to leave funds in the original currency or temporarily move them into another currency. For example, a company which expects to receive pounds on March 10 and must pay the same amount of pounds on March 24 might net these amounts and hold the pounds at interest rather than convert them into dollars and then back into pounds. If interest parity holds, nothing will be lost. If, however, the receivables and payables of pounds are separated by 2 months, the company might not net them; instead, it might convert these pounds into dollars. To avoid foreign exchange risk, the company would have to sell the receivables and buy the payables forward, and this involves transaction costs. We shall see later in this chapter some examples of the "cycle" or time period over which netting can be done.

Netting with Leading and Lagging

Leading and lagging are required when the payments and receipts are not for the same date. If, for example, the payment of £10 million to the denim-manufacturing subsidiary was due on April 10 and the British pound receipts for jeans supplied to the British sales subsidiary were due to be received on March 10, it would be advantageous to "lag" payment by the sales subsidiary, that is, delay it by a month. Alternatively, if receipts from the sales subsidiary were due on May 10, it could be advantageous to "lead" the sales subsidiary payment, that is, move it forward a month. While the gains from netting with the increased flexibility of leading and lagging are obvious, the practice of such a scheme can be difficult. Netting requires a well-managed international information network with a "currency center" into which all information on foreign payments and receipts flows.

We can illustrate potential methods for the netting of foreign exchange receipts and payments within the multinational enterprise by examining two actual cash management systems that have been in effect. Centralized working capital systems have been very carefully designed by Digital Equipment and International Harvester.

Digital Equipment Itself an advanced information processing company, Digital Equipment centralizes its cash management in two "currency centers."[2] The cash positions of European subsidiaries are monitored and managed from the European headquarters in Geneva. Cash management for other subsidiaries is handled by the company's principal headquarters, which is in Acton, Massachusetts. The subsidiaries and appropriate headquarters communicate via telex, and the movement of cash is facilitated by the use of a limited number of U.S. banks with offices in many countries. The cash management system works as shown in Figure 10.1.

Foreign exchange positions are established and adjusted on a weekly basis. Every Thursday, all subsidiaries send a report to the currency center at their headquarters. In their statements they give projected cash inflows and outflows in each foreign currency for the following week. They also give their bank account positions. The foreign sales subsidiaries are generally net receivers of foreign exchange. On the following Monday the subsidiary borrows its anticipated net cash inflow via an overdraft facility and transfers the funds to the headquarters' account at the same bank. For example, if the British sales subsidiary expects net receipts of £10 million and has no bank balance, it will call its banks for the best exchange rate. If the most favorable rate for buying dollars is $S(\$/£) = 2.0$, it will transfer $20 million to the Geneva currency center by borrowing £10 million and converting it into dollars. The selected bank—the one which offered the best rate on dollars—will debit the British subsidiary's account in London by £10 million and, on the same day, credit the Geneva headquarters' account with $20 million. The British subsidiary will pay the £10 million debt due to the overdraft as the receipts come in.

In order to ensure that it is able to make the same-day transfers and obtain the overdrafts, Digital maintains close ties with a limited number of multinational U.S. banks. The subsidiaries obtain funds only via overdrafts; they do not use other means of borrowing funds. Subsidiaries that are net users of foreign exchange instead of net receivers use the reverse procedure. The subsidiary reports its need for cash to the appropriate headquarters on Thursday, and beginning on the following Monday it uses overdraft lines as payments are met. On the following Friday the

[2] An excellent account of Digital Equipment's centralized cash management system can be found in "How Digital Equipment's Weekly Cash Cycle Mobilizes Idle Funds," *Money Report*, Business International, Jan. 30, 1981. A system that is similar to the Digital Equipment system and that uses a currency center in London is operated by RCA. The company adapted a system available from Citibank for large clients which keeps track of currency needs and netting. For a full account, see "Standard Netting System Remodelled to Suit RCA's Own Needs," *Money Report*, Business International, July 13, 1979. Chase Manhattan's system is known as Infocash, and the netting and information system available from the international financial advisory firm Business International in known as Xmis.

FIGURE 10.1
Digital Equipment's weekly cash cycle.

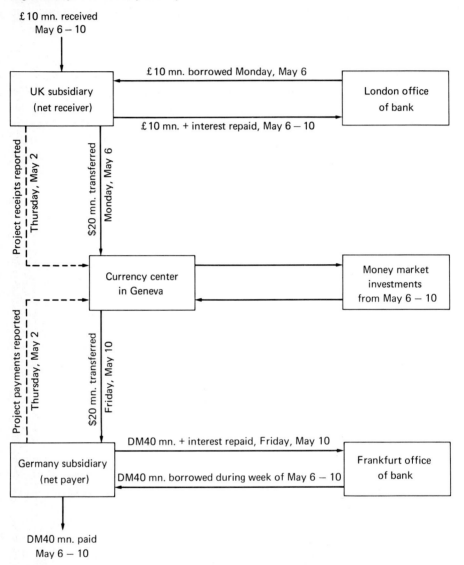

We will assume that the U.K. subsidiary is a net receiver of pounds and that the German subsidiary is a net payer of Deutsche marks. Both subsidiaries send their cash flow projections to the currency center on Thursday, May 2. On the following Monday the U.K. subsidiary borrows its expected cash needs and then transfers the dollar equivalent to Geneva. [It is assumed that S ($/£) = 2.0.] The debt is repaid in the currency of borrowing during the week of May 6–10. The German subsidiary borrows marks during the week of May 5–10 as its payments fall due. On Friday, May 10, the Geneva currency center transfers the dollar equivalent to the subsidiary. [Again it is assumed that S ($/£) = 2.0.] This is used to repay the overdraft on that day. During the week the currency center has $20 million to invest in the money market.

subsidiary receives funds from the parent company to pay off the overdraft and make up for any unanticipated disbursements that have been made.

There are occasions when a subsidiary will receive more funds than it anticipated and transfer them to headquarters more than once a week. Alternatively, a subsidiary may face unprojected disbursements or late receipts. It will then use backup overdrafts. Similarly, a subsidiary may face unusually large payments. It will have to telex its parent for extra funds. Digital uses post-office lock boxes in Canada and the United States in order to speed up the handling of receivables, and in Europe, Digital instructs customers to pay its bank directly rather than the local subsidiary itself. All investing or borrowing in currencies other than the U.S. dollar is hedged on the forward market to avoid foreign exchange risk.

Because the amount of cash handled by the two headquarters is so large, it can generally be invested more favorably than if each separate subsidiary placed it. Funds are invested in various money markets, including Eurodollars and dollar time deposits in the United States. The parent has the total amount of funds from its many subsidiaries to invest for a full week. A subsidiary will, however, repay the overdraft *during* the week. It follows that the interest costs on overdrafts are not as large as the interest earnings of the headquarters.

The major advantage of Digital Equipment's system is that there is no foreign exchange exposure for the subsidiary. This is because the payable on the overdraft is in the local currency, as is the receivable against which the funds have been borrowed. Local currency is paid out as it arrives. An additional advantage is that the currency centers handle large amounts of cash and can therefore get lower spreads when buying and selling foreign exchange. They can also take a broader perspective of investment and borrowing opportunities and consider the company's overall financial situation.

International Harvester   International Harvester (IH) is a leading U.S. multinational manufacturer of transportation and farm machinery with substantial sales outside the United States. The company has had a system of netting in effect since 1969 that includes many of its subsidiaries.[3]

The netting system is based on IH's currency clearing center, located in a finance company that IH owns in Switzerland. Prior to clearing IH's foreign exchange, the Swiss finance company had been responsible for Eurocurrency financing, investment, and other transactions involving foreign currencies. The netting scheme works on a monthly cycle, as illustrated in Figure 10.2. By the 15th day of each month, all the participating subsidiaries have sent information to the currency clearing center on payables and receivables existing at that time in local currencies. The clearing center converts all amounts into dollar terms at the current spot exchange rate and sends information to those subsidiaries with net payables on how much they owe and to whom. These paying subsidiaries are responsible for informing the net receivers of funds and for obtaining and delivering the foreign

---

[3]For a full account of International Harvester's scheme, see "Multilateral Netting System Cuts Costs, Provides Flexibility for International Harvester," *Money Report*, Business International, Dec. 20, 1979.

FIGURE 10.2
Example of International Harvester's foreign exchange netting system.

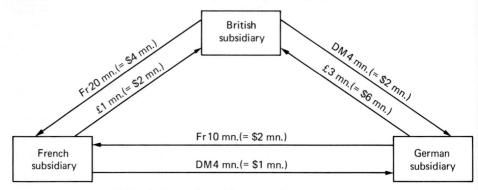

(*a*) Receivables and payables reported to currency center
before the 15th of month.

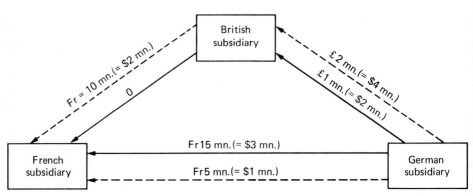

(*b*) Net payables/receivables (broken lines) and actual cash flows
(solid lines) made on the 25th of the month.

In this example it is assumed that on the 15th of the month $S\,(\text{DM}/\$) = 2.0$, $S\,(£/\$) = 0.5$, and $S\,(\text{Fr}/\$) = 5.0$. Information on receivables and payables is provided for the Swiss currency center on or before the 15th of the month. The currency center converts the amounts of foreign exchange into dollars at the going exchange rate (as shown in part *a*) and the net amounts owed between subsidiaries (as shown by the broken lines in part *b*). Rather than having the German subsidiary pay the British subsidiary the equivalent of $4 million while the British subsidiary in turn pays the French subsidiary $2 million, the German subsidiary will be instructed to add $2 million onto what it pays the French subsidiary and to reduce what it pays the British subsidiary by this amount. The British and French subsidiaries will receive no instructions to pay anybody. The total number of transactions will be reduced from six to only two. Transaction costs will be faced on only $5 million worth of transactions.

exchange. Settlement is on the 25th of the month or the closest business day, and the funds are purchased 2 days in advance so that they are received on the designated day. Any difference between the exchange rate used by the Swiss center on the 15th and the rate prevailing for settlement on the 25th gives rise to foreign exchange gains or losses, and these are attributed to the subsidiary.

The original clearing system was for intracompany use and did not include outside firms. After a decade with this system, IH introduced a scheme for foreign exchange settlements for payments to outsiders. There are two different dates, the 10th and the 25th or the nearest business day, on which all foreign exchange is purchased by and transferred from the Swiss center. The payment needs are telexed to the center from the subsidiary more than 2 days before the settlement date, and the center nets the amounts of each currency so as to make the minimum number of foreign exchange transactions. The subsidiary which owes the foreign exchange settles with the clearing center by the appropriate settlement date. According to the company, netting can cut the total number of transactions with outsiders in half, saving the company transaction costs.

More flexibility is given to International Harvester's cash management system by the use of interdivisional leading and lagging. If, for example, a subsidiary is a net payer, it may delay or lag payment for up to 2 months while compensating the net receiver at prevailing interest rates. Net receivers of funds may at their discretion make funds available to other subsidiaries at interest. In this way the need to resort to outside borrowing is reduced; the Swiss clearing center serves to bring different parties together. The netting with leading and lagging has allowed the company to eliminate intracompany floats and reduce by over 80 percent the amount that otherwise would have been transferred.[4]

There are obvious advantages to leading and lagging, particularly in moving profits between subsidiaries and over time to reduce total taxes. As a result, a number of countries have limits on leading and lagging, as shown in Table 10.2.

An alternative to the currency center is the "reinvoicing center." The reinvoicing center buys foreign currency accounts receivable for the local currencies of subsidiaries. The exchange rate used is an intracompany rate that is changed only infrequently, and so subsidiaries are isolated from foreign exchange risk. The problem is that many governments are concerned that multinationals will use internal exchange rates to artificially shift profits and thereby reduce taxes. As a result of government regulations and other accounting difficulties, reinvoicing centers are not common.

Natural Hedging

A netting system allows the currency center to compute the multinational's overall payables and receivables in each currency. When these are known, and intracompany settlement has taken place, the currency center must decide on whether overall corporate payables or receivables should be hedged via the forward market

---

[4]For a general account of the benefits of netting, see "Parent-Based Multicurrency Centers Provide Flexibility, Savings, in Managing Risks," *Money Report*, Business International, Feb. 20, 1981.

TABLE 10.2
LIMITS ON LEADS, LAGS, AND NETTING IN SELECTED COUNTRIES

Country	Export lag	Export lead	Import lag	Import lead	Netting
Argentina	360 days/no limit	360 days/no limit	Allowed—no limit	Allowed—no limit	Not allowed
Australia	180 days	30 days	180 days	30 days	Permission required
Belgium	180 days	90 days	180 days	30 days	Permission required
Brazil	Not allowed	Allowed—no limit	180 days	Not allowed	Not allowed
Canada	Allowed—no limit	Allowed—no limit	Allowed—no limit	Allowed—no limit	Allowed
Denmark	30 days	Allowed—no limit	Allowed—no limit	30 days	Allowed
France	180 days	Allowed—no limit	Allowed—no limit	Permission required	Permission required, yet hard to get
Germany	Allowed—no limit	Allowed—no limit	Allowed—no limit	Allowed—no limit	Allowed
Ireland	180 days	Allowed—no limit	Allowed—no limit	Not allowed	Permission required, but readily available
Italy	120 days	360 days	360 days	120 days	Not allowed
Japan	180 days	360 days	180 days	360 days	Not allowed
Korea	Allowed	180 days	180 days	Permission required, rarely given	Allowed
Malaysia	180 days	180 days	Allowed—no limit	Allowed—no limit	Allowed
Mexico	Allowed—no limit	Allowed—no limit	Allowed—no limit	Allowed—no limit	Allowed
Netherlands	Allowed—no limit	Allowed—no limit	Allowed—no limit	Allowed—no limit	Allowed
New Zealand	180 days	Allowed—no limit	Allowed—no limit	Not allowed	Permission required
Norway	Allowed—no limit	Allowed—no limit	Allowed—no limit	Allowed—no limit	Permission required
Pakistan	120 days	Allowed—no limit	Not allowed	Not allowed	Not allowed
Philippines	60 days	Allowed—no limit	90 days	Not allowed	Permission required
Singapore	Allowed—no limit	Allowed—no limit	Allowed—no limit	Allowed—no limit	Allowed
South Africa	360 days	Allowed—no limit	Allowed—no limit	Not allowed	Permission required
Spain	30 days	Allowed—no limit	90 days	90 days	Permission required, yet hard to get
Sweden	Allowed	Allowed	Allowed	Permission required	Permission required
Switzerland	Allowed—no limit	Allowed—no limit	Allowed—no limit	Allowed—no limit	Allowed
Taiwan	Allowed—no limit	Allowed—no limit	Allowed—no limit	Allowed—no limit	Allowed
United Kingdom	Allowed—no limit	Allowed—no limit	Allowed—no limit	Allowed—no limit	Allowed
United States	Allowed—no limit	Allowed—no limit	Allowed—no limit	Allowed—no limit	Allowed
Venezuela	Allowed—no limit	Allowed—no limit	Allowed—no limit	Allowed—no limit	Allowed

254

or via investing and borrowing. On the average, the multinational will do about as well by hedging as by not hedging, since forward exchange rates on the average do not differ substantially from eventually realized spot rates.[5] Of course, if there is no hedging, corporate performance will vary according to exchange rates, and many companies prefer to avoid this risk. However, the overall corporate risk from not explicitly hedging is, for two reasons, smaller than might appear from the variability of the individual foreign exchange receivables and payables.

First, a multinational will benefit from the statistical fact that the variance of a sum is smaller than the sum of individual variances. This is true even if the individual values are uncorrelated. Second, the presence of common comovements between certain currencies can add to the reduction in overall variance. This is different from netting, which involves the canceling of amounts of the same currency. We can show how natural hedging occurs from trading in many currencies by taking a straightforward example (see below) or by using some standard statistical results (see the appendix for this chapter).

An Example

Suppose that in its foreign operations, Aviva buys its cloth in France and sells its finished garmets in both France and Germany in the amounts shown below.

	Germany (DM)	France (Fr)
Denim purchase	0	8,000,000
Jeans sales	2,000,000	3,000,000

The timing of payments for French denim and the timing of sales of jeans are the same. Alternatively, we could think of the revenue from the export of jeans as receipts from foreign investments and the payment for imports of cloth as repayment on a debt.

One route open to Aviva is to sell forward DM2 million and buy forward Fr5 million. Aviva would then be covered against exchange rate risk. An alternative, however, is to consider how the French franc and the Deutsche mark move vis-à-vis the dollar and hence between themselves. Let us suppose, simply to reveal the possibilities, that because of the close economic association between France and Germany, when the Deutsche mark appreciates vis-à-vis the dollar, frequently the French franc does so also. In other words, let us suppose that the mark and the franc are positively correlated.

With net frame payables of Fr5 million, mark receivables of DM2 million, and spot exchange rates of, for example, $S(\$/DM) = 0.5$ and $S(\$/Fr) = 0.2$, the payables and receivables cancel out. The payable to France is $1 million at current

[5] On this see Dennis E. Logue and George S. Oldfield, "Managing Foreign Assets When Foreign Exchange Markets Are Efficient," *Financial Management*, vol. 6, summer 1977, pp. 16–22. Even the risk from changes in exchange rates can be diversified by shareholders, who will therefore pay no more for shares of companies which hedge.

rates, which is the same as the receivable from Germany. The risk is that exchange rates can change before payments are made and receipts are received. But what if both the franc and the mark move more or less together and the exchange rates become, for example, $S(\$/DM) = 0.55$ and $S(\$/Fr) = 0.22$? Then payments to France will be $1,100,000, and receipts from Germany will also be $1,100,000. What will be lost in extra payments to France will be gained in extra revenue from Germany. We find in this case that Aviva is quite naturally unexposed if it can be sure that the currencies will always move together vis-à-vis the dollar.[6]

In our example, we have, of course, selected very convenient circumstances and values. In general, however, there is safety in large numbers. If there are *receivables* in many different currencies, then when some go up in value, others will come down. There will be some canceling of gains and losses. Similarly, if there are many *payables*, they can also cancel. Moreover, as in our example, receivables and payables can offset each other if currency values move together. There are many possibilities that are not obvious, but it should be remembered that although some canceling of gains and losses might occur, some risk will remain. There is no certainty about how currency values will move vis-à-vis each other and no guarantee whatsoever that receivables and payables will come close to canceling. A firm should use forward contracts or some other form of hedging if it wishes to avoid all foreign exchange risk. But the firm with a large variety of small volumes of payables and receivables (that is, small volumes in many different currencies) might consider that all the transaction costs involved in the alternative forms of hedging are not worthwhile vis-à-vis the natural hedging from diversification.

Before we began describing the management of multiple cash positions by the multinational, we mentioned that the multinational corporation faces an internal problem of allocating receipts and costs as well as the problem of managing the flows of cash. The allocation problem requires the application of transfer prices, which is our next topic.

TRANSFER PRICING FOR MULTINATIONAL FIRMS

A *transfer price* is an internally used price; it is the price that a firm charges when goods or services are transferred from one corporate division or subsidiary to another. The transfer prices that are used influence the allocation of total corporate book profits. In a firm with purely domestic operations, the currency denomination of transfer prices does not matter. In the multinational firm, transfer prices must take into account the exchange rates to be applied to local prices. However, when goods or services are moved between divisions of a multinational, the foreign exchange gains and losses from movements in exchange rates offset each other, and

---

[6]If two different currencies move in opposite directions vis-à-vis the dollar, then natural hedging will exist with payables in both currencies or with receivables in both currencies rather than with offsetting payables and receivables in the two currencies. We can note that positive comovement of exchange rates vis-a-vis the dollar will be very common. It will occur, for example, with the European currencies, which have fixed exchange rates between themselves. Because of this, when the mark is gaining vis-à-vis the dollar, generally the franc will also be gaining, as in our example. Negative comovement is much more difficult to rationalize, and so it is excluded from the text.

so exchange risk considerations can be small for the overall operation. This means that the foreign exchange risks faced by the multinational firm are less than those faced by a firm that must meet actual rather than transfer prices in international business.

Transfer pricing, which requires only book entries, will make foreign exchange transaction costs lower than the transaction costs faced with actual payments, since it requires only netting—at the appropriate transfer prices. In addition, the size of the book entries for specific items that are transferred have important implications for overall corporate profitability. The ways that transfer prices can affect overall profits are not directly relevant to the cash management decision; instead, they are relevant for the allocation of income, for lowering tariffs and income volatility for the identification of profit centers and for taxes. Other transfer pricing considerations are more relevant for the capital budgeting decision described in Chapter 15. However, we will present an overview of the many facets of transfer pricing in this chapter so as to provide a unified treatment of the topic.

Strategic Considerations in Transfer Pricing

The repatriation of profits by a multinational firm from its overseas operations can be a politically sensitive problem. It is important that host governments do not consider the profit rate as being too high, or else the multinational is likely to face accusations of price gouging and lose favor with foreign governments. In order to give an appearance of repatriating a lower profit without reducing the actual profit brought home, the multinational can use transfer prices. It can set high transfer prices on what is supplied to a foreign division by the head office or by divisions in environments that are politically less sensitive. For example, it can extract high payments for parts supplied by other divisions or for general overheads. Alternatively, the multinational can lower the transfer prices of products which the foreign division sells to the head office or to other divisions. These methods of reducing foreign profits while repatriating income are particularly advantageous when foreign reinvestment opportunities are limited. It is a good idea to itemize all transfers between countries so as to make it clear to foreign host governments that not all flows are profits.

Transfer pricing to reduce overall corporate taxes can be advantageous. The multinational has an incentive to shuffle its income to keep profits low in high-tax countries and to keep profits relatively high in low-tax countries. There are complications if within a country there are different tax rates on retained versus repatriated income. The gains from profit shuffling via transfer prices are limited by the legal powers of the Internal Revenue Service, and of taxing authorities in some other countries, to reallocate income if it is determined that transfer prices have distorted profits.

The multinational firm is likely to be in a better position to avoid foreign exchange losses than a firm with only local operations. There have been times, especially under fixed exchange rates in the period before 1972, when the devaluation of certain currencies and the revaluation of others were imminent.

Because of extensive involvement by central banks, the interest rate differential between countries did not always reflect the anticipated changes in exchange rates, and so compensation was not offered for expected exchange movements. There were incentives for all corporations to reduce their holdings of the currencies which faced devaluation. However, an attempt to move from these currencies was viewed as unpatriotic when undertaken by domestic firms and as unfair profiteering when undertaken by multinationals. As a result considerable constraints were placed on moving funds in overt ways, but multinationals were in a better position than their domestic counterparts to internally move funds.

Transfer prices can be used to reduce import tariffs and to avoid quotas. When tariffs on imports are based on values of transactions, the value of goods moving between divisions can be artificially reduced by keeping down the transfer prices. This puts the multinational at an advantage over domestic firms. Similarly, when quotas are based on values of trade, the multinational can keep down prices to maintain the volume. Again the multinational has an advantage over domestic counterparts, but import authorities frequently adopt their own "value for duty" on goods entering trade to help prevent revenues from being lost through the manipulation of transfer prices.

Large variations in profits can be a concern to shareholders. In order to keep local shareholders happy, fluctuations in profits can be reduced via transfer prices. By raising the prices of goods and services supplied to foreign operations or lowering prices on the sales of foreign operations, unusually high profits can be brought down so that subsequent falls in profits are reduced.

Practical Considerations in Transfer Pricing

Transfer prices can be used to "window-dress" the profits of certain divisions of a multinational so as to reduce borrowing costs. The gains from having seemingly large profits by paying a subsidiary high transfer prices for its product must, of course, be balanced against the potential scorn of foreign host governments, higher taxes or tariffs that might result, and so on.

For the long-term survival of a multinational, it is important that interdivisional profitability be measured accurately. The record of profitability of different divisions is valuable in allocating overall spending on capital projects and in sharing other corporate resources. In order to discover the correct profitability, the firm should be sure that interdivisional transfer prices are the prices that would have been paid had the transactions been with independent companies—"arms-length prices." This can be particularly difficult in the international allocation of such items as research and consulting services or headquarters overheads; there is rarely a market price for research or other services of corporate headquarters. Profit allocation will usually be according to the distribution of corporate sales, with the sales valued at the "correct" exchange rate. The advantages of preventing distortions in transfer prices must be balanced against the potential gains from using distorted transfer prices to reduce tariffs, taxes, political risks, and exchange losses. This balance can be a difficult problem for multinational corporations.

SUMMARY

1 When overdrafts and extremely liquid financial instruments are available, working capital management in an international environment involves choosing between the financial securities of different countries. The objective is to maximize yields on temporary surpluses while maintaining desired liquidity or to minimize borrowing costs when funds are insufficient.

2 Where there are no forward markets, foreign exchange risk is reduced by keeping funds in currencies that will later be needed. With no forward markets and no funds already in the currencies that will be needed later, foreign exchange risk is reduced by investing in these currencies early on. Similarly, when funds are due to be received in a particular currency and there is no way to sell them forward, risk is reduced by borrowing in that currency to create an offsetting or matching payable. The borrowed funds are converted at the going spot rate, and the debt is repaid with the receivable.

3 Transaction costs must be considered in moving funds for the maximum yield or minimum cost. They can make it advisable to keep funds where they will be needed later.

4 Political risks can provide an incentive to keep funds at home. The extra exchange transaction costs that are met on liquidating foreign securities are a reason for keeping working capital in the currencies in which it is most likely to be needed.

5 Everything else being equal, working capital balances should be minimal in countries with no overdraft facilities or money markets. Because there are transaction costs, political risks, currency conversion delays, and restrictions on moving funds, some working capital should be held in each country of operation.

6 Cash budgeting can reduce the uncertainties in money inflows and outflows as well as the required cushion of working capital balances. Another reduction in overall cash needs comes from the centralized pooling of cash, because the unanticipated cash flows from subsidiaries in different countries tend to be offsetting.

7 Cash management problems are reduced if foreign sales, purchases, investments, and borrowings are denominated in a major currency. This can be achieved in many small countries which are used to using outside currencies, and it allows working capital to be maintained in a major financial center with a well-developed money market.

8 The netting of payments and receipts of different subsidiaries in different currencies is a highly rewarding activity in reducing transaction costs. When leading and lagging payments and receipts are also practised, the gains are even larger.

9 A currency center is a facility for computing net positions in different currencies and distributing information.

10 A reinvoicing center buys foreign currency receivables from subsidiaries at exchange rates that are changed only infrequently. There are tricky tax and legal problems in setting up a reinvoicing center.

11 Natural hedging occurs when there are payables and receivables in many different currencies. It occurs both because variances of sums are smaller than sums of individual variances and because there are correlations between certain exchange rates.

12 Transfer prices lower foreign exchange risks and external transaction costs. They can be used to reduce political risks, taxes, foreign exchange losses, tariffs, quotas, and shareholder frustration resulting from fluctuating profits. Offsetting the gains from distorting transfer prices are the losses from losing information on divisional profitability unless different sets of transfer prices are established for internal versus external use—a questionable and unethical practice.

QUESTIONS

1 If yields, on an annual basis, are similar on securities of all maturities, from 1 day to 20 years, does the firm that stays fully invested by keeping funds in short-term deposits and by using overdraft privileges bear any cost of remaining liquid?

2 Why does the fact that most trade is denominated in a major currency make it relatively simple to have low money management costs?

3 If interest parity holds, should a multinational move working capital if it expects changing exchange rates?

4 How do multinational banks help make it easier to manage working capital?

5 What is the difference between the implications of transaction costs and political risks for where working capital should be held? Is there a difference between the implications of transaction costs and liquidity?

6 What are the gains from pooling cash balances?

7 What is the difference between netting and natural hedging? How does it involve the number of currencies and correlations or connections between exchange rates?

8 What are the major differences between the ways Digital Equipment and International Harvester manage their working capital?

9 How does a currency center differ from a reinvoicing center?

10 How can conflicts exist when a firm sets transfer prices for maximizing overall profits? Could these conflicts arise from differential tax rates, import tariffs, imminent changes in exchange rates, and political risks?

BIBLIOGRAPHY

Ankrom, Robert K.: "Top-Level Approach to Foreign Exchange Rate Problem," *Harvard Business Review*, July–August 1974, pp. 79–90. Reprinted in Donald R. Lessard (ed.), *International Financial Management*, Warren, Gorham and Lamont, Boston, 1979, pp. 381–397.

Arpan, Jeffrey S.: *International Intracorporate Pricing*, Frederick A. Praeger, New York, 1972.

Goeltz, Richard K.: "Managing Liquid Funds Internationally," *Columbia Journal of World Business*, July–August 1972, pp. 59–65.

Horst, Thomas: "American Taxation of Multinational Firms," *American Economic Review*, vol. 67, June 1977, pp. 376–389.

Lall, Sanjaya: "Transfer-Pricing by Multinational Manufacturing Firms," *Oxford Bulletin of Economics and Statistics*, August 1973, pp. 173–195.

Lessard, Donald R., and Peter Lorange: "Currency Changes and Management Control: Resolving the Centralization/Decentralization Dilemma," *Accounting Review*, July 1977, pp. 628–637.

Prindl, Andreas R.: "Guidelines for MNC Money Manager," *Harvard Business Review*, January 1976, pp. 73–80.

Rutenberg, David P.: "Maneuvering Liquid Assets in a Multi-National Company: Formulation and Deterministic Solution Procedures," *Management Science*, ser. B, June 1970, pp. 671–684.

Sangster, Bruce: "International Funds Management," *Financial Executive*, December 1977, pp. 46–52.

Shapiro, Alan C.: "International Cash Management—The Determination of Multicurrency Cash Balances," *Journal of Financial and Quantitative Analysis*, December 1976, pp. 893–900.

Wunderlisch, Karl: "Centralized Cash Management Systems for the Multinational Enterprise," *Management International Review*, June 1973, pp. 43–57.

APPENDIX: Gains from Centralized Cash Management

In order to demonstrate the gains from centralized cash management, we need to define some terms.

Let us write the expected working capital requirements for a multinational operating in the United States and the United Kingdom as W_{US}^* and W_{UK}^*. Let the standard deviations of anticipated cash needs be σ_{US} and σ_{UK}.

W_{US}^* and W_{UK}^* are the amounts, in terms of U.S. dollars, that are most likely to be needed at any time. Let us assume that a multinational wants to be 95 percent sure of having sufficient cash on hand in each country and that working capital requirements for each country can be represented by a normal curve.

If cash is held separately in the two countries, then to be 95 percent sure of meeting needs in the United States, the multinational must hold as working capital this amount of dollars:

$$W_{US}^* + 1.64\,\sigma_{US}$$

We add $1.64\,\sigma_{US}$ to the most likely cash need because with a normal curve, 95 percent of the area under the curve falls to the left of 1.64 standard deviations.[7] Similarly, to be 95 percent sure of meeting needs in the United Kingdom, the company should hold this amount of dollars:

$$W_{UK}^* + 1.64\,\sigma_{UK}$$

[7]This can be shown diagrammatically:

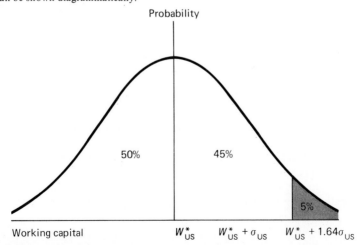

The shaded area is 5 percent of the total area, and so that area to the left of $W_{US}^* + 1.64\sigma_{US}$ is 95 percent of the area under the normal curve.

The total need for cash with the localized holdings of working capital is the sum of the two separate needs:

$$(W_{US}^* + W_{UK}^*) + 1.64\,(\sigma_{US} + \sigma_{UK}) \tag{10A.1}$$

This should be compared with total cash requirements when the funds are centrally held—in London *or* in New York—and moved to where they are required.

If the multinational pools its working cash balances, the most likely need is the sum of the separate needs:

$$W_{US}^* + W_{UK}^*$$

However, the standard deviation of the pooled needs is not the sum of the individual standard deviations. With total cash needs divided between the United States and the United Kingdom in the proportions θ_{US} and θ_{UK}, the standard deviation of the total need for working capital will be as follows:[8]

$$\sigma = \sqrt{\theta_{US}^2 \cdot \sigma_{US}^2 + \theta_{UK}^2 \times \sigma_{UK}^2}$$

$$\text{where} \quad \theta_{US} = \frac{W_{US}^*}{W_{US}^* + W_{UK}^*} \quad \text{and} \quad \theta_{UK} = \frac{W_{UK}^*}{W_{US}^* + W_{UK}^*}$$

It is assumed that cash needs in the two countries are mutually independent. The equation for the value of σ means that the multinational can be 95 percent sure of having sufficient cash by holding

$$(W_{US}^* + W_{UK}^*) + 1.64\,\sqrt{\theta_{US}^2 \cdot \sigma_{US}^2 + \theta_{UK}^2 \cdot \sigma_{UK}^2} \tag{10A.2}$$

dollars in its central location.

For example, let us assume that

$$W_{US}^* = \$2.8 \text{ million} \qquad W_{UK}^* = \$5.2 \text{ million}$$
$$\sigma_{US}^2 = \$1.0 \text{ million} \qquad \sigma_{UK}^2 = \$1.8 \text{ million}$$

Without pooled cash balances, the need—from Equation (10A.1)—for working capital is as follows:

$$(2.8 + 5.2) + 1.64(1.0 + 1.34) = \$11.84 \text{ billion}$$

If cash is pooled, the working capital need—given by Equation (10A.2)—is as follows:

$$(2.8 + 5.2) + 1.64\,\sqrt{(0.35)^2 \times 1.0 + (0.65)^2 \times 1.8} = \$9 \text{ billion}$$

We find that there are definite gains to be had from centralizing working capital and returning funds that are not immediately needed by local operations to a central pool that services the cash needs of the countries.

---

[8] This follows from the standard result in statistics for the variance of the sum of variables. It is shown in most if not all introductory statistics textbooks.

PART FOUR

REAL CHANGES IN EXCHANGE RATES: PRICING, PROFITABILITY, AND OUTPUT DECISIONS

CHAPTER 11

EXCHANGE RATE FORECASTING AND EFFICIENCY

Variations in the day-to-day value of foreign exchange are often wild enough to gain headline mention in the popular press. The forces behind these variations in exchange rates are complex and involve political events, pricing decisions of powerful cartels, news on the relative strengths of the world economies, surges of speculative activity, and virtually any major news item. It is not possible, other than in an ex post kind of way, to explain the daily ups and downs on the world exchange markets. But the long-term trends are much easier to explain. When the question concerns the reason why, for example, the Swiss franc or the Deutsche mark has made steady gains against the dollar or why the Italian lira or the Brazilian cruzeiro has incurred steady losses, the answer invariably lies either in relative rates of inflation or in interest rates.

Inflation affects the domestic buying power of money, and it is the exchange rate that measures the buying power of one kind of money versus the buying power of another. It should therefore be apparent that exchange rates depend on rates of inflation even though the day-to-day variations are determined by a host of other events. The most heavily discussed link between inflation and the rates of foreign exchange is the purchasing power parity condition (PPP), which was popularized by Gustav Cassell in the 1920s.[1] The PPP condition is essential for an understanding of long-term exchange rate trends under flexible exchange rates and even under fixed exchange rates. In this chapter, we will begin by describing the purchasing power parity condition and the evidence on how closely it holds. We will combine PPP with interest parity and obtain another important condition in international finance: the "Fisher-open" condition. Finally, we will see how the purchasing power

---

[1] See Gustav Cassell, *Money and Foreign Exchange after 1914*, The Macmillan Press, London, 1923.

parity, interest parity, and Fisher-open conditions have been used in exchange rate forecasting and in testing the efficiency of the foreign exchange market.

THE PURCHASING POWER PARITY CONDITION

The Absolute Form of PPP

Virtually every opportunity for profit will catch the attention of an enterpreneur somewhere in the world. One type of opportunity that will rarely be missed is the chance to buy an item in one place and sell it in another for a profit. For example, if you found that gold or copper was priced at a particular dollar price in London and that the price was simultaneously higher in New York, you would buy the metal in London and ship it to New York for sale. Of course, it takes time to ship physical commodities, and so at any precise moment, prices might differ a little between markets. Transportation costs are also involved. But if there is enough of a price difference, people will begin to take advantage of it by buying commodities in the cheaper market and then shipping them to and selling them in the more expensive market.

People who buy in one market and sell in another are known as commodity arbitragers. They arbitrage in goods, whereas the interest arbitragers of our earlier discussion arbitrage in money by borrowing where interest rates are low and placing funds where interest rates are high. Like the interest arbitragers, the commodity market arbitragers eliminate, through their actions, any profitable opportunities that may exist. They force up prices in the low-cost countries and lower them where commodity costs are higher. They cease their activities only when all profitable opportunities have been exhausted, which means that except for the costs of moving goods around, including any tariffs that might be involved, the prices in various markets are equalized.

In fact, prices of commodities should be the same in different countries even if there is no direct commodity arbitrage between countries themselves. This is because outside buyers will select the lowest price. For example, even if there was no arbitrage of wheat between Canada and the United States, the prices would need to be the same; otherwise, outside buyers would not buy from the more expensive supplier. So far we have ignored shipping and tariff costs.[2] However, since Canadian and American wheat ports are both the same distance away from Soviet receiving ports, differential shipping costs will not result in different selling prices. Similarly, even when there are tariffs, if they apply equally to both potential sources, they cannot explain price differences.

When prices in different countries are expressed in the *same* currency, the outcome of commodity market arbitrage—that particular commodity prices are everywhere equal—is easily seen. For example, we observe, as in Table 11.1, that dollar prices of an ounce of gold in London, Paris, Zurich, Hong Kong, and New York are very similar. But what does it mean to have arbitrage ensure that prices are

---

[2] We exclude quality considerations, dependability of continuous supply, and other political factors as well. We also exclude credit conditions and special deals that may be part of a contract.

TABLE 11.1
GOLD PRICES IN DIFFERENT CENTERS
(Wednesday, May 5, 1982; by the Associated Press)
Prices of commodities tend to be similar in different countries.
If they are not, profitable arbitrage can occur.

London: morning fixing	$341.75
afternoon fixing	$338.40
Paris: afternoon fixing	$345.02
Frankfurt: fixing	$343.99
Zurich: late fixing	$337.00
New York: Handy & Herman	
(only daily quote)	$338.40
New York: Engelhard	
(only daily quote)	
fabricated	$338.40

Source: *The New York Times*, May 6, 1982. (© 1982 by The New York Times Company. Reprinted by permission).

the same when they are expressed in different foreign currencies? The answer provides the "absolute" or static form of the purchasing power parity condition. This condition, like the interest parity condition, is called the "law of one price."

The price of an individual commodity—for example, wheat—will be the same in Britain and the United States if

$$p_{\text{wheat}}^{\text{US}} = S(\$/£)p_{\text{wheat}}^{\text{UK}} \tag{11.1}$$

where the p's are wheat prices within the United States and the United Kingdom. When the market prices differ markedly and this equation does not hold, those who arbitrage in commodities will profit from the opportunity and thereby help restore the equality. For example, if $p_{\text{wheat}}^{\text{US}} = \$4$ per bushel, $p_{\text{wheat}}^{\text{UK}} = £2$ per bushel, and $S(\$/£) = 2.20$, then an arbitrager could take $400,000 and buy 100,000 bushels of wheat in the United States. If this is sent to Britain, it will fetch £200,000, which at the going exchange rate will give the arbitrager $440,000 for an initial outlay of $400,000. Provided the costs are below $40,000, he or she will profit from the activity. Indeed, if we believe we can ignore costs, we know that for each commodity that arbitragers trade, their activity will continue until Equation (11.1) holds.

If Equation (11.1) was to hold for every item that people consume, then instead of writing the equation in terms of an individual good, we could write it in terms of prices in general. If P_{US} and P_{UK} represent the prices in the United States and Britain of a standard basket of wholesale goods, Equation (11.1) becomes

$$P_{\text{US}} = S(\$/£) \cdot P_{\text{UK}} \tag{11.2}$$

Equation (11.2) is the absolute or static form of the purchasing power parity condition. Because of differential shipping costs, differential tariffs on different suppliers, quotas, and other restrictions on free commodity arbitrage, the absolute form of this law of one price will not hold. However, we can put the purchasing power parity condition in a dynamic form which gives predictions with some limited validity. We will look at the relative form of PPP and then briefly examine the evidence.

The Relative Form of PPP

We can derive the relative form of PPP if we define some terms:

$\dot{S}(\$/£)$ is the percentage change in the spot exchange rate over a year, and $\dot{P}_{US}$ and $\dot{P}_{UK}$ are the annual inflation rates in the United States and Britain.

The definitions allow us to rewrite the absolute form of PPP for 2 successive years as

$$P_{US} = S(\$/£) \cdot P_{UK} \tag{11.2}$$

and

$$P_{US}(1 + \dot{P}_{US}) = S(\$/£) \cdot [1 + \dot{S}(\$/£)] \cdot P_{UK}(1 + \dot{P}_{UK}) \tag{11.3}$$

Taking the ratio of Equation (11.3) to Equation (11.2) gives

$$(1 + \dot{P}_{US}) = [1 + \dot{S}(\$/£)] \cdot (1 + \dot{P}_{UK})$$

that is,

$$\dot{P}_{US} - \dot{P}_{UK} = \dot{S}(\$/£) \cdot (1 + \dot{P}_{UK}) \tag{11.4}$$

Equation (11.4) is the PPP condition in its "relative" or "dynamic" form. We note that the relative form is necessary but not sufficient for PPP in its absolute form, Equation (11.2), to hold.

To take an example, if the United States experiences inflation of 10 percent ($\dot{P}_{US} = 0.10$) and Britain has 15 percent inflation ($\dot{P}_{UK} = 0.15$), then the dollar price of pounds should fall at a rate of 4.4 percent:

$$\dot{S}(\$/£) = \frac{\dot{P}_{US} - \dot{P}_{UK}}{(1 + \dot{P}_{UK})} = \frac{0.10 - 0.15}{1.15} = -0.044 \text{ or } 4.4 \text{ percent}$$

If the conditions hold in reverse, with the United States having higher inflation, then $\dot{S}(\$/£)$ is positive, and the dollar falls in value against sterling by 4.5 percent:

$$\dot{S}(\$/£) = \frac{0.15 - 0.10}{1.10} = 0.045 \text{ or } 4.5 \text{ percent}$$

Both values are relatively close to the 5 percent obtained from taking an approximation of Equation (11.4) and writing instead

$$\dot{P}_{US} - \dot{P}_{UK} = \dot{S}(\$/£) \tag{11.5}$$

What the PPP doctrine in this approximate form says is that the movement in the exchange rate is equal to the difference between inflation rates. Equation (11.5) is a good approximation whenever the foreign inflation rate is moderate.

Before we examine the evidence on PPP, we should note that we should not expect PPP to hold precisely within short time periods. With fixed exchange rates, purchasing power parity can be frustrated by central bank control of the exchange rate. Rapid inflation might not result in a devaluation for some time if the central bank borrows additional reserves or uses reserves accumulated in the past to defend its currency. We could expect that in the long run the central bank would give in and allow relative inflation rates to move the exchange rate, but this could take 5 or 6 years. We will therefore find long periods in which violations of PPP are persistently observed.

Even with a flexible exchange rate system, there are very many other factors that affect the exchange rate. In addition to being influenced by relative inflation rates, the exchange rate will be affected by interest rate differentials, relative growth rates of national income, resource discoveries, political developments, and other factors listed in Chapter 6. As with fixed rates, a number of years could pass before exchange rates move according to the PPP condition. It should therefore be no surprise that the statistical studies of PPP show mixed results. PPP is, at best, a long-run condition.

The Empirical Evidence on PPP

A considerable amount of evidence on the PPP condition is contained in a special volume of the *Journal of International Economics*.[3] We will examine a number of the studies in this volume as well as some other studies which use PPP as a forecasting device.

A major problem in testing the validity of the purchasing power parity condition is the need to use good price indexes for the measurement of $\dot{P}_{US}$ and $\dot{P}_{UK}$ or the inflation rates for the countries being studied. Price indexes cover many items, and what is happening to relative price within an index is not revealed. This is an important drawback because price increases in the export sector could hurt the exchange rate even if the overall price index is unchanged. In an effort to use as specific a set of prices as can be obtained and to avoid index number problems, J. David Richardson employed data on narrowly classified industrial items.[4] The

---

[3] "Purchasing Power Parity: A Symposium," *Journal of International Economics*, vol. 8, no. 2, May 1978.

[4] J. David Richardson, "Some Empirical Evidence on Commodity Arbitrage and the Law of One Price," *Journal of International Economics*, vol. 8, no. 2, May 1978, pp. 341–351.

classifications are as specific as "cement," "animal feeds," "bakery products," "chewing gum," "fertilizers," and so on. Richardson examined PPP between Canada and the United States,

$$\dot{P}_{US} - \dot{P}_{Can} = \dot{S}(\$/\text{Can}\$)(1 + \dot{P}_{Can}) \qquad (11.6)$$

and after fitting an equation somewhat like Equation (11.6) to the available data, he was forced to conclude that arbitrage was not apparent in many commodity categories. Moreover, he concluded that even when arbitrage is apparent, it is far from precise. It appears from Richardson's results that prices in Canada are more likely to move up or down after a change in the exchange rate—the $\dot{S}(\$/\text{Can}\$)$ in Equation (11.6)—rather than after a change in prices in the United States—the $\dot{P}_{US}$ in Equation (11.6).

Irving Kravis and Richard E. Lipsey extensively studied the relationship between inflation rates and exchange rates using different price indexes.[5] They used the "GNP implicit deflator" (which includes prices of all goods and services in the GNP), the consumer price index, and the wholesale price index. They also took care to distinguish between goods that enter into international trade (tradable goods) and those that do not (nontradable goods). They discovered, using these many prices and price indexes, that there were departures from purchasing power parity. They concluded, "As a matter of general judgement we express our opinion that the results do not support the notion of a tightly integrated international price structure. The record . . . shows that price levels can move apart sharply without rapid correction through arbitrage."[6] They did find that PPP holds more closely for tradable goods than for nontradable goods, but the departures from PPP even over relatively long periods were substantial even for traded goods.

Hans Genberg concentrated on testing to see whether PPP holds more precisely when exchange rates are flexible rather than fixed.[7] The most important aspects of his conclusion can be seen by comparing the two columns in Table 11.2. The table gives the average deviations, in percentages, from an estimated PPP condition. The estimates show departures from PPP for each country with its combined trading partners. The importance of each partner is judged by the share of that partner in the country's export trade. The PPP condition is then statistically fitted between the country, for example, Belgium, and the weighted average of its trading partners. The table shows, for example, that for the United States from 1957 to 1976, the actual difference between the inflation rate in the United States and the inflation rate in its (weighted) trading partners differed from the exchange rate change by, on the average, 3.8 percent per annum.

The second column of Table 11.2 includes the flexible exchange rate period which began in 1972. We find from the average deviations from PPP given at the

[5] Irving B. Kravis and Richard E. Lipsey, "Price Behavior in the Light of Balance of Payments Theories," *Journal of International Economics*, vol. 8, no. 2, May 1978, pp. 193–246.
[6] Ibid., p. 216.
[7] Hans Genberg, "Purchasing Power Parity under Fixed and Flexible Exchange Rates," *Journal of International Economics*, vol. 8, no. 2., May 1978, pp. 247–267.

TABLE 11.2
AVERAGE ABSOLUTE DEVIATIONS FROM PPP
(In Percentages)
There are larger departures from PPP for the years
1957–1976, which include a period of flexible exchange
rates. However, this could be because conditions
were more volatile during the 1967–1976 period.

	1957–1966	1957–1976
United States	1.2	3.8
United Kingdom	0.5	3.8
Austria	1.3	2.0
Belgium	1.4	2.1
Denmark	1.3	2.0
France	2.5	3.0
Germany	1.3	2.7
Italy	1.2	5.8
Netherlands	0.5	1.7
Norway	0.9	2.9
Sweden	0.7	1.4
Switzerland	0.7	5.8
Canada	2.0	3.3
Japan	1.9	3.8
Average	1.2	3.2

Source: Hans Genberg, "Purchasing Power Parity under Fixed and Flexible Exchange Rates," *Journal of International Economics*, North-Holland Publishing Company, vol. 8, no. 2, May 1978, p. 260.

bottom of the table that the addition of the flexible period makes the deviations increase. The implication is that there were greater violations during the flexible years, 1972 to 1976.[8]

Niels Thygesen has summarized the results of a study by the Commission of the European Communities, which set out to discover how long it takes for inflation rates to restore PPP after exchange rates have been artificially changed by the government to gain competitiveness for exports.[9] The idea is that a devaluation should raise the rate of inflation until PPP is restored. This could come about via higher import prices and consequent wage demands setting off reactions elsewhere in the economy. Using economic models of Britain and Italy, the study concluded that it took 5 to 6 years for inflation differentials to restore the PPP condition. However, Thygesen also observed that 75 percent of the return to PPP was achieved within 2 years.

Another study that examined how long it takes for PPP to be restored after being

[8] Genberg also discovered that most of the departures from PPP resulted from movements in exchange rates rather than from changes in price levels. This supports Richardson's conclusion. See also Mario Blejer and Hans Genberg, "Permanent and Transitory Shocks to Exchange Rates: Measurement and Implications for Purchasing Power Parity," unpublished manuscript, International Monetary Fund, 1981.

[9] Niels Thygesen, "Inflation and Exchange Rates: Evidence and Policy Guidelines for the European Community," *Journal of International Economics*, vol. 8, no. 2, May 1978, pp. 301–317.

disturbed is that of John Hodgson and Patricia Phelps.[10] They used a statistical model that allows lags and discovered that differential inflation rates precede the change in exchange rates with a lag of up to 18 months. A similar conclusion was reached by William Folks, Jr., and Stanley Stansell.[11] Their purpose was to forecast changes in exchange rates, and they discovered that exchange rates do adjust to relative inflation rates, but with a long lag.

A conclusion that is different from the conclusion of Hodgson and Phelps and Folks and Stansell was reached by Richard Rogalski and Joseph Vinso.[12] They chose a flexible exchange rate period, 1920 to 1924, and studied relative inflation for six countries.[13] Rogalski and Vinso concluded that there is no lag. This, they claim, is what would be expected in an efficient market (which we will shortly discuss) because relative inflation rates are publicly available information and should therefore be reflected in market prices such as exchange rates. This question of efficiency in the spot exchange rate has been tackled by Jacob Frenkel and Michael Mussa, who argue that even if we do observe departures from PPP, this does not imply that foreign exchange markets are inefficient. Exchange rates, they show, move like stock and bond prices. Indeed, Frenkel and Mussa find average monthly variations in exchange rates to be more pronounced than the variation of stock prices.[14] This is not itself evidence of efficiency, which refers more to the pattern of departures from PPP and will be discussed later.

Our survey of the empirical evidence and the conclusion that violations of PPP do occur should come as no surprise. Anyone who has traveled extensively and knows about prices abroad will probably feel that purchasing power parity rarely occurs. There are countries that are notoriously expensive, and they appear to stay this way over long periods. This proves, without any formal empirical evidence, that there are serious departures from PPP, at least in the absolute or static form, where price levels rather than inflation rates are compared. There are two major reasons that we can offer as to why this can occur.

Reasons for Departures from PPP

Restrictions on Movements of Goods   It is obvious that prices can differ between two markets by up to the cost of transportation without commodity market

---

[10] John A. Hodgson and Patricia Phelps, "The Distributed Impact of Price-Level Variation on Floating Exchange Rates," *Review of Economics and Statistics*, vol. 57, February 1975, pp. 58–64.

[11] William R. Folks, Jr., and Stanley R. Stansell, "The Use of Discriminant Analysis in Forecasting Exchange Rate Movements," *Journal of International Business Studies*, vol. 6, spring 1975, pp. 33–50.

[12] Richard J. Rogalski and Joseph D. Vinso, "Price Level Variations as Predictors of Flexible Exchange Rates," *Journal of International Business Studies*, vol. 8, spring 1977, pp. 71–81.

[13] This period was also studied by Jacob A. Frenkel, not because exchange rates were flexible but because the inflationary experience was so extreme. See Jacob A. Frenkel, "Purchasing Power Parity: Doctrinal Perspective and Evidence from the 1920's," *Journal of International Economics*, vol. 8, no. 2, May 1978, pp. 169–191.

[14] Jacob Frenkel and Michael Mussa, "Efficiency of Foreign Exchange Markets and Measures of Turbulence," Working Paper 476, National Bureau of Economic Research, Cambridge, Mass., 1981. We should also mention the extensive study by Richard Roll: "Violations of the 'Law of One Price' and Their Implications for Differential Denominated Assets," Conference on Multi-Currency Management and International Trade, Bergamo, Italy, October 1977.

arbitrage taking place. Clearly, if it costs $0.50 per bushel to ship wheat between the United States and Britain, the price difference must exceed $0.50 in either direction before arbitrage will occur. This means a possible deviation from the absolute form of purchasing power parity for wheat that spans a full dollar.[15] Tariffs and quotas will have a similar effect. If one country has, for example, a 15 percent import duty, prices within the country will have to move more than 15 percent above those in the other before it pays to ship and cover the duties that are involved.

The effect of duties is different from the effect of transportation costs. Duties do not have a symmetrical effect. As a result of duties, prices can move higher only in the country which has the import duties. But whether it be transportation costs or duties that must be paid, they explain departures from PPP only in its absolute or static form. Once the maximum price difference from shipping costs and duties has been reached, the PPP doctrine in its relative or dynamic form should explain movements through time that push against the maximum price difference. For example, suppose that prices at existing exchange rates are already 25 percent higher in one country because of a 15 percent import duty and 10 percent transportation costs. If that country has an inflation rate that is 10 percent higher than the inflation rate in another country, its exchange rate will have to fall, on the average, by 10 percent to prevent commodity arbitrage.

Quotas, which are limits on the amounts of different commodities that can be imported, generally mean that price differences can become quite sizable, because commodity arbitragers are limited in their ability to narrow the gaps. Like general duties, they provide a reason for persistent departures from PPP.

Price Indexes and Nontraded Outputs   We have already observed in describing the work of J. David Richardson and Irving Kravis and Richard E. Lipsey that many of the items that are included in the commonly used price indexes do not enter into international trade. We cannot, therefore, invoke the notion of commodity arbitrage to create an equivalent of Equation (11.1) for these items. Most difficult to arbitrage between countries are immovable items such as land and buildings; highly perishable commodities such as fresh milk, vegetables, eggs, and some fruits; and also services such as hotel accommodation and repair activities. These "untraded" items can allow departures from PPP to persist when we measure inflation from conventional market bundle price indexes.

To some extent, a tendency toward parity even in untraded items can be maintained by the movement of the buyers instead of the movement of the items themselves. For example, factories and office complexes can be located where land and rent are cheap. Vacationers can travel to places where holidays are less expensive. The movement of *buyers* tends to keep prices in different countries in line with each other.

The relative prices of traded versus nontraded outputs will not differ greatly

---

[15] As we mentioned, however, competitive pressures for similar prices to third countries equidistant from Britain and the United States will keep prices in a narrower range than would result from direct arbitrage between Britain and the United States.

between countries if *producers* within each country can move into the production of the nontraded outputs when their prices are very high. Consequently, if comparative advantages do not differ significantly between nations (that is, the nations have similar relative efficiencies in producing different goods), the relative prices of traded versus nontraded items will be kept similar between countries by the prospective movement of domestic producers. But if the prices of traded goods satisfy PPP, then so will the prices of nontraded items if they move with the prices of traded goods. However, we do require that the producers can move between traded and nontraded goods, which is frequently very difficult. And even when producers can move, the price adjustment can take a very long time, during which departures from PPP can persist.[16]

We should note that even if the price of each individual good were equalized between countries, price *indexes* could differ if the importance of each item in the indexes of different countries also differs. This would happen if the populations of different countries reveal different tastes.

COMBINING PPP AND INTEREST PARITY

Approximating the Interest Parity Condition

The purchasing power parity condition can be combined with a condition closely resembling the interest parity condition to obtain another important condition in international finance: the Fisher-open condition. We might like to combine PPP with the interest parity condition itself, as it is stated in Chapter 7, but this requires forward exchange rates, and these are hard to find for more than a few years ahead.[17] Since the PPP condition holds, at best, only in the long run it must be combined with a condition that is like interest parity but which uses expected exchange rates:

$$r_j = r_i + \dot{S}^*(j/i) \tag{11.7}$$

In the case of the United States and the United Kingdom, this is

$$r_{US} = r_{UK} + \dot{S}^*(\$/£) \tag{11.8}$$

In Equation (11.8)

$\dot{S}^*(\$/£)$ is the *expected* annual rate of change in the number of dollars per pound.

Positive $\dot{S}^*(\$/£)$ means an expected pound appreciation, and a negative value means a pound depreciation.

Equation (11.8) is a condition which is approximate and which we shall meet again in Chapter 14. There are two reasons why it is approximate.

---

[16]Mario Blejer and Ayre Hillman have provided a formal model with the costs of commodity arbitrage allowing temporary departures from PPP. See their article "A Proposition on Short-Run Departures from the Law of One-Price: Unanticipated Inflation, Relative Price Dispersion, and Commodity Arbitrage," in *European Economic Review* vol. 17, January 1982, pp. 51–60.

[17]Forward exchange contracts are occasionally as long as 5 years. However, these are drawn up for special customers of banks and are not common.

1 We should really write that

$$(1 + r_{US})^n = \frac{S_n^*(\$/£)}{S(\$/£)} (1 + r_{UK})^n \qquad (11.9)$$

where $S_n^*(\$/£)$ is the expected *level* of the spot rate—as opposed to the expected rate of *change*, $\dot{S}^*(\$/£)$. The two sides of the equation give the receipts from a dollar invested in the respective countries at compound interest for n years. The foreign receipts are an expected magnitude because they are converted back into dollars at the unknown exchange rate, $S_n^*(\$/£)$.

2 Since Equation (11.8) uses the expected spot exchange rate for n years in the future, there is risk in making investments abroad. Equation (11.8) and even the precise form in Equation (11.9) are hence conditions for investor or borrower indifference only if the investors or borrowers are risk-neutral.[18]

It is conventional to use a form of "interest parity" like Equation (11.8) in deriving the Fisher-open effect, and we shall do that here. We will, however, consider the precise condition and the question of introducing risk in Chapter 14.

We can interpret Equation (11.8) by saying that the expected yields or borrowing costs in two countries are equal if the interest rate at home equals the interest rate abroad plus the annual rate of appreciation (or minus the annual depreciation) of the foreign currency. For example, the expected yields on British and U.S. bonds are equal if U.S. rates are 10 percent, British rates are 12 percent, and the pound is expected to depreciate against the dollar by 2 percent per annum.

Combining the Two Parity Conditions

We have written the relative or dynamic form of the PPP condition in Equation (11.5) in terms of the actual rates of inflation and the actual change in the exchange rate. However, ex ante or before the event, if we believe that PPP will hold, then we can also put Equation (11.5) in an expectant form. We can say that we will expect the exchange rate to change by an amount that is equal to the difference between the two rates of inflation that we expect to occur. This can be written as

$$\dot{P}_{US}^* - \dot{P}_{UK}^* = \dot{S}^*(\$/£) \qquad (11.10)$$

where, as always, an asterisk means an expected amount. $\dot{P}_{US}^*$ and $\dot{P}_{UK}^*$ are, therefore, the expected rates of inflation in the United States and Britain.

Now, if we take the PPP equation in the expectant form of Equation (11.10) and compare it with the interest parity condition in Equation (11.8), we can note a clear similarity. We have

$$\dot{P}_{US}^* - \dot{P}_{UK}^* = \dot{S}^*(\$/£) \qquad (11.10)$$

$$r_{US} - r_{UK} = \dot{S}^*(\$/£) \qquad (11.8)$$

---

[18] Equations (11.8) and (11.9) are also approximate in that they exclude transaction costs, taxes, political risks, liquidity, and so on.

The right-hand sides of these two equations are equal. But if the right-hand sides are equal, so are the left-hand sides. This therefore means that

$$r_{US} - r_{UK} = \dot{P}^*_{US} - \dot{P}^*_{UK} \tag{11.11}$$

By rearranging this equation, we get

$$r_{US} - \dot{P}^*_{US} = r_{UK} - \dot{P}^*_{UK} \tag{11.12}$$

What we have on the two sides of this equation are the market interest rates less the expected rates of inflation in the two countries. The interest rate minus the expected inflation rate is the expected "real" rate of interest, popularized principally by Irving Fisher. As a result, Equation (11.12) could be dubbed the *Fisher-open condition.*[19]

The conventional Fisher condition or Fisher equation involves only an individual country. The condition comes from the following intuitively appealing argument. If we have zero inflation, the interest rate might be, say, 2 percent. But if people in general believe that prices will rise 8 percent over the next year, they are likely to demand 10 percent after taxes just to ensure that the return gives a 2 percent "real" compensation after inflation. Similarly, if borrowers expect prices to go up by 8 percent, they will be willing to pay 10 percent interest, because after inflation this is only 2 percent ($10\% - 8\% = 2\%$). This 2 percent (or whatever number is appropriate) is therefore called the *real interest rate.* Irving Fisher's argument suggests that in each country, such as the United States and Britain, we should find that

$$r_{US} = \rho_{US} + \dot{P}^*_{US} \qquad \text{and} \qquad r_{UK} = \rho_{UK} + \dot{P}^*_{UK}$$

The terms ρ_{US} and ρ_{UK} are the real interest rates in the United States and Britain, and $\dot{P}^*_{US}$ and $\dot{P}^*_{UK}$ are, as before, the expected rates of inflation. Fisher argued that within any country the real rate, ρ_j, and the expected inflation, $\dot{P}_j^*$, are independent of each other. With this added assumption the link between interest rates and inflation is called the *Fisher equation.*[20]

[19] Generally, economists refer to Equation (11.8), not Equation (11.12), as the Fisher-open condition. However, since Fisher spoke of real interest rates as actual rates minus the expected inflation rate, Equation (11.12) would be more appropriately labeled as Fisher-open. Equation (11.8) should perhaps be called the "interest-open" condition, where "open" means "open economy." For accounts of the Fisher-open condition, we can cite Robert Aliber and Clive Stickney, "Accounting Measures of Foreign Exchange Exposure: The Long and Short of It," *The Accounting Review,* January 1975, pp. 45–57, and Ian Giddy, "An Integrated Theory of Exchange Rate Equilibrium," *Journal of Financial and Quantitative Analysis,* December 1976, pp. 883–892.

[20] Fisher's own discussion of the link between expected inflation and interest rates can be found in Irving Fisher, *The Theory of Interest,* A. M. Kelley, New York, 1965. Some of the earlier econometric evidence on the Fisher equation appeared to indicate that ρ and $\dot{P}^*$ were not independent and that the real rate of interest fell at high rates of (generally expected) inflation. See, for example, William E. Gibson, "Interest Rates and Inflationary Expectations," *American Economic Review,* vol. 62, December 1972, pp. 854–865, and William P. Yohe and Denis S. Karnosky, "Interest Rates and Price Level Changes," *Review,* Federal Reserve Bank of St. Louis, vol. 51, December 1969, pp. 19–36. A test showing that Fisher's argument can be empirically verified is provided in Maurice D. Levi and John H. Makin, "Fisher, Phillips, Friedman and the Measured Impact of Inflation on Interest," *Journal of Finance,* vol. 34, March 1979, pp. 35–52.

By applying the Fisher equation to the Fisher-open condition in Equation (11.12), we can immediately see that the two sides of Equation (11.12) are the real rates of interest in the two countries. In other words, the Fisher-open condition is the condition that the real rates of interest are equal in different countries. From purchasing power parity and interest parity we have been able to derive an equality between ex ante real rates of return in different countries. We say ex ante because ρ_{US} and ρ_{UK} are the observed or nominal interest rates less the *expected* inflation rates, which are never known and are unlike actual or ex post inflation rates, which can be calculated after the inflation has occurred.

The equality of ex ante real interest rates can be considered as having an independent existence, one that does not have to be derived from PPP and interest parity. It follows from investors allocating their funds where real returns are highest. The real return is computed after movements in exchange rates are considered or after adjustment for forward hedging. This yield from abroad is adjusted for inflation in the investor's country. Investing according to highest yield will tend to reduce the marginal available returns where funds are sent—because of the greater supply of funds created. It will also tend to raise returns in the countries from which the funds are taken—because of the reduced supply of funds. The flow of funds will continue until the expected ex ante real returns in different countries are equalized. Thus the equality $\rho_{US} = \rho_{UK}$ itself follows directly.

If we write the ex ante forms of the variants of the interest parity, purchasing power parity, and Fisher-open conditions all together, that is,

$$\text{"interest parity": } \quad r_{US} - r_{UK} = \dot{S}^*(\$/\pounds)$$
$$\text{PPP: } \quad \dot{P}^*_{US} - \dot{P}^*_{UK} = \dot{S}^*(\$/\pounds)$$
$$\text{Fisher-open: } \quad r_{US} - \dot{P}^*_{US} = r_{UK} - \dot{P}^*_{UK}$$

we find that we can derive any one from the other two. This is left as an end-of-chapter problem for the reader. The conditions are shown in Figure 11.1, where we have used the Fisher-open condition as it appears in Equation (11.11). Each side of the triangle in Figure 11.1 represents a condition. The figure helps make it clear why satisfying any two conditions will mean that the remaining condition is satisfied.

None of the conditions will hold precisely. We gave many reasons for departures from interest parity and a couple of reasons for departures from purchasing power parity. Departures from the Fisher-open condition require differences in expected real yields between countries. This will occur when taxes exist. High-tax countries must offer higher before-tax expected real yields. Real yields will also differ according to political risks and other risk factors.[21]

---

[21] The relationship between security yields in different countries can be extremely complex because of taxes, regulations, currency risks, citizens' tastes, and so on. The problem has been tackled by F. L. A. Grauer, R. H. Litzenberger, and R. E. Stehle, "Sharing Rules and Equilibrium in an International Capital Market under Uncertainty," *Journal of Financial Economics*, vol. 3, June 1976, pp. 233–256, and Fisher Black, "International Capital Market Equilibrium with Investment Barriers," *Journal of Financial Economics*, vol. 1, December 1974, pp. 337–352. Little data exist on real rates in different countries. See, however, Robert Z. Aliber, "Real Interest Rates in a Multicurrency World," unpublished paper, University of Chicago.

FIGURE 11.1
The interdependence of exchange rates, interest rates, and
inflation rates.

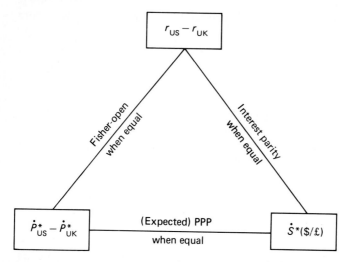

Interest parity, purchasing power parity, and the Fisher-open
condition are related. They can be derived from each other.

METHODS OF FORECASTING EXCHANGE RATES

The interest parity and purchasing power parity conditions reveal two possible ways
of forecasting the movement of exchange rates. First, the interest parity condition
shows that the expected change in exchange rates is given from the interest
differential because it states that

$$\dot{S}*(\$/£) = r_{US} - r_{UK}$$

Hence, if we look at market interest rates on securities with similar maturities and
risk in two countries, we can compute the *market expectation* of changes in foreign
exchange rates. For example, if the yields on 5-year government bonds are $r_{US} = 12$
percent and $r_{UK} = 16$ percent, we know that the market expects the dollar value of
sterling to fall by close to 4 percent per annum.[22] Secondly, if we individually hold
expectations about rates of inflation in two countries, we can form our *individual
expectations* of the future changes in exchange rates from PPP using

$$\dot{S}*(\$/£) = \dot{P}_{US}^* - \dot{P}_{UK}^*$$

---

[22]Since interest parity is known to hold only approximately, from computing the interest differential
we obtain a value that will generally not precisely equal the market expectation (because it is given from
market interest rates) of changes in exchange rates. In terms of our example, with $r_{US} = 12$ percent and
$r_{UK} = 16$ percent, we know that the market expects a decline in the dollar value of the pound of
approximately 4 percent per annum.

The market forecast that is based on the difference between comparable interest rates is readily available to any corporate executive who wishes to look at the relevant interest rates. The forecast of the path of exchange rates based on PPP as stated in Equation (11.5) is more problematic, since this requires that forecasts of inflation be obtained. Moreover, we have also observed that PPP does not hold very closely over short periods, and so in order to make a good forecast, there must clearly be other factors to consider. Most important, a forecaster must consider whether the central bank will permit the exchange rate to change and how long the central bank can prevent it from changing if market forces dictate that it should. However, the fact that market forces can build from the past, even with flexible exchange rates, is potentially helpful in making exchange rate forecasts from a model based on the PPP condition.

Forecasting with the PPP Condition

The potential lag after changes in prices until the PPP condition is restored has been used in the construction of an exchange rate forecasting device by Robert Everett, Abraham George, and Aryeh Blumberg.[23] Their method involves comparing the accumulated inflation differential between two countries with the accumulated change in the exchange rate. Figure 11.2 illustrates their approach. Let us assume that at the beginning of 1972, after the Smithsonian Agreement, PPP holds.[24] Suppose that from the first quarter of 1972 the quarterly rates of inflation in the United States have been 6.5 percent, 1.0 percent, 0.0 percent, and 1.0 percent higher than the inflation rates experienced in Germany. Thus the accumulated inflation differential at the end of each quarter is 6.5 percent, 7.5 percent, 7.5 percent, and 8.5 percent. This differential is the accumulated $\dot{P}_{US} - \dot{P}_{GY}$ and is plotted in Figure 11.2 as the "parity line."[25] If the depreciation (+) or appreciation (−) of the dollar against the Deutsche mark in the same quarters had been 2.0 percent, 0.5 percent, −0.5 percent, and 0.0 percent, the accumulated depreciation of the dollar would have been 2.0 percent, 2.5 percent, 2.0 percent, and 2.0 percent. In this case a +6.5 percent parity gap (8.5 percent − 2.0 percent) would have existed by the end of 1972.[26]

If a large parity gap accumulates, this indicates that a currency has become overvalued or undervalued. In our example in Figure 11.2, the dollar is becoming overvalued, and an adjustment could be considered imminent. Figure 11.3 shows that an adjustment indeed takes place. The dollar depreciates during 1973 so that

---

[23] Robert M. Everett, Abraham M. George, and Aryeh Blumberg, "Appraising Currency Strengths and Weaknesses: An Operational Model for Calculating Parity Exchange Rates," *Journal of International Business Studies*, vol. 11, no. 2, fall 1980, pp. 80–91.

[24] This is an assumption that may be incorrect. However, if an inappropriate starting date is selected, this will eventually be apparent as PPP is not restored, and a new starting date can be selected.

[25] The line giving the accumulated inflation differential is called the parity line because it gives the changes in exchange rates needed to preserve PPP; that is, $\dot{S}(\$/DM) = \dot{P}_{US} - \dot{P}_{GY}$. While our example uses quarterly data, Everett, George, and Blumberg use monthly data series.

[26] Because countries trade on a multilateral basis rather than merely on a bilateral basis, some further adjustments are needed to take account of how other countries can affect the U.S.-German exchange rate. This involves taking account of developments in other trading partners, but we do not need to bother with that here.

FIGURE 11.2
Plotting the accumulated parity gap.

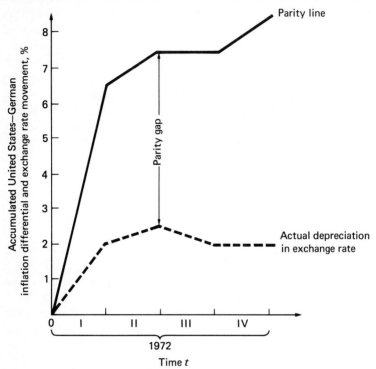

Actual inflation differentials determine the amount of movement in the exchange rate required to maintain PPP. The more the actual exchange rate deviates from the rate for PPP, the more likely it is to change toward its parity value. This can be seen by keeping track of the parity gap. An initial point of PPP is chosen and the gap is measured in each successive period.

PPP eventually is restored. In general, and as shown in Figure 11.4, the parity line and the actual exchange rate line do eventually meet. However, if these PPP-based forecasts can be made by anyone, they will not allow speculators to profit. The forward market and interest rates will reflect the likelihood of a change in exchange rates.

The calculations required to forecast exchange rates are often more complex than those we have just described. This has encouraged many companies to purchase forecasts from foreign exchange forecasting services. We might well expect that if the specialists' forecasts are frequently inaccurate, so will be those of the ordinary individual. It is therefore of value to examine the record of the forecasting services.

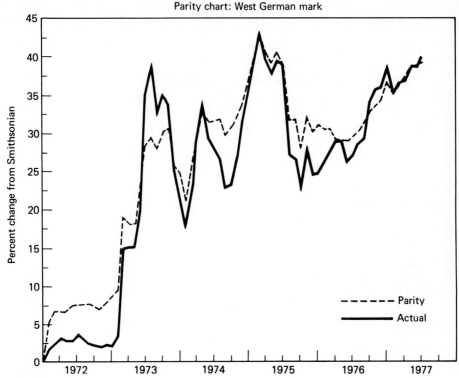

FIGURE 11.3
The appraisal chart for Germany. (*From Robert M. Everett, Abraham M. George, and Aryeh Blumberg, "Appraising Currency Strengths and Weaknesses: An Operational Model for Calculating Parity Exchange Rates,"* Journal of International Business Studies, *vol. 11, no. 2, fall 1980, p. 86.*)

The Performance of the Exchange Rate Forecasting Services

Table 11.3 gives a summary of the variety of exchange rate services that can be found.[27] The table shows that the costs, methods, scope, and scale of the different services are varied. But are these services worth it? Do they give their users a better idea of where exchange rates are going than can be obtained by looking at other generally available sources of information? The answer appears to be that the different services have different levels of success but in general do a poor job. We should examine how this conclusion is reached.

Stephen Goodman, a corporate executive with the Singer Company, performed a number of statistical tests on a large group of forecasting services.[28] He classified

[27] The table is from "A Guide to the Banks and Firms in the Foreign Exchange Advisory Business," *Euromoney*, August 1978, pp. 25–41.
[28] See Stephen H. Goodman, "No Better than the Toss of a Coin," *Euromoney*, December 1978, pp. 75–85.

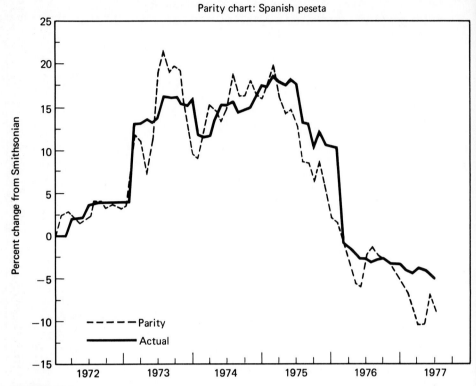

FIGURE 11.4
The appraisal chart for Spain. (*From Robert M. Everett, Abraham M. George, and Aryeh Blumberg, "Appraising Currency Strenghts and Weaknesses: An Operational Model for Calculating Parity Exchange Rates,"* Journal of International Business Studies, *vol. 11, no. 2, fall 1980, p. 87.*)

the services according to the techniques they employ. He separated those that use econometric (that is, statistical) techniques from those that use subjective evaluations and those that use technical decision rules. The econometric approach involves interest rates and inflation differentials and other explanatory variables. The previously described approach based on PPP would fit in this category. The technical rules are generally based on relating the future to the past path of exchange rates. The subjective approach is what you would think it is—forecasting by personal opinion. Goodman compared predictions made by the forecasting services with what eventually occurred. He examined the accuracy of predictions made between January and June in 1978.

Table 11.4 summarizes the results for the econometric forecasts in predicting trends and in predicting actual spot exchange rates ("point estimates"). The first column of results on predicting trends shows how often the forward rate was on the correct side of the current spot rate. Since any executive can look at the forward rate

TABLE 11.3
THE FOREIGN EXCHANGE ADVISORY SERVICES

Service	Fees		Method & length of forecast	Number of currencies	Number of customers
	Annual	**Other**			
Amex Bank	Negotiated individually		Kitchen sink* Up to 5 years informally	All major currencies; others on request	100+
Bank of America	No fee to bank's clients, except £750 for FX and exposure workshop, and negotiable fee for consulting service		Kitchen sink 1 week; 1, 3, and 12 months	15, others on request	Any bank clients
BI/Metrics	$12,000		Econometric Up to 18 months; planning 3- and 5-year	12	1
Brown Brothers Harriman	$18,000 to $45,000		Kitchen sink Up to 12 months	50, half in limited scope	55
Chase Econometrics	$12,000	$15,000 including time-share access to models	Econometric Up to eight quarters	8 monthly, 11 quarterly	n.a.
Chase Manhattan Bank	No fee for forecasts produced internally and available on request to bank's clients. Foreign exchange exposure management is separate service		Kitchen sink Up to 18 months, or 2 to 7 years, for general planning	12; others occasionally	Any bank clients on request, and staff
Chemical Bank	$2000 to $30,000		Kitchen sink 12 months and 4 years	26	111
Citibank	$25,000	Special project for negotiated fee	Kitchen sink Up to 12 months	All of interest to clients	60+

TABLE 11.3, cont.

Service	Fees		Method & length of forecast	Number of currencies	Number of customers
	Annual	**Other**			
ContiCurrency	$25,000	$15,000 to $20,000 for special projects or fewer demands	Kitchen sink 12 months and 5 to 10 years	33; others on request	52
Eurofinance	Fr1600 for 11 currencies, 1 year Fr5500 for six currencies, 5 years Fr50,000 for full corporate finance service		Econometric 1 year and 5 years	11	100, all services
European American Bank	$10,000 basic	$18,000 maximum; projects at $550 a day	Momentum for short term; kitchen sink for up to 5 years	All; emphasis on Europe	80
Forex Research	$10,000 for eight currencies $12,000 for 10 currencies		Kitchen sink Up to 18 months	10	80+
Harris Bank	$21,000 with renewal discounts		Kitchen sink Up to 12 months; informal longer	32	25
Gesellschaft für Trendanalysen		Monthly fee and 30% of net gains	n.a.	n.a.	31

IFC	$8000 for 10 currencies against the dollar $15,000 for above, plus eight currencies against Can$ and DM	Momentum	10 against US$; eight against Can$ and DM; yen against Sw Fr, £; £ against SKr	20+
Marine Midland	Marinfo, $2500 Projections and short-term consulting, $6000–$10,000 Major project, $75,000 $25,000	Kitchen sink 1, 3, 6, and 15 months	22: also special studies for longer	40+
Paine Webber Mitchell Hutchins	$1000 for monthly publications $3500 for above, plus 4/5 meetings a year	Kitchen sink 3, 6, 12, and 18 months	13	Five, and clients of parent brokerage firm
Morgan Guaranty: Foreign Exchange Services Group	No fee to bank's corporate clients	Kitchen sink	All leading currencies	Any of bank's corporate clients
Patterson, Little & Desmartin	$1500 (one currency) $1100 (2d to 4th currency) $7500 (all currencies)	Econometric 1, 2, 3, and 6 months	16	32
Predex	$5000 (Predex forecast) $4800 (short-term forecast)	Econometric	Predex forecast, 17, up to 18 months; Predex short-term forecast, 13, up to 6 months	56

TABLE 11.3, cont.

Service	Fees		Method & length of forecast	Number of currencies	Number of customers
	Annual	Other			
	$9000 (Predex forecast, plus simulations) $15,000 (Predex forecast, plus on-line services)				
N M Rothschild	$40,000 minimum		Kitchen sink Up to 5 years	55	18, plus "undisclosed number of Central Banks"
Waldner & Co	$30,000	$6000 (trial)	Momentum	7	23+

*Kitchen sink may include the use of econometric models, but it is mainly judgmental, taking economic, political, and psychological factors into account.
Source: "A Guide to the Banks and Firms in the *Foreign Exchange Advisory Business*," *Euromoney*, August 1978, pp. 25–41.

TABLE 11.4
THE PERFORMANCE OF ECONOMETRIC-ORIENTED SERVICES

Evaluation of econometric-oriented services: Accuracy in predicting trends
(Share of forecasts for which the exchange rate moved in the indicated direction in the subsequent 3-month period)

Currency	Forward rate	Berkeley Consulting Group	DRI	Forex Research	Predex	Service 5	Service 6	Arithmetic average (services only)
Canadian dollar	62	83	53*	n.a.	30	31	n.a.	49
French franc	37	63	43*	30	73	27	25*	44
Deutsche mark	67	57	77*	60	73	45	63	63
Yen	54	50	67*	67	47	37	n.a.	54
Swiss franc	80	n.a.	n.a.	n.a.	47	n.a.	10	29
Sterling	50	60	63*	60	43	37	29*	49
Arithmetic average	58	63	61	54	52	35	32	50

Evaluation of econometric-oriented services: Accuracy of point estimates of future spot rates
(Share of forecasts in which the predicted rate was closer to the spot rate than was the comparable forward rate)

Currency	Berkeley Consulting Group	DRI	Forex Research	Predex	Service 5	Service 6	Arithmetic average (services only)
Canadian dollar	60	27*	n.a.	13	37	n.a.	34
French franc	57	33*	48	40	38	57*	46
Deutsche mark	24	63*	57	41	33	53	45
Yen	37	60*	62	30	20	n.a.	42
Swiss franc	n.a.	n.a.	n.a.	30	n.a.	10	20
Sterling	70	33*	47	47	40	48*	48
Arithmetic average	50	43	54	34	34	42	43

*Based on part period data.
Source: Stephen Goodman, "No Better than the Toss of a Coin," *Euromoney*, December 1978, pp. 75–85.

TABLE 11.5
SPECULATIVE RETURN ON CAPITAL FROM FOLLOWING THE ADVICE OF ECONOMETRIC SERVICES
(In Percentages)

Currency		Buy and hold	Berkeley Consulting Group	DRI	Forex Research	Predex	Service 5	Service 6	Arithmetic average (services only)
Canadian dollar	Buy	(15.12)	2.52	(2.88)	n.a.	(4.96)	(0.60)	n.a.	(1.48)
	Sell		6.88	5.16*	n.a.	(2.08)	3.52	n.a.	3.37
	Total	(15.12)	4.40	1.64*	n.a.	(3.60)	0.28	n.a.	0.68
French franc	Buy	3.20	7.32	5.76*	2.40	7.20	3.24	10.08*	6.00
	Sell		2.28	(0.64)*	(3.16)	3.68	(2.68)	13.80*	(2.39)
	Total	3.20	4.20	1.40*	0.02	5.92	0.08	2.60*	2.37
Deutsche mark	Buy	6.80	5.72	13.00*	6.52	7.56	16.08	10.84	9.95
	Sell		(13.92)	(1.96)*	(7.00)	(4.40)	(4.04)	(4.88)	(6.03)
	Total	6.80	(1.56)	5.80*	(1.60)	4.68	0.64	0.36	1.39
Yen	Buy	12.52	7.36	15.56*	12.92	21.08	4.80	n.a.	12.34
	Sell		(16.40)	(13.68)*	(8.92)	(9.56)	(15.76)	n.a.	(12.86)
	Total	12.52	(5.32)	3.88	6.16	(2.40)	(7.96)	n.a.	(1.13)
Swiss franc	Buy	9.64	n.a.	n.a.	n.a.	18.80	n.a.	n.a.	18.80
	Sell		n.a.	n.a.	n.a.	(6.12)	n.a.	n.a.	(6.12)
	Total	9.64	n.a.	n.a.	n.a.	0.52	n.a.	n.a.	0.52
Sterling	Buy	0.12	14.04	4.56	8.40	2.76	2.16	6.20*	6.35
	Sell		10.48	(12.40)*	4.68	2.44	1.12	(9.32)*	(0.50)
	Total	0.12	12.04	(2.24)*	6.04	2.60	1.52	(2.52)*	2.91
Arithmetic average	Total	2.86	2.75	2.10	2.66	1.29	(1.09)	0.15	1.12

*Based on part period data.
Parentheses indicate a negative.
The total is the return on all transactions, both buy and sell; it is equal to the weighted average of the return on buys and on sells, where the weights are the share of transactions which are buys and sells respectively.
Totals for arithmetic average column represent horizontal sums; arithmetic average for arithmetic average column represents vertical sum of totals.
Source: Stephen Goodman, "No Better than the Toss of a Coin," Euromoney, December 1978, pp. 75–85.

(which speculators tend to move toward their expected future spot rate), it is a useful benchmark. It shows whether the forecasting services provide any information in addition to what is readily available without charge. We see that except in the case of the French franc, the forward rate is in the correct direction more than 50 percent of the time. The record of the forecasters is not correct 50 percent of the time. The accuracy of prediction is generally weak. The predictions of the forecasting services of point estimates, the levels of spot rates, are frequently further away from the realized rates than would be achieved by using forward rates.

Table 11.5 and Table 11.6 show the results of an additional test that Goodman performed. In order to compare forecasting success, Goodman computed the rates of return from following the advice of the different services. The rates of return from following the advice of the econometric-based services are given in Table 11.5. The performance of the advisory services can be compared with the strategy of just buying currencies and holding them. This practice offered gains on each currency other than the Canadian dollar, since the U.S. dollar weakened against most currencies in the study period. The econometric forecasters had a poor record. However, the technically oriented services, whose performances are summarized in Table 11.6, did a good job. Before adjustments for transaction costs or risk, the total returns from buying and selling according to their advice show an average yield of almost 8 percent. This means that if the advice of these services had been followed with the maintenance of a 5 percent margin, the return on the margin after adjusting for transaction costs would have been 145 percent. However, there would also have been periods of losses, and the follower of the advice might not have survived to enjoy the profit available to those currency speculators who did survive. Stated differently, we do not know whether the return of 145 percent is sufficient for the risk that is involved.

Richard Levich has also examined the performance of the advisory services, but his conclusions are rather different from the conclusions of Stephen Goodman.[29] While Levich also found the subjective and technical forecasts to be more accurate than econometric forecasts in the short run, he found the opposite for forecasts of a year (a period not checked by Goodman). Levich did find some gain from following the advice of the advisory services. However, as Levich pointed out, it is not clear whether the gain is sufficient to compensate for the risk of taking open exchange positions in order to follow the advice. It is clear from the results of both Goodman and Levich that the advisory services have at best a mixed record, and so it is unlikely that the average corporate executive who makes an individual forecast will be able to be correct more than 50 percent of the time.

Studying the success of forecasting services is one way to determine whether the foreign exchange markets are efficient. There have been more studies of the efficiency of foreign exchange markets, and these deserve attention.

---

[29] See Richard Levich, "Analyzing the Accuracy of Foreign Exchange Advisory Services: Theory and Evidence," in Richard Levich and Clas Wihlberg (eds.), *Exchange Risk and Exposure: Current Developments in International Financial Management*, D. C. Heath, Lexington, Mass., 1980.

TABLE 11.6
SPECULATIVE RETURN ON CAPITAL FROM FOLLOWING THE ADVICE OF TECHNICAL SERVICES
(In Percentages)

Currency		International Forecasting	Shearson Hayden, Stone	Waldner	Arithmetic average
Canadian dollar	Buy	0.99	4.61	2.50	2.70
	Sell	4.60	5.19	6.22	5.34
	Total	5.59	9.80	8.72	8.04
Number of transactions/yr.		5	17	11	11
French franc	Buy	(2.42)	n.a.	3.82	0.70
	Sell	(3.66)	n.a.	0.53	(1.57)
	Total	(6.08)	n.a.	4.35	(0.87)
Number of transactions/yr.		5	n.a.	15	10
Deutsche mark	Buy	10.49	8.78	7.53	8.93
	Sell	2.46	3.02	1.19	2.22
	Total	12.95	11.80	8.72	11.16
Number of transactions/yr.		5	25	13	14
Yen	Buy	12.42	10.95	11.78	11.72
	Sell	(1.73)	(1.63)	(1.52)	(1.63)
	Total	10.69	9.32	10.26	10.09

Number of transactions/yr.		5	21	12	13
Swiss franc	Buy	9.52	12.99	2.76	8.42
	Sell	2.07	3.11	(10.28)	(1.70)
	Total	11.60	16.10	(7.52)	6.73
Number of transactions/yr.		5	22	14	14
Sterling	Buy	6.70	2.62	9.24	6.19
	Sell	5.55	2.64	9.93	6.04
	Total	12.25	5.26	19.17	12.23
Number of transactions/yr.		4	24	12	13
Arithmetic average	Total	7.83	10.46	7.28	7.90
Number of transactions/yr.		5	22	13	13

Parentheses indicate a negative.
Total is the return on all transactions, both buy and sell.
Totals for arithmetic average column represent horizontal sums; arithmetic average for arithmetic average column represents vertical sum of totals.
Source: Stephen Goodman, "No Better than the Toss of a Coin," *Euromoney*, December 1978, pp. 75–85.

EFFICIENCY OF FOREIGN EXCHANGE MARKETS

We should begin by explaining what we mean by an efficient market.

A efficient market is a market in which all available information is reflected in market prices. As a result, no abnormal profit vis-à-vis the risks involved can be obtained from utilizing the available information.[30]

The definition of market efficiency is generally put into a testable form by computing the excess (or abnormal) return on a particular asset. The excess return is the actual return minus the return that would be expected, given the level of risk, if all available information concerning the asset had been utilized. Excess returns are examined over time to determine whether, on the average, they are equal to zero and serially uncorrelated.[31] Since we must specify the expected returns, tests of market efficiency are really joint tests of both the model used to generate the expected returns and market efficiency.

Efficiency can take on different meanings according to which type of information we wish to include in the set that is assumed to be available to decision makers. If information only on historical prices or returns on the particular asset is included, we are testing for "weak-form efficiency." With all publicly known information included, we are testing for "semistrong efficiency," and with all information, including that available to insiders, we are testing for "strong-form efficiency." Because of central bank involvement with foreign exchange rates, tests of the efficiency of exchange markets are not as straightforward as tests of the efficiency of stock markets. Nevertheless, some tests are possible.[32]

If profits can consistently be made by interest arbitrage, then we can be led to believe that the foreign exchange (or money) markets are inefficient. Profits are made when there are departures from interest parity, and so we can test for inefficiency by examining, for example,

$$\epsilon = (r_{US} - r_{UK}) - \left[\frac{F_1(\$/\pounds) - S(\$/\pounds)}{S(\$/\pounds)} \right] \cdot (1 + r_{UK}) \qquad (11.13)$$

where ϵ is interest disparity, and it is understood that the forward premium/discount

---

[30] On the concept of market efficiency and the tests in the context of the stock market, see Eugene Fama, "Efficient Capital Markets: A Review of Theory and Empirical Work," *Journal of Finance*, vol. 25, June 1970, pp. 383–417.

[31] By having no serial correlation we mean that excess returns to successive periods are not related to each other. If an excess return in one period means a likelihood of further excess returns in an adjacent or subsequent period, the excess returns are serially correlated.

[32] An excellent survey of the tests can be found in Richard Levich, "On the Efficiency of Markets for Foreign Exchange," in Rudiger Dornbusch and Jacob Frenkel (eds.), *International Economic Policy: Theory and Evidence*, Johns Hopkins Press, Baltimore, 1979. This section draws on Levich's survey.

is annualized. If ϵ is large enough to allow a profit to be frequently made from interest arbitrage, we can claim that the foreign exchange market is inefficient. Tests by E. Wayne Clendenning and by Jacob Frenkel and Richard Levich show that ϵ is generally too small for a profit to be made consistently from interest arbitrage *within* the Eurocurrency market. However, Frenkel and Levich find some opportunity for earning a profit, even after adjustments for transaction costs, from arbitrage *between* countries.[33] As we have explained, this appearance of a potential for profit could persist because of exchange controls, liquidity differentials, political risk of foreign versus domestic investments, or taxes, and it might not mean that an actual risk-adjusted profit can be made.

A common notion of efficiency suggests that exchange rates should follow a "random walk," that is, that they should be serially uncorrelated. Tests indicate that exchange rates do not change randomly.[34] However, this is no surprise, since we would expect randomness only if interest rates were similar in the two countries. When interest rates are different, exchange rates should be expected to change in a particular direction.

Similar to the test of randomness is the test of whether profits can be made by using technical trading rules, such as "buy if a currency goes up 2 days in a row." Michael Dooley and Jeffrey Shafer, and also Dennis Logue, Richard Sweeney, and Thomas Willett, found that profitable rules could be devised, and this suggests market inefficiency.[35] Even though profits persist after adjustments for transaction costs, it is not clear whether they are sufficient to compensate for the risks involved. Moreover, it is important that the rules be known in advance and not discovered by going over the existing data to find what *would have* worked. Given a sufficiently extensive search, *some* profitable rules will always emerge, but they are not likely to help in the future.

The forward exchange market has also been studied to see whether it is efficient. The tests have generally been done to determine whether the forward rate is an unbiased predictor of the future spot rate. By "unbiased" we mean that the forward

[33] See E. Wayne Clendenning, *The Eurodollar Market*, Clarendon Press, Oxford, 1970. See also Jacob Frenkel and Richard Levich, "Covered Interest Arbitrage: Unexploited Profits?" *Journal of Political Economy*, vol. 83, April 1975, pp. 325–338, and Jacob Frenkel and Richard Levich, "Transaction Costs and Interest Arbitrage: Tranquil versus Turbulent Periods," *Journal of Political Economy*, vol. 85, December 1977, pp. 1007–1024.

[34] See the results in William Poole, "Speculative Prices on Random Walks: An Analysis of Ten Time Series of Flexible Exchange Rates," *Southern Economic Journal*, vol. 33, April 1967, pp. 468–478, and John Burt, Fred Kaen, and Geoffrey Booth, "Foreign Exchange Market Efficiency under Flexible Exchange Rates," *Journal of Finance*, vol. 32, December 1977, pp. 1325–1330. In fact, efficiency implies only that forward contracts do not offer abnormal returns, and when we have inflation, efficiency does not imply a random movement of the spot rate.

[35] See Michael Dooley and Jeffrey Shafer, *Analysis of Short-Run Exchange Rate Behavior: March 1973 to September 1975*, International Finance Discussion Paper 80, Federal Reserve System, Washington, D.C., and Dennis Logue, Richard Sweeney, and Thomas Willett, "Speculative Behavior of Foreign Exchange Rates during the Current Float," *Journal of Business Research*, vol. 6, 1978, pp. 159–174. The discovery of profitable trading rules has been carried into the forward market by Paul Boothe ("Estimating the Structure and Efficiency of the Canadian Foreign Exchange Market," unpublished Ph.D. dissertation, University of British Columbia, 1981).

TABLE 11.7
FORWARD EXCHANGE RATES AND THE ACTUAL (REALIZED) RATES FOR POUNDS VIS-À-VIS DOLLARS, 1977–1981

Date of forward rate		3-month forward rate	Realized rate	Annualized error (%)	12-month forward rate	Realized rate	Annualized error (%)
1976	IV	1.6560	1.7172	−14.78*	1.5635	1.9180	−24.95
1977	I	1.6923	1.7195	−6.43	1.6262	1.8630	−14.56
	II	1.7023	1.7475	−10.62	1.6510	1.8610	−12.72
	III	1.7498	1.9180	−38.45	1.7475	1.9735	−12.93
	IV	1.9207	1.8630	+12.02	1.9180	2.0370	−6.20
1978	I	1.8621	1.8610	+0.24	1.8630	2.0650	−10.84
	II	1.8090	1.9735	−36.37	1.8610	2.1810	−17.20
	III	1.9559	2.0370	−16.59	1.9735	2.2015	−11.55
	IV	2.0324	2.0650	−6.42	2.0370	2.2340	−9.67
1979	I	2.0581	2.1810	−23.89	2.0650	2.1700	−5.08
	II	2.1625	2.2015	−7.21	2.1810	2.3485	−7.68
	III	2.1943	2.2340	−7.24	2.2015	2.3905	−8.59
	IV	2.2227	2.1700	+9.48	2.2340	2.3700	−6.09
1980	I	2.1755	2.3455	−31.81	2.1700	2.2265	−2.60
	II	2.3060	2.3905	−14.66	2.3485		
	III	2.3755	2.3700	+0.93	2.3905		
	IV	2.3910	2.2265	+27.52	2.3700		
1981	I	2.2405			2.2265		

*A minus sign means that $S(\$/£)$ is underestimated.

rate will not overestimate or underestimate the spot rate.[36] Virtually every test finds the forward rate to be an unbiased predictor of the eventual spot rate. However, it is a poor predictor and will provide very large errors. This is shown, for example, in Table 11.7. The table shows the 3-month and 12-month forward rates for the British pound and the actual spot rates that existed at the maturity of the contracts. While it might be true that the errors over substantial periods are, on the average, zero (but not in the period covered in the table), the deviation of the forward rate from the eventually realized spot rate is so large that those who failed to avail themselves of the forward market would have experienced great variations in incomes. Of course, those who allowed themselves to be long in British pounds would generally have done well in this period.

Market efficiency and the effects of transaction costs, shipping costs, political and exchange risks, taxes, nontraded goods, and so on, which prevent interest parity and purchasing power parity from holding are most important in determining whether real or effective changes in exchange rates occur—the topic of the next chapter. The size of real changes in exchange rates must be determined if we are to continue with an evaluation of investment and borrowing performance and the consequences of changes in exchange rates for the economic risk of the exporting or importing firm.

SUMMARY

1 Virtually any newsworthy economic or political development can affect spot exchange rates. However, in the long run, a most important factor influencing spot exchange rates is the rate of inflation.
2 Countries that have high inflation will experience a reduction in the values of their currencies. This follows from the purchasing power parity doctrine, PPP.
3 Evidence on PPP has been provided from studies on narrowly classified commodities and on traded goods only. Most of the evidence supports PPP only in the long run.

[36] There are numerous studies of the efficiency of the forward market. We can cite Michael Porter, "A Theoretical and Empirical Framework for Analyzing the Term Structure of Exchange Rate Expectations," *IMF Staff Papers*, vol. 18, September 1971, pp. 613–645; David Kaserman, "The Forward Rate: Its Determination and Behavior as a Predictor of the Future Spot Rate," *Proceedings of the American Statistical Association*, 1973, pp. 417–422; Robert Aliber, "Attributes of National Monies and the Independence of National Monetary Policies," in Robert Aliber (ed.), *National Monetary Policies and the International System*, University of Chicago Press, Chicago, 1974; Steven Kohlhagen, "The Performance of the Foreign Exchange Markets: 1971–74," *Journal of International Business Studies*, vol. 6, fall 1975, pp. 33–39; Ian Giddy and Gunter Dufey, "The Random Behavior of Flexible Exchange Rates," *Journal of International Business Studies*, vol. 6, spring 1975, pp. 1–32; W. Bradford Cornell and J. Kimball Dietrich, "The Efficiency of the Market for Foreign Exchange under Floating Exchange Rates," *Review of Economics and Statistics*, vol. 60, February 1979, pp. 111–120; Jacob Frenkel, "The Forward Exchange Rate, Expectations and the Demand for Money: The German Hyperinflation," *American Economic Review*, vol. 67, September 1977, pp. 653–670, and "Purchasing Power Parity: Evidence from the 1920's," *Journal of International Economics*, vol. 8, May 1979, pp. 161–169; Alan Stockman, "Risk, Information and Forward Exchange Rates," in Jacob Frenkel and Harry Johnson (eds.), *The Economics of Exchange Rates: Selected Studies*, Addison-Wesley Publishing Company, Boston, 1978; and the summary of these and other papers in Richard Levich, "On the Efficiency of Markets for Foreign Exchange," in Rudiger Dornbusch and Jacob Frenkel (eds.), *International Economic Policy: Theory and Evidence*, Johns Hopkins Press, Baltimore, 1979.

4 Departures from PPP can be caused by transportation costs, import duties, and quotas on the one hand and by price differences for nontraded outputs on the other hand. However, even the prices of nontraded outputs will not move far apart if the users of these outputs can move, and if producers move between traded and nontraded outputs when relative prices make one group more profitable.

5 The PPP condition and a condition closely resembling the interest parity condition can be used to derive the equality of ex ante real interest rates between countries. This latter relationship is the Fisher-open condition, a condition that has an independent rationale.

6 Purchasing power parity, interest parity, and the Fisher-open condition represent ways in which the economies of different countries are linked. In addition, they are crucial in judging the size of real changes in the exchange rates, which we will do in the next chapter.

7 Interest differentials provide market predictions of changes in exchange rates. Using interest rates for different pairs of countries and for different maturities gives market forecasts for different exchange rates over different periods. Individual forecasts can be made if the individuals hold expectations on rates of inflation in the two countries. These individual forecasts are not very accurate in the short run because PPP holds very poorly over shorter periods.

8 Because it frequently takes some time after inflation differentials occur for exchange rates to change and restore the PPP condition, the PPP condition can be used as an exchange rate forecasting device. We can base future exchange rate movements on the gap between accumulated inflation differentials (adjusted for trade elsewhere) and the accumulated change in exchange rates.

9 Some forecasting services use econometric methods, and others are more technical or subjective. They all tend to look at factors such as PPP and interest rate differentials along with other economic and political conditions. The record of the forecasters is mixed. The technical or subjective forecasters have tended to outperform the econometric forecasters.

10 Closely connected to the issue of the ability to make useful forecasts is the subject of foreign exchange market efficiency. Tests of efficiency have involved the examination of covered interest differentials, the randomness of exchange rate movements, and the accuracy of the forward rate as a predictor of the spot rate. In general, markets appear to be efficient when judged by the randomness of exchange rates and the accuracy of the forward rate in predicting the spot rate. The efficiency is less obvious from covered interest differentials, but this could be because of risks, taxes, liquidity, and so on.

QUESTIONS

1 Which commodities do you think fit the purchasing power parity condition most closely? Are they valuable, widely traded, durable, homogeneous in quality, and so on?

2 Distinguish between direct arbitrage between countries and the "arbitrage" that occurs when buyers look for the cheapest market. How will the latter tend to ensure PPP even if there are shipping costs and import tariffs, and how must these shipping costs and tariffs apply for perfect PPP?

3 What are the differences between the movement of goods and the movement of factors of production in taking us toward PPP? Does the answer have to do with the speed of returning to PPP and comparative advantage?

4 Why do you think PPP is violated by a larger amount during periods of flexible rather than fixed exchange rates? Wouldn't you think a priori that PPP would be violated by a larger amount when exchange rates are fixed?

5 Write the PPP, interest parity, and Fisher-open conditions. Derive each one from the other two.

6 Why is Equation (11.8) not an interest parity condition? If investors and borrowers are neutral toward risk, would it be a precise representation of interest indifference, and if not, what condition would be?

7 Once the limit of deviation from PPP in absolute or static terms, because of transportation costs, tariffs, and so on, is reached, must the relative or dynamic PPP condition begin to hold? At the limit of possible deviation from the absolute PPP condition, is there an asymmetry in the relative condition from faster inflation at home versus abroad on the one hand, and from slower inflation at home versus abroad on the other hand?

8 Assume that you are given the following:

r_{US}	r_{UK}	$\dot{P}^*_{US}$	$\dot{P}^*_{UK}$
13%	15%	10%	12%

All the variables are measures of per annum rates over 5 years, and the inflation expectations are your own.

  a What is the implicit market prediction of the per annum future change in exchange rates?

  b What is your prediction?

  c Given that you believe that interest parity almost always holds to within 1 percent, how sure are you of the market prediction, $\dot{S}^*(\$/£)$?

  d Does a knowledge of $\dot{S}^*(\$/£)$ tell you what the actual $\dot{S}(\$/£)$ will be?

9 How would you use PPP in a statistical forecast of the foreign exchange value of the Canadian dollar over the next 10 years?

10 What would prevent real rates of return from becoming equal? Could different intertemporal trade-offs in different countries explain persistently differing real returns?

BIBLIOGRAPHY

Aliber, Robert Z.: *Exchange Risk and Corporate International Finance*, The Macmillan Press, London, 1978.

Aliber, Robert Z., and Clyde P. Stickney: "Accounting Measures of Foreign Exchange Exposure: The Long and Short of It," *Accounting Review*, January 1975, pp. 44–57.

Balassa, Bela: "The Purchasing-Power-Parity Doctrine: A Re-Appraisal," *Journal of Political Economy*, vol. 73, December 1964, pp. 584–596. Reprinted in Richard N. Cooper (ed.), *International Finance: Selected Readings*, Penguin Books, Middlesex, United Kingdom, 1969.

Dornbusch, Rudiger, and Dwight Jaffee: "Purchasing Power Parity and Exchange Rate Problems: Introduction" and the collection of papers they introduce in "Purchasing Power Parity: A Symposium," *Journal of International Economics*, May 1978, pp. 157–351.

Gaillot, Henry J.: "Purchasing Power Parity as an Explanation of Long-Term Changes in Exchange Rates," *Journal of Money, Credit and Banking*, August 1970, pp. 348–357.

Giddy, Ian H.: "An Integrated Theory of Exchange Rate Equilibrium," *Journal of Financial and Quantitative Analysis*, December 1976, pp. 883–892.

Goodman, Stephen H.: "No Better than the Toss of a Coin," *Euromoney*, December 1978, pp. 75–85.

Levich, Richard M.: "On the Efficiency of Markets for Foreign Exchange," in Rudiger Dornbusch and Jacob A. Frenkel (eds.), *International Economic Policy: Theory and Evidence*, Johns Hopkins Press, Baltimore, 1979.

Officer, Lawrence H.: "The Purchasing Power Parity Theory of Exchange Rates: A Review Article," *IMF Staff Papers*, vol. 23, March 1976, pp. 1–60.

Schadler, Susan: "Sources of Exchange Rate Variability: Theory and Empirical Evidence," *IMF Staff Papers*, vol. 24, July 1977, pp. 253–296.

CHAPTER 12

REAL CHANGES IN EXCHANGE RATES

This chapter is concerned with the effects that changes in exchange rates have on the financial statements of a firm and whether the measured effects give an accurate picture of what has really happened to the value of assets and liabilities. The uncertainty of the value of existing foreign assets and liabilities because of changes in exchange rates is what we referred to as "translation risk" in the introduction. This chapter is also concerned with the effects of exchange rates on the international competitiveness of exporters and importers and hence on income not yet received. This is the "economic risk" described in Chapter 1. Finally, this chapter shows the difference between the levels of concern for domestic and international financial managers caused by economic risk.

NORMAL EFFECTS OF EXCHANGE RATES

Generally, one might believe that, for example, an appreciation of the pound sterling against the dollar would be welcomed by management in a U.S. firm that

1 Holds existing pound-denominated assets, including receivables from exports. These will be worth more U.S. dollars when their value is translated at the higher sterling exchange rate.

2 Sells goods that compete with British products. This is because the extra cost of pounds brings economic benefits in terms of increasing the competitiveness of U.S. firms.

The first of these effects is a beneficial result of translation/transaction exposure, while the second is a beneficial result of economic exposure.

The same appreciation of the British pound would be expected to be a source of concern to financial executives in a U.S. firm that

1 Has existing liabilities denominated in pounds, including payables on imports. The debt repayments will require more dollars when translated in U.S. accounts.

2 Buys goods from Britain. Higher import prices will reduce profitability if the goods are for sale to the public or are inputs for production.

The first of these is a harmful effect of translation/transaction exposure, and the second is a harmful effect of economic exposure.

While generally accurate, this list of gainers and losers from translation exposure and economic exposure can give a misleading impression. As we shall discover in this chapter, if, for example, exchange rate movements mirror relative rates of interest according to a condition that closely resembles the interest parity condition, exchange rate changes can mean very little for the translated value of financial assets and liabilities. Whether the relevant condition holds turns out to depend on whether expected interest yields are equal in different countries and whether changes in exchange rates have been expected. We will also discover in this chapter that changes in exchange rates will have little effect on the translated values of foreign fixed assets—such as factories or inventory—if purchasing power parity holds exactly.

A full and accurate picture of the effects of exchange rates will not be obtained from financial statements which show only translation effects. The economic effects on future profitability of changes in exchange rates are not recorded in accounting statements. Only after additional profits materialize from the extra competitiveness of, for example, U.S. exporters after a dollar depreciation will these effects resulting from economic exposure be recorded in the income statement. Similarly, any potentially smaller future profits resulting from higher import prices which, for example, raise future production costs are not recorded until the lower future profits occur. The nature of the change in exchange rates that will have these effects on profitability turns out to be the same as the type of change that has an effect on the translated value of foreign fixed assets.

We will take the viewpoint of a financial manager who is trying to determine what the changes in exchange rates mean for his or her firm. In particular, we wish to show how the manager can determine whether there has been a real change in

1 The true value of assets and liabilities
2 The level of international competitiveness

We can define the "real change in exchange rates" in this way:

The real change in exchange rates is the change that alters the value of domestic versus foreign assets/liabilities or the level of international competitiveness.

We will see that in a world of highly different inflationary experiences, a measure of the real change in the exchange rate will often be more meaningful than the nominal change.

EXCHANGE RATES AND TRANSLATION RISK

It is the nature of an internationally oriented firm to have assets and liabilities denominated in different currencies. American firms often borrow in Europe in units of local currencies. Foreign firms frequently borrow in U.S. dollars. Many firms make direct investments in controlled subsidiaries or hold a noncontrolling share of an enterprise in a foreign country. When exchange rates change, the values of these liabilities and assets when translated into domestic currency are likely to change, and it becomes an important matter to discover by how much. This determination takes on a different character for financial assets as opposed to fixed assets. Financial assets are money market securities and bonds, while fixed assets include plant and inventory, the values of which move with general inflation.

Financial Assets and Liabilities

Suppose that Aviva Corporation has invested in some British bonds. Let us assume that these are long-term bonds. Clearly a depreciation of the British pound will decrease the dollar value of these financial securities when they are translated (that is, converted into dollars) at the new exchange rate. But would we want to consider Aviva as being worse off by holding sterling bonds rather than dollar-denominated bonds? Alternatively, would an appreciation of the pound make Aviva better off?

A depreciation of a currency that is compensated for in terms of higher interest yields on financial assets should not be considered a real depreciation from the point of view of these assets. For example, if the pound fell in value against the dollar by 10 percent but British interest rates were 10 percent higher than those in the United States, the firm would be no worse off from British versus U.S. investments. According to our definition of a real change in exchange rates, that is, a change which affects the value of foreign versus domestic assets, we might therefore define the real change for financial assets held for a year as follows:[1]

$$\text{Real percentage change in } (\$/£) = \frac{S_1(\$/£) - S(\$/£)}{S(\$/£)} - (r_{US} - r_{UK})$$

$S_1(\$/£)$ is the actual spot rate at year-end, and r_{US} and r_{UK} refer to interest earnings during that year. The definition consists of the actual percentage increase in the value of the pound minus the extent to which higher interest rates in the United States have compensated for this. Because translation gains are made on the interest earned in Britain as well as on the principal, a more precise definition is

$$\text{Real percentage change in } (\$/£) = \frac{S_1(\$/£) - S(\$/£)}{S(\$/£)} \cdot (1 + r_{UK}) -$$
$$(r_{US} - r_{UK}) \qquad (12.1)$$

[1]We might alternatively refer to this as the "effective change" in the exchange rate.

A positive value of Equation (12.1) will signify a real pound appreciation. This is because the increased value of the pound has not been offset by higher U.S. interest rates. For example, if $S(\$/£) = 2.00$, $S_1(\$/£) = 2.10$, $r_{US} = 0.16$, and $r_{UK} = 0.12$, the value of Equation (12.1) is $[(2.10 - 2.00)/2.00] \times 1.12 - (0.04) = 0.016$. This real appreciation of 1.6 percent is smaller than the actual appreciation of 5 percent because higher U.S. interest rates have compensated the holder of U.S. bonds, and so the gain from holding British bonds has been reduced.

A negative value of Equation (12.1) will mean a real pound depreciation, and this holds in reverse for the dollar.[2]

In the special case when the left-hand side of Equation (12.1) is equal to zero, we have

$$r_{US} = r_{UK} + \frac{S_1(\$/£) - S(\$/£)}{S(\$/£)} (1 + r_{UK}) \qquad (12.2)$$

This is similar to the interest parity condition and differs only in that it uses the actual future spot rate, $S_1(\$/£)$, rather than the forward rate, $F_1(\$/£)$. When forward hedging takes place and covered yields are equalized, the difference between earnings from investment at home and earnings from investment abroad is known at the time of investment, and changes in exchange rates will have no effect. The real change in exchange rates in evaluating investment in domestic versus foreign bonds will be zero.

When investment in foreign securities is not hedged so that changes in exchange rates can have an effect, the *expected* yield from investing abroad for 1 year can be computed as follows:

$$\text{Expected yield from U.K. investment} = r_{UK} + \frac{S_1^*(\$/£) - S(\$/£)}{S(\$/£)} (1 + r_{UK}) \qquad (12.3)$$

In Equation (12.3) we have used the expected exchange rate at year-end, $S_1^*(\$/£)$. The expected yield differs from the yield from local investment, r_{US}, by the difference between Equation (12.3) and r_{US}; that is,

$$\text{Extra } expected \text{ yield from U.K.} = \frac{S_1^*(\$/£) - S(\$/£)}{S(\$/£)} (1 + r_{UK}) - (r_{US} - r_{UK}) \qquad (12.4)$$

There will be no extra *expected* yield from investment in Britain if investment there occurs until interest rates and exchange rates are such that Equation (12.4) has

---

[2]If the firm has hedged the British asset in the forward exchange market, then the change in exchange rates will mean no change in the translated foreign value versus the domestic value, and so according to our definition, the real change is zero. When an asset is hedged against exchange risk, we should say that foreign exchange transaction gains (losses) on the asset are exactly offset by the translation losses (gains) on the forward contract.

a value of zero. If this occurs and

$$S_1(\$/\pounds) = S_1^*(\$/\pounds)$$

that is, the eventually realized spot rate equals the expected rate so that expectations were correct, then Equation (12.1) also has a value of zero. Hence when there is an expected interest parity [Equation (12.4) has a value of zero] and when expected spot exchange rates are realized, there will be no real change in the exchange rate. When *expected* yields in Britain and the United States are equal, that is, Equation (12.4) has a value of zero, but expectations are incorrect, with

$$S_1(\$/\pounds) > S_1^*(\$/\pounds)$$

the zero value of Equation (12.4) from the equating of expected yields will mean a positive value for Equation (12.1) and a real appreciation of the pound. The increased value of the pound is not fully expected when $S_1(\$/\pounds) > S_1^*(\$/\pounds)$, and it is this that has meant incomplete compensation in interest rates and the real appreciation.

When international investment equalizes overall expected yields and

$$S_1(\$/\pounds) < S_1^*(\$/\pounds)$$

the zero value of Equation (12.4) means a negative value of Equation (12.1). We will have experienced a real depreciation of the pound.

We have discovered that when interest differentials compensate for the expected change in exchange rates, only unanticipated changes in exchange rates can leave investors better or worse off from foreign versus domestic investment. But can a judgment of relative investment performance be made from a company's financial statements? We will see that a judgment is possible so that we do not have to apply Equation (12.1) to decide whether foreign investment was a good idea. However, the method of making this judgment from financial statements depends on the accounting procedures that are in effect. We should therefore begin by examining U.S. accounting practices.

U.S. International Accounting Principles

Until 1982, the United States used an accounting standard generally known as FASB 8. This was a highly controversial standard and is well worth describing.[3] Under FASB 8, a company was required to show all foreign exchange translation

---

[3]See *Statement of Financial Accounting Standards,* no. 8, Financial Accounting Standards Board, Stamford, Conn., October 1975. The general outline of the new accounting system which has replaced the so-called FASB 8 system is presented in *Foreign Currency Translation: Exposure Draft,* revised, Financial Accounting Standards Board, Stamford, Conn., June 30, 1981, and *Statement of Financial Accounting Standards, no. 52—Foreign Currency Translation,* Financial Accounting Standards Board, Stamford, Conn., December 1981.

gains or losses (those from converting foreign assets or liabilities into dollar amounts) in the current period income statement. Different treatment was given to current operating receipts and expenditures and to financial assets/liabilities on the one hand and to fixed or real assets on the other hand. This was referred to as a temporal distinction, and the rules were as follows:

FASB 8 Rules

1 Revenues and expenses from foreign entities (overseas operations) were translated at the average exchange rate prevailing during the period, except for assets valued on a historical basis such as depreciation. These assets were translated at historical exchange rates. Financial assets and liabilities were translated at the average exchange rate during the period.

2 Other assets, primarily fixed or real assets, were translated at historical exchange rates. Historical costs were used in terms of local (foreign) currency.

What FASB 8 therefore required was that if local currency values were measured at current cost, they were to be translated at current exchange rates, and if they were measured at historical cost, they were to be translated at historical exchange rates.

The FASB 8 accounting procedure required that all translation adjustments had to appear in the income statement. This made income appear highly volatile and caused numerous corporate treasurers to take permanently hedged positions to prevent adverse shareholder reaction. The procedure which has replaced FASB 8 is called FASB 52, and this involves two principal changes:

FASB 52 Rules

1 The *functional currency* is selected for the subsidiary. This is the primary currency of the subsidiary. For example, a British subsidiary of a U.S. parent firm will declare that the pound is its functional currency. Any foreign currency income of the subsidiary (for example, marks or francs earned by the British subsidiary) is translated into the functional currency according to the FASB 8 rules. After this, *all* amounts are translated from the functional currency into dollars at the *current* exchange rate.

2 Translation gains and losses are to be disclosed and accumulated in a separate account showing shareholders' equity. Only when foreign assets or liabilities are liquidated do they become transaction gains or losses and appear in the income statement.

The rule on using current exchange rates on all items is relaxed when there is extremely high inflation in the country whose currency is being translated. Extremely high inflation means a cumulative amount of over 100 percent during the preceding 3 years. If this condition is met, the temporal distinction used in FASB 8 still applies. This means that in circumstances of extreme inflation, current exchange rates are used for current-cost items such as financial assets and liabilities, and historical rates are used for historical-cost items.

The best way to illustrate the effects of these accounting procedures is to take examples. The examples should distinguish between financial assets and fixed assets.

Financial Assets and Financial Statements

Suppose that in the previous year, $1 million had been placed in a U.S. long-term bond yielding 12 percent ($r_{US} = 0.12$), and $1 million had been placed in a British long-term bond yielding 20 percent ($r_{UK} = 0.20$). Suppose that last year the spot rate had been $S(\$/£) = 2.0$ and that during the year the pound depreciates or is devalued to $S_1(\$/£) = 1.8$.

The actual pound depreciation or devaluation is 10 percent. However, interest rates make up for some of this. The real depreciation of the pound given by Equation (12.1) is computed as follows:

$$\text{Real change in } (\$/£) = \frac{1.8 - 2.0}{2.0}(1.20) - (-0.08) = -0.04$$

The negative value means a real depreciation of the pound of 4 percent, which is a real appreciation of the dollar. The 10 percent decline in the value of the pound is not fully compensated by the higher British interest rate.

In terms of the financial accounts, after placing $1 million in the U.S. bond for 1 year, there will be $120,000 in interest appearing in the income statement, and if interest rates do not change, there is no change in the value of financial assets. This is shown in Table 12.1.

Placing $1 million in Britain at the initial exchange rate $S(\$/£) = 2.0$ means investing £500,000. At $r_{UK} = 0.20$, this will earn £100,000. At the exchange rate of $1.8/£, the £100,000 will be translated into $180,000 of income.

The £500,000 British asset is worth only $900,000 at the rate of $1.8/£.[4] Since the initial value was $1 million, there is a translation loss of $100,000. Under FASB 8 this would have appeared in the income account, but with the FASB 52 accounting procedure this will appear separately. This is shown in the second row of Table 12.1. Under FASB 8 the declared income on the British bond would have been $180,000 − $100,000 = $80,000 with $S(\$/£) = 1.8$, and under the FASB 52 system, which has replaced FASB 8, there is a declared income of $180,000 if the translation loss is not realized, that is, if the bond is not sold.

Under FASB 8, there is a relative loss on the British bond of $40,000 ($80,000 − $120,000 = −$40,000), or 4 percent of the original investment, compared with the $120,000 in earnings from the U.S. bond. In the same way, when using the FASB 52 procedure and combining the shareholder equity account with income, we have an absolute income on British bonds of $180,000 − $100,000 = +$80,000. Compared with the $120,000 that would have been earned on the U.S. bond, this involves a relative loss of $40,000. The real depreciation or devaluation of 4 percent found from both the FASB 8 procedure and the FASB 52 procedure agrees with what we found in the definition, Equation (12.1). But we note that with the FASB 52 accounting procedure, we must include shareholder equity effects if we are to make a good judgment of investment performance with financial assets.

---

[4] We see the problem of using an average exchange rate rather than the end-of-year rate which is truly current, as used here. The advantage of averages exists when income flows continue throughout the year and when we want a smoother translation.

TABLE 12.1
EARNINGS ON DOMESTIC VERSUS BRITISH BONDS

	Interest earnings	Translation gain or loss	Declared income, FASB 8	Declared income, FASB 52
U.S. bond	+$120,000	–	–	+$120,000
$S_1(\$/\pounds) = 1.8000$	+$180,000	–$100,000	+$80,000	+$180,000
$S_1(\$/\pounds) = 1.8667$	+$186,667	–$66,667	+$120,000	+$186,667
$S_1(\$/\pounds) = 1.9000$	+$190,000	–$50,000	+$140,000	+$190,000

If the exchange rate after a year of investment had moved to $S_1(\$/£) = 1.8667$, then the real change in the exchange rate would have been zero, since the definition, Equation (12.1), tells us that

$$\frac{1.8667 - 2.0}{2.0}(1.20) - (-0.08) = 0.0$$

This result occurs because the end-of-year exchange rate of $\$1.8667/£$ corresponds to the expected spot rate that would have created an equality between expected yields.[5]

In terms of the entries in the financial accounts, $1 million in Britain at $S(\$/£) = 2.0$ is £500,000, which as before earns £100,000. At $S_1(\$/£) = 1.8667$, this is worth a total of $186,667. The translation loss at this realized exchange rate is $66,667 [$1,000,000 - ($1.8667 \times 500,000)]$. If we use FASB 52, this gives total earnings of $120,000 ($186,667 - $66,667) if we are careful to aggregate the appropriate interest earnings from the income account and the foreign exchange loss that is given in the shareholder equity account. FASB 8 provides the same answer. We obtain the same earnings at home as abroad, $120,000, and the actual fall in the value of the pound means no real change in the exchange rate.

If the pound falls in actual value by only 5 percent to $S_1(\$/£) = 1.9$, then the £100,000 in earnings from Britain will be worth $1.9 \times 100,000 = \$190,000$, and the translation loss will be $50,000 [$1,000,000 - ($1.9 \times 500,000)]$. The total earnings are therefore $140,000 ($190,000 - $50,000) if we are careful to include all earnings. This is $20,000 more than the earnings from the U.S. bond. Even though the pound has fallen in value, the overcompensation in the British interest rate is a real gain from British bonds of 2 percent. This will be found as the real percentage change in the exchange rate from the definition, Equation (12.1), but we again note that if our accounts are to give the correct result, they must be integrated so that equity effects are added to income earned.

General Statement of Accounting Effects of Exchange Rates on Financial Assets/Liabilities*

In the previous section we used an example to show how U.S. accounting procedures provide statements of the effects of changes in exchange rates. Here we will show these effects in general terms.

For each dollar invested for a year at home, an investor will receive as income $\$r_{US}$. The full amount will appear as interest income in the income statement no

---

[5]With $r_{UK} = 0.20$, $r_{US} = 0.12$, and $S(\$/£) = 2.0$ we can rearrange the interest parity condition

$$S_1^*(\$/£) = S(\$/£)\frac{(1 + r_{US})}{(1 + r_{UK})}$$

to find $S_1^*(\$/£) = 1.8667$. As we claimed earlier, the real change in exchange rates is zero if expected yields are equalized and the realized rate, $S_1(\$/£)$, is equal to the expected rate.

matter what accounting principle is used, and if interest rates remain constant, there will be no change in the value of the bond.

For each dollar invested for a year in Britain, an investor who is unhedged will receive interest earnings, measured in terms of dollars of

$$\frac{S_1(\$/£)}{S(\$/£)} r_{UK}$$

This amount, which will appear in the income statement, is, however, only part of the earnings on the British long-term bond.

What must be added to or subtracted from the interest earned in Britain is the change in the capital value of the British security in terms of dollars. If interest rates in Britain, as in the United States, do not change, the sterling value of the British bond will also remain unchanged. The value when translated *in terms of dollars* will, however, change by

$$\frac{S_1(\$/£)}{S(\$/£)} - 1$$

This is a translation loss or gain. With FASB 8 accounting it was included as income, but under the new procedure it is included separately in the shareholder equity account. It is counted as income only when the asset is sold; then the translation gain or loss becomes a transaction gain or loss.

To conform to the definition of a real change in exchange rates for financial assets and liabilities as given in Equation (12.1), we must combine the interest income and the translation gain or loss because these are both legitimate parts of earnings. The combined interest income and translation gain or loss (if necessary, combined from the separate parts of the financial accounts) give total earnings of

$$\$\frac{S_1(\$/£)}{S(\$/£)} \cdot r_{UK} + \frac{S_1(\$/£)}{S(\$/£)} - 1 = \$\frac{S_1(\$/£)}{S(\$/£)}(1 + r_{UK}) - 1 \tag{12.5}$$

The difference between accounting entries for total domestic earnings and accounting entries for total foreign earnings corresponds to the definition of the real change in exchange rates given in Equation (12.1). The difference between domestic earnings and total foreign earnings is

$$r_{US} - \left[\frac{S_1(\$/£)}{S(\$/£)}(1 + r_{UK}) - 1 \right] \tag{12.6}$$

where the second term is obtained from Equation (12.5) above. The difference in Equation (12.6) can be reduced to

$$\frac{S_1(\$/£) - S(\$/£)}{S(\$/£)}(1 + r_{UK}) - (r_{US} - r_{UK}) \tag{12.7}$$

which is the same as our definition in Equation (12.1). We find that we must combine the interest income and the translation gain or loss to know the real effect of changes in exchange rates. With FASB 8 this was done automatically, but with FASB 52 we must be careful to aggregate the income and shareholder equity accounts.

Judging the borrowing decision, which means judging financial liabilities, is the reverse of judging the investment decision, and we must reverse the interpretation of condition (12.1). When borrowing is hedged in the forward market, there is no real change in exchange rates. When it is unhedged, real borrowing costs are the same at home and abroad as long as the depreciation in the value of a currency is compensated with higher interest payments. There is an ex post real advantage to borrowing abroad instead of at home if the realized depreciation of the foreign currency is more than the extra interest rate that is paid abroad versus at home.

Fixed Assets and Real Changes in Exchange Rates

We might believe that if, for example, Aviva Corporation owned some assets in Britain such as a subsidiary with land, buildings, capital equipment, and inventory, then a depreciation of the pound would make ownership of these assets less desirable than the ownership of similar assets back in the United States. However, the depreciation of the pound might merely reflect higher inflation in Britain, which would raise the pound market value of the fixed assets in that country. For example, if British inflation is 10 percent higher than U.S. inflation and the pound falls 10 percent against the dollar, the U.S. and British assets will both be worth 10 percent more in dollar amounts. This requires, of course, that the asset values move in line with general inflation.[6] We find in such a situation that domestic and foreign real assets do not change in value vis-à-vis each other, and so the real change in exchange rates is zero.

The changes in U.S. accounting procedures have helped reduce volatility in reported income. However, neither FASB 8 nor its replacement, FASB 52, uses the current market or replacement value for foreign-currency-denominated assets in the translation into dollars at current exchange rates. Instead, historical costs of fixed assets are used. We have seen that as long as we include all the components, we still obtain an accurate picture of the effects of changes in exchange rates on financial assets/liabilities. However, when we are dealing with fixed assets and inflation rates differ between countries, U.S. accounting procedures provide a distorted picture of the effects of exchange rates.

It can be shown, as we will do by example, that the correct and accurate accounting procedure uses not only the current exchange rate for translation (as

---

[6]Common stocks have not generally kept pace with inflation, and so we might not wish to consider them as "real." The values of land, buildings, machines, and inventory do keep pace with general inflation over long periods. We note that we abstract from tax implications. Implicitly, as with financial assets, we are taking tax rates on income and on foreign exchange gains to be the same, whereas in fact taxes on exchange gains can often be postponed or be at the more favorable capital gains rate.

does the FASB 52 procedure) but also the current market value of fixed assets.[7] We will therefore compare the FASB 52 procedure not only with its predecessor, FASB 8, but also with the correct procedure for dealing with fixed assets. We will begin by providing a workable definition of the real change in exchange rates for fixed assets that is comparable to the definition, Equation (12.1), used for financial assets.

Defining the Real Change in Exchange Rates for Fixed Assets

If fixed-asset prices have risen at the rate $\dot{P}_{US}$ and the real rate of return in the form of profits on the assets has been ρ_{US}, then the total amount received after a year from each dollar of fixed or real assets held at home is[8]

$$\$(1 + \rho_{US} + \dot{P}_{US}) \tag{12.8}$$

What is received from a dollar in real assets is the original dollar, the real profit on that dollar (ρ_{US}), and the inflation in the value of the asset, P_{US}.

Each dollar placed abroad in real assets that rose with inflation at $\dot{P}_{UK}$ with a rent or profit rate of ρ_{UK} will produce, when translated in the financial accounts at the exchange rate $S_1(\$/£)$, earnings of

$$\$ \frac{S_1(\$/£)}{S(\$/£)} (1 + \rho_{UK} + \dot{P}_{UK}) \tag{12.9}$$

This is because the original dollar will purchase $1/[S(\$/£)]$ in British fixed assets on which profits are ρ_{UK} and inflation is $\dot{P}_{UK}$ and which can be translated into dollars at $S_1(\$/£)$. Real investment yields in Britain and the United States will be equal if Equations (12.8) and (12.9) are equal, that is, if

$$\rho_{US} + \dot{P}_{US} = \frac{S_1(\$/£)}{S(\$/£)} \rho_{UK} + \dot{P}_{UK} + \frac{S_1(\$/£) - S(\$/£)}{S(\$/£)} (1 + \dot{P}_{UK}) \tag{12.10}$$

The left-hand side is the total return in the United States, and the right-hand side is the return in Britain. When Equation (12.10) holds, we can say that there has been no real change in exchange rates for fixed assets. This is because a change in exchange rates still leaves returns from foreign investments equal to returns at home.

In order to put Equation (12.10) in more familiar terms, we might assume that the translated real return from Britain in terms of profit, that is $[S_1(\$/£)/S(\$/£)]\rho_{UK}$, is

---

[7] Britain uses the correct procedure. The reason why it is not used in the United States is that there is no rule on how to account for inflation.

[8] It is not entirely by chance that we call the real return on fixed or real assets ρ_{US}, the term used earlier with the Fisher equation. If real returns on fixed assets are similar to those on financial assets, the ρ_{US} used here will be the same as that in the previous chapter. We can note that a more precise definition of total return would involve the product $\rho_{US} \cdot \dot{P}_{US}$. This should, however, be small and we do not consider it in our analysis here.

equal to ρ_{US}.[9] Then Equation (12.10) can be written as

$$\dot{P}_{US} = \dot{P}_{UK} + \dot{S}(\$/\pounds)\,(1 + \dot{P}_{UK})$$

This is the purchasing power parity condition of the previous chapter in its exact form, that is, Equation (11.4). We discover that if PPP holds and market values of real assets in local currencies move at the same rates as the general rates of inflation, there is no difference between the earnings on domestic fixed assets and the earnings on foreign fixed assets. According to our definition of the real change in exchange rates, an actual change in exchange rates that merely offsets differential inflation in market asset values will not be a real change. For a real change in exchange rates that makes foreign assets an ex post poorer investment than domestic assets, we need this condition:

$$\dot{P}_{US} > \dot{P}_{UK} + \dot{S}(\$/\pounds)\,(1 + \dot{P}_{UK}) \tag{12.11}$$

and vice versa. In other words, we need departures from purchasing power parity in its relative form for real changes in exchange rates on fixed or real assets.

We can provide a more precise definition of the real appreciation of the pound (depreciation of the dollar) for real assets:

Real percentage change in $(\$/\pounds) =$

$$\frac{S_1(\$/\pounds) - S(\$/\pounds)}{S(\$/\pounds)}(1 + \dot{P}_{UK}) - (\dot{P}_{US} - \dot{P}_{UK}) - (\rho_{US} - \frac{S_1(\$/\pounds)}{S(\$/\pounds)}\rho_{UK}) \tag{12.12}$$

This definition is very similar in form to the definition of the real change in exchange rates for financial assets or liabilities given in Equation (12.1). For *financial* assets or liabilities, a real change in exchange rates requires an actual change that is not compensated by interest rate differentials. For fixed or real assets, a real change in exchange rates requires an actual change that is not compensated by inflation differentials in market prices of assets or in real asset yields in terms of profit. (The effect of exchange rates on the translated value of ρ_{UK} is included additively in the final term.)

Fixed Assets and Financial Statements

When we examine the financial accounts in order to judge the performance of domestic versus foreign fixed investments, we are up against even more problems than we have with financial assets and liabilities. With financial assets and liabilities we can obtain the correct judgment as long as we are sure to include both income

---

[9]The total real return from Britain includes a translation gain/loss, since ρ_{UK} is multiplied by $S_1(\$/\pounds)/S(\$/\pounds)$. Equality of real yields is a better assumption in the long run than in the short run.

and the separate shareholder equity effect within total earnings. With fixed assets this is not sufficient. Indeed, by including shareholder equity effects as they are measured with the FASB 52 accounting procedure, we might distort the picture even more than by leaving these effects out of the calculations. These points are by no means obvious, so we will show them by taking an example.

Suppose that in the previous year, $1 million was invested in U.S. fixed assets that provided a 5 percent real rate of profit, and $1 million was invested in British fixed assets which provided a 5.5556 percent real rate of profit. Suppose that over the previous year, inflation in the United States was 10 percent, and inflation in Britain was 16 percent, with fixed or real asset market prices and general prices moving at the same rates. Suppose that in the previous year the exchange rate was $2.0/£ and that by the end of the year it was $1.8/£. We have

$$\rho_{US} = 0.0500 \qquad \rho_{UK} = 0.05556 \qquad \dot{P}_{US} = 0.10 \qquad \dot{P}_{UK} = 0.16$$
$$S(\$/£) = 2.0 \qquad \text{and} \qquad S_1(\$/£) = 1.8$$

What we want to know from the example is what we will find in a company's accounts.

The actual pound depreciation or devaluation is 10 percent. However, the higher inflation in asset values in Britain has made up for some of this. The real pound depreciation (dollar appreciation) against which to judge the measured accounting effects is calculated with Equation (12.12) which gives

$$\text{Real percentage change in } (\$/£) = \frac{(1.8 - 2.0)}{2.0}(1.16) - (-0.06)$$

$$- (0.05 - \frac{1.8}{2.0} 0.05556) = -0.056 \text{ or } -5.6\%$$

Since the change is negative, we call it a real pound depreciation. It is lower than the actual depreciation because the actual fall has been partially compensated by higher inflation in the market value of British fixed assets. But what will the different accounting procedures show?

In terms of the financial accounts, the $1 million in the U.S. real assets earned a profit of $\rho_{US} \times \$1,000,000 = \$50,000$. In addition, the 10 percent inflation in the United States raised the dollar value of the fixed assets by $100,000, which is a "gain" to the company even if it does not show in accounts until it is realized.

The $1 million sent to Britain at $S(\$/£) = 2.0$ had an initial value of £500,000. At $\rho_{UK} = 0.05556$, the £500,000 earned $\rho_{UK} \times £500,000 = £27,778$. When translated into U.S. dollars at the current exchange rate $S_1(\$/£)$, as a current earnings, this £27,778 becomes $1.8 \times 27,778 = \$50,000$ in the income statement. This is true no matter what accounting procedure is used. The $50,000 is shown as the first item in Table 12.2. Translation gains and losses—those resulting from converting foreign asset values into units of local currency—require more careful treatment than fixed-asset income.

TABLE 12.2
EARNINGS ON BRITISH FIXED ASSETS WITH DIFFERENT STANDARDS

	Rental or profit income	Translation gains			Income plus *declared* translation gains			Income plus actual translation gains		
		FASB 8	FASB 52	Correct method	FASB 8	FASB 52	Correct method	FASB 8	FASB 52	Correct method
$S_1(\$/£) = 1.8000$	+$50,000	0	−$100,000	+$44,000	+$50,000	+$50,000	+$94,000	+$50,000	−$50,000	+$94,000

Let us begin with the FASB 8 accounting standard. This required that the historical values of real assets had to be translated at historical exchange rates and that any changes in these values had to be declared in the income statement. Only in special circumstances will this procedure provide the correct answer, and in this case it will not. The historical real-asset market value of the British fixed asset is £500,000, and the historical exchange rate is $S(\$/\pounds) = 2.0$. This gives a balance sheet entry of $2.0 \times 500,000 = \$1,000,000$. Since the original cost is also $1,000,000, there is no exchange gain or loss. The current income, as for all the procedures we are comparing, is $50,000 when $S_1(\$/\pounds) = 1.8$, and so the declared income, which is the sum of the current income and the translation loss (of zero), is $50,000. This is shown with the FASB 8 entries in Table 12.2 and is the same as the *declared* income on the U.S. fixed asset but smaller than the true income.

Under the FASB 52 procedure, which replaced FASB 8, the income on the British fixed asset is still $50,000. However, with FASB 52, the values of fixed assets are translated at current exchange rates, but historical costs are used for the value of the assets in units of the local currency. The current exchange rate is $S_1(\$/\pounds) = 1.8$, and the historical cost is £500,000, and so the value is recorded as $900,000. There is a translation loss of $100,000 from the original $1 million value of the British real asset. This is excluded from current income and goes only into the separate shareholder equity account, and so the declared income with FASB 52 is the same as with the FASB 8 procedure, and it is the same as domestic income.[10] However, if exchange rates do not return to the previous levels before the British real asset is sold, the $100,000 will appear as income when it becomes a transaction loss, showing a loss of $50,000 ($50,000 - \$100,000 = -\$50,000$).

As we pointed out earlier, the correct method for handling foreign fixed assets uses the current exchange rate and the current market value of assets. This is different from the FASB 52 procedure and the older FASB 8 procedure. We note that by the year-end, the initial £500,000 invested in the British fixed asset has increased with 16 percent inflation to £580,000. At the current exchange rate of $S_1(\$/\pounds) = 1.8$, this is translated into $1,044,000 on the balance sheet, and so there is a translation gain of $44,000. If this is included as income, the total earnings from Britain are $50,000 + \$44,000 = \$94,000$, compared with the total return from U.S. fixed assets of $150,000. The relative loss from the change in exchange rates is $56,000 ($94,000 - \$150,000 = -\$56,000$), which is 5.6 percent of the original investment, the same as the real percentage change in exchange rates computed with Equation (12.12). This correct result is in contrast with the outcomes of FASB 8 and FASB 52, which show no loss in the income statement in relation to declared U.S. income. When the shareholder equity effect is included with FASB 52 and the total return from the British fixed assets is compared with the total return from the U.S. asset, we have a relative loss on the British asset of $200,000 ($-\$50,000 -

---

[10]Our treatment is valid for countries which do not suffer from extreme inflation and for which the straightforward forms of FASB 52 rules apply. Countries with extreme inflation (over 100 percent in three years) continue to use the temporal distinction found in FASB 8 and will have accounts like those shown for FASB 8 rather than for FASB 52.

$150,000 = -\$200,000$). No matter how we look at it, we cannot obtain the correct picture from the new FASB 52 procedure, or the old FASB 8 procedure. We will not do so until we use a current cost–current exchange rate translation procedure.

EXCHANGE RATES AND ECONOMIC RISK

Measuring Changes in International Competitiveness*

The measurement of the real change in exchange rates that affects the international competitiveness or profitability of a firm because of its economic exposure is similar to the measurement of the real change in exchange rates for judging investments in foreign fixed assets. Again, we will see that a real change in exchange rates will occur only if there is a change which constitutes a departure from PPP.

Let us define the dollar profits of a U.S. exporting firm as π where from the definition of profits as revenue minus costs we can write

$$\pi = S(\$/\pounds)p_{UK}q - C_{US}q$$

or

$$\pi = [S(\$/\pounds)p_{UK} - C_{US}]q \qquad (12.13)$$

In Equation (12.13), p_{UK} is the pound price of the U.S. firm's export good in Britain, and C_{US} is the (constant) per-unit U.S. dollar production cost of the export. The product, $S(\$/\pounds)p_{UK}$, is the export sales price of the company's product in terms of dollars, and so the difference between $S(\$/\pounds)p_{UK}$ and C_{US} is the dollar profit ("markup") per unit sold. By multiplying this difference by the quantity of total sales, q, we get the U.S. exporter's total profit in dollar terms, or π.

In order to see the conditions under which changes in exchange rates will raise or lower a U.S. exporter's profits, we will write the annual rates of change in exchange rates and profits as $\dot{S}$ and $\dot{\pi}$. As before, the dot over a variable signifies a rate of change. Let us assume that the market selling price of the company's product in the United Kingdom grows at the British general rate of inflation, which we have written as $\dot{P}_{UK}$. Let us also assume that the production cost of the product, which is made in the United States, grows at the general rate of inflation in the United States, $\dot{P}_{US}$. For the given output level, q, we can write the U.S. exporter's profit at the end of the year as follows:

$$\pi(1 + \dot{\pi}) = [S(\$/\pounds)p_{UK}(1 + \dot{S})(1 + \dot{P}_{UK}) - C_{US}(1 + \dot{P}_{US})]q \qquad (12.14)$$

Equation (12.14) is obtained from Equation (12.13) merely by replacing π with $\pi(1 + \dot{\pi})$, $S(\$/\pounds)$ with $S(\$/\pounds)(1 + \dot{S})$, and so on.

Subtracting Equation (12.13) from Equation (12.14) gives

$$\dot{\pi} = \{S(\$/\pounds)p_{UK}[\dot{S}(1 + \dot{P}_{UK}) + \dot{P}_{UK}] - C_{US}\dot{P}_{US}\}q/\pi$$

Profits will grow after, for example, a depreciation or devaluation of the dollar (when $\dot{S}$ is positive) if $\dot{\pi} > 0$, that is, if

$$S(\$/\pounds)p_{\text{UK}}\left[\dot{S}(1 + \dot{P}_{\text{UK}}) + \dot{P}_{\text{UK}}\right] - C_{\text{US}}\dot{P}_{\text{US}} > 0$$

If the devaluation or depreciation takes place when the profits are zero $[S(\$/\pounds)p_{\text{UK}} = C_{\text{US}}]$, we can rewrite this as

$$S(\$/\pounds)p_{\text{UK}}\left[\dot{S}(1 + \dot{P}_{\text{UK}}) + \dot{P}_{\text{UK}} - \dot{P}_{\text{US}}\right] > 0$$

Since $S(\$/\pounds)$ and p_{UK} are positive, a devaluation or depreciation of the dollar will raise a U.S. exporter's profits if

$$\dot{S}(1 + \dot{P}_{\text{UK}}) > \dot{P}_{\text{US}} - \dot{P}_{\text{UK}} \tag{12.15}$$

More generally, we can define the real change in exchange rates affecting international competitiveness or the profitability of trade as follows:

$$\text{Real percentage change in } (\$/\pounds) = \dot{S}(\$/\pounds)(1 + \dot{P}_{\text{UK}}) - (\dot{P}_{\text{US}} - \dot{P}_{\text{UK}}) \tag{12.16}$$

When the real change is positive, there is a real or effective appreciation of the pound (depreciation of the dollar), and when the real change is negative, there is a real or effective depreciation of the pound (appreciation of the dollar).

We see immediately from our condition that the U.S. exporter's profits from the British market are improved if there is a violation of purchasing power parity as stated in Equation (11.4). In particular, we learn that profitability is improved if the devaluation/depreciation, $\dot{S}$, is greater than the extent to which U.S. inflation exceeds inflation in Britain.

An Intuitive Explanation and Summary

We would expect a U.S. exporter's product to gain in competitiveness in Britain if it falls in price vis-à-vis competing goods made in Britain. If, for example, a U.S. exporter's dollar price rises 10 percent from increasing U.S. production costs while British producers' prices rise only 8 percent, a U.S. dollar devaluation of more than 2 percent will make U.S. exporters more competitive in Britain. Alternatively, if the United States has 5 percent inflation and Britain has 15 percent inflation, it will take an increase in the value of the dollar of more than 10 percent to lower the competitiveness of U.S. exporters. It is clear that changes in competitiveness require departures from purchasing power parity. In general, if depreciation is greater than the extent to which domestic inflation exceeds foreign inflation, exporters in the country of depreciation will gain.

We can summarize our conclusions by saying that real changes in exchange rates on financial assets or liabilities require departures from a condition similar to interest parity. Real changes in exchange rates on real or fixed assets and in international competitiveness require departures from purchasing power parity. We have provided evidence that both types of departures do exist, and so we should be careful to compute these more meaningful measures of real changes in exchange rates when judging performance. We should also be careful to note that the need for financial managers to watch (real) exchange rates and the effect these have on the competitiveness of operations makes international finance a trickier and more extensive discipline than conventional domestic finance. This is because exchange rates affect both the financial and operational performance of the firm.

INTERNATIONAL VERSUS DOMESTIC FINANCE

In the study of domestic finance, events taking place in the financial markets, such as changes in interest rates or dividend payments, affect cash flows originating in the financial markets themselves. There would be no obvious change in the cash flow from sales of jeans or payments for denim cloth in Aviva Corporation if, for example, bond prices or interest rates were to change.[11] The finanical manager can therefore to a large extent take events on the production side of the firm as being quite independent of events taking place in the financial markets. However, in the study of international finance, the problem for the financial manager is different. Changes taking place in the international financial markets have an important bearing on the cash flows from the manufacturing or operating side of a firm.

The central variable in our consideration of international finance, namely, the exchange rate, has a joint effect upon the financial situation and international competitiveness and hence on the manufacturing situation. For example, a real devaluation of the currency used in the country in which Aviva produces jeans will lower jeans prices and affect the sales of jeans abroad and at home. A devaluation will also affect the cost of imported denim cloth. Cash receipts and cash payments stemming from the production side of the firm will clearly be dependent on the financial market conditions reflected in the exchange rate. Failure to take account of the effects on the operating side of the firm of events in financial markets can result in financial errors.[12]

The difference between the job of the financial manager of a strictly domestic firm and the job of the financial manager of an internationally oriented firm is shown in Figures 12.1 and 12.2. The financial manager of a truly domestic firm can accept outside projections of sales revenues and production costs. Little in the manager's department and of which he or she should have knowledge other than interest rates and general economic conditions will have a direct bearing on cash flows associated with sales or production costs. The financial manager can therefore

---

[11]To the extent that interest rates reflect expected inflation according to the Fisher equation, cash flows from sales and production costs will move with interest rates. In this sense, the financial and production sides of the firm are linked even in conventional domestic finance.

[12]Of course, if PPP always holds, then the exchange rate is unimportant. Indeed, it could be said that it is the need to consider the implications of departures from PPP and interest parity—along with political risks and taxes—that makes the study of international finance a separate discipline.

be concerned with the problems of estimating only the values of financial cash flows generated in the rectangles in Figure 12.1.

Since real variations in exchange rates affect revenues from sales and production costs, as well as revenues from assets and payments on liabilities, the financial manager of an internationally oriented firm has much broader concerns. He or she must be concerned with what real exchange rates might do and how they will affect all the cash flows shown in the rectangles of Figure 12.2. Even the quantity produced and sold will depend on exchange rates and could become part of an important estimating task.

There are a multitude of factors which must be considered in the estimation. We will consider these in the next chapter but give a brief list here.

1 *Whether the firm is an importer or an exporter.* A real devaluation of a country's currency will in general raise the home price of imports and reduce the foreign currency price of exports. Importers generally lose from their economic exposure, while exporters gain.

2 *The degree of competition faced by the firm.* We must consider whether or not any extra profitability that might arise from real changes in exchange rates will be canceled by competition from new market participants. Economic exposure depends on the elasticity of demand for products.

3 *Which currency is used in the analysis.* This will, in turn, depend on the

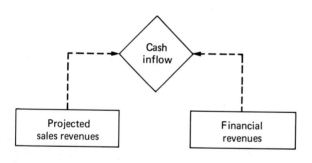

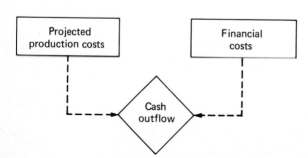

FIGURE 12.1
The strictly domestic firm.

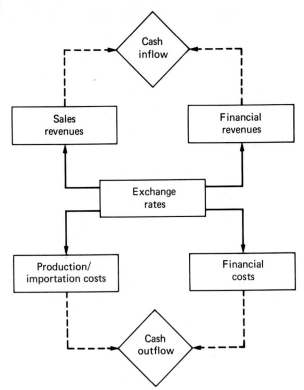

FIGURE 12.2
The internationally oriented firm.

currency that is relevant and of interest to the firm. For example, the higher dollar price an exporter can charge a foreign customer after a dollar devaluation might represent a lower foreign currency price.

4 *Whether payment for goods lags the sales/buying agreement.* When an agreement to buy or sell is in effect, the effect of a change in exchange rates depends on whether the agreement fixes the price in the home currency or in the foreign currency. For example, when the sales price is fixed in the domestic currency, it is actually possible for an exporter to lose from a devaluation of his or her own currency.

5 *Whether a sales agreement has been offset in the forward or money market.* As we have already seen, translation or transaction risk or exposure resulting from payment being made after the delivery price has been set can be avoided by using the forward exchange or money markets. Economic exposure cannot so easily be avoided.

We will examine the various factors listed above, and we should always remember that we are concerned with real changes in exchange rates as defined by departures from PPP [Equation (12.16)]. If a depreciation or devaluation in the exchange rate merely reflects higher general inflation at home rather than abroad, there is no real cheapening of a firm's exports and no real increase in the relative prices of imports.

SUMMARY

1 The common view is that a devaluation helps exporters but hurts importers and also helps holders of foreign assets but hurts holders of foreign liabilities. This is true provided we talk of real rather than nominal devaluations or depreciations.
2 A real devaluation of a foreign currency makes those who invested in assets denominated in that currency wish they had kept their funds at home. Real changes in exchange rates on financial assets and liabilities can be measured from the extent to which ex post changes in exchange rates do not compensate for the interest differential.
3 When expected spot rates are realized, and when expected yields on financial assets or liabilities in different countries have been equalized, real exchange rate changes are zero. This is much like interest parity.
4 When making judgments of past financial investments or debts from financial accounts of a firm, we must compare interest earnings at home with interest and translation gains from abroad. FASB 8 used current exchange rates and required the reporting of gains or losses as they occurred. With the existing FASB 52 procedure, translation gains and losses are accumulated in a shareholders' equity account. The change in this account must be added to income to judge relative investment or borrowing performance at home versus abroad.
5 Inflation in local market values of foreign fixed assets frequently compensates for changes in actual exchange rates. The real change in exchange rates for foreign fixed assets is obtained by measuring the departure from purchasing power parity modified for real profit differentials.
6 FASB 8 used historical costs and historical exchange rates if the assets were usually valued at historical rates, as with fixed or real assets. The FASB 52 procedure uses historical costs and current exchange rates but puts translation gains or losses in a separate account. Both FASB 8 and its successor produce incorrect measures of fixed-asset investment performance even if we aggregate accounts. With the correct method, current market or replacement costs are used, and the current exchange rate is used for translation.
7 International competitiveness or profitability is affected by exchange rates only if the changes do not merely reflect differential general rates of inflation. As with foreign fixed assets, real changes in exchange rates require departures from purchasing power parity.
8 Exchange rates are financial variables. However, they affect production and sales levels and thereby increase the scope of international financial management compared with the extent of domestic financial management. The financial manager of an internationally oriented firm must be concerned with the production effects of exchange rates.

QUESTIONS

1 Would the distinction between real and actual changes in exchange rates be important if inflation and interest rates were everywhere the same and were also small?
2 Suppose you had invested $500,000 for 6 months in the United States and in Italy and interest rates and exchange rates turn out to be as follows:

r_{US}	r_{IY}	S ($/Lit)	$S_{1/2}$ ($/Lit)
15%	28%	0.0010	0.0009

$S(\$/\text{Lit})$ is the exchange rate when the investment was made, and $S_{1/2}(\$/\text{Lit})$ is the actual rate 6 months later.

a Was foreign investment a good idea?

b What would appear under FASB 8 as foreign income?

c What values will appear in the income account and the shareholder equity account with the FASB 52 accounting procedure?

d What value of $S(\$/\text{Lit})$ would create equal returns for domestic and foreign investment?

3 Suppose you had invested $1 million in U.S. fixed assets and in Italian fixed assets under the following conditions:

ρ_{US}	ρ_{IY}	$\dot{P}_{US}$	$\dot{P}_{IY}$	$S(\$/\text{Lit})$	$S_1(\$/\text{Lit})$
2%	4%	10%	25%	0.00100	0.00085

Assume that fixed-asset prices in local currency have kept pace with prices in general.

a Which investment yielded higher returns over the year?

b What would appear in an FASB 8 income statement for foreign investment income?

c What will appear in the income statement and the shareholder equity account under the FASB 52 procedure?

d What should appear as income?

e Why do both your answer to **b** and your answer to **c** (where income and shareholder equity are aggregated) not agree with your answer to **d**?

4 What has been the real change between 1975 and 1982 in the value of the dollar against the pound on bonds? Use quotations of 1982 and 1975 spot rates and 1975 government bond interest rates in Britain and the United States. What has been the real change in the exchange rate for dollars against pounds with regard to the international competitiveness of U.S. versus British manufacturers? What has been the real change in exchange rates for stocks, assuming that these are real assets and earnings given from price earnings ratios and values given from New York and London stock exchange indexes?

5 Redo the analysis in the text of a real change in exchange rates for financial liabilities instead of assets. Describe how a declining value of a currency retires debt.

6* Redo the analysis in the text for measuring real exchange rate changes relevant for judging the international competitiveness of an exporter so that it applies to an importer instead. Assume that the importer competes with local producers of similar goods and that production costs and prices move with inflation.

7* Redo the analysis of exchange rate changes and the international competitiveness of an exporter by allowing the quantity sold, q, to change with the exchange rate instead of holding it constant. Use calculus to make the problem easier, and note that p_{UK} and q should be at profit-maximization levels in every period. [This is a very difficult question.]

8 Select a recent annual financial statement for a multinational firm. Do the reported data give a fair picture of what you think has happened over the year to this firm's financial assets/liabilities, its real assets, and its competitiveness?

BIBLIOGRAPHY

Barrett, M. Edgar, and Leslie L. Spero: "Accounting Determinants of Foreign Exchange Gains and Losses," *Financial Analysts Journal,* March–April 1975, pp. 26–30.

Burns, Joseph M.: *Accounting Standards and International Finance,* American Enterprise Institute, Washington, D.C., 1976.

Choi, Frederick D.S., and Gerhard G. Mueller: *An Introduction to Multinational Accounting*, Prentice-Hall, Inc., Englewood Cliffs, N.J., 1978.

Corporate Foreign Exchange Exposure Management, Citibank Counseling Department, New York, 1975.

Foreign and U.S. Corporate Income and Withholding Tax Rates, Ernst and Whinney, New York, January 1980.

Foreign Currency Translation: Exposure Draft, revised, Financial Accounting Standards Board, Stamford, Conn., June 30, 1981.

Rhomberg, Rudolf R.: "Indices of Effective Exchange Rates," *IMF Staff Papers*, March 1976, pp. 88–112.

Ring, Tony: "The Impact of Taxation on Foreign Exchange Exposure," *Euromoney*, January 1976, pp. 82–84.

Shank, John K.: "FASB Statement 8 Resolved Foreign Currency Accounting—Or Did It?" *Financial Analysts Journal,* July–August 1976, pp. 55–61.

Shapiro, Alan C.: "Defining Exchange Risk," *The Journal of Business*, January 1977, pp. 37–39.

Statement of Financial Accounting Standards No. 52—Foreign Currency Translation, Financial Accounting Standards Board, Stamford, Conn., December 1981.

Wyman, Harold E.: "Analysis of Gains and Losses from Foreign Monetary Items: An Application of Purchasing Power Parity Concepts," *The Accounting Review*, July 1976, pp. 545–558.

CHAPTER 13

ECONOMIC EXPOSURE

This chapter shows what changes in exchange rates imply for the cash flows of exporting and importing firms and is hence concerned with their economic rather than translation or transaction exposure. It is concerned with the effects of exchange rates on, for example, an exporter's product price and sales—which affect cash inflows—as well as on production costs—which affect cash outflows. It shows how the elasticity of demand and the nature of production influence the extent to which profits are affected by changes in exchange rates. We will discover how the effects of exchange rates depend on such things as the time span considered and the degree of competition from other firms. We will consider a number of situations.

We reach the important conclusion in this chapter that even if a company has hedged its foreign exchange receivables and payables and has no foreign assets or liabilities—that is, no translation or transaction exposure—there is still an important element of foreign exchange exposure. This is the economic exposure which occurs because the future profits from operating as an exporter or importer depend on exchange rates.

The techniques of matching receivables and payables with forward exchange contracts, money market borrowing and lending, and so on, are not designed to help eliminate economic exposure; instead, they help eliminate translation and transaction exposure. Indeed, because economic exposure is so difficult to eliminate, it has been called "residual foreign exchange exposure." We will discover that the extent of economic or residual exposure depends on such factors as the elasticity of demand for the product, production cost conditions, the currency relevant for measurement, and whether inputs are produced domestically.

Before beginning, we should point out that some firms face economic or residual foreign exchange exposure without even dealing in foreign exchange. For example, restaurants in Miami, Florida, that are visited by foreign tourists gain or lose customers according to the exchange rate. This happens despite the fact that they are generally paid in U.S. dollars and even though they pay for food, labor, rent, and interest in U.S. dollars. Even industries which compete with imported goods face economic exposure. For example, U.S. firms that supply beef to U.S. supermarkets and that never see foreign exchange can find competition from foreign beef suppliers—in Canada and Latin America—more fierce when the U.S. dollar gains against other currencies, lowering prices of the non-U.S. product.

Since the links in the economic chain of interdependence are many, industries that, for example, supply Miami hotels, U.S. beef producers, or other industries more directly involved in international trade will find themselves affected by changes in exchange rates. It should therefore be apparent that economic exposure makes the required perspective of management extremely broad. It should also be apparent that economic exposure is difficult to avoid with the exposure-reducing techniques we have met so far. But let us begin by examining what influences the extent of economic exposure. We will consider separately the exporter and the importer.

THE EXPORTER

Competitive Markets in the Short Run

The most straightforward situation of economic exposure involves a perfectly competitive market, which by definition is a market where any one firm can sell all it wishes without affecting the market price. To put this in context, let us suppose that before a devaluation of the U.S. dollar, Aviva Corporation was able to sell all the jeans that it wished to produce at the price of $p_1^\$$ a pair. The dollar sign denotes that the price is in terms of Aviva's home currency. After a devaluation, Aviva Corporation will be able to sell the jeans it wishes to produce at a higher price, $p_2^\$$. This is because with the U.S. dollar cheaper to foreigners, Aviva can charge a higher U.S. dollar price and yet leave the foreign exchange price unchanged or cheaper.

We can go further and say precisely how much higher the new price, $p_2^\$$, will be after a devaluation. To determine this, we define $p_1^£$ as the price of Aviva's jeans in Britain before the devaluation and $S(\$/£)$ as the predevaluation exchange rate. We can write the number of pounds that Aviva gets for each pair of jeans sold in Britain as $p_1^£$ and say that

$$p_1^£ = \frac{1}{S(\$/£)} \cdot p_1^\$ \tag{13.1}$$

This equation merely defines the relationship between the price charged in Britain in pounds and the price in dollars. If Aviva is operating in a competitive market, there are many other firms—at home, in Britain, and around the world—that are prepared to supply similar jeans. There is no reason for the foreign suppliers to change their pound price just because the United States has experienced a depreciation/devaluation.

After a devaluation/depreciation to an exchange rate of $S'(\$/£)$, the pound and dollar prices are related as follows:

$$p_2^£ = \frac{1}{S'(\$/£)} \cdot p_2^\$$$

If the price of jeans in Britain is changing in line with the British inflation rate, $\dot{P}_{UK}$, and we can write $p_2^£ = p_1^£(1 + \dot{P}_{UK})$, then

$$p_1^£(1 + \dot{P}_{UK}) = \frac{1}{S'(\$/£)} \cdot p_2^\$ \tag{13.2}$$

That is, after the exchange value of the dollar falls to $S'(\$/£)$, the price that Aviva should charge in Britain will move in line with the prices of other jeans suppliers. Prices of these other suppliers are assumed to change at the rate of British inflation. Equation (13.2) follows because Aviva can sell all it wishes at the price charged by other suppliers, and there is therefore no advantage to lowering its price after a devaluation.

Taking the ratios of Equation (13.1) and Equation (13.2), we get

$$(1 + \dot{P}_{UK}) = \frac{S(\$/£)}{S'(\$/£)} \cdot \frac{p_2^\$}{p_1^\$}$$

or

$$\frac{p_2^\$}{p_1^\$} = \frac{S'(\$/£)}{S(\$/£)}(1 + \dot{P}_{UK})$$

This tells us that after a devaluation of the dollar or an increase in the price of foreign exchange to $S'(\$/£)$, the U.S. dollar price of jeans in Britain will rise by the combined rate of devaluation and British inflation. This is true no matter what the rate of inflation is in the United States. For example, if the dollar falls in value by 5 percent and Britain has 10 percent inflation affecting jeans (and other) prices, the dollar price that Aviva charges will go up 15 percent. Of course, the rate of inflation in the United States will determine production cost increases and the extent to which the 15 percent gain in the dollar price of the product represents an increase in profitability.

The predevaluation and postdevalution prices, $p_1^\$$ and $p_2^\$ = [S'(\$/£)/S(S/£)](1 + \dot{P}_{UK})p_1^\$$, are shown in Figure 13.1, where the price axes are drawn in home currency ($) units. To keep the diagrams straightforward, we take the U.S. inflation to be zero so that the marginal cost curve, MC, does not shift. Since the firm is a

FIGURE 13.1
Exporter and devaluation in a competitive market.

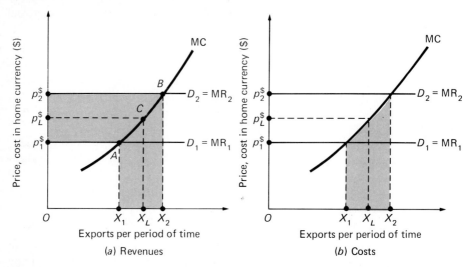

(a) Revenues

(b) Costs

A depreciation or devaluation raises the price an exporter can charge in terms of his or her
own currency. In the perfectly competitive situation the price rises by the percentage of
devaluation/depreciation plus the percentage of inflation in the United Kingdom. This raises
profit-maximizing output, sales revenues, and the total cost of production. In the long run,
new firms and the expansion of older firms reduce selling prices, output, and profits to
original levels. If the country's exporters are a small part of the overall market, some benefits
will remain.

perfectly competitive firm, the demand curve is a horizontal line at the relevant
price. Further, since additional units can be sold at a constant price, the horizontal
demand curve is also the marginal revenue (MR) curve.[1] The marginal cost, MC, is
assumed to increase as output increases.

In Figure 13.1, before the devaluation our firm, Aviva Corporation, would have
produced and sold X_1 units per period by seeking its optimum output where
marginal revenue, MR_1, equals marginal cost, MC. This is the point of maximum
profit. If output is less than X_1, $MR > MC$, and profit is increased by producing
more and adding more revenue than costs. At an output greater than X_1,
$MC > MR$, and profit is increased by producing less and thereby reducing costs by
more than revenue.

If we are dealing with a situation without U.S. inflation, where all inputs such as
the denim cloth are produced domestically, we can expect—at least in the short
run—that MC will remain as before the devaluation. Foreign inputs will probably
become more expensive after the devaluation, raising production costs and hence
MC, but when inputs are all domestic there is no immediate reason for domestically

---

[1] In the long run newly entering firms will shift the demand or MR curve. We will deal with this
situation shortly.

produced inputs to cost more.[2] With the price and hence marginal revenue of jeans in dollar terms rising to $p_2^\$ = [S'(+\$/\pounds)/S(\$/\pounds)](1 + \dot{P}_{UK})p_1^\$$ after the devaluation and the marginal cost remaining as the MC curve, Aviva will want to raise its production to X_2 per period. This is the new profit-maximizing output, where $MR_2 = \text{MC}$. We find that a higher price in dollars and a higher level of sales have resulted from the devaluation.

Part *a* of Figure 13.1 shows how revenues in units of domestic currency have increased because the price is higher and the sales are greater. Revenues will increase by the shaded area in part *a*. There is an unambiguous increase in cash inflows in terms of home currency after a devaluation. A simple reversal of interpretations in the diagram to determine the effects of a revaluation/appreciation will similarly show that there is an unambiguous decrease in cash inflows for an exporter when they are measured in terms of the home currency.

In the short run, with no U.S. inflation and per-unit costs of production unaffected by the devaluation, the total production cost will rise by only the cost of producing the additional quantity that is sold. Since MC is the cost of producing each additional item, the area under MC between X_1 and X_2 will be the additional cost incurred in providing the extra goods sold, $X_2 - X_1$. Hence, the total manufacturing cost will rise by the shaded area in part *b* of Figure 13.1. We can see that with revenues rising by the shaded area in part *a* and costs rising by the shaded area in part *b*, profits, which rise by the difference between revenues and costs, will rise by the area $p_2^\$ BAp_1^\$$ in part *a*. After a devaluation, the increase in cash outflows for production costs will always be less than the increase in cash inflows from revenues.

How do we determine the amount by which total profits will increase? We note that with $p_2^\$$ exceeding $p_1^\$$ by the U.K. inflation and the percentage of the devaluation, the increase in profits—even if output remains at X_1—will be equal to the sum of the U.K. inflation rate and the percentage of the devaluation multiplied by the original revenues. For example, with a 10 percent devaluation and 5 percent U.K. inflation, $p_2^\$$ exceeds $p_1^\$$ by 15 percent, and so if initial revenues were \$1000, profits will rise by at least \$150. With output increasing, profits will rise by an even bigger percentage. This is clear from part *a* of Figure 13.1 by comparing the size of the extra profit, area $p_2^\$ BAp_1^\$$, with the original revenues given by the unshaded rectangle, $Op_1^\$ AX_1$. We can notice, also, that the flatter MC is, the greater is the increase in profit.

Long-Run Effects; Imported Inputs

Since the accurate forecasting of cash flows is an important job for the financial manager, we should not limit our discussion to only the immediate effects of

---

[2]Later we do allow for U.S. inflation and for imported inputs with consequent movement in the long run. It should be clear that if the U.S. inflation and U.K. inflation are related according to PPP, that is, if $\dot{P}_{US} = \dot{P}_{UK} + \dot{S}(1 + \dot{P}_{UK})$, then MC will move by $\dot{P}_{US}$, which is as much as the vertical movement in $D = \text{MR}$, that is, $\dot{P}_{UK} + \dot{S}(1 + \dot{P}_{UK})$. Therefore the devaluation is not real and has no lasting effect.

devaluation on flows of revenues and production costs. When we are dealing with a firm in perfect competition with others, as we are here, it is important to appreciate that any increase in profits that will accompany a devaluation or depreciation will probably be temporary. A perfectly competitive market, by definition, involves the free entry of new firms. The additional profit that might be available after a real devaluation/depreciation (that is, one that does not just make up for differences in inflation) will serve as an incentive for new firms to get involved and existing firms to expand. This can bring the rate of profit back to its predevaluation/pre-depreciation level. It is likely that only in the interim will the higher-than-normal profits be made. Hence, if Aviva is operating in a competitive market, it should not be too excited after falls in the exchange value of the dollar, even if they are real. The long-run effect on cash flows and profit can be far less favorable.

We have shown that profits in our export-oriented industry will rise immediately after a devaluation. This will induce firms in purely domestic endeavors to move into this export sector until the "last" firm to enter can reap a profit equal to the best it could achieve in some alternative endeavor. Competition from new firms might tend to move the price that the original firms such as Aviva can gain for their product back toward $p_1^\$$.[3] As a result, we would move back toward the predevaluation situation of price p_1 and output X_1 with original cash flows. Extra profits will last only as long as it takes new firms to get involved, which will depend largely on the nature of the product.

We might want to note that if the devaluing country produces only a small fraction of the world's output of a particular good, then the free entry of firms within the country will have a limited impact when cutting into the extra profit from devaluation. This will be true because many new firms might enter the industry within the devaluing country without significantly affecting the world price. Prices might move back very little from $p_2^\$$, perhaps only to $p_L^\$$ in Figure 13.1. Output would be X_L. Profits would remain abnormally high and are given by the shaded area $p_L^\$ CA p_1^\$$. Fortunately for Aviva Corporation, other countries also manufacture jeans.

There is another route that is possible through rising costs that can also limit the period of obtaining extra profit after a real devaluation and hence limit the postdevaluation/postdepreciation celebrations of the exporter. This involves the eventual reduction in the real devaluation via the inflation that an actual devaluation itself sets up. This will work in all market settings, not only in competitive markets, and so we will consider the effect separately. The effect will come about even if none of the inputs used by the firm under consideration are imported; in this case, after the devaluation there will be no immediate increase in costs. Cost increases will nevertheless take place eventually.

General import prices tend to rise after a depreciation or devaluation. To the extent that imports figure in the cost-of-living index, a devaluation will increase the

---

[3] The price will move back below $p_1^\$(1 + \dot{P}_{UK})$ because with no U.S. inflation, this price is higher than the original price, and so abnormal profits will still remain. Of course, $p_1^\$$ is a dollar price, and so after the devaluation of the dollar, the same dollar price, $p_1^\$$, means a *cheaper* pound price.

cost of living and thereby reduce the buying power of wages. If efforts to maintain real or price-adjusted wages result in wage increases to compensate for the higher cost of living, the production costs will rise. This is shown in Figure 13.2.

In part *a* of Figure 13.2, we show the marginal cost of production rising from MC to MC_L. Every unit is shown to cost more to produce as money wages rise. We can think of MC moving up by the U.S. inflation rate, and so we have

$$\frac{MC_L}{MC} = (1 + \dot{P}_{US})$$

at each output level. In order to retain an effective (or real) devaluation, we draw a smaller vertical shift in MC than in the demand curve, which, as we have already stated, shifts by

$$\frac{p_2^\$}{p_1^\$} = \frac{S'(\$/£)}{S(\$/£)} (1 + \dot{P}_{UK})$$

Indeed, the real extent of the devaluation/depreciation is the difference between the percentage shift in the price line, $D = MR$, and the percentage shift in the MC

FIGURE 13.2
Exporter and devaluation in a competitive market: effect of cost increases.

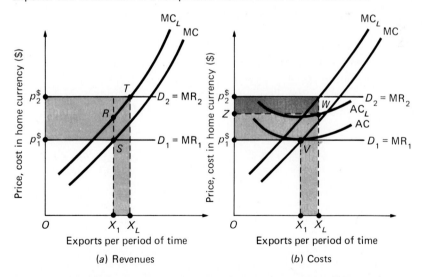

(a) Revenues   (b) Costs

A devaluation will raise import costs and the costs of production. This means a reduction in the extent of real devaluation. Profit-maximizing output and profits will return to original levels. However, as long as some real devaluation remains, there will be extra sales and profits.

curve, since from the equations above this is

$$\frac{p_2^\$}{p_1^\$} - \frac{MC_L}{MC} = \frac{S'(\$/£)}{S(\$/£)}(1 + \dot{P}_{UK}) - (1 + \dot{P}_{US})$$

$$= \frac{S'(\$/£) - S(\$/£)}{S(\$/£)}(1 + \dot{P}_{UK}) - (\dot{P}_{US} - \dot{P}_{UK})$$

or the real devaluation/depreciation defined in Equation (12.16).

A word is in order as to why we might expect costs to rise less than the product price after a dollar devaluation. Only a fraction of the goods purchased by workers is produced abroad. Let us say, for example, that this fraction is 25 percent. If a 10 percent devaluation were to occur, this might at worst raise the price of imported goods by the same 10 percent. The price index of *all* goods and services purchased by workers would rise by about 2.5 percent as a result of a 10 percent increase in prices of only 25 percent of the goods.[4] If workers received wage increases to compensate completely for the price-level increase resulting from the devaluation, wages would rise by 2.5 percent, and this would be the extent of the upward shift in the cost curves (MC to MC_L and AC to AC_L). We see that the vertical shift in costs should be less than the amount of devaluation that determines the size of the shift in demand from D_1 to D_2. Because we can move MC and AC and the demand lines, $D =$ MR, by any amounts relative to each other, Figure 13.2 can be used to show the effects of inflation *induced* by a devaluation/depreciation. It is also a valid representation when there is an *original* real devaluation with inflation in both countries.

If costs rise in the long run to MC_L and AC_L, output will end up only at X_L, where $MC_L =$ MR$_2$, although the price will remain at the same level, $p_2^\$$, as before the increase in costs. Total revenues will rise from $Op_1^\$SX_1$ to $Op_2^\$TX_L$ as a result of the higher home currency price and the larger number sold. The total cost is AC multiplied by output, which before the devaluation was $Op_1^\$VX_1$. After the devaluation, at the output of X_L, the total cost is area $OZWX_L$, which exceeds the predevaluation cost by the lightly shaded area in part *b* of Figure 13.2. Since revenues rise by the shaded area in part *a*, or the entire shaded area in part *b*, and costs rise by the lightly shaded area in part *b*, profits rise by the difference, the darkly shaded area in part *b*.[5]

The dampening effect on profits from the competition-induced price reduction shown in part *a* of Figure 13.1 must be added to the profit reduction from higher costs. The effects will both contribute to a smaller profit increase from devaluation, but even firms that do not face extra competition from other producers will find

---

[4]Clearly, in a small "banana republic," where only masses of "bananas" are produced, perhaps as much as, say, 90 percent of the goods used could come from abroad, and these would be paid for with revenues from the sale of bananas. Then, the overall price index would rise by about as much as the devaluation, and the vertical shift of MC and AC would be the same as that of the demand curve.

[5]To simplify the argument, we have drawn area $Op_1^\$SX_1$ so that it is equal to area $Op_1^\$VX_1$. This means that before the devaluation, revenues equal costs, and profits are zero. Any profit after the devaluation is a result of the devaluation itself. We have also simplified the argument by ignoring the long-run envelope of AC curves.

profits shrinking because of rising costs brought about by the devaluation/depreciation that reduces the real changes in exchange rates.

The effect of having imported inputs is, diagrammatically, precisely the same as the effect of general inflation through wage pressure that we have just discussed. Figure 13.2 will consequently also describe the effect of having imported inputs. If some of the inputs going into the production of our export good come from abroad—that is, they are re-exports—a devaluation will probably make these inputs immediately more expensive to our exporting firm. As a result, MC and AC will both shift upward to the extent that imported inputs figure in production. We know that this vertical shift will be less than the shift in the selling price when at least some inputs are domestic. As before, the shift is given in Figure 13.2 by the MC_L and AC_L curves, and we see that the output increase is smaller than it would be without imported inputs—that is, output increases to X_L, where MC_L cuts D_2. Profits rise by the darkly shaded area in part b of Figure 13.2.

The difference between the effect of imported inputs and our previous case of general devaluation-induced inflation is only in the immediateness of effect, with input prices probably rising much more quickly than with the link through wages. We should remember, however, that input and general inflation effects can both work together in the long run. From this point on, we shall consider only the short run. We shall see that this can become complicated enough.

The Case of Imperfect Competition

There are a large number of imperfect market settings, but in general we can say that in an imperfect market, a firm will still sell some of its product even if it raises the price. This will be the case when perfect substitutes are not available. It will occur frequently, since products of different firms generally have different characteristics.

Frequently, in imperfect markets, gains in profits can be maintained because new firms can be prevented from moving into a profitable firm's market. Devaluation gains, then, will be offset only to the extent that inputs are imported and through the general inflation route, not through the influx of new firms.[6] We shall not consider imported inputs or general inflation, and the gains in profit that we show will be permanent in the absence of these cost-increasing effects.

To examine a firm like Aviva in an imperfect market setting, we allow for some inelasticity in demand; that is, we draw a conventional downward-sloping demand curve.[7] When, as before, we have the home currency on the vertical axis, what is the effect on this firm's demand curve when there is a devaluation/depreciation? We will see that it will move vertically upward, just as in a competitive market. Indeed, the

---

[6] All that is necessary for the devaluation to have a lasting effect is that other firms *within our firm's own country or other devaluing countries* cannot easily enter our firm's market. This is why we claimed that Aviva was fortunate that jeans are produced in many different countries, which allows devaluation benefits to be long-lasting with *dollar* prices remaining higher.

[7] Of course, in a competitive market, the *industry* demand curve is also downward-sloping. Competitive market *firms* were given horizontal demand because each is a small part of the market.

argument will differ little from the argument we used in the discussion of competitive markets.

Let us consider any particular sales volume on demand curve D_1 in Figure 13.3, for example, X_1. Now when the demand curve is at the predevaluation level, D_1, volume X_1 can be sold at the domestic currency price of $p_1^\$$. With the exchange rate of $S(\$/\pounds)$, this means a foreign currency price of $p_1^\pounds = [1/S(\$/\pounds)]p_1^\$$ *at this output* of X_1.

After the devaluation, the same amount—that is, X_1—will be sold abroad if the foreign currency price is raised in line with prices of other suppliers to $p_2^\pounds = p_1^\pounds (1 + \dot{P}_{UK})$. It is the foreign currency price that always matters, and if Aviva keeps its pound prices in line with prices charged by other producers in the British market (which are assumed to rise at the U.K. inflation rate), it will remain competitive. This is because the British do not look at the price tag of a pair of U.S.-made jeans on sale in Britain in terms of the U.S. dollar. Rather, they consider the number of British pounds that must be paid for the jeans, just as a U.S. car buyer considers the dollar price of an imported vehicle. It is the monetary unit of the country where the product is sold that influences the buyer's purchase decision. But at the devalued/depreciated exchange rate of $S'(\$/\pounds)$, the new pound price of $p_2^\pounds = (1 + \dot{P}_{UK})p_1^\pounds$

FIGURE 13.3
Devaluation and the demand curve.

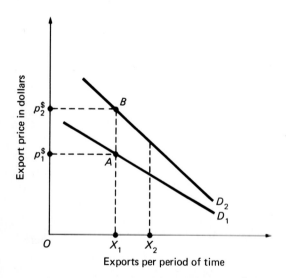

For each sales level, the price that can be charged after the devaluation with sales unchanged rises by the percentage of the devaluation. This means that the demand curve shifts vertically by the percentage of the devaluation (plus any foreign inflation).

means a dollar price of

$$p_2^\$ = S'(\$/£)p_2^£ = S'(\$/£)(1 + \dot{P}_{UK})p_1^£ \tag{13.3}$$

In other words, if, when the exchange rate changes from $S(\$/£)$ to $S'(\$/£)$, the dollar price changes from $p_1^\$$ to $p_2^\$$, as in Equation (13.3), sales will remain unchanged at X_1. In terms of Figure 13.3, we are saying that before the devaluation at price $p_1^\$$, we will sell X_1 abroad and hence be at point A. After the devaluation, we will sell the same amount, X_1, abroad only if the dollar price is $p_2^\$ = S'(\$/£)$ $(1 + \dot{P}_{UK})p_1^£$. Therefore we obtain point B. We find that the demand curve after the devaluation is moved upward to $p_2^\$ = [S'(\$/£)/S(\$/£)](1 + \dot{P}_{UK})p_1^\$$; that is, the vertical shift is equal to the devaluation plus the U.K. inflation.

We can now take another sales volume, say X_2, and follow precisely the same argument. Each and every point on the new demand curve, D_2, will be vertically above the old demand curve, D_1, in proportion to the devaluation and the U.K. inflation.

We should think of vertical movements of demand rather than a "rightward shift" along the lines that "more is sold for the same dollar price after a devaluation." Although this is true, it does not tell us "how much," whereas our argument in the text makes it clear that the vertical shift is in exactly the same proportion as the change in the exchange rate and U.K. inflation. Of course, we notice that since the vertical shift is always in the same *proportion* as the change in the exchange rate and the U.K. inflation, the *absolute* shift is less at lower prices on the demand curve. This is shown in Figure 13.3, with demand curve D_2 closer to D_1 at lower prices.

Part a of Figure 13.4 shows the vertical shift in the demand curve (D_1 to D_2) from a U.S. dollar devaluation, along with the corresponding shift in the MR curve. We have assumed that costs are constant in part b by drawing a flat MC.[8] It would complicate matters only a little to allow for increasing costs by also considering AC curves. Rising costs would tend to reduce the effects of devaluation on profits, but they would not eliminate these positive effects.

We see from Figure 13.4 that before the devaluation, the firm will produce X_1 per period, which is where $MC = MR_1$, and it will be able to sell this output at the price $p_1^\$$. After the devaluation, the firm will produce X_2 per period and sell this at the price $p_2^\$$. The increase in revenue from $Op_1^\$ A X_1$ to $Op_2^\$ A' X_2$ is represented by the total shaded area in part a of Figure 13.4. An important point to realize is that with a downward-sloping curve, the price increase from $p_1^\$$ to $p_2^\$$ is less than the vertical shift in the demand curve ($AC < AB$). We discover that export prices when stated in the domestic currency rise *less than* the combined percentage of the devaluation and the U.K. inflation. This is different from the case of perfect competition, where we found the product price rising by an amount *equal* to the devaluation and the U.K. inflation.

---

[8] As in the case of perfect competition, for a given change in the exchange rate, U.S. inflation will change production costs but not the U.K.-based demand curve. To keep our diagrams straightforward, we assume that there is no U.S. inflation.

FIGURE 13.4
Exporter and devaluation in an imperfectly competitive market.

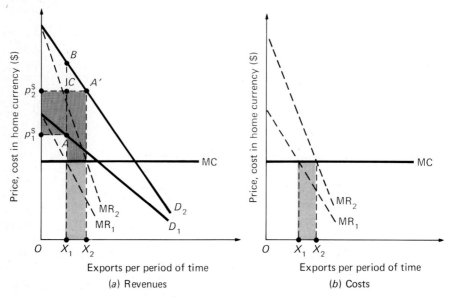

(a) Revenues   (b) Costs

In an imperfectly competitive market the home currency price of exports will increase by a smaller percentage than the devaluation. Sales will increase by a smaller fraction than in the case of perfect competition.

With output rising from X_1 to X_2, costs will rise by this amount times the cost of manufacturing each of the units. Since each unit costs the manufacturer an amount given by the height of the MC curve, the total cost will rise by the lightly shaded area in part b of Figure 13.4 (shown also in part a). Profits will rise by the difference between the change in total revenue, given by the total shaded area in part a, and the change in total cost, given by the lightly shaded area. The change in profits is therefore represented by the darkly shaded area in part a, which is the difference between the total shaded area and the lightly shaded area.

The extent to which prices will rise, output increase, and profits be affected will depend on the slope (elasticity) of the demand curve and the slope of the MC curve, which we have made horizontal so that profits can be easily computed. The reader might note that if the firm is up against a rigid constraint in raising output, then MC can be vertical, and a devaluation will leave output and sales unchanged, with domestic currency prices rising by the full percentage of devaluation and U.K. inflation—just as in the case of perfect competition. It has been observed, for example, that auto exporters have raised their home currency prices in proportion to any depreciation/devaluation; that is, they have left foreign prices unchanged. This has been attributed to their inability to raise output in the short run. Why lower your foreign-currency selling price if you cannot satisfy any extra demand that this might create? The slopes of the demand and cost curves become vital parameters for effective financial planning in an exporting firm. The demand sensitivity of the firm should be estimated, and the degree of capacity utilization should be measured to determine the response that the production side should make to real changes in exchange rates. This is part of the broader job of financial management in export versus domestically oriented firms.

Analysis in Foreign Currency Units

So far we have measured all the vertical axes in our diagrams in units of the home or domestic currency, which we have taken as the U.S. dollar. By drawing our diagrams in terms of home currency units, we have been able to examine the effects of exchange rates changes when these effects are measured in these same units. Our revenue, cost, and profit changes that result from devaluations or revaluations are, therefore, U.S. dollar amounts; in general, they are amounts that are relevant for U.S. firms. Some firms that are operating within a country, however, will be concerned with revenues, costs, and profits, in some particular foreign currency unit. For example, a British firm with a manufacturing operation in the United States may not be happy if a devaluation/depreciation of the U.S. dollar raises its U.S. dollar earnings. Since the dollar is less valuable, the higher U.S. dollar earnings may bring fewer pounds than before the devaluation. Similarly, a U.S. firm with a subsidiary in, for example, Canada, may not be thrilled if a depreciation of the Canadian dollar raises the Canadian dollar earnings of its subsidiary. These higher earnings could be worth less in U.S. dollars. Such possibilities should be of concern to the financial manager of any firm with branches or subsidiares abroad.

Interest in the effects of a devaluation or revaluation, when measured in terms of foreign currency units, should not be limited to firms with subsidiaries abroad. Any firm that denominates borrowing in some foreign currency—even if it enjoys only one location—will care about the effect of exchange rate changes on its operating revenues, measured in units of the currency of its debt. For example, a U.S. firm that has borrowed in British pounds will care very much about its trading revenues as measured in pounds after the exchange rate change. This is because the firm has payables in British pounds. Canadian firms that borrow in New York in U.S. dollars will care about their U.S. dollar revenues, since they are required to service U.S. dollar debts. Any non-U.S. firms issuing Eurobonds or borrowing in the Eurodollar market will care about U.S.-dollar-denominated revenue, no matter where they are located. For all these reasons, we should consider the effects of exchange rate changes on revenues, costs, and profits when measured in units of foreign currency. We will limit our discussion to an imperfect market, but the competitive case, with a flat demand curve and an upward-sloping MC, is extremely similar and is left as an exercise for the reader.

As we said, the price that is relevant to a buyer is the price he or she has to pay in terms of his or her own currency. When there is no inflation and the price of Aviva jeans in Britain remains unchanged in terms of British pounds but changes in terms of U.S. dollars, there is no reason for sales in Britain to change. It follows that when there is, for example, a devaluation of the U.S. dollar, there is no reason for the

FIGURE 13.5
Exporter and devaluation in an imperfectly competitive market: Foreign currency units.

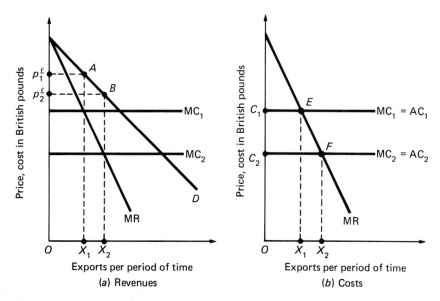

(a) Revenues

(b) Costs

The relevant price for demanders is the price denominated in the buyers' currency. When we measure the vertical axis in the buyers' currency, the demand and MR curves are unaffected by changes in exchange rates. If production costs are unchanged in the producers' currency, a devaluation of that currency will lower costs denominated in the buyers' currency. The export price will decline in the buyers' currency after a devaluation.

demand curve for Aviva's jeans to shift if it is drawn against the pound price. At the same pound price as before, the same monthly volume of jeans will be sold. The demand curve in Figure 13.5, and hence also the MR curve, is the same both before and after the devaluation.[9]

The effect of changes in exchange rates on the cost curves is different from the effect on the demand curve. When our diagrams are drawn in units of foreign currency and there is an exchange rate change, the cost curves will move vertically in proportion to the exchange rate. Why is this so?

If it costs, say, MC_1 to produce an extra pair of Aviva's jeans and no inputs are imported, then after a devaluation the production cost should still be MC_1 if the devaluation has not induced general inflation. However, before the devaluation, with an exchange rate of $S(\$/£)$, the cost in units of foreign exchange was

$$MC_1^£ = \frac{1}{S(\$/£)} \cdot MC_1^\$$$

[9] With inflation in Britain we could move the demand curve vertically upward by the U.K. inflation rate. There is no need to do this to make our point.

After the devaluation to $S'(\$/\pounds)$, with the dollar cost the same, the foreign exchange cost becomes

$$\text{MC}_2^\pounds = \frac{1}{S'(\$/\pounds)} \cdot \text{MC}_1^\$$$

By simply taking ratios, we get

$$\frac{\text{MC}_2^\pounds}{\text{MC}_1^\pounds} = \frac{S(\$/\pounds)}{S'(\$/\pounds)}$$

That is, the MCs, in terms of British pounds, change in proportion to the exchange rate. Since a devaluation of the dollar means that $S'(\$/\pounds) > S(\$/\pounds)$, the MC, in terms of British pounds, falls as the dollar is devalued. In Figure 13.5, this is shown with MC moving downward from MC_1 to MC_2. Since we have drawn Figure 13.5 with a constant MC, we know that $\text{MC} = \text{AC}$, and so the AC curve moves downward with the devaluation of the dollar when the vertical axis is in terms of British pounds.

With profit maximization requiring that MC = MR, we see from Figure 13.5 that a devaluation of the U.S. dollar should raise Aviva's jeans output from X_1 to X_2. With the demand curve remaining at D, the pound price will fall from $p_1^\pounds$ to $p_2^\pounds$. We see that even with the demand curve unshifted by a devaluation, the devaluation lowers the foreign exchange price of exports and raises the amount sold.[10] With lower prices and higher sales, what has happended to revenues in terms of the British pound?

The answer clearly depends on whether sales have risen by a larger or smaller proportion than the reduction in price. If the increase in sales is greater than the price reduction, revenues will be higher. Such a situation requires that the elasticity of demand exceed unity, which we know to be the case by making a straightforward observation. Since MC is positive, and the firm produces where MR = MC, MR must also be positive. But with MR positive, an extra unit of sales, even though it requires a fall in price, must raise total revenue. We know, therefore, that pound revenues must rise, with $Op_2^\pounds BX_2$ necessarily greater than area $Op_1^\pounds AX_1$.

Part b of Figure 13.5 gives the required curves for considering the effect of a devaluation on total costs. Since total costs are given by AC multiplied by the output, whether costs have increased depends on the slope of MR. Costs have changed from area OC_1EX_1 to area OC_2FX_2. Have costs increased, and if so, by how much? Well, continuing at this point without the help of mathematics is difficult. Mathematics helps us show that total costs, in terms of pounds, will increase after the dollar is devalued, but by a smaller amount than the increase in revenues. In terms of pounds, profits are therefore increased. This, along with the other results we have reached, is demonstrated in the appendix for this chapter.

---

[10] By referring back to the equivalent home currency diagram, Figure 13.4, the reader will see that while the pound price *falls*, devaluation *raises* the export price in terms of dollars (from $p_1^\$$ to $p_2^\$$). Figures 13.4 and 13.5 are, however, consistent.

THE IMPORTER

It would generally be presumed that importers would lose from a devaluation/ depreciation and gain from a revaluation/appreciation—the opposite of the effects for exporters. This presumption would normally be correct, with the exact magnitude of effect of exchange rates depending on such factors as the degree of competition and which currency we use for our analysis. The amount of change in cash flows would be important information for the financial manager of an importing firm, whether the firm is importing finished goods for sale at home or some of the inputs used in producing its local output. If the goods are finished goods for sale, determining the effects of changes in real exchange rates requires that the financial manager know the elasticity of the market demand for the product. The financial manager must also decide on the relevant currency for measurement. We will begin by measuring in dollar amounts.

Analysis in Home Currency Units

Let us again consider Aviva Corporation and assume that it has decided to import finished jeans that are manufactured in Britain for sale in the United States. The most straightforward case is one in which Aviva can import whatever quantity of jeans it wishes at the same cost per pair. Being able to buy jeans at the constant cost $MC_1^\$$ means that we have the horizontal cost curve $MC_1 = AC_1$ shown in parts a and b of Figure 13.6. We can think of two sets of circumstances where jeans could be imported at a constant cost per pair. These make our discussion of very general use.[11]

Assume that Aviva faces market demand conditions that are less than perfectly elastic in selling the imported British jeans in the U.S. market. This requires that there are not many other *sellers* of the same jeans. This could very easily be the case in practice if, for example, Aviva is licensed as the sole importer of these particular jeans in the United States.[12] This situation is very common. Many of the products produced in foreign countries are distributed and sold in each market by licensed firms.[13]

The demand curve is shown along with the associated MR and cost curves in Figure 13.6. Before the devaluation, Aviva Corporation will import and sell M_1 pairs of jeans per period, which is the profit-maximizing quantity where MR =

---

[11] The cost curve for jeans will be flat if shipping and production costs in Britain are constant. The cost curve will also be flat if Aviva buys somebody else's jeans and it is one of the many buyers of these jeans. Every buyer, if sufficiently small, will be able to obtain whatever quantity it wants at the going price. This will mean that no buyer has any monopsony power. In fact, however, an assumption of constant costs is not necessary and only aids in computing total costs and profits.

[12] If the import was freely available to any importer or potential importer, any one firm would face a flat demand curve for the good at the going price. This perfect competition would put the demand curve at the level of the cost curve, and so no profit would be made above the normal return on the capital and enterprise involved.

[13] Our analysis is equally valid for a U.S.-based sales subsidiary of a foreign firm where we are specifically concerned with the profits of the subsidiary and not the foreign parent (for which the analysis of the exporter is applicable). Sales subsidiaries are common for automobiles, TVs, stereos, cameras, computers—and branded denim jeans.

FIGURE 13.6
The importer and a devaluation.

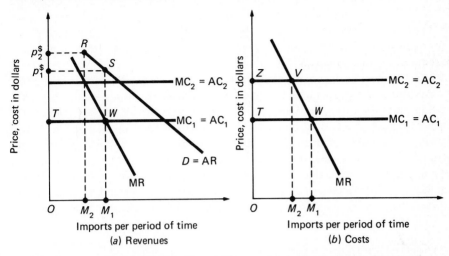

If the importer's buying costs are unchanged from a devaluation in terms of the foreign supplier's currency, cost curves will move up by the percentage of devaluation when measured against the importer's currency. Demand curves will not be affected if they are drawn against the demander's currency. Only the amount demanded—a move along the curve—will be affected rather than the position of the curve. A devaluation will raise import prices and lower sales. The importer's profits will decline.

MC_1. The jeans will be sold at the price $p_1^{\$}$ per pair, giving a total revenue in dollars of area $Op_1^{\$} SM_1$. The cost of the jeans of $MC_1 = AC_1$ per unit gives a total cost of $OTWM_1$ dollars. The initial profit is the difference between total revenue and total cost, which is area $Tp_1^{\$} SW$ in Figure 13.6.

After a devaluation of the dollar to $S'(\$/£)$, there is no reason for the British pound production cost to be affected. With the British pound cost unchanged at $MC_1^{£}$ but the exchange rate now at $S'(\$/£)$, the new dollar cost must increase in proportion to the exchange value of the British pound against the dollar. The cost curves in parts a and b of Figure 13.6 shift vertically upward by the percentage of the dollar devaluation/depreciation.[14] The importer will reduce the amount imported and sold to M_2 per period, where $MR = MC_2$, and will sell this new amount, with the demand curve $D = AR$, at the price $p_2^{\$}$. We see that the effect of a dollar devaluation is to reduce imports and sales and raise prices.

The effect on revenues, costs, and profits of the importer is less obvious from Figure 13.6 than the effect on quantities and prices. Revenues have changed from $Op_1^{\$} SM_1$ dollars to $Op_2^{\$} RM_2$ dollars. However, we know from the straightforward observation made for the exporter that as a result of a dollar devaluation, revenues have fallen for the importer. All profit-maximizing firms sell at a point where the

[14] If we wish to allow for inflation in Britain, the vertical shift in MC can include this. We can keep the diagrams more straightforward by concentrating on the devaluation rather than inflation.

demand curve for their product is elastic. This is because they choose to be where MR = MC, and since MC must be positive, MR is positive—that is, revenues are increased by additional sales, even though higher sales require lower prices. With the importer on an elastic part of his or her demand curve, the percentage reduction in the quantity sold must exceed the percentage increase in price—that is, revenues are reduced by a devaluation.

To determine the effect of a devaluation on profits, we must determine the effect on costs and compare this with the effect on revenues. This is not easily done with the diagrammatic analysis of Figure 13.6. However, as the mathematics in the appendix reveals, a devaluation also reduces the total costs of the import; that is, area $OZVM_2$ is less than area $OTWM_1$. The appendix also reveals that provided we begin with positive profits, the reduction in costs is smaller than the reduction in revenues, and so the dollar profits of the importer fall from a devaluation/ depreciation. The effects of a devaluation in terms of British pounds are more easily obtained from a diagrammatic analysis than the effects in terms of dollars.

Analysis in Foreign Currency Units

The effects of a dollar devaluation in terms of British pounds are shown in Figure 13.7. With the cost of the jeans to Aviva Corporation at $MC^{£}$ and the demand curve at $D_1 = AR_1$, Aviva will import and sell M_1 pairs of jeans per period at the price $p_1^{£}$ per pair. The volume and the price are obtained by choosing the profit-maximizing position, where MC = MR_1. We note, of course, that $p_1^{£}$ must equal $[1/S(\$/£)]p_1^{\$}$ and that $MC^{£} = MC_1^{\$}/S(\$/£)$ where $p_1^{\$}$ and $MC_1^{\$}$ are the amounts in Figure 13.6.

Now, if the British pound cost of the import does not change from a dollar devaluation, as previously argued, MC = AC will remain in its original position. The amount of the item our importer can sell, however, will depend on the dollar price charged. At any level of sales—for example, M_1—the same amount will be sold after the devaluation only at the same dollar price. This must mean a lower British pound price (lower by the percentage of the devaluation), and so the dollar price is unchanged. In terms of British pounds, the demand curve of the American buyers of Aviva's imported jeans must shift vertically downward by the percentage of the dollar devaluation. This is shown with a move from $D_1 = AR_1$ to $D_2 = AR_2$, with the associated MR curves moving from MR_1 to MR_2 in Figure 13.7.

Figure 13.7 tells us that a devaluation will reduce the profit-maximizing amount of imports from M_1 to M_2 (the same reduction as in Figure 13.6) and result in a lower British pound price for the jeans (which, nevertheless, is a higher dollar price, as is seen in Figure 13.6). With both the quantity and price falling, the British pound revenue must fall by the total shaded area in part *a* of Figure 13.7.

With the British pound cost of the jeans unaffected by a devaluation/ depreciation, but with a smaller amount imported, the total cost is reduced by the shaded area in part *b* of Figure 13.7. Profits will fall by the difference between the reduction in British pound revenues and the reduction in British pound costs. This fall in profits is shown by the heavily shaded area in part *a* of Figure 13.7. We conclude that an importer's profits are reduced from a devaluation/depreciation of

FIGURE 13.7
Importer and devaluation in foreign currency units.

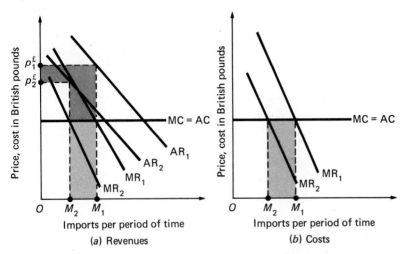

(a) Revenues   (b) Costs

After a devaluation of the dollar the same number of imported goods will be sold at the same dollar price. This requires a lower pound price. The demand and MR curves therefore shift downward. Import costs in terms of pounds should be unaffected by a devaluation. The quantity and pound price of imports will decline along with profits.

the importer's currency. This occurs whether we measure these profits in terms of the domestic currency or in terms of the foreign currency.

Imported Inputs

Suppose that instead of importing finished jeans, Aviva is importing the denim cloth or perhaps cut denim that is ready for final manufacture in the United States. When a firm imports unfinished goods or some of the inputs for production, a devaluation of the domestic currency will raise production costs at each level of output.

When a firm is engaged in production, marginal costs and average costs will rise with output. The effect of a dollar devaluation will be to shift upward the rising cost curves, as shown in Figure 13.8. The amount by which costs increase depends on the importance of the inputs and on whether alternative sources of inputs are available and can be substituted. As Figure 13.8 shows, the effect of the dollar devaluation is to raise the product price and reduce the quantity manufactured and sold. In these circumstances the effect on profits becomes difficult to determine.

Summary of Effects of Exchange Rates on Exporters and Importers

Before we add the complications of forward hedging and the invoicing of exports or imports in different currencies, we will find it useful to summarize what we have learned.

FIGURE 13.8
Importer of inputs and devaluation.

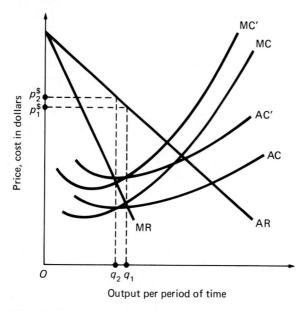

When inputs are imported, a devaluation will raise
production costs. Higher production costs will lower the
output of goods sold domestically and raise prices.

1 Even with no foreign assets or liabilities or current payables or receivables, changes in exchange rates will affect firms engaged in exporting or importing. This is called economic or residual risk and is very difficult to avoid.[15]

2 Devaluations raise export prices in home currency terms and at the same time raise export sales. The reverse is true for revaluations.

3 Devaluations raise an exporter's profits. However, when the exporter is in a competitive environment, these profits exist only in the short run. The gains are reduced by using imported inputs and are in any case removed in the long run by the free entry of new firms into the industry. When the exporter is in an imperfectly competitive industry, the benefits of a devaluation can remain. However, even in the imperfectly competitive environment additional profits can be partially eliminated by general inflation brought about by a devaluation.

4 Foreign-owned companies or companies with foreign currency debts will care about receipts and payments in units of foreign currency. A devaluation will lower prices in foreign currency units (while raising prices in units of the devalued

---

[15] It is difficult to hedge against residual or economic exposure because it depends on factors such as the elasticity of demand, the importance of imported inputs, and so on.

currency) and raise an exporter's sales. For firms in imperfect competition, revenues will increase because the percentage sales increase exceeds the price reduction. This follows because imperfectly competitive firms sell where demand is elastic. Production costs will also increase, but it can be shown mathematically that revenues will rise more than costs, and so profits will increase.

5 Import prices rise in units of the devalued currency and fall in units of foreign currency. The quantity of imports will fall from a devaluation. In an imperfectly competitive environment the importer's sales revenues will fall in terms of the devalued currency because price increases are smaller than quantity reductions. Costs will also fall, but not by as much as revenues. The profits of importers therefore decline from a devaluation. This is true whether we measure in terms of the local currency or in terms of foreign currency.

EFFECT OF CURRENCY OF INVOICING AND FORWARD HEDGING

In our discussion of economic risk we have so far allowed the quantity sold and the price the exporter receives or the importer pays to vary as the exchange rate changes. These variations in quantity and price do not always occur immediately. Often the quantity to be purchased or supplied and the price are fixed for a certain period into the future. This temporarily postpones some of the effects of economic risk, causes additional risks, causes a translation/transaction risk to be faced in addition to the economic risk, and results in conclusions that are potentially different from those reached earlier. For example, exporters can lose from devaluations and importers can gain—the reverse of the normal effects.

The effect of changes in exchange rates depends on whether sales or inputs are included in previous agreements and on which currency is used in the agreements. We will consider the following cases for exporters:

1 A fixed volume of exports has been promised for future delivery at prices fixed in terms of dollars (or in pounds, with these sold on the forward market), but inputs are subject to inflation or are at pound-contracted prices. This situation involves what is in effect a translation or transaction exposure on payables and the removal of this exposure on export revenues.

2 A fixed volume of exports has been promised for delivery at prices stated in pounds sterling, and the pounds have *not* been sold on the forward market. This situation involves a translation or transaction exposure on receivables.

We should note that what we will be discussing involves the precontracting of prices and/or quantities. So far in this chapter we have taken price determination, production, and settlement as being contemporaneous. Clearly, there is then no transaction or translation risk on exposed receivables or payables, even though exchange rates do change profitability and therefore do leave economic risk. When we have the precontracting of prices and quantities, we have translation or transaction exposure and postponed economic risk. Since this occurs frequently, we will sketch the potential consequences.

FIGURE 13.9
Exporter with payables exposure: Dollar accounting.

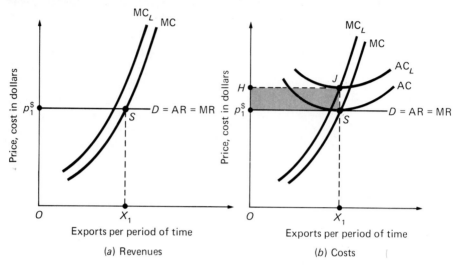

(a) Revenues   (b) Costs

If a fixed number of goods are sold at a fixed dollar price, revenues will be unchanged after devaluations. We can think of economic risk on revenues as being postponed. If a devaluation raises input costs, total costs will rise. This is because of transaction risk if the prices of imported inputs are denominated in pounds. The higher input costs could reduce profits, and so exporters can lose from a devaluation.

The Exporter with Exposed Inputs

Dollar Accounting Assume that Aviva Corporation has fixed the dollar price from exports of a fixed number of pairs of jeans, either by selling foreign exchange proceeds forward or by invoicing in dollars. With the dollar receipts per unit and the quantity supplied fixed, total revenues are fixed, and the gains/losses from economic exposure are temporarily eliminated.

While total dollar revenues will not change from a devaluation, costs could rise either via the route of general inflation, induced by rising import prices, or because some inputs are imported at prices denominated in pounds which are not bought forward. Let us take input prices to be fixed in pounds so that we have payables exposure on pounds and the situation shown in Figure 13.9.

The total revenue from sales is represented by area $Op_1^\$ SX_1$. However, costs could increase to $OHJX_1$. If Aviva's profits were minimal before the devaluation, the devaluation will result in losses equal to the area $p_1^\$ HJS$. We can see that a U.S. exporter might lose from a devaluation.[16] Of course, the loss is temporary and exists only while sales revenues are fixed and while more is paid for inputs.

If production costs as well as revenues from sales are fixed by buying forward

---

[16] Aviva would prefer to reduce output and sales to the level where MC_L cuts $p_1^\$$. Losses would be reduced a little if this were done, but with an agreement to deliver X_1, this might not be possible.

foreign exchange for imported inputs and arranging a period of fixed dollar wages, then, of course, both costs and revenues will be unaffected by exchange rates while the various agreements are in effect. The exporting firm can therefore avoid temporary losses from a devaluation when foreign exchange is sold forward or invoicing is in dollars by trying also to fix dollar input costs, including wages, for the same period.

We should note that the temporary decline in profits from a devaluation as a result of the precontracted importation of inputs for production is exactly analogous to the temporary worsening of the balance of payments—known generally as the *J-curve effect*. The balance of payments temporarily worsens because precontracted imports with prices in foreign currency will cost more in dollars, and this might offset any extra revenues from exports. Our analysis in this chapter therefore shows for an individual firm the J curve that is usually shown for the entire economy. The reason for the name "the J-curve effect" is obvious from Figure 13.10. If a devaluation takes place at time t_0, profits could temporarily fall or the balance of payments temporarily worsen because of the extra burden of payables denominated in foreign currency, but eventually the economic effects of the devaluation will begin to improve both profits and the balance of payments.

FIGURE 13.10
The J curve.

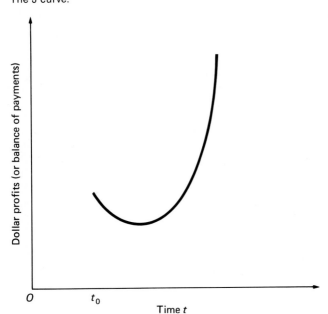

When the prices of imports are denominated in foreign currency, a devaluation can lower the profits of firms and worsen the balance of payments of nations. The negative effects are temporary, and eventually the beneficial effects of a devaluation will begin to dominate.

Pound Accounting With the prices of jeans fixed in dollars from selling export proceeds forward or dollar invoicing, these contracted dollars will represent fewer pounds. Production costs which are in dollars will also represent fewer pounds, but as long as some inputs are imported and become more expensive, revenues will fall more than costs. With revenues falling by more than the reduction in costs, profits will decline, or losses will increase. We find that exporters might lose not only in dollar terms but also in terms of pounds. This is no surprise, since lower profits in dollars are certainly lower profits in pounds after a dollar devaluation, because there are fewer pounds for each dollar.

The Exporter with Receivables Exposure

We have considered the case where the dollar receipts are fixed, either by selling foreign-currency-invoiced receivables forward or by invoicing in dollars. This eliminated economic risk on revenues but left transaction exposure on payables. We can now consider what will happen when prices are precontracted but foreign currency is not sold forward. This postpones the economic risk and causes a transaction exposure on receivables.

It is relatively easy to compute the effect of Aviva's having precontracted to supply jeans to Britain at a fixed pound-per-pair price when the pounds have not been sold forward. A dollar devaluation would make these pounds more valuable by the percentage of devaluation—a gain on pound receivables—but postpone the effect of economic exposure. Production costs might also rise because of imported inputs or wage pressure from devaluation-induced inflation, but this effect is likely to be smaller than the effect on revenues, and so dollar profits will rise. This gain on receivables in pounds for jeans that have already been sold will be followed by gains on jeans not yet sold, resulting from the economic exposure described earlier.

The Importer /

If Aviva has agreed to purchase a given quantity of jeans at a dollar invoice price, or at a pound price when the pounds are bought forward, there is no immediate effect of a dollar devaluation in dollar terms. Aviva's costs are in dollars and are unaffected by exchange rates, as are Aviva's revenues. Only after the period during which dollar prices were fixed will a devaluation have the economic exposure effect described earlier in this chapter. A revaluation of the dollar will also leave costs, revenues, and profits unaffected in dollar terms. We have a case where there is no translation or transaction exposure and where the effects of economic exposure have been postponed.

If Aviva has agreed to purchase a given quantity of imports at pound prices, there is a fixed payable in pounds and hence payables transaction exposure. A dollar devaluation will increase the dollar value of this payable. For a given total revenue in dollars received on the contracted quantity, we have a reduction in dollar profits. The losses on payables will be followed by the importer's losses from economic exposure when prices are again raised.

A Reminder: Importance of Lags

If sales, delivery, and payment could all occur simultaneously, there would be no need to worry about the contract currency or the presence of forward agreements. There would be no receivables or payables in trade, and the only effects of changes in exchange rates would be those from the economic exposure described earlier in this chapter. The currency used for sales invoicing and forward market covering are important only when price agreements and payments are separated in time. This, however, frequently happens to be the case. We then have the combined effects of translation/transaction exposure and economic exposure.

An Example

Suppose that Aviva has agreed to sell 100 pairs of jeans to Britain over the next 2 years at $24 per pair and to buy 200 yards of denim from Britain in this same period for £2 per yard. Suppose that 2 yards of denim is required per pair and that the labor cost for each pair is $8.

Suppose that at the time of contracting the exchange rate is $S(\$/£) = 2.0$ and that the dollar is then devalued to $S(\$/£) = 2.5$. Suppose also that the elasticity of demand for Aviva jeans in Britain is -2 and that after the devaluation Aviva raises the price of jeans to $25 per pair.

1 What are the gains/losses from the devaluation on the jeans sold and on the denim bought at the precontracted prices? (That is, what are the gains/losses from transaction exposure on payables and receivables?)

2 What are the gains/losses from the extra competitiveness of Aviva's jeans, that is, from economic exposure?

Assume that Aviva can buy all the denim it wishes at £2 per yard and that wages are not increased after the devaluation.

Effect of Transaction Exposure

Before the devaluation:

Expected total revenue/year = 100 pairs × $24/pair = $2400

Expected total cost/year = 100 pairs × 2 yd/pair × £2/yd × $2/£ + 100 pairs
× $8/pair = $1600

∴ Expected profit = $2400 − $1600 = $800/year

After the devaluation:

Total revenue = 100 pairs × $24 pair = $2400

Total cost = 100 pairs × 2 yd/pair × £2/yd × $2.50/£ + 100 pairs × $8/pair
= $1800

∴ Expected profit = $2400 − $1800 = $600/year

We find that the exporter's profit on contracted quantities and prices of jeans supplies and denim purchases is *reduced* by $200 per year for 2 years because of the transaction exposure.

Effect of Economic Exposure

Before the devaluation:

$$\text{Expected profit} = \$800/\text{year (as we just showed)}$$

After the devaluation:

When the dollar price of jeans rises from $24 per pair to $25 per pair, the pound price falls from $24 \times £0.5/\$ = £12$ to $25 \times £0.4/\$ = £10$. This is a 16.67 percent price reduction. With a demand elasticity of -2, it will result in sales increasing by 33.33 percent to 133 pairs per year. It follows that after the devaluation of the dollar

$$\text{Expected revenue} = 133 \text{ pairs} \times \$25/\text{pair} = \$3325$$
$$\text{Expected cost} = 133 \text{ pairs} \times 2 \text{ yd}/\text{pair} \times £2/\text{yard} \times \$2.5/£ + 133 \text{ pairs} \times \$8/\text{pair} = \$2394$$
$$\text{Expected profit} = \$3325 - \$2394 = \$931$$

We find that the exporter's profit is increased by $131 per year from the devaluation because of economic exposure.

In this specific example the firm is likely to feel happy about the devaluation because in the long run it will come out ahead. It should be clear, however, that temporary setbacks from transaction exposure on payables could be serious.

SUMMARY

1 An exporting firm in a competitive market will experience a temporary increase in sales revenues and production costs after a real devaluation/depreciation of its currency. Revenues will rise by more than the increase in costs, and so net profit flows will increase.
2 The higher temporary profit for a competitive firm will encourage new firms to get involved. This might limit the period of extra profit for any particular pre-existing firm.
3 Higher input costs associated with the devaluation/depreciation can also limit profit improvements. Increases in input costs can result from the effect of the devaluation on wages via a general inflationary impact or from the need to import inputs.
4 The home currency price of an exporter's product will rise by the percentage of the devaluation/depreciation and the foreign inflation rate when the product is sold in a competitive market.
5 An exporting firm in an imperfectly competitive market will experience an increase in revenues and costs after a devaluation/depreciation when amounts are measured in terms of the firm's home currency. Revenues will rise by more than the increase in costs, and so profits will increase. The higher profits can persist if they are not offset by higher input costs. Revenues, costs, and profits that are measured in terms of foreign exchange will also increase from a devaluation.

6 The price of the goods sold by an exporter will, after a devaluation of the home currency, rise in terms of the home currency but fall in terms of the amount of foreign exchange. This happens because the home currency price rises by a smaller percentage than the devaluation.

7 A devaluation raises the prices of imports in terms of the devalued currency and reduces the quantity that is imported and sold. Revenues and costs in terms of dollars will fall, and so will the importer's profit. A revaluation lowers input prices and raises an importer's dollar revenues, costs, and profits.

8 A devaluation lowers the prices of imports when these prices are measured in terms of the foreign currency.

9 A dollar devaluation lowers revenues, costs, and profits in terms of the foreign currency. A revaluation will raise them.

10 When an agreement exists to export to a foreign buyer a stated quantity at a price fixed in the home currency (or in foreign exchange that is sold forward), a devaluation can temporarily hurt the exporter through the route of fixed revenues with rising costs. This is true in both dollar and foreign currency units.

11 If prices in an export sales agreement are stated as foreign currency amounts and these are not sold forward, a devaluation will raise the dollar revenues, costs, and profits of the U.S. exporter.

12 An importer buying an agreed-upon quantity at an agreed-upon price in dollars (or with foreign exchange proceeds bought forward) will experience no change in dollar revenues, costs, or profits. An importer buying an agreed-upon quantity at prices invoiced in foreign exchange will experience no change in dollar revenues, increased dollar costs, and reduced profits.

QUESTIONS

1 Rank the following export industries according to the amount of increase in sales volume you would expect to result from a fall in the value of the U.S. dollar.
   a Wheat farming
   b Automobile production
   c Foreign travel to the United States
   d Computer hardware
   Use diagrams in your answers.

2 Rank the industries in question 1 according to the effects of a devaluation/depreciation on profits. You may assume that there are different amounts of imported inputs, different elasticities of demand, and so on.

3 Do you think that the United States is a sufficiently large importer of products in general so that the effect of a dollar depreciation would be eliminated by pressure on nominal wages from import price increases? How about Canada, Fiji, or Iceland?

4 Assume that the elasticity of demand for Aviva's jeans is -2.0. Assume that production costs are constant and that there is a 10 percent dollar depreciation.
   a By how much will the quantity sold increase?
   b By how much will dollar revenues increase?
   c By how much will foreign exchange revenues increase?
   d By how much will costs increase?
   e By how much will profits increase?

5 As in question 4, assume that Aviva's jeans face an elasticity of demand of -2.0 with constant costs, and assume also that approximately half the total cost is accounted for by

denim cloth, which is imported. To an approximation, what will this mean for your answers in question 4?

6 Redraw Figure 13.2 to show the *short-run effect* of a dollar *revaluation* on the profits of a U.S. exporter who sells in a competitive market.

7 Redraw Figure 13.2 to show the *long-run effects* of a dollar *revaluation* on the profits of a competitive U.S. exporter.

8 Redraw Figure 13.4 to show the effect of a *revaluation* of the dollar on a U.S. exporter in an imperfectly competitive market.

9 Redraw Figure 13.2 to show the effect of devaluation induced cost increases when amounts are measured in units of foreign exchange.

10 Why does a devaluation simultaneously raise export prices as measured in home currency and lower them in terms of foreign currency?

11 Redraw Figure 13.6 and Figure 13.7 to show the effect of a *revaluation* on revenues, costs, and profits.

12 Reconcile a rising domestic currency price and a falling foreign currency price for an imported good after a devaluation of the domestic currency. Why does this mean that the domestic currency price rises by less than the percentage of the devaluation/depreciation?

13 What would the availability of very close substitutes for an import mean for the elasticity of demand of the firm that exports our imports? Who will bear the burden of devaluation in this case?

14 Why does an exporter or importer face foreign exchange risk even if the firm has no foreign currency receivables or payables? Would it be difficult to hedge against this risk on the forward market?

15 Draw the revenue and cost diagrams for a British-owned firm which produces in and exports from the United States and cares about the British pound amounts of sales, costs, and profits after a U.S. dollar devaluation. Assume that the firm enters into a long-term sales agreement to provide X_1 per period at a fixed U.S. dollar price. [*Hint*: You need £ on the vertical axes and a horizontal AR line that will shift downward in terms of pounds after the devaluation. In the cost diagram, the MC and AC curves should be shifted downward.]

BIBLIOGRAPHY

Dufey, Gunter: "Corporate Finance and Exchange Rate Changes," *Financial Management*, vol. 6, summer 1977, pp. 23–33.

Heckerman, Donald: "The Exchange Risk of Foreign Operations," *The Journal of Business*, January 1972, pp. 942–948.

Makin, John H.: "Portfolio Theory and the Problem of Foreign Exchange Risk," *Journal of Finance*, May 1978, pp. 517–534.

Shapiro, Alan C.: "Exchange Rate Changes, Inflation and the Value of the Multinational Corporation," *Journal of Finance*, May 1975, pp. 485–502.

———: "Defining Exchange Risk," *Journal of Business*, January 1977, pp. 37–39.

APPENDIX: Exchange Rates and the Exporter and Importer—A Mathematical Treatment

THE EXPORTER

Consider the situation of a U.S. firm that exports to the British market. We will present the effects of a change in the value of the dollar, first in terms of dollar amounts and then in terms of British pounds.

Effects in Terms of Home Currency (Dollars)

The total dollar revenue, TR, of our U.S. firm from selling its entire output in Britain can be written as

$$\text{TR} = Sp^{\pounds}q \tag{13A.1}$$

where S is the number of dollars per British pound, $p^{\pounds}$ is the sales price in British pounds in Britain, and q is the number of units sold. The total cost of production for the quantity, q, if each unit costs the same, can be written in U.S. dollars as

$$\text{TC} = cq \tag{13A.2}$$

where c is the cost per unit in home currency.

A profit-maximizing firm will always equate marginal revenue and marginal cost in determining the amount to sell or, alternatively, in determining what price to charge. That is, it sets

$$d(\text{TR})/dq = d(\text{TC})/dq$$

By taking Equation (13A.1) and Equation (13A.2) and differentiating, using the fact that $dS/dq = 0$, since changes in the production of our firm could have no effect on the exchange rate, we have

$$Sp^{\pounds} + Sq\,\frac{dp^{\pounds}}{dq} = Sp^{\pounds}\left(1 + \frac{q}{p^{\pounds}}\frac{dp^{\pounds}}{dq}\right) = c \tag{13A.3}$$

The definition of elasticity of demand is that it is the percentage change in quantity, dq/q, divided by the percentage change in the price the buyer pays, $dp^{\pounds}/p^{\pounds}$. Writing η as the absolute value of the elasticity, since the elasticity is otherwise negative, allows us to write Equation (13A.3) as

$$Sp^{\pounds}\left(1 - \frac{1}{\eta}\right) = c \tag{13A.4}$$

so that

$$p^{\pounds} = \frac{c}{S\left(1 - \dfrac{1}{\eta}\right)} \tag{13A.5}$$

Equation (13A.5) tells our U.S. firm how to set its price abroad in terms of pounds according to the cost of production, the prevailing exchange rate, and the elasticity of demand. We recall that firms with some control over price will always sell at a point where $\eta > 1$, that is, where MR is positive. This follows, since the firm produces and sells where MR = MC, and we know that extra units always have positive costs (that is, MC > 0), so MR must also be positive. Relationship (13A.5) consequently makes sense only when $\eta > 1$.

If we differentiate Equation (13A.5) with respect to S, since η and c are constants, we obtain

$$\frac{dp^£}{dS} = -\frac{c}{S^2\left(1 - \frac{1}{\eta}\right)} = -\frac{p^£}{S} \tag{13A.6}$$

Since we know that $p^£$ and S are both positive, we know that $dp^£/dS < 0$. This negative derivative means that a devaluation of the dollar (an increase in S, the price of a British pound) will lower the profit-maximizing British pound price that a U.S. firm exporting to Britain should charge. This is seen in the text from Figure 13.5.

To determine what changes in the exchange rate do to U.S. dollar revenues, we can find $d\,TR/dS$. We have

$$\frac{d\,TR}{dS} = p^£q + Sp^£\frac{dp}{dp^£}\frac{dp^£}{dS} + Sq\frac{dp^£}{dS} = p^£q + Sq(1-\eta)\frac{dp^£}{dS} \tag{13A.7}$$

but Equation (13A.6) gives us $dp^£/dS$, which when used in Equation (13A.7) gives

$$\frac{d\,TR}{dS} = p^£q - Sq(1-\eta)\,\frac{p^£}{S} = \eta p^£q \tag{13A.8}$$

Expression (13A.8) tells us that $d\,TR/dS > 0$, since every element in the expression is positive. This means that a devaluation of the dollar (an increase in S) will increase the U.S. dollar revenues of our firm from sales to Britain. In general, a devaluation/depreciation of a firm's own currency will raise the total revenue in domestic currency units from sales abroad. This is consistent with the finding in part a of Figure 13.1, part a in Figure 13.2, and part a of Figure 13.4 in the text.

To determine the effect of exchange rates on profits arising from trade, we must first examine the effect on costs, $d\,TC/dS$. Since c is constant,

$$\frac{d\,TC}{dS} = c\frac{dq}{cS} = c\frac{dq}{dp^£}\frac{dp^£}{dS} = -c\frac{dq}{dp^£}\cdot\frac{p^£}{S} \tag{13A.9}$$

In Equation (13A.9) we use $dp^£/dS$ from Equation (13A.6). By introducing $\eta = -\dfrac{dp}{dp^£}\cdot\dfrac{p^£}{q}$ we have

$$d\,TC/dS = \eta cq/S \tag{13A.10}$$

Again, since the elements in Equation (13A.10) are all positive, $d\,TC/dS > 0$, and we know that a devaluation of the dollar (an increase in S) will raise the dollar cost of production. This is consistent with the finding in part b of Figure 13.2 and part b of Figure 13.4 in the text.

We have learned that a devaluation/depreciation of the dollar will raise dollar revenues and dollar costs. The impact on profits will depend on which has risen more. Since dollar profits, ϕ, are given by

$$\phi = TR - TC$$

so that

$$d\phi/dS = d\,TR/dS - d\,TC/dS$$

we get

$$d\phi/dS = \eta p^{\pounds} q - \frac{cq\eta}{S} = \eta q\left(p^{\pounds} - \frac{c}{S}\right)$$

where the term in parentheses is the "markup" per unit in terms of pounds. Since this is positive if profits were originally made, a devaluation of the dollar unambiguously raises dollar profits.

Effects in Terms of Foreign Currency (British Pounds)

In terms of British pounds, we can write

$$\mathrm{TR}^{\pounds} = p^{\pounds} q \quad \text{and} \quad \mathrm{TC}^{\pounds} = cq/S$$

Equating MR and MC, that is, equating $d\mathrm{TR}^{\pounds}/dq$ and $d\mathrm{TC}^{\pounds}/dq$, again gives, as in Equation (13A.5),

$$p^{\pounds} = \frac{c}{S\left(1 - \dfrac{1}{\eta}\right)}$$

and, therefore, as in Equation (13A.6),

$$\frac{dp^{\pounds}}{dS} = -\frac{c}{S^2\left(1 - \dfrac{1}{\eta}\right)} = -\frac{p^{\pounds}}{S}$$

Now,

$$\frac{d\mathrm{TR}^{\pounds}}{dS} = p^{\pounds}\frac{dq}{dS} + q\frac{dp^{\pounds}}{dS} = q(1 - \eta)\frac{dp^{\pounds}}{dS}$$

and so using $dp^{\pounds}/dS$ from Equation (13A.6) allows us to write

$$d\mathrm{TR}^{\pounds}/dS = cq\eta/S^2 \tag{13A.11}$$

Since $d\mathrm{TR}^{\pounds}/dS$ is unambiguously positive, a devaluation of the dollar will raise revenues in terms of British pounds. This is what we concluded in the text from Figure 13.5 and the added knowledge that demand must be elastic at chosen outputs of an imperfectly competitive firm. Also,

$$\frac{d\mathrm{TC}^{\pounds}}{dS} = c\frac{d(q/S)}{dS} = \frac{c}{S}\frac{dq}{dS} - \frac{cq}{S^2}$$

But

$$\frac{dq}{dS} = \frac{dq}{dp^£}\frac{dp^£}{dS} = -\frac{dq}{dp^£}\frac{p^£}{S} = \frac{q\eta}{S}$$

Therefore,

$$\frac{d\,TC^£}{dS} = \frac{cq\eta}{S^2} - \frac{cq}{S^2} = \frac{c(\eta - 1)q}{S^2} \tag{13A.12}$$

Since (13A.12) is clearly positive, a devaluation of the dollar will raise production costs in terms of British pounds, even though this was not clear from part *b* of Figure 13.5 in the text. The effect on British pound profits is given by

$$\frac{d\phi^£}{dS} = \frac{d\,TR^£}{dS} - \frac{d\,TC^£}{dS} = \frac{cq\eta}{S^2} - \frac{c(\eta - 1)q}{S^2} = \frac{cq}{S^2}$$

We discover that the British pound value of profits for a U.S. firm selling in Britain will increase from a devaluation of the U.S. dollar.

THE IMPORTER

Effects in Terms of Home Currency (Dollars)

The total dollar revenue, TR, for a U.S. importer is

$$TR = p^\$ q \tag{13A.13}$$

and the total cost, if each unit costs the same is

$$TC = Sc^£ q \tag{13A.14}$$

where $p^\$$ is the dollar sales price, q is the quantity imported and sold, $c^£$ is the fixed cost of the import in terms of pounds, and S is the number of dollars per pound.

A profit-maximizing importer equates marginal revenue and marginal cost to determine the quantity to import and sell. By differentiating Equation (13A.13) and Equation (13A.14), we have

$$MR = \frac{d\,TR}{dq} = p^\$ + q\frac{dp^\$}{dq} = p^\$\left(1 - \frac{1}{\eta}\right)$$

where η is the absolute value of $\dfrac{p^\$}{q}\cdot\dfrac{dq}{dp^\$}$, and

$$MC = d\,TC/dq = Sc^£$$

Equating MR and MC gives

$$p^\$ = \frac{Sc^\$}{\left(1 - \dfrac{1}{\eta}\right)} \tag{13A.15}$$

and so since $c^£$ is fixed,

$$\frac{dp^\$}{dS} = \frac{c^£}{\left(1 - \dfrac{1}{\eta}\right)} = \frac{p^\$}{S} > 0 \tag{13A.16}$$

That is, a dollar devaluation (an increase in S) will raise the dollar price of the good that is sold. We note that since firms always choose the elastic part of demand, our results make sense only when $\eta > 1$.

To determine the effect of exchange rates on U.S. dollar revenues, we need $d\,TR/dS$. We have

$$\frac{d\,TR}{dS} = p^\$ \frac{dq}{dS} + q \frac{dp^\$}{dS} = q(1 - \eta)\frac{dp^\$}{dS}$$

which, when we use Equation (13A.16), gives

$$\frac{d\,TR}{dS} = \frac{p^£ q}{S}(1 - \eta) < 0 \tag{13A.17}$$

since $\eta > 1$ for any profit-maximizing firm. We learn that a devaluation of the dollar (an increase in S) must reduce U.S. dollar revenues, since the derivative is negative with $\eta > 1$. This is what we found in part a of Figure 13.6.

The effect of exchange rates on U.S. dollar costs is given by $d\,TC/dS$. Since $c^£$ is constant,

$$\frac{d\,TC}{dS} = c^£ q + Sc^£ \frac{dq}{dS} = c^£ q + Sc^£ \frac{dq}{dp^\$} \cdot \frac{dp^\$}{dS}$$

which, when we use Equation (13A.16), gives

$$\frac{d\,TR}{dS} = c^£ q - c^£ q\eta = c^£ q(1 - \eta) < 0 \tag{13A.18}$$

since $\eta > 1$. We learn that a devaluation reduces dollar costs (expenditures on imports), which is what we claimed but were unable to demonstrate directly in part b of Figure 13.6.

With revenues and costs in dollar terms both falling for our importer from a devaluation, the effects on profits will depend upon which falls by a larger amount. We learn, from Equation (13A.17) and Equation (13A.18), that

$$\frac{d\phi}{dS} = \frac{d\,TR}{dS} - \frac{d\,TC}{dS} = q(1 - \eta)\left(\frac{p^\$}{S} - c^£\right)$$

If the imported good is sold at a profit, then $p^\$/S$, which is the selling price in the United

States in terms of pounds, must exceed $c^£$, the cost in pounds; that is, $[(p^$/S) - c^£] > 0$. Since $(1 - \eta) < 0$, because $\eta > 1$ for a profit maximizer, we can conclude that $d\phi/dS < 0$, that is, that the dollar profits of an importer are reduced from a dollar devaluation or depreciation. This was claimed but not proved in the text. Similarly, dollar profits rise from a dollar revaluation or appreciation. Of course, it is important that there be an initial profit. If there are initial losses—that is, if $[(p^$/S) - c^£] < 0$—profits will fall from a currency appreciation.

Effects in Terms of Foreign Currency (British Pounds)

In terms of British pounds, we can write $TR^£ = p^$q/S$, where as before $p^$$ is the dollar price of the imported good, which is what is relevant to the buyer. We can also write $TC^£ = c^£q$, where $c^£$ is the constant pound cost of the import. Equating MR and MC, that is, $dTR^£/dq$ and $dTC^£/dq$, again gives

$$p^$ = \frac{Sc^£}{\left(1 - \dfrac{1}{\eta}\right)} \tag{13A.19}$$

and therefore

$$\frac{dp^$}{dS} = \frac{c^£}{\left(1 - \dfrac{1}{\eta}\right)} = \frac{p^$}{S} \tag{13A.20}$$

We know that

$$\frac{dTR^£}{dS} = \frac{d(p^$q)/dS - p^$q}{S^2} = \frac{p^$q(1-\eta)}{S^2} - \frac{p^$q}{S^2}$$

when we use the result of Equation (13A.17). This gives

$$\frac{dTR^£}{dS} = -\frac{p^$q\eta}{S^2} < 0 \tag{13A.21}$$

We can see that a devaluation/depreciation of the dollar will unambiguously reduce British pound revenues. This is inevitable, since dollar revenues are known to fall, as we have shown, and also since there are fewer pounds to the dollar after a devaluation. The pound value of revenues must fall for both reasons. The effect of exchange rates on British pound costs is

$$\frac{dTC^£}{dS} = c^£ \frac{dq}{dp^$} \frac{dp^$}{dS} = -\frac{c^£q\eta}{S} < 0 \tag{13A.22}$$

when we use $dp^$/dS$ from Equation (13A.20). We see that like the British pound value of revenues, the British pound value of the total costs of the imports must fall after a devaluation/depreciation.

The effect of exchange rates on profits is as follows:

$$\frac{d\phi}{dS} = \frac{d\text{TR}}{dS} - \frac{d\text{TC}}{dS} = -\frac{p^{\$} q\eta}{S^2} + \frac{c^{\pounds} q\eta}{S} = \frac{q\eta}{S}\left(c^{\pounds} - \frac{p^{\$}}{S}\right)$$

That is, if the imported item sold at a profit so that, just as before, $[(p^{\$}/S) - c^{\pounds}] > 0$, we know that $d\phi/dS < 0$. In other words, an importer loses from a devaluation/depreciation. Since we have already learned that dollar profits are reduced by a devaluation, and since we know that there are fewer pounds per dollar after a devaluation, the lower pound profit from a devaluation should come as no surprise. Nor should the gains from a revaluation or appreciation.

PART FIVE

CAPITAL DECISIONS

CHAPTER 14

INTERNATIONAL ASPECTS OF LONG-TERM FINANCING

There are numerous aspects of the long-term financing decision which are unique to the international arena. This chapter deals with these peculiar international aspects of the financing problem and their impact on equity versus debt considerations. Many of the problems multinational firms encounter in making long-term financing decisions are different from those met in short-term money market financing (Part 3). This is because the risk of changes in exchange rates is readily avoidable in the money market via forward contracts and because regulations on foreign ownership and hence on equity positions are generally more onerous than regulations on the short-term capital flows of money markets. We must therefore introduce a number of new aspects of international financing criteria when we deal in this chapter with the long-term capital market.

We shall begin by looking at long-term financing with debt capital when transaction or translation exposure is unavoidable. This requires that we extend the money market criteria of Chapter 7. We will look also at the different types of bonds that a firm might issue and the way risk is avoided with bond financing. We will then move on to equity financing. The required expected yield on equity depends on the extent to which risk can be reduced by international diversification. Dealing with this leads us into the capital asset pricing model, CAPM. After considering the effect of international diversification on the cost of capital, we will look at some of the methods that have been devised to avoid government restrictions on flows of capital and dividends. Finally, we will examine conventional debt/equity ratios in different countries.

BOND FINANCING

The Criteria

As a natural extension of what we learned in the money market, if a firm disregards foreign exchange risk and other considerations and $\dot{S}*(\$/\pounds)$ is the firm's expected change in the exchange rate, the firm should borrow in the British bond market when[1]

$$r_{US} > r_{UK} + \dot{S}*(\$/\pounds) \tag{14.1}$$

On the other hand, if

$$r_{US} < r_{UK} + \dot{S}*(\$/\pounds) \tag{14.2}$$

there is an incentive to sell or issue bonds in the United States.

For example, suppose that the borrowing costs and the expected change in the exchange rate are as follows:

r_{US}	r_{UK}	$\dot{S}*(\$/\pounds)$
10%	14%	−5%

That is, the financial manager sees a higher borrowing cost for the firm in the United Kingdom but also expects a decline in the exchange value of sterling against the dollar of 5 percent per annum over the life of the bond. It would be advantageous to borrow in Britain, if this particular borrower is not averse to risk involving exchange rates, because

$$r_{US} > r_{UK} + \dot{S}*(\$/\pounds)$$

The criteria in Equations (14.1) and (14.2) use the executive's *expected* change in the exchange rate rather than the forward premium, which we used in Chapter 7. This is because forward cover is generally not available for the life of bonds, which can be 10 or more years.[2]

Ex post, the actual exchange rate will often change by a considerable amount over the life of a bond, creating a potential for sizable gains or losses. In other words, actual changes can deviate markedly from the changes which had been expected by the financial executive. History is full of examples of currencies which have changed in value against the dollar by hundreds of percentages. Even some of the major

---

[1] While the criteria we give are probably as close to providing an exact decision rule as the criteria of most decision makers, they are approximate and can lead to errors. For a more precise rule, see the appendix for this chapter.

[2] Forward contracts are written for periods of up to 5 years in certain leading currencies. Contracts for periods that are longer than 5 years are virtually nonexistent because banks cannot offset the two sides of buying and selling a currency that far forward.

currencies have moved considerably in value over a number of years. Relatively small annual changes in exchange rates build up into very large changes over the life of long-term bonds.

To show how great the mistake can be, we can examine the results of a survey by William R. Folks, Jr., and Josef Follpracht. These results are shown in Table 14.1. Folks and Follpracht examined the cost of a number of foreign-currency-denominated bonds issued by U.S.-based multinational firms over the period July 1969 to December 1972. The table allows us to compare the coupon rates with the

TABLE 14.1
COSTS OF FOREIGN CURRENCY BONDS

Currency	Issue	Coupon rate/yr	Before-tax cost of borrowing/yr
Deutsche mark	Studebaker-Worthington	7¼	14.69
	International Standard Electric	7	12.31
	TRW	7½	12.38
	Tenneco	7½	12.33
	Tenneco	7¾	12.77
	Kraftco	7½	12.27
	Continental Oil	8	15.83
	Transocean Gulf	7½	12.50
	Firestone	7¾	11.83
	Philip Morris	6¾	9.87
	Goodyear	7¼	10.44
	Teledyne	7¼	10.44
Swiss franc	Burroughs	6¼	12.31
	Standard Oil (California)	6¼	12.42
	Goodyear	7	13.69
	American Brands	6½	13.08
	Texaco	6¾	13.37
	Cities Service	7¼	19.27
Dutch guilder	General Electric	8¼	20.08
	GTE	8¼	19.44
	IBM	8	16.46
	Cities Service	8	17.65
	International Harvester	8	17.65
	Philip Morris	7½	12.67
	Sperry Rand	6½	10.44
	Holiday Inns	6½	10.62
	Teledyne	6¼	10.27
	Standard Brands	6½	10.85
	Textron Atlantic	6¾	11.21
Pound sterling	Amoco	8	5.29
Luxembourg franc	International Standard Electric	6½	7.85

Source: William R. Folks, Jr., and Josef Follpracht, "The Currency of Denomination Decision for Offshore Long-Term Debt: The American Experience," working paper, Center for International Business Studies, University of South Carolina, 1976.

eventual effective annual costs computed as of March 1976 or at the bonds' maturities. We can see that the appreciation of the Deutsche mark, Swiss franc, Dutch guilder, and Luxembourg franc made the borrowing cost of bonds considerably higher than the rate given by the coupons. We cannot tell whether the costs were high compared with the dollar rates that were available when the bonds were originally sold, but there is good reason to believe that they were. The only foreign currency bond which turned out to be advantageous as of March 1976 was the pound sterling bond. The fall in value of the pound sterling reduced the effective dollar repayment cost by over 2.7 percent per annum. The conclusion depends on where the examination ends, but it does show that what may appear to be a cheap debt may end up being expensive borrowing.

Because of the potential for large unanticipated costs when borrowing by issuing bonds in currencies that steadily appreciate, some nontrivial advantage could be required before the risk is considered worthwhile. In such a case, our criteria in Equations (14.1) and (14.2) need some modification. For example, if management determines that the risk will be worth taking only with an expected 2 percent interest saving, we must revise Equation (14.1) to the following:

$$r_{US} > r_{UK} + \dot{S}^*(\$/\pounds) + 0.02 \tag{14.3}$$

Only when inequality (14.3) holds will the expected borrowing cost be sufficiently lower in Britain to warrant borrowing in that market. For example, if r_{US} is 10 percent, r_{UK} is 14 percent, and $S^*(\$/\pounds)$ is -5 percent (a 5 percent per annum expected depreciation of the pound), this will not be sufficient to warrant the risk of borrowing in Britain, for although the criterion in inequality (14.1) is met, the revised criterion in inequality (14.3) is not.

It should be remembered that the adaptation of the criteria in (14.1) and (14.2) is required because in the short-term money market a firm can choose between covered and uncovered borrowing. In the long-term bond market, generally only uncovered borrowing is available.

The required risk premiums on international bond decisions would have to be established by management. During times of greater economic uncertainty and potential volatility in foreign exchange markets, higher premiums should generally be required to compensate for the greater risk. Borrowing or investing abroad involves risk because the actual rate of change of the exchange rate, $\dot{S}(\$/\pounds)$, will in general differ from the ex ante expectation, $\dot{S}^*(\$/\pounds)$. If $\dot{S}(\$/\pounds) > \dot{S}^*(\$/\pounds)$, this will make the ex post borrowing cost greater than the ex ante cost.

For example, if as before we have $r_{US} = 10$ percent, $r_{UK} = 14$ percent, and $\dot{S}^*(\$/\pounds) = -5$ percent, then by using the straightforward ex ante criteria in inequalities (14.1) and (14.2), we know that the U.S. borrower facing these particular conditions should borrow in the United Kingdom. Suppose that this is done and that ex post we discover that $\dot{S}(\$/\pounds) = -2$ percent. The actual cost of borrowing in the United Kingdom will be

$$r_{UK} + \dot{S}(\$/£) = 0.14 - 0.02 = 0.12 \text{ or } 12 \text{ percent per annum}$$

Having borrowed in the United Kingdom will in retrospect turn out to have been a bad idea via-à-vis the 10 percent U.S. rate.

In general, if it turns out that $\dot{S}(\$/£)$, the actual per annum change in the exchange rate, has been such that

$$r_{UK} + \dot{S}(\$/£) > r_{US}$$

then we know that borrowing in the United Kingdom was a mistake. We see that it is necessary to compare the actual, not the expected, per annum change in the exchange rate with the interest differential. A management-determined risk premium such as the 0.02 premium we used in writing the revised criteria in inequality (14.3) will help to ensure that correct decisions are made. The larger the required premiums, the more often the decision will in retrospect appear correct, but larger premiums also mean missing many opportunities, and they will never guarantee ex post correct decisions.

Borrowing with Foreign-Source Income

There is *less* risk involved in borrowing abroad rather than at home when the borrower is receiving income in foreign exchange, and these foreign currency receivables can require a *negative* premium when borrowing abroad. We have already pointed out in Part 3 that firms receiving foreign income can hedge by borrowing foreign funds in the money market. The point is even more valid with long-term borrowing and is extremely important for firms which have sizable foreign operations. When a steady and relatively predictable long-term income is received in foreign currency, it makes sense to denominate some long-term payments in that same currency. The closer the balancing within each currency between what is received in income and what is paid out in interest, the lower the foreign exchange risk.

An example of a situation where the sale of bonds denominated in foreign exchange will reduce foreign exchange risk involves a Canadian firm that sells Canadian resources in world markets at contracted amounts in U.S. dollars.[3] If lumber or coal is sold by the Canadian firm to, for example, the U.S. or Japanese market at prices stated in U.S. dollars, it makes good sense for the Canadian firm to borrow in New York or Europe in U.S. dollars. Then the repayments on the debt can come out of the firm's U.S. dollar revenues. Similarly, if an Australian manufacturer is selling to Japan in yen, it makes sense to borrow with yen-denominated bonds, or if a Venezuelan oil exporter is selling to Chile in dollars, it

---

[3] Virtually all natural resource exports—oil, coal, gas, ore, and lumber—are sold at U.S. dollar prices. This reduces the foreign exchange problem for U.S.-based firms that sell or buy natural resources.

makes good sense to borrow in U.S. dollar denominations. The exact matching of debt repayments and foreign currency income is difficult, but it is generally possible to achieve some risk reduction at a small cost.[4]

The degree of foreign exchange exposure is, according to some definitions, related to the gap between the income and the payments in each currency, and reducing exposure requires reducing this gap. It is with this in mind that many suggest that firms borrow where they operate, in the host country. As we have seen in Chapter 13, the situation might not be quite as simple as this. While an accountant sees foreign exchange exposure as a translation risk that depends on actual changes in exchange rates and can be hedged against by reducing net foreign exchange flows, to an economist foreign exchange exposure involves economic risk, which is more difficult to avoid. Economic risk depends on the elasticity of demand for exports, the importance of imported inputs, and so on, and cannot be eliminated merely by matching current flows.

Other Debt Capital Considerations: Foreign Bonds versus Eurobonds

Even when interest rates and exchange rate expectations have been taken into account, along with any required advantage to encourage foreign borrowing, there are still other factors that must be considered. Among these are the size of the bond issue and the brokerage or underwriting costs that are involved in issuing the bond.

The New York and London capital markets can handle very large individual bond issues. In many of the other capital markets of the world, a $50 million bond issue would be considered large, and a $200 million bond issue would be huge. In New York or London, such issues are not uncommon. Indeed, the volume of funds handled by some of the bigger institutions such as the pension funds and insurance companies is such that these institutions can often buy an entire bond issue that is privately placed with them. The bond-issue size that the New York and London markets can handle and the lower costs of issuing bonds under private placement make New York and London attractive markets for large American and foreign borrowers, even when the interest cost of funds might seem a little higher than elsewhere.[5]

Foreign Bonds   Many borrowers, including U.S. corporations and foreign governments, attempt to reduce their borrowing costs by issuing "foreign-pay bonds," which are often given the name *foreign bonds.* For example, a Canadian

---

[4]Like Canadian resource exporters in the forestry and mining industries, many Canadian utility companies borrow in U.S. dollars even when only a small fraction of their revenues comes from sales to the United States. In terms of simply avoiding risk, this is not a good idea. These firms should limit the proportion of their debt in U.S. dollars to the fraction of their income derived from the United States. In the case of utilities, this could be quite small.

[5]The importance of transaction costs and the size of borrowing in encouraging Canadian borrowers to look to the United States capital market is examined by Karl A. Stroetmann in "The Theory of Long-Term International Capital Flows and Canadian Corporate Debt Issues in the United States," unpublished Ph.D. dissertation, University of British Columbia, 1974.

firm or a provincial government might sell bonds in New York that are denominated in U.S. dollars. A Brazilian company might denominate a bond in Deutsche marks and sell it in Germany. With foreign bonds, the borrowers rather than the lenders must bear the foreign exchange risk. By not denominating in their local currency, the borrowers are able to sell their bonds in a market which they believe will be cheaper.

There are periods when certain currencies are viewed as particularly attractive For example, during the 1970s there were many lenders looking for Deutsche mark assets. Borrowers can try to take advantage of what lenders view as attractive currencies, if they do not share this view, by issuing their bonds in these units. For example, in the 1970s many firms issued Deutsche-mark- and Swiss-franc-denominated bonds, as we saw in Table 14.1.

In the context of our criteria in (14.1), we have the following situation. Certain borrowers may have a relatively low expectation for $\dot{S}^*(\$/DM)$, for example, and so for them

$$r_{US} > r_{GY} + \dot{S}^*(\$/DM)$$

They might therefore wish to borrow, if they are not averse to the exchange risk, in Deutsche marks. At the same time, certain lenders (investors) may have a particularly favorable view of Deutsche marks and a higher expectation for the value of $\dot{S}^*(\$/DM)$, reversing the inequality. They might therefore be willing to buy the Deutsche-mark-denominated bonds. This will not be true of all borrowers and lenders, but as long as there are some of each, Deutsche mark bonds will be issued and bought.

An example of an apparent interest saving from issuing a sterling-pay bond involves ACONA N.V., which is the offshore financing subsidiary of the large Associated Corporation of North America. In 1980 ACONA N.V. sold £20 million worth of 5-year, 14 percent coupon bonds. The bonds sold at a small-issue discount at 99.5 percent of their par value to yield 14.15 percent. The bonds were sold by the Merrill Lynch International Bank, which hedged both the interest payments and the principal with forward contracts. A saving from the sale of sterling bonds was made clear with another sale just 2 days after the closing of the sterling bond sale. At this time, Associated sold $100 million worth of 13.875 percent, 10-year bonds in the U.S. market at a price which when corrected for the form in which interest was paid (semiannually in the United States and annually in Great Britain) provided a yield of 14.6 percent.[6]

Eurobonds   A bond that is sold in countries which do not use the currency of denomination of the bond is a *Eurobond*. For example, a U.S.-dollar-denominated

---

[6]The forward premium or discount was not disclosed, but it seems to have been almost "flat" (zero) because according to the bank, the claims of a gain of 45 points (that is, 14.60% − 14.15%) "were in the ballpark." The two bonds are not strictly comparable because the maturities and other features differ. However, the fact that the corporation went ahead with the sterling issue indicates that some saving was achieved. For a further account of these bond sales, see "Swap/Forward Deal: MNC Saves by Borrowing Dollars through Sterling," *Money Report*, Business International, Nov. 21, 1980.

TABLE 14.2
EUROBOND CURRENCIES OF DENOMINATION, 1979

Denomination currency	Total issues, US $ equivalent, billions	Percentage of total Eurobonds
U.S. dollar	10.54	58.9
German mark	4.96	27.7
Canadian dollar	0.47	2.6
Composite currencies	0.41	2.3
Other	1.52	8.5
Total	17.90	

Source: Organization for Economic Co-operation and Development, 1980.

bond sold outside of the United States—in Europe or elsewhere—is a Eurobond, a Eurodollar bond. A sterling-denominated bond offered for sale outside of Britain is a Eurobond—a Eurosterling bond—and so on. A Eurobond differs from a foreign bond, which is sold in the country in whose currency it is issued. (For example, a U.S.-dollar bond issued by a Canadian borrower for sale in the United States is a foreign bond.)

Foreign bonds are usually sold by a broker within the country in which they are issued. Eurobonds are sold by international syndicates of brokers because they are directed at simultaneous sales in a number of different countries. Eurobonds are the long-term equivalent of the money market Eurocurrencies. The absolute importance of Eurobonds versus foreign bonds is indicated in Table 14.2 and Table 14.3.

The Eurobond comes not only in a straightforward form, denominated in one currency and containing the standard provisions in domestic bonds, but also in a variety of other forms. Some Eurobonds are "multicurrency" bonds. A multicurrency bond gives the lender the right to request repayment in one of two or more

TABLE 14.3
SOURCES OF INTERNATIONAL DEBT CAPITAL

	1979		1980	
	Billions, US $ equivalent	%	Billions, US $ equivalent	%
Eurobonds	17.35	15	20.05	17
Foreign bonds	19.98	17	17.93	15
Special placement	1.60	1	1.44	1
Bank loans	78.26	67	78.42	67
	117.19		117.84	

Source: Organization for Economic Co-operation and Development, *Financial Statistics*, July 1981.

currencies. The amounts of repayment are often set equal in value at the exchange rates in effect when the bond is issued. If, during the life of the bond, exchange rates change, the lender will demand payment in the currency that has appreciated the most or depreciated the least. This reduces the risk to the lender in that it can help him or her avoid a depreciating currency. It does, however, add to the borrower's risk.

A variant of the multicurrency Eurobond using special exchange rates is the "unit of account bond," such as the European unit of account (EUA) bond. This type of bond has a unit of account established as a reference unit. The exchange rates vis-à-vis the unit are changed only infrequently. These might be DM2.0 per EUA, £0.40 per EUA, and so on. The borrowers borrow a certain number of EUAs. Clearly, the funds will be taken in the currency that has the highest current market premium over the parity exchange rate within the unit. But what the borrowers gain in their option of taking the borrowed funds in the currency of choice is lost in making interest payments and repaying the principal. Here the lender has the option of selecting the currency; the lender will also take the currency at the highest premium vis-à-vis the parities of the unit of account.[7]

To take a straightforward situation, suppose that the EUA is defined only in Deutsche marks and sterling as DM2.00 per EUA and £0.50 per EUA and that a borrower sells EUA 1 million worth of bonds. Suppose that when the bonds are sold, there are DM3.60 per pound. The borrower can take DM2 million or £500,000 at his or her discretion. At DM3.60/£, the DM2 million will buy £555,556, and so the borrower will take marks. Suppose that at the time of repaying the principal the spot rate is DM5.00/£. The lender can receive either DM2 million or £500,000. Since DM2 million will buy only £400,000 at DM5.0/£, the lender will take the £500,000. The same criteria will be used to select the currency for interest payments.

There are other multicurrency types of borrowing that are even more involved than borrowing with EUAs. There are units of account with currency components that are weighted by the volume of international trade, GNP, and so on, of the various countries. These include "currency cocktails" such as the SDR unit. Each SDR involves US$0.54, DM0.46, ¥34.00, Fr0.74, and £0.071. Another cocktail is the Eurco.

Currency cocktails can offer significant savings. For example, in January 1981 the rate on a 5-year SDR-denominated bond offered by Nordic Investment Bank was approximately 11.5 percent, while at the same time the rate on a straight 10-year U.S.-dollar bond offered by Du Pont of Canada was 13.69 percent, and the rate on a 7-year bond offered by GM's offshore finance subsidiary, General Motors Acceptance Corporation (or GMAC) Overseas Finance N.V., was 12.87 percent. While the rates are not strictly comparable, the lower rate on the SDR bond shows that investors value the diversification of currency cocktails. They will be

---

[7]There are prescribed procedures for revising conversion rates between EUAs and the component currencies. Some of these have been described by Peter Lusztig and Bernhard Schwab in "Units of Account and the International Bond Market," *Columbia Journal of World Business*, spring 1975, pp. 74–79.

particularly desirable during unstable times. SDR-denominated bonds date back to 1975.[8]

While on the topic of the multicurrency denomination of financial contracts, we can note an interesting use of a currency cocktail outside of the bond market. In 1980, the Australian carrier Qantas Airlines used a multicurrency lease for paying the owners of two Boeing 747s that it was using. The lease required payment in Deutsche marks, guilders, Australian dollars, and pounds sterling—all currencies that the airline received in its business. With this arrangement, Qantas could match the multicurrency nature of its income with the payments on the lease. If Qantas had bought rather than leased the planes, it could have matched the currencies of income and payments by financing the planes with a currency cocktail Eurobond requiring repayment in the various currencies of income. Lease contracts or bonds can help firms avoid *all* transaction exchange risks only if an exact matching is achieved. However, even when no attempt is made to match currencies of income and payments, multicurrency denominations will still help a firm reduce risk, for exchange rate movements can be averaged along the lines demonstrated in conventional portfolio theory.

The risk on bonds that comes from potential changes in interest rates can be removed if the bonds are given floating interest rates, that is, if the rates are revised, as in the money market, according to the much-used London Interbank Offered Rate, LIBOR. Rates are often revised every 6 months, and in 1979, 48 percent of the Eurobonds offered a floating rate.

In order to sell Eurobonds, many U.S. firms have established an "offshore finance subsidiary." Because it is incorporated abroad, this subsidiary does not have to withhold taxes. Taxes are withheld on income paid abroad—generally at a rate of 15 or 30 percent—and there are some lenders who cannot get the withheld amount credited against the taxes they pay at home. To attract these lenders, the bonds are sold by the specially created offshore finance subsidiary. ACONA N.V. and GMAC Overseas Finance N.V., which we met in previous examples, are offshore finance subsidiaries. The "N.V.," or "Nammloze Vennootschap," indicates that the subsidiary is located in a popular home for offshore finance subsidiaries: the Netherlands Antilles.

Political Risks and Bond Financing

The freezing or seizing of assets by inhospitable governments should not be a worry to those who borrow abroad. Instead, it should be a concern to the investors whose assets are lost. It might therefore be thought that while political risks are important in the investment decision, they are relatively inconsequential in the borrowing decision. However, some firms may borrow abroad *because* they fear confiscation

---

[8]For more on SDR bonds, see "Slimmed-Down SDR Makes Comeback: Techniques Include Opening Up Market for Negotiable SDR C.D.'s," *Money Report*, Business International, Jan. 16, 1981.

or expropriation. If assets are seized, these firms can refuse to repay local debts and thereby reduce their losses.

Not only are losses from actual confiscations reduced by having foreign debt, but even the probability of confiscation is reduced. Foreign host governments may prefer to avoid the anger of people at home who are holding the debt of a foreign corporation.

EQUITY FINANCING

A number of non-U.S. corporations have raised equity capital in the U.S. equity market. At the close of 1980, the 38 foreign companies that were listed on the New York Stock Exchange were worth about 15 percent of the total market. However, while many large U.S. companies raise debt capital in different countries, equity is generally raised at home.[9] The international financial question raised by the equity part of capital markets from a U.S. perspective is hence not where companies should sell shares. Rather, it concerns how the existence of equity markets in different countries affects the potential extent of portfolio diversification by shareholders and hence the required rate of return to compensate for risk. Much of this is a natural extension of the standard theory of diversification, which we will review briefly below.

Considerable evidence has been produced which shows that the ability to buy stocks in different countries allows the formation of portfolios with lower risk and thereby reduces the expected yield that companies must offer on stock. In this section we will describe the nature of this evidence and show why internationally open equity markets reduce the cost of capital. But first it will be instructive to look at the relative and absolute market sizes shown in Tables 14.4 and 14.5. These tables show that while the United States has the largest market, there are significant markets elsewhere. An opportunity for international diversification should clearly be present.

International Diversification of Security Portfolios

Risk reduction via diversification is generally considered in connection with decisions on equities. However, because of exchange rate risks, default risks, and risks to bond values from changes in interest rates, risk reduction via diversification can easily apply to bonds. Whenever there is some independence of returns on different securities, risks are reduced by maintaining only a portion of wealth in any asset. This will mean missing the maximum overall expected rate of return, because some wealth will be invested in assets with lower expected yields. However, given

---

[9]The shares of some large U.S. corporations such as IBM and General Motors are traded in foreign stock markets, but this is done in order to satisfy foreign governments or for the convenience of foreign stockholders. For statistics on the size of foreign equities trading in the United States, see *Fact Book 1981*, New York Stock Exchange, June 1981.

TABLE 14.4
MARKET VALUE OF SELECTED FOREIGN MARKETS
(December 31, 1980)

	Market capitalization, $ billion
Europe:	
United Kingdom	$ 189.7
Germany	71.3
France	52.8
Switzerland	45.5
Italy	25.0
The Netherlands	24.5
Spain	16.3
Sweden	12.2
Belgium/Luxembourg	10.0
Denmark	4.0
Norway	2.6
Austria	1.9
Total	$ 455.8
Far East:	
Japan	$ 356.6
Hong Kong	37.6
Singapore	24.3
Total	$ 418.5
Australia	$ 59.7
Europe + Far East + Australia	$ 934.0
United States	$1240.0

Source: Perspective, Capital International, Geneva, Switzerland, 1981.

some degree of risk aversion on the part of an investor, having less risk will compensate for lower expected returns. This is an established part of portfolio theory originally developed separately by Harry Markowitz and James Tobin.[10]

Within an economy there is independence of movement of asset returns, and this provides some diversification opportunities without the need to venture abroad. However, there is a tendency for the various segments of an economy to commonly feel the influence of overall domestic activity. This limits the independence of individual security returns and therefore also limits the gains to be made from

[10] See Harry Markowitz, *Portfolio Selection: Efficient Diversification of Investments*, John Wiley & Sons, New York, 1959, and James Tobin, "Liquidity Preference as Behavior toward Risk," *Review of Economic Studies*, vol. 25, February 1958, pp. 65–86. Reviews of the major discoveries of portfolio theory can be found in, for example, J. Fred Weston and Eugene Brigham. *Managerial Finance*, 5th ed., The Dryden Press, Hinsdale, Ill., 1975; James Van Horne, *Financial Management and Policy*, 4th ed., Prentice-Hall, Inc., Englewood Cliffs, N.J., 1977; and Richard Brealey and Stewart Myers, *Principles of Corporate Finance*, McGraw-Hill Book Company, New York, 1981.

TABLE 14.5
COMPARISON OF THE MARKET VALUE OF LISTED SECURITIES WITH GNP

	GNP—1980, $ billion	Market capitalization as of 12/31/80, $ billion	Market capitalization as percentage of GNP
Belgium	$ 70.1	$ 10.0	14.3%
France	398.4	52.8	13.3
Germany	501.4	71.3	14.2
Italy	232.0	25.0	10.8
The Netherlands	93.7	24.5	26.1
United Kingdom	249.8	189.7	75.9
Japan	663.0	356.6	53.8
United States	1811.4	1240.0	68.5

Source: *Perspective*, Capital International, Geneva, Switzerland, 1981, and OECD, *Main Economic Indicators*, April 1981.

diversification. Because of different policy actions and internal developments, there are reasons for having greater independence of returns across different coutries. A number of studies show how much independence has occurred.

Table 14.6 gives the correlations between monthly returns on a number of stock markets; the correlations were computed by Bertrand Jacquillat and Bruno H. Solnik.[11] The presence of some independence between markets is apparent with correlations as low as .335 in the case of the U.S. and German markets. Even lower correlations with the U.S. market were found in an extensive study by Donald Lessard.[12] These are shown in Table 14.7. We should expect clear gains from a diversified stock portfolio.

An indication of the size of the gains from including foreign stocks in a portfolio has been provided by the research of Bruno Solnik.[13] Solnik computed the risk of portfolios of n securities for different values of n in terms of the variance of these portfolios. The variance of a portfolio was compared with the variance of a typical stock (that is, $V_n = \sigma_n^2/\sigma_1^2$), and it was found that the risk declines as more stocks are added. Solnik discovered that an international portfolio of stocks from numerous markets has about half as much risk as a portfolio of comparable size of only U.S. stocks. This result is shown in Figure 14.1. We see that the risk of U.S. stocks for portfolios of over about 20 stocks is approximately 20 percent of the risk of a typical security, whereas the risk of a well-diversified international portfolio is only about 12 percent of the risk of a typical security. When Solnik considered other countries which have far smaller markets, he found that the gains from international

[11] Bertrand Jacquillat and Bruno H. Solnik, "Multinationals Are Poor Tools for Diversification," *Journal of Portfolio Management*, winter 1978, pp. 8–12.
[12] Donald R. Lessard, "World, Country and Industry: Relationships in Equity Returns," Sloan School working paper, January 1975.
[13] Bruno H. Solnik, "Why Not Diversify Internationally Rather Than Domestically?" *Financial Analysts Journal*, July–August 1974, pp. 48–54.

TABLE 14.6
CORRELATIONS BETWEEN MONTHLY RETURNS ON NATIONAL STOCK MARKET INDEXES, 1974–1976

	United Kingdom	Belgium	France	Germany	Netherlands	Switzerland	United States
United Kingdom	1.000	.671	.635	.387	.708	.612	.578
Belgium		1.000	.717	.599	.816	.798	.621
France			1.000	.566	.740	.751	.542
Germany				1.000	.632	.602	.335
Netherlands					1.000	.807	.583
Switzerland						1.000	.685
United States							1.000

Source: Bertrand Jacquillat and Bruno H. Solnik, "Multinationals Are Poor Tools for Diversification," *Journal of Portfolio Management*, winter 1978, pp. 8–12.

TABLE 14.7
CORRELATIONS WITH THE U.S.
MARKET, 1959–1973

Australia	.23
Austria	.12
Belgium	.46
Canada	.80
Denmark	.04
France	.25
Germany	.38
Italy	.21
Japan	.13
Netherlands	.61
Norway	.17
Spain	.04
Sweden	.33
Switzerland	.49
United Kingdom	.29

Source: Donald Lessard, "World, Country and Industry: Relationships in Equity Returns," Sloan School working paper, January 1975.

diversification were, not surprisingly, much larger. The gain from diversification from holding equities of different countries turned out to greatly exceed the gain from holding different equities within a country.

Solnik constructed the portfolios that produced these results so that they were hedged against foreign exchange risk. To see if exchange rate risk would significantly reduce the gains from international diversification, he also constructed portfolios that were not hedged against exchange risk. The unhedged portfolios had only a little more risk than the portfolios that were hedged. This is shown graphically in Figure 14.2. It is clear that the gain from having securities of different

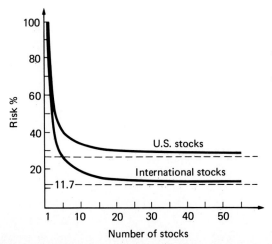

FIGURE 14.1
The advantages of international diversification. (*From Bruno H. Solnik, "Why Not Diversify Internationally Rather Than Domestically?"* Financial Analysts Journal, *July–August 1974, pp. 48–54.*)

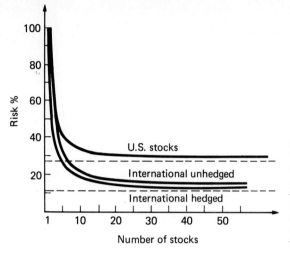

FIGURE 14.2
The advantage of international diversification with and without exchange risk. (*From Bruno H. Solnik, "Why Not Diversify Internationally Rather Than Domestically?"* Financial Analysts Journal, *July–August 1974, pp. 48–54*).

TABLE 14.8
INTERNATIONAL PORTFOLIO VERSUS NEW YORK MARKET,
MARCH 24, 1971–June 30, 1975

Total international portfolio return	+30.8%
S & P 500—total return	+11.6%
NYSE composite—total return	+ 8.4%
Standard deviation of international portfolio	2.0% per week
Standard deviation of NYSE composite	2.7% per week

Source: Gary F. Bergstrom, "A New Route to Higher Returns and Lower Risks," *Journal of Portfolio Management*, autumn 1975, pp. 30–38.

countries more than offsets any foreign exchange risk that this implies, even if hedging does not take place.[14]

The advantage of international diversification has been used by, for example, the Putnam Management Company to achieve improved yields and lower risk. The performance of Putnam's international portfolio as reported by Gary F. Bergstrom is shown in Table 14.8. Between March 24, 1971, and June 20, 1975, a higher return and a lower variance were experienced with the international portfolio as opposed to the New York market.[15] Putnam has shown that the independence of the markets of different countries can be valuable in portfolio management.

[14] The value of diversifying internationally among different stock markets has been demonstrated by other researchers. Some of the earliest work is by Herbert Grubel, ("Internationally Diversified Portfolios: Welfare Gains and Capital Flows," *American Economic Review*, vol. 59, December 1968, pp. 1299–1314) and Haim Levy and Marshall Sarnat ("International Diversification of Investment Portfolios," *American Economic Review*, vol. 60, September 1970, pp. 668–675).

[15] See Gary F. Bergstrom, "A New Route to Higher Returns and Lower Risks," *Journal of Portfolio Management*, autumn 1975, pp. 30–38.

The ability to more effectively allocate wealth when more investment opportunities are available allows investors to reduce the risk they must bear. In the standard theory of finance the unavoidable risk is known as the *undiversifiable* or *systematic risk*. If the risk that must be borne is reduced, the equilibrium yields required on the securities will be reduced. This means a lower cost of capital for use in evaluating capital investment projects. These concepts are not straightforward and are perhaps best explained by using the framework provided by the capital asset pricing model.

THE CAPITAL ASSET PRICING MODEL (CAPM)

The domestic variant of the capital asset pricing model, familiar from the so-called beta analysis used in security selection, can be written as follows:[16]

$$(r_j^* - r_f) = \frac{\text{cov}(r_j, r_m)}{\text{var}(r_m)} \cdot (r_m^* - r_f) \tag{14.4}$$

where
r_j^* = equilibrium or required rate of return on security/portfolio j
r_f = risk-free rate of interest
r_m^* = expected return on the market in which the security is traded
$\text{cov}(r_j, r_m)$ = covariance between security j and the market, m
$\text{var}(r_m)$ = variance of the market portfolio

The intuitive explanation of the capital asset pricing model is that a security or portfolio will offer an equilibrium risk premium, $(r_j^* - r_f)$, vis-à-vis that of the market, $(r_m^* - r_f)$, that is related to the risk that the asset or portfolio contributes to the market as a whole, $\text{cov}(r_j, r_m)/\text{var}(r_m)$. This is the part which cannot be diversified away—systematic risk. *If* a security compensated for more than the systematic risk, it would be a bargain, and investors would buy it and combine it with other securities, leaving the risk it contributes to be small relative to the compensation for risk. The buying of the security would raise its market price and lower its yield until it was no longer a bargain, even within a diversified portfolio.

The international variant of the capital asset pricing model has been developed by Bruno Solnik and extended by Piet Sercu.[17] It considers the implications of an international view of investment opportunities, and while the mathematics is difficult, it can be stated verbally along lines similar to the explanation of the domestic capital asset pricing model.

---

[16] For the derivation of the capital asset pricing model, see William Sharpe, "Capital Asset Pricing: A Theory of Market Equilibrium under Conditions of Risk," *Journal of Finance*, vol. 19, September 1964, pp. 424–447. The model is explained in many finance textbooks and is only stated here.

[17] See Bruno H. Solnik, "An International Market Model of Security Price Behavior," *Journal of Financial and Quantitative Analysis*, September 1974, pp. 537–554, and Piet Sercu, "A Generalization of the International Asset Pricing Model," *Review Français de Finance*, June 1980, pp. 91–135.

The equilibrium risk premium vis-à-vis the relevant risk-free rate consists of both the expected cost of hedging the security against exchange rate risk and a premium for systematic risk such as that in Equation (14.4).

The cost of hedging involves the return on a bundle of forward exchange contracts or local-currency borrowings designed to make asset prices independent of exchange rates. The CAPM-like risk premium involves the systematic risk that is the result of all factors other than exchange rate risk. In other words, when we allow for international diversification, equilibrium returns require compensation for the cost of hedging against foreign exchange risk and for any undiversifiable risk with the hedged international market.

In order to understand the nature of the international capital asset pricing model conclusion, suppose that after a period of restricted movement of capital, free movement is suddenly allowed. We have shown that because of the diversity of the stock markets of different nations and their relative performances, investors will be able to diversify more non-exchange-rate risk; that is, the correlation with the hedged international portfolio will be smaller than with the narrower-based domestic markets of the investors. If, in addition, the cost of hedging against exchange rate risk is small, the ability of investors to diversify internationally will lower equilibrium risk premiums. For a given risk-free rate, this means a lower equilibrium yield on a security. Allowing free international movement of capital therefore lowers the cost of capital.

Whether shareholders can diversify internationally and thereby lower systematic risk depends on government regulations on the flow of capital. However, even when regulations do exist, vehicles are frequently available for moving funds abroad. For example, while individuals might be prevented from moving funds, they might be able to invest in companies or investment funds which can move funds.[18] The gains from diversification with other equity markets will depend on the diversity offered at home. As Table 14.4 has already revealed, the U.S. market constitutes a substantial part of the world market, and so reductions in risk from U.S. investors diversifying internationally are considerably smaller than for residents of smaller countries.

Conceptually, the capital asset pricing model can be used in determining the required rate of return on capital projects. In order to do this, we must consider the covariance between the *project* and the relevant market portfolio. The interpretation of the capital asset pricing model is that a project should yield the riskless rate of interest plus a risk premium given by the cost of hedging and the undiversifiable shareholder risk of the project with the relevant market.[19] We have already made it clear that the presence of international diversification will in general reduce the

---

[18] For market-based evidence on whether shareholders have universal or local investment opportunities, see Richard Stehle, "An Empirical Test of the Alternative Hypotheses of National and International Pricing of Risky Assets," *Journal of Finance*, May 1977, pp. 493–502. The evidence is inconclusive.

[19] The relevant market will be the international market when shareholders can diversify internationally. We speak of *project* risk rather than *company* risk, as it is the project risk that is added by the capital spending.

equilibrium return, and so the opportunity for shareholders to diversify internationally will frequently mean that they need lower risk premiums on a project than if they could diversify only domestically.[20]

In practice, the computation of the required shareholder return on a particular *project* is an extremely difficult or impossible task. While the company will have a past record of returns (and the industry provides an even larger collection of returns), there is no record of returns for the project, and so the required non-exchange-rate risk premium cannot be calculated. In addition, we need to compute the cost of hedging against foreign exchange risk.[21] Furthermore, before we can use estimates of the cost of equity, we must adjust for debt. Some of these problems are among the questions which remain unresolved in the area of domestic finance, and we can say little about them in the more complicated area of international finance.[22]

BANK FINANCING, DIRECT LOANS, ETC.

So far we have examined international aspects of offshore bond financing and the benefits of international diversification on equity financing. We have stated that bonds may be sold in a foreign currency denomination in the country using that currency (foreign bonds) or in countries not using the denomination currency (Eurobonds). The ability to select the market of issue can lower borrowing costs but could introduce foreign exchange risk because forward markets are generally not available for hedging on bonds. However, a firm might actually reduce foreign exchange risk by borrowing offshore if it has a long-term foreign currency income. We have also concluded that the ability of shareholders to diversify internationally lowers the equilibrium return on equity and thereby lowers the firm's cost of equity capital.

For a large part of the financing of foreign subsidiaries of multinational firms, neither bonds nor equity is used. According to a survey by the U.S. Department of Commerce of foreign direct investors, approximately half of the financing was generated inside the corporation.[23] The results of the survey are summarized in

---

[20] Shareholders can diversify by themselves by holding different securities, or they can diversify by holding the shares of a diversified company. There is some evidence from share price behavior that shareholders value the diversified firm; this implies that they themselves cannot directly diversify. See the paper by Tamir Agmon and Donald Lessard, "Investor Recognition of Corporate International Diversification," *Journal of Finance*, vol. 32, September 1977, pp. 1049–1055, and the paper by John Hughes, Dennis Logue, and Richard Sweeney, "Corporate International Diversification and Market Assigned Measures of Risk and Diversification," *Journal of Financial and Quantitative Analysis*, vol. 10, November 1975, pp. 627–637. A different conclusion on the value of diversification by firms is reached by Bertrand Jacquillat and Bruno H. Solnik, "Multinationals Are Poor Tools for Diversification," *Journal of Portfolio Management*, winter 1978, pp. 8–12. Further evidence is provided by Azmi D. Mikhail and Hany A. Shawky, "Investment Performance of U.S.-Based Multinational Corporations," *Journal of International Business Studies*, spring/summer 1979, pp. 53–66.

[21] We might, however, believe that this is small.

[22] For an excellent account of the many difficulties in a domestic context, see Richard Brealey and Stewart Myers, *Principles of Corporate Finance*, McGraw-Hill Book Company, New York, 1981.

[23] U.S. Department of Commerce, Office of Foreign Direct Investments, *Foreign Affiliate Financial Survey, 1966–1969*, July 1971. This study has not been revised because the office that prepared it was eliminated, but the proportion of funds generated within the corporation has probably not changed greatly.

TABLE 14.9
SOURCES OF FUNDS FOR SUBSIDIARIES

		$ Billion		Percentage
From within the multinational enterprise		6.1		60
Internally generated by affiliate	4.7		46	
Depreciation	2.9		29	
Retained earnings	1.7		17	
From parent	1.4		14	
Equity	1.0		9	
Loans	0.5		5	
From outside the multinational enterprise		4.0		40
Loans	3.9		39	
Equity	0.2		2	
Total		10.1		100

Source: U.S. Department of Commerce, Office of Foreign Direct Investments, *Foreign Affiliate Financial Survey, 1966–1969*, July 1971, p. 34.

Table 14.9. If anything, the true percentage of internally generated funds is probably larger than the percentage shown. According to a different survey by Sidney Robbins and Robert Stobaugh, lending and borrowing by different subsidiaries are significant but net out in the Commerce Department's financial survey. Robbins and Stobaugh estimated that the total for outstanding loans was $14 billion. This amount is much larger than the amount quoted for loans outstanding to the parent company in the Commerce Department's survey. We can note from Table 14.9 that subsidiaries raise little equity. The debt incurred by subsidiaries is almost 20 times the equity they themselves raise.

According to Robbins and Stobaugh, most multinational corporations prefer to use intracompany credit rather than discretionary loans. This is because credit requires more limited documentation, and when repayment is made on intracompany credit, foreign host governments are not as likely to intervene. There are also potential gains from interest avoidance on credit advances that are unavailable on interdivisional loans.

Some of the debt raised outside the company takes on a character which is peculiarly international. For example, only in the international arena do we find so-called back-to-back or parallel loans.

Back-to-Back or Parallel Loans

A *back-to-back* or *parallel loan* involves an exchange of funds between firms in different countries, with the exchange reversed at a later date. For example, suppose that a U.S. company's subsidiary in Britain needs sterling while a British company's subsidiary in the United States needs dollars. The British firm can lend pounds to the U.S.-owned subsidiary in Britain while it borrows an approximately equivalent amount of dollars from the U.S. parent in the United States. After an agreed-upon term, the funds can be repaid. There is no exchange rate risk in either case because each is borrowing and repaying in the same currency.[24] Each side can pay interest within the country where funds are lent according to the going market rates.[25]

The advantages of back-to-back loans versus bank loans are that they can circumvent restrictions on the movement of funds and help avoid banks' spreads on foreign exchange transactions. The problem with back-to-back loans is locating the two sides of the deal. As in other "barter" deals, the needs of the parties must be harmonious before a satisfactory contract can be achieved. While the banks might well know of financing needs which are harmonious, they have little incentive to initiate a deal which avoids their spreads. Consequently, the majority of back-to-back loans are arranged by brokerage houses on behalf of their clients and do not involve banks.

Credit Swaps

A credit swap involves the exchange of currencies between a bank and a firm rather than between two firms. It is an alternative method of obtaining debt capital for a foreign subsidiary without sending funds abroad. In a credit swap the parent makes funds available to a bank at home. For example, a Canadian firm may place Canadian dollars in an account in Toronto. The Canadian bank then instructs one of its foreign subsidiaries to lend foreign currency to a subsidiary of the parent. For example, an office of the Canadian bank in London might lend pounds to a subsidiary of the Canadian firm operating in Britain. The advantage of the credit swap is that the parent does not have to exchange its local currency for the foreign exchange that is needed and face foreign exchange risk when the debt is repaid.

If the foreign exchange appears likely to depreciate, the bank will pay less interest on the deposited currency than it charges on the funds which are borrowed. Indeed, if the differential between the rates on the deposited currency and the borrowed currency equals the eventual change in the exchange rate according to the interest parity condition, there will be no advantage to the firm from a credit swap over sending dollars to Britain. This is because the change in the exchange rate will compensate for the interest differential. However, the credit swap does reduce the risk for the parent and for the subsidiary. The parent deposits and receives Canadian dollars in our example, while the subsidiary borrows and receives pounds. The credit swap is hence a device for helping firms avoid foreign exchange transaction risk.

OTHER FACTORS AFFECTING FINANCIAL STRUCTURE

We have presented a number of international financial considerations affecting the bond and equity decision and decisions involving bank loans and direct loans. There

---

[24] The loan agreement could just as well involve the subsidiaries of British and U.S. firms in a different country. For example, the U.S. firm could lend the British firm dollars in New York while the German subsidiary of the British firm lends the German subsidiary of the U.S. firm Deutsche marks in Germany.

[25] When no interest is paid, the exchange of currencies is called a swap rather than a parallel loan. Clearly, swaps are unlikely to occur when interest rates differ substantially.

are, however, a number of other factors which can affect the financing decision. Frequently these are based on the politically sensitive nature of a large amount of foreign investment. Sometimes, however, they are based on convention or restrictions on the movement of capital. We will quickly mention some of the more notable factors.

Generally, the more financing that is denominated in local currency, the lower the danger from changing exchange rates.[26] Because local financing is not usually available in equity form, many firms tend to use minimal equity financing for foreign subsidiaries. Reinforcing the tendency toward using high debt/equity ratios is the greater political sensitivity with regard to repatriating income on equity, as opposed to paying interest on debts. However, offsetting the factors leading to more debt is the fact that if equity is kept small, profits can look unreasonably high on the equity invested in foreign operations. The profit rate on equity can be used in a claim of exploitation by foreign governments.

Certain governments require that a minimum equity/debt ratio be maintained, while some banks also set standards to maintain the quality of debt.[27] According to survey work by Sidney Robbins and Robert Stobaugh, U.S. firms have generally kept their equity well above that required by local regulations.[28]

Some of the earliest work in financing subsidiaries by Edith Penrose revealed a varying financial structure the multinationals maintained as their subsidiaries grew larger.[29] Penrose argued that after receiving initial help from the parent company, subsidiaries move onto an independent growth path using funds from retained earnings and local borrowing. This has allowed some small foreign investments to grow into substantial foreign operations. E. R. Barlow and Ira Wender have hypothesized that the very high fraction of earnings retained by foreign subsidiaries stems from the view of these earnings as windfalls that can be reinvested even when the parent would not normally be investing in the subsidiary.[30] We might alternatively hypothesize that the high fraction of reinvested earnings is required to help convince the host governments of the benefits in the form of further investment that the foreign company can bring, thereby reducing political risk.

When earnings are retained abroad, U.S. corporations can postpone the payment of U.S. corporate income taxes and withholding taxes. According to

[26]This is because the currency of payments will match the currency of income. It has been pointed out by Rudiger Naumann-Etienne ("A Framework for Financial Decisions in Multinational Corporations— A Summary of Recent Research," *Journal of Financial and Quantitative Analysis*, November 1974, pp. 859–874) that in making borrowing decisions, the firm should consider the risk reduction that comes from borrowing in numerous currencies as well as the risk reduction from matching the currency of payment to the currency of income.

[27]Restrictions on the amount of equity or debt can be handled in a linear programming approach to financing. An example of this has been shown by Walter L. Ness, Jr., "A Linear Programming Approach to Financing the Multinational Corporation," *Financial Management*, winter 1972, pp. 88–100.

[28]Sidney M. Robbins and Robert B. Stobaugh, "Financing Foreign Affiliates," *Financial Management*, winter 1973, pp. 56–65.

[29]Edith T. Penrose, "Foreign Investment and the Growth of the Firm," *Economic Journal*, June 1956, pp. 220–235. This was reprinted in John H. Dunning, *International Investment*, Penguin Books, Harmonsworth, England, 1972.

[30]E. R. Barlow and Ira T. Wender, *Foreign Investment and Taxation*, Prentice-Hall, Inc., Englewood Cliffs, N.J., 1955.

Walter Ness, the savings from the deferral of tax payments lower the cost of equity capital for multinational corporations and induce the corporations to have a lower debt/equity ratio in financing foreign subsidiaries.[31] This tax advantage to equity runs counter to the frequently mentioned advantage to debt from the tax deductibility of interest but not dividends. However, since many countries offer a tax deduction for interest, this cannot explain the greater reliance on debt for financing foreign subsidiaries unless the advantage to debt in the foreign countries exceeds the advantage at home. Furthermore, according to Ian Giddy and Alan Shapiro, the alternatives for repatriating income via transfer pricing, royalties, fees, and so on, override any advantage from deferred tax payments encouraging the use of equity capital.[32]

When internally generated funds are insufficient, the debt ratios of subsidiaries can be increased without affecting the entire corporation by borrowing from other subsidiaries. This is not liked by banks, since it can increase the risk of individual subsidiaries and reduce the control the banks can exercise on debt ratios.

CAPITAL STRUCTURE IN DIFFERENT COUNTRIES

The financing of subsidiaries generally involves a higher debt/equity ratio than is used in financing the parent company. This is because foreign exchange risk is reduced by the matching of the currencies of payment and income and because paying interest is not as politically sensitive as taking home profits. The reductions in foreign exchange risk and political risk outweigh the advantages of equity financing, such as the potential postponement of the payment of U.S. taxes and a politically attractive lower rate of return. While the arguments favoring debt appear to dominate, we cannot give any straightforward rule for the optimal debt structure of foreign subsidiaries. As a result, some writers claim that subsidiaries should use norms within the country of operation, while other writers claim that companies should consider each case separately to minimize their overall cost of capital.[33]

Financing norms do vary widely. As Table 14.10 shows, the use of debt versus equity in the United States is smaller than in most other countries. According to a survey of factors behind debt ratio norms in five different countries, the French establish their capital structure in a way that offers the borrower the best guarantee of the future availability of capital.[34] This tends to be done even if it means, for

[31] Walter L. Ness, Jr., "U.S. Corporate Income Taxation and the Dividend Remittance Policy of Multinational Corporations," *Journal of International Business Studies*, spring 1975, pp. 67–77.

[32] Alan C. Shapiro, "Financial Structure and the Cost of Capital in Multinational Corporations," *Journal of Financial and Quantitative Analysis*, June 1979, pp. 211–226, and Ian H. Giddy, "The Cost of Capital in the Multinational Firm," unpublished paper, Columbia University, 1976.

[33] On the use of local norms for capital structure, see Lee Remmers, "Some Determinants of Financial Structure in Foreign Subsidiaries," paper given at the Financial Management Association Meetings, Atlanta, October 1973, and Arthur I. Stonehill and Thomas Stitzel, "The Financial Structure of Multinational Corporations," *California Management Review*, fall 1969, pp. 91–96. For the case-by-case approach, see Sidney M. Robbins and Robert B. Stobaugh, *Money in the Multinational Enterprise*, Basic Books, Inc., New York, 1973.

[34] See Arthur Stonehill, Theo Beekhuisen, Richard Wright, Lee Remmers, Norman Toy, Antonio Pares, Alan Shapiro, Douglas Egan, and Thomas Bates, "Financial Goals and Debt Ratio Determinants: A Survey of Practice in Five Countries," *Financial Management*, autumn 1975, pp. 27–41.

TABLE 14.10
CAPITAL STRUCTURE IN DIFFERENT COUNTRIES

Country	D/E*	D/A
Australia	0.87 : 1	0.43 : 1
Canada	1.16 : 1	0.54 : 1
France	2.42 : 1	0.71 : 1
Germany	2.03 : 1	0.67 : 1
Italy	4.00 : 1	0.58 : 1
Japan	5.13 : 1	0.83 : 1
Netherlands	1.49 : 1	0.60 : 1
Saudi Arabia	1.63 : 1	0.62 : 1
Sweden	1.78 : 1	0.64 : 1
Switzerland	1.25 : 1	0.49 : 1
United Kingdom	1.36 : 1	0.58 : 1
United States	0.95 : 1	0.49 : 1

*D = total debt, E = shareholders' equity, A = total assets.
Source: *Money Report*, Business International, Feb 1, 1980, p. 41.

example, that the debt ratio will be lower than the ratio that would minimize the company's cost of capital. The Japanese also attach considerable importance to the future availability of capital. Here, however, the intimate links between the banks and other firms allow companies to use a considerable amount of debt before they substantially reduce future borrowing prospects.

In the Netherlands the capital market is small, and banks are the primary source of capital, as they are in Japan, although ownership is separated. Dutch financial executives appear to place heavy emphasis on meeting cash flows and avoiding financial risks. Their view is shared by Norwegian executives, who face a system based heavily on bank debt. Even U.S. firms show an important tendency toward avoiding financial risk by selecting a debt structure that allows them to meet future financial commitments. In foreign operations, however, U.S. firms make an effort to select a financial structure that minimizes foreign exchange risk, and this means more debt.[35]

SUMMARY

1 Bond investment and borrowing criteria involve comparing domestic interest rates with foreign rates plus the expected annual appreciation/depreciation of the foreign currency. Because hedging is difficult, mistakes can be extremely costly or beneficial, and so some firms will require large advantages before borrowing abroad.

2 When a firm has a relatively stable long-term income in a foreign currency, foreign exchange risk is reduced by borrowing in that currency. Since a large part of international

[35] For more on debt ratio norms in other countries, see Norman Toy, Arthur Stonehill, Lee Remmers, Richard Wright, and Theo Beekhuisen, "A Comparative International Study of Growth, Profitability, and Risk as Determinants of Corporate Debt Ratios in the Manufacturing Sector," *Journal of Financial and Quantitative Analysis*, November 1974, pp. 875–886.

trade is denominated in U.S. dollars, there is an incentive to borrow in U.S. dollars in the United States (foreign bonds) and in Europe (Eurodollar bonds).

3 Foreign bonds are sold in the market that uses the currency in which the bonds are denominated. For example, a U.S.-dollar-denominated bond sold by a Canadian firm in New York is a foreign bond. A Eurobond is sold in markets which do not commonly use the currency of denomination. For example, a U.S.-dollar-denominated bond sold by a U.S. or Canadian firm in London is a Eurobond. Similarly, a sterling-denominated bond sold in New York is a Eurobond. Eurobonds are sometimes multicurrency bonds; the lender can choose the currency. Some are unit of account bonds; these are denominated in a unit such as the EUA against which exchange rates are fixed. Eurobonds are generally sold by syndicates, while foreign bonds are sold by local brokers.

4 Political risk should not discourage subsidiaries from borrowing where they are located. Indeed, when there are local creditors, the risk of damaging political action is reduced.

5 Securities from different countries tend to exhibit more independence than purely domestic securities. There are therefore more gains from international diversification than from domestic diversification.

6 Because with international diversification a greater reduction of total risk is possible, the systematic risk in an internationally diversified portfolio is less than that for a domestically diversified one. The ability of shareholders to internationally diversify therefore reduces the cost of equity capital to the firm.

7 A back-to-back or parallel loan involves an exchange of funds between firms in different countries, with the exchange later reversed. This kind of loan is advantageous when there are restrictions on the movement of capital between countries. A credit swap is an exchange of currencies between a bank and a firm. The parent makes funds available to the bank at home, while the bank makes a foreign currency available to a subsidiary.

8 In general, risk is reduced if subsidiaries borrow locally, although some equity is required to maintain a sufficiently low return so that the foreign government will not complain about exploitation. Self-financing tends to replace equity financing from the parent in the typical growth scenario.

QUESTIONS

1 With $r_{US} = 12.50$ percent, $r_{UK} = 14.00$ percent, $S(\$/£) = 2.25$, and $S_{10}^*(\$/£) = 1.50$, where would you borrow? What is the total gain on each $1 million borrowed from making the correct choice?

2 If $r_{US} = 12.50$ percent, $r_{UK} = 14.00$ percent, and $S(\$/£) = 2.25$, what must the actual exchange rate be after 10 years, $S_{10}(\$/£)$, in order to make borrowing in Britain a good idea?

3 Why does having an income in foreign currency reduce required borrowing risk premiums? What type of risk—translation/transaction risk or economic risk—is reduced?

4 What determines whether you would issue a Eurosterling bond or a sterling bond (that is, a foreign bond) in Britain?

5 What are the limitations in applying the traditional capital asset pricing model in an international context?

6 If the reduction in the cost of debt capital exceeds the reduction in the cost of equity when shareholders and the firm can use the international capital market, what will happen to the optimum capital structure?

7 What types of companies will have the greatest reduction in systematic risk when foreign equity markets are available?

8 (*Based on the appendix for this chapter.*) Explain why a comparison of yields or costs should include the fact that coupons are paid at the end, rather than at the beginning of periods, when exchange rates change rapidly. What additional complication arises when the delay in payments results in gains (losses) from a depreciating (appreciating) currency?

BIBLIOGRAPHY

Adler, Michael, and Bernard Dumas: "Optimal International Acquisitions," *Journal of Finance*, March 1975, pp. 1–19.

Agmon, Tamir, and Donald R. Lessard: "Investor Recognition of Corporate International Diversification," *Journal of Finance*, September 1977, pp. 1049–1055.

Black, Fisher: "International Capital Market Equilibrium with Investment Barriers," *Journal of Financial Economics*, December 1974, pp. 337–352.

Cohen, Kalman, Walter Ness, Robert Schwartz, David Whitcomb, and Hitoshi Okuda: "The Determinants of Common Stock Returns Volatility: An International Comparison," *Journal of Finance*, May 1976, pp. 733–740.

Cohn, Richard A., and John A. Pringle: "Imperfections in International Financial Markets: Implications for Risk Premia and the Cost of Capital to Firms," *Journal of Finance*, March 1973, pp. 59–66. Reprinted in Donald R. Lessard (ed.), *International Financial Management: Theory and Application*, Warren, Gorham and Lamont, Boston, 1979.

Frankel, Jeffery A.: "The Diversifiability of Exchange Risk," *Journal of International Economics*, August 1979, pp. 379–393.

Grauer, Frederick L., Robert H. Lizenberger, and Richard E. Stehle: "Sharing Rules and Equilibrium in an International Capital Market under Uncertainty," *Journal of Financial Economics*, June 1976, pp. 233–256.

Grubel, Herbert G.: "Internationally Diversified Portfolios: Welfare Gains and Capital Flows," *American Economic Review*, December 1968, pp. 1299–1314.

Hughes, John S., Dennis E. Logue, and Richard J. Sweeney: "Corporate International Diversification and Market Assigned Measures of Risk and Diversification," *Journal of Financial and Quantitative Analysis*, November 1975, pp. 627–637.

Lessard, Donald R.: "World, Country, and Industry Relationships in Equity Returns: Implications for Risk Reduction through International Diversification," *Financial Analysts Journal*, January–February 1976, pp. 2–8.

Levy, Haim, and Marshall Sarnat: "International Diversification of Investment Portfolios," *American Economic Review*, September 1970, pp. 668–675.

Rugman, Alan M.: "International Diversification by Financial and Direct Investment," *Journal of Economics and Business*, fall 1977, pp. 31–37.

Sercu, Piet: "A Generalization of the International Asset Pricing Model," *Review Français de Finance*, June 1980, pp. 91–135.

Shapiro, Alan C.: "Financial Structure and Cost of Capital in the Multinational Corporation," *Journal of Financial and Quantitative Analysis*, June 1979, pp. 211–226.

Solnik, Bruno H.: "Why Not Diversify Internationally Rather Than Domestically?" *Financial Analysts Journal*, July–August 1974, pp. 48–54.

———: "An International Market Model of Security Price Behavior," *Journal of Financial and Quantitative Analysis*, September 1974, pp. 537–554.

APPENDIX: Comparing the Bond-Life Borrowing Costs

In the text we offered the rule that if borrowers are neutral toward risk and $\dot{S}*(\$/£)$ is the expected appreciation of the pound vis-à-vis the dollar, then if

$$r_{US} > r_{UK} + \dot{S}*(\$/£)$$

the borrowers should borrow in Britain, and if

$$r_{US} < r_{UK} + \dot{S}*(\$/£)$$

they should borrow in the United States. This rule neglects not only risk aversion but the fact that coupon payments are generally made periodically and begin some time after the borrowing has occurred.

To obtain a more accurate comparison of borrowing costs, we can note that the repayment per dollar borrowed via bonds with n years of end-of-year coupon is

$$\$(1 + nr_{US}) \tag{14A.1}$$

Each dollar borrowed in the United Kingdom gives $1/[S(\$/£)]$ in pounds, on which interest is paid at the rate r_{UK}. This is $r_{UK}/[S_i*(\$/£)]$ in pounds in each future period of expected coupon payments. The total amount of interest plus principal that the borrower expects to pay is

$$\$\left[\frac{r_{UK}}{S(\$/£)} \sum_{i=1}^{n} S_i*(\$/£) + \frac{S_n*(\$/£)}{S(\$/£)} \right] \tag{14A.2}$$

because repayment is on $1/[S(\$/£)]$ in pounds in each period at the interest rate r_{UK} and the expected exchange rate $S_i*(\$/£)$. If the spot exchange rate is expected to change at a steady rate, $\dot{S}*$, we can write that

$$S_i*(\$/£) = (1 + \dot{S}*)^i S(\$/£) \tag{14A.3}$$

This gives the expected spot rate for i years into the future on the basis of today's rate and the expected annual rate of change. By substituting (14A.3) into (14A.2), we get the total bond-life repayment per dollar borrowed in Britain:

$$\$\left[r_{UK} \sum_{i=1}^{n} (1 + \dot{S}*)^i + (1 + \dot{S}*)^n \right] \tag{14A.4}$$

This is the expected total repayment to compare with (14A.1). This comparison should not be affected by computing total payments rather than the present values of payments.

For example, when $r_{UK} = 14$ percent and $\dot{S}* = -0.04$, a total of only $1.80 will be repaid on each dollar obtained via Britain with a 10-year bond, whereas $r_{US} = 10$ percent, a total of \$2 will be repaid per dollar borrowed in the United States. By comparison, the rule offered in the text showed the U.S. and U.K. costs to be equal under these conditions. There is a difference between the rule in the text and the rule offered here of comparing the sums in (14A.1) and (14A.4) because each payment to the British lender will have the advantage of being made after a full year of currency depreciation. The difference is reduced if coupon payments are made more frequently.

The effect we have shown is reversed when the foreign currency is appreciating. For example, when $r_{UK} = 6$ percent and $\dot{S}^* = +0.04$, then a total of \$2.23 will be repaid on each dollar obtained via the United Kingdom; this is obtained by using (14A.4). However, on the dollar borrowed in the United States at $r_{US} = 10$ percent, the payment will be \$2. More is paid on funds borrowed in Britain because of the delay in making payments. This delay costs the borrower in terms of appreciating pounds that must be purchased.

CHAPTER 15

CAPITAL BUDGETING AND MULTINATIONAL ENTERPRISE

The massive multinational corporations (MNCs) whose names are household words in numerous languages and which have power that is the envy and fear of almost every government grew by making direct investments overseas. The criteria used for making these direct investments will be presented here as we develop a principle of capital budgeting that can be used in evaluating foreign capital investments. In the international arena, capital budgeting involves complex problems that are not shared in a domestic context. These include, for example, the dependence of cash flows on capital structure because of cheap loans from foreign governments, exchange rate risks, political risks, multiple tiers of taxation, and restrictions on repatriating income. We will show the conditions under which some of the more complex problems in the evaluation of overseas investments can be reduced to manageable size. We will also give some commonly cited reasons for the growth of multinational corporations and briefly venture beyond strictly financial concerns to give an account of the problems and benefits these supernational bodies have brought.

There are a number of approaches to capital budgeting for traditional domestic investments, including net present value (NPV), adjusted present value (APV), internal rate of return, and pay-back period. We shall use the adjusted present value technique, which has been characterized as a "divide and conquer" approach, for each difficulty is tackled as it occurs. This technique involves accounting separately for the complexities found in foreign investments as a result of such factors as subsidized loans and restrictions on repatriating income. Before we show how the difficulties can be handled, we will give explanations of the difficulties themselves. Our explanations will show why the APV approach has been proposed for the evaluation of overseas projects rather than the traditional NPV approach, which is used extensively in evaluating domestic projects.

DIFFICULTIES IN EVALUATING FOREIGN PROJECTS[1]

Introductory textbooks in finance tend to advise the use of the NPV technique, and NPV is defined as follows:

$$NPV = -C_0 + \sum_{t=1}^{T} \frac{CF_t^*(1 - \tau)}{(1 + \bar{r})^t} \tag{15.1}$$

where C_0 = capital cost
CF_t^* = expected before-tax cash flow in year t
τ = tax rate
$\bar{r}$ = weighted average cost of capital
T = life of the project

The weighted average cost of capital, $\bar{r}$, is in turn defined as follows:

$$\bar{r} = \frac{E}{E + D} r^e + \frac{D}{E + D} r(1 - \tau)$$

where r^e = equilibrium cost of equity capital reflecting only the systematic risk
r = before-tax cost of credit
E = total market value of equity
D = total market value of debt
τ = tax rate

We see that the cost of equity and the cost of debt are weighted by the importance of equity and debt as sources of capital and that an additional adjustment is made to the cost of debt, since interest payments are generally deductible against corporate taxes. The adjustment of $(1 - \tau)$ gives the effective cost of debt after the fraction τ of interest payments has been saved from taxes. While not universally accepted, this NPV approach has enjoyed a prominent place in finance textbooks.[2]

There are two categories of reasons why it is difficult to apply the traditional net present value technique to overseas projects and why an alternative framework such as the adjusted present value technique is required. The first category of reasons involves the difficulties which cause cash flows—the *numerators* in NPVs—to be seen from two different perspectives: that of the investor's home country and that of

[1]Our account of the adjusted present value technique draws heavily on a paper by Donald Lessard: "Evaluating Foreign Projects: An Adjusted Present Value Approach," in Donald R. Lessard (ed.), *International Financial Management: Theory and Application*, Warren, Gorham & Lamont, Boston, 1979. A revised version of this paper appears in Roy L. Crum and Frans G. Derkinderen (eds.), *Capital Budgeting under Conditions of Uncertainty*, Martinus Nijhoff, The Hague, 1980.

[2]For the traditional textbook account of the NPV approach with the weighted average cost of capital, see James C. Van Horne, *Financial Management and Policy*, 5th ed., Prentice-Hall, Inc., Englewood Cliffs, N.J., 1980. For an account of the alternative APV approach using an adjusted cost of capital, see Richard Brealey and Stewart Myers, *Principles of Corporate Finance*, McGraw-Hill Book Company, New York, 1981.

the country in which the project is located.[3] The correct perspective is that of the investor's home country, which we assume to be well identified. The second category of reasons involves the degree of risk of foreign projects and the appropriate discount rate—the *denominator* of the NPV. We will begin by looking at why cash flows differ between the investor's perspective and the perspective of the country in which the project is located; later we will turn to the appropriate discount rate.

FACTORS AFFECTING INVESTORS' CASH FLOWS

Blocked Funds   If funds that are "blocked" or otherwise restricted can be utilized in a foreign investment, the capital cost to the investor may be below the local project construction costs. From the investor's perspective there is a gain from activated funds equal to the difference between the face value of those funds and the present value of the funds if the next best thing is done with them. This gain should be deducted from the capital cost of the project to find the cost from the investor's perspective. For example, if the next best thing that can be done is to leave blocked funds idle abroad, the full value of the activated funds should be deducted from the capital cost. Alternatively, if half of the blocked funds can be returned to the investor after the investor pays taxes or uses an internal funds transfer system, then half of the value of the blocked funds should be subtracted from the cost of the project.

Effects on the Sales of Other Divisions   From the perspective of the manager of a foreign project, the total value of cash flows generated by the investment is relevant. However, factories are frequently built in countries in which sales have previously taken place. If the multinational corporation exports to the country of the project from the home country or some other preexisting facility, only the increment in the MNC's corporate income is relevant. Sales will often decline or be lost in the absence of a project, and this is why the investment is made. However, we must net out whatever income would have otherwise been earned by the multinational corporation in order to take care of the so-called synergy or interdependence between subsidiaries.

Remittance Restrictions   When there are restrictions on the repatriation of income, only those flows that are remittable to the parent are relevant from the MNC's perspective. This is true whether or not the income is remitted. When remittances are legally limited, sometimes the restrictions can be circumvented to some extent by using internal transfer prices, overhead payments, and so on. If we include only the income which is remittable via legal and open channels, we will obtain a conservative estimate of the project's value. If this is positive, we need not add any more. If it is negative, we can add income that is remittable via illegal

---

[3]Michael Adler has tackled the challenging problem of having no clear home base. See Michael Adler, "The Cost of Capital and Valuation of a Two-Country Firm," *Journal of Finance*, March 1974, pp. 119–132.

transfers, for example. This two-step potential is a major advantage of the APV approach. A two-step procedure can also be applied to taxes.

Different Levels of Taxation   The cash flows for the investor depend on the total amount of taxes paid and not on which government collects the taxes. For a U.S.-based multinational, when the U.S. tax rate is above the foreign rate, the effective tax rate will be the U.S. rate if full credit is given for foreign taxes paid. For example, if the foreign project is located in Singapore and the local tax rate for foreign-based corporations is 40 percent, while the U.S. corporate tax rate is 46 percent, then after the credit for foreign taxes paid is applied, only 6 percent will be payable in the United States. If, however, the project is located in the United Kingdom and faces a tax rate of 52 percent, full credit will not be available, and the effective tax rate will be 52 percent. This means that when we deal with foreign projects from the investor's point of view, we should use a tax rate, τ, which is the higher of the home country and foreign rates.

Taking τ as the higher of the tax rates at home and abroad is a conservative approach. In reality, taxes are often reduced to a level below τ through the appropriate choice of transfer prices, royalty payments, and so on. These techniques can be used to move income from high-tax countries to low-tax countries and thereby reduce overall corporate taxes. In addition, the payment of taxes can be deferred by leaving remittable income abroad, and so if cash flows are measured as all remittable income whether or not remitted, some adjustment is required, since the actual amount of taxes paid will be less than the cash-flow term suggests. The adjustment can be made to the cost of capital or included as an extra term in an adjusted present value calculation.[4]

Concessionary Loans   While governments do offer special financial aid or other kinds of help for certain domestic projects, it is very common for foreign investments to carry some sort of assistance. This may come in the form of low-cost land, reduced interest rates, and so on. Low-cost land will merely be reflected in capital costs, but concessionary lending is more problematic in the NPV approach. However, with the APV technique we can add a separate term to include the subsidy. This is particularly important, since the special concessionary loan will be available to the corporation but not directly to the shareholders. This will make the appropriate cost of capital for foreign investment projects differ from that for domestic projects, which is what happens in segmented capital markets.

---

[4]A method for valuing foreign investments that is based on net present value and the weighted average cost of capital that takes care of taxes has been developed by Alan C. Shapiro ("Financial Structure and the Cost of Capital in the Multinational Corporation," *Journal of Financial and Quantitative Analysis*, November 1978, pp. 211–226). In general, the NPV and APV approaches will be equivalent if they take care of all complexities. This has been shown by Lawrence D. Booth ("Capital Budgeting Frameworks for the Multinational Corporation," unpublished manuscript, University of Toronto, 1980). Preference for APV rather than NPV is based on the more explicit nature of allowance for complexities and the ability to use APV to see whether projects are profitable even before an allowance is made for complexities. If they are profitable before positive allowances are added, we know they will be profitable after the allowances are added.

The various difficulties encountered in the evaluation of foreign projects can be incorporated within the APV approach, which we have not yet presented. We need not delay any more.

THE ADJUSTED PRESENT VALUE TECHNIQUE

The APV for a foreign project can be written as follows:[5]

$$\text{APV} = -S_0 K_0 + S_0 \text{AF}_0 + \sum_{t=1}^{T} \frac{(S_t^* \text{CF}_t^* - \text{LS}_t^*)(1-\tau)}{(1+\text{DR}_e)^t} + \sum_{t=1}^{T} \frac{\text{DA}_t \tau}{(1+\text{DR}_a)^t}$$

$$+ \sum_{t=1}^{T} \frac{r_g \text{BC}_0 \tau}{(1+\text{DR}_b)^t} + S_0 \left[\text{CL}_0 - \sum_{t=1}^{T} \frac{\text{LR}_t}{(1+\text{DR}_c)^t} \right]$$

$$+ \sum_{t=1}^{T} \frac{\text{TD}_t^*}{(1+\text{DR}_d)^t} + \sum_{t=1}^{T} \frac{\text{RF}_t^*}{(1+\text{DR}_f)^t} \qquad (15.2)$$

where S_0 = spot exchange rate, period zero
S_t^* = expected spot rate, period t
K_0 = capital cost of project in foreign currency units
AF_0 = restricted funds activated by project
CF_t^* = expected remittable cash flow in foreign currency units
LS_t^* = profit from lost sales, in dollars
τ = higher of U.S. and foreign corporate tax rates
T = life of the project
DA_t = depreciation allowances in dollar units
BC_0 = contribution of project to borrowing capacity in dollars
CL_0 = face value of concessionary loan in foreign currency
LR_t = loan repayments on concessionary loan in foreign currency
TD_t^* = expected tax savings from deferrals, intersubsidiary transfer pricing
RF_t^* = expected illegal repatriation of income
DR_e = discount rate for cash flows, assuming all-equity financing
DR_a = discount rate for depreciation allowances
DR_b = discount rate for tax saving on interest deduction from contribution to borrowing capacity
DR_c = discount rate for saving on concessionary interest rate
DR_d = discount rate for saving via intersubsidiary transfers
DR_f = discount rate for illegally repatriated project flows
r_g = market borrowing rate at home

[5]The definition of APV is that of Donald R. Lessard in "Evaluating Foreign Projects: An Adjusted Present Value Approach," in Donald R. Lessard (ed.), *International Financial Management: Theory and Application*, Warren, Gorham and Lamont, Boston, 1979.

We can describe each of the terms in the APV equation and show how these terms take care of the difficulties in evaluating foreign investment projects.

$-S_0 K_0$ The capital cost of the project is assumed to be denominated in foreign currency and incurred in year zero only. It is converted into dollars at S_0.

$S_0 AF_0$ We reduce the capital cost by the value, converted into dollars, of the blocked funds activated by the project. AF_0 is the face value of the blocked funds minus their value in the next best use.

$$\sum_{t=1}^{T} \frac{(S_t^* CF_t^* - LS_t^*)(1 - \tau)}{(1 + DR_e)^t}$$ CF* represents the expected legally remittable

project cash flows on sales from the new project, with these beginning after a year.[6] From this is subtracted the lost income on sales from other facilities which are replaced by the new facility. If the lost income is measured in U.S. dollars, as it will be if sales are lost to the U.S. parent company, we do not multiply the lost income by S_t^*. If the lost income is measured in units of foreign currency, S_t^* applies to LS_t^*. Other funds remitted via intersubsidiary transfer pricing and other ways that are illegal are included in a later term. The cash flows are adjusted for the effective tax rate, which is the higher of the domestic and foreign corporate rates. Any reduction from this level that results from moving funds from high-tax countries to low-tax countries can be added later. We assume here that the same tax rate applies to lost income on replaced sales as well as to new income. If the lost income would have faced a different tax rate, LS_t^* must be considered separately from CF_t^*. The discount rate is the all-equity cost of capital that reflects all systematic risk, including unavoidable political risk and exchange rate risk.[7]

$$\sum_{t=1}^{T} \frac{DA_t \tau}{(1 + DR_a)^t}$$ Depreciation is allowed against corporate taxes for projects

located abroad as well as for those at home. The benefits of the depreciation allowances are the amounts of allowances times the corporate tax rate against which they are applied. We have given DA_t in dollar amounts and therefore have not included S_t^*. This will be appropriate if the higher tax rate is the rate in the United States; in this case allowances will be deducted against U.S. taxes. If the higher tax rate is the rate in the foreign country, DA_t will probably be in foreign currency units, and we will need S_t^*.

$$\sum_{t=1}^{T} \frac{r_g BC_0 \tau}{(1 + DR_b)^t}$$ When debt is used to finance a project at home or abroad, the

interest payments are tax-deductible. Whether or not the project in question fully

---

[6] As before in the book, asterisks stand for expected values. Terms without asterisks are assumed to be known at the time of the investment decision.

[7] We are not yet ready to give a full account of the factors determining the discount rates. We will therefore concentrate on the numerator terms.

TABLE 15.1
VALUE OF A £1 MILLION CONCESSIONARY LOAN

Year	Loan outstanding	Principal repayment	Interest payment	Total payment	Present value of payment
1	£1,000,000	£100,000	£100,000	£200,000	£173,913
2	900,000	100,000	90,000	190,000	143,667
3	800,000	100,000	80,000	180,000	118,353
4	700,000	100,000	70,000	170,000	97,198
5	600,000	100,000	60,000	160,000	79,548
6	500,000	100,000	50,000	150,000	64,849
7	400,000	100,000	40,000	140,000	52,631
8	300,000	100,000	30,000	130,000	42,497
9	200,000	100,000	20,000	120,000	34,111
10	100,000	100,000	10,000	110,000	27,190
					£833,959

utilizes its borrowing capacity and consequent tax savings, the tax savings on the amount that *could* be borrowed should be included as a benefit.[8] The annual benefit equals the interest payments that are saved from the tax reduction, with the interest rate being the market borrowing rate at home. For example, if the project has a value of $1 million and the firm likes to maintain 50 percent of its value in debt, the project will raise borrowing capacity by $BC_0 = \$500,000$, and the interest payment on this amount, that is, $r_g BC_0$, should be included each year. This will be true even if the actual amount borrowed is larger or smaller than $500,000. For example, if $200,000 is borrowed on the $1 million project, an additional amount of $300,000 can be borrowed elsewhere in the corporation, with consequent tax offsets on the interest on $300,000. If $800,000 is borrowed, the project will reduce the capacity to borrow for other activities by $300,000, and the lower tax reductions elsewhere will offset the tax deductions on $300,000 worth of borrowing for the project. This leaves the interest on only $500,000 appropriate for inclusion as BC_0.

$$S_0 \left[CL_0 - \sum_{t=1}^{T} \frac{LR_t}{(1 + DR_c)^t} \right]$$ The current value of a concessionary loan is the

difference between the face value of the loan and the present value of the repayment on the loan discounted at the rate of interest that would have been faced in the absence of the concessionary financing. This must be converted into dollars. For example, if a 10-year loan with a 10 percent interest rate and 10 equal principal repayments is made available when the market rate would have been 15 percent, the present value of the repayment on a £1 million loan is £833,959. This is shown in Table 15.1. The value of the subsidy is hence £166,041. This amount has a current dollar value of $332,082 if, for example, $S_0 = 2.0$.

---

[8]Borrowing capacity is not a limit imposed on the firm from outside. It results from the firm's decision on how much debt it wishes to carry.

We should note that subsidized debt has potential effects on the tax shield from interest payments. We have considered corporate tax savings from debt in the previous term. This uses borrowing capacity and the market interest rate in the home country. This term will do whenever subsidized debt leaves total interest payments as without the subsidy. This might not, however, be so. For example, if total debt capacity is constrained by total face value of debt being constant rather than by interest payments being constant, then the tax shield for the corporation will be smaller than shown.[9]

$$\sum_{t=1}^{T} \frac{TD_t^*}{(1 + DR_d)^t}$$ By using the higher of the domestic and foreign tax rates for τ

we have taken a conservative approach. In practice, a multinational is likely to be able to move funds from high-tax locations to low-tax locations and defer the payment of taxes, thereby reducing the effective rate to a level below τ. Cash flows can be moved by adjusting transfer prices, head office overhead, and so on, and the payment of taxes can be deferred by reinvesting in low-tax countries. The APV technique allows us to include these tax savings as a separate term. As we have mentioned, a two-step approach is possible. We can evaluate APV without a TD_t^* and see if it is positive. If it is, we need not do anything else. If it is not, we can see how much of a tax saving will be required to make APV positive and determine whether such a saving can reasonably be expected.

$$\sum_{t=1}^{T} \frac{RF_t^*}{(1 + DR_f)^t}$$ The cash flow we use for CF_t^* is, like the tax rate, a conservative

estimate. CF_t^* includes only the flows which are remittable when transfer prices, royalties, and so on, reflect their appropriate market values. However, a multinational might manipulate transfer prices or royalty payments to repatriate more income (as well as to reduce taxes). Any extra remittable income from international (and illegal) channels can be included after the APV from the legal cash flows has been computed, if the APV is negative. This two-step procedure can be applied simultaneously to both the extra remittable income and the extra tax savings that might be obtained through internal price and income tinkering.

We have described the numerators of the APV formula and shown how they take care of many of the difficulties in evaluating foreign investment projects which we cited earlier. We have not yet said much about the denominators in the APV formula.

SELECTING THE APPROPRIATE DISCOUNT RATES

So far we have said little about the discount rates other than that cash flows should be discounted at an all-equity rate that reflects risk. As we noted in Chapter 14, only

---

[9]The appropriate approach depends on whether, for example, the firm fixes the amount of debt it will bear or the annual interest payments. A general account of the valuation of subsidized financing can be found in Richard Brealey and Stewart Myers, *Principles of Corporate Finance*, McGraw-Hill Book Company, New York, 1981.

the systematic component of total risk matters, and this risk requires a premium in the discount rate to reflect the firm's cost of capital. To some extent the additional risks of doing business abroad are mitigated by the extent to which cash flows from foreign projects are independent and therefore reduce the variance of corporate income. If there is risk reduction from having some independence of cash flows from different countries, but the pooling of flows from different countries is not directly available to shareholders, the diversification offered by the MNC should be reflected in discount rates as well as in the market value of the stock.[10] This is because the pooling of cash flows reduces the business risk.

The risks faced with foreign investments that are not explicitly faced with domestic investments are those from foreign exchange and political events.[11] These risks provide a reason, in addition to those previously cited, why the NPV technique is difficult to apply to foreign capital projects. Both political risk and exchange rate risk can, for example, make the optimal capital structure change over time. This is difficult to incorporate within the weighted average cost of capital used in the NPV technique. However, in the APV technique, where we use an all-equity cost of capital (DR_e) to discount cash flows, the capital structure matters only because of the effect on taxes, treated in a separate term.

Political risk and foreign exchange risk, like business risk, can be diversified if a firm invests in a portfolio of securities of different countries which are denominated in many different currencies. This means that the risk premium on the discount rate which reflects only the systematic risk might not be very large.[12] In the previous chapter we argued that knowing the systematic risk requires that we have a covariance for the project with the market portfolio. We also stated how difficult it is to obtain a project covariance. Moreover, the relevant risk premium for the APV approach must be for an all equity investment. This adds even more difficulty when any existing risk premium reflects the company's debt. But these are only some of the problems in selecting appropriate discount rates. We have already mentioned the problem of the shareholder perspective, which is difficult when shareholders are from different countries and when capital markets are segmented. Yet another problem is inflation and the connected question of the nature of the cash flows.

The primary question concerning how to treat inflation in the evaluation of

---

[10]The ability of the corporation to do what its shareholders cannot requires segmented markets that the corporation can circumvent. The extent to which this might be the case has been studied by Tamir Agmon and Donald Lessard ("Investor Recognition of Corporate International Diversification," *Journal of Finance*, September 1977, pp. 1049–1055).

[11]We recall from Chapter 13 that foreign exchange risk can exist for a completely domestic firm with local sales and production when competition from imports depends on exchange rates. This is why we say "explicitly."

[12]In Appendix 15.2 we show that instead of including the risk of political events in the discount rate, we can incorporate it within the cash-flow term. This procedure, which can also be followed with other types of risk, involves putting cash flows into their "certainty equivalents." A method of dealing with risk that avoids the need to find certainty equivalents or risk premiums is to deduct from cash flows the cost of political insurance or a foreign exchange risk management program. This is the recommendation of Arthur I. Stonehill and Leonard Nathanson in "Capital Budgeting and the Multinational Corporation," *California Management Review*, summer 1968, pp. 39–54. The ability of shareholders to diversify foreign exchange risk has been examined by Jeffery A. Frankel ("The Diversifiability of Exchange Risk," *Journal of International Economics*, vol. 9, August 1979, pp. 379–393).

foreign investments is whether we should discount at the "nominal" interest rate or the "real" interest rate—where the real rate is the nominal rate minus the expected rate of inflation. This distinction between nominal interest and real interest is explicit in the Fisher equation presented in Chapter 11:

$$r = \rho + \dot{P}*$$

where ρ is the real rate, r is the nominal rate, and $\dot{P}*$ is the expected rate of inflation. The answer to the question of which of the discount rates to use is that it does not matter provided we are consistent. That is, we will reach the same conclusions if we discount nominal cash flows by the nominal rate or real cash flows by the real interest rate. We can also note that if capital markets are not segmented, that is, if there is a free flow of capital, the real interest rates in different countries will be similar.

It is frequently the case that we form an idea of the expected cash flow at today's prices. This is a "real" cash flow, and it is often adjusted upward at the expected rate of inflation to yield the expected "nominal" cash flow. If we use inflated values, we should discount at the nominal rate. Alternatively, we can avoid inflating future cash flows (and then deflating them at the nominal discount rate) and instead leave cash flows in today's prices and discount at the real discount rate. The latter is in many ways a more straightforward procedure.

The advantage from using today's prices and the real rate extends to the use of today's exchange rates with foreign currency cash flows. This is so because if PPP can be expected to hold, exchange rates will mirror the inflation differential, and we will obtain the same home currency cash flows from converting today's flows at today's exchange rates as we will by converting future (inflated) amounts at future (depreciated) exchange rates.

When foreign currency cash flows are predetermined or *contractual* we do not have a choice between real and nominal discount rates and between current and future expected exchange rates. Examples of contractual cash flows are revenues from exports sold at fixed prices and depreciation allowances based on historical costs. The contractual amounts are fixed in nominal terms and should therefore be discounted at the nominal rate and converted into dollars at the expected future exchange rate. Contractual flows do not, therefore, lend themselves to simplification through the use of today's cash flows of foreign exchange at today's exchange rates. These conclusions can be derived by using the PPP condition and the Fisher equation.

Using Real Interest Rates and Today's (Real) Cash Flows and Exchange Rates*

We will concentrate on the CF_t^* term of Equation (15.2), but our conclusions are valid for any other noncontractual terms in the computation. The cash flow term is

$$\sum_{t=1}^{T} \frac{S_t^* \text{CF}_t^*(1-\tau)}{(1+\text{DR}_e)^t}$$

Since the numerator gives the expected U.S.-dollar cash flow, DR_e should be the nominal U.S. discount rate, reflecting the project's systematic risk and all-equity financing (with the effects of debt included later in APV). Using the Fisher equation and taking a U.S. perspective, we can write $(1 + DR_e)^t$ as

$$(1 + DR_e)^t = (1 + \rho_{US} + \dot{P}_{US}^*)^t \qquad (15.3)$$

where ρ_{US} is the real rate of return. We can write definition (15.3) more precisely as

$$(1 + DR_e)^t = (1 + \rho_{US} + \dot{P}_{US}^* + \rho_{US}\dot{P}_{US}^*)^t = (1 + \rho_{US})^t (1 + \dot{P}_{US}^*)^t \quad (15.4)$$

This is similar to (15.3), since $\rho_{US}\dot{P}_{US}^*$ is the product of two small amounts—for example, $0.02 \times 0.10 = 0.002$—and is therefore unimportant.

If we think that exchange rates will be changing at a steady forecasted rate, $\dot{S}^*$, we can write

$$S_t^* \equiv S_0(1 + \dot{S}^*)^t \qquad t = 1, 2, \ldots, T$$

This condition is used in Chapter 11. If, in addition, we believe that cash flows in the foreign currency will grow at the foreign rate of inflation, we can write

$$CF_t^* = CF_1^*(1 + \dot{P}_{UK}^*)^{t-1} \qquad t = 1, 2, \ldots, T$$

where $\dot{P}_{UK}^*$ is the annual rate of inflation and CF_t^* is the initial cash flow, which we assume is unknown. Using this, our definition of S_t^*, and the Fisher equation, we have

$$\sum_{t=1}^{T} \frac{S_t^* CF_t^*(1 - \tau)}{(1 + DR_e)^t} = S_0 \frac{CF_1^*}{(1 + \dot{P}_{UK}^*)} \sum_{t=1}^{T} \frac{(1 + \dot{S}^*)^t (1 + \dot{P}_{UK}^*)^t (1 - \tau)}{(1 + \rho_{US})^t (1 + \dot{P}_{US}^*)^t} \quad (15.5)$$

The expressions S_0 and $CF_1^*/(1 + \dot{P}_{UK}^*)$ have been placed in front of the summation because they do not depend on t.[13] We can reduce Equation (15.5) to a straightforward expression if we invoke the PPP condition.

We have been writing the precise form of purchasing power parity as

$$\dot{P}_{US} = \dot{P}_{UK} + \dot{S}(1 + \dot{P}_{UK})$$

If the best forecast we can make is that PPP will hold—even though we know that in retrospect we could well be wrong—we can write PPP in the expected form:

$$\dot{P}_{US}^* = \dot{P}_{UK}^* + \dot{S}^*(1 + \dot{P}_{UK}^*)$$

---

[13] We remove $CF_1^*/(1 + \dot{P}_{UK}^*)$ rather than just CF_1^* because we wish to have all expressions in the summation raised to power t. The interpretation of $CF_1^*/(1 + \dot{P}_{UK}^*)$ is that it is the value of the initial foreign cash flow at today's prices.

By adding unity to both sides, we get

$$(1 + \dot{P}_{US}^*) = (1 + \dot{P}_{UK}^*) + \dot{S}^*(1 + \dot{P}_{UK}^*) = (1 + \dot{P}_{UK}^*)(1 + \dot{S}^*)$$

or

$$\frac{(1 + \dot{S}^*)(1 + \dot{P}_{UK}^*)}{(1 + \dot{P}_{US}^*)} = 1$$

By using this in expression (15.5), we can write the APV cash-flow term in Equation (15.2) in the straightforward form:

$$\sum_{t=1}^{T} \frac{S_t^* CF_t^*(1 - \tau)}{(1 + DR_e)^t} = S_0 \frac{CF_t^*}{(1 + \dot{P}_{UK}^*)} \sum_{t=1}^{T} \frac{(1 - \tau)}{(1 + \rho_{US})^t} \qquad (15.6)$$

All we need to know to evaluate expression (15.6) is the initial exchange rate, S_0; the initial cash flow at today's prices, $CF_t^*/(1 + \dot{P}_{UK}^*)$; the tax rate, τ; and the real discount rate that reflects the systematic risk. In reaching this conclusion, we assumed only that cash flows could be expected to grow at the overall rate of inflation, that PPP can be expected to hold, and that Fisher's equation does hold. Any noncontractual term can be handled in this straightforward way; we avoid forecasting inflation and exchange rates at which to convert the foreign currency amounts. Our conclusion is based on the view that inflation and changes in exchange rates are offsetting—requiring PPP—and that local inflation and inflation premiums in interest rates are also offsetting—requiring the Fisher equation.

While it is reasonable to *expect* PPP and the Fisher equation to hold, when events are *realized*, it is very unlikely that they will have held. However, the departures from the conditions are as likely to be positive as negative. This is part of the risk of business. The risk is that realized changes in exchange rates might not reflect inflation differentials, and the interest rate might poorly reflect the level of inflation. This risk should be reflected in DR_e or ρ_{US}, which, as we have stated, should contain appropriate premiums.

When we are dealing with contractual values, we cannot use the real interest rate with uninflated cash flows. This is because the foreign currency streams are nominal amounts that must be converted at the exchange rate at the time of payment/receipt and discounted at the nominal rate. What we have if the cash flows are contractual is

$$\sum_{t=1}^{T} \frac{S_t^* CF_t^*(1 - \tau)}{(1 + DR_e)^t} = \sum_{t=1}^{T} \frac{S_0(1 + \dot{S}^*)^t CF_t^*(1 - \tau)}{(1 + DR_e)^t}$$

We cannot expand CF_t^* in order to cancel terms, since all values of CF_t^* are fixed contractually. We are left to discount at the nominal rate of interest, DR_e. We discount the nominal CF_t^* converted into the investor's currency at the forecasted exchange rate.

When the profiles of cash flows or incremental effects such as tax shields vary in real terms and do not grow at the inflation rate (perhaps they initially increase in real terms and later decline), we cannot use PPP and the Fisher equation to reduce the complexity of the problem, even for noncontractual cash flows. We must instead use the APV formula—Equation (15.2)—with forecasted nominal cash flows and the nominal discount rate.

Discount Rates for Different Items

Now that the method or methods for handling inflation with the discount rate has been explained, we are ready to describe the nature of the discount rates in the APV formula.

DR_e This should be nominal for contractual cash flows resulting from sales made at fixed future prices. Since the cash flows are converted into dollars, the rate should be the nominal rate for the United States. DR_e should also be the all-equity rate, reflecting the project's systematic risk, including the risk from exchange rates. When the cash flows are noncontractual, as they will most generally be, we can use a real rate, today's actual exchange rate, and initial-period expected cash flows at today's prices, $CF_1^*/(1 + \dot{P}_{UK}^*)$. This makes the calculations more straightforward.

DR_a Since in many countries depreciation is based on historical costs, DA_t will be contractual, and DR_a should therefore be the nominal rate. Since we have written DA_t directly in dollar terms, we should use the U.S. rate. The only risk premium should be for the chance that the depreciation allowances will go unused. If the investor feels very confident that the project will yield positive cash flows, this risk is small, and so DR_a should be the riskless nominal rate of the United States. This is true even if DA_t is measured in foreign currency units, provided we convert them into U.S. dollars.

DR_b If the project's contribution to borrowing capacity is measured in nominal U.S. dollar terms—and it is very likely that it will be—we should discount at the U.S. nominal rate. The risk is that the tax shield cannot be used, and if this is considered small, we can use the riskless rate.

DR_c The value of a concessionary loan depends on the interest rate that would otherwise be paid. If the loan repayments will be nominal foreign exchange amounts, we should use the foreign interest rate that would have been paid.

DR_d and DR_f Tax savings, additional repatriated income via transfer prices, and the deferment of tax payments via reinvestment in low-tax countries could be estimated at either today's prices or future prices. If the estimates of TD_t^* and RF_t^* are at today's prices and are therefore real, we must use a real rate, and if they are at future inflated prices, we must use a nominal rate. If the estimates are in U.S. dollars, as they probably will be, we must use a U.S. rate. Since the risk is that of not being able to find techniques for making these tax savings and additional remittances, the appropriate discount rate requires a risk premium. Donald Lessard advises the use of the same rate used for cash flows, DR_e.[14]

POLITICAL RISK

Political risk involves the chance of overseas investments being "confiscated"—which refers to a government takeover without any compensation—or "expropriated"—which refers to a government takeover with compensation.[15] Besides confiscation and expropriation, there are the political risks of wars and revolutions. While these are not the result of action by the foreign government specifically directed at the firm, they could damage or destroy an investment. In addition, there are the risks of currency inconvertibility and restrictions on the repatriation of income beyond those already reflected in the CF_i^* term. The treatment of these risks requires that we make adjustments in the APV calculation and/or allowances for late compensation payments for expropriated capital. The required adjustment can be made to the discount rate by adding a risk premium or to the expected cash flows by putting them into their certainty equivalents.[16]

We know that when we view the adjustment for risk in terms of the inclusion of a premium in the discount rate, only systematic risk needs to be considered. Since by investing in a large number of countries it is possible to spread out the risks and therefore reduce them, the systematic risk of political developments could be small enough to be irrelevant. Risk diversification requires only a degree of political independence between countries. It is made even more effective if the political misfortunes from events in some countries provide positive benefits in other countries. For example, a war or a revolution in African countries that produce copper might raise the income of South American producers of copper.

There are a number of ways in which political risks can be reduced or avoided other than by diversification, and so required risk premiums will be small. We will consider a number of these methods.

Methods of Reducing Political Risk

The Purchase of Investment Insurance Many countries will insure their companies that invest overseas against losses from political events such as currency inconvertibilities, expropriation, wars, and revolutions. In the United States this insurance is offered by the Overseas Private Investment Corporation (OPIC). The

---

[14]See Donald R. Lessard, "Evaluating Foreign Projects: An Adjusted Present Value Approach," in Donald R. Lessard (ed.), *International Financial Management: Theory and Application*, Warren, Gorham and Lamont, Boston, 1979. As we have already mentioned, this paper forms the basis of the APV technique explained here.

[15]It is possible for expropriation to involve generous compensation. If the compensation is likely to reflect market values and be received very promptly, no adjustment should be made for risk, since the "risk" is zero.

[16]We have already mentioned that the two methods are conceptually equivalent. This is shown in Appendix 15.2.

Overseas Private Investment Corporation has been in operation since the early 1970s, having replaced programs in effect since the Economic Co-operation Act of 1948. OPIC will insure U.S. private investments in the underdeveloped countries. Since there tends to be more risk in the underdeveloped countries, the insurance is particularly important. Over 60 percent of non-oil-related investments in the underdeveloped countries are covered by OPIC.

In addition to investment insurance, OPIC offers project financing. The project financing involves assistance in finding sources of funds, including OPIC's own sources, and assistance in finding worthwhile projects. Reimbursement for losses on loans is also offered. There is no coverage for losses due to changes in exchange rates, but there is also no need for such coverage because of the private means that are available, such as the forward and futures markets. OPIC charges a fee for complete coverage that is between 1 and 2 percent per annum of the amount covered on the insurance policy. Insurance must generally be approved by host governments and is available only on new projects. Since 1980, OPIC has joined with private insurance companies in the Overseas Investment Insurance Group. This has been done to move the insurance into the private sector of the economy.

In Canada, foreign investment insurance is provided by the Export Development Corporation (EDC). The Canadian EDC will insure against losses due to war, insurrection, confiscation, expropriation, and events which prevent the repatriating of capital or the transfer of earnings. This role of the EDC is similar to the role of OPIC. The EDC also offers insurance against nonpayment for Canadian exports, a function performed by the Export-Import Bank in the United States. The insurance coverage offered in the United Kingdom is very similar to the coverage offered by OPIC and the Canadian EDC, and similar programs exist in Australia, Denmark, France, Germany, Holland, Japan, Norway, Sweden, and Switzerland.

If the compensation provided by project insurers (1) is received immediately and (2) covers the full value of the project, the availability of insurance means that the only required adjustment for political risk is a deduction for insurance premiums from cash flows. We can deduct available premiums even if insurance is not actually purchased, since the firm will be self-insuring and should deduct an appropriate cost for this.[17]

Keeping Control of Crucial Elements of Corporate Operations Instead of hoping for compensation *after* losses have been incurred, many companies take steps to reduce the probability that losses will be incurred. A popular method is to ensure that foreign operations cannot run well without the investor's cooperation. This can frequently be achieved if the investor maintains control of a crucial element of operations. For example, food or soft-drink manufacturers keep secret their special ingredients. The auto companies can produce vital parts, such as engines, in

---

[17]As we mentioned earlier, this is the approach recommended by Arthur I. Stonehill and Leonard Nathanson in "Capital Budgeting and the Multinational Corporation," *California Management Review*, summer 1968, pp. 39–54.

some other country and can refuse to supply these parts if their operations are seized.[18] The multinational oil companies have used refining capacity coupled with alternative sources of oil to reduce the probability that their oil wells will be expropriated. Similarly, many companies have kept key technical operations with their own technicians, who can be recalled in the event of expropriation or confiscation. This has not always been an effective deterrent, as more mercenary technicians can often be found if the salary is sufficient—or technicians can be provided by the communist bloc. Moreover, given sufficient time, local people can pick up the important skills.

Programmed Stages of Planned Divestment   An alternative technique for reducing the probability of expropriation is for the owner of a foreign direct investment to promise to turn over ownership and control to local people in the future. This is sometimes required by the host government. For example, the Cartagena Agreement of 1969 requires the foreign owners of enterprises in the Andean countries of South America to lower their ownership, over time, to below 50 percent.

Joint Ventures   Instead of promising shared ownership in the future, an alternative technique for reducing the risk of expropriation is to share ownership with foreign private or official partners from the very beginning. The shared ownerships are known as *joint ventures*, and these have been tried by U.S., Canadian, European, and Japanese firms with partners in Africa, Central and South America, and Asia. Joint ventures as a means of reducing expropriation risks rely on the reluctance of local partners, if private, to accept the interference of their own government. When the partner is the government itself, the disincentive to expropriation is the concern over the loss of future investments. Joint ventures with multiple participants from different countries reduce the risk of expropriation, even if there is no local participation, if the government wishes to avoid being isolated simultaneously by numerous foreign powers.

Even if joint ventures with government-controlled enterprises work well while that government remains in power, they can backfire if the government is overthrown by the opposition in a polarized political climate. Extreme changes in governments have been witnessed so many times that the risks of siding with a government that falls are well known. In addition, even when the local partner is a private corporation, if expropriation means more ownership or control for the partner, there is likely to be muted local opposition at best. It is these reasons which may explain the observation that the risk of joint ventures has been greater than that of ventures with total U.S. ownership. A study of U.S. affiliates in the 1960–1976 period showed that joint ventures with host governments were expropriated 10

---

[18] According to Roy E. Pederson, who cited the case of IBM, the risk can be reduced by keeping all research and development at home. See Roy E. Pedersen, "Political Risk: Corporate Considerations," *Risk Management*, April 1979, pp. 23–32.

times more often" than fully U.S.-owned ventures and that joint ventures with private firms were expropriated 8 times more often.[19]

Local Debt   The risk of expropriation as well as the losses from expropriation can be reduced by borrowing within the countries where investment occurs. If the borrowing is denominated in the local currency, there is the additional reduction of foreign exchange risk. These obvious gains from engaging in local debt are limited by the opportunities. Those countries where expropriation is most likely tend to be the countries with the most highly undeveloped capital markets and host governments unwilling to make loans. The opportunities for reducing risk by having local people hold equity in the firm are also limited by the frequent shortage of middle-class shareholders in the high-risk countries and by the absence of a viable market in which to sell the primary issue.

Despite the techniques for reducing risk, some danger may remain.[20] Some researchers have tried to obtain measures of the relative amounts of risk in different locations.

The Measurement of Political Risk

Some idea of political risk can be obtained from an index such as the Political System Stability Index defined by Dan Haendel, Gerald West, and Robert Meadow.[21] This index uses data on socioeconomic characteristics, social conflicts, and government processes and considers ethnic fractionalization, the rate of economic growth, the frequency of public demonstrations, riots, coups d'état, and the power of the government to control civil disorder. Objective proxy measures are defined, and the index which is formed from these ranks countries by their stability. An index of country risk based on a financial market evaluation in the form of interest rates in the Eurobond market (with the higher rates presumably reflecting higher risks) has been formed by the staff at *Euromoney*, a financial magazine.[22] This is called the Business Environment Risk Index and is not unlike the index published frequently by Business International.

Harald Knudsen has computed political risk by comparing national aspirations with achievements.[23] When aspirations run ahead of actual achievements, there is

[19]See David Bradley, "Managing Against Expropriation," *Harvard Business Review*, July–August 1977, pp. 75–83. For a survey of work on political risks, see Stephen Kobrin, "Political Risks: A Review and Reconsideration," *Journal of International Business Studies*, spring/summer 1979, pp. 67–80.

[20]For different types of risk, see Stephen Kobrin, "When Does Political Instability Result in Increased Investment Risk?" *The Columbia Journal of World Business*, fall 1973, vol. 13, pp. 123–134. See also Part II of David Eitman and Arthur I. Stonehill, *Multinational Business Finance*, 2d ed., Addison-Wesley Publishing Company, Reading, Mass., 1979.

[21]The construction of the index is described in Dan Haendel, Gerald West, and Robert Meadow, *Overseas Investment and Political Risk*, Foreign Policy Research Institute, Philadelphia, 1974, published in association with Lexington Books, D. C. Heath.

[22]See, for example, *Euromoney*, October 1979, pp. 130–138.

[23]Harald Knudsen describes his methodology in his article "Explaining the National Propensity to Expropriate: An Ecological Approach," *Journal of International Business Studies*, spring 1974, pp. 51–71.

national frustration. When a high degree of foreign ownership is present, this may trigger expropriation or destruction of foreign capital.

The various studies all suffer from being unable to distinguish the different risks of different industries; they measure only the risk of the country. Yet a number of studies show that some industries, especially those involving natural resources or utilities, involve a greater political risk.[24]

A study of political risk which considers a specific project, an oil company venture in a developing country, has been done by Derek Bunn and M. M. Mustafaoglu.[25] The authors gave a group of experts a set of political events, such as war and civil disorder, and a set of political risk factors, such as the visibility of foreigners in the country and the availability of technology, and obtained the probability of each political event.

While the measurement of political risk can be helped by some scientific methods, an evaluation will frequently have to rely on a company's people on the spot and information supplied by diplomats and bankers. A tour of the site for the investment could help in gathering more information, but ultimately the risk evaluation will be subjective. Sometimes it might be believed that the risk is not constant. For example, risk could rise with time if a nationalistic party was gaining in popularity. This can make the selection of discount rates that reflect risk an extremely difficult task.

Fortunately for the project evaluators, the variety of techniques available for reducing political risks and the ability of shareholders to diversify the remaining risks by holding assets from numerous countries allow the use of relatively small risk premiums. The same conclusion applies to foreign exchange risk, which can be reduced by borrowing from foreign sources and diversified by shareholders in nonsegmented capital markets.

With the nature of the terms in the APV formula carefully defined and the factors influencing the risk premiums also explained, we are ready to consider a realistic example of capital budgeting. We will consider whether Aviva Corporation should build a jeans-manufacturing factory in Italy.

AN EXAMPLE

Suppose that as a result of the imminent entry of new firms into the Italian jeans market, Aviva is considering opening an Italian factory. Aviva hopes that by being on the spot it can be more responsive to local preferences for style and thereby avoid steadily losing sales to the new entrants. The construction costs of the plant have been estimated at Lit 2 billion, and it is believed that it will add $1 million to Aviva's

[24]It is apparent from the results of J. Frederick Truitt that there are different risks in different industries. See J. Frederick Truitt, "Expropriation of Foreign Investment: Summary of the Post World War II Experience of American and British Investors in Less Developed Countries," *Journal of International Business Studies*, vol. 1, fall 1970, pp. 21–34. See also Robert Hawkins, Norman Mintz, and Michael Provissiero, "Government Takeovers of U.S. Foreign Affiliates," *Journal of International Business Studies*, vol. 7, spring 1976, pp. 3–16.

[25]Derek W. Bunn and M. M. Mustafaoglu, "Forecasting Political Risk," *Management Science*, vol. 24, November 1978, pp. 1557–1567.

borrowing capacity.[26] Because of taxes on remitted earnings from Aviva's previously established sales subsidiary in Italy, the proposed factory can be partially financed with Lit600 million, which, if it had been returned to the United States, would have faced taxes of Lit400 million in Italy. Of this amount, credit for only Lit 280 million would have been received in the United States.[27] The funds would have been returned to the United States because nothing better could have been done with them.

The current exchange rate between the lira and the U.S. dollar is Lit1000/$, and so $S_0 = 0.00100$, and the spot rate is expected to move at a rate given by the relative inflation according to PPP. Italian inflation is expected to proceed at 25 percent, while U.S. inflation is expected to be 10 percent.

Jeans sales, which will begin when the plant is completed, after a year, are expected to average 50,000 pairs per year. At the beginning of the year of construction, the jeans have a unit price of Lit20,000 per pair, and this is expected to rise at the general rate of inflation. The average production cost at material prices at the time of construction is Lit15,000 per pair, and this cost is likely to keep in line with general Italian inflation.

The Italian market had previously been supplied by Aviva's main plant in California, and recent sales to the Italian market were 10,000 pairs per year. The most recent profit on U.S.-manufactured jeans was $5 per pair, and this can be expected to keep pace with general U.S. inflation. However, it was expected that in the absence of an Italian factory, Aviva would have lost 8.9 percent of its Italian sales per annum to the new entrants. This is why Aviva is considering opening an Italian plant of its own. It has learned that it must be in touch with local styles when local firms enter the market.

The factory is expected to require little in the way of renovation for 10 years. The market value of the plant in 10 years is extremely difficult to estimate, and Aviva is confident only in the belief that it will have some substantial value.

Aviva has by great art and ingenuity managed to arrive at an all-equity cost of capital that reflects the project's systematic risk (including the risk of political events that are not covered by insurance, the deviation of exchange rates from predicted levels, and so on) of 20 percent. This allows for the fact that much of the risk can be diversified by the shareholders and/or avoided by insurance, forward cover, and so on.

In return for locating the factory in an area of heavy unemployment, Aviva will receive from the Italian government Lit600 million of the Lit1400 million it needs in addition to the previously blocked funds at the subsidized rate of 10 percent. The principal is to be repaid in equal installments over 10 years. If Aviva had been required to borrow competitively in Italy, it could have expected a 35 percent borrowing cost, as opposed to its 15 percent borrowing cost in the United

---

[26] We assume that overdraft facilities are available in Italy so that cash balances do not have to be provided along with the construction costs. Banking service costs are included in operating costs.

[27] The Italian government restricts remittances on "nonproductive" enterprises—hence the high cost of remitting earnings. We will assume that the factory is a productive enterprise and therefore subject only to appropriate corporate taxes.

States. This is a little above the U.S. riskless rate of 12 percent. The remaining Lit 800 million that is needed for construction will be provided as equity by Aviva U.S.A. Income on the project is subject to a 25 percent tax in Italy and a 46 percent tax in the United States, and Italian taxes are fully deductible against U.S. taxes.

The U.S. Internal Revenue Service will allow Aviva to write off 10 percent of the dollar equivalent of the historical construction cost each year. By using carefully arranged transfer prices and royalties, Aviva thinks it can reduce taxes to a level below the legal level by about $5000 in the initial year of operation, and it expects this to hold steady in real terms, but it does not expect to be able to remit more income than the amount declared.

We can show below that in terms of the notation used in defining APV in Equation (15.2), Aviva faces the following:

K_0 = Lit 2,000,000,000
BC_0 = $1,000,000
AF_0 = Lit 600,000,000 − (Lit 600,000,000 − Lit 400,000,000) = Lit 400,000,000
S_0 = 0.00100
S_t^* = 0.00100$(1 − 0.12)^t$
CF_t^* = Lit 500,000(20,000 − 15,000)$(1 + 0.25)^t$ + scrap value when t = 10
LS_t^* = $10,000(5)$(1 + 0.10)^t (1 − 0.089)^t$ = $50,000
CL_0 = Lit 600,000,000
LR_t = see Table 15.2
DA_t = $200,000
TD_t = $5000(1 + 0.10)^t$
RF_t = 0
  τ = 0.46
DR_e = DR_d = DR_f = 0.20
DR_a = DR_b = 0.12
DR_c = 0.35
  r_g = 0.15

We will solve the problem by using all nominal values for cash flows and all nominal discount rates.

Many of the values attached to the terms of the APV formula are self-evident. For example, the construction cost is Lit 2,000,000,000, and the borrowing capacity is $1,000,000. The value of activated funds, AF_0, is their face value minus their value in their next best use. If the next best use is to bring them home and face taxes, the next best value is Lit 600,000,000 − Lit 400,000,000. We exclude the tax credit in the United States *on repatriated restricted funds* because it is smaller than the taxes paid in Italy; thus the effective tax rate is the Italian rate. If the credit cannot be applied against other income, it has no value. This means that if the blocked funds had been brought back, Lit 200,000,000 would have been received after taxes. We substract this from the Lit 600,000,000 used in the project to get Lit 400,000,000 for AF_0.

The expected exchange rates are obtained from the definition $S_t^* = S_0(1 + \dot{S}^*)^t$. We obtain $\dot{S}^*$ from the PPP condition; that is,

$$\dot{S}^* = \frac{\dot{P}_{US}^* - \dot{P}_{IT}^*}{(1 - \dot{P}_{IT}^*)} = \frac{0.10 - 0.25}{1.25} = -0.12$$

The cash flow, CF_t^*, is obtained by multiplying the expected sales of 50,000 pairs per annum by the expected profit per pair. The profit per pair during the construction year, when prices and costs are known, would be Lit 20,000 − Lit 15,000 if production could begin immediately, but by the initial year of operation the profit per pair is expected to rise to (Lit 20,000 − Lit 15,000)(1 + 0.25). The profit is expected to continue to rise at 25 percent per annum, with an expected cash flow by year t of

$$(\text{Lit } 20,000 - \text{Lit } 15,000)(1 + 0.25)^t$$

from each of the 50,000 pairs. The value of this is shown in Table 15.2. The present value of the cash flow at Aviva's chosen cost of capital of $DR_e = 0.20$ is also shown.

The scrap value of the project is uncertain. As a result, we can take a two-step approach to see whether the project is profitable without estimating a scrap value, since if it is, we can save time in our evaluation.

Replaced sales, LS_t^*, have most recently been producing a profit for Aviva U.S.A. of $5 × 10,000 = $50,000 per year. With the profit per unit expected to grow at the U.S. inflation rate of 10 percent and the number of units expected to decline by 8.9 percent, expected profits from replaced sales remain at their current level of $50,000 per year.

The amount of the concessionary loan is $CL_0 = \text{Lit } 600,000,000$. The repayments for the principal are at Lit 60,000,000 each year, with interest computed on the unpaid balance at 10 percent per annum. This is discounted at the market rate in Italy of $DR_c = 0.35$. The values of the discounted loan repayments are given in Table 15.2. The table also gives the values of the discounted net-of-tax depreciation allowances of $200,000 per year. This is 10 percent of the historical cost in dollars, $S_0 K_0$. We use the dollar cost because the depreciation is effectively against U.S. corporate taxes. These are at the rate $\tau = 0.46$.

The debt or borrowing capacity of the project is such that Aviva can borrow $1,000,000 (which is half the dollar cost of construction) to obtain tax shields somewhere within its operations. The interest rate Aviva would pay if it took the tax shields by borrowing more at home is $r_g = 0.15$. This will save taxes on 0.15 × $1,000,000 at the tax rate $\tau = 0.46$. We have discounted the saving from the tax shield at the riskless dollar rate, $DR_b = 0.12$. We have also discounted depreciation allowances at this riskless dollar rate.

The extra tax benefits of $5000 are assumed to keep pace with U.S. inflation. We have discounted $TD_t^* = $5000 at Aviva's cost of equity of 20 percent.

We can form an opinion concerning the feasibility of the jeans factory if we use the values of the terms as we have stated them, including the totals from Table 15.2, in the APV formula, Equation (15.2):

$$\begin{aligned} APV = & -(0.001 \times 2,000,000,000) + (0.001 \times 400,000,000) + 749,545 \\ & + 519,767 + 389,866 + 0.001 \times (600,000,000 - 287,779,550) \\ & + 29,054 + 0 = \$400,452 \end{aligned}$$

We discover that the APV is positive. In general, this means that the project is

TABLE 15.2
ADJUSTED PRESENT VALUE TERMS FOR ITALIAN JEANS FACTORY

Year	S_i^* ($/Lit)	CF_i^* (Lit)	$S_i^* CF_i^*$ ($)	$S_i^* CF_i^* - LS_i^*$ ($)	$(1 - \tau)\dfrac{S_i^* CF_i^* - LS_i^*}{(1 + DR_e)^i}$ ($)
1	0.0008800	312,500,000	275,000	225,000	101,250
2	0.0007744	390,625,000	302,000	252,000	94,500
3	0.0006815	488,281,250	332,764	282,764	88,364
4	0.0005997	610,351,560	366,028	316,028	82,299
5	0.0005277	762,939,450	402,603	352,603	76,520
6	0.0004644	953,674,320	442,886	392,886	71,051
7	0.0004087	1,192,092,900	487,208	437,208	65,889
8	0.0003596	1,490,116,120	535,846	485,846	61,016
9	0.0003165	1,862,645,150	589,527	539,527	56,465
10	0.0002795	2,328,306,440	648,433	598,433	52,191
					749,545

TABLE 15.2
CONTINUED

Year	$\dfrac{DA_{t,\tau}}{(1 + DR_a)^t}$ ($)	$r_g BC_{0\,\tau}$ ($)	$\dfrac{r_g BC_{0\,\tau}}{(1 + DR_b)^t}$ ($)	TD_t^* ($)	$\dfrac{TD_t^*}{(1 + DR_d)^t}$ ($)	Outstanding loan (Lit)	Loan interest (Lit)	LR_t (Lit)	$\dfrac{LR_t}{(1 + DR_c)^t}$ (Lit)
1	82,143	69,000	61,607	5,000	4,167	600,000,000	60,000,000	120,000,000	88,888,889
2	73,342	69,000	55,007	5,500	3,819	540,000,000	54,000,000	114,000,000	62,551,440
3	65,484	69,000	49,113	6,050	3,501	480,000,000	48,000,000	108,000,000	43,895,750
4	58,466	69,000	43,851	6,655	3,209	420,000,000	42,000,000	102,000,000	30,708,959
5	52,203	69,000	39,153	7,321	2,942	360,000,000	36,000,000	96,000,000	21,409,296
6	46,610	69,000	34,957	8,053	2,697	300,000,000	30,000,000	90,000,000	14,867,567
7	41,616	69,000	31,212	8,858	2,472	240,000,000	24,000,000	84,000,000	10,270,812
8	37,157	69,000	27,868	9,744	2,266	180,000,000	18,000,000	78,000,000	7,070,082
9	33,176	69,000	24,882	10,718	2,077	120,000,000	12,000,000	72,000,000	4,834,244
10	29,570	69,000	22,216	11,790	1,904	60,000,000	6,000,000	66,000,000	3,282,511
	519,767		389,866		29,054				287,779,550

worthwhile, but since the APV is relatively small vis-à-vis the $2 million construction cost, we would be wise to exercise caution. However, the APV does not yet include any estimate for the market value of the factory and land at the end of 10 years. If Aviva feels that while it cannot estimate this value, it should exceed half the original cost in real terms, it can take a more confident position. Half the original project cost is $1 million, and since this is a real value, it should be discounted at the real interest rate relevant for dollars. Using Aviva's risky rate, this is DR_e minus the U.S. expected inflation rate of 10 percent; that is, $DR_e = 0.20 - 0.10 = 0.10$. At this rate the present value of $1 million in 10 years is $385,543, which makes the APV clearly positive. The $385,543 would be subject to a capital gains tax if it were to be realized because the entire project has been depreciated, but even after taxes the project would seem to be worthwhile.

ACTUAL PRACTICE OF CAPITAL BUDGETING

The adjusted present value approach using the correct discount rate to reflect the contractual or noncontractual nature of cash flows and the systematic risk of the investment project requires management to take a very scientific view. We can expect that constraints on the knowledge of managers and the time available to make decisions result in approaches that are more pragmatic than the approach we presented. According to a survey of multinational corporations this does appear to be the case. The survey was made of 10 U.S. multinationals by Business International to see how they analyze acquisitions.[28] The survey showed that only 7 of the 10 corporations used any sort of discounting method at all.

Only one of the respondents in the Business International survey said that it looked at synergy effects, that is, the effects the acquisition would have on other subsidiaries. Five of the ten firms used the same hurdle discount rate for all acquisitions, whatever the country. Projected exchange rates were used by five of the respondents, while two used the projected rate if they considered a currency to be unstable and the current rate if they considered it to be stable. The remainder used current rates to convert all currency flows, but it was not clear from the survey whether these flows were measured in current price terms. At least one company assumed that exchange rate movements would be reflected in relative interest rates and therefore used the U.S. interest rate on cash flows converted into dollars at the current exchange rate.

THE GROWTH OF MULTINATIONAL CORPORATIONS

It is foreign direct investments which have taken place in the past that have resulted in the growth of the multinational corporation. In our example the investment was a result of the movement of indigenous firms into Aviva's market. This reason for

---

[28]See "BIMR Survey Reveals How U.S. Multinationals Analyze Foreign Acquisitions," *Money Report*, Business International, Nov. 28, 1980. See also "Stress on Currency Fluctuations as MNCs Analyze Foreign Acquisitions," *Money Report*, Business International, Nov. 5, 1980.

overseas investment can be considered as strategic. It is especially important in dynamic and changing markets, such as publishing and fashion clothing, where subsidiaries must keep in line with local needs and where shipping time is vital. The nature of dynamic markets might help explain the relatively large number of small or medium-sized firms found in a study by the Conference Board of U.S. multinational firms; 26 of the 107 companies in the survey had total sales below $100 million per annum.[29] Besides strategic reasons for direct investment, numerous other reasons have been put forward, and while these are not strictly financial, they deserve some mention in this book.

Reasons for the Growth of MNCs

Availability of Raw Materials If there are mills producing denim cloth in other countries and the quality is good and the price is attractive, why should a firm like Aviva Corporation buy the material abroad, ship it to the United States, manufacture the jeans, and then ship the finished garments? Clearly, if the ability exists to manufacture the jeans in the foreign market, the firm can eliminate two-way shipping costs—for denim in one direction and jeans in the other—by directly investing in a manufacturing plant abroad.

Many industrial firms, most particularly mining companies, have little choice but to locate at the site of their raw materials. If copper or iron ore is being smelted, it often does not make sense to ship the ore when a smelter can be built near the mine site. The product of the smelter—the copper or iron bars, which weigh much less than the original ore—can be shipped out to the market. But we still have to ask why it would be a foreign firm rather than an indigenous firm that would carry out the enterprise. With an indigenous firm there would be no foreign direct investment. One reason why foreign firms have an edge has to do with know-how and technical factors concerning integration of operations.

Integrating Operations and Enforcing Quality and Secrecy Standards When there are advantages to vertical integration in terms of assured delivery between various stages of production and the different stages can be performed better in different locations (as with the smelting of ores), there is good reason to invest abroad. This reason for direct investment has been advanced by Charles Kindleberger, who along with Richard Caves has done some of the earlier work on direct investment.[30]

It is often possible for firms to sell their knowledge in terms of patent rights and to advance a license to a foreign producer. This relieves a firm of the need to directly

---

[29]See *International Letter*, no. 442, Federal Reserve Bank of Chicago, Feb. 27, 1981.

[30]We refer to Charles P. Kindleberger, *American Business Abroad*, Yale University Press, New Haven, Conn., 1969. See also Richard E. Caves, "International Corporations: The Industrial Economics of Foreign Investment," *Econometrica*, 1971. A number of papers on direct investment are contained in John H. Dunning (ed.), *International Investment*, Penguin Books, Harmonsworth, U.K., 1972. For factors affecting the initial decision, the reader could consult J. David Richardson, "On Going Abroad: The Firm's Initial Foreign Investment Decision," *Quarterly Review of Economics and Business*, winter 1971, pp. 7–22.

invest abroad. However, sometimes the firm that has a production process or product patent can make a larger profit by doing the foreign production itself. This is because there is some knowledge which cannot be sold and which is the result of years of experience. Aviva, for example, might be able to sell patterns and designs, and it can license the use of its name, but it cannot sell a foreign firm its experience in producing and marketing the product. This points to another reason why a firm might wish to do its own foreign production.

Products develop good and bad names, and these are carried across international boundaries. Even people in the Soviet bloc, for example, know the names of certain brands of jeans. It would not serve the good name of Aviva Corporation to have a foreign licensee do a shoddy job in producing jeans with the Aviva label. We find that there can be solid reasons for direct investment rather than selling a license in terms of transferring expertise and ensuring the maintenance of a good name.

Along similar lines, another reason for direct investment rather than selling a patent license involves the protection of the patent rights. This point has been raised by Erich Spitaler, who argues that a firm can be motivated to choose direct investment by a feeling that while a licensee may take every precaution to protect any patent rights, it might be less conscientious than the original owner of the patent.[31]

The Product Life Cycle Hypothesis   It has been argued, most notably by Raymond Vernon, that opportunities for further gains at home eventually dry up.[32] To maintain the growth of profits, the corporation must venture abroad to where markets are less well penetrated and where there is perhaps less competition. This makes direct investment the natural consequence of being in business for a long enough time and doing well at home. There is an inevitability in this view that has concerned those who believe that American firms are further along in their life cycle development than the firms of other nations and are therefore dominant in foreign expansion.[33] However, even when U.S. firms do expand into foreign markets, their activities are often closely scrutinized by the host governments. Moreover, the spread of U.S. multinationals has been matched by the inroads of foreign firms into the United States, especially since the 1970s. Particularly noticeable have been auto and auto-parts producers such as Volkswagen of America and Michelin Tires. Foreign firms have an even longer history as leaders in the U.S. food and drug industry (Nestlé, Hoffman-Loroche); in oil and gas (Shell, British Petroleum—as BP, Sohio, and so on); in insurance, banking, and real estate development; and in other areas.

---

[31]See Erich Spitaler, "A Survey of Recent Quantitative Studies of Long-Term Capital Movements," *IMF Staff Papers*, March 1971, pp. 189–217.

[32]Raymond Vernon, "International Investment and International Trade in the Product Life-Cycle," *Quarterly Journal of Economics*, May 1966, pp. 190–207.

[33]An inevitable U.S. domination of key businesses in Europe and the world was a popular view in parts of Europe in the 1960s and 1970s. Particularly influential was J. J. Servain-Schreiber's *The American Challenge*, Hamish Hamilton, London, 1968.

Capital Availability and Organizational Factors   Robert Aliber has suggested that access to capital markets can be a reason why firms themselves move abroad.[34] The smaller one-country licensee might not have the same access to cheaper funds as the larger firm, and so larger firms are able to operate within foreign markets with a lower discount rate.

Richard Cyert and James March emphasize reasons given by organization theory, a theme that is extended to direct foreign investment by E. Eugene Carter.[35] The organization theory view of direct investment emphasizes broad management objectives in terms of the way management attempts to shift risk by operating in many markets, achieve growth in sales, and so on, as opposed to concentrating on the traditional economic goal of profit maximization.

Taxes, Regulation, and Foreign Subsidies   Another reason for producing abroad instead of producing at home and shipping the product concerns the import tariffs that might have to be paid. If import duties are in place, a firm might produce inside the foreign market in order to avoid them. We must remember, however, that although this will be true, tariffs protect the firm engaged in production in the foreign market, whether it be a foreign firm or an indigenous firm. Tariffs cannot, therefore, explain why foreign firms move abroad, and yet the movement of firms is the essence of direct investment. Nor, along similar lines, can tax write-offs, subsidized or even free land offerings, and so on, explain direct investment, since foreign firms usually are not helped more than domestic ones. We may rely on our other listed reasons for direct investment and the overriding desire to make a larger profit, even if that means moving abroad rather than into alternative domestic endeavors.

There have been cases where the threat of tariffs or quantitative restrictions on imports in the form of quotas have prompted direct investment overseas. For example, a number of foreign automobile and truck producers considered opening or opened plants in the United States to avoid restrictions on selling foreign-made cars. The restrictions were designed to protect jobs in the U.S. industry. Nissan Motors built a plant in Tennessee and Honda built a plant in Ohio. Volkswagen began assembling automobiles and light trucks in the United States and Canada. Other companies making direct investments included Renault, Daimler-Benz, Volvo, and Fiat.

It can be argued that some firms have moved abroad so as to be able to produce in a less heavily regulated environment. There is little about this that can be stated with certainty, but a case might be made that some firms have moved to escape standards set by, for example, the U.S. Environmental Protection Agency, the Occupational

---

[34]Robert Aliber, "A Theory of Direct Foreign Investment," in Charles P. Kindleberger (ed.), *The International Corporation: A Symposium*, M.I.T. Press, Cambridge, Mass., 1970.

[35]Richard M. Cyert and James G. March give an account of organization theory in *The Behavioral Theory of the Firm*, Prentice-Hall, Inc., Englewood Cliffs, N.J., 1963. E. Eugene Carter extends the theory to direct investment in "The Behavioral Theory of the Firm and Top Level Corporation Decisions," *Administrative Science Quarterly*, December 1971, pp. 413–428.

Safety and Health Administration, and other agencies. Some of the foreign countries which have lower environmental and safety standards offer a haven to firms using dirty or dangerous processes. The items that are produced might even be offered for sale back inside the United States, especially chemicals and drugs. Financial institutions, primarily banks, also have an incentive to locate some of their operations in an environment with less regulation and control. Certain Caribbean islands have attracted branches of American, Canadian, and British banks, as well as branches of other European banks, and these are well beyond the size that the local markets could support. We have already mentioned this in explaining the growth of the Eurodollar market. The temptation to escape home regulation and control has made banks leaders among the multinational enterprises.

Problems Arising from Multinational Enterprises

It is often difficult to classify a truly multinational corporation because in reality there is a continuum of extent or sphere of international operation and influence. At what point a corporation moves into the multinational category is unclear. Nevertheless, there are corporations that are clearly multinational and which have brought about specific problems and considerations that should be mentioned here. Many of these considerations are more political than financial in nature and are therefore mentioned only briefly. They stem from the size of the multinational corporations and the difficulty in regulating them.

Multinational corporations can indeed be large. The profits of some of the larger corporations can exceed the operating budgets of the governments in some smaller countries. It is the power that such scale can give that has led to the greatest concern. Can the MNCs push around their host government to the advantage of the shareholders and the disadvantage of the citizens of the country of operation? This has led several countries and even the United Nations to investigate the influence of MNCs. The host governments are, however, in a difficult position. On the one hand, they want to protect their citizens, but on the other, they want the jobs, taxes, foreign exchange, technology, and other benefits that the MNCs can bring. Moreover, their own citizens might be shareholders.

It can be difficult to manage economies in which multinationals have extensive investments, such as the economies of Canada and Australia. Since MNCs often have ready access to external sources of finance, they can blunt local monetary policy. When the host government wishes to constrain economic activity, multinationals might nevertheless expand through foreign borrowing. Similarly, efforts at economic expansion might be frustrated if multinationals move funds abroad and search for yield advantages elsewhere. You do not have to be a multinational to frustrate plans for economic expansion—integrated financial markets will always produce this effect—but MNCs are likely to participate in any opportunities to gain profits. The multinationals can also "shift" profits to reduce their total tax burden; they can show larger profits in countries with lower tax rates. This can make the MNC a slippery animal for the tax collector, even though it uses many local public goods provided from general tax revenues.

It has been argued that multinationals can make foreign exchange markets volatile. For example, it has been claimed that when the U.S. dollar is moving rapidly against the European currencies, the Canadian dollar swings even further. In particular, a declining value of the U.S. dollar against, for example, the Deutsche mark or sterling has been associated with an even larger decline of the Canadian dollar against the same European currency. Although the existence of this phenomenon has not been formally verified, MNCs have been given "credit" for such an effect. It has been claimed that when U.S. parent companies are expecting an increase in the value of Deutsche marks, sterling, and so on, they buy these foreign currencies and instruct their Canadian subsidiaries to do the same. With a "thinner" market in the Dominion currency, the effect of this activity could be greater movement in the value of the Canadian dollar than in the value of the U.S. dollar.

Concern has been expressed, especially within the United States, that U.S.-based multinationals can defy foreign policy objectives of the U.S. government through their foreign branches and subsidiaries. A firm might break a blockade and avoid sanctions by operating through overseas subsidiaries. This could cause even greater concern within some host countries. Why should companies operating within their boundaries have to follow orders of the U.S. government or any other foreign government? Multinational corporations present a potential for conflict between national governments. There is even potential for conflict within international/ multinational trade unions. For example, in 1980 and 1981 Chrysler Corporation was given loan guarantees to help it continue in operation. The U.S. government insisted on wage and salary rollbacks as a condition. Chrysler workers in Canada did not appreciate the instruction from the U.S. Congress to accept a reduced wage.

Multinationals tend to concentrate and specialize their "good" and "bad" activities within certain locations. This can mean doing the research and development (R&D) within the home country. Highly trained university and technical school graduates who find their employment and promotion opportunities diminished in their own country by the small scale of local operations would prefer locally owned and managed enterprises. This has been a controversial problem in countries that consider themselves "branch plant" economies. Canadian and Australian scientists and engineers have been particularly outspoken.

Accusations have been made, most notably with regard to the oil industry, that multinationals can use monopoly power to withhold output to effect price increases for their products. Because the multinationals have such extensive operations, much of the data on which the governments must rely is often data collected and reported by the MNCs themselves. There is no guarantee that the data are accurate, and there is no easy way to enforcing controls and punishing culprits. This has become one of the leading political issues of the 1980s.

There is little doubt that MNCs spread a common culture. Chain hamburger outlets become the same on every Main Street in Iowa and on the Champs Elysées in Paris. Soft-drink bottles with a familiar shape can wash up on any beach, and there is no obvious way of telling from which country they came. Hotel room・'re alike everywhere. The same corporate names and product names appear in every major western language. Even architecture shows a common influence—the "international style." Many have decried this development, complaining that it is robbing the world of a good deal of its variety and local interest. Yet the local people demand the products of the MNCs. This is all part of the unending love-hate relationship between concerned people everywhere and the multinational corporation.

SUMMARY

1 The net present value technique is difficult to use in the case of foreign investment projects. The adjusted present value technique is frequently recommended instead.

2 Cash flows from foreign investments can be seen in two different ways: from the investor's perspective and from the perspective of the project managers in the foreign countries. It is the investor's perspective which is relevant. Factors which can make a difference between cash flows from the different perspectives include blocked funds (which reduce capital costs to investors), reduced sales from other corporate divisions, restrictions on remitting earnings, extra taxes on repatriated income, and concessionary loans. These factors can be included in the adjusted present value, APV.

3 The APV technique allows a two-step evaluation. The first step involves a conservative estimate that includes only easily estimated benefits of the project. The second step, including other benefits, is needed only if the first step gives a negative estimate.

4 The calculation of APV includes cash flows net of taxes and reduced earnings elsewhere, depreciation allowances, tax shields, the value of concessionary loans, and other potential benefits. Each item must be discounted at an appropriate discount rate.

5 Discount rates should reflect only the systematic risk of the item being discounted. Doing business abroad can help reduce overall corporate risk when incomes are more independent between countries than between operations within a particular country, and this can mean lower discount rates for foreign projects.

6 Discount rates can, however, be higher on foreign investment projects because of political risk and exchange rate risk. These risks can be diversified by shareholders if they invest in a number of countries, and this reduces risk premiums.

7 We must be consistent when we take care of inflation in foreign project evaluation. We can use either real values of cash flows, and so on, and real interest rates or nominal cash flows and nominal interest rates.

8 When we are dealing with noncontractual flows, we can choose the method of handling inflation that we prefer. However, with contractual flows which are nominal amounts, we must use nominal discount rates. The choice of approach with noncontractual flows exists because of the PPP condition and the Fisher equation. These help ensure that inflation in cash flows will be offset by movements in exchange rates, and so on. However, the fact that PPP, and so on, are imprecise contributes risks. These should be incorporated in selected discount rates.

9 Only systematic or unavoidable political risk needs to be reflected in discount rates. Risk can be reduced by buying investment insurance, by keeping control of key elements of operations, by planning to eventually turn over the investment to local people, by establishing joint ventures, and by having local debt or local shareholders.

10 When some political risk is unavoidable, we need to estimate how large it is. Political stability indexes have been devised to at least rank risks.

11 Multinational corporations have grown by discovering opportunities and making direct investments overseas. The reasons why the MNCs have moved abroad include the

entrance of indigenous or foreign firms into markets, the availability of heavy raw materials, the opportunity to integrate operations, the need to protect patents, the continued need to expand when domestic market opportunities are fully exhausted, the greater availability of capital to MNCs, and the desire to avoid tariffs and regulations.

12 MNCs have brought numerous problems. They can make it difficult to manage an economy; they may be able to defy the political directions of their own or foreign governments; and they can concentrate skilled jobs within certain locations, manipulate prices, and spread a common culture.

QUESTIONS

1 Will withholding taxes that are at rates below domestic corporate tax rates affect direct investment when full withholding tax credit is available? How will withholding tax rates affect the distribution of total tax revenues between countries?

2 A U.S. automobile manufacturer, National Motors, is considering building a new plant in Britain to produce its sports car, The Sting. The estimated construction cost of the plant is £50,000,000, and construction should be completed in a year. The plant will raise borrowing capacity by about $40,000,000. National Motors can reinvest £20,000,000 already held in Britain. If these funds were repatriated to the United States, they would face an effective tax rate of 46 percent. Inflation in Britain is expected to be at a 15 percent rate, while inflation in the United States is expected to be 10 percent. The current exchange rate is $S(\$/£) = 2.00$, and it is believed that PPP is likely to hold.

National Motors expects to sell The Sting with only minor modifications for 5 years, and after this period the plant will require remodeling. The value of the plant for future use is expected to be £40,000,000 in nominal terms after 5 years. The Sting will have an initial sticker price of about £8000, and it is expected that 10,000 will be sold each year. Production costs are estimated at £6000. These values are expected to move in line with the general price level in Britain.

National Motors also builds a two-seater car in Germany called the Racer and expects 4000 Racers to be replaced by The Sting. Since Racers are in short supply, 2000 of the 4000 Racers can be sold in Japan at the same profit as in Germany. The before-tax profit on the Racer during the initial year of producing The Sting is expected to be DM5000 per car, with $S(DM/£) = 4.00$. This is expected to keep in line with German inflation and PPP is expected to prevail between Britain and Germany.

Because National Motors will be building The Sting in Merseyside, an area of heavy unemployment, the British government has offered the company a loan of £20,000,000 at a 10 percent interest rate. The principal is to be repaid in five equal installments, with the first installment due at the beginning of the initial year of production. The competitive market rate in Britain is 20 percent, while in the United States, National Motors faces a borrowing rate of 12 percent and a riskless rate of 10 percent. The balance of the capital will be provided as equity. The tax rate in Britain is 50 percent, which is higher than the 46 percent rate in the United States. British tax law allows car plants to be depreciated over 5 years.

The British and U.S. tax authorities are careful that appropriate transfer prices are used so that no taxes can be saved by using intercompany pricing techniques. National Motors believes a 20 percent discount rate is appropriate for the project.

Should The Sting be built?

3 Which items in the previous question are contractual, and which are noncontractual? Could you discount the cash flows with a real rate of interest?

4 If political risk insurance is purchased but the settlement of claims is likely to take 2 years,

how would you make an allowance for political risk? If you deduct insurance premiums from cash flows, will you still need a risk factor in the discount rate?

5 Assume that you are thinking about building an automobile-manufacturing plant in Egypt.

  a What steps would you take to reduce foreign exchange risk?

  b What steps would you take to reduce or avoid political risk?

6 What examples can you list of foreign multinationals operating in the United States?

7 Which of the reasons for the growth of MNCs do you think are the primary reasons for the development of multinationals in the following industries?

  a Drugs and pharmaceutical manufacture

  b Automobile manufacture

  c Metal refining

  d Hotel operation

  e Commercial banking

  f Energy development

  g Fast food

  h Fashion clothing

8 Do you think the standard of living overseas has been raised by the investments of multinationals? Does this offer a reason for offering MNCs concessionary loans?

BIBLIOGRAPHY

Adler, Michael: "The Cost of Capital and Valuation of a Two-Country Firm," *Journal of Finance*, March 1974, pp. 119–132.

Dunning, John H. (ed.): *International Investment*, Penguin Books Ltd., Harmondsworth, U.K., 1972.

———: *Economic Analysis and the Multinational Enterprise*, Frederick A. Praeger, New York, 1975.

Kobrin, Stephen J.: "The Environmental Determinants of Foreign Direct Investment: An Ex Post Empirical Analysis," *Journal of International Business Studies*, fall 1976, pp. 29–42.

Lessard, Donald R.: "Evaluating Foreign Projects: An Adjusted Present Value Approach," in *International Financial Management: Theory and Application*, Warren, Gorham and Lamont, Boston, 1979.

Magee, Stephen P.: "Information and the Multinational Corporation: An Appropriability Theory of Direct Foreign Investment," in Jagdish N. Bhagwati (ed.), *The New International Economic Order*, M.I.T. Press, Cambridge, Mass., 1977, and reprinted in Donald R. Lessard (ed.), *International Finance Management: Theory and Application*, Warren, Gorham and Lamont, Boston, 1979.

Ragazzi, Giorgio: "Theories of the Determinants of Direct Foreign Investment," *IMF Staff Papers*, July 1973, pp. 471–498. Reprinted in Donald R. Lessard (ed.), *International Financial Management: Theory and Application*, Warren, Gorham and Lamont, Boston, 1979.

Shapiro, Alan C.: "Capital Budgeting for the Maintenance Corporation," *Financial Management*, spring 1978, pp. 7–16.

Stonehill, Arthur I., and Leonard Nathanson: "Capital Budgeting and the Multinational Corporation," *California Management Review*, summer 1968, pp. 39–54.

Vernon, Raymond: *Storm Over the Multinationals: The Real Issues*, Harvard University Press, Cambridge, Mass., 1977.

APPENDIX 15.1: A Survey of International Taxation

International taxation is a complex subject, and we can do little more than explain variations in the types of taxes encountered and the methods that can be used to help reduce them. We will view taxation questions in the most general terms.[36]

TAXES FACED IN INTERNATIONAL TRADE

Corporate Taxes

Income taxes are the chief source of revenue for the U.S. government, and the corporate income tax is an important component of the total of income taxes. Income taxes are direct taxes, and the United States is dependent on direct taxes for a greater proportion of its total revenue, compared with the percentage of total revenue accounted for by direct taxes in most countries. Members of the European Economic Community (Common Market) collect direct taxes, but these are augmented by a value-added tax or VAT, which is an indirect tax.[37] Many poorer countries have a tax on imports as their primary revenue source. Other taxes that are found are based on wealth, sales, turnover, employees, and so on. Despite variations in the proportion of total tax receipts derived from corporate and other income taxes, the corporate tax rates are remarkably similar in industrialized countries. Table 15A.1 shows, for example, that the rates are between 40 and 56 percent in a large number of nations. Outside the industrialized countries the rates that are charged vary considerably, with some "tax havens" charging no corporate tax at all. Countries with zero rates include the Bahamas and Bermuda. The absence of corporation taxes is designed to encourage multinationals to locate offices for sheltering income from abroad.

The United States considers that is has jurisdiction over all the income of its citizens and residents wherever it is earned. However, credit is given for taxes paid elsewhere as long as the credit does not cause taxes to fall below what would have been paid had the income been earned in the United States. While citizens and residents of the United States are taxed on their full income wherever it is earned, nonresidents are taxed only on their income in the United States. This is the practice in other countries. The resident versus nonresident status of a corporation is determined by where it is incorporated.

Some countries that appear to have low corporate tax rates have more normal rates when local corporate taxes are added. For example, while Switzerland has federal corporate rates below 10 percent, the local authorities, called *cantons*, have tax rates of between 5 and 40 percent. Different provincial rates in Canada can effectively add anything from 0 to 5 percent to the national rate. Further variation and complication are introduced by the fact that some national tax authorities give full credit for local taxes, while others do not. In addition, there is considerable variation between countries according to what expenditures are deductible in determining taxable income and the amount of deductions.

---

[36] For more detailed descriptions of international taxation in the United States, see Elizabeth A. Owens, *Bibliography on Taxation of Foreign Operations and Foreigners, 1968–75,* International Tax Program, Harvard Law School, Cambridge, Mass., 1976.

[37] By definition, direct taxes cannot be shifted and are borne directly by those on whom they are levied. In contrast, indirect taxes can be shifted in part or in full to somebody who is not directly taxed. For example, corporate and personal income taxes are paid by those on whom they are levied. On the other hand, sales taxes and import duties charged to firms are at least in part paid by consumers. The consumer therefore pays indirectly.

TABLE 15A.1
CORPORATE INCOME TAX RATES
(Percentages)

Australia	46	Netherlands	48
Belgium	48	New Zealand	45
Canada	46	Singapore	40
Denmark	40	South Africa	42
France	50	Sweden	40
Ireland	45	United Kingdom	52
Japan	40	United States	46
Mexico	42	West Germany	57

Source: Ernst & Whinney, *Foreign and U.S. Corporate Income and Withholding Tax Rates*, January 1981.

Value-Added Tax (VAT)

A value-added tax is similar to a sales tax, and each seller can deduct the taxes paid at previous stages of production. If, for example, the VAT rate is 25 percent and a company cuts trees and sells $100 worth of wood to a furniture manufacturer, the tax is $25, since there are no previous stages of production. If the wood is made into furniture that is sold for $240, the furniture manufacturer must pay $60 minus the already collected VAT. Since the wood producer paid $25, the VAT of the manufacturer is $35. Since the eventual effect is the collection of 25 percent of the final selling price, the VAT is like a sales tax that is collected at each stage of production rather than only at the final retail stage.[38]

Because each payer receives credit for taxes paid at previous stages of production, there is an incentive to get complete records from suppliers. This reduces evasion but can give rise to complaints about burdensome, costly paperwork. The value-added tax has partially replaced income taxes on individuals in the European Economic Community. It has been promoted because it is a tax on spending and not on income. Taxes on income are a disincentive to work, while taxes on spending can be considered a disincentive to spend, that is, an incentive to save. Another advantage of VAT to countries promoting exports is that the rules of the General Agreement on Tariffs and Trade allow rebates of VAT to exporters, while a potential drawback is that VAT can distort patterns of output.

Import Duties

Before income tax and value-added tax became primary sources of revenue, import duties or tariffs (two terms for the same thing) were major sources of fiscal receipts.[39] Since goods entering a country are shipped to specific ports where policing can be intensive, import duties are a good source of revenue when income or sales records are poor. This partly explains why some underdeveloped countries depend on tariffs. Also, tariffs can explain why an automobile or refrigerator can cost 5 times more in some countries than in others. Because tariffs can be levied more heavily on luxuries than on necessities, they do not have to be regressive.[40]

[38] For more on VAT, see *Value Added Tax*, Price Waterhouse, New York, November 1979.
[39] Tariffs are also called excise taxes. These can be based on value (ad valorem) or on the weight of imports.
[40] With a regressive tax, the poor pay a larger *fraction* of their income or spending than do the rich. A tax can be regressive even if the rich pay a larger absolute *amount*.

Tariffs can explain why some firms move production facilities abroad. For example, if automobiles made in the United States and sold in Britain face a tariff and this can be avoided if the vehicles are produced in Great Britain, a British plant may be opened. Tariffs are used to protect jobs that are believed to be threatened by cheap foreign imports. For example, if sales of imported footwear or automobiles increase while domestically produced goods face sluggish sales, there may be lobbying to impose tariffs or quantitative restrictions (quotas) on imports. Tariffs tend to distort the pattern of international trade because countries may produce goods and services for which they do not have a comparative advantage but on which they can make profits behind protective barriers. Duties have been imposed by the U.S. government in the form of "countervailing tariffs" when it was believed that foreign competitors were *dumping* (selling at lower prices abroad than at home) or receiving "unfair" export help from their governments.

Withholding Taxes

Withholding taxes are collected from foreign individuals or corporations on income they have received from sources within a country. For example, if a U.S. resident earns dividends in Canada, taxes will be withheld and paid to Revenue Canada. Credit is generally received on taxes withheld, and so the level of withholding primarily affects the amount of total taxes received by the respective tax authorities. For example, if the U.S. resident has 10 percent withheld in Canada and is in a 35 percent tax bracket in the United States, the tax payable will be reduced to 25 percent of the income after credit for the 10 percent is given. Higher withholding rates therefore generally mean that more is collected by the foreign authorities and a smaller amount by the domestic government.

There are some circumstances in which the level of withholding does matter. Clearly, if the rate of withholding exceeds the effective tax rate at home, full credit may not be obtained. This can happen even if the tax *rate* at home is higher than the withholding rate if the definition of income or eligible deductions differs between the countries. For example, if little depreciation is deductible in the foreign country but generous allowances exist at home, the taxable income may differ, and more taxes may be paid abroad than are payable at home. There is an overall limitation on credit for taxes withheld that equals taxes payable in the United States, but when tax returns for a number of countries are combined, full credit may be obtained even when on an individual country basis there would have been unused credit.[41]

Many countries have treaties with others which establish especially favorable withholding rates. Table 15A.2 gives an idea of how many tax treaties have been signed by the United States.

Branch versus Subsidiary Taxes

An important element in corporate tax planning is deciding whether to operate abroad with a branch or with a subsidiary. A branch is a foreign operation that is incorporated at home, while a subsidiary is incorporated in the foreign country.

If a foreign activity is not expected to be profitable for a number of years, there may be an advantage to starting out with a branch structure so that negative earnings abroad can be

---

[41] When high levels of withholding are combined with low levels, the unused credit on the low levels of withholding is utilized by the high levels of withholding within the combined tax return. Even if the combined return does not provide full credit, unused credit can be carried back 2 years or forward 5 years.

TABLE 15A.2
U.S. TAX TREATY WITHHOLDING RATES

Country	Dividends, %	Interest, %	Patent and know-how royalties, %
Australia	15	N/A*	N/A
Austria	10	E†	E
Belgium	15	15	E
Canada	15	15	15
Denmark	15	E	E
France	15	10	5
Greece	N/A	E	E
Ireland	N/A	E	E
Italy	15	N/A	E
Japan	15	10	10
Luxembourg	7.5	E	E
Netherlands	15	E	E
New Zealand	N/A	15	15
Norway	15	E	E
South Africa	N/A	N/A	N/A
South Korea	15	12	15
Sweden	15	E	E
Switzerland	15	5	E
Trinidad and Tobago	25	15	15
United Kingdom	N/A	E	E
West Germany	15	E	E

*N/A: treaty does not limit withholding on this type of income.
†E: exempt from withholding tax.
Source: Ernst & Whinney, Foreign and U.S. Corporate Income and Withholding Tax Rates, December 1981.

used to offset profits at home in a consolidated tax return. U.S. tax laws and the tax laws of a number of other countries allow branch income to be consolidated. If a company expects positive foreign income and this income is not to be repatriated, there may be an advantage to a subsidiary structure. Foreign branches pay taxes on income as it is earned, while subsidiaries do not pay U.S. taxes until the income is repatriated. Whether this is sufficient reason to form an overseas subsidiary depends on relative tax rates and on whether the company wishes to repatriate earnings.

ORGANIZATIONAL STRUCTURES FOR REDUCING TAXES

Domestic International Sales Corporations (DISCs)

The ability to form a Domestic International Sales Corporation was introduced in the United States in 1971 to provide a tax incentive for U.S. corporations to raise exports. A DISC can be established by, for example, a U.S. manufacturing company for handling exports to foreign subsidiaries or to unrelated foreigners. The exports give the DISC export earnings. DISCs can also engage in leasing and in providing architectural and engineering services to gain export earnings. A DISC itself is not subject to U.S. taxes. Rather, its shareholder(s) is (are) taxed, but only on actual or "deemed" distributions. Since the DISC is deemed by the Internal Revenue Service to distribute the larger of actual distributions, or 50 percent of taxable income, it can defer taxes on half its export earnings even when it distributes the full amount.

To qualify as a DISC, a U.S. nonmanufacturing corporation must meet the following requirements.

1 More than 95 percent of its receipts must be from export earnings.
2 More than 95 percent of it assets must be in the form of "export assets"—property held for sale abroad, property used in selling abroad, accounts receivable, stock in related foreign corporations, capital, and other assets relating to export sales.
3 More than $2500 worth of capital must be available on each day of the year.
4 The intention to be a DISC must be stated in the 90-day period before the beginning of the tax year.

80-20 Subsidiaries

If 80 percent or more of a corporation's income is earned abroad, dividends and interest paid by the corporation are considered foreign-source income by the U.S. Internal Revenue Service. An 80-20 subsidiary is formed to raise capital for the parent, since it is considered foreign by the IRS and therefore does not need to deduct withholding taxes. Payments made to 80-20 corporations may well be taxed by foreign governments, but when the income is consolidated, credit will be obtained. If an 80-20 corporation is incorporated in the Netherlands Antilles or in another country with a treaty with the United States permitting no withholding taxes, then when interest is paid by the U.S. parent to the 80-20 subsidiary, the parent can also avoid having taxes withheld. This means that a company can avoid withholding taxes completely by having an 80-20 corporation in a treaty country.

Internal Pricing

In our discussion of transfer pricing in Chapter 10 we mentioned that it is possible for a corporation to shift profits from high-tax countries to low-tax countries in order to reduce its overall taxes. The potential for U.S. corporations to do this is reduced by an important section of the U.S. Internal Revenue Code. Section 482 allows the Treasury to reallocate income and/or expenses to prevent evasion of taxes within commonly owned entities. The IRS requires internal prices to be as if they had been determined competitively. This is known as a requirement for arms-length pricing.

Tax Havens

Some countries charge extremely low corporate taxes to encourage corporations to locate within their jurisdiction, bring jobs, and so on. These countries include the Bahamas, Bermuda, the Cayman Islands, and Granada, and they are all endowed with delightful climates. The ability of U.S. corporations to take full advantage of tax havens is limited by Section 882 of the U.S. Tax Code. This says that foreign corporations doing business in the United States are taxed at U.S. rates. There is therefore no obvious advantage to locating the corporate headquarters in the tax haven for doing business at home.

TAX RATES IN VARIOUS COUNTRIES

We conclude this appendix with a list of corporate tax rates, subsidiary rates, branch rates, withholding rates, and so on, as shown in Ernst & Whinney's *Foreign and U.S. Corporate Income and Withholding Tax Rates*, January 1981. Finer details on the tax situation can be found in the original publication.

TABLE 15A.3
TAX RATES IN VARIOUS COUNTRIES

Argentina	
	Rate (%)
Corporate income tax	
Domestic corporation—taxable income	33
Branch of foreign corporation—taxable income	45
Withholding tax	
Dividends	17.5
Interest	11.25
Royalties from patents, know-how, and like property	18
Branch tax	0
	Years
Net operating losses	
Carried back	0
Carried forward	10

Australia	
	Rate (%)
Corporate income tax	
Domestic corporation and branch of foreign corporation—taxable income	46
Withholding tax	
Dividends	30
Interest	10
Royalties from patents, know-how, and like property	46
Branch tax	5
	Years
Net operating losses	
Carried back	0
Carried forward	7

TABLE 15A.3
CONTINUED

Austria		
	Basic rate (%)	+ Percentage on amount in excess of lower limit
Corporate income tax		
Domestic corporation and branch of foreign corporation—taxable income		
S 0 to S 200,000	30	–
S 200,001 to 250,000	30	50
250,001 to 400,000	40	–
400,001 to 500,000	40	50
500,001 to 1,000,000	50	–
1,000,001 to 1,142,800	50	40
Over 1,142,800	55	
		Rate (%)
Withholding tax		
Dividends and royalties from patents, know-how, and like property		20
Interest		0
Branch tax		0
		Years
Net operating losses		
Carried back		0
Carried forward		5

Bahamas

The Bahamas impose no corporate income taxes and require no withholding of tax on remittances abroad.

Belgium	
	Rate (%)
Corporate income tax	
Domestic corporation—taxable income	48
Branch of foreign corporation—taxable income	54
Withholding tax	
Dividends, interest, and royalties from patents, know-how, and like property	20
Branch tax	0
	Years
Net operating losses	
Carried back	0
Carried forward	5

TABLE 15A.3
CONTINUED

Bermuda

Bermuda imposes no corporate income taxes and requires no withholding of tax on remittances abroad.

Brazil

	Rate (%)
Corporate income tax	
Domestic corporation and branch of foreign corporation—taxable income	35
Taxable income above NC$46,500,000	+ 5
Withholding tax (nontreaty countries)	
Dividends	25
Interest	25
Royalties from patents, know-how, and like property	25
Branch earnings after income tax	25
	Years
Net operating losses	
Carried back	0
Carried forward	4

Canada

	Rate (%)
Corporate income tax	
Domestic corporation and branch of foreign corporation—taxable income	46
Withholding tax	
Dividends, interest, and royalties from patents, know-how, and like property	25
Branch tax	25
	Years
Net operating losses	
Carried back	1
Carried forward	5

Cayman Islands

The Cayman Islands impose no corporate income taxes and require no withholding of tax on remittances abroad.

TABLE 15A.3
CONTINUED

Chile	
	Rate (%)
Corporate income tax	
Domestic corporation and branch of	
foreign corporation—taxable income	14.762
Withholding tax	
Dividends	40
Interest	40
Royalties	40
Branch tax	40
Net operating losses	*Years*
Carried back	0
Carried forward	5

Columbia	
	Rate (%)
Corporate income tax	
Domestic corporation—taxable income	40
Domestic limited liability company—	
taxable income	20
Withholding tax	
Dividends	20
Interest	0
Royalties from patents, know-how,	
technical assistance, and like	
property	47.2
Branch tax	52
	Years
Net operating losses	
Carried back	0
Carried forward	5

Denmark	
	Rate (%)
Corporate income tax	
Domestic corporation and branch of	
foreign corporation—taxable income	40
Withholding tax	
Dividends	30
Interest and royalties from patents,	
know-how, and like property	0
Branch tax	0
	Years
Net operating losses	
Carried back	0
Carried forward	5

TABLE 15A.3
CONTINUED

France	
	Rate (%)
Corporate income tax	
Domestic corporation and branch of foreign corporation—taxable income	50
Withholding tax	
Dividends	25
Interest	$33\frac{1}{3}$
Royalties from patents, know-how, and like property	$33\frac{1}{3}$
Branch tax	25
	Years
Net operating losses	
Carried back	0
Carried forward	5

Germany (West)	
	Rate (%)
Corporate income tax	
Domestic corporation—taxable income	
Undistributed profits	56
Distributed profits	36
Branch of foreign corporation—taxable income	50
Withholding tax	
Dividends and royalties from patents, know-how, and like property	25
Interest	0
Branch tax	0
	Years
Net operating losses	
Carried back	1
Carried forward	5

Greece	
	Rate (%)
Corporate income tax	
Domestic corporation and branch of foreign corporation—taxable income	43.396
Withholding tax	
Dividends	38–47
Interest	43.396
Royalties from patents, know-how, and like property	17.25
Branch tax	0
	Years
Net operating losses	
Carried back	0
Carried forward	3 or 5

TABLE 15A.3
CONTINUED

Hong Kong	
	Rate (%)
Corporate income tax	
Domestic corporation and branch of foreign corporation—taxable income	17
Withholding tax	
Dividends	0
Interest	15
Royalties from patents, know-how, and like property	17
Branch tax	0
	Years
Net operating losses	
Carried back	0
Carried forward	Unlimited

India	
	Rate (%)
Corporate income tax	
Domestic corporation—taxable income	
Public	
Up to Rs 100,000	45
Over Rs 100,000	55
Private	
Up to Rs 200,000	55
Over Rs 200,000	60
Branch of foreign corporation—taxable income	70
Withholding tax	
Dividends	25
Interest	75.25
Royalties from patents, know-how, and like property	75.25
Branch tax	0
	Years
Net operating losses	
Carried back	0
Carried forward	
Depreciation	Unlimited
Other business losses	8

TABLE 15A.3
CONTINUED

Ireland	
	Rate (%)
Corporate income tax	
Domestic corporation and branch of foreign corporation—taxable income	45
Withholding tax	
Dividends	0
Interest and royalties from patents, know-how, and like property	35
Branch tax	0
	Years
Net operating losses	
Carried back	1
Carried forward	Unlimited

Italy	
	Rate (%)
Corporate income tax	
Domestic corporation and branch of foreign corporation—taxable income	25
Withholding tax	
Dividends	10 or 30
Interest	20
Royalties from patents, know-how, and like property	0 to 14
Branch tax	0
	Years
Net operating losses	
Carried back	0
Carried forward	5

TABLE 15A.3
CONTINUED

	Japan	
	Distributed income rate (%)	Undistributed income rate (%)
Corporate income tax		
Domestic corporation and branch of foreign corporation—taxable income		
For fiscal periods ending after May 1, 1975		
Corporations with capitalization of ¥100 million or less:		
Up to ¥7 million	22	28
Excess over ¥7 million	30	40
Corporations with capitalization in excess of ¥100 million	30	40
		Rate (%)
Withholding tax		
Dividends, interest, and royalties from patents, know-how, and like property		20
Branch tax		0
		Years
Net operating losses		
Carried back		1
Carried forward		5

	Jordan	
		Rate (%)
Corporate income tax		
Domestic corporation and branch of foreign corporation—taxable income		
Banks and financial, insurance, and exchange companies		45
Industrial shareholding companies		38.5
Other shareholding and private companies		40
Withholding tax		
Dividends		0
Interest, royalties from patents, know-how, and like property paid to a nonresident		20
Know-how and design fees paid by a Jordanian branch to its foreign head office, holding company, or fellow subsidiary		Negotiable
Branch tax		0
		Years
Net operating losses		
Carried back		0
Carried forward		6

TABLE 15A.3
CONTINUED

Kenya	
	Rate (%)
Corporate income tax	
Domestic corporation—taxable income	45
Branch of foreign corporation—taxable income	52.5
Withholding tax	
Dividends	20
Interest	20
Royalties from patents, know-how, and like property; management and professional fees	30
Rents and other income from use of property	40
Branch tax	0
	Years
Net operating losses	
Carried back	0
Carried forward	Unlimited

Korea (South)	
	Rate (%)
Corporate income tax	
Domestic corporation—taxable income	
Publicly held corporation in which a major shareholder owns less than 35% of total issued shares	
Up to W50 million	25
In excess of W50 million	33
Other corporations	
Up to W50 million	25
In excess of W50 million	40
Withholding tax	
Publicly held corporation	10
Others	25
Interest and royalties from patents, know-how, etc.	25
Interest on bank deposits	10
Branch profit remittance	0
Branch tax	
Up to W50 million	25
In excess of W50 million	40
	Years
Net operating losses	
Carried back	0
Carried forward	3

TABLE 15A.3
CONTINUED

Lebanon

	Rate (%)
Corporate income tax	
Domestic corporations, limited liability partnerships (so far as limited partners are concerned), and branches of foreign corporations	22 + 15 municipal tax on corporation tax
Withholding tax	
Dividends	12
Interest	
Paid to nonresidents	0
Paid to residents	10
Royalties	1.18
Branch tax	0
	Years
Net operating losses	
Carried back	0
Carried forward	3

Luxembourg

	Rate (%)	
	Tax on lower limit	+ *Percentage on amount in excess of lower limit*
Corporate income tax		
Domestic corporation and branch of foreign corporation—taxable income		
Up to Lux Fr 400,000	–	20
Lux Fr 400,001 to 600,000	80,000	50
600,001 to 1,000,000	180,000	30
1,000,001 to 1,312,000	300,000	72
Over 1,312,000	524,640	40

	Rate (%)
Withholding tax	
Dividends	15
Interest	0
Royalties from patents, know-how, and like property	12
Branch tax	0
	Years
Net operating losses	
Carried back	0
Carried forward	5

TABLE 15A.3
CONTINUED

Malaysia	
	Rate (%)
Corporate income tax	
Domestic corporation and branch of	
foreign corporation—taxable income	45
Withholding tax	
Dividends	0
Interest	15
Royalties from patents, know-how, and	
like property	15
Branch tax	0
	Years
Net operating losses	
Carried back	0
Carried forward	Unlimited

Malta	
	Rate (%)
Corporate income tax	
Domestic corporation and branch of	
foreign corporation—taxable income	32.5
Withholding tax	
Dividends	0
Royalties from patents, know-how, and	
like property and interest	32.5
Branch tax	0
	Years
Net operating losses	
Carried back	0
Carried forward	Indefinite

Mexico	
	Rate (%)
Corporate income tax	
Domestic corporation and branch of	
foreign corporation—taxable income	42
Withholding tax	
Dividends	21
Interest	42
Royalties from patents and like	
property	42
Know-how	21
Branch tax	21
	Years
Net operating losses	
Carried back	1
Carried forward	4

TABLE 15A.3
CONTINUED

Netherlands	
	Rate (%)
Corporate income tax	
Domestic corporation and branch of foreign corporation—taxable income	48
Withholding tax	
Dividends	25
Interest and royalties from patents, know-how, and like property	0
Branch tax	0
	Years
Net operating losses	
Carried back	2
Carried forward	8

New Zealand	
	Rate (%)
Corporate income tax	
Domestic corporation—taxable income	45
Branch of foreign corporation—taxable income	50
Withholding tax	
Dividends, interest, and royalties from patents, know-how, and like property	15
Branch tax	0
	Years
Net operating losses	
Carried back	0
Carried forward	Unlimited

Nigeria	
	Rate (%)
Corporate income tax	
Domestic corporation—taxable income	45
Branch of foreign corporation	Foreign branches not permitted
Withholding tax	
Dividends	12.5
Interest and royalties from patents, know-how, and like property	45
Branch tax	Foreign branches not permitted
	Years
Net operating losses	
Carried back	0
Carried forward	4

TABLE 15A.3
CONTINUED

Norway	
	Rate (%)
Corporate income tax	
Domestic corporation and branch of foreign corporation—taxable income	
Distributed profits	23
Undistributed profits	50.8
Withholding tax	
Dividends	25
Interest and royalties from patents, know-how, and like property	0
Branch tax	0
	Years
Net operating losses	
Carried back	0
Carried forward	10

Peru	
	Rate (%)
Corporate income tax	
Domestic corporation and branch of foreign corporation—taxable income	
Up to S/ 1,000,000	20
On next 49,000,000	30
On next 450,000,000	40
On next 500,000,000	50
Excess over 1,000,000,000	55
Withholding tax	
Dividends	30
Interest	40
Royalties from patents, know-how, and like property	30
Branch tax	30
	Years
Net operating losses	
Carried back	0
Carried forward	5

TABLE 15A.3
CONTINUED

Philippines	
	Rate (%)
Corporate income tax	
Domestic corporation and branch of foreign corporation—taxable income	
Up to ₱100,000	25
Excess over 100,000	35
Withholding tax	
Dividends and royalties from patents, know-how, and like property	35
Interest	15
Branch tax	15
	Years
Net operating losses	
Carried back	0
Carried forward	0

Portugal	
	Rate (%)
Corporate income tax	
Domestic corporation and branch of foreign corporation—taxable income	
Up to Esc 1 million	31.5
Esc 1 million to Esc 5 million	37.8
Over Esc 5 million	42.0
Withholding tax	
Dividends	18.0
Interest	
Loans	30.0
Bank deposits	15.0
Debentures	12.0
Royalties	15.0
Branch tax	0
	Years
Net operating losses	
Carried back	0
Carried forward	5

TABLE 15A.3
CONTINUED

Puerto Rico	
	Rate (%)
Corporate income tax	
Domestic corporation and branch of foreign corporation—taxable income	45
Withholding tax	
Dividends	25
Interest and royalties from patents, know-how, and like property	29
Branch tax	0
	Years
Net operating losses	
Carried back	1
Carried forward	5

Singapore	
	Rate (%)
Corporate income tax	
Domestic corporation and branch of foreign corporation—taxable income	40
Withholding tax	
Dividends	0
Royalties from patents, know-how, and like property	40
Interest	40
Branch tax	0
	Years
Net operating losses	
Carried back	0
Carried forward	Unlimited

South Africa (Republic of)	
	Rate (%)
Corporate income tax	
Domestic corporation and branch of foreign corporation—taxable income	42
Withholding tax	
Dividends	15
Interest	10
Royalties from patents, know-how, and like property	12.6
Branch tax	0
	Years
Net operating losses	
Carried back	0
Carried forward	Unlimited

TABLE 15A.3
CONTINUED

Spain

	Rate (%)
Corporate income tax	
Domestic corporation and branch of foreign corporation—taxable income	33
Withholding tax	
Dividends	15
Interest	15
Royalties from patents, know-how, and like property	15
Branch tax	0
	Years
Net operating losses	
Carried back	0
Carried forward	5

Sweden

	Rate (%)
Corporate income tax	
Domestic corporation and branch of foreign corporation—taxable income	40
Withholding tax	
Dividends	30
Interest and royalties from patents, know-how, and like property	0
Branch tax	0
	Years
Net operating losses	
Carried back	0
Carried forward	10

Switzerland

	Rate (%)
Corporate income tax	
Domestic corporation and branch of foreign corporation—taxable income	3.63–9.8, federal; 5–40, canton
Withholding tax	
Dividends	35
Interest	35
Royalties from patents, know-how, and like property	0
Branch tax	0
	Years
Net operating losses	
Carried back	2, federal
Carried forward	0–5

TABLE 15A.3
CONTINUED

Taiwan	
	Rate (%)
Corporate income tax	
Domestic corporation and branch of foreign corporation—taxable income	
NT$ 0 to NT$ 50,000	0
50,000 to 100,000	15
100,000 to 500,000	25
Over 500,000	35
Withholding tax	
Dividends	35
Interest and royalties from patents, know-how, and like property	20
Branch tax	Remittances generally not permitted
	Years
Net operating losses	
Carried back	0
Carried forward	3

United Kingdom	
	Rate (%)
Corporate income tax	
Domestic corporation and branch of foreign corporation—taxable income	52
Withholding tax	
Dividends	0
Interest and royalties from patents, know-how, and like property	30
Branch tax	0
	Years
Net operating losses	
Carried back	1
Carried forward	Unlimited

United States	
	Rate (%)
Corporate income tax	
Domestic corporation and branch of foreign corporation—taxable income	46
Withholding tax	
Dividends, interest, and royalties from patents, know-how, and like property	30
Branch tax	0
	Years
Net operating losses	
Carried back	3
Carried forward	7

TABLE 15A.3
CONTINUED

Uruguay	
	Rate (%)
Corporate income tax	
Domestic corporation and branch of foreign corporation—taxable income	25
Withholding tax	
Dividends	0
Interest	0
Royalties from patents, know-how, and like property	25
Branch tax	20
	Years
Net operating losses	
Carried back	0
Carried forward	5

Venezuela	
	Rate (%)
Corporate income tax	
Domestic corporation and branch of foreign corporation—Tariff 2	
Taxable income	
On first Bs 300,000	18
On next 2,200,000	30
On next 2,500,000	35
On next 15,000,000	45
On excess over 20,000,000	50
Withholding tax	
On payments to foreign recipients:	
Professional fees	
Royalties	90% subject
Technical assistance	to tax
Technological services	
Interest to banks	15
Interest to others	Normal Tariff 2
Branch tax	20
	Years
Net operating losses	
Carried back	0
Carried forward	3

APPENDIX 15.2: Political Risk and Discount Rates

Let us define CF_t^* as the cash flow if confiscation does not occur and let us assume that the probability that complete confiscation will occur in any year is a constant.[42] We will write this probability as λ. With λ as the probability that confiscation will occur, $(1 - \lambda)$ is the probability that it will not occur. With $(1 - \lambda)$ as the probability that income will continue in each individual year, the probability that it will continue for 2 years is $(1 - \lambda)^2$, and for t years it is $(1 - \lambda)^t$. For example, if there is a 0.95 probability of nonconfiscation in any individual year, the probability of nonconfiscation for 2 years is $0.95 \times 0.95 = 0.90$. With CF_t^* as the cash flow if the investment has not been confiscated, the expected cash flow adjusted for the probability that the investment will survive is

$$(1 - \lambda)^t CF_t^* \tag{15A.1}$$

We see from expression (15A.1) that because CF_t^* is the cash flow if the investment is not lost, the expected cash flow that is adjusted for the probability of losing the investment is the smaller amount, $(1 - \lambda)^t CF_t^*$. For example, if the expected cash flow is £100 if confiscation has not yet occurred and the probability of confiscation in each year is 0.02, then the probability-weighted expected cash flow after 5 years is $(0.98)^5 \times 100$, that is, £90, and after 10 years it is £82.

If we assume that the cash flow is a constant, $\overline{CF}$, (15A.1) can be written as follows:

$$V = \sum_{t=1}^{T} \frac{(1 - \lambda)^t CF_t^*}{(1 + DR_e)^t} = \overline{CF} \sum_{t=1}^{T} \frac{(1 - \lambda)^t}{(1 + DR_e)^t} \tag{15A.2}$$

$\sum_{t=1}^{T} \dfrac{(1 - \lambda)^t}{(1 + DR_e)^t}$ is a geometric series. By writing it in full as

$$G = \frac{(1 - \lambda)}{(1 + DR_e)} + \frac{(1 - \lambda)^2}{(1 + DR_e)^2} + \cdots + \frac{(1 - \lambda)^T}{(1 + DR_e)^T}$$

we have

$$\frac{(1 - \lambda)}{(1 + DR_e)} G = \frac{(1 - \lambda)^2}{(1 + DR_e)^2} + \cdots + \frac{(1 - \lambda)^T}{(1 + DR_e)^T} + \frac{(1 - \lambda)^{T+1}}{(1 + DR_e)^{T+1}}$$

By subtracting, we get

$$G - \frac{(1 - \lambda)}{(1 + DR_e)} G = \frac{(1 - \lambda)}{(1 + DR_e)} - \frac{(1 - \lambda)^{T+1}}{(1 + DR_e)^{T+1}}$$

As T approaches infinity on a project with an infinite life, we find that

$$\frac{DR_e + \lambda}{1 + DR_e} G = \frac{1 - \lambda}{1 + DR_e}$$

[42] An analysis that considers more events, not just confiscation, has been provided by Alan Shapiro. See Alan C. Shapiro, "Capital Budgeting for the Multinational Corporation," *Financial Management*, spring 1978, pp. 7–16.

That is,

$$G = \frac{1 - \lambda}{DR_e + \lambda}$$

We can therefore write Equation (15.2) as follows:

$$V = \frac{\overline{CF}(1 - \lambda)}{(DR_e + \lambda)}$$

This can be compared with the value for the constant cash flow without political risk:

$$V' = \overline{CF} \sum_{t=1}^{T} \frac{1}{(1 + DR_e)^t}$$

By repeating the method for summing a geometric series, we get

$$V' = \frac{\overline{CF}}{DR_e}$$

as T approaches infinity. We find that we can allow for the risk of confiscation by multiplying the cash flows by the probability that the firm will survive each year and dividing by the sum of the discount rate and the probability of confiscation.

NAME INDEX

SUBJECT INDEX